D1609762

Hungary in the Thirteenth Century

Z.J. Kosztolnyik

*Non venit ante suos
prudentia nobilis annos.*
Horace

EAST EUROPEAN MONOGRAPHS, BOULDER
DISTRIBUTED BY COLUMBIA UNIVERSITY PRESS, NEW YORK
1996

EAST EUROPEAN MONOGRAPHS, No. CDXXXIX

Copyright 1996 by Z.J. Kosztolnyik
ISBN 0-8803-336-7
Library of Congress Catalog Card Number 95-83816

Printed in the United States of America

To Mother
R.i.p.

CONTENTS

LIST OF ABBREVIATIONS   vii

PREFACE   ix

THE ÁRPÁDS IN THE THIRTEENTH CENTURY   xi

CHAPTER ONE
  EARLY YEARS OF THE THIRTEENTH CENTURY
     1. The Chronicle on the Reign of King Emery   1
     2. King Emery and the Fourth Crusade   24

CHAPTER TWO
  DOMESTIC TURMOIL
     1. The Early Reign of Andrew II   38
     2. The Crusade of Andrew II   60

CHAPTER THREE
  THE MONARCH OF THE DECREES WITH GOLDEN SEALS
     1. The *Decretum* of 1222   77
     2. Andrew II and the German Knights   93
     3. The Church in Hungary During the Early 1230's   103

CHAPTER FOUR
  THE TARTARS ARE COMING!   121

CHAPTER FIVE
  THE MONGOL INVASION
     1. The Engagement at Mohi, 1241   151
     2. The Tartars Take Over the Country   165

CHAPTER SIX
  THE AFTERMATH: THE 1240'S
     1. Béla IV Cries to the Roman Pontiff for Help   180
     2. Béla IV Caught in the Political Web
       Between Halich and Vienna   200

CHAPTER SEVEN
  BÉLA IV'S LAW OF 1251, AND THE PROBABLE IMPACT
  UPON IT BY AURELIUS AUGUSTINUS' CONCEPT OF
  "QUI IMPERANT,...NEQUE IMPERANT...PRINCIPANDI
  SUPERBIA, SED PROVIDENDI MISERICORDIA"
  (*De Civitate Dei*, XIX, 14)   223

CHAPTER EIGHT
THE END OF BÉLA IV'S REIGN: THE LAW OF 1267   239

CHAPTER NINE
LADISLAS IV THE CUMAN
    1. Struggle for the Throne   255
    2. The Synod of Buda, 1279   272
    3. The Assassination of Ladislas IV   284

CHAPTER TEN
THE CULTURAL BACKGROUND
    1. Literary Remains and Chronicles   302
    2. Towns and Townships   318
    3. Cultural Conditions in Hungary in the
       Reports of Western Chronicles   332

CHAPTER ELEVEN
THE LAST OF THE ÁRPÁDS: THE KINGSHIP OF
ANDREW III   342

CHAPTER TWELVE
ANDREW III: THE FIRST CONSTITUTIONAL MONARCH
    1. Constitutional Developments   374
    2. The Anjou Claim to the Árpád Throne   390

APPENDIX I
A THIRTEENTH CENTURY WOMAN:
ST. ELIZABETH OF HUNGARY   404

APPENDIX II
MEDIEVAL HUNGARIAN THEOLOGIANS   409

BIBLIOGRAPHY   426

INDEX   498

LIST OF ABBREVIATIONS

ASS	*Acta sanctorum Bollandiana*
ÁUO	Wenczel, *Árpádkori új Okmánytár*
CD	Fejér, *Codex diplomaticus Hungariae ecclesiasticus ac civilis*
FRA	*Fontes rerum Austricarum*
HO	I. Nagy, *Hazai Okmánytár*
Hodinka	Hodinka, *Orosz évkönyvek*
HJb	*Historisches Jahrbuch*
HZ	*Historisches Zeitschrift*
ItK	*Irodalomtörténeti Közlemények*
Kukuljevic	*Codex diplomaticus Croatiae, Dalmatiae, Slavoniae*
Mansi, *Concilia*	Mansi, *Sacrorum conciliorum collectio*
MKSz	*Magyar Könyvszemle*
MIÖG	*Mitteilungen des Institutes für österreichische Geschichts- forschung*
MGHLL	*Monumenta Germaniae historica, Legum collectio*
MGHSS	*Monumenta Germaniae historica, Scriptores*
MPH	*Monumenta Poloniae historica*
Monumenta Zagrabiae	Tkalcic, *Monumenta historica liberae regiae civitatis Zagrabiae*
MPG	Migne, *Patrologia graeca*
MPL	Migne, *Patrologia latina*
MHSM	*Monumenta spectantia historiam Slavorum meridionalium*
RA	Szentpétery, *Regesta*
RASS	Rauch, *Rerum Austricarum scriptores*

RHM	Endlicher, *Rerum Hungaricarum monumenta Arpadiana*
RISS	Muratori, *Rerum Italicarum scriptores*
SIE	*Szent István Emlékkönyv*
Smiciklas	*Codex diplomaticus regni Croatiae, Dalmatiae et Sloveniae*
SSrG	*Scriptores rerum Germanicum in usum scholarum*
SSH	Szentpétery, *Scriptores rerum Hungaricarum*
Teutsch-Firnhaber	*Urkundenbuch zur Geschichte Siebenbürgens*
VMH	Theiner, *Vetera monumenta historiam Hungariae sacram illustrantia*
Wenczel, *Anjoukori*	Wenczel, *Anjoukori diplomácia emlékek*
Závodszky	Závodszky, *A Szent István, Szent László és Kálmán korabeli törvények és zsinatok határozatai*
Zimmermann-Werner	*Urkundenbuch zur Geschichte der Deutschen in Siebenbürgen*

PREFACE

The thirteenth century has been characterized, and it is known today, by various adjectives. J.J. Walsh described it as the greatest of centuries. To H.K. Sedwick, it was the age of expanding knowledge and social progress. Friedrich Heer regarded it as the time of change, the period of religious and intellectual revolt. Jaroslav Pelikan, who dealt with the theology of St. Thomas Aquinas, St. Bonaventure, and Duns Scotus, viewed it as the century of religious thought - the age of divine wisdom.

In the Hungarian historians' point of view, the idea formulated by Bálint Hóman has validity. The 1200's were, he observed, the time of constitutional development for the country, when the monarchs had three times, though on every occasion differently, issued the document that assured the lesser nobility a firm representative slot in the public life of the kingdom. One may agree with Gyula Kristó, who wrote that the thirteenth century was the century of Golden Bulls.

The constitutional developments in the country peaked under Andrew III (1290-1301), the last Árpád scion, who received a western education in his youth, and had successfully applied the representative principle to government during his reign. In the process, he became the country's first constitutional monarch.

The author wishes to thank our daughter Elizabeth Irene of Boulder, Colorado, for her editorial assistance in preparing the manuscript.

Z.J. Kosztolnyik
Texas A&M University

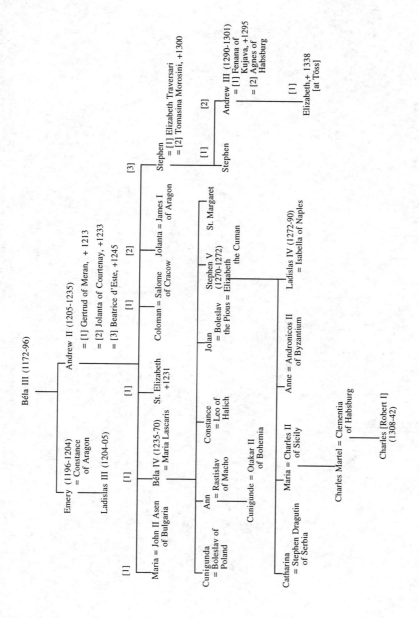

The Árpáds in the Thirteenth Century

CHAPTER ONE

EARLY YEARS OF THE THIRTEENTH CENTURY

1. *The Chronicle on the Reign of King Emery*

> Cui successit Emericus...et regnavit annis VIII-o, mensibus VIIe, diebus VI. Huius uxor Constantia filia regis Aragonie cesari Frederico per consilium apostolici copulatur.
>
> *Chronicon pictum*, c. 172

The *Chronicon pictum* is, indeed, brief in its report on the reigns of Emery I (1196-1204), and Ladislas III (1204-05), the son and the grandson, respectively, of King Béla III (1172-96).[1] The compiler's record of the Chronicle on Béla III was also short, barely a paragraph, starting with a "P" initial. The illumination of the initial depicted the monarch standing, with a royal crown on his head, wearing a shirt of mail, holding the orb in his right hand, and a striped red and white standard in his left.[2] Under the caption "Emericus coronatur," (mere reference to the contents of the next paragraph), King Emery was, once again, depicted in a drawing of simple frame on the same codex leaf; in the center of this drawing the king sat on the throne holding the sceptre in his right hand, and the orb in his left, as two bishops placed the crown upon his head.[3] (Incidentally, the crown drawn was identical with the circlet in the "P" initial.) On the same leaf of the codex there is a nine line report[4] - it makes up six lines in print[5] - on the reign of Emery, proceeded by a "C" initial picturing the monarch standing tall, with the crown on his head, holding the orb in his left, the sceptre in his right hand. Besides the brief entry in the Chronicle, writs issued by Emery provide a guide as to his activities and accomplishments - his struggle with brother Andrew (later Andrew II), trouble in the Balkans, his contacts with Serbia and Bulgaria, and the Fourth Crusade.[6]

The nine (in print, six) line text recorded that Emery had followed his father (Béla III) on the throne, and reigned for eight years, seven months, and six days. Upon his death, his Queen Constance had married, upon advice received from the pope, Emperor Frederick II. The compiler-chronicler established the date of Emery's death as of Tuesday, November 30, 1200.[7] However, on the grounds of the compiler's report that November 30, "Pridie Kal. Decembris," fell on a Tuesday, *feria tertia*, the correct date would be the year 1204.[8] The chronicler ended his report by saying that they buried King Emery in the cathedral of Eger.[9]

It may merit some interest to note that the "Poson Chronicle," c. 64, carried the same general report with the difference that it recorded only the eight years of Emery's reign, and said nothing about the second marriage of the widowed queen. (Evidently the scribe did not consider the matter important enough to be mentioned; or, he regarded it as humiliating for the royal family to record it.) It, too, rendered the year 1200 as the date of the king's death.[10] On the other hand, von Mügeln's *Ungarnchronik* rather crudely followed the text structure of the *Chronicon pictum*, but spelled Emery (Emericus) as "Demetricus," the son of Béla III, "... sein sun."[11] Emery's queen, and it is worth noting the crude phrasing of the German text - "... des selben hausfrawe" - was Constance.[12] They had buried the ruler at Fehérvár (Weyssenburg), von Mügeln stated, unlike the Chronicle's record of Eger - "in ecclesia Agriensi."[13] The information supplied by von Mügeln must have originated in the fact that Ladislas III, heir and son of King Emery, had been interred at Fehérvár, "... cuius corpus Albe quiescit,"[14] as von Mügeln himself correctly recorded it;[15] von Mügeln must have misread a line of the Chronicle text he was copying from. It is only a small matter of misplaced entry a few lines below in the text.

One ought to note that the six and a half lines in the Chronicle[16] (less the four lines in actual print)[17] devoted to Ladislas III were proceeded by a drawing in a simple frame in the body of the text, with a caption on top of it that read: "The coronation of Ladislas II [sic!]."[18] The drawing pictured Ladislas III standing, though a little bent forward, in front of the throne, while a bishop placed the crown upon his head; on the left side of the bishop was another bishop, and between them stood a nobleman, probably a courtier. The other bishop and the noble appeared to witness the event (requiring two witnesses - "unus testis nullus testis!"). The rather curious characteristic of the drawing is that at the time he was crowned, Ladislas III was still a child, perhaps five years old, but the miniaturist portrayed him as a grownup. It was customary of that age.[19]

Interesting also is the caption of the drawing - or the title to the next paragraph in the text - in red, that spoke of Ladislas II[20], probably on the grounds that the chronicler did not previously refer to anti-king Ladislas (*ob.* 1163), and spoke instead of the son of Emery as Ladislas II.[21] The scribe (copyist) of this line (title) written in red ink might have been the miniaturist-illuminator, though it could have been the chronicler as well.[22] In the "P" initial of this portion of the text, "Post eum regnavit...," there stood Ladislas III with a circlet on his head, bent a little forward, holding the orb in his right hand, and in the left the sceptre.[23] In both of these drawings, Ladislas was depicted wearing red shoes, and like his father in the "C" initial, standing on rocky terrain.[24]

Anonymus *P. dictus magister* wrote with loving affection about Béla III, whose notary he once (*"quondam"*) had been.[25] If the king named by Anonymus was indeed Béla III, and the latest research implies that was clearly the case,[26] then the first sentence of Anonymus' *Gesta Ungarorum* bore witness that, at the succession of Emery to the throne, Anonymus the chronicler had lost his office of royal notary. He had fallen out of the king's grace, probably on grounds that he did not agree with the young monarch who, perhaps irresponsibly but systematically, had defended what he must have regarded as royal prerogatives (such as, to rule by fiat) during his short reign.[27] Anonymus the chronicler, educated abroad and proud of his acquired French culture,[28] held different values and opinions as to what the essence of royal power and the office of the king ought to be.[29] Anonymus was the first and only medieval Hungarian chronicler who recorded the Hungarian blood-oath taken by the tribal chiefs in the late 880s that cited, in fact, the responsibilities of the *elected* Hungarian ruler; he summarized, in five entries, the meaning and significance of that oath.[30]

In the introductory paragraph of his *Gesta*, Anonymus made a twofold observation; first, it was the leader of the Hungarian (Magyar) conquest of the mid-Danubian region during the mid-890s, Árpád, a descendant of Prince Álmos, and his headmen of noble blood who had acquired everything together during the conquest, and had equally shared everything with one another after the conquest of the land had been completed.[31] Second, the headmen of noble blood had, on their own, elected Álmos, and later his son Árpád, as their chief.[32] Anonymus therefore argued that their descendants must not be left out of the meetings and deliberations of the Royal Council, nor exempted from participation in the administration of their country's public business.[33]

The chronicler Anonymus, in other words, was strongly critical; in his point of view, the nobles of King Emery, and of his predecessors, were the offspring of the electors, who had chosen Álmos as their lord, just as, indeed, King Emery was a descendant of Álmos. But the monarch and his predecessors had frequently transferred their nobles away from the court, preventing them from serving as court advisors, or officials in public administration.

The king, Anonymus claimed, created the impression - rather, he seemed to have expressed the idea - that he would not share jurisdiction and administrative powers on equal terms with the nobles; and, if he had excluded his nobles (headmen) from wholly participating in the conception and execution of more important decisions, the king, had, in fact, prevented them from playing an equal role in the royal council and in governmental affairs.[34] The king's attitude, Anonymus wrote -and he most probably had Emery in mind, although he could have written about Béla III as well[35] - had totally contradicted the text and the meaning (of the third paragraph) of the "Blood Oath" their predecessors took, and which he, Anonymus, committed to writing.[36]

By comparing the last line of Anonymus' introduction to his *Gesta* - "felix igitur Hungaria, cui sunt dona data varia"[37] - with the five articles of the Blood Oath (as interpreted by him),[38] "fusis propriis sanguinibus in ubnum vas ratum fecerunt iuramentum"[39] (probably after Solinus, c. 15,[40] though C.A. Macartney says it could also have been a Scythian custom, which the Magyars had adopted[41]), this writer, for one, is under the impression that Anonymus wished to exploit the domestic condition created by a young monarch's succession to the throne,[42] so that the chronicler may define, in writing, his constitutional concept acquired during his student days in Paris and state that, in contrast to the strong-handed reign of Béla III, one expected a constitutional decentralized rule from young King Emery.[43] In the process, Anonymus lost his game, and the new king's good will as well.

The observation reached by this writer may, incidentally, determine the date of Anonymus' authorship of his *Gesta*. He was the notary of Béla III, and wrote his composition during the reigns of the sons of Béla III, especially of Andrew II.[44] This may make it clear why the nobles revolted against King Emery and threw their support to Prince Andrew - the latter had promised them that he would keep the articles (especially the third article) of the Blood Oath.[45]

King Emery's father had already taken the cross, prior to his death,[46] and so did Archbishop Jób of Esztergom;[47] Palatine Mak (Magh; Moch) had also made plans to go to the Holy Land.[48] But Béla III died unexpectedly; chronicler Albericus, who wrote the correct year, but the wrong day of his death, could not resist mentioning that a Bishop Kalán had him poisoned.[49] Before he died, Béla III had designated his son Emery as his heir to the throne,[50] who had previously, in the summer of 1194, succeeded Bishop Kalán as governor of the region beyond the Drave river,[51] and who was crowned for a second time already during the lifetime of his father.[52] Béla III had bequeathed a good deal of wealth to his younger son, Andrew, because he wanted to enable him to go on a crusade, thereby fulfilling the vow his father had made.[53]

The prince, however, failed to fulfill his father's command.[54] Why was it necessary, he had thought, for the Hungarian king to go on a crusade? Not even Saint Ladislas I went on the first crusade, even though the Chronicle recorded that he was expected to go and play a role in it. Did his father, Béla III, the former heir to the Byzantine throne, plan to go because he wished to gain, thereby, the throne of Byzantium?[55] The prince had led an irresponsible life while his inheritance lasted; then, his evil friends encouraged him to ask his brother, King Emery, for his share of the realm's territory that legally belonged to him, where he could rule freely and independently of his brother.[56]

Hostilities broke out between King Emery and Prince Andrew; the prince had the upper hand, and Rome intervened. In referring to a letter sent by his predecessor, Celestine III, the new pontiff, Innocent III, forbade the Hungarian nobles to support Andrew against their king.[57] The papal curia especially warned the prince to fulfill his father's crusading vow (instead of causing mischief at home), under pain of excommunication and disinheritance from succession to the throne.[58]

What Prince Andrew and his advisors must have been unable to comprehend was that by their behavior they actually aided the diplomacy of the Holy See; they provided the very determined new pontiff with the opportunity to intervene in the domestic quarrels of the realm - in fact, to take charge of its foreign policy. Rome could not have done this during the reign of Béla III.[59] Nor did King Emery improve the situation by letting his brother enjoy the support of Leopold IV of Austria (who was a great patron of the arts)[60]; the king made another bad move in his game of diplomatic chess by handing over to his brother the "Region Beyond the Drave River" as an autonomous area.[61]

The prince could now conduct his own affairs in accordance with his own policies and judgment on his own territory. He could, and did, assume the title "Dux Chulmie;" he curtailed the expansionist tendencies of the Serb court toward the north, and interfered in ecclesiastical policies.[62]

In order to counterbalance the growing influence of the prince, the king granted full legislative and judicial powers to Bishop Dominic of Zagreb over the "faithful" (i.e., Christian inhabitants) of the region controlled by the prince.[63] King Emery further confirmed the Knights of the Hospital in their possessions located in the area,[64] and acknowledged the prerogatives of the archbishop of Esztergom to collect one-tenth of the toll, paid and collected at Pozsony and at Szepes, that formed a portion of royal revenues.[65]

On the grounds that the metropolitan had remained loyal to him during his controversy with Andrew, the king donated the royal palace, still under construction, to the archbishop of Esztergom with the understanding that during an official visit or prolonged stay in Esztergom, the monarch would reside there as a guest of the archbishop.[66] The question may be raised, of course, whether King Emery thus wanted to pay his respects to Archbishop Jób, or simply free himself of the expense of maintaining another royal residence? The king's gift to the archbishop, and his permission to Zerzowoj *iobagio* (a lesser noble in royal service) at Pozsony, so that the latter could freely move about in the royal curia, as a reward for his loyalty to the king during his troubles with Andrew, might be looked upon as an open provocation of Andrew.[67]

If one were to consider the fact that, as early as 1191, during the days of Béla III, Rome had already confirmed the "Hungarian" archbishop of Spaleto (an area under the secular governorship of Bishop Kalán of Pécs) in all of his archiepiscopal rights and that the archbishop had held jurisdiction over twelve bishoprics in Dalmatia - some of which existed in name only,[68] contrary to the claims of the established Croatian-Dalmatian hierarchy,[69] as if thereby to limit the expansionist plans of the cunning Nemanja of Serbia[70] - can one really comprehend how much power Prince Andrew wanted to possess after his victory over the king's forces in 1197.[71] From circumstantial evidence the prince reasoned that Emery, still a prince, had been governor of the "Region Beyond the Drave" when Emery, crowned for the second time, had succeeded to the throne. One can rationalize on psychological grounds that it was imperative for Andrew to possess the area - to assure his right of succession to the crown.[72]

Therefore, it was not without reason that Emery complained to Rome that his opponents wanted war, not peace.[73] Andrew took up arms; he had aspirations to the crown.[74] Nor did the papal warning delay him; three Hungarian bishops had sided with him - John of Veszprém,[75] Boleslav of Vác (founder of the house of canons of Prémontré at Lelész),[76] and his brother, Elvin of Várad, a simonist who had been sued by his own cathedral chapter in a court of law.[77] The writ of Pope Innocent III addressed to Andrew, asking him that he respect and love his royal brother, may be placed here in context with developing events;[78] but the papal curia had to warn the prince again during Lent, 1197, that he may not, under the threat of excommunication to be pronounced over him by the two archbishops of Esztergom and Kalocsa, take up arms against king and country.[79]

The continued threat of civil war, and the catastrophic condition of the treasury wore out the health and the nerves of King Emery; he saw everyone as an enemy. When he had found out, for example, that Bishop Boleslav had played an intermediary role between the prince and his supporters and had, in fact, collected money for the conspirators (keeping it in the sacristy of his cathedral at Vác), the monarch lost self-control.[80] On an Ember Day during the first week of Lent, 1199, he suddenly made an appearance at

Vác; and although the cathedral chapter had correctly paid respects to him, he insisted, before the canons, that the bishop open the sacristy to him. Bishop Boleslav, however, denied the king's request.[81]

The refusal of Boleslav further angered the king. On the evening of the same day he appeared for a second time at the cathedral, summoned the bishop, and demanded that he hand over the keys to the sacristy. Because the bishop made no appearance, the king had forced his entry into the church and ordered the sacristy to be opened. When the bishop dared to protest, the king physically got a hold of him, and after the bishop stumbled over the steps of the high altar, the king had him dragged from the sanctuary, and ordered him to be thrown out of his cathedral.[82]

According to the letter Emery sent to Rome, the canon in charge, *custos*, was willing to open the sacristy by this time; the king had the money counted, appropriated the bishop's share of it, and took charge of some of the bishop's "dubious" correspondence (such as compromising letters pertinent to the presumed conspiracy).[83] When the deeply humiliated and physically insulted ordinary forbade church functions to be held in the cathedral on the grounds of this sacrilege, Emery, who must have been very concerned about the results of this confrontation, ordered that the payment of the tithe be withheld from the bishop of Vác, and threatened to blind anyone who dared to spread news about the affair.[84]

At this point, the simmering domestic upheaval erupted - the lands and goods of Bishop Dominic of Zagreb, a loyal supporter of King Emery, were devastated by Prince Andrew,[85] whose armed retainers now clashed with the king's forces.[86] The king, however, with regained self-confidence, behaved more carefully; the prince, too, may have become overconfident. In the encounter near Rád, between Lelle and the Szemes creeks, not too far from Lake Balaton, the king held the upper hand.[87] The prince fled to the court of Leopold VI of Styria, and the king, out of sheer frustration, devastated the Hungarian-Styrian border.[88] It may be the irony of fate that the monarch understood only after the battle that it was his palatine who had urged Andrew to turn against him.[89]

The king now designated Miko, his loyal steward, as the next palatine; however, Elvin, the simonist bishop of Várad had Miko excommunicated on a trumped up charge that Miko, as royal reeve, had arrested one of the bishop's men in transit because that man acted as a courier between Andrew and the insurgents supporting him.[90]

There must have been a tremendous outcry against the bishop, because Rome intervened - one must not excommunicate the king's trusted officer without due process of the law. Were a royal office holder to be excommunicated without proper canonical process, any bishop could violate the ban numerous times.[91] Pope Innocent III made it clear that the king's counselors and his trusted persons may only be placed under church punishment within due process of the law.[92]

Andrew's fortunes started to decline before the battle at Rád; the royal writ issued at Zagreb, in March 1199, referred to him without mentioning his princely title.[93]

Pope Innocent III also had to react in a most diplomatic manner to the complaints of the bishop of Vác: the Holy See always had the highest regard for Hungary, and King Emery's father had shown respect for the papal curia; may King Emery follow his father's example by rendering satisfaction to the humiliated high priest, and pay him indemnity for damages, under the pain of a papal ban.[94] In referring to the example of Heliodorus in the Book of Maccabees, the pontiff warned the monarch to repent - on account of the expected canonical punishment, the Lord may strike heavily at him and at his realm.[95] Rome ordered Archbishop Saul to have a frank discussion with the king and to impress the idea upon him that he had committed a grave sin.[96]

King Emery did not inherit the patience and personal diplomatic tact of his father. He did not receive the archbishop, and wrote a letter instead to the papal curia to excuse himself. Later, he did compensate the bishop of Vác for damages and showed reconciliation toward the archbishop of Kalocsa, but in a manner, and at a time, when he saw fit. This must have been the sole occasion when King Emery displayed any independence in his dealings with the curia.[97]

In the spring of 1200, Rome, undaunted, interfered again in Hungarian politics. The crusade had to begin, and Innocent III was determined to bend the spiteful monarch to obedience to the Holy See;[98] furthermore, a reconciliation had to take place between the two brothers, King Emery and Prince Andrew.[99] Both brothers had to go on a crusade, the papal curia stipulated, and the duke of

Austro-Styria was to take over the government of the kingdom during their crusade abroad.[100] Were one of the two brothers to die during the campaign, the other would keep, or receive, the crown.[101] Andrew would regain his princely territory beyond the Drave river, but the king would have to exercise limited authority in ecclesiastical matters in the region.[102] When the archbishopric of Spaleto, held by Bernard, Emery's former tutor, fell vacant,[103] the first task of the new archbishop was to have the holdings of Dominic, the bishop of Zagreb, surveyed, to compensate him for all the harassment and damages he had to endure during the earlier confrontation between the king and his brother. In fact, the prince had to donate an island in the Sava stream to the bishop of Zagreb.[104]

The king was expected, under the terms of this commitment, to go on a crusade - on the condition, however, that the pontiff exempt twelve Hungarian nobles, whose services were needed for the defense of the kingdom, from participating in the crusade.[105] Emery had no confidence in Leopold of Austria, nor did he believe in the necessity of another crusade.[106] When political turmoil developed in Serbia, south of the Hungarian border, Emery used it as a convenient excuse to indefinitely delay his taking the cross.[107]

What had happened south of the border was that Nemanja, ruler of Serbia, became a monk, and his son Stephen succeeded him as the Grand Steward of Serbia. However, Stephen, married to a daughter of Alexius III Angelos of Byzantium, was a habitual drunkard, who accused his wife of infidelity and pushed her aside. Thereupon Vulk (Vulcanus), Stephen's brother, who had claimed the title of King of Dalmatia, publicly criticized his brother's behavior and the mistreatment of his sister-in-law. Although both brothers turned to Rome for intervention, a vicious war broke out between them.[108]

King Emery interfered in the political-family quarrel south of the border by aiding Vulk against Stephen; he made Vulk the new Grand Steward of Serbia, provided that Vulk acknowledge him as "King of Serbia" and pressured his people into spiritual submission to the Roman See. In fact, Emery authorized Archbishop John of Kalocsa (the former bishop of Csanád; now, Saul's successor in the see of Kalocsa) to take charge of the Catholic mission in Serbia.[109] Emery cleverly suggested to Vulk that he turn to Rome for official recognition of his position by requesting a royal circlet from the curia, thereby to ease the conversion among his people to the Roman Church without, however, lessening Emery's royal title in Serbia.[110]

Emery remained King of Serbia only in name.[111] The papal curia approved the approach of the monarch and of his game of diplomacy. Were the Roman Catholic "mission" in Serbia to become successful, it would evolve under the supervision of the Hungarian ("Serb") monarch; were it to falter, however, the Grand Steward would carry the blame for the disaster. One may conclude from the papal letter that only upon a successful completion of missionary work could Vulk obtain the royal circlet; and yet, the missionary effort had to be carried out under the initiative of the Hungarian ruler.[112]

John Casmaris, papal legate, had reached an agreement with the Bogomils in Bosnia, who had submitted to Rome on April 8, 1203, in the presence of the Hungarian Grand Reeve Kulin, at a location designated as "near the Bosnian stream." The legate took the signed agreement to King Emery's summer residence on Csepel island for approval. There, two Bogomil monks read out loud the text of the already approved and publicly announced document in front of King Emery, the papal legate, the archbishop of Kalocsa, Bishop Kalán of Pécs (under whose jurisdiction came the "southern portion" of the realm), and, rather curiously, before the son of Grand Reeve Kulin.[113]

The previous text of the agreement might have been unclear; perhaps it served as a working draft that needed revision. But it is also possible that the monarch, jealously guarding his powers,[114] wanted to make it known that it was he who signed the writ, witnessed by his archbishop and bishop.[115] King Emery wanted to make it clear that it was he, and not the papal legate, who conducted Hungarian foreign policy of a politico-religious nature.[116] Furthermore, the king wanted it known that he would not separate himself of the already converted Bogomils; he had the transcript of the signed writ handed to the son of Kulin and admonished him that he refrain from protecting "heretic" Bogomils under the pain of royal disfavor - a fine of one thousand silver marks,[117] of which, incidentally, only one half would be forwarded to the royal court.[118] Upon the death of Grand Reeve Kulin, his son succeeded him in office, being in charge of the "southern regions" of the realm.[119]

The coin might have another side to it. Expansion of the influence of the Roman curia into Serb territory, initiated by the Hungarian monarch, put an end to any Bogomil attempt to expand in the area; the threat of growing Bogomil influence in Serbia might also have turned Vulk's attention toward the Holy See. Were the missionary activity of the Roman clergy on Serb soil initiated by the Hungarian court to turn out positively, and Vulk to gain a royal diadem from the Roman pontiff, Vulk, once crowned with a circlet from Rome, might not tolerate the continued predominance of the Hungarian court in the area any longer. Was it not King Emery who held the title "King of Serbia?"[120]

It may be the reason why Grand Reeve Kulin displayed firm tolerance of the Bogomils in the territory, contrary to the official instructions of the king (or because of the secret message included in those instructions), on the grounds that the Bogomils represented a politically powerful counter-force against a Serbia that had grown in strength and political prestige, thereby possibly endangering the diplomatic intents of the Hungarian court.[121]

A successful campaign against the Bogomils, even one carried out by peaceful means, might have disturbed the ecclesiastical and diplomatic goals of the Bulgarian court in the Balkans. The authority of the Hungarian court now extended to the southern border of Serbia. Confrontation with Bulgaria seemed to be unavoidable because the court of Bulgaria exercised religious-spiritual authority over certain parts of Serbia.[122] The Bulgarian leader, wild and forceful "Little John" (Kajolan; Ioannitius Caloioannes), followed in the footsteps of his two murdered brothers, John Asen and Peter, and continued their policy of expansion.[123] The only problem with this policy was that John also incorporated the town of Nis into his territorial acquisitions, although Béla III of Hungary had handed over Nis, as dowry for his daughter, to the Byzantine court of Isaac Angelos.[124]

In referring to the earlier diplomacy of his father, who had actually asserted ecclesiastical authority over the bishoprics, several of which lay in Bulgaria,[125] King Emery made similar demands on his own behalf and caused an unavoidable rift, in terms of both diplomacy and personal relations, with Kajolan.[126] Emery had even taken, albeit temporarily, the title of the "King of Bulgaria,"[127] in spite of the fact that he had, as late as 1203, demonstrated his good will toward the court of Bulgaria.[128] The behavior of Kajolan voided any further cooperation with the Bulgarian court; King Emery's claim to certain bishoprics in Bulgaria had changed the attitude of Kajolan toward the Hungarian curia.[129]

The Roman See supported King Emery. The papal court not only permitted him to delay his crusade, but also authorized him to take proper military action against Bulgaria. It is not sinful, wrote the pope to Emery, to fight with the pagan, or even with Christians over what was considered to be a just cause.[130]

And yet, King Emery's inconsistent and thoughtless behavior toward the end of his reign, and his warped personality, created a depressive image in the public mind. He greeted with friendship, for instance, the papal legate, Cardinal Leo, who had carried with him the royal diadem destined for John, new ruler of Bulgaria, to extend papal recognition to the new Catholic monarch of that country, in the face of rather hostile opposition from the Byzantine court.[131] King Emery held Cardinal Leo in high regard because the legate had, through negotiations, arranged for the union of the Church of Bulgaria with the Roman See. In fact, the king went as far as to recall and demobilize the armed forces he had sent against Bulgaria, in order to facilitate the outcome of the talks between the legate and John of Bulgaria.[132]

By an unexpected decision, however, Emery recalled the legate from the Hungarian-Byzantine border,[133] and demanded from him that he make certain that John of Bulgaria would, before receiving the diadem, make amends for war damages to the Hungarian court.[134] On the grounds that Emery had earlier acted as mediator between the curia and Bulgaria (and had assumed the title "King of Bulgaria" during that time), he did have a reason for making such an undiplomatic move.[135] But Cardinal Leo saw it differently and made a protest; he could not rely on coercion, nor could he establish preconditions for the conversion of the people of Bulgaria. The legate refused to cooperate with Emery.[136]

The king would not listen to reason. He ordered his reeve (named Keve) to surround the house on the border where the legate spent the night, and to place him under house arrest. The Cardinal had the incident reported to Rome.[137] The king also wrote to the papal court, recording events from his point of view. Emery argued that the Roman See had been ill-advised during the negotiations with

Bulgaria, and had humiliated him by assuring diplomatic recognition to John of Bulgaria. He still had diplomatic misunderstandings to settle with the ruler of Bulgaria, because the latter had not paid indemnity for damages caused during previous military encounters in the area.[138]

Pope Innocent III had, in his response of October 4, 1204, pointed out that he had a clear overview of the Hungarian-Bulgarian controversy, and understood only too well the political background of the confrontation. It was not the papal intent to insult the Hungarian king, but the pontiff had to keep political reality in sight. On the grounds that King Emery wished to have his young son crowned for a second time, the pontiff asked him to yield to the papal curia on the Bulgarian question.[139]

With diplomatic tact King Emery declared his support for Kajolan,[140] and Innocent III sent the pallium to Bulgarian Archbishop Vazul of Tyrnovo.[141] Cardinal Leo, the papal legate, took the diadem to Kajolan,[142] ordained Archbishop Vazul primate of Bulgaria, together with two archbishops and four bishops, anointed and crowned Kajolan king.[143] It was in such a manner that Kajolan became king of Bulgaria, and made his peace with King Emery in 1204.[144]

NOTES

1. Cf. *Chronicon pictum*, cc. 171 and 172, in Emericus Szentpétery (ed.), *Scriptores rerum Hungaricum*, 2 vols. (Budapest, 1937-1938), cited hereafter as *SSH*, I, 462f; on the Chronicle, see Elemér Mályusz, "A Képes Krónika kiadásai [Editions of the Illuminated Chronicle]," in János Horváth and György Székely (eds.), *Középkori kútfőink kritikus kérdései* [Critical Problems Concerning the Medieval Hungarian Historical Sources], vol. I of *Memoria saeculorum Hungariae* (Budapest, 1974), cited hereafter as *Kútfőink*, 167ff; Gyula Kristó, *História és kortörténet a Képes Krónikában* [History and the Contemporary Record in the Chronicle] (Budapest, 1977); C.A. Macartney, *The Medieval Hungarian Historians* (Cambridge, 1953), 133ff., and his observations on the "Buda Chronicle," *ibid.*, 111ff.; Cyril Horváth, *A régi magyar irodalom története* [History of Old Hungarian Literature] (Budapest, 1899), 26ff.; on the background of the mid-fourteenth century Chronicle, see Desző Dercsényi, *Nagy Lajos kora* [The Age of Louis the Great of Hungary] (Budapest, n.d. [1941]; reprint 1990), 61ff.; M. Ferdinándy, "Ludwig I von Ungarn, 1342-82," *Südost Forschungen*, 21 (1972), 41ff.

2. See Desző Dercsényi (ed.), *Chronicon pictum: Képes Krónika*, 2 vols. (Budapest, 1963), vol. I (facsimile), fol. 61b.

3. *Ibid.*, fol. 61. Depiction of the coronation scenes in the Chronicle seems to be schematic; it is always two high clergymen who place the crown upon the king's head. See Ilona Berkovits, *La miniatura ungherese nel periodo degli Angioni* (Rome, 1947), 6ff. Drawings and text do not always coincide; the miniaturist had to be aware of details in Hungarian history, such as historic legends that were only preserved in oral tradition, and he painted illuminations not necessarily coherent with the preserved (i.e., written) text. Cf. D. Dercsényi, "The Treasures of Louis the Great [of Hungary]," *Hungarian Quarterly*, 6 (1940), 120ff; idem, *Nekcsei Dömötör bibliája a washingtoni Library of Congress-ben* [D. Nekcsei's Bible in the Library of Congress] (Budapest, 1942) - a repr. from *MKSz*, 1942, 113ff. The illuminator's country background scenes remind one of the approach taken by Giotto; cf. G. Holmes, *Florence, Rome, and the Origins of the Renaissance* (Oxford, 1986), 216ff.; Heinrich Wölfflin, *Classic Art*, trans. Peter and Linda Murray, 5th ed. (London, 1994), 5f., and 5, n. 1. The illuminator drew mountain scenes in a cubistic, dreary manner; the terrain was dried out, broken up, as if shattered by an earthquake; he used vegetation and plants as decorative elements in a manner similar to the painters in Siena in the thirteenth century. Cf. Julius Herrmann, *Die italienischen Handschriften des Dugento und Trecento* (Vienna, 1930), 288ff.

4. Dercsényi, *Chronicon pictum*, I, fol. 62a.

5. *SSH*, I, 463,8-13.

6. Dercsényi, *Chronicon*, I, fol. 62a. For the royal writs, cf. E. Szentpétery and I. Borsa (eds.), *Regesta regum stirpis Arapdianae critico-diplomatica*, 2 vols. (Budapest, 1923-1987), cited hereafter as *RA*, nn. 168 to 212, though n. 212 is only known from an answer of Pope Innocent III to the Hungarian king; nn. 213-216a were writs reissued by Andrew II. Only one writ, *RA*, n. 209, referred to the Fourth Crusade - where Emery thanked the pontiff for reprimanding the crusaders for

having taken Zara by force; the king also asked for a compensation, Gusztáv Wenczel (ed.), *Árpádkori új Okmánytár* [New Collection of Documents of the Árpád Age], 12 vols. (Pest, 1860-74), cited hereafter as *ÁUO*, VI, 239f.

7. *SSH*, I, 463,11-12.

8. *Ibid.*, I, 463, note 4; "Chronicon Zagrabiense," c. 16, *ibid.*, I, 211,5-9; Macartney, 109f.

9. "... in ecclesia Agriensi;" *SSH*, I, 463,12-13.

10. *Ibid.*, II, 41,19-22 - not the be confused with the "Annales Posonienses," *ibid.*, I, 127; it carries no entries on this. Macartney, 32f., and 84f.; Polycarp Radó, *Libri liturgici manuscripti bibliothecarum Hungariae* (Budapest, 1947), 40, fol. 9-9', and note 2.

11. Henrici von Müglen, "Ungarnchronik," c. 60, *SSH*, II, 205,5; Macartney, 144ff.

12. *SSH*, II, 205,6.

13. *Ibid.*, II, 205,8; compare with Chronicle, *ibid.*, I, 463,13.

14. *Ibid.*, I, 646,4.

15. *Ibid.*, II, 205,10.

16. Dercsényi, *Chronicon*, fol. 62b.

17. *SSH*, I, 463,17 - 464,2.

18. Dercsényi, *Chronicon*, fol. 62a; Z.J. Kosztolnyik, "A View of the History in the Writings of Gerhoch of Reichersberg and in the Medieval Hungarian Chronicles," *Die ungarische Sprache und Kultur in Donauraum: Vorlesungen des II Internationalen Kongresses für Hungarologie, Wien, 1986* (Vienna-Budapest, 1989), 513ff.

19. Letter of Pope Innocent III, dated November 5, 1203, in August Potthast (ed.), *Regesta pontificum Romanorum*, 2 vols. (Berlin, 1875), n. 2017; for text, cf. J.P. Migne (ed.), *Patrologiae cursus completus, series latina*, 221 vols. (Paris, 1844-55), cited hereafter as *MPL*, 215, 170d, and in Georgius Fejér (ed.), *Codex diplomaticus Hungariae ecclesiasticus ac civilis*, 44 vols. (Budae, 1829-44), cited hereafter as *CD*, II, 415. Helene Tillman, *Papst Innocenz III* (Bonn, 1954), 62ff.

20. *SSH*, I, 463,15.

21. Cf. Chronicle, cc. 160, 167, and 169, *SSH*, I, 446,23; 460,13; and 461,4-5 and 20, respectively; compare with "Zagreb Chronicle," c. 12, *ibid.*, II, 210,5 and with the "Annales Posonienses," anno 1172, *ibid.*, I, 127,7. Interestingly, Simon de Keza, *Chronica Ungarorum*, c. 67, depicted Ladislas II as anti-king - *ibid.*, I, 183,17-18: "Ladislaus dux dibi usurpat regnum et coronam," and made no mention of Ladislas III: "Post Belam vero regnavit Emiricus [sic] filius eius. Sed post hunc regnavit Andreas;" *ibid.*, I, 184,1-2.

22. Dercsényi, *Chronicon*, II, 22ff.

23. *Ibid.*, I, fol. 62b.

24. *Ibid.*, I, fol. 62a.

25. Cf. Anonymus [P. dictus magister], *Gesta Ungarorum*, prologus, *SSH*, I, 33,43; Macartney, 59ff; Loránd Szilágyi, "Az Anonymus-kutatás eredményei és problémái [The Outcome and Remaining Questions in Search of the Hungarian Anonymus]," *Századok*, 123 (1989), 273ff. - scheduled for publication in 1948!

Jenő Pintér, *Magyar irodlomtörténet* [History of Hungarian Literature], 8 vols. (Budapest, 1930-41), I, 211ff.; János Horváth, *Árpádkori latinnyelvü irodalmunk stílusproblémái* [Stylistic Questions Concerning the Latin Language Literature of the Árpádian Age] (Budapest, 1954), 196ff.

26. Péter Váczy, "Anonymus és kora [Anonymus and his Age]," Horváth and Székely, *Kútfőink*, 13ff.; Gy. Kristó, "Szempontok Anonymus gestájának megitéléséhez [Some Remarks on Anonymus' Gesta]," *Acta historica Szegediensis*, 66 (1979), 45ff.

27. Cf. *CD*, II, 358; the reply from Emery, *ÁUO*, VI, 198ff.: "iniurias Maiestatis nostrae a falsi principibus nostris."

28. *SSH*, I, 33,5-10; Kosztolnyik, art. cit., 516ff.

29. He writes about relations between king and nobles, *SSH*, I, 33,10-12, basing his data on written evidence, he says, *ibid.*, I, 34,2-4.

30. *Ibid.*, I, 40,19, and c. 6; Macartney, 68.

31. "VII principalis personae ... viri nobiles genere;" *SSH*, I, 40,14-15; "per genere," *SSH*, "labores eorum acquire possent ... nemo eorum expers fieret;" *ibid.*, I, 40,26-27.

32. *Ibid.*, I, 41,1.

33. "... quod ipsi et filii eorum nunquam a consilio ducis et honore regni omnino privarentur;" *ibid.*, I, 41,2-3.

34. The reason why he remained so stubborn may be seen from one of his writs, dated 1199, to Rome - cf. *ÁUO*, VI, 198ff.; *RA*, n. 187, and from his letter, dated 1204, to Innocent III, *RA*, n. 212, the contents of which may be derived from a papal writ, Potthast, n. 2284; August Theiner (ed.), *Vetera monumenta Slavorum meridionalium historica*, vol. I (Rome, 1863), 35.

35. On Béla III's self-assured attitude, see, for example, his assize of 1181 on written petitions to be submitted to his court, *RA*, n. 130.

36. Compare Anonymus, c. 57, with art. 3 of the "Blood Oath," - *SSH*, I, 113ff., and I, 40f.

37. *Ibid.*, I, 34,4-5.

38. Anonymus, c. 6.

39. *Ibid.*, I, 40,19.

40. If the "Blood Oath" was a Scythian custom, the Magyars, too, could have lived by it - Macartney, 68.

41. On Scythian background, see F.K. Prümm, *Religionsgeschichliches für den Raum der altchristlichen Welt* (Rome, 1954), 799f., and György Györffy, *Napkelet felfedezése: Julianus, Plano Carpini és Rubruk utijelentései* [In Search of the Orient: The Traveler Accounts of Julian, Plano Carpini and Rubruck] (Budapest, 1965), 73; R. Hennig, *Terrae incognitae*, 4 vols. (Leiden, 1944-56), III, 24ff. and 47ff.

42. Emery's private tutor was Bernard of Perugia, a learned person, who had visited Hungary before as a papal legate - cf. Thomas of Spaleto, *Historia Salonitarum*, in J.G. Schwandtner (ed.), *Scriptores rerum Hungaricum vetera ac genuini*, 3 vols. (Vienna, 1746-48), III, 532ff., esp. 567, c. 23; *Monumenta spectantia historiam Slavorum meridionalium*, 48 vols. (Zagreb, 1868-1918), cited

18

hereafter as *MSL*; also, in G.H. Pertz (ed.), *Monumenta Germaniae historica, Scriptores*, 30 vols. (Hannover, 1854, etc.), cited hereafter as *MGHSS*, XXIX, 575 (c. 24!), who must have given Emery a good education - cf. I. Nagy (ed.) *Hazai Okmánytár* [Domestic Documents], 8 vols. (Györ-Budapest, 1865-91), cited hereafter as *HO*, II, 1f.

43. E.H. Kantorowicz, *The King's Two Bodies: A Study in Medieval Political Theology* (Princeton, 1957), 87ff.

44. F.G. Karsai dated it mid-thirteenth century - see his "Ki volt Anonymus? [Anonymus' Identity]," Horváth and Székely, *Kútfőink*, 39ff. On the French background, see Karl Hampe, *Das Hochmittelalter*, 5th rev. ed. (Cologne-Graz, 1963), 253ff.; Kosztolnyik, art. cit., 517.

45. See, for example, the writ of Andrew II of 1206, *RA*, n. 225; text in *HO*, VI, 6, or *CD*, III-2, 464 (abbr.).

46. Cf. Albericus clericus Austriensis, "Gesta Friderici," in *Fontes rerum Austricarum*, Abt. 1: *Scriptores*, 10 vols. (Vienna, 1855 etc.), cited hereafter as FFRA, V, 88, though the work attributed to him "gar kein einheitliches Werk sei, sondern aus drei Teilen bestehe," the third part of which was incorporated into the "Chronicle of Magnus of Reichersberg," - Alfons Lhotsky, *Quellenkunde zur mittelalterlichen Geschichte Österreichs* (Cologne-Graz, 1963), 226.

47. Cf. Ferdinandus Knauz (ed.), *Monumenta Ecclesiae Strigoniensis*, 2 vols. (Strigonii, 1873-74), I, 139ff., 148, 157; since 1185, he was the archbishop of Esztergom, *RA*, n. 129.

48. In a 1188 writ of Béla III, Moch was listed as reeve of Nyitra, *RA*, n. 147, and in a falsified writ of the same year, he was named as the royal Palatine, *RA*, n. 152; *ÁUO*, VI, 183.

49. Albericus Trium Fontium, "Chronicon," anno 1196: "moritur in coena Domini, ... de cuiys potiontione contra quendam episcopum Calanum orta suscipio;" *MGHSS*, XXIII, 873; on Alberic, see W. Wattenbach, *Deutschlands Geschichtsquellen im Mittelalter*, 2 vols., 6th ed. (Berlin, 1893-94), II, 461ff.; Z.J. Kosztolnyik, *From Coloman the Learned to Béla III (1095-1196): Hungarian Domestic Policies and Their Impact Upon Foreign Affairs* (New York, 1987), 217f.

50. "Zagreb Chronicle," c. 15, *SSH*, I, 211,3-4, and c. 16; *MGHSS*, XXV, 354,31-36; Lhotsky, 196f.; Spaleto, c. 23. On the last days of Béla III, cf. the letters of Innocent III, *CD*, II, 311ff. and 412; the pontiff praised the memory of Béla III - Potthast, n. 2900; *MPL*, 214, 227ac. For recent editions of earlier portions of the register, see O. Hageneder and A. Haidacher (eds.), *Die Register Innocenz' III, 1 Pontifikatsjahr (1198-99)*, Publikationen des österreichischen Kulturinstitutes in Rom, Abt. II, Reihe 1, vol. I (Graz-Cologne, 1964), cited hereafter as *Register 1*, n. 270; and O. Hageneder, W. Maleczek, and A. Strnad (eds.), *Die register Innocenz' III, 2 Pontifikatsjahr (1199-1200)*, II - 1, vol. II (Rome-Vienna, 1979), cited hereafter as *Register 2*. See further F. Kempf, *Die Register Innocenz' III, eine paläographisch-diplomatische Untersuchung*, vol. IX of *Miscellanea historiae pontificae* (Rome, 1945), 45ff.; W. Imkamp, *Das Kirchenbild Innocenz' III (1198-1216)*, vol. 22 of *Päpste und Papsttum* (Stuttgart, 1983), 71ff.

51. See J. Koller, *Historia episcopatus Quinqueecclesiarum*, 3 vols. and vol. 7 (Posonii, 1782-8‹ Pest, 1812), I, 304; St. Katona, *Historia critica regum Hungariae stirpis Arpadianae*, 7 vols. (Pest-Buda, 1779-81), IV, 372f.

52. On Emery's previous coronation, see *MGHSS*, XVII, 202, anno 1182; on the second coronation, Katona, IV, 369 and T. Smiciklas (ed.), *Codex diplomaticus regni Croatiae, Dalmatiae et Slavoniae*, 14 vols. (Zagreb, 1904-16), II, 267.

53. Cf. *Chronica regia Coloniensis*, ed. G. Waitz, SSrG (Hannover, 1880; reprinted 1978), 168, anno 1199; Wattenbach, II, 441ff.

54. Innocent III to Andrew, January 29, 1198, Potthast, n. 4; *Register 1*, n. 10; Katona, IV, 477; a chronicler spoke of "rege Hungariae et regina," to imply that Béla III had already been dead, and Emery still not married - *MGHSS*, XXVI, 509, anno 1197; O. Hageneder, "Exkommunikation und Thronfolgerlust bei Innocenz III," *Römische historische Mitteilungen*, 2 (1959), 9ff.

55. *SSH*, I, 417,15-27; Z.J. Kosztolnyik, *Five Eleventh Century Hungarian Kings: Their Policies and Their Relations with Rome* (New York, 1981), 104. Did Béla III, former heir of the Byzantine throne, plan to go on a crusade because he wanted to gain thereby the Byzantine throne? Idem, *From Coloman*, 207 ff.

56. Béla II had died in 1196 - "Continuatio Cremifanensis," anno 1196, *MGHSS*, IX, 549; Guilelmus abbas S. Thomae, "Geneologia Ingeburgis reginae," *ibid.*, XXIX, 165; the "Zagreb Chronicle" gave the wrong date, *SSH*, I, 211,1-2. In 1198, Prince Andrew defeated King Emery - cf. I. Kukuljevic (ed.), *Codex diplomaticus Croatiae, Dalmatiae, Slavoniae*, 2 vols. (Zagreb, 1874-75), II, 192.

57. Potthast, n. 16; *Register 1*, n. 7.

58. *Ibid.*, n. 10; Potthast, n. 4; *CD*, II, 313; Katona, IV, 477 and V, 300 (fragment only).

59. Potthast, nn. 256 and 290, further, nn. 283 and 285; *Register 1*, nn. 251 and 270; further, nn. 269 and 271; on papal relations with monarchs, see F. Kempf, *Papsttum und Kaisertum bei Innocenz III*, vol. XIX of *Miscellanea historiae pontificiae* (Rome, 1954), 231ff.; M. Maccarone, "Innocenzo III prima del pontificato," *Archivio della Romana di Storia Patria*, 66 (1943), 59ff.

60. "Chronicon Austriacum," anno 1174, in A. Rauch (ed.), *Rerum Austricarum Scriptores*, 3 vols. (Vienna, 1793-94), cited hereafter as *RASS*, II, 225; "Continuatio Claustroneuburgensis II," *MGHSS*, IX, 616; Erna Patzelt, *Österreich bis zum Ausgang der Babenbergerzeit* (Vienna, 1947), 145ff.

61. *Chronica regia*, 169, anno 1199; *CD*, II, 319; A. Huber, "Studien über die Geschichte Ungarns im Zeitalter der Árpáden," *Archiv für österreichische Geschichte*, 65 (1883-84), 153ff., esp. 156ff.

62. *CD*, II, 318; Kukuljevic, II, 199; Katona, IV, 488. Again, Kukuljevic, I, 193 - in favor of Zagreb, though one is to recall that in 1198, King Emery had also confirmed the privileges of Zagreb that originated with his predecessor! Cf. *RA*, n. 178, in ref. to *CD*, II, 343; also, Potthast, n. 760 (Pope Gregory IX), and *ÁUO*, I, 231.

63. *RA*, n. 84; *CD*, II, 363; Katona, IV, 560f., and, compare to *RA*, n. 193, *CD*, II, 386; Katona, IV, 613.

64. *RA*, n. 173; *CD*, II, 329.

65. *RA*, n. 175; *CD*, II, 325.

66. *RA*, n. 177; *CD*, II, 324; Prince Andrew also issued such a writ - Knauz, I, 156.

67. *RA*, n. 169; *CD*, II, 308; Katona, IV, 466.

68. Spaleto, c. 24; *ÁUO*, VI, 179ff.; *CD*, II, 272ff.

69. Kukuljevic, I, 162; according to a writ of Kulin, Bosnia was, really, not that independent - *ÁUO*, I, 349f.

70. "... in terra regis Ungarici, videlicet in Bosnia," to quote Wolkan, ruler of Serbia - see Kukuljevic, II, 216; Theiner, I, 204 (anno 1247!); *CD*, II, 372.

71. Perhaps, as a countermeasure, Emery affirmed the privileges of the Spaleto cathedral chapter - *RA*, n. 171; Katona, IV, 489.

72. Next to the kingdom, Béla III "dedit et filiam principis Antiochiae" to his son Emery - *Chronica regia*, 168; Katona, IV, 336ff.

73. See the letter of Innocent III of January 29, 1198, Potthast, n. 4; *Register 1*, n. 4.

74. Innocent III on June 15, 1198, *ibid.*, n. 271; Potthast, n. 285; *CD*, II, 312.

75. *RA*, n. 187; *ÁUO*, IV, 198ff.

76. Innocent III had referred to him in his writ of June 21, 1199 - see Potthast, n. 748 and n. 749; *Register 2*, n. 89 and nn. 96, 97; *CD*, II, 358ff.; Katona, IV, 552f.

77. Archbishop Saul of Kalocsa had Elvin excommunicated, but the latter pretended submission, whereupon the archbishop sent him to Rome - Potthast, n. 283; *Register 1*, n. 269; Katona, IV, 517f.

78. *CD*, II, 313f.

79. Based upon a papal writ addressed to Emery, dated February 4, 1199, in Potthast, n. 591; *Register 1*, nn. 546 and 549; A. Luchaire, *Innocent III*, 6 vols. (Paris, 1904-08), V, 66, with the wrong date - as if it were sent to Emery.

80. *ÁUO*, VI, 198ff., esp. 199f.

81. *Ibid.*, VI, 199,3-17.

82. *CD*, II, 358.

83. *ÁUO*, VI, 199,18-21; "quicquid itaque contra Deum et honorem Ecclesiae idem episcopus nos commissione vobis dixerit, non credatis." *Ibid.*, VI, 199,21-23.

84. *Ibid.*, VI, 200; *CD*, II, 358f.

85. *RA*, n. 184; *CD*, II, 363.

86. *Ibid.*, III-2, 440f.

87. "... ib valle Raad;" *ibid.*

88. "Chronicon Austriacum," in Rauch, *RASS*, II, 229; "Cont. Lambacensis," *MGHSS*, IX, 556, anno 1199; "Cont. Claustroneoburgensis III," *ibid.*, IX, 634, anno 1199; further, *ibid.*, IX, 634, 629, anno 1199.

89. *RA*, n. 181, and mentioned by Innocent III, Potthast, n. 16; *Register 1*, n. 7; *CD*, II, 316.

90. Emery to Rome, *RA*, n. 187; *ÁUO*, VI, 198ff.

91. Innocent III to Abbot John of Pannonhalma, Potthast, n. 16; *supra*, n. 89.

92. *ÁUO*, VI, 200f.

93. *CD*, II, 369f. and 376; Kukuljevic, II, 202 and 205, issued at Zara, in the name of Emery, with reference to "atque Andreae incliti viri," without his princely title.

94. Potthast, n. 290; *Register 1*, n. 270.

95. Potthast, nn. 748 and 749; *Register 2*, nn. 89, 96, and 97.

96. Potthast, n. 749; *Register 2*, nn. 89, 96, 97; *CD*, II, 361; on Heliodorus, see II Maccabees, 3. See also Carolus Péterffy (ed.), *Sacra concilia Ecclesiae Romanae Catholicae in regno Hungariae celebrata*, 2 vols. (Vienna, 1742), I, 84ff.

97. "De eo autem, quod Colochensis Archiepiscopus, ut audivimus, conqueritur, quia ipsum ad praesentiam nostram cum litteris vestris accedere non permissimus; ... non in contemptum Romanae Ecclesiae hoc facimus;" *RA*, n. 187; *ÁUO*, VI, 200.

98. Potthast, n. 972; August Theiner (ed.), *Vetera Monumenta historiam Hungariae sacram illustrantia*, 2 vols. (Rome, 1859-60, reprinted in Osnabrück, 1968), cited hereafter as *VMH*, n. 19; Vilmos Fraknói, *Magyarország és a Szentszék* [Hungary and the Holy See], 3 vols. (Budapest, 1901-03), I, 37ff. On V. Fraknói (1843-1924), see Olga R. Takács, "Róma ellenállhatatlan ... Vonások két századvégi pap-tudós portréjához [Rome is Irresistible. Some Remarks on the Profiles of Two Priest Scholars of the End of the Century]," *Vigilia*, 57 (1992), 437ff.; the other scholar was Arnold Ipolyi (1823-86).

99. Truce negotiated by the learned papal legate, Gregory of Sancta Maria in Aquino, with the aid of Archbishop Conrad of Mainz - *ÁUO*, I, 88; August Theiner (ed.), *Vetera monumenta Slavorum meridionalium*, vol. I (Rome, 1863), cited hereafter as VMSM, I, 47, implied that the writ cannot be located. On the negotiations, see also *MGHSS*, IX, 620, anno 1200, and Rauch, *RASS*, II, 229.

100. Potthast, nn. 1845 and 2283; *MPL*, 215, 160c, and 413ff., and 215, 197c.; *Chronica regia*, 169.

101. VMSM, n. 156.

102. *Ibid.*, n. 19.

103. *RA*, n. 186.

104, *MGHSS*, XXIX, c. 24; Horváth and Székely, *Kútfőink*, 156ff.

105, *RA*, n. 193; *CD*, II, 386ff., confirmed by Gregory IX in 1227 - cf. Potthast, n. 7960; *VMH*, n. 152.

106. Innocent III permitted King Emery to temporarily retain twenty noble knights at home, Potthast, n. 290; *Register 1*, n. 270.

107. See the identical texts in *MGHSS*, IX, 620 and 634, and compare with Innocent III's letter of January 1, 1200, Potthast, n. 934; *ÁUO*, VI, 205ff.

108. *MPL*, 215, 240ac; *RA*, n. 208; further, Potthast,, n. 1797; *MPL*, 214, 971bc; *CD*, II, 389.

109. Innocent III on March 11, 1203, Potthast, n. 1864; *MPL*, 215, 29; and the papal writ to Bernard of Spaleto, dated June 21, 1202, Potthast, n. 1768; *MPL*, 214, 1108f.; *ÁUO*, VI, 225ff. On background, see I. Bekker (ed.), Nicethae Choniatae *Historia* (Bonn, 1835), cited hereafter as *CB*, 704f., or I.A. van Dieten (ed.), Nicethae Choniatae *Historia* (Berlin-New York, 1975), 531,72 - 532,20; Gy. Moravcsik (ed.), *Fontes Byzantini historiae Hungaricae aevo ducum et regum ex stirpe Arpad descendentium* (Budapest, 1984), 295f. and 296, note 40; K.

Krumbacher, *Geschichte der byzantinischen Literatur*, 2nd ed. (Munich, 1897), 91ff. and 281ff.

110. Vulkan, king of Dalmatia, to Pope Innocent III, referring to their family relationship, "vestri generosi sanguinis affinitatem habere cognovimus;" Smiciklas, II, 333, and compare with Potthast, n. 2283; *MPL*, 215, 413ff., esp. 415b.

111. *ÁUO*, VI, 85f.

112. A. Huber, *Österreichische Rechtsgeschichte*, revised ed. Alfons Dopsch (Vienna, 1901), 122.

113. *ÁUO*, VI, 226f., closing paragraph.

114. *RA*, n. 208 (anno 1203); *CD*, II, 410f.; further, Innocent III to Archbishop Basilius of Zagora, Potthast, n. 1776; *ÁUO*, VI, 232ff. Thomas of Spaleto became quite irritated at the Bogomils at Zara - "Chronica," c. 26, *MHSM*, XXVI, 93ff., c. 26 (in Schwandtner, III, 244ff., c. 25!).

115. Anonymus, *Gesta*, that he "quondam ... Bele [III] regis Hungarie notarius," fell out of the good graces of the king's son and successor - *SSH*, I, 33f.

116. *RA*, n. 187; *ÁUO*, VI, 198ff., may reflect the king's frame of mind.

117. "Quicquid itaque contra Deum et honorem Eccelesiae idem episcopus nos commisisse vobis dixerit, non credatis;" *ibid.*, VI, 199, and compare to the king's letter to Innocent III, *ibid.*, VI, 239f.; Kantorowicz, 207ff.; a similar concept expressed in a letter of Gerbert of Reims to Otto III - cf. J. Havet (ed.), *Lettres de Gerbert* (Paris, 1889), 178, epistola 183.

118. *RA*, n. 208.

119. *CD*, II, 437.

120. *RA*, n. 208.

121. Innocent III to Emery, "qui terram megaiupani ad suum dominium revocavit;" Potthast, n. 1797; *MPL*, 214, 971bc; Choniates, Dieten, 531f. (*CB*, 704f.).

122. Papal complaints addressed to Emery, Potthast, nn. 1142, 2183; *CD*, II, 378f., and *MPL*, 215, 413ff., respectively; Emery's letter, *RA*, n. 208, as cited above, was probably his reply to the papal writ of November 21, 1202, Potthast, n. 1768; *MPL*, 214, 1108; C. Baronius et al, *Annales ecclesiastici*, ed. A. Theiner, vols. XIX-XXIII (Barri Ducis, 1869-80), anno 1202, implied that Emery wrote his letter in 1202. On Baronius, cf. C.K. Pullapilly, *Caesar Baronius, Counter-Reformation Historian* (Notre Dame - London, 1975), 144ff.

123. *ÁUO*, VI, 227f; Fraknói, I, 39f.; M.F. Font, "Ungarn, Bulgarien und das Papsttum um die Wende vom 12 zum 13 Jahrhundert," repr. from *Hungaro-Slavica*, 188, 259ff.

124. Caloioannes - written as Gubanus, see the letter of King Emery, *RA*, n. 201, though only known from the papal response, Potthast, n. 1755, and compare to n. 1775; *ÁUO*, VI, 229ff.

125. Choniates, Dieten, 368,38-46; *CB*, 481; Georgius Acropolita, *Annales*, c. 11, in J.P. Migne (ed.), *Patrologiae cursus completus, series graeca*, 166 vols. (Paris, 1854-57), cited hereafter as MPG, 140, 1007f.; Moravcsik, *Fontes*, 297f.; Krumbacher, 286ff.

126. Choniates, Dieten, 371ff.; *CB*, 458ff.; for background, compare with Potthast, n. 2282; *CD*, II, 432ff.; *MPL*, 215, 410ff.; Katona, IV, 716f.

127. Knauz, I, 163. Hún-Pázmány, (*CD*, III-2, 263), Thomas (*ÁUO*, XI, 31f.), and Alexander Győr (*CD*, III-1, 62) were mentioned as the king's military commanders.

128. *CD*, II, 409f.

129. King Emery claimed five "Bulgarian" bishoprics "de confinio Bulgariae," *ÁUO*, VI, 281ff., esp. 283, though the bishopric of Nis was definitely Bulgarian - *ibid.*, VI, 281.

130. Letter of Innocent III, dated November 9, 1202, *CD*, II, 393, though Potthast, n. 3820, dated it 1209, and made a correction: "ubi perperam ad a. 1209, deleatur regestum 3820" (II, 2045).

131. Cf. L.A. Muratori (ed.), *Rerum Italicarum Scriptores*, 28 vols. (Milan, 1723-51, and recent reprint), cited hereafter as Muratori, III, 524, "ad quartum." Potthast, nn. 2282 and 2283; *MPL*, 215, 410f.; and the papal reply to Emery's previous writ, Potthast, n. 2284; *CD*, II, 435ff.; and the papal letter addressed to Joannitius, *ÁUO*, VI, 201f.

132. As it might be concluded from the letter of "Little John," Joannitius, to Rome, and the papal reply, *ÁUO*, VI, 281ff. and 284f.; Potthast, nn. 2284 and 2229.

133. Katona, I, 726, in reference to Potthast, n. 2284.

134. Katona, IV, 714ff.

135. Cf. King Emery's letter, in Katona, IV, 628f., anno 1204.

136. Potthast, n. 2282, and the letter of Archbishop Basil of Ternova on being consecrated by Cardinal Leo, *ÁUO*, VI, 294f.

137. Potthast, n. 2283.

138. Muratori, *RISS*, III, 523ff, "ad tertium;" and the papal bull, making arrangements for a royal coronation, *ÁUO*, VI, 265ff.; letter from Joannitius requesting the diadem, *ibid.*, VI, 292ff.

139. Potthast, n. 2290; *MPL*, 215, 427ac; Katona, IV, 731f., and Potthast, n. 2284; Muratori, *RISS*, III, 524, "ad tertium."

140. *ÁUO*, VI, 227; *MPL*, 215, 229ff.; Potthast, n. 1775; *MPL*, 214, 1112f., and 214, 1113f.

141. Potthast, n. 1775; *ÁUO*, VI, 288; *MPL*, 215, 294ab+*CD*.

142. *ÁUO*, VI, 292ff.; VMSM, I, 39f.

143. *ÁUO*, VI, 294f.; *MPL*, 215, 553f.

144. *ÁUO*, VI, 281f.; *MPL*, 215, 290ff.; for a different papal point of view, cf. Potthast, n. 3109; *MPL*, 215, 1162. Vulk's son George held the title "King of Zeta and Dioclea" until 1208, though real power rested with Grand Reeve Stephen, who had been acknowledged as king by the curia in 1217 - *ÁUO*, VI, 281ff.

2. *King Emery and the Fourth Crusade*

> ...dux Veneciarum, vir prudentissimus,
> eosdem adiit, plurima munera optulit
> et omnem inopiam illorum sublevare
> promisit, si ad expugnandam quandam
> civitatem regis Ungarie nomine Izarim
> cum eo proficisci dispenerent.
>
> *Chronica regia, Cont. III, a. 1201*

In order to understand the background of events discussed here, one has to realize that the German emperor, Henry VI, had himself entertained the idea of a crusade against Byzantium. The anti-Byzantine plan of the German imperial court did not result from a hastily conceived concept; it was his father's intention that Henry VI wished to carry out, as it may be perceived from a letter, dated 1189, of Frederick Barbarossa addressed to him from Philiopolis.[1]

During the reign of Isaac II Angelos of Byzantium, the emperor had already requested the surrender of the region from Dyarrachium to Thessalonica by the Byzantine court, an area that had previously been held by the Normans in Sicily, but afterwards reconquered by the Byzantines.[2] As if to underline the serious nature of the German request, Philip of Swabia, the younger brother of Henry VI, had married Irene, daughter of Isaac II Angelos.[3] Isaac II had, however, been dethroned and blinded, and his brother, Alexios (now, Alexios III) had justifiably feared the wrath of the German court.[4]

The aim of the German crusade was the conquest of what was still known as the Byzantine Empire, as well as occupation of the near East. According to a German chronicler, the petition made by the ruler of Cyprus to Henry VI for a royal title - the ruler of Cyprus had promised perpetual loyalty to the German emperor's court - served the emperor's interests.[5] What the German court had not taken into consideration, however, was the change in papal politics initiated by the succession of Innocent III to the throne of St. Peter.[6]

The papal curia now became an ally of the Byzantine emperor, as if the "Greek problem" had lost its significant ecclesiastical and religious character.[7] It was imperative from the papal point of view to retain an interest in the survival of what had been the Byzantine state.[8]

The German court made serious demands on Byzantium. Only for the payment of an immense sum of money were they prepared to relinquish their goal - rather, to delay their planned invasion of the city. In order to gain time to redeem his cause, Alexios III levied a forced special tax, *alemanikon*, upon his subjects, a portion of which had to be used for rebuilding the military defenses of the shrunken empire.[9] But Henry VI had unexpectedly died the night before the German fleet had gathered at Messina in preparation of the naval attack on Byzantium, in the summer of 1197.[10]

The result of this tense development was that the Comneni dynasty had also aimed at gaining "world" predominance in the eastern half of, or even in the entire Mediterranean basin. The Comneni wanted to replace the Hohenstaufen family in European politics. As Alexios III wrote to Rome, *they* (the Roman See and the Byzantine empire, which had been in continuous existence since Justinian the Great) must unite against their common opponent, the upstart Hohenstaufen court.[11]

The new pontiff, Innocent III, held a different opinion. He did not wish to cooperate with the temporal ruler of the schismatic Greek Church, and proposed a church union instead.[12] Were Alexios III to oppose him, the pontiff would seek contact with the dethroned Greek emperor;[13] the wife of the Duke of Swabia was the daughter of Isaac II Angelos.[14] Alexios III, however, showed neither concern, nor much understanding in the matter; in another letter addressed to Pope Innocent III, he argued that the Byzantine emperor represented a higher authority than the Roman pontiff.[15]

During the execution of the papal plan for a crusade,[16] an uninvited third party had made its appearance on the diplomatic scene in the person of Enrico Dandalo, Doge of Venice.[17] The doge had made demands to Byzantium, partly because he wanted to reinstate trading privileges that had been previously held in Byzantium by the Venetian republic and partly for the reason that he had to ascertain that Pisa, the commercial rival of the republic, as well as Genoa, received no preferential trading status with the Byzantine court.[18]

The crusading force that consisted mostly of Franks - Fulk of Neuilly, wandering preacher and papal legate, had done good work[19] - had already assembled near Venice,[20] and Geoffrey of Villa-hardouin signed an agreement with the republic, in that the latter had consented to placing ships and provisions at the disposal of the crusaders for a negotiated sum of money.[21] And yet, when the agreed upon whole amount could not be paid at all by the crusaders, and the doge refused to provide ships and supplies for the crusaders, the latter, lacking financial means and condemned to inactivity, were quite eager to accept a compromise deal from Doge Enrico. Before their scheduled departure for their destination to the Holy Land, the crusaders would take military action against Fort Zara on the Adriatic shore, a fortified Christian city, at that time under the rule of the Christian king of Hungary. They would have to occupy it for the republic. In turn, the doge of Venice would provide services for the crusaders by transporting (and feeding) them across the sea to their destination.[22]

King Emery had been preoccupied with organizing and establishing church influence in Bosnia and Serbia,[23] when the "crusaders" boarded ships at Venice, attacked and occupied Zara - to the great consternation of the Hungarian monarch and the frustrated anger of the papal curia.[24] Although the "crusaders" - at this time the paid mercenaries of Venice - had soon moved away, and the Venetians had cleared the city of Zara after they had demolished its fortifications, and had Zara returned to the Hungarian monarch,[25] the unprovoked and undeclared act of war terminating in the conquest of Zara by a Christian foreign power permanently spoiled the desire of King Emery ever to support the crusading cause of the Roman See.[26]

Although King Emery must have had some satisfaction when the papal curia took a stand against the Frankish military adventurers at Zara,[27] he soon had to realize that only statements were made, because the promised indemnity was not paid, and the curia insisted that the Hungarian king go on a crusade. Rome instructed Arch-bishop Ugrin of Esztergom to crown Ladislas, Emery's son, because the king had to be readied for going on a crusade;[28] in fact, the pontiff warned members of the Hungarian hierarchy to encourage the population to keep faith with, and remain loyal to, the child-king. Evidently, Innocent III had distanced himself from his earlier idea that the Duke of Austria would act as Hungarian regent during the absence of the king (and his brother) from the country; Emery's crowned son would represent royal presence in the country, through the cooperation of trusted nobles, who were loyal to him and to King Emery.[29]

The historian has to take note, though, that Boniface of Montferrat, commander of the crusaders assembled at Venice, took no part in the military operation involving the conquest of Zara.[30] Only two weeks after the event did he arrive in the crusaders' camp with the intention to persuade the republic of Venice to grant a hearing to Alexios, son of Isaac II, the dethroned and blinded emperor of Byzantium. Alexios had been asking for help to restore his father to the imperial throne.[31]

Alexios had great plans and made many promises. He promised, in return for such aid, to redeem the debt the crusaders owed to Venice; to submit to the spiritual jurisdiction of the Roman See; and to richly reward those who had volunteered to fight for his father's restoration to the imperial throne.[32] On the other hand, one should note the statement in the Novgorod Chronicle that said that the "Franks" liked the gold and silver that had been promised them by the son of Isaac, and they had ignored, in the process, the interests of the pope and of the empire - as if to clear the argument that, though the papal curia and the Greek imperial court instigated the crusade, it was the doge of Venice who gained control of its operation.[33]

May the historian also remark that since the participants of the crusading forces were mainly "Franks," not "Germans," and not even Venetians, and since the "Fourth Crusade" had gone astray at its very beginning with the capture by a Christian force of a Christian stronghold, the whole undertaking may be looked upon as a Frankish military move aimed at promoting Franco-Byzantine political-diplomatic and commercial business interests - in the instance identical with those of the previously dethroned Byzantine emperor, Basil II.[34]

The record has it that King Emery and Prince Andrew were not opposed to the restoration of Isaac II to his throne, and Alexios was permitted to travel freely during his sojourn from Swabia to Zara, on territories under Hungarian administration. But Simon de Montfort, his brother Guy, and the Abbot of Vaux-Cerny decided to leave the crusaders; they made their peace with King Emery and journeyed through Hungary to the Holy Land.[35]

Relations between the king of Hungary and the papal curia continued to deteriorate.[36] Rome was prepared and by this time determined to pursue a policy in Serbia and Bulgaria - a policy that undermined the political and diplomatic interests of King Emery.[37] Innocent III would not help the king in gaining ascendancy over the peoples in the Balkans, although he had protected the monarch from his greedy relative, his brother Andrew,[38] and handled with care the king's personal relations with Bishop Boleslav of Vác and Cardinal Leo, the papal legate.[39] But it remained the curia's policy to establish Catholic kingdoms in both Serbia and Bulgaria, thereby to assure religious and political peace in the Balkans under the aegis of the Holy See.[40] Was King Emery's unwillingness to cooperate with the curia the reason why Vulk could not realize his political dream of kingship, and the reason why the papal policy to establish Rome's politico-religious presence in the Balkans had backfired? The Hungarian monarch had lost interest, and made no further attempt at exploiting political-economic and diplomatic options still at his disposal in the Balkans.[41]

Emery followed closely the developments in the German empire. He aided Otto IV against Philip of Swabia, probably under the influence of Otakar I of Bohemia, who was the son of the Czech Vladimir II, because Otakar I had married Constance, a sister of King Emery, in 1199.[42] Earlier, in 1198, Philip of Swabia had named Otakar King of Bohemia, a title Philip soon withdrew,[43] however, on the grounds that Otakar I had turned against him.[44] Certain units of Emery's armed forces had merged with the military forces of Otakar I near the Thuringian border, whereupon Philip staged a counterattack on the Czech ruler in the summer of 1203.[45]

A German chronicler noted that there were some Polish and Russian volunteers (Polowci[orum]; Plawci), and Cumans (Valve) among the army units "sent" by King Emery.[46] The chronicler wrote "volunteers" (*nec deferit ibi illud*), meaning that they were not members of the regular army units of the monarch. They may have been un-rewarded and over-employed mercenaries in the king's service, who paid little attention to their existence.[47]

King Emery had kept delaying his pilgrimage to the Holy Land. He married an Aragonese princess, Constance, the daughter of

Alfonso II;[48] her brother, Peter II the Catholic, was a great troubadour who had died fighting heretics in southern France in 1213.[49] The Hungarian king had offered, as dowry, two royal counties in Hungary to his queen. Were he to die before her, she would inherit both counties, on the condition that she remained in Hungary. Were she to decide to leave the realm, she would receive twelve thousand silver marks in compensation.[50]

Andrew, the king's jealous brother, had also decided to marry. He took Gertrud to wife, a daughter of Bertold IV of Istria-Carinthia, a proud descendant of the Andechs family near Munich; the family had allies and friends at the emperor's court.[51] In reaching a marriage agreement with the leaders of the anti-papal party in the German empire, Prince Andrew had hoped to undermine the power of his royal brother. His father-in-law was the duke of Dalmatia-Croatia, though he referred to himself as the Duke of Meran (seashore of the Adriatic).[52] Bertold's sister was married to Omnod, the Hungarian Grand Reeve. Gertrud's sister, Hedwig, had married a Polish prince.[53] The daughter of Hedwig, Agnes, was the wife (*recte*: according to Canon law, the mistress) of Philip II Augustus of France; she bore him two children.[54]

Another confrontation between Emery and Andrew thus became unavoidable, because Gertrud was a determined woman who cared only for her own family. She had gained full control over her weak husband and persuaded him to behave heedlessly toward his brother, the king.[55] Gertrud wanted to become queen, and encouraged her husband to reach out for the Hungarian crown.[56] When a son, Ladislas (III) was born to Emery and Constance in 1201, Gertrud influenced Andrew to establish the claim that, in accordance with ancient Hungarian constitutional custom, it was the ruling king's grown younger brother - and not the king's own son - who had the right to succeed to the throne.[57]

Pope Innocent III had been aware of the domestic turmoil in Hungary. He wanted to preempt a probably far-spread constitutional-political upheaval in that land by writing to the prince that, were King Emery to die, the successor would have to be Emery's crowned infant son.[58] The papal curia further instructed the archbishop of Esztergom to crown Ladislas during his father's reign, and to compel the king to take the loyalty oath to Rome for his infant son.[59]

Did His Holiness want to make it certain that Emery's son become the political-spiritual vassal of the Holy See?[60] Because of his position as the protector of orphans,[61] and, in the canonical sense, since his father had taken the loyalty oath for him, as the feudal overlord of Ladislas III,[62] Innocent III warned Prince Andrew that upon the death of Emery, the coronation insignia must be available for the coronation of Ladislas III. The pontiff wished to prevent the emergence of unknown pretenders to the throne.[63]

Did Innocent III go too far by writing to the members of the Hungarian hierarchy to remind them that they had to protect the rights of the infant king from any usurper, and to take most seriously the loyalty oath they took to Ladislas (III)?[64]

Two conclusions may be drawn from these papal admonitions. One, King Emery was seriously ill by 1201. The attitude he had assumed toward the Bogomils, and the behavior he had displayed during the papal negotiations with Bulgaria, can only be explained as related to his serious illness.[65] Therefore, the papal curia had to insist that Emery's son and heir inherit the throne, and claim full jurisdiction over the realm under the Hungarian Crown.[66] Second, Rome had no confidence in Prince Andrew, nor did it trust Andrew's German wife and her relatives, among whom the curia had cause to suspect active political opposition to Pope Innocent III.[67] Could this have been the reason why Pope Innocent III encouraged Andrew to leave the realm, and begin the long overdue crusade his father, Béla III, had planned and promised to do?[68]

According to the dates in the papal correspondence, these events had taken place when King Emery was still alive. It is known from a non-papal source that Andrew had, again, revolted against his brother toward the end of Emery's reign, but the king, in order to avoid unnecessary bloodshed, visited, alone, with only a rod in his hand, the camp of the rebels,[69] took Andrew by the hand, led him away from his stunned supporters, then had shackled and imprisoned him in a nearby fort named Kene.[70] Later, he had the princely prisoner transferred to Esztergom, and had Gertrud, Andrew's wife, who most probably had instigated the entire affair, sent back home.[71]

The question remains whether the chronicler had previously used the terminology, and the same scenery, depicting the late confrontation between the two brothers?[72] Had the king, unarmed and unattended, with a bare stick in his hand, actually arrested his brother in a region ("Region Beyond the Drave") that came directly under the administrative control of the prince? In his letter dated November 5, 1203, Innocent III recorded nothing about a confrontation between the king and the prince,[73] although ten months later, in a writ of September 15, 1204, the pontiff had expressed concern about the king, who took the prince captive in a dishonest manner (and without a fight).[74]

King Emery had been ill by this time.[75] He may have suffered a psychological breakdown or from ulcers. Because of his unruly nature, he could not spend even the last few months of his earthly life in peace. In filling the vacancy created by the death of Archbishop Ugrin, the cathedral chapter of Esztergom chose John, archbishop of Kalocsa, as its metropolitan.[76] The king, however, regarded John's suffragan bishop, Kalán of Pécs, as a personal enemy, whom he had also accused of publicly maintaining illicit relations with one of his female relatives.[77] Although Rome responded to the charge, the papal writ sent to Kalán that described the accusations brought against him as untenable, fell into the hands of the monarch, who had the writ confiscated, and the bishop placed under close surveillance.[78]

Emery evidently misunderstood the contents of the papal writ - he seemed to be more concerned with its tone than with the fact that the accusation he had brought against the bishop merited no serious attention by the papal curia - and demanded that Rome conduct a full-scale inquiry. He further instructed the bishops about the case, and asked his boyhood tutor, Bernard, archbishop of Spaleto, to intervene in Rome against Bishop Kalán.[79]

Emery did not live to see the results of the papal inquiry. The papal letter, dated November 22, 1204, had referred to him without actually saying whether he was still alive.[80] Before he had died, Emery had his son, Ladislas, crowned by the archbishop of Kalocsa,[81] although, as if to express doubts about the legality of this coronation, Emery had his brother, Prince Andrew, recalled from exile.[82]

A word of explanation will be in order here. Upon the death of King Emery, Bishop Kalán and his colleagues, Boleslav of Vác and Kalanda of Veszprém, had met to publicly question the canonical status of Archbishop John of Esztergom, on the grounds that earlier, while he was still archbishop of Kalocsa, John had severely attacked the prerogatives of the See of Esztergom.[83]

On his deathbed, Emery had asked Andrew to be the guardian of his son Ladislas (III) during his years of minority.[84] The king developed paranoid schizophrenia: he also had withdrawn all the accusation he had raised against Cardinal Leo, the papal legate, even before the papal curia had made a final decision on this, the Hungaro-Bulgarian question.[85] The dying monarch had assigned from his treasury two-thirds of the money to the disposal of the Knights of the Temple and the Knights of the Hospital;[86] he left one-third of his fortune to the Cistercian abbey at Pilis, with the request that the money remain at the personal disposal of his widow and their son.[87]

The final arrangements made by Emery were completely irrational. They were, in part, reminiscent of his reign, and, in part, served as evidence that he could not grasp and judge political and personal matters clearly toward the end of his life.[88] He was buried at Eger.[89] (Mügeln's record that Emery was buried at Fehérvár is erroneous, based on a misread entry.)[90]

Andrew, acting as regent, had his wife recalled from exile,[91] and withheld the money deposited by Emery for his widow and their son at the Cistercian abbey at Pilis.[92] Because of the oath he took to the deceased monarch, Archbishop John of Esztergom supported the claims of the child king, Ladislas III, to the throne.[93] For that reason - as evidenced by two papal writs addressed to the Hungarian court - Andrew had publicly displayed preference for Kalán, bishop of Pécs, who was the arch-opponent of the archbishop of Esztergom.[94]

Although in his writ of April 27, 1205, Pope Innocent III threatened everyone who dared to oppose Queen Constance and her son, Ladislas III, with excommunication,[95] the dowager Queen had realistically appraised her situation - she and her son fled the country, seeking refuge with Leopold VI of Austria.[96]

Andrew, acting as regent, now demanded that the king, Ladislas III, and the Crown be extradited to him, but Ladislas III had died in Austria, on May 5, 1205.[97] Bishop Peter of Győr had the young king's body taken to Fehérvár for interment.[98] Upon his death, Archbishop John of Esztergom found no legal impediment for crowning Andrew king with the Crown that had been returned by the Duke of Austria to Esztergom.[99]

NOTES

1. See *Chronica regia*, 156f.; J.F. Böhmer (ed.), *Acta imperii selecta* (Innsbruck, 1870), 152; Choniates, *Historia*, in *CB*, 631f.; in Dieten, 478.; G. Ostrogorsky, *Geschichte des byzantinische Staates*, 2nd ed. (Munich, 1952), 330f.

2. Choniates, *CB*, 627f.; Dieten, 475f.

3. *Chronica regia*, 157; W. Norden, *Das Papsttum und Byzanz* (Berlin, 1903, repr. New York, n.d.), 128 and 133; the continuator of Otto of Freising, Otto of Sanblasien (de Sancto Blasio), *Chronica*, ed. A. Hofmister, SSrG (Hannover-Leipzig, 1912), 63 and 66, saying that upon his dethronement, Isaac II had already taken the possibility of German aid into account. Sanblasien is reliable, except his time schedule; see Wattenbach, II, 284f. See further, *Annales Marbacenses*, ed. H. Bloch, SSrG (Hannover-Leipzig, 1907), 64 and 77; Wattenbach, II, 480ff.

4. *Chronica regia*, 203f., and 208ff.; Choniates, *CB*, 593ff.; Dieten, 450,58-452,29.

5. *Annales Marbacenses*, 198f.

6. *Ibid.*, 161f.; see the *Gesta* of Pope Innocent III, *MPL*, 214, vii-ccviii, esp. cc. 7-9, 60-64; see below, note 15. See the papal letter of February 7, 1204, Potthast, n. 2122; *MPL*, 215, 159f.; Norden, 122.

7. *Ibid.*, 122, 130, and 132; *Chronica regia*, 202ff.; Arnold of Lübeck, *Chronica Slavorum*, ed. G.H. Pertz, SSrG (Hannover, 1868; repr. 1978), 241ff. and 245ff.; on Henry VI, *ibid.*, 198f.; Karl Hampe, *Deutsche Kaisergeschichte in der Zeit der Salier und Staufer*, 12th rev. ed., ed. F. Baethgen (Heidelberg, 1968), 232; Th. Toeche, *Kaiser Heinrich VI* (Leipzig, 1867), 352 f.; *VMH*, I, 410.

8. Lübeck, *Chronica*, 241ff.; *Chronica regia*, 199f. and 208ff.; Leo of Armenia had addressed a similar request to Henry VI, but by the time they had crowned him, the emperor was dead, Sanblasien, 51.

9. Choniates, *CB*, 627 and 632; Dieten, 475,76-479,43.

10. *Ibid.*, 479,44-481,94; *CB*, 633 and 635; Sanblasien, 71; L. Bréhier, *L'eglise et l'orient au moyen age: les croisades*, 5th ed. (Paris, 1928), 143; Henry VI died on September 28, 1997 - his death was a tragedy for the Germans - cf. Sanblasien, 71; Hampe, *Kaisergeschichte*, 233: Henry VI might have died of malarial fever; Burchardis Usurpegiensis *Chronicon*, ed. O. Holder-Egger and B. v. Simon, SSrG (Leipzig, 1916), 69, 70, spoke of poison: "interfecisse veneno procurante uxore sua." L. Bréhier, *Vie et mort de Byzance* (Paris, 1946), 365ff.; W. Kienast, *Deutschland und Frankreich in der Kaiserzeit (900-1270)*, vol. IX in 3 parts, 2nd rev. ed., in K. Bosl *et al.* (eds.), *Monographien zur Geschichte des Mittelalters* (Stuttgart, 1974-75), 228ff. and 673f.

11. Cf. the letter, dated February, 1199, of Alexios III to the Roman pontiff, in *Register 2*, n. 201 (210); see further, Potthast, n. 349; *Register 1*, n. 353; G.L. Tafel and G.M. Thomas (eds.), *Urkunden zur älteren Handels- und Wirtschaftsgeschichte der Republic Venedig*, 3 vols., FFRA, Dipl. XII (Vienna, 1856-57), I, 236ff., n. 83; C.M. Brand, *Byzantium Confronts the West, 1180-1204* (Cambridge, MA, 1968), 225f., in answer to the papal writ of mid-August to mid-September, 1198, Potthast, nn. 349 and 359; *Register 1*, n. 353 (and n. 354); Norden, 134; F. Dölger (ed.), *Regesten der Kaiserurkunden des oströmischen Reiches*, Reihe A, Abt. 1-2 (Munich-Berlin, 1924-25), n. 1643; Norden, 134; A. Luchaire, *Innocent III: la question l'orient* (Paris, 1907), 61ff.

12. Pope Innocent III had to instruct the Greek emperor that Alexios III had to defend the Holy Land out of his own resources; the pontiff had asked the Byzantine emperor to send the patriarch, or his representative, to the next church synod (where they also may discuss church union); cf. Potthast, nn. 862 and 863; *Register 2*, nn. 200 (209) and 202 (211); Tafel-Thomas, I, 241ff., n. 84.

13. Potthast, n. 1763; *MPL*, 214, 1123ff., esp. 1124d-1125a; Burckhard, *Chronicon*, 68; A. Hauck, *Der Gedanke der päpstlichen Weltherrschaft bis auf Bonifaz VIII* (Leipzig, 1904), 43; M. Maccarone, "«Potestas directa» e «potestas indirecta» nei teologi del XIIe-XIII secolo," *Sacerdozio e regno da Gregorio VII a Bonifacio VIII*, vol. XVIII of *Miscellanea historiae pontificiae* (Rome, 1954), 27ff. and 33ff.

14. *MPL*, 214, 1124ab; Choniates, *CB*, 635; Dieten, 481; also, *CB*, 548f.; Dieten, 419,91-10; Burckhard, *Chronicon*, 81, 219; Lübeck, *Chronica*, 219; Sanblasien, 63, 70, and 77; *Chronica regia*, 137, 157; Patzelt, 167ff.; Erich Zöllner, *Geschichte Österreichs*, 4th ed. (Munich, 1970), 75ff.; Hugo Hantsch, *Geschichte Österreichs*, 2 vols., 5th rev. ed. (Vienna, 1969), I, 86f.

15. *Register 2*, n. 201 (210); Potthast, nn. 862 and 863; *Register 2*, nn. 209 and 211; "Gesta Innocentii III," in Muratori, *RISS*, III-1, 486ff., or *MPL*, 214, cxxff.; Dölger, *Regesten*, n. 1648; Zöllner, 125.

16. Potthast, n. 347; *Register 1*, n. 334; *ÁUO*, I, 86; Potthast, n. 2473, *MPL*, 215, 595f.; *CD*, II, 455ff.; Tafel-Thomas, XII, 228ff.; H. Grégoire, "The Question of the Diversion of the Fourth Crusade," *Byzantion*, 15 (1940-41), 152ff.

17. Choniates, *CB*, 713f.; Dieten, 538f.; Potthast, n. 347; *Register 1*, n. 336; Ch. Diehl, *Byzance, grandeur, decadence* (Paris, 1920); idem, *Une republique patricienne Venice*, 2nd ed. (Paris, 1928), 17f.; H.E. Mayer, *Geschichte der Kreuzzüge*, 3rd ed. (Stuttgart, 1973), 173; H.E. Queller, *The Fourth Crusade* (Philadelphia, 1977), 36ff.

18. Ricardi "Historia Ducum Venetum," *MGHSS*, XIV, 92ff.; A. Dandalo, "Chronica," Muratori, *RISS*, XII, 321ac; Brand, 200ff.

19. Cf. Roger of Hoveden, *Chronica*, ed. W. Stubbs, R.S. (London, 1868-71), IV, 76f.; Norden, 152ff.; F. Cerone, "Il papa ed i Veneziani nella quarta crociata," *Archivio Veneto*, 36 (1888), 57ff. and 287ff.

20. H. Kretschmayr, *Geschichte von Venedig*, vol. I (Gotha, 1905), 290; Queller, 6f.; Grand, 234; on background, *Chronica regia*, 199f.; Innocent III's *Gesta*, c. 83; Potthast, nn. 359 and 363; *Register 2*, nn. 270 and 271.

21. Cf. E. Faral (ed.), Geoffrey of Villehardouin, *La conquete Constantinople*, 2 vols. (Paris, 1938-39), I, lvi-lxvii; II, 18ff.; Tafel-Thomas, I, 363ff. and 442f.; Muratori, *RISS*, XII, 326f.; *Chronica regia*, 199.

22. *Chronica regia*, 199f.; Burckhard, *Chronica*, 81; Faral, Villehardouin, I, 58ff.; Lübeck, *Chronica*, 241, vi:19; Katona, IV, 536ff., collected the facts and all the evidence most adverse to the "conquerors" of Zara.

23. *ÁUO*, VI, 225ff.; VMSM, I, 15f.

24. Faral, Villehardouin, I, 58ff.; A.J. Andrea and Ilona Motsiff, "Pope Innocent III and the Diversion of the Fourth Crusade," *Byzantinoslavica*, 33 (1972), 6ff.; Brand, 232ff.; T.F. Maden, "Vows and Contracts in the Fourth Crusade: The Treaty of Zara and the Attack on Constantinople in 1204," *International History Review*, 15 (1993), 441ff.

25. *Chronica regia*, 199f.; Faral, Villehardouin, 76ff.; *ÁUO*, VI, 298ff.; Tafel-Thomas, I, 421ff., and compare with Potthast, n. 1948; *ÁUO*, VI, 242ff.; S. Runciman, *A History of the Crusades*, 3 vols. (Cambridge, 1954), III, 114ff.

26. *Chronica regia*, 200; *RA*, n. 212; Potthast, n. 2284; E. Gerland, "Der vierte Kreuzzug und seine Probleme," *Neue Jahrbücher für das klassiche Altertum*, 12 (1904), 505ff.

27. *RA*, n. 209; *ÁUO*, VI, 239f.

28. Potthast, n. 2196; *MPL*, 215, 340; *CD*, II, 431.

29. Potthast, n. 1839 (already in 1203!); *CD*, II, 401.

30. Choniates, *CB*, 711ff.; Dieten, 536,27-542,63.

31. Faral, Villehardouin, 76ff.; *ÁUO*, VI, 298ff.

32. *Chronica regia*, 203ff.; Lübeck, *Chronica*, vi:19, p. 241ff.; Robert of Auxerre, "Chronicon," *MGHSS*, XXVI, 265,23-26 and 266,1-3.

33. *ÁUO*, VI, 254; Tafel-Thomas, I, 436; C. Hopf (ed.), *Chronista Novorodensis*, in *Chroniques gréco-romanes inédites* series (Berlin, 1873), 93ff.; R. Mitchell and F.N. Forbes (eds.), *Chronicle of Novgorod*, Camden Society, 3rd ser. (London, 1914), 43ff.

34. Grégoire, *art. cit.*, 152ff.

35. Cf. *Chronica regia*, 206ff.; "Annales Herbipolenses," a. 1203, *MGHSS*, XVI, 10,45-55; Innocent III's *Gesta*, c. 83.

36. *RA*, n. 212; Knauz, I, 156.

37. Potthast, n. 1797; *CD*, II, 389.

38. As it may be seen from a royal writ, in *RA*, n. 187; cf. *ÁUO*, VI, 198ff., 265ff., and 268ff.

39. *Ibid.*, VI, 292ff.

40. *Ibid.*, VI, 278f., 279f., 281, 281ff., and 284f.; Potthast, n. 2135; *MPL*, 215, 280ff., 288f., and 290ff.

41. Potthast, nn. 2140 and 2143; *ÁUO*, VI, 286f. and 289f.; further, Potthast, n. 2144; *MPL*, 215, 297a; Katona, IV, 706. The king and Archbishop Jób of Esztergom were not on speaking terms; the king had the tithe withdrawn from the archbishop and suspended the deaneries from his jurisdiction. Potthast, n. 1845; *CD*, II, 403, though earlier, he had referred to the archbishop as "dilecti et fidelis nostri;" *ÁUO*, VI, 224f. The monarch also had expressed his displeasure with the monks at Somogyvár, who were still electing French monks as abbots of their community - Potthast, n. 2280; *MPL*, 215, 417f.; *CD*, II, 446f.

42. "Chronicon Bohemiae," c. 67, *MGHSS*, XI, 283; Lübeck, *Chronica*, vi:5; F. Palacky, *Geschichte von Böhmen*, II-1, 3rd ed. (Prague, 1866), 57ff. and 63ff.; on background, B. Gebhardt, *Handbuch der deutschen Geschichte*, 4 vols., 8th ed. (Stuttgart, 1954-60), I, 348ff.

43. "...a precibus nostis inductus, rege Bohemiae a Philippi consortio separato, et regi Othoni coniuncto, cum ipso pro isto validum contra illum exercitum destinasti;" Potthast, n. 2284; *CD*, II, 435ff.

44. "...ut regnum sive ducatum Bohemiae Odackero adulterio auferet et ad Tehobaldum puerum...transferret;" Pribico Pulkava de Tradenina, "Chronica Bohemorum," anno 1201, *MGHSS*, XXX, 41. It is revealing that Innocent III had referred to him as "zhupan," *Supponis Boemiae* - cf. Potthast, n. 2040; *MPL*, 216, 1097.

45. Lübeck, *Chronica*, vi:5; though Palacky accused him of spreading lies, *op. cit.*, II-1, 65, note 101; were one to agree with Lübeck's assertion of "...sunt enim Boemi natura pravi, actu scelerati," one could understand Palacky's anger.

46. "...nec defuit ibi illud perditissimum hominum genus, qui Valwen dicuntur;" Lübeck, vi:5, p. 224, note 5.

47. Palacky, II-1, 64, n. 100, expressed a negative opinion.

48. Cf. H. Svrita (J. Zurita), *Indices rerum ab Aragoniae regibus gestarum ab initiis regni ad annum MCDX* (Caesaraugustae, 1578), I, 84; Katona, IV, 496, dated the marriage 1198, probably erroneously, since Henry of Bohemia, who was, presumably at the wedding, had died on June 16, 1196 - Palacky, I (repr. Prague, 1844), 491.

49. *Chronica regia*, 234; H.J. Chaytor, *A History of Aragon and Catalonia* (London, 1933), 78f.; G. Jackson, *The Making of Medieval Spain* (New York, 1975), 82 and 118; Hampe, *Hochmittelalter*, 356.

50. *CD*, III-1, 297f. The Lady-in-waiting of the Aragonese bride was Tota - *RA*, n. 198; *CD*, III-1, 318; and, *RA*, n 362, *CD*, III-1, 316f. Peire Vidal, known troubadour and poet, had also accompanied her - W.T.H. Jackson, *The Literature of the middle ages* (New York, 1960), 251f., 273f.; G. Sebestyén, Adalékok a középkori

36 HUNGARY IN THE THIRTEENTH CENTURY

énekmondók történetéhez [Additional Remarks on the History of Medieval Troubadours] (Budapest, n.d.,), 8ff. and 19ff.

51. "Chronicon rythmicum Austriacum," lines 241-51, *MGHSS*, XXV, 349ff.; Lhotsky, 190f.

52. Zöllner, 73ff. and 88f.; Hantsch, I, 79 and 139f. Sanblasien, 54, c. 36, to the effect that Richard of England had humiliated the Duke of Austria, and the latter had him captured on his return from the Holy Land; Hantsch, I, 80; Toeche, *Heinrich VI*, 558ff.

53. See "Vita s. Hedwigis patronae et ducissae Silesiae," c. 1, in A. Bielowski (ed.), *Monumenta Poloniae historica*, 6 vols. (Lvov-Cracow, 1864-93; repr. Warsaw, 1960-61), cited hereafter as *MPH*, IV, 513; *Acta Sanctorum Ungariae* ex Bollandi, *et al.*, excerpta, 2 vols. (Tyrnaviae, 1743-44), cited hereafter as ASH, II, 250ff.; Gábor Tüskés and Éva Knapp, "Europäische Verbindungen der mittelalterlichen Heiligenverehrung in Ungarn," *Analecta Bollandiana*, 110 (1992), 31ff.

54. William of Newburgh, *Historia regum Anglicanae*, R.S. (London, 1856), ii:16; F.X. v. Funk and K. Bihlmeyer, *Kirchengeschichte*, 2 vols., 8th ed. (Paderborn, 1926-30), II, 185f.; Johannes Haller, *Das Papsttum: Idee und Wirklichkeit*, 5 vols., rev. ed. (Stuttgart, 1962), III, 345ff. and 539; F.X. Seppelt, *Geschichte der Päpste*, 5 vols. (Munich, 1952-59), III, 360ff.

55. *Chronica regia*, 186.

56. *Ibid.*; Katona, V, 15f.

57. "Chronicon Admontense," in H. Pez (ed.), *Scriptores rerum Austricarum*, 3 vols. (Regensburg, 1721-45), cited hereafter as SSRA, II, 195f., as if to refer to Iohannes Cinnamus, *Epitomae rerum ab Iohanne et Manuele Comnenis gestarum*, ed. A. Meineke (Bonn, 1836), cited hereafter as Cinnamus, v:1, *CB*, 203: "lex enim est apud Hungaros, ut semper ad fratres supertites diadema transmittatur;" Kosztolnyik, *Five Kings*, 74 and 176, n. 17; on Cinnamus, cf. Krumbacher, 279ff.

58. Potthast, n. 2473 (April 25, 1205): "Andreas regni gubernator;" *CD*, II, 455f. and 415; Katona, IV, 759f., and compare with "Continuatio Admontensis," anno 1203, *MGHSS*, IX, 590; Kantorowicz, 336ff.

59. Potthast, n. 2196 (April 24, 1204); *MPL*, 215, 340bc; *CD*, II, 431; Katona, IV, 712.

60. Potthast, n. 2197; *MPL*, 215, 340cd; *CD*, II, 423f.; Katona, IV, 666.

61. Haller, III, 319ff.

62. Potthast, n. 1839 (February 25, 1203); *MPL*, 215, 13; *CD*, II, 401.

63. Potthast, n. 2476 (April 25, 1205); *CD*, II, 457f.; Katona, I, 763f.

64. Potthast, nn. 1864 and 1863; *CD*, II, 409f. and 417ff., respectively; Katona, IV, 670ff., and compare with the papal writ of September 15, 1204, written in the interest of Cardinal Leo, Potthast, n. 2282; *CD*, II, 432f.; Katona, IV, 714ff.; see further, Potthast, nn. 2143 and 2283.

66. Potthast, n. 2284; Katona, IV, 726ff.; Potthast, nn. 2196 and 2197; *RISS*, III, 523ff.

67. See, for example, the papal letter addressed to Andrew II, dated June 7, 1206, Potthast, n. 2793; *CD*, III-1, 29.

68. Potthast, nn. 2015 and 2017; DC, II, 412 and 415f.

69. *MHSM*, I, 81; Schwandtner, III, 569f.

70. Spaleto wrote about "quoddam castrum," *ibid.*; "...et cathenis constrictum, perpetualiter incarceravit," in Rauch, *RASS*, II, 229, where? - at Kené (Kneginec), near Varasd; *CD*, III-1, 82.

71. *MGHSS*, IX, 590, anno 1203. One may note that in the days of Béla II (1131-41), the Hungarians also had to rely upon intrigue to defeat Boleslav III of Poland - cf. Otto of Freising, *Chronica sive Historia de duabus civitatibus*, SSrG, ed. Adolfus Hofmeister (Hannover-Leipzig, 1912; repr. 1984), vii:21; on Béla II, cf. Kosztolnyik, *From Coloman*, 99ff.

72. "Emericus...fratrem suum dolo captum;" *MGHSS*, IX, 620, anno 1203; also, *ibid.*, IX, 634, anno 1203.

73. Potthast, n. 2016; *CD*, II, 413; Katona, IV, 690.

74. Potthast, n. 2284; *CD*, II, 435ff.; *RA*, n. 212; Muratori, *RISS*, III, 523ff., esp. "ad primum," c. 80; Katona, IV, 726ff.

75. One may conclude from the papal writ, dated April 25, 1205, that Emery's death had occurred earlier than expected, Potthast, n. 2475; *CD*, II, 457; Bálint Hóman and Gyula Szekfű, *Magyar történet* [Hungarian History], 5 vols., 6th ed. (Budapest, 1939), I, 432f.

76. Potthast, n. 2328 (November 22, 1204); *MPL*, 215, 463ac.

77. *RA*, n. 211; Potthast, n. 2837; *MPL*, 215, 931ff.; *CD*, III-1, 38ff.

78. Potthast, n. 2086; *MPL*, 215, 221f.; *CD*, II, 444f.; J. Koller, *Historia episcopatuus Quinqueecclesiarum*, vols. 1-3 and 7 (Pest, 1782-84 and 1812), I, 312.

79. Potthast, n. 2281; *MPL*, 215, 417f.

80. *CD*, II, 451ff., as above, note 75.

81. See Thomas of Spaleto, c. 24, *MHSM*, XXVI, 81; *MGHSS*, IX, 590,18-24; *ibid.*, IX, 620,48-50, the latter in contradiction with the writ from the papal curia that said that the pontiff *mandat* Archbishop Ugrin of Esztergom to crown Ladislas, King Emery's son - Potthast, n. 2196; *CD*, II, 430ff.

82. SSRA, II, 229, and Pez, SSRA, I, 800f., anno 1203.

83. Potthast, n. 2328; *MPL*, 215, 463c.

84. Andrew - "Hungariae gubernator;" Potthast, n. 2473; *MPL*, 215, 595f.; Katona, IV, 759f.

85. Potthast, n. 2290; *MPL*, 215, 427ac.

86. Potthast, n. 2474; *MPL*, 215, 596d; on April 24, 1204, Rome called upon the archbishop of Esztergom to crown Emery's son - Potthast, n. 2195 -- that he show good will! - *MPL*, 215, 340bc; Luchaire, *Innocent III*, V, 66f.

87. Potthast, n. 2475; *MPL*, 215, 596bc.

88. "...Rex Henricus insanible genus languoris incurrit;" Spaleto, c. 24, *MHSM*, xxvi, 82.

89. *SSH*, I, 463,12-13. A letter by Andrew II, written in September, 1233, was dated "Regni nostri anno XXX" - *ÁUO*, VI, 518, and so was the writ dated, *ibid.*, VI, 519ff., meaning that Emery had died in 1204. Andrew II issued a writ, dated September 21, 1233, "in the 32nd year of his reign," so the death of Emery must be dated before September 21, 1204. Cf. Knauz, I, 310.

90. *SSH*, II, 205,8.

91. *MGHSS*, XXV, 355,4-15 (lines 240-51) and 355,18-23 (lines 254-59).

92. As it is evident from Potthast, n. 2478; *MPL*, 215, 598f.

93. To be concluded from a papal writ addressed to Andrew, "dux regni Hungariae gubernator;" Potthast, n. 2473; *MPL*, 215, 595f.; Katona, IV, 759.

94. Potthast, nn. 2478 and 2479; *CD*, II, 458 and 459; *MPL*, 215, 598ab. In Potthast, n. 2484, the pontiff "mandat" the archbishop of Kalocsa and the bishop of Várad, *MPL*, 215, 597f.

95. Potthast, n. 2479.

96. "Anonymi Leobensis Chronicon," anno 1205, in Pez, I, 801; "Anonymi Bavarii monachi Capilatio chronologica rerum Boicarum," anno 1205, in Oefele, *Scriptores Boicarum*, II, 335; "Chronicon Austriacum," anno 1205, in Rauch, *RASS*, II, 230.

97. *Ibid.*; *MGHSS*, IX, 591,5-7; 621,20-21; 634,47-53.

98. *Ibid.*, IX, 590f.

99. *Ibid.*, IX, 591,7-10. See the letter of Andrew II, in Knauz, I, 185, transcribed at the papal curia, and dated April 20, 1209 - see Potthast, n. 3712; *MPL*, 216, 39f.; *CD*, III-1, 90f.

Chapter Two

Domestic Turmoil

1. The Early Reign of Andrew II

> Huic successit Andreas filius Bele tertii,...cuius uxor fuit domina Gertrudis de Alamania, de qua genuit Belam, Colomanum, Andream et beatam Elyzabeth.
>
> *Chronicon pictum*, c. 174

In his letter of July 27, 1205, Pope Innocent III addressed Andrew as king of Hungary;[1] in the letter of June 26 of the same year, the pontiff spoke to him as governor of the kingdom;[2] and in a June 24, 1205, communication, the pope referred to him as "Master" of Hungary.[3]

The coronation of Andrew II might have taken place in early summer of that year; his first issued charter was dated August 1, 1205.[4] The date of the coronation will not be altered by the circumstantial evidence that Andrew II's *Decretum Primum* (The Golden Bull) of 1222 was promulgated in the seventeenth year of his reign. It can only mean that the Decree had been issued in early July, 1222, at the latest.[5] Archbishop John of Kalocsa, now the ranking prelate in the realm, performed the coronation.[6] (A word of explanation is in order here. It is a matter of record that the papal writ, dated October 6, 1205, confirmed [*prefecit*] John of Kalocsa as the new archbishop of Esztergom, and the papal letter of October 14, 1205, addressed to the Canons of Kalocsa cathedral, explained to them that the elevation of their archbishop to the see of Esztergom did not threaten their position and future.[7])

Andrew II took a new coronation oath.[8] According to the wording of three papal documents, he swore to preserve his royal privileges [*perpetuitates*] intact; and, with the permission of the curia, he promised to revoke previous grants he had unconstitutionally made,[9] as his son and heir (the future Béla IV) would reclaim them.[10]

On the basis of these papal documents, one may understand how Andrew II had copiously wasted donations of land and office on unworthy friends, frivolous ecclesiastics, even religious orders; how he gave spontaneous gifts without any reason, and how he reclaimed almost every gift and/or donation he had made. The curia authorized him to repossess everything he had given away - contrary to, in fact, the breach of his coronation oath.[11] One is unwillingly reminded here of his early contemporary, the English king John Lackland, who had easily affixed his seal to the Great Charter because he knew that Rome would, at any time, void that document.[12]

The Hungarian monarch took two oaths. At the altar in the church he took the first one in accordance with the Roman *Pontificale*, that he defend and protect the Church, orphans, widows and persecuted persons, and maintain justice and peace in the realm. Outside of the church, he swore to secure and preserve the inheritance of the Crown - what it may lose, he would recover.[13]

The coronation oaths of Andrew II changed the laws of King St. Stephen (*ob*. 1038) which stated that anyone could freely possess everything one had.[14] It was by this coronation oath that Andrew II defended himself from the demands, based upon the late ninth century "Blood Oath" which was particularly emphasized at this time, that county reeves of certain families inherit their offices.[15] Were he to accept, or to identify himself with these demands, he could lose a major portion of good quality territorial holdings of the royal domain. According to the construed text of the coronation oath, the royal lands were looked upon as property of the Crown; out of these lands individuals received for life - though not always permanently - holdings by their families, personal grants for usufruct for services rendered to king and country.[16]

As long as a grantee family had remained loyal to the king and provided men for the Crown's military defenses, the grant[s] of land, or of office, remained in the hands of the family; were the loyalty to be broken, however, the grant[s] could be terminated before or with the death of the grantee and revert to the Crown. The crown-held lands were identical, still, with the territorial royal possessions held by King St. Stephen.[17]

The papal curia tacitly approved of repossession by the Crown of lands that were given to the Church, if the donation violated the royal coronation oath.[18] The abbot of Pannonhalma, on the other hand, at the 1221 dedication of the church of the abbey, obtained the official return of the fisheries and fishing privileges at Gönyő that had earlier belonged to the abbey.[19] Andrew II failed in keeping his coronation oath when, after that, he donated Gora county near Zagreb to the Cistercians at Toplica, whose acquaintance he had made when he was Prince of Slovenia.[20] Incidentally, one may note that the first Gothic church in Hungary was constructed at Toplica during this time.[21]

The monarch also donated the area along the Barca stream - where later the town of Brassó would be built - to the German Knights, with the understanding that they would construct wooden forts in the region and open a path south of the Carpathians to bring the Christian faith to the Cumans, thereby expanding even further the Hungarian king's political jurisdiction.[24] Was it a politically sound idea? Did Andrew II know anything about the German Knights? Did he have assurances that the Order would live up to expectations?[25] The Barca region in southeastern Transylvania lay far away from the administration of the Hungarian court.[26]

After the receipt of a land-grant, it was only his feudal ties that bound the recipient to the monarch - a situation that did not seem to perturb the king.[27] He had argued in one of his pronounce-ments that he, as the ruler, was under no obligation to limit the amount, or the extent of his gifts,[28] and it could happen that he would re-donate the same land (or office) to another person.[29] Or, was the royal chancellor so disorganized an individual that he could not, as he did not, remember former transactions involving particular grants of land and/or office?[30]

It was characteristic of Andrew II's grandiose pretenses that when he sent his daughter Elizabeth to the court of her fiancé, the Duke of Thuringia, in 1221, he sent with her, as dowry, a silver crib, a silver bathtub, jewelry and silk garments, and at least eight thousand marks of silver.[31] It must have been the vanity of Queen Gertrud to represent her husband's riches to her important German relatives; nor did Andrew II wish to remain behind his wife's generosity.

When their son Béla was born in 1206, the king had been on a hunting party around Nagyvázsony near Veszprém; in his sudden joy over receiving the news, he gave the village to the local bishop - but soon reclaimed it, and gave it to his head official named Salamon.[32] And, to insult the bishop of Veszprém even more, he asked the bishop of Vác to be his son's godfather.[33]

Queen Gertrud was the daughter of Berthold IV of Merania, and a sister of Otto, Count of Andechs, Lord of Merania (on the Adriatic shore),[34] whose younger brother Berthold was, since 1206, archdean at the cathedral of Bamberg.[35] But the cathedral of Kalocsa requested from Pope Innocent III that Berthold become the archbishop of Kalocsa to succeed Archbishop John, who had been elevated to the see of Esztergom. Andrew II gave a strong endorsement for the request of the Kalocsa chapter of canons, who wanted to appease the Queen, but the curia handled the case more cautiously.[36]

The Holy See authorized the archbishop of Salzburg to meet with archdean Berthold to convince himself (to the satisfaction of the papal curia) of the spiritual qualifications and the religious-educational background of the archdean. The meeting must have taken place at the border, and ended with unsatisfactory results. The archbishop reported to Rome that although Berthold could read the Bible fairly well, translate it easily into his native tongue, and could acceptably answer questions concerning Latin grammar, he knew nothing about Canon law, nor of speaking effectively in public.[37]

Berthold did not receive papal confirmation as a candidate for an archiepiscopal see;[38] however, the canons of Kalocsa expressed such indignation at the outcome of the interview that Rome had to acknowledge the election, *postulatio*, of Berthold under the condition that, as soon as he reached canonical age, it would confirm him as archbishop of Kalocsa.[39] It is worth noting that although the canons had argued that Berthold was a well-educated person, versed in all branches of knowledge, the "learned" archbishop-elect had, upon obtaining papal confirmation, to go to Vicentia to pursue further studies - to no littler consternation of Pope Innocent III.[40]

The papal curia thought it well to void the treaty signed by John, at that time sill the archbishop of Kalocsa, and Berthold, the archbishop-elect of Kalocsa, an agreement that stated that the young monarch previously crowned, would have to be, when actually ascending the throne, anointed and crowned for a second time by the archbishop of Kalocsa, i.e., Berthold.[41] Pope Innocent III stressed the point of view that there could develop a dangerous situation in the country were more than one high priest was permitted to perform the royal coronation.[42] In the same writ, the pontiff denied the request of Andrew II for permission to have the archdean of Szeben ordained as bishop of Transylvania (on the grounds that the new bishop would be a suffragan of the archbishop [Berthold] of Kalocsa).[43]

Was it because Berthold could not be expected to crown kings that he had to be promoted *ban[us]* by Andrew II,[44] and *ban[us]* of Slavonia?[45] The answer might partly be found in the fact that Berthold had soon after been named Voyvoda (grand reeve, or steward) of Transylvania - evidently a political family appointment made by the king under instigation from his wife.[46] Or, the answer may partly lie in the fact that, at this time, the monarch had called upon the Teutonic Knights to settle in Barca land (in the southeastern part of the realm). The king had hoped that by promoting Berthold as head official in Transylvania, he could, through him, carefully monitor the activities of the German Knights, thereby also extending his authority over western Wallachia, the area south of the Carpathians down to the lower Danube.[47]

There had existed a need for Andrew II to expand into Wallachia because he had lost the Adriatic southwest for his country. Venice had gained control of Zara, a fortified Hungarian outlet to the sea; the count of Zara and its archbishop had become subjects of the Republic of Venice, who were expected to aid the republic in the forthcoming power struggle with Hungary over Dalmatia.[48] Thirty citizens of Zara had to serve as hostages in Venice to guarantee the loyalty of their city to the republic.[49] Andrew II could do little else but attempt to at least retain Spaleto and nearby Almissa, a pirates' nest, under his rule.[50]

After the events of 1204, the political star of Venice reached its zenith because no Byzantine empire that would have checked the political influence of the republic existed at that time.[51] At the same time, the [Catholic] Latin empire established in former Byzantine territories had an impact upon the court of Andrew II. Even if the Hungarian court, as the Latin one, looked down upon John Kajolan of Bulgaria,[52] Kajolan had shown good will toward the Hungarian court on the very day of his coronation as the Catholic ruler of Bulgaria.[53] But John II had turned against the Latin emperor, who was Andrew II's blood relative, defeated him in April, 1205,[54] taken him prisoner of war, and laid siege to Thessalonica; John II was murdered before he could take city.[55]

In spite of the diplomatically friendly attitude of the Bulgarian court, Andrew II continued his expansionist policy toward Bulgaria.

He now aimed at recovering Fort Baranch, under the secretly reached understanding with the grand steward of Serbia.[56] The king and the grand steward had met in 1208, and the grand steward also began to make territorial demands from Bulgaria - even at the risk of a new conflict with Andrew II.[57]

In the field of church diplomacy, the king seemed to have followed the policy of his brother, King Emery, but mainly of their father, Béla III, by supporting his brother-in-law, Otakar of Bohemia - who, incidentally, enjoyed papal diplomatic support - during the confrontation between the German emperor, Otto IV of Brunswick and the Holy See.[58] In the summer of 1213, Frederick II, papal protégé for the German throne, supported by Hermann of Thuringia and Otakar I of Bohemia, was engaged in a struggle with Otto IV for imperial recognition.[59] Among the troops of the Czech Otakar one could find Hungarian army units under the command of Thomas of Huntpázmány.[60] Andrew II had shown loyalty to Rome by such a gesture in permitting a small Hungarian force to war on German soil under his Czech brother-in-law against the opponent of the pope. Regardless of the outcome of the confrontation, the monarch had made a gesture, and by providing troops he proved his support of the Roman See.[61]

One may assume that Andrew II wished to establish a diplomatic base in Rome, and to handle with Rome's support what he regarded as unacceptable developments in Halich. Although the dates rendered by the Russian annals (in this instance, the Volina [Volhyna] Annals) are not reliable - they place events some three years ahead of their actual occurrence[62] - one accepts their information if it can be supported by papal correspondence. For instance, a letter of Innocent III, dated July 7, 1206, provides information on the military expedition of Andrew II to Halich.[63]

Vladimir Jaroslavich, who had retaken Halich from Béla III, died in 1198. Roman of Ladomer, with Polish aid, occupied Halich; he had been notorious for savagely decimating the ranks of the boyars who dared to oppose him.[64] He was, however, an ally of Andrew II - were one of them to die a natural death, or in battle, the other would support the dead man's family.[65] When he was killed in warring with the Poles (who were rather taken aback by the atrocities committed during his occupation of Halich),[66] Roman's widow and two children requested protection from the Hungarian monarch. Andrew II met with the widow at Sanok; he named Roman's four and a half year old son, Danilo, as the new ruler of Halich and provided him with a Hungarian body guard for protection.[67] Andrew II reserved for himself, however, the use of the title, "King of Halich-Ladomer."[68]

Understandably, the nobles of Halich rebelled against such an arrangement, perhaps not so much on account of Hungarian wardship of Danilo, but on the grounds that Andrew II, by naming himself king of Halich, could easily attach the region to his kingdom. To complicate matters, the widow of Roman did not trust Andrew II; she fled to the court of Boleslav of Poland, son of Casimir, to request his support. The Polish ruler sent her back to the court of Andrew II with the suggestion that the Hungarian court aid her in the recovery of Halich.[69]

There remained no alternative to the Hungarian king but to marry his daughter to Danilo and to restore his son-in-law to the throne of Halich.[70] At this stage of events, rather unexpectedly, Vladimir Igorevich had surprised Andrew II with a large monetary gift (Andrew II always had chronic financial problems because of his fiscal irresponsibility), and with the proposal that he not marry his daughter to Danilo.[71] Igorevich himself had designs on Halich. He did have a brief military encounter with Vladimir Roman, which he lost, but needed the support of Andrew II to make good his claim.[72] All of these political moves took place in the year 1206.[73] The Volynian Annals recorded, however, that Igorevich's rule over Halich had been brief - by 1208, the Hungarian court had to send Benedict, the son of Korlát, grand reeve of Transylvania, to recapture Halich by force.[74]

The strong-willed grand reeve took the government of Halich into his own hands. He had Vladimir Roman exiled to Hungary. Benedict's inconsistent behavior, and his uncivilized attitude toward women, created ill feeling among the boyars - they referred to him as antichrist.[75] Vladimir Roman, who by then escaped from Hungary, had, with the help of the boyars, removed the over-confident grand reeve from office.[76] Vladimir Roman paid the humiliated Hungarian court a given sum of money in lieu of compensation, but in Halich, he sought revenge. He had five thousand boyars, the "trouble makers," executed in cold blood. Some of the boyars escaped to Hungary and asked Andrew II to make Danilo their ruler again.[77]

In 1211, therefore, another Hungarian armed force moved toward Halich under the command of Palatine Pot (Path) of the clan of Győr[78] (the one who had the abbey at Lébény built[79]). The palatine had Danilo accompany him. During the campaign the palatine occupied Prezemysl, captured Prince Sviatoslav, but met strong resistance east of Halich. Although some of the nobles supported Pot and Danilo, the majority of the boyars remained quite hostile - for example, the Povloci Cumans, who supported Vladimir Roman. In spite of these problems, Pot overcame their resistance, placed Danilo on the throne in the cathedral of Halich dedicated to the Mother of God.[80] The "people" (boyars? Galicians?) in Halich meanwhile had murdered Vladimir Igorevich and his son,[81] and Volodislav (Volodimer?), who called himself the leader of the boyars, took over the government.[82]

Soon thereafter, Andrew II had gathered his forces again and marched on Halich. He had planned to recall the mother of Danilo from exile, and to punish the rebellious boyars. His plans did not materialize because the king had to leave Halich in a hurry, as Mistislav "the Numb" took over the reins of power in the area, and Danilo with his mother had to return to Hungary.[83] One is under the impression that the army Andrew II took with him on this campaign consisted of mercenaries, not his regular forces provided by his nobility, and the commander of the mercenaries saw no reason for warring in Halich; he must have observed how unpopular the Hungarian king and his protégé were among the population.[84]

It is to be feared that the "diplomatic efforts" of Andrew II had collapsed exactly at the time when his domestic "innovations" also failed. Troubles developed when the king's inconsistent governing policy caused greater and deeper resentment and public discontent with him began to peak. Some nobles had already thought of Géza, the younger brother of the deceased Béla III (and an uncle of Andrew II), as the one who ought to take over the government of the realm. Their conspiracy did not materialize because the king had spies everywhere; the delegates sent to Géza were captured by the king's men.[85]

Another conspiracy had been organized against the king and his queen in 1213. Berthold, the queen's younger brother who had already been referred to earlier as the archbishop-elect of Kalocsa and royal head official in Transylvania, had been representing the king at public functions at this time.[86] Some nobles resented this sign of Berthold's growing influence in public, and conspired against the royal family.[87] The conspirators were not even afraid of committing regicide - they directed their frustrated anger at Queen Gertrud of foreign birth and her brother, who, in their opinion, unworthily held a high ecclesiastical position and illegally occupied prominent public offices in the kingdom.[88] The aim of their conspiracy was not so much directed at assassinating the king, but to remove him forcefully from power, and to place his seven year old son Béla on the throne.[89]

Archbishop John of Kalocsa might have played a key role in this grand-scale conspiracy, even though he did not directly belong to the inner group of conspirators.[90] The archbishop must have been quite unhappy with the reign of Andrew II - partly because he had to constantly endure the monarch's ill humor,[91] and partly because he had been forced to play a secondary role in matters of church administration and policy making, on account of the predominant position held by the king's incompetent relative/protégé, Berthold.[92] Bánk, a nobleman, belonged to the group of malcontents also; Bánk, together with Palatine Pot (Path), took part in the prolonged Halich wars of Andrew II, and in 1213, Bánk succeeded Pot as Palatine[93]

In the fall of 1213, when Andrew II again departed for Halich,[94] the royal reeve Peter stayed at the court with the Queen and Berthold; Leopold IV of Austria was a house guest.[95] On September 28, Queen Gertrud went hunting to the Pilis Hills with Berthold, Duke Leopold, and Reeve Peter. He,[96] another royal reeve named Simon,[97] a noble (also known as Simon),[98] and Palatine Bánk (who later became the brother-in-law of Reeve Simon), attacked the Queen, Archbishop Berthold, and Duke Leopold, who were inside a tent resting, perhaps with the intent to murder the archbishop.[99] But Berthold and the duke escaped, and the conspirators had, with great difficulty, murdered the Queen, cutting off both of her arms with a knife.[100] It was the two royal reeves, Peter and Simon, who had delivered the deadly blows.[101] After this terrible deed, the Cistercian monks at Pilis buried the horribly mutilated body of Queen Gertrud at their abbey.[102]

King Andrew II was en-route toward Halich when, at Lelész, they handed him a bloody piece of the queen's clothing. His aimless life now turned purposeful. He immediately returned home to prevent the outbreak of what he must have regarded as a political-social uprising in the country aimed at him and his government.[103]

A word of explanation is in order here. What might be regarded as the background of the horrible murder of Queen Gertrud had been referred to before. Berthold, as the younger brother of Queen Gertrud,[104] received, at a very young and uncanonical age, the archiepiscopal see of Kalocsa;[105] soon after, he had been promoted to Grand Steward of the realm,[106] and to Grand Reeve (Voyvoda) of Transylvania.[107] His promotions had occurred under the persuasive influence and politicking of the Queen. Berthold's ecclesiastical career had not been without drawbacks, because Pope Innocent III had on various occasions expressed to Andrew II his displeasure over the undignified behavior of the young archbishop and his too quick advancement in the hierarchy.[108] The pope wrote to Andrew II that he had made a master out of someone who was still a pupil, and a poor pupil at that.[109]

Rome further declared as void the agreement that had been forced by the king upon John of Esztergom - an agreement that had been firmly contested by the canons of the Esztergom cathedral chapter[110] - according to which it would have to be the archbishop of Kalocsa (that is, Berthold) who would perform the second coronation of Béla, the king's son and heir, when Béla had actually succeeded his father on the throne, instead of the archbishop of Esztergom, who since ancient times alone had the right to crown the kings of Hungary.[111]

Were Esztergom unwilling to crown the prince as Junior King during his father's lifetime, Kalocsa would carry out the act (as there had been a precedent set for this during the twelfth century).[112] The papal decision was clear: it would create a most dangerous political situation for the country if two archbishops had the right to crown the king.[113]

The dissatisfied nobles played a decisive role in the assassination of the Queen.[114] Queen Gertrud's heavy-handed nepotism made them angry. In their view, the monarch was unduly under the influence of his wife, and they saw no alternative but to rely on physical force. Altering the situation by legal means was impossible, for the monarch did not listen to them.[115] When the royal reeve of Sebenico captured the envoy the nobles had sent to Byzantium to recall the sons of Béla III's younger brother, Géza, from exile and to offer the crown to them, the malcontents caught in the web of conspiracy had no alternative but to take preemptive steps by striking out first.[116]

Andrew II's latest military adventure in Halich provided the conspirators with a golden opportunity - Berthold and the Queen could be politically neutralized and removed from influencing and directing government politics.[117] Mainly on account of a statement with double meaning attributed to Archbishop John of Esztergom, one can assume that the conspirators did not intend to murder the Meranians, though the thought of political assassination must have entered their minds.[118] Perhaps it was the behavior of the Queen during the onslaught of the conspirators; perhaps the sight of human blood caused them to behave as they did and commit the thoughtless and most irresponsible murder.[119]

Andrew II returned home at once, and had the case tried immediately at his court. The trial included the active participants in the murder and their supporters.[120] The Assembly of Nobles served as the court of law: it found Reeve Peter guilty as charged of murder,[121] and since he had resisted arrest, the court ordered that he be captured and quartered.[122] The others, too, had to be captured and executed.[123] Several of the conspirators fled to Poland.[124]

The death of the Queen remained undiscussed by the court. Reeve Simon, brother of Grand Reeve Nicholas, was only referred to in a writ dated 1228.[125] Nicholas, the son of Barcza, Judge of the Queen's Court, replaced Bánk as palatine,[126] though Bánk himself had not been punished; by 1217, four years after the murder, he was Grand Steward again.[127] As a matter of fact, Bánk became Judge of the King's Country Court of Law in 1221.[128] It was only in 1240, during the fifth year of his reign, that King Béla IV, son of Andrew II and Queen Gertrud, confiscated the land holdings of Bánk in the Sáros, Kishont, and Szabolcs regions.[129]

Did the king's court and the nobles find the charge of conspiracy against the Queen and her relatives justifiable?[130] It is known that Berthold, who had escaped the bloodbath and fled abroad, returned to Hungary, though was given no public office.[131] Alberic's Chronicle did not mention Bánk among the conspirators (murderers) involved in the case.[132] Alberic stated, however, that when Berthold had left the country under the pretext of going on a crusade, he illegally took seven thousand silver marks with him.[133]

The remark made by the Austrian Rhymed Chronicle, anno 1212,[134] that Queen Gertrud had the wife of Bánk handed over to the personal pleasures of her brother, and for her guests' entertainment, cannot be taken seriously.[135] What might be more curious is that Keza - as one has access to his text today[136] - wrote nothing about the affair,[137] and it was only the chronicler of Óbuda who inserted it into his narrative, anno 1347, placing a terrible curse upon Bánk.[138]

After the assassination of the Queen, Reeve Salomon of Bács took Béla under his personal protection;[139] the rights of the prince to succeed his father to the throne were guaranteed by his father's coronation oath, so Andrew II could not waste away his son's inheritance.[140] And, in order to prevent the formation of another political faction (and perhaps conspiracy), Andrew II took preventive steps.

First, he had Prince Béla crowned Junior King in 1214, and provided him with his own court and officials. He appealed to Rome to excommunicate any individual who wished to make Béla king during his, Andrew II's, lifetime.[141]

Secondly, he requested from the papal curia that Archbishop John of Esztergom be allowed to crown his younger son, Coloman, as King of Halich.[142] Within a few months, he again requested that the curia send a royal diadem for Coloman.[143]

Third, Andrew II turned to Innocent III with the petition that Archbishop John of Esztergom govern the realm, together with the bishops of Győr and Pécs, and the cooperation of the royal chancellor, during his forthcoming journey to the Holy Land.[144] He also petitioned that the papal curia prepare a transcript of the papal writ on the privileges of the Esztergom archbishop to crown the kings of Hungary - the letter that had been lost after the assassination of Queen Gertrud.[145]

And finally, the monarch established a stipend during his sojourn at the abbey in Lelész for masses to be said for the repose of the soul of his murdered wife.[146] In 1215, the king had agreed to take Jolánta, daughter of the Duke of Flanders, and younger sister of Henry the Brave, the Latin emperor of Byzantium, to be his wife. The emperor was the nephew of Philip II Augustus of France.

Bishop Peter of Győr had Jolánta accompanied to the Hungarian court, and Andrew II deposited eight thousand silver marks as dowry for the new queen.[147] Were the king to die before her, the Roman curia guaranteed the rights of the queen.[148]

The supporters of Béla Junior King now turned to Rome with the request that the king (Andrew II) may legally revoke the land and office grants he had previously made or wasted on unworthy recipients - in actual breath of his oath of coronation.[149] Indeed, organized teams comprising three judges each began to conduct investigations in every county.[150] Personnel deployed at the royal forts maintained the area under the administration of the county (district) fort, that is, under the king's jurisdiction. At this time, new expressions began to emerge in legal usage, such as *civiles*, *castranses*, *regi civiles*, designating the fort personnel, whose "iobagiones" were elevated to regional superintendents: *maior* (*gazdatiszt*), with political-economic responsibilities, and baronial rankings.[151]

The courts of law based their legal decisions on written data concerning royal grants of land, or of office, though any fort or county official (the reeve or fort office holder) could claim and repossess land or office that had been given away unmerited by the monarch. In cases concerning the fort (county, district) domain, the reeve of the fort and his officials passed judgment. It was within their jurisdiction to send, in a company of *pristaldus*, the party involved in a land or office grant legal suit before the cathedral chapters in Buda and/or in Várad, where members of the parties involved could take the oath over the validity of their claim, or were to undergo the ordeal of fire. Individuals considered innocent were ordered to submit to an ordeal by fire.[152]

The almost constant need for making military and diplomatic decisions in Halich kept Andrew II busy. Volodislav himself wanted to become ruler in Halich and expelled Mistislav, the descendent of Saint Vladimir. The Hungarian court supported Volodislav, and ordered Danilo and his mother to leave Halich again, asking the Polish Prince Lesko to look after them. Prince Lesko saw the matter differently - he wanted to drive Volodislav out of Halich, but did not wish to ruin his relationship with the Hungarian court. He granted Danilo some territory in Ladomer, and proposed to Andrew II that his younger son Coloman marry Lesko's three year old daughter, and that they govern Halich together.[153] Halich had become a political issue at both the Hungarian and Polish courts. Through the marriage between the Hungarian prince and the Polish princess, the Hungarian monarch could free himself from further political and military involvements in that region.[154]

Neither the Hungarian monarch nor the Polish prince had considered, however, the possible hostile reaction of the boyars of Halich. The boyars were furious, and turned to the Roman See for help. They were ready, they said, to accept the religious primacy of Rome were the curia to permit them to retain their Greek-Byzantine liturgical rite, and were it to send a crown for their ruler, a Russian prince. The requested papal recognition would, they thought, extend and strengthen ties between the papal curia and the Hungarian court, by separating Halich from the common world of other Russian principalities.[155]

The Hungarian governor in Halich, Demeter, son of Sükösd (Sixtus) de genere Alba, was a virtuous man with good manners, but unable to control the political and military anarchy in the region.[156] For example, when Andrew II had requested that Rome send a diadem to enable the archbishop of Esztergom to crown his son, Coloman, King of Halich - a most bizarre move on his part; it only proved the thoughtless analysis by the Hungarian court of the prevailing political and military situation in and around Halich[157] - Mistislav of Novgorod could not restrain his emotions - he attacked Governor Demeter, invaded Halich, and forced the Hungarians to leave the area immediately.[158]

Mistislav of Novgorod had made arrangements with the other Russian princes that allowed Danilo to retain the Polish territory he had earlier received (regardless of the expected hostile reaction from the Polish nobility),[159] on the grounds that Danilo's wife, Ann, was the daughter of Mistislav.[160] But Mistislav held a short-sighted policy that actually aided the Hungarian court by driving the Poles into King Andrew II's camp. In 1216, the Hungarian king, supported by a new Hungarian-Polish army, restored Danilo and his wife to the throne of Halich, as Archbishop John of Esztergom had crowned them King and Queen.[161] Thereafter, Mistislav withdrew his forces from Halich permanently, moved to Novgorod, and Danilo established a firm foothold in Ladomer.

In order to characterize these developments in detail, one might observe that Mistislav had previously captured the seventeen year old Coloman and his fourteen year old wife at Halich,[162] and requested that Andrew II's youngest son, Prince Andrew, marry Mistislav's daughter.[163] In 1226, Prince Andrew actually occupied the throne of Halich, but Danilo sent the helpless prince back home.[164] In 1231, Andrew returned to Halich, but only in 1234 could Danilo reclaim the area.[165]

These rather confusing developments involving Halich prevented high-ranking Russian ecclesiastics from attending the Fourth Lateran Synod, scheduled by Pope Innocent III to gather in Rome in November, 1215.[166]

NOTES

1. Cf. Potthast, n. 2567; *MPL*, 215, 702; *CD*, III-1, 22.
2. Potthast, n. 2553; *CD*, II, 463.
3. "Dominus Hungariae," Potthast, n. 2550; *MPL*, 215, 661; *CD*, II, 460.
4. Cf. *RA*, n. 217; *RHM*, 400ff.
5. See *RA*, n. 417; Marczali, *Enchiridion*, 143; *RHM*, 417; the altered version of 1231 was published in the 29th year of his reign - *RA*, n. 479; Marczali, *Enchiridion*, 142; *RHM*, 433, therefore, his coronation might have taken place in 1206.
6. *RA*, n. 224; *CD*, III-a, 31, and compare with *CD*, II, 32; Knauz, I, 185 - a papal transcript of April 20, 1209, Potthast, n. 3712; *MPL*, 216, 391; *CD*, III-1, 90f.
7. Potthast, n. 2558; *MPL*, 215, 717; see further, Knauz, I, 184ff.; Fraknói, *Magyarország és a Szentszék*, I, 42f.; and Potthast, n. 2591; *CD*, III-1, 29. Andrew II nominated Bishop Kalán of Pécs, and persuaded certain members of the Esztergom chapter to accept the nomination; however, Rome asked for a new election - Potthast, n. 2550, as cited above, n. 3. The right of the Roman curia to intervene in this type of election would be defined anew by the IV Lateran Council, 1215, ca. 23-26, in Ae. Friedberg (ed.), *Corpus Iuris Canonici*, 2 vols. (Leipzig, 1879-81; reprint, Graz, 1959), II, 88ff.; or J.D. Mansi (ed.), *Sacrorum concilorum nova et amplissima collectio*, 31 vols. (Florence-Venice, 1759-98), XXII, 1011ff.
8. Kantorowicz, 355, note 144, commenting on Andrew II's coronation oath; see further Potthast, n. 8305, by Gregory IX; *VMH*, n. 191; *CD*, III-2, 314.
9. Potthast, n. 6318; *CD*, III-1, 294; Katona, V, 338.
10. *RA*, nn. 583, 584, 585, 589; *CD*, III-1, 220 and III-2, 194, 195; *ÁUO*, XI, 215; Knauz, I, 271.
11. Potthast, n. 7352; *CD*, III-2, 17; see also the papal writ addressed to Béla Junior King, dated July 15, 1225, in Potthast, n. 7443; *VMH*, n. 126.
12. Potthast, nn. 4990 and 4991; *Bullarium magnum Romanum*, editio Romano (reprint Graz, 1963-64), III, 172ff.; C.R. Cheney, *Innocent III and England*, vol. IX of *Päpste und Papsttum*, ed. G. Denzler (Stuttgart, 1976), 382ff.; Matthew of Paris, *Historia maiora*, 7 vols. R.S. (London, 1872-83), III, 166ff.; C.H. McIlwain, *The Growth of Political Thought in the West* (New York, 1932), 231f.; Maccarone, 27ff.
13. His coronation oath might have been similar to the Prologue of the Laws of Ladislas IV, 1279 - Marczali, *Enchiridion*, 175; *RHM*, 555f.; or, with the oath taken by Vladislas I, cf. Schwandtner, I, 463f.; Kantorowicz, 355, note 144, referred to the coronation of Charles I Anjou of Hungary in 1310 - see Marczali, *Enchiridion*, 205ff.
14. King St. Stephen's Laws, aa. i:35 and ii:5-6, *ibid.*, 69ff.; *RHM*, 310ff.; Kosztolnyik, *Five Kings*, 111ff.
15. Anonymus, cc. 5-6; *SSH*, I, 40f.; Macartney, 68.
16. See *ÁUO*, VI, 341ff.; and an earlier royal grant, *ibid.*, VI, 324f. On royal grants given without merit, see *RA*, n. 592; *ÁUO*, VI, 486f., and compare to the Bull of 1222, art. 17, Marczali, *Enchiridion*, 139; *RHM*, 415.
17. King St. Stephen's Laws, aa. ii:2, *ibid.*, 321; Marczali, *Enchiridion*, 77f.; also, Laws of Coloman the Learned, aa. i:20 and 21, *ibid.*, 107; Kosztolnyik, *From Coloman*, 46ff.
18. Potthast, n. 7444; *VMH*, n. 126; compare to Potthast, n. 7443; Katona, IV, 469f.
19. "... ut autem hec nostra donacio ... salva semper et inconcussa permaneat;" *ÁUO*, VI, 410 (dated 1222).
20. Cf. *RA*, n. 231, and n. 220; *ÁUO*, XI, 82, and consult Kantorowicz, 42ff., who referred to the Norman Anonymus, "De consecratione pontificum vel regum," in E. Dümmler (ed.), *MGH Libelli de lite*, 3 vols. (Hannover, 1891-97), cited hereafter as LdL, III, 642ff., esp. 664,32-38, and 665,28-30 [-31]; also, H. Böhmer, *Kirche und*

Staat in England und in Normandie im 11 und 12 Jahrhundert (Leipzig, 1899), 177ff.
21. *RA*, n. 258 (anno 1211); *CD*, III, 103ff.; Katona, V, 129.
22. *RA*, n. 243; *CD*, III-1, 76.
23. Katona, V, 91.
24. *RA*, n. 261; *VMH*, n. 106; re-written by Pope Gregory IX, on April 23, 1231, in Potthast, n. 8278; *VMH*, n. 169.
25. *CD*, III-1, 370ff.
26. Potthast, n. 8723; *VMH*, n. 170; *CD*, III-2, 246.
27. Hóman-Szekfü, I, 456ff.
28. *RA*, n. 240; *ÁUO*, VI, 333f. (anno 1209), and compare to a writ of Béla IV, dated July 27, 1267, *RA*, n. 1528.
29. See *CD*, IV-1, 105, where Béla IV mentioned "immensae donationes," and compare to Rogerius, *Carmen miserabile*, cc. 3 and 9; *SSH*, II, 554 and 557f.
30. The chancellor is a disorderly man, who cannot remember anything - Knauz, I, 185; Katona, V, 33, transcribed by Innocent III, Potthast, n. 3712; *MPL*, 216, 39.
31. On this, see J. Thalcic (ed.), *Monumenta historica episcopatus Zagrabiensis*, 2 vols. (Zagreb, 1874-74), I, 25; Antal Schütz (ed.), *Szentek élete az év minden napjára* [Lives of the Saints for Every Day of the Year], IV (Budapest, 1933), 229ff.; Sándor Bálint (ed.), *Ünnepi Kalendárium* [Almanac for Holy Days] (Budapest, 1977), 475ff.; see also Gábor Barna's remembrance of Sándor Bálint on his 90th birthday, in *Vigilia* 59 (1994), 577ff.; further, Mária Püskely, *Arpádházi Szent Erzsébet* [Saint Elizabeth of the House of Árpád] (Rome, 1981), 6ff.
32. *CD*, III-1, 155; IV-3, 387f.
33. Katona, V, 15f.
34. Cf. Thomas Ebendorf, 109,8-13 and 109, note 6; 110,6-12; *Monumenta Erphesfurtensa*, ed. O. Holder-Egger, SSrG (Hannover, 1899), 757f.; *Annales Marbacenses*, ed. H. Bloch, SSrG (Hannover-Leipzig, 1907; reprint 1979), 79,5-6 and 85,5-14; also, "Chronicon rhytmicum Austriacum," *MGHSS*, XXV, 355, lines 246-75; there is an "überprüft und verbessert" version of the text by Gerlinde Stiassni, "Anonymi clerici Chronicon rythmicum: ein Beitrag zur Historiographie des XIII Jahrhunderts," Doctoral dissertation, Vienna, 1955, 115ff.; Lhotsky, *Quellenkunde*, 190f.
35. *MGHSS*, XXV, 355,16-17 (lines 252-53); and, *ibid.*, XVII, 173,24-26; see further the writ of Innocent III to Andrew II, on May 5, 1207, Potthast, n. 3037; *MPL*, 215, 1332; Huber, art. cit., AföG, 65, 16ff.
36. Potthast, n. 2793; *MPL*, 215, 893; *Annales Marbacenses*, 79,22-25; Fraknói, I, 43.
37. Katona, V, 68 - as recorded by Pope Innocent III in his writ to Andrew II, dated May 5, 1207, in Potthast, n. 3037; *MPL*, 215, 1132.
38. *CD*, III-1, 49.
39. Potthast, n. 3252; *MPL*, 215, 1266; *CD*, III-1, 53; in one of his letters, Andrew II referred to him as the archbishop of Kalocsa and *ban(us)*, cf. *RA*, n. 243; *CD*, III-1, 76 (anno 1209); earlier, *RA*, n. 242 referred to him as the archbishop-elect of Kalocsa; *RA*, n. 244 spoke of him as elected archbishop and *ban(us)*.
40. Potthast, n. 3617; *MPL*, 215, 1534, and compare to Potthast, n. 3252.
41. *Ibid.*, n. 4378; *MPL*, 216, 515ff.; *ÁUO*, VI, 351ff.; *RA*, n. 265. In referring to John as the former archbishop of Kalocsa, see Potthast, n. 2588, on October 6, 1205, and Potthast, n. 2591, on October 14, 1205.
42. Potthast, n. 4282, July 15, 1211; *MPL*, 216, 447; Kosztolnyik, *From Coloman*, 244 and 260, n. 134, and 279.
43. Potthast, n. 4378, in ref. to *RA*, n. 257; *ÁUO*, VI, 351f.

44. *RA*, n. 225, anno 1206, on Berthold [spelled Pertold!], "ban(us)" and archbishop of Kalocsa; *RA*, n. 227 referred to him as archbishop-elect; *RA*, n. 243, anno 1209, as archbishop and "ban(us)"; *CD*, III-1, 76.
45. *RA*, n. 269.
46. Potthast, n. 4871; *RA*, n. 272, named Michael ban(us), and Bánk as the palatine; *CD*, III-1, 121f. Ignatius de Batthyány (ed.), *Leges ecclesiasticae regni Hungariae et provinciarum adiacentium*, 3 vols., rev. ed. (Claudipoli, 1824, etc.), II, 299f.
47. *RA*, n. 261; *VMH*, n. 106, as it might be evident from a letter of Pope Gregory IX, dated April 26, 1231, see Potthast, n. 8729; see further, A. von Bethlen (ed.), *Geschichtliche Darstellung des Deutschen Ordens in Siebenbürgen* (Vienna-Leipzig, 1831), 97f., though the Order had sought, and obtained, protection from the Holy See; cf. Potthast, n. 7115 (December 12, 1223); *VMH*, n. 87; the Knights wanted to have their territorial rights recognized as "property" of the Holy See - Potthast, n. 7232 (April 30, 1224); *VMH*, nn. 105 and 107.
48. According to the text taken from the *Liber pactorum* [Venetian State Documents], cf. G.L.F. Tafel and G.M. Thomas (eds.), *Urkunden zur älteren Handelsgeschichte der Republik Venedig*, 2 vols. (Vienna, 1856), I, 421ff.; Zara became Venetian territory in 1203!
49. Cf. Thomas of Spaleto, c. 25 (*MHSM*; *MGHSS*, XXIX, 576f.); remarks made by Pope Innocent III, *MPL*, 214, 1178f.; Choniates, *CB*, 757ff.; Dieten, 572,79 - 575,78; Nicholas Mesarites' "Funeral Oration," in A. Heisenberg, *Neue Quellen zur Geschichte des lateinischen Kaisertums*, 2 vols. (Munich, 1932), I, 41ff.
50. *RA*, n. 229; *ÁUO*, VI, 313ff.; *RA*, n. 228; Katona, V, 59f.
51. Dandalo, x:3-4; in Muratori, *RISS*, XII, 315ff.; Margrave Boniface married Margaret, the widow of Isaac Angelos, and sister of Andrew II - Choniates, *CB*, 793; Dieten, 599; Moravcsik, *Fontes*, 296; Georgios Acropolita spoke of the beauty of Margaret - "Annales," cc. 8 and 11, *ibid.*, 298.
52. Choniates, *CB*, 323; Dieten, 248f.
53. On November 8, 1204, see Kajolan's letter to Innocent III, *ÁUO*, VI, 281ff. and 292ff.; *MPL*, 215, 290ff., and 551.
54. A. Gardner, *The Lascarids of Nicea: The Story of an Empire in Exile* (London, 1922), 66; E. Gerland, *Geschichte des lateinischen Kaiserreichs von Konstantinople*, vol. I (Hamburg, 1905), 92.
55. Choniates, *CB*, 709; Dieten, 534f.; R.L. Wolff, "The Second Bulgarian Empire to 1204," *Speculum* 24 (1949), 167ff. On the hostile relationship, see the pope's letter of May 25, 1207, Potthast, n. 3109; *MPL*, 216, 1162; *ÁUO*, VI, 316f.; Geoffrey de Villehardouin, *La conquete de Constantinople*, ed. Edmund Faral, 2 vols. (Paris, 1938-39), cc. 138 and 206; Ostrogorsky, 342.
56. In 1232, Baranch must have been under Hungarian administration - cf. the papal letter, dated March 21, 1232, in Potthast, n. 8901; *CD*, III-2, 276; *VMH*, n. 179, in referring to Bishop Bulcsú of Csanád that stated that one of the two bishops he reported on happened to be the bishop of Baranch [Brundisi!].
57. In about 1212, Andrew II took up arms against the "Gubatos," that is, Bulgarians - *ÁUO*, I, 132; in 1217 he made a donation to Uruz [Vruz?], *iobagio* of Zala county, who had distinguished himself in the battle "iuxta castrum Bronch;" cf. *RA*, n. 336; *ÁUO*, XI, 141, implying that the region had come under his rule during the reign of Asen II.
58. *Chronica regia*, 232; *ÁUO*, II, 441f.; F.M. Mayer and R. Kaindl, *Geschichte und Kulturleben Österreichs*, 5th rev. ed., ed. H. Pirchegger, I (Vienna, 1958), 63ff.; Gebhardt, *Handbuch*, I, 350ff.
59. Burckhard, *Chronicon*, anno 1210.
60. In 1216, Andrew II had renewed, *RA*, n. 304, a donation he had earlier made to royal Reeve Thomas, *RA*, n. 234; however, Thomas died in 1216 and the king had to confirm Alexander, the royal cup-bearer, son of Thomas and the younger

brother of Alexander, Reeve Sebes, in their possession of the now divided land-grant; cf. *RA*, n. 308; *CD*, III-1, 176,

61. This is evident from a letter of the pope written on another occasion - *RA*, n. 355, anno 1219; its date can be determined from a writ of Pope Honorius III, March 5, 1219, in Potthast, n. 6001; *VMH*, n. 33.

62. See Hodinka, 84ff., and 279f.

63. Potthast, n. 2837; *MPL*, 215, 931ff., esp. 933b; *ÁUO*, I, 41f.

64. Hodinka, 304; M.F. Font, "Politische Beziehungen zwischen Ungarn und der Kiever Rus' im 12 Jahrhundert," *Ungarn Jahrbuch* 18 (1990), 1ff.

65. Hodinka, 308a; *GVC*, 187 (anno 1203).

66. Hodinka, 308a, Gustin recorded the year 1202, that is, 1205! *GVC*, 17 and 18; he fell on June 19, 1205.

67. The Russian record mentioned a mighty giant, the one-eyed Makó (Valpo), as the commander of the Hungarian guard - Hodinka, 304af.; *GVC* 18; he may have been Makó [Mica; Mike], the palatine of King Emery - *RA*, nn. 193, 194, (dated 1201), and 195.

68. *RA*, n. 219, does not, as yet, mention this title: "Galiciae Ladomerieque;" *ÁUO*, VI, 300, but a writ dated 1026 does - *ÁUO*, VI, 307f.; Knauz, I, 181.

69. Hodinka, 308af.

70. *Ibid.*, 312af. and 312bf; *GVC*, 20.

71. Hodinka, 314bf.; *GVC*, 19.

72. Hodinka, 314bff.

73. *RA*, n. 227; on the husband of Tota, see *CD*, III-1, 316.

74. Hodinka, 310a; *GVC*, 20.

75. Hodinka, 310f.

76. *Ibid.*, 312af.

77. *Ibid.*, 314af.

78. *Ibid.*, 316a; Peter (Petur; Pator), landowner in Valkó-Szerém-Bács counties, and royal reeve of Kirné - *RA*, n. 384; Bánk, castle reeve at Pozsony, and Reeve of the Queen's Court - *RA*, n. 258; *ÁUO*, VI, 349; see further, *RA*, nn. 262 and 269.

79. On Lébény, cf. *RA*, nn. 1231 and 1372; *ÁUO*, XII, 492, and VIII, 50f.; K. Bosl et al, *Eastern and Western Europe in the Middle Ages* (London, 1970), 105f., recorded on a similar abbey at Zsámbók, and on the monastic church at Ják, *ibid.*, 189.

80. Hodinka, 320a-322a, and 322b; *GVC*, 22.

81. Hodinka, 322a.

82. *Ibid.*, 322a.

83. *Ibid.*, 324a-326a; 324b; *GVC*, 23.

84. Hodinka, 324b-326b, and his remarks that Marcel (*RA*, n. 258) had lost his standards in battle, Hodinka, 320a.

85. *CD*, III-1, 100.

86. His title was "ban(us)," - *RA*, nn. 262 (anno 1211), 269, 270 (anno 1212); Albericus, *Chronicon, MGHSS*, XXIII, 872f.; "Ungarnchronik," *SSH*, II, 205f.; "Chronicon Knauzianum," *ibid.*, II, 338af.; on this, Macartney, 149; "Chronicon Posoniense," *SSH*, II, 41,24-26; Macartney, 146; and the "Chronicle of Leutschau," *SSH*, II, 281,23-25; Macartney, 147. Berthold did receive a landgrant - *CD*, III-1, 135. Keza, c. 94, made mention of landgrants given to "foreigners;" he made no mention of Berthold, however, cf. *SSH*, I, 192.

87. From the standpoint of the papal curia, Berthold was unqualified for an ecclesiastical position - Potthast, nn. 3073, 3117, 3252.

88. His title was "Woyvoda" (Grande Reeve, or Steward) - *CD*, III-1, 114ff., 129, archbishop of Kalocsa, and royal reeve of Bács and Bodrog counties, *CD*, III-1, 148; *RA*, nn. 272, 273, 274, 275, 282, 282, 283; *SSH*, I, 464f.; Alberic, in *MGHSS*, XXIII, 873,7-9. Gyula Kristó, "Magyar öntudat és idegenellenség az Árpád-korban

[Hungarian Ethnic Consciousness and Hatred Toward Foreigners in the Árpád Age], *ItK*, 94 (1990), 425ff.

89. According to the *Chronica regia*, 186, the purpose of the conspirators was to murder the king, "regem occidere conati sunt, ... in castra regis irruunt, ad occidendum regem inquirunt." *SSH*, I, 464f., on the conspiracy of the Hungarian nobles; Alberic, in *MGHSS*, XXIII, 898,24-25.

90. Archbishop John's dubious answer:"Reginam interficere nolite timere bonum est, si omnes consenserint, eo solus non contradico," *MGHSS*, XXIII, 898,25-30, and compare, *ibid.*, IX, 780,17-18, as if to imply that the conspiracy was aimed at the royal "protégés;" the chronicler of Salzburg hinted, though, that "litterae amfibolicae, duplicem habentes constructionem;" *ibid.*, IX, 780,14-18; I. Victoriensis, *Liber certarum historiarum*, SSrG, ed. F. Schneider (Hannover-Leipzig, 1909), 128f.; *CD*, III, 269ff.

91. See the request of Andrew II to the papal curia, *RA*, n. 257; *ÁUO*, VI, 352.

92. The monarch respected the archbishop, *RA*, n. 224, and granted him land, *RA*, n. 226, although the behavior of the Queen and members of her family might have become a sty in the archbishop's eye - *RA*, n. 243.

93. The question remains, of course, who was responsible for the information in this portion of the Chronicle? In *RA*, n. 281 (a. 1213), Bánk had signed as the palatine, but in n. 282, anno 1213, Nicholas, reeve of Csanád had signed in that capacity.

94. *MGHSS*, IX, 780,15-18, mentioned "expeditionem contra Ruthenos;" Hodinka, 326a.

95. See A. Huber, "Studien über die Geschichte Ungarns inder Zeit der Arpáden," *Archiv für österreichische Geschichte*, 65 (1883-84), 153ff.; esp. 170ff.

96. *Annales Marbacenses*, 85, 11-13: "a comite quoam Petro et a quibusdam aliis trucidatur." Also, *MGHSS*, XXV, 355,27-37, lines 263-273.

97. It was of this Simon that King Stephen V had remarked that it was he "qui aviam nostram intrfecit," *RA*, n. 1907; *ÁUO*, VIII, 260.

98. There were two Simons; as late as 1270, the son-in-law of Bánk was described as being "sine herede decedente," *ibid.*

99. "... in odium Teutenicorum," in "Annales Gotwicenses," anno 1213, *MGHSS*, IX, 602,42-43; another source spoke of the Hungarian lords as the conspirators, "omnium malorum auctores erant comites, qui matrem regis occiderant." It is to be noted, though, that the entry is from the year 1242! Cf. "Continuatio Sancrucensis II," *ibid.*, IX, 640,36-37. The Hungarian source mentioned Bánk by name, *SSH*, I, 464f.

100. *Chronica regia*, 186f.

101. *MGHSS*, IX, 780,15-18.

102. Ebendorfer, 198,22-24; *SSH*, I, 465,3-4, mentioned also by Béla IV, *RA*, n. 621; *ÁUO*, VII, 27ff.; Gy. Székely and A. Bartha, *Magyarország története: előzmények és magyar történet 1242-ig* [History of Hungary: Prehistory and Hungarian History until 1242] (Budapest, 1984), 1284ff.

103. Prince Coloman was in command - Hodinka, 326a, 336a, and 338a; *MGHSS*, IX, 592,13-15; XVII, 526,52-53; XVII, 632,13.

104. *Ibid.*, XXIII, 873,1-13.

105. On *RA*, n. 225, Berthold signed as archbishop of Kalocsa; on *RA*, n. 227, as the archbishop-elect; *ÁUO*, VI, 307f.

106. *RA*, n. 243; *CD*, III-1, 76.

107. In 1207, as grand reeve of Slavonia, *RA*, n. 269; *HO*, VIII, 12, and, "Woyvoda" on *RA*, n. 272; Batthyány, *Leges*, II, 299.

108. Letter of Innocent III, Potthast, n. 3073; the pontiff yielded slowly, *ibid.*, n. 3252 (December 24, 1207); *CD*, III-1, 53.

109. Potthast, n. 3617.

110. *Ibid.*, n. 4378; *ÁUO*, VI, 351ff.; Knauz, I, 193f.
111. Potthast, n. 3725; *MPL*, 216, 51a, and 216, 50c, a-d; Kosztolnyik, *From Coloman*, 244 and 279.
112. Cf. W. Holtzmann, "Papst Alexander III und Ungarn," *Ungarische Jahrbücher*, 6 (1926), 397ff., esp. 401f.; for the text of the papal writ taken from the Tortosa Kapitelbibliothek, MS 144, fol. 24.
113. *MPL*, 215, 413c.
114. *MGHSS*, XXIII, 898,24-30.
115. *Ibid.*, IX, 592,13-19. The royal seal must have been lost during the assassination scene; previous royal writs, as, e.g. *RA*, nn. 175 and 178, had to be reconfirmed because of this - *ÁUO*, XI, 134f.
116. This seems to be evident from a letter of Andrew II to Rome, *RA*, n. 294; *VMH*, I, 1f., esp. 2,1-3; *CD*, III-1, 163ff.; Katona, V, 209f.; *MPL*, 216, 950; quoted by J. Horváth, *Irodalmi kezdetek*, 267; Kristó, art. cit. (1990).
117. *Chronica Magni, Cont.*, *MGHSS*, XVII, 526,52-53, Peter who did it, was the Reeve of the Queen's Court, *RA*, n. 254; it also listed Bánk in the same capacity, although on *RA*, nn. 255 and 258,, he appeared as reeve of Bihar and as the reeve of Bihar and of the Queen's Court. On *RA*, nn. 272, 273, 275, and 283, Bánk appeared as palatine (and reeve of Keve; reeve of Pozsony); on n. 283, though Jula (Gyula; Julius) was named as *bán* (grand steward); on *RA*, n. 314, Bánk was once more named as ban(us), while Jula as palatine; see also *RA*, nn. 317 and 318.
118. "Reginam occidere nolite timere bonum est, et si omnes consenserint, ego non contradico;" the Salzburg chronicler, *MGHSS*, IX, 780,15018. See above, note 90. the chronicler(s) most probably gained his (their) information from the Cistercian monks at Pilis abbey; the fact that he (they) also recorded the double-dealings of the archbishop may mean that the monks did not like the archbishop! Cf. Wattenbach, II, 461ff. Somogyvár abbey was founded by French Cistercians - *RA*, n. 24; and Béla III had reassured the French monks settling down in Hungary of the same privileges they had enjoyed in France - *RA*, n. 137; Katona, IV, 288f.; Kosztolnyik, *From Coloman*, 219f.
119. *RA*, n. 254, on Peter, reeve of Bács.
120. *Chronica regia*, 187.
121. *CD*, IV-1, 68.
122. *Annales Marbacenses*, 85,11-13; *MGHSS*, IX, 780,17-18.
123. *Annales Marbacenses*, 85,12-14.
124. Katona, V, 204f.
125. *RA*, n. 441; *CD*, III-2, 129f.
126. *RA*, n. 289.
127. *RA*, nn. 314, 317, 318, etc.
128. *Ibid.*, n. 364 - reeve of the court and of Fehérvár, *CD*, III-1, 329f.
129. *RA*, n. 676; *HO*, VIII, 35.
130. In a royal writ, dated 1216, Bánk was listed as "iobagio fides" - *ÁUO*, XI, 139f. Keza, c. 97, reminds one of the original meaning of *iobagio*, *SSH*, I, 193,32-34.
131. Innocent III ordered the Hungarian hierarchy to punish anyone who would speak out against Berthold - Potthast, n. 4871.
132. *MGHSS*, XXIII, 898,24-30.
133. "... nobis nescientibus abtulisse, quod nobis iniuste sublatum est;" *CD*, III-1, 163ff., letter of Andrew II to Rome, *VMH*, n. 1, last paragraph.
134. Lhotsky, *Quellenkunde*, 190f.; see above, note 34.
135. *MGHSS*, XXV, 355,25-31, and note 7; Ebendorfer, 109,8-13.
136. Jenő Szűcs, "Kézai problémák [Questions Concerning Chronicler Keza]," *Kútfőink*, 187ff.; L.J. Csóka, *Latinnyelvű történelmi irodalmunk kialakulása Magyarországon a XI-XIV században* [Development of Latin Language Hungarian

DOMESTIC TURMOIL   59

Historical Literature During the Eleventh Through Fourteenth Centuries] (Budapest, 1967), 599ff.
137. Keza, c. 71, *SSH*, I, 184.
138. See the Chronicle, *ibid.*, I, 465,4-6 - as if the treacherous example of Felicián Zách, who had attempted to murder the king, Louis the Great of Hungary in 1330, came to life in the expanded text of the chronicler, c. 206, *ibid.*, I, 493f.; A. Domanovszky's introduction, *ibid.*, I, 219 and 220; Hóman-Szekfű, II, 71ff.; Dercsényi, *Nagy Lajos*, 143.
139. *RA*, n. 291; *ÁUO*, VI, 367f.
140. *RA*, n. 293 concerning the loyalty of Simon; *CD*, III-1, 393.
141. *RA*, n. 294; *VMH*, I, 2,1-3.
142. *Ibid.*, I, 1.
143. *RA*, n. 302; *ÁUO*, VI, 374f.; see further the writ issued in 1217, *ibid.*, VI, 383ff. and 550f.; *MGHSS*, XXVI, 765. Rome will see to it that members of the Hungarian hierarchy will be properly educated - Potthast, n. 6337; *VMH*, n. 41.
144. *VMH*, n. 1 (*RA*, n. 294).
145. "... anno ante preterite suo per iure coronationis ad ecclesiam Strigoniensem pertinenti;" *ibid.*, I, 2,3-6; A. Theiner (ed.), *Cardinal Baronius, Annales ecclesiastici*, XX (Barri Ducis, 1869), 332f.
146. *RA*, n. 321; *VMH*, n. 22.
147. In order to strengthen his public position, the king requested aid from Rome, and, in his characteristic manner, cast an eye on the Byzantine throne! Cf. R. Röhricht, *Studien zur Geschichte des Fünften Kreuzzuges* (Innsbruck, 1891), 23; Hóman-Szekfü, I, 437f.
148. Potthast, n. 6328; *VMH*, n. 50.
149. Potthast, n. 6318; *CD*, III-1, 294; also, Potthast, n. 7443; *VMH*, nn. 126 and 127; Potthast, n. 8305 (December 30, 1228); *VMH*, n. 191, dated anno 1233!
150. As if witnessed by a papal writ, Potthast, n. 7443; Katona, V, 469f.
151. See, e.g., *VMH*, nn. 187 and 190, for phrase such as these: "camerae et publicis officiis;" "iobagionibus et servientibus genti nostri;" "super domos vel villae servientium;" "curiales comites parrochiani" - among his *iobagiones* some occupied higher ranks, "iobagionum, quantum cumque magnus."
152. *VMH*, I, 108f.
153. Hodinka, 330v-332b; 330a (anno 1211!).
154. *Ibid.*, 336b.
155. According to the letter of Andrew II to Rome, *ÁUO*, VI, 374f.; *RA*, n. 302.
156. *RA*, n. 294; *VMH*, n. 1 (introductory paragraph); Hodinka, 330ab-332ab; 332a.
157. Letter of the king to Demeter de genere Alba, *RA*, n. 529; *ÁUO*, VI, 545ff., and compare with the letter of Béla IV, *RA*, n. 608.
158. Pope Honorius III to Andrew II, Potthast, n. 6777; *VMH*, n. 65; Hodinka, 328a-330a.
159. Regardless of the expected hostile attitude of the nobles - *ibid.*, 328af.
160. *Ibid.*, 334a; 334b.
161. *Ibid.*, 332b-334b; *ÁUO*, VI, 545ff.
162. Hodinka, 342a.
163. *Ibid.*, 342a-348a.
164. *Ibid.*, 362a-370a.
165. *Ibid.*, 332a.
166. On the Fourth Lateran Council, 1215, see, e.g., "Reineri Leodiensis Annales," *MGHSS*, XVI, 674; "Annales Ceccanses," *ibid.*, XIX, 330; Muratori, *RISS*, VII, 893; Haller, *Papsttum*, III, 465ff. and 555; Seppelt, *Päpste*, III, 386ff.

2. The Crusade of Andrew II

> Post autem Andreas Terram Sanctam
> visitavit ad mandatum domini papae.
>
> *Chronicon pictum*, c. 175

The "crusade" of Andrew II has been described by some historians as the Fifth Crusade, in spite of the fact that the monarch's expedition to the Holy Land was not a serious military undertaking.

Why did Andrew II go to the Holy Land in 1217? Officially, he had followed the papal summons to realize the promise his father, Béla III, had made, thereby to show his political-religious loyalty to the Roman See. But that was only a pretense on his part, because he had made almost no preparation to carry out such a large scale military maneuver in the Holy Land. The real reason for him to go must have been that it was at that time that the Byzantine-Latin throne fell vacant, and Andrew II regarded himself as a candidate for the Greek imperial throne. The king boarded ships to cross the sea to the Near East with the resolution in mind that, by imitating the political circumstances that had surrounded the Fourth Crusade, he could realize his goal of gaining great power and predominance in Byzantium - by use of physical force if necessary.

The plans of Andrew II were ruined by the election of his relative to the Byzantine throne, and the coronation of that relative by the pontiff as Byzantine-Latin emperor, which was carried out with papal approval. Since Andrew II had no alternative, he visited the Holy Land "in fulfillment of the vow his father had made," made his presence known, and departed quickly. But during his journey home, he established political-diplomatic ties with various ruling families in Asia Minor. He had, for example, his son Béla engaged to Maria, the daughter of the ruler of Nicea.

Andrew II had assumed that if not he, then someone else from among his descendants would gain access to the Byzantine throne on account of these family contacts. He did not consider that Rome would not have tolerated the formation of a new political-diplomatic configuration through the establishment of a Buda-Byzantine axis. Nor did Andrew II reckon with the tolerance level of his people;

they were not willing to support a policy so foreign to their minds and liking, and they protested against its very concept.

In accordance with its motto, "Reformatio tam in capite, quam in membris,"[1] the Fourth Lateran Council proclaimed the necessity of another crusade; let there be a truce for four years; let one-twentieth of all ecclesiastical income be spent on the organization and operation of the crusade.[2]

The new pontiff, Honorius III, would not tolerate any further delay by Andrew II of Hungary in taking command of the crusade.[3] Politics and military events in Halich must not draw the attention of the Hungarian court away from the realization of the undertaking, the pontiff wrote warningly to the king - much as his predecessor, Innocent III, had to do on a previous occasion.[4] As lenient as he might have been - or, because he had been - with the German emperor,[5] the less tolerance Honorius III displayed toward Andrew II, who had no alternative but to make some pretense of preparation for the campaign.[6]

In order to understand the background of this political and military maneuvering, one needs to realize that Pope Innocent III had earlier attempted to persuade Sultan al-Adil (Saphadin) to reach an agreement with the Christians instead of fighting them. He requested that the sultan return Jerusalem peacefully to him and exchange his Christian prisoners of war for Arabs held captive by the Franks. Thereby, the fate of Christians in the East would not be worse than that of the Moslems in the West!

The pontiff had asked al-Adil to understand that he was only a tool in the hands of the Almighty; the Lord permitted his brother to capture Jerusalem only because He wanted to punish the godless inhabitants of that city. Innocent III held the opinion that the sultan was identical with the Beast of the Book of Revelations, but the six hundred and sixty-six years allowed to the beast were about to expire. It was now time to take action. The chronicler ought to mention that al-Adil had taken action - a man of practical sense was he, who had prepared for war.[7]

The Fourth Lateran Council had declared that participants of the new crusade were to be ready for departure by June, 1217.[8] Were they to journey by sea, they were to embark at Brundisi or at Messina, and the pope would be there to bless them. Were they to go by a land route (*recte*: those who went on land to their destination), they would be looked after by the papal legate, who would also provide spiritual comfort and political advice for them, if needed. The pontiff promised to issue from the papal treasury thirty thousand pounds of silver marks, and place a ship from the Roman port at their disposal. The curia offered ten percent of its annual income for the coverage of expenditures of the crusade, and called upon the clergy to pledge one-twentieth of their annual income for the next three years for the same purpose.[9]

The Hungarian court made the arrangement that, for the duration of the monarch's absence from the realm, Archbishop John of Esztergom would be acting governor or regent. Were the king to die on the crusade, his son, Béla, would inherit the throne and his younger son, Coloman, would remain ruler in Halich. Were both sons to die, Andrew, their youngest brother, would claim the inheritance. Since Andrew was a minor, Alice (Ahalys), a lady-in-waiting to Queen Jolánta, would look after him.[10] The archbishop would have to share the government of the country with Gyula the Palatine, Grand Reeve Raphyan of Transylvania, Grand Reeve (ban[us] Bánk, and Oghuz [Agyasz], Judge of the King's Court.[11] Berthold, the brother of the assassinated Queen Gertrud, would protect Prince Béla. (As a matter of fact, Berthold had immediately dispatched Béla to Stein, a Meranian residence near Laibach.[12]) Were the monarch to die during the campaign, Queen Jolánta would receive eight thousand silver marks from her dowry.[13]

Did Andrew II formulate a foreign policy different from that of his predecessor? Did he earlier, before the Fourth Lateran Council, express willingness to forge ahead with a pledge to realize the vow his father had made, so that he might merit, on his own terms, the trust and good will of the Holy See?[14] Did the king have any money in 1217 to organize and go on a crusade? Did he have any plans or military strategy for the campaign? Did he have a desire to go?[15] The Hungarian clergy were not at all happy about the payment of one-twentieth of their annual income for the expenses of the king's crusade,[16] with the exception of Bishop Kalán of Pécs, who had taken the cross, and left upon his death in 1218 an amount of money for continued military action in the Near East.[17]

Andrew II's first choice was to travel on land with his crusaders, a cheap and perhaps more convenient way for the journey, but for one reason. Upon the death in 1216 of Henry the

Brave, Latin emperor of Byzantium, many of the barons of the empire advocated the election of the Hungarian monarch to the Latin-Byzantine throne, on the two-fold ground that he was the husband of the niece of the deceased emperor and he was the brother of the Queen of Thessalonica.[18]

One may indeed draw the conclusion from a papal letter addressed to Andrew II informing him that the "Greeks" had messengers dispatched to Rome with intelligence that they intended to elect the Hungarian king, or his brother-in-law, emperor of Latin, Byzantium. The papal writ stressed the point of view that the election must not cause a delay in the recovery of the Holy Land, though Andrew II might, if he pleased, leave *early* for the crusade - before the set departure date in early June, 1217. The papal letter further created the impression - in the mind of the addressee; and in the mind of this researcher - that the curia was willing to permit Andrew II to obtain the Byzantine throne with the help of his armed crusaders, or at least influence the outcome of the election.[19]

And yet, another group of barons in the Latin empire voted for Peter Courtenay, the brother-in-law of Henry the Brave, and vote they did, with the full consent of the pope. As the result of papal intervention, Peter and his queen were crowned emperor and empress in Rome on April 9, 1217.[20] Andrew II must have been greatly disappointed, as he must have taken the outcome of the election for granted. Had he been elected Byzantine emperor, he would have chosen the land route; hence the absence of ships in the harbor at Spaleto. The idea of land travel now feel by the wayside; the king chose the sea route.[21]

Did he, understandably, lose interest and initiative to go on with the crusade after de Courtenay had been elected Latin emperor of Byzantium and the papal curia solemnly approved of the election? Only in the summer of 1217 did the king summon his troops to gather at Spaleto - an area under his administrative jurisdiction - and not in the harbor of Rome. It must have been in such a manner that Andrew II wanted to emphasize that although he performed services for Rome, he carried them out according to his own ideas.[22]

Andrew II had to rent, for three thousand marks, ten ships from Venice for the transport of his forces across the sea; he further had to surrender to Venice his claim to Zara on the seashore, and reduce the import-export tax for Venetian merchants engaged in business in regions under his administration from 3.33% to 1.12%; further, he had to grant the Venetian merchants tax exemptions on gold and silver products, silk, and precious stones.[23]

It was during the summer of 1217 that the Hungarian monarch began his journey to Spaleto to board ships with his men.[24] En-route to the seacoast, the canons of the Zagreb cathedral had asked him to confirm them in the privileges their chapter had previously obtained from King Ladislas I.[25]

Spaleto was filled with "crusaders" (one would be tempted to call them adventurers, on the grounds that they had no religious motivation), and the king decided to live in his tent outside of the town walls. The bishops of Győr and of Eger, the abbot of Pannonhalma, and Ugrin, his chancellor, accompanied him, with some ten thousand troops (although this writer, for one, suspects that the number was closer to five thousand, particularly when one thinks of the space on the ships, the food and supplies for that number of men).[26] Leopold of Austria also went along with his brothers-in-law, Otto of Meran, and Bishop Eckbert of Bamberg, the dukes of Hehenberg and Ottingen. The bishops of Münster and Utrecht had also joined the crusade.[27]

Duke Leopold had departed earlier and reached the Holy Land in sixteen days; Andrew II, as it was his custom, was in no hurry, nor did he have enough ships to have all of his troops ferried across the sea. Many of the men had to return home, and only a small number of them went with him to the Near East.[28]

It seems curious that the curia was concerned about the crusaders who were stranded at Messina, Brundisi, and at other Italian seaports, because of the discipline problems caused by the men. The Holy See had warned their leaders not to fail to meet with the Hungarian king and the Austrian duke on the island of Cyprus, where they were expected to attend a council, together with King John of Jerusalem and delegates of the crusading Orders, in order to determine their invasion plan.[29] Hugh of Lusignan of Cyprus joined forces with Andrew II, and in mid-October, 1217, they arrived in Acre.[30]

In 1217, only a narrow strip of land on the shore, stretching from Jaffa to Beirut, remained in Christian hands. Famine and hardships had prevailed, and the price of food was extremely high. An increasing number of Franks had already departed for home from the region. Prior to the arrival of the Hungarian king, some sixty ships of pilgrims had left the area.[31] The arriving Hungarians - the small number of men who had accompanied the king - must not have created a good impression on the native population. The Hungarians shaved their beards in the Frankish manner, wore French arms and helmets, carried triangular shields decorated with the royal Hungarian coat of arms - that is, nine white stripes on a red base with lions in between the stripes. The influence of his second wife - she was a French princess - of King Béla III, father of Andrew II, must have left a mark upon the attitude and behavior of the king's armed contingents.[32]

On November 3, 1217, a war council was held at Accon in the royal tent of Andrew II. It was attended by King Hugh of Cyprus, the King of Jerusalem, and the Patriarch of Jerusalem, and they decided to plan ahead for the capture of Damietta in Egypt (!). The council accepted the military plan of the Palestinian princes for maneuvers: they were to divert the attention of the Sultan from their original and final goal - the conquest of Egypt - by calling for a sham invasion of Syrian territory, despite the fact that they did not have enough ships to sail to Egypt and lacked trained personnel to man the ships.

In such a manner of planning, what had originally been an ideal of a papal crusade, had been turned into a personal military adventure of the princes of Palestine - and of the Hungarian monarch - in their efforts to realize their own selfish (and undefined) interests. Worse still, Andrew II remained under the false impression that he would be offered command of the entire crusading operation. He had not realized that Syria was, as it had been, in the sphere of political-diplomatic interest and the military fighting ground of King John of Jerusalem.

King John took over the military high command of the entire operation, on the grounds that he was familiar with the terrain and warring tactics prevalent in the region; he was a more qualified leader for the campaign. Besides King Andrew II, Leopold of Austria, Bohemund IV of Antioch, Hugh of Cyprus, King John Birenne of Jerusalem, the Patriarch Ralph Merancourt of Jerusalem, William of Chartres, Grandmaster of the Templars, Henry of Salza, Grandmaster of the Teutonic Knights, Otto of Meran, Archbishop

Berthold of Kalocsa, and Bishop Jacob de Vitry of Acre participated in the council.[33]

On November 3, the patriarch of Jerusalem appeared in the Christian camp, bringing with him the relic of the Holy Cross that had been rescued from the Battle at Hattin (1187). Contemporary sources indicate that the operation could not have been regarded as a serious and purposeful military undertaking, as it lacked foresight and precise planning. Indeed, the new arrivals failed to establish a theater of military operations at their destination. In great heat during early November, the "crusading force" of some ten (others say twenty) thousand men marched toward Lake Tiberias, crossed the Jordan river, and captured, without a fight, the entire supply depot of their Arab opponents.[34] The seventy-four year old Coradinus (al-Adil), lord of Egypt, Syria, and Mesopotamia, had expected the "westerners" to invade from the direction of Jerusalem.[35] In spite of the advice he received from his son, al-Adil refused to mount a defensive counterattack against the Christian forces; it may be that their great number and seemingly strong performance made the sultan overcautious.[36]

After a three day rest, the Christian forces marched, it seems, from the southeastern shore of Lake Genezareth toward the north, instead of moving toward Damascus, and devastated the uninhabited region along the Jordan. Because of a bad harvest in Syria, the invaders could not requisition supplies of food; they were also short of horses, and, without a sufficient number of horses and available food supplies, they could not march very fast nor very far. They would not even think of a major military operation in the area. On the bridge at "Jacob's Well," they crossed the river at Haluvett Lake, marched southward on the right hand side of the Jordan. At Kafarnaum, they circled Like Tiberias, and returned to Acre.[37]

What were the results of this marching operation? Perhaps some booty and many fallen enemy left behind unburied, but no tangible political or military accomplishments.[38] It must have been out of a sense of sheer frustration that they attacked the fortification on Mount Tabor, defended by some two thousand men.[39]

Dénes (Dionysius), commanding officer of Andrew II's men, led the attack on a gray, foggy day, the first Sunday of Advent. Dénes carried the day, but did not exploit his victory. He hesitated too long before ordering the final assault on the fort and suffered a bloody defeat at the hands of the defenders. Humiliated, he withdrew to Acre. It might have been an irony of fate that later, after this disastrous attempt at taking the fort, the Arab leader himself ordered the destruction of the fort on Mount Tabor, on the grounds that its existence had caused resentment among Christians in the area.[40]

The attack on the fort on Mount Tabor must have exhausted Andrew II's expedition to the Near East. The entire affair was a full-scale military and diplomatic disaster. Or, did the king want it to happen, in order to fulfill the letter of the promise his father made to the curia about undertaking a crusade - without actually realizing that promise? The king's written report sent to Rome might imply such a conclusion.[41]

In January, 1218, Andrew II boarded a ship for his journey back home.[42] The nobles in Acre had begged him in vain to remain; in vain, the Patriarch of Jerusalem had him excommunicated for not staying, but the king left the Holy Land where he did not wish to harvest any military glory.[43] From among his nobles, only Bishop Thomas of Eger remained in Syria, who would take part in the siege of Damietta, and only return home in the fall of 1219. It is recorded that during the siege of Damietta, two Hungarian bishops died.[44]

During his journey home, Andrew II visited Tripoli, where Bohemund IV was his friend and relative; Bohemund had been served well by the Knights of the Hospital from their fort, the Krak-des-Cheveliers.[45] The monarch paid a call on the Grandmaster of the Knights, and after consultation with his nobles, decided to pay them an annual subsidy of five hundred silver marks - out of the royal income derived from the salt mines at Szalacs.[46] The king further promised to both the garrison at Krak[47] and that of Margitia to pay each one hundred marks.[48]

According to the royal writ issued by Chancellor Ugrin - a copy of which was to be retained by the Knights at Tripoli; a transcript to be sent to the Knights in Hungary - the monarch granted them the region in Jánász in Hungary, as far as Csurgó, exempted them from the jurisdiction of regional administrators, and placed the Knights under the supervision of the Judge of the King's Court.[49]

Andrew II had further engaged his younger son, Andrew, to the daughter of the ruler of Galicia on his return voyage, thereby to make Prince Andrew an heir to the Armenian throne.[50] The Sultan of Iconium told the king that he expected to marry a member of the

Árpád dynasty, and in order to accomplish that, he was willing to convert to the Catholic faith.[51] Theodore Lascaris of Nicea had his own daughter engaged to Béla, the first born and heir of Andrew II.[52] One may note that previously Lascaris had married the daughter of Peter of Courtenay, the sister-in-law of the Hungarian king.[53]

John II Asen (Kajolan), son of Asen I, occupied the throne of Bulgaria and asked, in Tirnovo, for the hand in marriage of Maria, a daughter of Andrew II.[54] It was there that Andrew II received news about the outbreak of revolution in Hungary. Archbishop John of Esztergom, the regent, could not quell the uncontrollable situation. It is an irony of fate that the archbishop did not belong to the king's inner circle; in fact, he was quite unpopular with the members of that circle. The archbishop was a law-abiding person, who had served the interests of his country well.[55] The rebels attacked him, devastated his home, and forced him into exile. Only upon his arrival could the monarch recall him and compensate him for the damages suffered with a donation of the Whyncy estate along the Maros river.[56]

What particular event had triggered the revolution in the country during the king's sojourn in the Near East? Could it have been the fact tat Andrew II had taken the crown of Queen Gisela - the Queen of King St. Stephen - with him? This diadem of the Hungarian queens had been preserved and guarded at Veszprém. Together with the crown jewels and other precious treasures that belonged to the abbey of Tihany,[57] had the crown caused, or contributed to, the outbreak of the uprising?

Andrew II must have had an emotional urge to impress his new acquaintances abroad with his personal wealth, because it is a matter of record that, for example, Pontius, Grandmaster of the Templars, had earlier helped the king out of his financial difficulties.[58] Andrew II had been so deeply in debt that he could not even afford to send a gift with his personal delegate that he dispatched to the papal curia.[59] Queen Constance, the widow of King Emery, and crowned Empress of Frederick II since November 20, 1220,[60] had to seek diplomatic help from Rome to recover payment of the thirty thousand marks that had been left to her by her deceased first husband.[61]

In his dispatch to Rome, Andrew II complained to the curia that upon his arrival at home from the Holy Land, some awful conditions existed in his country; his personal and political enemies had paralyzed the realm's economy for the next fifteen years, he reported to Rome.[62] It was common knowledge among contemporaries, however, that it was the monarch who had surrounded himself with irresponsible and unbalanced individuals as personal advisors and office holders, and it was their unqualified advice that had "unreadied" the king in domestic and economic matters.[63]

On the other hand, even though Andrew II had the nerve to boast to Rome about his accomplishments during the "crusade," he had achieved a good deal for the Church in Armenia and Nicea, in that he had his niece marry the Sultan of Iconium, thereby converting him and his people to the faith and cause of the Roman Church.[64] From this point of view, the "crusade" of Andrew II must have been a success. He had fulfilled his promise, and his father's vow, to go on a crusade, and returned home with some of the most valuable relics from the Holy Land - or so he claimed. His "relics" included the head of Saint Stephen, the First Martyr of Christianity, and one of the six water jars from the marriage feast at Caana.[65]

Although the Patriarch of Jerusalem excommunicated him on account of his early departure from Acre, he explained to Rome that he had to leave the area early because of the increasingly difficult situation at home.[66] More importantly, several Hungarian prelates had taken the cross in 1219,[67] Bishop Robert of Veszprém and royal chancellor, by birth a Frenchman of Luttich, among them.[68]

It was more than likely, however, that Archbishop John of Esztergom had opposed the king's crusading venture from its very beginning on the grounds that monarch had been too involved in Byzantine politics. Before Peter of Courtenay could gain possession of his throne, the Byzantines imprisoned him, and he died in prison.[69] Peter's son, Robert Courtenay, spent the winter of 1220-21 in Andrew II's court, and in the spring of 1221, Béla, Andrew II's son and heir, accompanied Robert to be crowned the new emperor of Byzantium.[70]

Had these diplomatic developments continued, and had Emperor Robert died unexpectedly - of natural or unnatural causes - the king could have, the archbishop suspected and feared, become a candidate for the Byzantine throne. The king suspended the archbishop from exercising his functions on the grounds that he had ordained an unlearned cleric of Burgundy as the bishop of Pécs; however, the real cause of the suspension had been that Archbishop John dared to question publicly the personal behavior of the monarch and the orders given by him.[71]

The Hungarian monarch evidently wasted too much attention on realizing a political-diplomatic game of chess for the Latin Crown of Byzantium; that could have been the reason why the people of his own country had rebelled against him.[72] When Andrew II had named his son Béla governor of Croatia and Dalmatia, the whole country rose against him in support of the prince,[73] publicly demanding that the king publicly and officially recognize the rights of his subjects, including the rights of the clergy, most probably on the grounds of a reference to article 14 of Alberic's *Decretum* promulgated during King Coloman's reign, that stated that the monarch cannot order a bishop to elevate any unqualified candidate from among the royal servants to clerical status.[74]

The people of the country demanded that the law forbid a Jew or Moslem to hold public office.[75] Jews and Moslems had taken charge of collecting taxes and public revenues, acted as overseers of the salt mines and sales, and occupied positions of public trust as stewards of the royal chamber.[76] They firmly adhered to their religious faith and cultural inheritance; still, they played an increasingly important role in fiscal policy-making at the royal court. Their growing political and economic influence in and over the realm stood in sharp contrast with the laws of the land.[77]

In its response to Andrew II's report to Rome, the curia had to warn the Hungarian court of King Andrew II and Queen Jolánta that they must not permit "pagans" to enjoy any predominant role in Christian business concerning the country's Catholic population.[78] Still, one may conclude from the royal response that it was the monarch's country-wide opponents who must have been afraid that the king who, by taking up the cause of the non-Christian ("pagan") element in society, could assure himself of the adherence of a loyal administrative social stratum, whose social and administrative function would easily undermine the established but aging class of officials holding public office.[79]

The "Saracen" Islamic subjects of Queen Jolánta, who had been schooled at Aleppo, but were living in the country, spoke Hungarian like natives, and fought, if and when called upon, in wars for Hungarian goals and interests. The public roles they played, and the educational background they possessed, made them a thorn of jealousy in the sides of many officials, who claimed to be the king's most loyal subjects.[80]

Could it be further concluded from the aforementioned papal letter - and so stated for the record - that it was what might be referred to as reliance upon the loyalty of the non-Christian ("pagan") officials of the realm that encouraged Andrew II to go on his sham-crusade so as to prove to his opponents, and to the papal curia, that the Hungarian king could always count on the support of a certain social element of his country's population?[81]

Andrew II had seriously misjudged his people's aversion to "foreign" ventures - the king's "crusade" - and to "foreigners" living in their midst, serving as royal officials in their society.

NOTES

1. On the IV Lateran Council, see *MGHSS*, XVI, 674,1-15; XVI, 356,14-25; XIX, 151,20-22; XIX, 300,33-40; Mansi, *Concilia*, XXII, 1081; Ordericus Raynaldus, *Annales ecclesiastici*, 15 vols. (Lucca, 1738-56), anno 1215, par. ii:4-7; Innocent III's opening remarks, in Friedberg, *Corpus*, II, 5ff., with the seventy canons printed selectively, arranged by subject in various collections of Canon Law, *ibid.*, II, xii. The question is, of course, whether one has access to the full text of the resolutions? - cf. H. Jedin (ed.), *Handbuch der Kirchengeschichte*, 10 vols. (Freiburg i. Br., 1962, etc.), III-2, 206; Haller, III, 465ff.

2. Directives on the crusades were summarized by Potthast, nn. 5012, 5048, and 5050a; Mansi, *Concilia*, XXII, 1057ff.; circumstances surrounding the death of the pope were recorded by Honorius III on July 25, 1216 - cf. Potthast, n. 5317; P. Presutti (ed.), *Regesta Honorii papae III* (Rome, 1888), nn. 2-7; Raynaldus, *Annales*, anno 1216, n. 9.

3. See the papal writ of January 30, 1217, Potthast, n. 5440; *VMH*, n. 5; domestic troubles prevented the king from earlier departure - Thuróczy, *Chronica*, c. 100 (in Galántai and Kristó, 136f; in Schwandtner, I, 149, ii:73). Were the king to die, his son would succeed him, although Archbishop John of Esztergom would exercise royal powers at first, and the seashore would be controlled, in the king's name, by the General of the Order of Templars - Potthast, n. 5456; *VMH*, n. 6; A.L. Tautu (ed.), *Acta Honorii III et Gregorii IX* (1216-27; 1227-41) (Rome, 1950); *CD*, III, 189.

4. In 1213, the curia granted a three year delay to Andrew II, Potthast, n. 4669; *MPL*, 216, 757 has a different date. The Holy See formed no legal claim for intervention, Potthast, nn. 347, 924, and 4725; *MPL*, 214, 308bc-309ab, 214, 180ab, 216, 817ff. Innocent III set 1217 as the date for the crusade, Potthast, n. 4669; *MPL*, 216, 757ac. R. Röhricht, "Der Kreuzzug Königs Andreas II von Ungarn," *Forschungen zur deutschen Geschichte*, 16 (1876), 139ff., esp. 142; on the papal attitude toward the crusade(s), see A. Keutner, *Papsttum und Krieg unter dem Pontifikat des Papstes Honorius III (1216-1227)* (Munster, 1935), 13ff.

MPL, vols. 214-217 is still the main source collection of Innocent III's Register, with the exception of O. Hageneder and A. Haidacher (eds.), *Die Register Innocenz' III, 1 Pontifikatsjahr (1198-1199)*, Publikationen des Österreichischen Kulturinstituts in Rom, Abt. II, Reihe I, vol. I (Graz-Cologne-Vienna, 1964); and O. Hageneder, W. Maleczek, and A. Strnad (eds.), *Die Register Innocenz' III, 2 Pontifikatsjahr (1199-1200)*, Abt. II, Reihe I, vol. II (Rome-Vienna, 1979); vols. xvii-xix of the Register were lost - *MPL*, 216, 991b, and the abbreviated summary is less reliable - cf. H. Röscher, *Papst Innocenz III und die Kreuzzüge* (Göttingen, 1969), 140; and yet, Potthast, nn. 5127-5314, based his data on the summary assuming that the list of addresses might render the needed information - see A. Haidacher, "Beiträge zur Kenntnis der verlorenen Registerbände Innocenz' III," *Römische Mitteilungen*, 4 (1960-61), 37ff. The Register was prepared from original documents, or from concepts contained in the documents - on this, see F. Kempf, *Die Register Innocenz' III: eine paläographische-diplomatische Untersuchung* (Rome, 1945), 65ff.; on the meaning and importance of the Register, *ibid.*, 102ff.; on the officials who put it together, *ibid.*, 119ff.

5. He had been the emperor's tutor, later papal chamberlain for years - cf. Gebhardt, I, 355; Hampe, *Hochmittelalter*, 317; idem, "Kaiser Friedrich II," *HZ*, 83 (1899), 1ff., esp. 15f., and 39f.

6. On February 11, 1217, in Potthast, n. 5456; *VMH*, n. 6; neither had the curia shown much understanding for John of England, who had delayed taking the cross; Potthast, n. 4960; *MPL*, 217, 245; C.R. Cheney and W.H. Simple (eds.), *Selected Letters of Innocent III Concerning England* (London, 1953), 194ff., nn. 72,

74. King John had to face a domestic opposition - see Cheney and Simple, n. 80. The pope had argued that he was acting as John's feudal overlord - King John had been a papal vassal since 1213, Potthast, nn. 4842 and 4843, dated November 4, 1213; *MPL*, 216, 922f. and 924b; but as the visible head of the Church, see writs of August 24, 1215, Potthast, nn. 4990 and 4991; Cheney and Simple, nn. 82, 83, he had taken action - McIlwain, 231; as Röscher, 161, remarked, "der Ordinatio charakterisiert das Charakter der geistigen Körperschaft." Sidney Painter, *The Reign of King John* (Baltimore, 1949), 285ff.; H. Conrad, "Gottesdienst und Heereverfassung in der Zeit der Kreuzzüge," *Zeitschrift der Savigny Stiftung für Rechtsgeschichte*, kan. Abt., 61 (1941), 71ff.

7. The papal appeal, dated April 26, 1213, Potthast, n. 4719; *MPL*, 216, 832ff.; Raynaldus, *Annales*, anno 1213, n. 3. The papal delegation sent to the Sultan was mentioned by R. Röhricht, *Geschichte des Königreichs Jerusalem* (Innsbruck, 1898), 718, note 6. Al-Adil, The Beast of the Book of Revelations - Potthast, n. 4706; *MPL*, 216, 818b. On the military readiness of the sultan, see Raynaldus, *Annales*, anno 1214, n. 7. The crusade had its share of preachers from abroad, with the problem remaining, in what language did they sermonize? Did they use interpreters? How effective were the sermons delivered through interpreters in Hungary? On the role of non-native preachers, see R. Röhricht, "Zur inneren Geschichte des Kreuzzuges," in his *Studien*, 5ff.. On preaching in the thirteenth century, see W. P. Ker, *Medieval English Literature* (Oxford, 1948, a reprint of the 1912 edition), 154ff., and G. R. Owst, *Preaching in Medieval England* (Cambridge, 1926), 96ff., and 222ff.

8. The papal writ of December 5, 1216, addressed to the French-German clergy and the faithful, supported the crusade - Potthast, n. 5381; Presutti, n. 151; C.A. Horoy (ed.), *Honorii III Romani Pontificis opera omnia*, 5 vols. (Paris, 1879-82), I, n. 184; Röscher, *Innocenz III*, 140ff. On the small number, but deep faith of the crusaders, see Potthast, n. 5622; Presutti, n. 885. T.C. VanCleve, "The Fifth Crusade," in R.L. Wolf and H.W. Hazard (eds.), *The Later Crusades, 1189-1311*, vol. II of *A History of the Crusades*, ed. K.S. Setton, 4 vols., 2nd ed. (Madison, 1969, etc.), 377ff., who briefly referred to the participation of Andrew II in the crusade.

9. On taxing the clergy for the crusade, see Presutti, nn. 101 and 102; Horoy, I, nn. 57, 58, and 65; see further the papal warning to John of Esztergom and the archbishop of Spaleto, Potthast, nn. 5362 and 5365; *CD*, III-1, 183. The curia also made comments on the king of Norway, Presutti, n. 399; domestic troubles had delayed Andrew II from departing earlier, Thuróczy, *Chronica*, c. 100 (Schwandtner, I, 149, ii:73).

10. Potthast, n. 5456; *VMH*, n. 6.

11. *RA*, n. 313; *VMH*, n. 7.

12. Pauler, II, 58.

13. *RA*, n. 321; *VMH*, n. 22; *ÁUO*, VI, 383 (and 550f.); also, *MGHSS*, XXVI, 765; the family background of Jolanta is discussed by Röhricht, *Studien*, 23; Hóman-Szekfü, I, 437f.

14. Innocent III's encouraging letter, dated January 29, 1198, Hageneder, *Register 1*, n. 10. In 1213, the curia granted a three year delay, Potthast, n. 4669; *MPL*, 216, 757, with a different date; Röhricht, in *Forschungen*, 139ff. Röscher, 262, noted that before Innocent III, there had been no papal intervention in the crusades; Innocent III saw it differently, *ibid.*, 265 and 268ff.; still, judged by the correspondence, one may conclude that the pontiff had formed no legal claim for intervention, Potthast, nn. 347, 924, and 4725!

15. In contrast to the papal point of view, "firmum habuisti propositum ... peregrinationis arripere;" *VMH*, n. 5; Presutti, I, n. 218.

16. *VMH*, n. 8.

17. Potthast, n. 5970; *VMH*, n. 29; Czínár, *Monasterologii*, I, 69ff.; *CD*, III-1, 277.

18. Potthast, n. 5440; *VMH*, n. 5; Röhricht, *Studien*, 23.
19. King Andrew II's departure is dealt with in the papal writ of January 30, 1217, Potthast, n. 5440; on conditions at Spaleto, see Thomas of Spaleto, c. 26, or R. Röhricht (ed.), *Testimonia minora de quinto bello sacro chronicis orientalibus exercitiis* (Genoa, 1882), 229; Röhricht, *Forschungen*, 142, commented on the chronicler's report of ten thousand horse and an immense multitude of troops.
20. *MGHSS*, XIX, 301; "Chronicon fossae novae," Muratori, *RISS*, VII, 895; see also, "Catalogus pontificum et imperatorum Romanorum Casiensis," *MGHSS*, XXII, 362.
21. Cf. the papal writ of April 24 (25), 1217, Potthast, n. 5586; *VMH*, n. 12. It is very likely that had Andrew II been elected emperor, he would have taken the land route, as indicated by the absence of ships at Spaleto. The king must have taken the outcome of election for granted.
22. For remarks on the number of ships that were at the disposal of the monarch, cf. *MGHSS*, XXIX, 578,33-35.
23. *ÁUO*, VI, 380ff.; Dandalo, in Muratori, *RISS*, XII, 339.
24. Röhricht, *Testimonia*, 229.
25. *RA*, n. 323; *RHM*, 409ff.; *VMH*, I, 83f., third paragraph; also, *RA*, n. 325; *VMH*, I, 73ff.
26. Röhricht, *Forschungen*, 142; Thomas of Spaleto, c. 26; also in *MGHSS*, XXIX, 577,44; Katona, V, 262f.
27. Potthast, n. 5585; *VMH*, n. 12; Raynaldus, *Annales*, anno 1217, n. 26. On the earlier departure of Leopold, see "Annales Clausterneoburgenses," *MGHSS*, IX, 622,35-39; *Chronica regia*, 238f.; Ebendorfer, 198f., and 108,11-22; Jacob de Vitry's *Epistolae*, n. 3 (dated September, 1218), in R. Röhricht's edition, *Zeitschrift für Kirchengeschichte*, 15 (1895), 568; *Annales Marbacenses*, anno 1217, 87,12-21.
28. de Vitry, letter 3; papal writ of November 24, 1217, Potthast, n. 5622; *CD*, III-1, 230f.; J.R. Sweeney, "Hungary in the Crusades, 1169-1218," *International History Review*, 3 (1981), 467ff.
29. The letter of Honorius III to the Master and the members of the Order of St. John of the Hospital, Potthast, n. 5585; *VMH*, n. 13; papal writ addressed to the archbishop of Genoa and other Italian bishops, Potthast, n. 5586. The papal letter mentioning "P. Albanensem episcopum, Apostolicae Sede legatum," spoke of "Pelagio Albanensi episcopo," alias Pelagius, the papal legate - cf. Potthast, n. 5583; J.P. Donovan, *Pelagius and the Fifth Crusade* (Philadelphia, 1950), 29ff.
30. de Vitry, letter 3. Hans Eberhard Mayer, *Geschichte der Kreuzzüge*, 3rd ed. (Stuttgart, 1973), 195, spoke of "österreichisch-ungarischen Truppen."
31. "Annales Ceccanses," *MGHSS*, XIX, 302,15-22.
32. Thuróczy, *Chronica*, c. 100, actually said that Andrew II had become the commander in chief of the crusading force; in Schwandtner, I, 148, ii:72.
33. On the war council, see *Chronica regia*, 242f.; "Oliveri Relatio de expeditione Damiatina," *ibid.*, 325; and "De expeditionibus in Terra Sancta factis," *ibid.*, 343f.; also recorded by L'estoire d'Eracles, cf. *Historiens occidentaux*, 5 vols. (Paris, 1841-95), II, 321ff., a part of *Recueil des historiens croisades*, 16 vols. (Paris, 1841-1906), cited hereafter as RHC Hist. orientaux; compare with Raynaldus, *Annales*, anno 1217, n. 31., and de Vitry, letter 3.
34. de Vitry, letter 3; Röhricht, *Geschichte*, 725f., follows the letter in his interpretation; idem, art. cit., "Kreuzzug Andreas." See "Oliveri Relatio," c. 1, in *Chronica regia*, 325.
35. Coradinus, cf. *Chronica regia*, 242f. Oliver of Cologne (Paderborn), *Historia Damiatina*, ed. Hermann Hoogweg, vol. 202 of *Bibliothek des Literarischen Vereins in Stuttgart* (Tübingen, 1894), 163ff.; Mayer, 197.
36. A bad harvest and scarcity of horses had slowed down the operation - de Vitry, letter 3; *Bullarium Romanum*, 24 vols. (Turin, 1857-72), III, 333.

37. "Oliveri Relatio," c. 1, in *Chronica regia*, 325; also, *ibid.*, 243.
38. See the letter of the Grandmaster of the Templars to Rome, *ÁUO*, I, 144ff.; *CD*, III-1, 230ff. R. Grousset, *Histoire des croisades du royaume Franc de Jerusalem*, 3 vols. (Paris, 1936), III, 202, made Andrew II responsible for anything bad that had happened; Thomas of Spaleto, c. 26, acknowledged the king's faults, but absolved him by saying that he might have been poisoned, and therefore could not think clearly; also, *MGHSS*, XXIX, 578,46-48.
39. The fort with seventy-seven towers, constructed by Coradinus himself - *Chronica regia*, 243; "Oliveri Relatio," c. 2, *ibid.*, 325f.; RHC Hist. orientaux, II-1, 113f.
40. *Ibid.*
41. *Ibid.*, II-1, 321ff.; *Chronica regia*, 244; also, 343, 344. Andrew II would not take part in further expeditions - de Vitry's letter 3; Oliver, c. 3, in *Chronica regia*, 326; Röhricht, *Forschungen*, 148; J.M. Powell, *Anatomy of a Crusade, 1213-1221* (Philadelphia, 1986), 132ff.
42. See his letter to Rome, *RA*, n. 355; *VMH*, n. 32; *CD*, III-1, 250ff.; on the excommunication by the patriarch, see Dandalo, "Chronicon," x:4,29-35, in Muratori, *RISS*, XII, 339f.
43. *Chronica regia*, 243; Oliver, c. 4, *ibid.*, 326; Röhricht, *Quinti scriptores*, II, 133.
44. Cf. "Chronicon Rheinhardbrunnensis," *MGHSS*, XXX-1, 592,44-47.
45. *Chronica regia*, 243; Röhricht, *Forschungen*, 148.
46. *RA*, n. 329; *VMH*, n. 23; *CD*, III-1, 233ff.
47. *RA*, n. 331; *VMH*, n. 26; Röhricht,, *Regesta regni Hierosolymitani*, n. 241; *CD*, III-1, 233ff.
48. *RA*, n. 330; *VMH*, n. 24; Katona, V, 287f.; the king's letter to Rome is recorded by Potthast, n. 6845.
49. *RA*, n. 328; *VMH*, n. 25; *CD*, III-1, 239ff.
50. Andrew II's writ to Rome, *RA*, n. 355, and the papal response, dated March 5, 1219, Potthast, n. 6001; *VMH*, n. 33.
51. *VMH*, I, 21, last paragraph.
52. "... filiam Comnini Theodori Lazcari filio nostro duximus in uxorem;" *VMH*, I, 21,3-4.
53. See A. Gardner, *The Lascarids of Nicea: The Story of an Empire in Exile* (London, 1922), 53f.; Ostrogorsky, 343.
54. "... cum Azeno Bulgariae ... nostra filia patrimonium celebravimus;" *VMH*, I, 21-45.
55. *RA*, n. 354; *ÁUO*, VI, 399ff.
56. Grand Reeve Nevke had arranged a truce between the archbishop and the canons of the Esztergom chapter - *ibid.*; Knauz, I, 221f.; *MGHSS*, IX, 622.
57. *RA*, nn. 340 and 383; *HO*, V, 8 and 9; further, Gregorius Pray, *Dissertatio de sancto Ladislao rege Hungariae* (Posonii, 1774), 109.
58. *RA*, n. 353; *VMH*, n. 143 (anno 1226!); on the background, cf. Hóman-Szekfű, I, 439ff., and Székely, 1309ff.
59. "Porro vestra non miretur Sanctitas, si de bonis regni nostri ad praesans iuxta honorem vestrum et nostrum vobis cathecizare non possumus;" *VMH*, I, 21, concluding paragraph.
60. See "Annales Cavenses," iii:193, in Muratori, *RISS*, VII, 926; "Annales Sense," anno 1220, *MGHSS*, XIX, 227; Richardi de s. Germano "Chronicon," in Muratori, *RISS*, VII, 992; *Annales Marbacenses*, 84,17-18 and 89,8-12.
61. Cf. Svrita (Zurita), *Indices*, 103; Gebhardt, I, 340 and 352; the Salzburg archbishop conducted the inquiry - letter of Pope Honorius III to Eberhard of Salzburg, November 23, 1220, Potthast, n. 6409.

62. *RA*, n. 355.
63. Of whom he did not speak too highly, "quam plurimi potentum et nobilium regni, satellites Sathanas, regiam non verentes offendere maiestatem;" *ÁUO*, VI, 400; also, the tone and content of papal writs, cf. Potthast, nn. 6328 and 6329; *VMH*, nn. 40 and 42.
64. *VMH*, I, 21f.; Thuróczy, *Chronica*, c. 100, to prove that he had no clear idea about the king's Near Eastern adventure.
65. Thuróczy, *Chronica*, c. 100.
66. *Ibid.*; *Chronica regia*, 243.
67. *MGHSS*, XXX-1, 592,44-47. It should be noted that between 1217 and 1219, various individuals signed writs as bishops of Györ and Várad - see *RA*, nn. 338 to 354.
68. Thomas of Spaleto, c. 27.
69. *CD*, III-1, 187; Gardner, 94; W. Miller, *The Latins in the Levant: A History of Frankish Greece, 1204-1566* (London, 1908), 82f.
70. Robert Courtenay became emperor in 1219; he died in 1228, cf. Ostrogorsky, 345.
71. Cf. Knauz, I, 217, 218, and 221; *MGHSS*, IX, 622.
72. *VMH*, n. 85.
73. See the papal writ of March 13, 1224, Potthast, n. 7190; also, n. 7192; *VMH*, nn. 98 and 101.
74. *RA*, n. 404; Potthast, n. 7189; *VMH*, n. 97; Alberic's Decrees, in *RHM*, 362; Kosztolnyik, *From Coloman*, 46ff.; Katona, V, 431f.
75. See Alberic's Decrees, aa. 74 and 75, *RHM*, 368f.; also, Coloman's *Lex Iudaeis data, ibid.*, 371f.; Kosztolnyik, *From Coloman*, 54, n. 43; 55, n. 67; see further Coloman's First Synod of Esztergom, art. 60, *RHM*, 356f., or Marczali, *Enchiridion*, 113; Kosztolnyik, 58ff., and Decrees I and II of Andrew II, aa. 24 and 31, Marczali, *Enchiridion*, 141a and b; *RHM*, 415 and 432.
76. There will be more detailed data available by the time of Béla IV - *CD*, IV-1, 174 and 272f.; Knauz, I, 550.
77. See Sámuel Kohn, in *Történelmi tár*, 106 and 108.
78. See papal writ of December 15, 1222, in Potthast, n. 6900; *VMH*, n. 73.
79. Potthast, n. 6639; *VMH*, n. 58.
80. For details, see Röhricht, *Beiträge*, II, 260f., and 260, note 35.
81. The provisions of the Decree (Golden Bull) of 1222, aa. 11 and 24 concerning Jews and foreigners had to be repeated, and slightly rephrased, in the Decree of 1231, aa. 23 and 31; cf. Marczali, *Enchiridion*, 138ab and 141ab; Katona, V, 355.

CHAPTER THREE

THE MONARCH OF THE DECREES WITH GOLDEN SEALS

1. *The Decretum I of 1222*

> ... libertas tam nobilium regni nostri, quam etiam aliorum, instituta a sancto Stephano rege...
>
> Andrew II's *Decretum I*

In his writ of December 15, 1222, Pope Honorius III called upon the bishop of Eger, and the abbots of Egres and of Szentgotthárd, to warn the multitude of Hungary, lest they break the law by committing treason against king and crown, or disturb the nobility's wealth and the status-quo power. His Holiness had heard, "cum igitur, sicut accepimus," that in accordance with the country's new law, the monarch, henceforth, had to appear twice a year before the people's public assembly, where the people made unfair and hardly justifiable demands on him.

The people asked the king to divest the hated nobles of their dignity and public offices, and distribute their wealth among the population. Had the surprised and unreadied king given in to those demands, he would have ignored the country's laws and undermined his own royal powers; had he denied them, he would have exposed himself and his loyal supporters to danger from the people.[1] The warning words of the pontiff undoubtedly referred to the *Decretum I* of Andrew II, the Hungarian Decree with the Golden Seal (Hungarian Golden Bull), issued prior to May 7 of that year.[2]

In the beginning of the thirteenth century, one may observe earth-shattering social upheavals all over Europe. The social thinkers of the time, the Albigensians, who had succeeded the already forbidden Waldensians, and the Patari were in revolt; superiors turned against inferiors; the poor assailed the rich.[3] No wonder, indeed, that Pope Innocent III urged renewal in the interest of the Church, and in support of a society undergoing a crisis.[4]

The great reformer of the age, Dominic Guzman from Spain, urged ecclesiastical reforms through a rational and spiritual approach: the ones who would not accept the teaching of the Church must be convinced to the contrary by reasoning and humility, arguing not from horseback, he said, but standing on bare feet.[5] Francis of Assisi, son of a rich cloth merchant and a man of his society, changed his living habits and chose the life of a beggar - he became a preacher for his "little brethren," as if to imitate Christ, in order to pacify the stratum of society that so deeply hated the rich and powerful.[6]

In England, the barons of King John Lackland were unhappy with their monarch's poor behavior and unsuccessful politics.[7] The fulfillment of their demands, the Magna Carta, had, however, been voided by Rome within a few months after its issue. In the judgment of the Holy See, the barons' greed for power was, *ratione peccatae*, unjustified against the monarch who represented his country's interests. (The question remains, of course: is greed ever justified?)[8]

In Hungary, the servant stratum had begun to move up on the social scale; the swineherds of the Zsilic Woods, whose predecessors were placed by King Ladislas I (*ob.* 1095) under the abbot of Pannonhalma[9] (and, who had, during the last hundred and fifty years, grown to some three hundred families living in the villages), refused to acknowledge the wardship of the abbot. The Palatine had to take physical action in 1218 to force them to adhere to the original charter, the terms of which their forefathers must have agreed to but could not possibly have understood because of their illiteracy.[10]

Other servant strata had moved against their landlords, and reform-minded clergymen. According to a writ of the pontiff, they met twice a year, demanding evil things from their ruler.[11] "Evil things" - such as? Were they really evil? Or did their poverty make them desperate? They did have legitimate reasons for their demands. Could they have been the participants of an agro-social upheaval in the country?

During the latter half of the twelfth century, and in the early decades of the thirteenth century, the large estates increased in importance. This led to an increase in land values. Land became a valuable commodity, agriculture began to develop, and produce of the land grew in both quality and quantity. The abolishment of the earlier frontier zones (*gyepü*) on the borders freed land for agriculture, and multiplied the greed for individual landholdings.

Was the aim of the king's irrational economic policy to meet this greed for agricultural holdings by satisfying it? Sale and purchase of land became more frequent; it called for a growth of written documentation of transactions, in that landgrants had to be ascertained in writing to replace earlier oral agreements made in good faith and under oath. The increasing number of writs issued by the *loci credibiles* ascertaining land sales and purchases bears further testimony to the changes in law governing the holding, or ownership of individual lands.[12]

King Andrew II's powers of government decreased on account of his parceling out goods from the royal domain to less deserving recipients, in order to bribe them into obtaining their political support. The king allotted the nobles much potential power; he must have felt intimidated by them, or he must have acted out of sheer laziness. Many of the king's reeves became permanent officeholders in the process. Royal privileges had to be shared with the landholding nobles who, in terms of the economy and the common law of the land, had challenged the interests of the lesser nobility, and of the king's *servientes* (the service, or lesser, nobles).

The new landholders (landowners?) could execute laws in a western feudal fashion on the territory under their jurisdiction; the monarch, who had surrendered his rights to them, had to seek more and different sources of revenue elsewhere. He had to rent out *régale* - the collection of salt tax, tolls, and of the "one-thirtieth," the collection of which lay in the hands of greedy and careless collectors, who made the lives of the country's poor classes unbearable.[13]

At the same time, there was not written law or documentation available to support the claim to landholdings by a great number of the members of the higher nobility: they had gained access to their lands by word of mouth from the monarch. Consequently, they had, in the early 1200s, grouped themselves into family clans, as if to prove thereby the legality of their holdings or ownership of their land. The use of the name of the clan could mean that its bearer had an old and responsible tradition behind it. When, during the earlier part of the century, smaller families had emerged on the lands of the larger estates, they had kept the family name and connection intact, on the grounds of belonging to the same clan.[14]

The king's service nobility, *servientes regis*, were identical with the landholding common free element in society,[15] and with the formerly wealthy stratum that served the king, but had declined in social importance (though its members were still characterized by the term *liber*).[16] The more wealthy stratum of the common free element, the *miles*, may also have been a distant forerunner of the royal service noble, whose distant predecessors had performed services for the royal court.

One may take note that in 1212, Andrew II had introduced at his curia the son of a certain Alykon of foreign *hospes* background; the son became a royal *iobagio* - a reminder of the Hungarian Anonymus's remark that the "servientes" in the time of Attila had also served Árpád.[17]

In the Várad Register, a document collection that provided reliable information on Hungarian society of the age, the king's service nobles were not mentioned at all; instead, the Register spoke of *homo liber*, *omnino liber*, and *vir militaris*.[18] If Anonymus had, in his late-twelfth century narrative, preserved the social stratification of the realm of his age, then, in his point of view, the royal service nobles (*serviens regis*) must have been, as late as the 1190s, closely ranked with the peasant (*rusticus*), and therefore far beneath the *nobilis* on the social scale.[19]

During the reign of Andrew II, the royal service noble, as indicated by his "royal" designation, owed duties directly to the monarch, and he was not under the jurisdiction of the royal regional fort or county reeve. He held property, which instilled in him a sense of social responsibility, and held him back from a social backslide. He was allowed to increase the number of people - i.e., landless peasants and serfs - in his service. But he still remained on the "accepted" edge of the noble class - away from the barons' social circle - and he had to serve his king faithfully in order to retain his position.[20]

The *iobagio castris* (royal vassal/knight) assigned to the defense of the royal forts had to protect the king and uphold his authority on the same grounds in order to retain his position in society.[21] He might have been a "bound" *liber* at first, a landholder since the days of King St. Stephen, of lands that had been taken from the regions that had surrounded the royal forts, and provided for the upkeep of the fort's personnel.[22]

The *iobagio's* social status remained on the periphery of the nobles' class, like that of the royal *serviens*, or the *iobagio exemptus*, detached from the social stratum of fort-knights, holding a place below on the social ladder, though within the structure of the nobility. He could not inherit land, and the lands he held in usufruct were small.[23] Therefore, the king's landgrant policy must have concerned both the freemen and members of both the *iobagio* classes, even though it may have left the *servientes regis* (service, or lesser, nobles) less perturbed in their worry about their social belonging. Were the service noble, however, to question, or to publicly protest the king's landgrant policy, he could not be prevented from doing so.[24]

Did a "palace revolution" take place in the country during the early months of 1222, when the monarch *new* opponents had gained temporary control of the government by forcing the king's *old* allies from office?[25] Some individuals must have bitterly complained - were one to read correctly the introductory statement of the 1222 Decree, that the king had unexpectedly listened to bad advice. They claimed that, guided by personal greed, the monarch had curtailed their social standing by giving lands he had reclaimed from them to the castle knights and to members of the service nobility (to whom King St. Stephen had already granted freedom) because the king wanted to appease those knights. This might point toward such a hypothesis.[26]

One has only to compare the royal resolution, in which Andrew II rewarded his supporters who had aided him during the humiliations he had to go through during the reign of his brother, King Emery, in order to obtain the throne,[27] with royal writs logged in the Register, where Andrew II attempted to appease Archbishop John of Esztergom (a transcript of this writ had been prepared at the papal curia),[28] to understand that Andrew II had, upon his succession to the throne, dismissed his father's loyal advisors.[29]

Those advisors, in turn, must have thought it appropriate to fight back, causing a social upheaval in early 1222. One might gain this notion from the prefatory paragraph of the Golden Bull, and from other royal resolutions logged in the Register,[30] where, for instance, the monarch, wanting to appease the high churchmen, compensated the Esztergom archbishop and his cannons with landgrants for damages they had sustained during his sojourn to the Holy Land.[31]

Who, however, aided the service nobles in their reaching out for the rectification of the status? Was it the adherents of deceased King Emery - nobles who had been forced out of public office; individuals excluded from gaining commissions - who now supported the justifiable demands of the service nobles - justifiable in that they claimed to have possessed them since the early eleventh century (actually, since the late ninth century) - and the request of the fort knights for an improvement in their social position?

It seems to be quite clear from the various articles of the Golden Bull that its very issue was necessary because of the confrontation between the nobles who had been driven from power and the various interest groups vying for predominance in political decision-making.

The following provisions might support such a hypothesis:

a) the decision that only four *iobagiones* - in this instance, the Palatine, the Grand Reeve, the Reeve of the King's Court, and the Reeve of the Queen's Court - may hold more than one office simultaneously;[32]

b) the resolution that nobody may receive a whole county (fort district), or high commission, on a perpetual basis from the monarch;[33]

c) that no one may be forced to surrender against his will, "aliquo tempore ne priuetur," a landgrant or commission received from the Crown on account of the ill humor of the monarch;[34]

d) no foreigner may obtain land or commission, and he did, return it[35] - meaning that a *hospes* (foreigner) may be given no land, nor a commission, without the consent of the King's Council.[36]

The concluding paragraph of the Golden Bull of 1222, that only mentioned ten bishops by name, and nobody from among the king's officials,[37] would imply that, to quote Pope Honorius III, the "multitude" that had gathered at Fehérvár had made use of its right to remove (indict?) royal officials from the King's Council.[38] Indeed, on the royal writ issued June 3, 1222, for the Teutonic Knights, the names of previous advisors of the deceased King Emery appeared as co-signers: they were the most bitter opponents of King Andrew II.[39]

To cite but one example in support of this hypothesis, one may refer to a late document issued by King Emery, on which the name of Reeve Tiborc of Bodrog appeared as one of the co-signers;[40] the same Tiborc had signed, as the reeve of Pozsony, on a writ dated shortly after the issuance of the "Golden Bull" by Andrew II.[41] Therefore, one can reason that it was the confrontation between the king, his *nobiles* (landholding upper nobility), and the various interests groups in the land that led to the promulgation of the "Golden Bull." In his previously referred to letter of December 15, 1222, Pope Honorius III spoke not so much of the pronounced resolutions of the "Bull," but about the social upheaval that had broken out in the realm during that year.[42]

The *Decretum* ("Golden Bull") of 1222 dealt, first of all, with the right of inheritance of the royal *serviens* (lesser or service noble) who died without a male heir.[43] With the exception of the one-fourth of the estate (or chattel) that was to be inherited by a female relative,[44] the three-fourths of the inheritance went to male relatives of the deceased. If there were no male heirs, or they had previously died, the inheritance (estate) reverted to the royal *fiscus*.[45]

This resolution confirmed the Laws of King St. Stephen, and it was one of the main articles of the Bull, because it assured the right of *dominium* by the royal service noble.[46] From this it followed that, if the monarch went to war abroad, the service noble would go with him only for pay; were he to decide not to accompany the king, he would not be punished, nor would he pay a fine. However, he had to accompany the king at his own expense, were the enemy to invade the realm.[47]

Were a noble to fall in battle, his son obtained a reward; were a service noble to die in a military action with the king, his son would also receive a reward.[48] The service noble did not pay taxes, nor was he obligated to provide food and lodging for the king, and/or for the king's entourage (the latter being members of the high nobility).[49] Individuals who had formed the monarch's ambulatory household, such as the stable personnel, hunters, and hawkers, could not spend a night in the village of a service noble without paying for it;[50] nor could villagers of the service noble provide grazing land for royal swineherds, or pay the one-tenth to the high noble in the king's company.[51]

The service noble did not come under the jurisdiction of the regional royal reeve, nor of that of the county reeve, except when the new currency was issued annually; nor did the fort reeve have any authority over him.[52] In other words, the service noble only "served" his king and country when called upon. The king was responsible for the maintenance of public law and order in the realm. The royal *billogus* (itinerant justice) persecuted thieves and robbers, pronouncing sentence at the feet of the fort reeve,[53] but without any interference from the region's inhabitants; the people may indict, but must not judge a thief or robber in the court of law.[54]

The interests of the country, and of social order, demanded that a widow whose husband had been executed for a crime, of had fallen in judicial combat, retain her husband's property.[55] The king would leave alone the property of the service noble, and guarantee the latter's personal safety, even if the noble were under a court investigation. The court of law would not indict or begin proceedings against a service noble only to try to appease the mighty. Nor would the service noble suffer a disadvantage if, or when, he transferred his case from the court of law of the king to that of the Junior King, assuming the transfer occurred before the start of the court process.[56]

According to the first paragraph of the Bull, the service nobles assemble at Fehérvár on the feast of King St. Stephen (August 20), to meet with the king, or with his palatine, face to face; the king or the palatine was obligated to hear them out.[57] Needless to say, the new role assigned to the palatine only increased the prestige of his position countrywide.

Article 23 of the Bull confronted the fiscal policy of the monarch by saying that "new" money issued every year had to be worth the money issued by his father, Béla III (*ob.* 1196); Andrew II had to establish an honest financial policy by minting and issuing good currency.[58] In order to prevent further economic abuse, the king must gain his share of income derived from the sale of raw skins (leather) - mostly in the area south of the Drave river - in accordance with the customs that dated back to the days of King Coloman the Learned (*ob.* 1116).[59] The county reeve may retain for himself one-third of the collected tax, be it sales tax, toll money, or payment of any kind, as, for example, number of oxen offered in payment, from everywhere in the county.[60]

The law protected the public. Were the reeve to prove to be unworthy of his office, he would lose it, and the income from it.[61] The king's *iobagio* (nobleman) must not oppress the poor and the fatherless;[62] and the law would protect from any illegal demand the property a widow had inherited from her husband.[63] The lower class did have some benefits and protection, and yet they were discontented; their well-being depended a good deal upon the enforceability of the law.

The question remains, of course, had Andrew II promulgated the "Golden Bull?" Its seven copies, that, according to the concluding paragraph, had to be prepared,[64] have not been preserved. The text came down to posterity in a 1318 transcript, authenticated by a bishop's seal.[65] Another version of the text appeared in the 1351 Decree of Louis the Great of Hungary (*ob.* 1382).[66] The already cited letter of Pope Honorius III (of December 15, 1222) did not directly refer to the issue of the Decree, thought it spoke of a new law[s] of the land.[67] What is clear, however, from the signatures on royal writs dated after the issuance of the Decree is that the king had re-organized his council, and the Decree, as its text is available today, did not list any of the high officials who served in the King's Council by name.[68]

On the other hand, the resolutions of the Decree that forbade churchmen to actively participate in commercial undertakings, business transactions, and did not tolerate the ordination of serfs, or of one's servants, to the priesthood, may show some influence of the Fourth Lateran Council on the thinking of the king's advisors who, presumably, had drafted the document.[69]

Neither law, order, nor peace were restored, peace not secured in the realm in the year 1222.[70] The monarch turned to Rome complaining that his country's inhabitants had denied him their obedience! Under the pretense that they had crowned his eldest son, Béla Junior King, the estates looked upon the prince as their ruler.[71] According to the information preserved in the papal register, the pontiff took immediate action: in his writ of July 4, 1222, he called upon the members of the Hungarian hierarchy to apply church sanctions against anyone who dared to cause a revolt; "non fuerit ipsius regis intentio,...ut eo vivente alius dominaret in regno."[72]

The nobles might have, of course, attempted to prevent the resolutions of the Decree to be realized, and caused a rift between the monarch and his son who, incidentally, had opposed his father's wasteful policies;[73] however, their efforts remained fruitless.[74] Prince Béla, crowned Junior King, maintained a separate court in Croatia and held certain royal privileges.[75] That is to say, according to Article 18 of the Decree, the nobles had free access to Béla, and to his younger brother, Coloman; "possint libere ire ad filium nostrum, seu a maiori ad minorem."[76] Were Béla to punish a nobleman, the latter could not appeal to the royal court; legal court proceedings begun before Béla could only be completed at the court of Béla. Furthermore, court cases initiated in front of the monarch could be terminated only by the king himself.[77]

Personal relations between the prince and his father remained strained. It is from a papal writ, once again, that it is known that the marriage of Béla that caused a personal rift with his father, came to the attention of the papal curia. As mentioned above, in 1218, when he had returned from his expedition to the Holy Land, Andrew II, still in transit, had engaged his son to Maria, daughter of Theodore Lascaris, ruler of Nicea. Andrew II took the bride home with him, had her raised at his court in Hungary, but later the royal father changed his mind. Perhaps a more prestigious, diplomatically more "correct" marriage would assure wider recognition of his family and of the country, he thought. From the king's point of view, or in the opinion of some of his advisors, the daughter of the rule of Nicea was too insignificant a match for the heir to the Hungarian throne. Andrew II persuaded Béla to break off the engagement, and the prince asked the papal curia to annul the marriage that had been arranged for him by his parent during the years when Béla was still a minor.[78]

Pope Honorius III now instructed the bishops of Eger, Vác, and Várad to conduct an investigation in the case.[79] During the inquiry, the archbishop of Kalocsa and eight other bishops informed the Holy See that the appeal of Béla asking for annulment had little legal foundation, as it did not correspond to reality. They stated that, when Béla and Maria came of age, they were properly married, and lived peacefully with one another for two years. It was only upon the advice of "certain evil persons," the chronicler said, that Béla separated from his lawful spouse, thereby creating a nationwide

scandal. "Ut ad consummationem matrimonii...fideliter laborarent....
Nunc autem quorundam malivolis suggestionibus pervesorum, vir
legitimam...in totius regni scandalum...dimisit uxorem."[80]

Rome suggested that Béla retake his wife.[81] The Junior King
obeyed the papal command, thereby making his father angry. Béla
had to flee to Austria, together with his wife, and with Reeve Buzárd
of Pozsony, who remained loyal to him.[82]

Leopold of Austria rejoiced at this turn of events because he
had an almost constant border dispute with the Hungarian court.[83]
Many Hungarian nobles, including the bishop of Veszprém,
supported Béla, and contributed to weakening the father's bargaining
position.[84] Rome emerged as peacemaker between father and son,[85]
in that the pontiff warned Béla to be respectful toward, and careful
with, his father. At the same time, the curia called upon the
supporters of Béla to tone down the controversy between the prince
and king.[86]

The Holy See now asked Andrew II to be patient and forgiving
with his son, and treat him as the heir to the throne, assuring him of
the need of constitutional dignity, and to allow the supporters of the
prince, who had left the country with him, to peacefully return
home, without the threat of further punishment.[87]

The misunderstanding between Andrew II and Prince Béla
mush have perturbed the pontiff because he sent letters regarding
this matter to the Czech duke,[88] and the duke of Austria;[89] he
dispatched a special writ addressed to members of the Hungarian
hierarchy concerning the controversy.[90]

The papal intervention had not been fruitless: King Andrew
made peace with his son.[91] In the summer of 1224, Béla, Junior
King, once again headed the royal administrative districts of Croatia-
Dalmatia. Now it was the king's turn to support the efforts of his son
to reclaim the royal lands he had wastefully given away. It was also
King Andrew II, who had an agreement reached with the Teutonic
Knights, inviting them to settle down within the administrative
borders of his country.[92]

NOTES

1. Cf. Potthast, n. 6900; *VMH*, n. 73; *CD*, III-1, 390f.; Hóman-Szekfü, I, 490f.; A. Huber, *Österreichische Rechtsgeschichte*, rev. ed., ed. Alphons Dopsch (Vienna-Leipzig, 1901), 135ff.; T. Bogyay, "A 750 éves Aranybulla" [The Golden Bull is 750 Years Old], *Katolikus Szemle*, 24 (1982), 289ff.

2. Cf. *RA*, n. 379; Marczali, *Enchiridion*, 134aff.; *RHM*, 412ff.; Hóman-Szekfü, I, 491f.; Hóman, *Ungarisches Mittelalter*, II, 85ff.; Székely, *Magyarország története*, 1320ff.; Géza Érszegi, "Az Aranybulla" [The Golden Bull], *Fejér megyi történeti évkönyv*, 6 (1972), 5ff., esp. 14f.; F. Eckhart, *Magyarország története* [A History of Hungary] (repr. Buenos Aires, 1952), 82ff. and 319.

3. Friedrich Heer, *Europäische Geistesgeschichte*, 2nd ed. (Stuttgart, 1965), 122ff.; Hampe, *Hochmittelalter*, 314ff.; on the Albigensians, see the report of Abbot Arnold of Citeaux to Pope Innocent III, in *MPL*, 216, 139; Funk-Bihlmeyer, II, 146ff. and 148ff.

4. Innocent III, "Gesta," cc. 33 and 40; A. Fliche and V. Martin, *Histoire de l'Eglise depuis de Origenes a nos Jours*, vol. X (Paris, 1950), 156ff. and 188ff.; M. Maccarone, *Chiesa e stato nella dottrina di Innocenzo III* (Rome, 1940), 26ff. and 37ff.; on Maccarone, see the review essay by T.F.X. Noble in *Catholic Historical Review*, 80 (1994), 518ff.

5. Funk-Bihlmeyer, II, 214ff.; J. Loserth, *Geschichte des späten Mittelalters*, part. II of *Handbuch der mittelalterlichen und neueren Geschichte*, ed. G. v. Below and F. Meinecke (Munich-Berlin, 1903), 15ff.; Jordan of Saxony, "Libellus de principiis Ordinis Praedicatorum," ed. H.C. Scheeben, in *Monumenta Ordinis Fratrum Praedicatorum historica*, vol. XVI (Rome, 1935), n. II; H.C. Scheeben, *Der hl. Dominkus* (Freiburg, 1927); M. Heimbucher, *Orden und Kongregationen der katholischen Kirche*, 2 vols., 3rd ed. (Paderborn, 1933), I, 469ff.; *ASS*, Aug. I, 558ff., esp. cc. 202, 210-211, and 320-36 - with data pertinent to Hungary; and the "Primitive Life of Dominic" by P. Ferrand, in *Analecta s. Ordinis Fratrum Praedicatorum*, vol. IV (Rome, 1893, etc.), 296ff., esp. 306; M.H. Vicaire, *Saint Dominic and His Times*, trans. K. Pond (New York-London, 1964), 187ff.; Bede Jarrett, *Life of Saint Dominic* (New York: Image Books, 1964), 72ff.

6. *ASS*, Oct. II, 556ff.; J.J. Walsh, *The Thirteenth: Greatest of Centuries*, 5th ed. (New York, 1913), 254ff.; H.D. Sedgwick, *Italy in the Thirteenth Century* (Boston-New York, 1912), 74ff. and 86ff.; G.K. Chesterton, *St. Francis of Assisi* (New York: Image Books, 1957), 38ff.; Funk-Bihlmeyer, II, 209ff.; Heer, *Geistesgeschichte*, 138ff.; J. Jörgensen, *St. Francis of Assisi* (New York: Image Books, 1955), 60ff.; W. Dettloff, "Die Geistigkeit des hl. Franziskus in der Theologie der Franziskaner," *Wissenschaft und Weisheit*, 19 (1956), 197ff.

7. Bryce Lyon, *A Constitutional and Legal History of Medieval England* (New York-London, 1960), 310ff.; A.L. Poole, *From Domesday Book to Magna Carta*, 2nd ed. (Oxford, 1955; repr. 1970), 468ff.; J.C. Holt, *Magna Carta* (Cambridge, 1969), 105ff. and 313ff.; S.E. Thorn, "What Magna Carta Was," in E.N. Griswold (ed.), *The Great Charter* (New York-Toronto: Mentor Books, 1965), 11ff.

8. See the papal bull of August 24, 1215, in Potthast, n. 4990; *Bullarium Magnum Romanum*, vol. III-1 (Rome, 1733; repr. Graz, 1963, etc.), 172f.; Cheney-Simple, 212ff.; Innocent III's writs addressed to the English barons, in *MPL*, 217, 248, and 245f.; Funk-Bihlmeyer, II, 181ff., esp. 186; McIlwain, 231f., in reference to the bull "Per venerabilem," Potthast, n. 1794; Friedberg, II, 714ff.; also, Lyon, 306ff.

9. *RA*, n. 29; Erdélyi, *Rendtörténet*, I, 590ff., with facsimile, *ibid.*, I, 75; *ÁUO*, VI, 360ff., esp. 361.

10. *Ibid.*, VI, 360ff.; *RA*, n. 396, and compare with *RA*, n. 283; Katona, V, 403.

11. Potthast, n. 6900; *VMH*, n. 73; *CD*, III-1, 390ff.; Székely, *Magyarország története*, 1330f.

12. *Ibid.*, 1012ff.; Hóman-Szekfű, I, 473ff.; Gy. Györffy, *Wirtschaft und Gesellschaft der Ungarn um die Jahrtausenwende* (Vienna-Graz, 1983), 102ff.

13. *Ibid.*; J.R. Strayer, "Feudalism in Western Europe," *Feudalism in History*, ed. R. Coulborn (Princeton, 1956), 15ff.

14. See Anonymus, *Gesta Ungarorum*, cc. 6, 8, and 40; Macartney, 72f.; compare with Constantine VII Porphyrogenitus, "De administrando imperio," cc. 39 and 40, in Marczali, *Enchiridion*, 37ff.; Gy. Moravcsik (ed.), Konstantinos Porphyrogennetos, *De administrando imperio* (Budapest, 1949); new ed., with English translation by R.J.H. Jenkins (London, 1962; revised, Washington, D.C., 1967), cc. 38 and 40.

15. Anonymus, c. 21, *SSH*, I, 62,27, and compare with I. Szekfű, "De servientibus et familiaribus," *Dissertationes hist. Academiae Scientiarum Hungaricae*, xxiii-3 (Budapest, 1912), 5ff. Anonymus's remark that in the tent of Attila the *servientes* were being served food on silver plates, while the *nobiles* on gold plates, *SSH*, I, 94,19-20, may be compared to the Chronicle, c. 102: "...qui fuit serviens," *ibid.*, I, 367,8 and note 2; also, *ibid.*, I, 401,24 and note 1.

16. *Ibid.*, I, 367,42-44.

17. *Ibid.*, I, 62,28-29; and I, 401,21-22; on Alykon, see *RA*, n. 279; *ÁUO*, I, 22f.

18. *RHM*, 640; Kosztolnyik, *From Coloman*, 258, n. 97, and 284, n. 10; E. Jakubovich and D. Pais (eds.), *Ó-magyar Olvasókönyv* [Old Hungarian Reader] (Pécs, 1929), 81ff.; I.G. Bolla, "Az Aranybulla-kori mozgalmak a Váradi Regestrum megvilágításában" [Early Thirteenth Century Social Movements in Hungary in the Light of Entries in the Várad Register], *Acta Universitatis Budapestiensis*, sectio hist., 1 (1959), 84ff.

19. "...fercula, pocula portabantur servientibus et rusticis in vasis argenteis," *SSH*, I, 94,19-20.

20. *RA*, n. 379, that is, *Decretum I* (Golden Bull) of 1222, Marczali, *Enchiridion*, 134aff., aa. 2-3; *RHM*, 412ff.; K. Csíky et al. (eds.) *Corpus Iuris Hungarici: Magyar Törvénytár, 1000-1895* , vol. I (Budapest, 1899), 13ff.; also, D. Márkus et al. (eds.), *Corpus Iuris Hungarici: Magyar Törvénytár*, 10 vols. (Budapest, 1896, etc.), I, 130ff.; Gy. Bónis, "A székesfehérvári törvénynaptól az ország szabadságáig" [The Road from the Law Days Held at Fehérvár to the Country's Freedom], *Székesfehérvár évszázadai* [Centuries of the History of Székesfehérvár], ed. J. Fitz and A. Kralovanszky, 2 vols. (Székesfehérvár, 1967-72), II, reprint; Hóman-Szekfű, I, 458f.; also, *RA*, n. 219; *ÁUO*, VI, 300; *RA*, nn. 222 and 223; *HO*, VII, 2; *ÁUO*, XI, 83; E.H. Kantorowicz, "Kingship Under the Impact of Scientific Jurisprudence," *Twelfth Century Europe and the Foundations of Modern Society*, ed. M. Clagett et al. (Madison, WI, 1966), 89ff.

21. Anonymus, C. 22, *SSH*, I, 64,13 and note 3; also, cc. 11 and 52; "...iobagiones castri sunt pauperes nobiles, qui ad regem veniens, terram eis tribuit de castris terris,...et castrum guerre tempore custodirent," Keza, c. 97, *ibid.*, I, 193,32-34. Also, Chronicle, c. 149, *ibid.*, I, 428,28 and note 4.

22. *Decretum I*, a. 19; and *Decretum II* (1231), a. 26 - Marczali, *Enchiridion*, 140ab; and Keza, c. 97.

23. Várad register, *RHM*, 640ff., aa. 10, 11, mainly 42, 111, 123, 158, 194, etc.

24. Cf., for example, *RA*, nn. 230, 234, 235, 236, 240.

25. *Ibid.*, n. 225; a donation of Andrew II for his supporters who had aided him during the reign of his brother, King Emery - *ÁUO*, VI, 6.

26. Marczali, *Enchiridion*, 134a.

27. *RA*, n. 225.
28. *Ibid.*, nn. 227 and 224; *CD*, III-1, 31.
29. Potthast, n. 3712; *CD*, III-1, 90; *ÁUO*, VI, 307; Katona, V, 33.
30. *RA*, nn. 373 and 378; *CD*, III-2, 224f.
31. *RHM*, 417ff.; Katona, V, 397.
32. *Decretum I*, a. 30; Érszegi, *art. cit.* (1972); W. Näf, "Herrschaftsverträge des Spätmittelalters," *Quellen zur neueren Geschichte* (Bern, 1951), 7ff.; Kantorowicz, *The King's Two Bodies*, 355, note 144 and 143, quoting Henry Bracton: "...rex infra et supra legem."
33. *Decretum I*, a. 16.
34. *Ibid.*, a. 17.
35. *Ibid.*, a. 26.
36. *Ibid.*, a. 11.
37. *Ibid.*, a. 31 (Marczali, *Enchiridion*, 143a; *RHM*, 417).
38. Potthast, n. 6900; *VMH*, n. 73; *CD*, III-1, 390ff.
39. *RA*, n. 378; *RHM*, 417ff.; *VMH*, n. 190.
40. *RA*, n. 210; *ÁUO*, I, 91f.
41. *RA*, n. 380; Zimmermann-Werner, I, 18.
42. *VMH*, n. 73.
43. *Decretum I*, a. 4.
44. *Ibid.*, and compare to King St. Stephen's Laws, a. ii:2, Marczali, *Enchiridion*, 77f.; *RHM*, 321. On the "filial quarter," see A. Murarik, *Az ősiség alapintézményének eredete* [Origins of "aviticitas'] (Budapest, 1938), 163ff., deduced from Roman Law, *lex falcidia*; on this, F. Eckhart, "Vita a leánynegyedről" [Debate on the 'filial quarter'], *Századok*, 66 (1932), 408ff.; J. Holub, "La 'quarta puellaria' dans ancien droit hongrois," *Studi in memoria di Aldo Albertoni*, vol. 3 (Padua, 1935), 275ff. The arguments are based on Emperor Justinian's *Corpus Iuris Civilis*, eds. P. Krueger, Th. Mommsen, and R. Schoell, 3 vols. (Berlin, 1895-99), III: *Institutiones*, i:16. Kantorowicz, *The King's Two Bodies*, 339, on King St. Stephen; J. Kárpát, "Die Lehre von der hl. Krone Ungarns im Lichte des Schrifttums," *Jahrbücher für die Geschichte Osteuropas*, 6 (1941), 1ff.; and, Lipót Hütter, *Korszerű-e a szentistváni világnézet?* [Is the Political Outlook of King St. Stephen Up to Date?] (Székesfehérvár, 1938), 49ff.
45. *Decretum I*, a. 4.
46. Stephen's Laws, a. ii:2; László Feketekúty, *Christentum und Staat* (Cologne, 1953), 10ff. and 48ff.
47. *Decretum I*, a. 7; and *Decretum II* (1231), aa. 15-16.
48. *Decretum I*, a. 10.
49 *Ibid.*, a. 3; *Decretum II*, a.6.
50. *Decretum I*, a. 15; *Decretum II*, aa. 8-10.
51. *Decretum I*, a. 22; *Decretum II*, a. 30.
52. *Decretum I*, a. 5a; *Decretum II*, aa. 12-13.
53. *Decretum I*, a. 5b; *Decretum II*, a. 13b.
54. *Decretum I*, a. 6; *Decretum II*, a. 14.
55. *Decretum I*, a. 12; *Decretum II*, aa. 24-25.
56. *Decretum I*, a. 17 (and, a. 18).
57. *Ibid.*, a. 1; *Decretum II*, aa. 1-3.
58. *Decretum I*, a. 23; Peter Spufford, *Money and Its Use in Medieval Europe* (Cambridge, 1988), 123 and 136.
59. *Decretum I*, a. 27, explained in more depth in *Decretum II*, a. 33.
60. *Decretum I*, a. 29; more detail in *Decretum II*, aa. 34-35.
61. *Decretum I*, a. 14.
62. *Ibid.*, a. 13.

63. *Ibid.*, a. 12.

64. *Ibid.*, a. 31; Ákos von Timon, *Ungarische Verfassungs- und Rechts-geschichte*, trans. Felix Schiller, 2nd ed. (Berlin, 1904), 124ff.; Feketekúty, 114ff.; Gaines Post, "The Theory of Public Law and the State in the Thirteenth Century," *Seminar*, 6 (1948), 42ff.

65. *RA*, n. 379; Székely, *Magyar történet*, 1329.

66. From the text of the 1351 *Decretum* of Louis the Great of Hungary (*ob.* 1382), cf. Marczali, *Enchiridion*, 216ff.; Csíky, *Corpus Iuris*, I, 166ff.; F. Dőry (ed.), *Decreta regni Hungariae* (Budapest, 1976), 124ff., provided a better reading of the text, esp. of art. IX. Ferenc Somogyi and F.L. Somogyi, "The Constitutional Guarantees of 1351: The Decree of Louis the Great," *Louis the Great of Hungary and Poland*, ed. B.S. Vardy (New York, 1986), 429ff.; Hóman-Szekfű, II, 247ff.; Dercsényi, *Nagy Lajos*, 61ff.

67. Potthast, n. 6900.

68. Marczali, *Enchiridion*, 142a; Gy. Kristó, *Az Aranybullák évszázada* [The Century of Golden Bulls] (Budapest, 1981).

69. "...universi et singuli...;" *Decretum I*, a. 31; *Decretum II*, a. 21, and compare with a statement of the Fourth Lateran Council, 1215: "Una vero est fidelium universalis ecclesia;" Const. 1: de fide Catholica, in Friedberg, II, 5; Mansi, *Concilia*, XXII, 981; further, J. Gerics, "Az Aranybulla ellenállási záradékának értelmezéséhez" [Interpreting the 'ius resistendi' Clause of the Golden Bull], *Ünnepi tanulmányok Sinkovics István 70 születésnapjára* [Studies in Honor of István Sinkovics on his 70th Birthday], ed. Iván Bertényi (Budapest, 1980), reprint; Z.J. Kosztolnyik, "*De facultate resistendi*: Two Essential Characteristics of the Hungarian Golden Bull of 1222," *Studies in Medieval Culture*, 5 (1975), 97ff.

70. The curia knew about political events in Hungary - cf. letter, dated March 3, 1231, of Gregory IX, in Potthast, n. 8671; *VMH*, n. 168.

71. Potthast, n. 6870; *VMH*, n. 70.

72. *Ibid.*

73. Rogerius, "Carmen," c. 4, in *SSH*, II, 554f.; I. Rákos, "IV Béla birtokrestaurációs politikája" [The Reconstructive Policy of Béla IV], *Acta historica Szegediensis*, 47 (1974), 3ff.

74. Potthast, n. 6974; *VMH*, n. 78: "...comites et barones ac populus...ut...cum ea integritate qua usque modo conuenerunt, persolvant;" and, the writ of Pope Honorius III, dated July 4, 1222, in Potthast, n. 6870.

75. See writ concerning lands in Slavonia, *CD*, III-1, 403, anno 1223 - though Smiciklas, *Codex diplomaticus*, III, 244, dated it 1225; the writ may be a forgery, *RA*, n. 401, but its transcript is authentic, *RA*, n. 713.

76. "...possint libere ire ad filium nostrum, seu a maiori ad minorem;" Marczali, *Enchiridion*, 139a, art. 18.

77. *Ibid.*, 140a.

78. Thomas of Spaleto, c. 26; Thuróczy, *Chronica*, c. 100; in Schwandtner, I, 149, ii:73.

79. Potthast, n. 6845; *VMH*, n. 67.

80. *VMH*, n. 85 - no date!

81. From a papal writ, February 21, 1224, Potthast, n. 7124; *VMH*, n. 93.

82. The pontiff praised Leopold of Austria for giving shelter, "benigne et honeste" to Béla - Potthast, n. 7177; *VMH*, n. 94; also, the pope's letter to the king, Potthast, n. 7173; *VMH*, n. 92.

83. *Ibid.*, and the writ cited earlier, Potthast, n. 7171; *VMH*, n. 91.

84. Potthast, n. 7175; *CD*, III-1, 432.

85. The curia to the bishop of Vác, Potthast, n. 7178; *VMH*, 95.

86. Potthast, n. 7174; *VMH*, n. 93.

87. Potthast, n. 7189; *CD*, III-1, 435.
88. Potthast, n. 7179, warning him not to take a stand toward Béla who, because of his strained relations with the king, had to flee to Austria; let the duke behave honestly toward Béla, "sui honeste valeat commorari," - cf. Potthast, n. 7152; *CD*, VII-5, 234.
89. Potthast, n. 7177; *VMH*, n.94; Raynaldus, *Annales*, anno 1224, par. 34; and Potthast, n. 7193; *VMH*, n. 100.
90. Potthast, nn. 7175, 7176, 7178, and 7192; *VMH*, nn. 90, 95, and 101. Compare with *RA*, n. 1312 (a. 1262).
91. Raynaldus, *Annales*, a. 1224, par. 35; Katona, VI, 431, in ref. to a papal writ addressed to Andrew II - Potthast, n. 7189, and, to Béla, in Potthast, n. 7192; *VMH*, n. 99.
92. See papal writ of June 22, 1224, in Potthast, n. 7274; *RA*, n. 261; *CD*, III-1, 106f.

2. *King Andrew II and the German Knights*

> ...fideles hospites nostri Theutonici
> Ultrasilvani universi ad pedes maiestatis
> nostrae humiliter nobis conquerentes...
>
> Andrew II's *Andreanum*

In his charter of 1211, King Andrew II placated Teutonic Knights in the southeastern segment of his realm - the Barca region in Transylvania. He gave them the "Borza Land Beyond the Forest" adjacent to the territory that was previously settled by the Cumans. The knights were required to remain within the defined borders of their [assigned] district. The king determined their privileges in mining rights of gold and silver, the right to hold fairs, to construct forts and towns, and exempted them from forced lodging, or from any further "exactiones."[1]

The purpose of this settlement was related to the defense of the country against the Cumans. The king stated in one of his writs, dated 1212, that the Teutonic Knights were exposed to constant attacks from the Cumans in their territory (a writ of which Pope Gregory IX had made a transcript, dated April 26, 1231).[2] But the main objective for the settlement of the Order had been "missionary work" among the pagans, as referred to by Pope Honorius III in his correspondence of late 1222, and or January 13, 1223.[3] This objective seemed to give credence to the expressed motive for the Knights' existence in the late first quarter of the century; they stood for "defensione Christianos contra paganos."[4]

As recipients of the donation of land from the Hungarian monarch, the Knights enjoyed the rights of a landlord over a particular area in the realm, with all privileges and obligations. This is evident from the 1222 renewal of the charter by the king to Hermann, Grandmaster of the Teutonic Knights (assuming, of course, that the writ was not a forgery), that restricted anew their district within their assigned boundaries.[5] The renewal of the grant to the Grandmaster was necessary on the grounds that the king had, in one of his fits of angry outburst, withdrawn his original grant to the Order. In 1222, the king had reduced the area under the Knights' jurisdiction (*confinium*), even though he had, in 1222, donated Fort

Crucpurg (Kreuzberg - Hill of the Cross) to the Knights, with the surrounding meadows, and forbade anyone to disturb them in their possession of both the fort and of the meadow.[6]

The lands received by the Knights were populated by new settlers, and the Knights maintained a civilized way of life in the area.[7] The Knights, however, wanted independence by establishing a firm territorial base in the region, thereby exempting it from the spiritual and political jurisdiction of the regional bishop. They wanted to place the territory directly under the jurisdiction of the Roman See - "nullum praeter Romanum Pontificem habent episcopum."[8]

In response to the request of the Knights, the papal curia had to assure itself of direct control of the land;[9] oddly enough, the curia acted with the knowledge of the Hungarian court, as the latter evidently assumed its interests would remain unharmed. The court of Andrew II must have assumed that the Knights would continuously meet the terms of their obligations toward the king. This did not happen. In the spring of 1225, Andrew II had to lead a military expedition against the Knights, thus exiting from the area.[10]

As recorded in direct correspondence between the king and the curia (and additionally through the bishop of Port, who was a special envoy on a mission in the empire), strong protests appeared on behalf of the Knights.[11] Andrew II had even expressed some willingness to make concessions. However, the Knights remained unsatisfied and refused the king's proposal.[12] Thereupon the monarch had no alternative but to expel them permanently from his territory.

Had Andrew II been afraid that the Knights would set up an "ecclesiastic" state in Barca land? Consider the reasoning of Alphons Dopsch that the receiver of a landgrant possessed full jurisdiction over the land given to him. Thus, the "ecclesiastic" state to be established by the Knights could easily have brought with it the expansion of imperial German interests in the region.[13] It was this threat that the king had suddenly been concerned about.[14]

It is evident from the papal responses dated October 27, 1225, and February 17, 1226, that the Knights had appealed to the Roman curia; however, the Hungarian court had remained adamant in its refusal: it did not permit a resettlement of the Knights in the realm, and had the Barca region attached to the territory of German settlers in southern Transylvania.[15] Andrew II further granted the *Adrianum* - a charter for the German settlers in order to confirm them in their privileges in the territory.[16] The king acted like this in accordance with article 19 of his Decree of 1222, which stated that migrants (*hospites*) who had arrived and remained within the borders of the realm were to retain the rights they had, or had obtained, since their arrival.[17]

In the 1224 *Adrianum*, Andrew II had redefined the privileges of his German "guests" in Transylvania in matters of government, rights and obligations in paying taxes, "forced lodging" in time of war, (draft) quotas in terms of military service, and made no mention of the Teutonic Knights. The text of the document - "fideles hospites nostri Theutonici Ultrasilvani universi" - had expressed the idea that the king had remained the actual overlord of the territory given to the "hospites."[18] It is noteworthy, though, that the royal writs dealing with German settlers in Transylvania, be it the German Knights or the "hospites," did not contain the term "Saxon;" only a writ, dated 1232, mentioned "Saxons" for the first time, when the archbishop of Esztergom had regained access to the town "once inhabited by Saxons," and authorized the royal reeve Lampert to carry out the transaction.[19]

According to the terms laid down in the *Adrianum*, the king unified the administration of the area inhabited by German settlers east of Szászváros (Saxontown) with the region of the Széklers, that further included the Sebes area Székler settlement in southern Transylvania, south of the Maros and Nagy-Küküllő streams, and placed it under the administrative jurisdiction of the royal reeve of Szeben. Only the monarch and his reeve held jurisdiction over the population of the region.[20]

The settlers were free to elect their officials from among themselves, and they were to be regarded as free landholders (of the Crown); they also held common rights over the woods and the waters - that is, they held forestry and fishing rights that were previously held by the Petchenegs and the Cumans. The king was not allowed to donate any of these lands to his lesser, or service, nobles. The German merchants, or merchants living among them, paid no toll, and were free to market their goods, or hold markets everywhere. They had to pay an annual amount of five thousand silver marks in lieu of *lucrum cameare* - the exchange fee paid for the "new money" (currency) issued by the king (royal mint) once a year.[21]

In time of war, were an enemy to invade the country, the settlers were obligated to send five thousand trained and equipped knights for the king's service. Were the king to conduct military operations abroad, the settlers were obligated to dispatch only one hundred knights for his service; and were the monarch not to conduct the operation of his forces in person, the military quota of the settlers was to be reduced to fifty knights.[22]

During the latter half of the 1220s, the organized settlement of the Kézdi and Sepsi Széklers took place. [23] Prince Béla must have assumed the governorship of Transylvania in 1226, because it was his younger brother Coloman who, after August 1, 1226, had made land grants in Slavonia,[24] and Coloman had referred to himself as "Dux totius Sloveniae."[25]

Available earlier documents bear witness to the presence of Széklers in the region.[26] The Széklers had served as fort- and border guards, and originally came from the Telegd region in Bihar county.[27] In 1228, the record made mention of the first Székler royal reeve by the name of Bagamér.[28] Reeve (ispán) Bagamér of the Széklers supported the king during his Bulgarian campaign in that year, as the Székler detachment formed part of the military force of Grand Reeve (Governor) Béla of Transylvania during that military expedition.[29] In fact, in 1244, King Béla IV had rewarded Bagamér for his participation in that campaign.[30]

During the 1220s, the German settlers began to construct Brassó - the "Town of the Hungarian Crown," or Kronstadt.[31] In 1226, when Béla had assumed the governorship of Transylvania, and Coloman became the governor of Slavonia,[32] Prince Andrew, the youngest of the three brothers, laid claim to Halich; however, because of the intrigues of Mistislav, Andrew only gained access to the area surrounding Przemysl,[33] and his father, the king, had to lead another military campaign against Halich in 1226.[34]

In order to pay for the expenses of this campaign, Andrew II broke the promises he had made in his Decree of 1222, by farming out the collection of royal revenue to Moslems and Jews.[35] On the home front, the population revolted against what they considered greed on the part of the non-Hungarian tax collectors, who, in the popular view, had been abusing their authority.[36] Worse still, the king lost the campaign in Halich, but Mistislav, following his advisors' recommendation, made peace with him.[37]

Prince Béla, as governor of Transylvania, urged the royal court to enforce the conversion of Cumans to the Christian faith, and took the matter into his own hands, requesting the cooperation of Franciscan and Dominican friars to carry out that objective.[38] The royal court took action; in order to organize the Cuman mission, the court had authorized Archbishop Robert of Esztergom to travel, as papal legate, to Cuman territory in both Transylvania and Moldavia.[39] Barc, the leader of the Cumans, had expressed willingness to convert to the Christian faith, and he, with his family and some fifteen thousand people, were baptized.[40]

Archbishop Robert named Theodore, a Dominican, as the first bishop of the new diocese beyond the Carpathians, and established his See at Milkovia. Theodore's jurisdiction also included the Barca land, formerly held by the Teutonic Knights, in the southeastern corner of Transylvania.[41] Prince Béla had assured the Cumans that they would retain their freedom, ancient liberties and customs, after their conversion to the Christian faith.[42]

Archbishop Robert's Cuman mission that led to the establishment of the bishopric of Milkovia served a political purpose as well. The Szörény region - that is, western Wallachia from the Orsova Straits to the mouth of the Olt stream - was under the *de facto* rule of the Hungarian court, but was uninhabited, and had to be populated by Rumanian shepherds settling down in tribal groups under the *kenéz*, their ethnic self-elected leaders.[43] The king had changed the administration of the region into a *banate*, and obligated the old and new inhabitants to pay regular taxes.[44] Furthermore, he obliged them to provide him with military service if, and when, it became necessary. In time of war, every third or every fifth male in the population of the area had to report under the royal standard.[45]

Béla, Grand Reeve of Transylvania, had planned, out of military consideration, to occupy Bulgaria and in 1228, he moved with his military force, which included the Székler detachment of Transylvania, commanded by Reeve Bagamér, against the Bulgarians.[46] The campaign, however, remained unsuccessful; they could not occupy Bodon, a border fort. And yet, in one of his letters, the prince had referred to his father as "King of Bulgaria," and to himself as the "Son of the King of Bulgaria."[47]

The intention of the royal court to reclaim and repossess part of the royal domain that had been wastefully given away by Andrew II during the early years of his reign had to be scaled down by the court because of the events that took place in Halich.[48] Mistislav regretted the promise concerning the succession to the throne of Halich he had made to Andrew, Béla's youngest brother, and called upon Danilo to take charge of the region. When Mistislav died, the nobles of Halich had called for Danilo, who, in alliance with Conrad of Masova, took possession of Halich. Prince Andrew had to go home.

Under these circumstances, the Hungarian court had no alternative but to order Béla to take countermeasures for the recapture of Halich. Béla's hastily gathered forces included many converted Cumans, but they were unable to repossess the region. Mainly on account of bad weather, the entire expedition ended in failure. Béla's forces had suffered heavy losses in men and supplies.[49]

The king could not find peace of mind. In 1231, he himself took to arms, when the news reached him that Halich had been unhappy under Danilo's rule. Andrew II was successful: he restored his youngest son Andrew to the throne of Halich, left behind a strong garrison for his protection, then turned on Ladomer, and took possession of the area also.[50] These unexpected victories encouraged Béla to make a serious effort to repossess former royal estates that had been wastefully given away in the recent past. His attempts were successful; as his chancellor noted admiringly, the "Junior King" was able to preserve royal dignity and reclaim respect for the crown.[51]

On the other hand, Béla's serious attitude had caused him to have many enemies;[52] they even organized a conspiracy against him - and against his father. But the conspirators were discovered in time; they fled the realm and the court confiscated their possessions.[53] And yet, it can be concluded from the data available on the first decades of his reign that Andrew II failed to economize on the time and opportunities that had been at his disposal.

The king had made a thoughtless decision in inviting the German Knights to settle down in his realm; he ought to have known that the Knights had to have political motives in acquiring new territory. And, when he realized the real purpose of the Knights' arrival in Barca land, he, in a likewise reckless manner, expelled them from his territories instead of pursuing a more persuasive approach, and behavior, toward them. Through diplomacy, Andrew II could have convinced the grudging Knights to willingly submit to his rule - and to the country's laws - or arrange for their more orderly departure.

The monarch also behaved in a similarly irresponsible manner toward Mistislav and Danilo in Halich. As is evident from the record, the good will displayed by Mistislav would have enabled Andrew II to handle the Halich question more convincingly, and tactfully, through personal negotiations. Instead of leading expensive, countless, and time-consuming military expeditions against Halich, Andrew II ought to have gained information beforehand about the religious, political, social, and diplomatic conditions that prevailed in that territory. Evidently, the Hungarian king must have had little use for organized military intelligence.

In the manner he had displayed during his military venture to the Holy Land in 1217-18, Andrew II behaved irrationally in Halich. A more personal approach through relatives or family channels could have informed him that his "family plan" regarding Halich was really quite unrealistic. In involving himself with the Halich question for years, Andrew II had only wasted precious time, energy, and opportunities he ought to have far more efficiently used in improving the political and socio-economic conditions in his own country.

NOTES

1. Cf. *RA*, n. 261 (anno 1211); *CD*, III-1, 106f.; F. Zimmermann, C. Werner, and G. Müller (eds.), *Urkunden zur Geschichte der Deutschen in Siebenbürgen*, 3 vols. (Hermannstadt, 1892-1902), I, 11f.; G.D. Teutsch and F. Firnhaber (eds.), *Urkundenbuch zur Geschichte Siebenbürgens*, vol. I (Vienna, 1857), 8f.; L. Hanzó, "A barcaság betelepítése és a Német Lovagrend" [Settlement of the Barca Region and the German Knights], *Századok*, 123 (1989), 359ff. - an article scheduled for publication in 1948! - see *ibid.*, 237; and the scholarly monograph by F. Teutsch, *Geschichte der Siebenbürger Sachsen für das Sächsische Volk* (Hermannstadt, 1907), passim, and his remark on "objectivity," or the lack of it, *ibid.*, 359f.; Otto Mittelstrass, *Beiträge zur Siedlungsgeschichte Siebenbürgens im Mittelalter* (Munich, 1961); Gebhardt, *Handbuch*, I, 487f.; K. Schünemann, *Die Entstehung der Städtewesen in Südosteuropa* (Bresslau, 1929).

2. *RA*, n. 275 (anno 1212) - transcribed by Gregory IX on April 26, 1231, see Potthast, n. 8728; *VMH*, n. 169; Teutsch-Firnhaber, I, 46.

3. Potthast, nn. 6910 and 6922.

4. Cf. Th. Hirsch, M. Töppen, and E. Strehlke (eds.), *Scriptores rerum Prussicarum: Die Geschichtsquellen der Preussischen Vorzeit bis zum Untergang der Ordenherrschaft*, 5 vols. (Leipzig, 1861-74), I, 676; M. Perlbach, "Der Deutsche Orden in Siebenbürgen", *MIÖG*, 26 (1905), 415ff.; M. Tumler, *Der Deutsche Orden im Westen, Wachsen und Wirken bis 1400, mit einer Abriss der Geschichte des Ordens von 1400 bis zur neuesten Zeit* (Vienna, 1954).

5. *RA*, n. 380 (anno 1222) - most probably composed from royal writs listed under *RA*, nn. 261, 275, and 391; it might not be authentic! On the German Knights, see Funk-Bihlmeyer, II, 163f.; on the privileges of the landlord, see Alphons Dopsch, *Wirtschaftsgeschichte der Karolingerzeit*, 3rd rev. ed., ed. Erna Patzelt, 2 vols. (Cologne-Graz, 1962), I, 131f., and 402ff.; II, 111 and 131.

6. *RA*, n. 391 (anno 1222), and transcribed by Pope Gregory IX on April 30, 1231, cf. Potthast, n. 8732; *VMH*, n. 170; Teutsch-Firnhaber, I, 46; according to Zimmermann-Werner, I, 14f., it was only a postscript to the previous 1212 document - logged as *RA*, n. 275 - but it was not! Its composition showed similarities with royal writs in *HO*, V, 11, and *ÁUO*, VI, 315. Assuming that the writ logged under *RA*, n. 380 was authentic, n. 391 had to be issued in early 1222; it did scale down the size of the "confinium" - cf. E. Jekelius (ed.), *Das Burzenland*, 4 vols. (Kronstadt, 1928-29), III-1, 51; IV, 78f.

7. Potthast, n. 6918; *VMH*, n. 76; Perlbach, *art. cit.*

8. Potthast, n. 7115; *VMH*, n. 87; J. Schütze, "Bemerkung zur Berufung und Vertreibung des Deutschen Ordens durch Andras II von Ungarn," *Siebenbürgisches Archiv* (Archiv des Vereins für siebenbürgische Landeskunde), 3rd. ser., VIII (Cologne-Vienna, 1971), offprint.

9. Potthast, nn. 7274 and 7232; *VMH*, n. 105; G. Eduard Müller, "Die Ursache der Vertriebung des Deutsche Ordens aus dem Burzenland im Jahre 1225," *Korrespondenblatt des Vereins für Siebenbürgische Landeskunde* (Hermannstadt, 1925), xeroxed reprint.

10. Potthast, n. 7431; *VMH*, n. 124; compare with Potthast, n. 7531; *VMH*, n. 136; *CD*, III-2, 74.

11. Potthast, n. 7472; *VMH*, n. 130; Raynaldus, *Annales*, anno 1225, par. 19-20.

12. Potthast, n. 7470; *VMH*, n. 128; Béla Köpeczy (ed.), *Erdély története* [History of Transylvania], 3 vols. (Budapest, 1986), I, 295ff., and my review of this opus in *Austrian History Yearbook*, 22 (1991), 170ff.

13. Potthast, n. 7494; *VMH*, n. 135; *CD*, III-1, 58; Dopsch, II, 111 and 131.

14. Cf. *RA*, n. 380; *CD*, III-1, 370f.; Zimmermann-Werner, I, 18f.; Potthast, n. 7232; *VMH*, n. 105; Hanzó, *art. cit.*, 378f.

15. *RA*, n. 413 (anno 1224); Potthast, nn. 7494 and 7531.

16. *RHM*, 420ff.; Marczali, *Enchiridion*, 145ff.: "...fideles hospites nostri Theutonici Ultrasilvani universi ad pedes maiestatis nostrae humiliter nobis conquerentes;" Zimmermann-Werner, I, 34ff.; Köpeczy, *Erdély*, I, 296f.
17. For art. 19 of the Decree of 1222, cf. Marczali, *Enchiridion*; see also art. 26 of the Decree of 1231 - *ibid.*, 140b.
18. *RA*, n. 491; *ÁUO*, XI, 242; Knauz, I, 288; Hanzó, *art. cit.*, 354; Köpeczy, *Erdély*, 295ff. and 593f.
19. *RA*, n. 491; this writ also applied, for the first time, the term "Saxon," in the year 1232. Further, see map in Köpeczy, I, 384; on the Széklers, see *ibid.*, I, 291ff.; György Györffy, "A székelyek eredete" [In Search of the Széklers], in Elemér Mályusz (ed.), *Erdély és népei* [Transylvania and its Peoples] (Kolozsvár, 1941); Siculus (*sic!*), "A székelyek eredetéhez" [Remarks on the Origins of the Széklers], *Emlékkönyv a Székely Múzeum 50 éves jubileumára* [Memorial Volume on the 50th Anniversary of the Székler National Museum], ed. V. Csutak (Sepsiszentgyörgy, 1929; repr. Budapest, 1988), 641ff.
20. *RA*, n. 413; Marczali, *Enchiridion*, 146, art. 1.
21. *Ibid.*, 146f.; Spufford, 123 and 136.
22. *RA*, n. 413; József Deér, "Közösségérzés és nemzettudat a XI-XIII századi Magyarországon" [Communal Identity and National Consciousness in Hungary During the Eleventh-Thirteenth Centuries], *Klébersberg Kúnó Történetkutató Intézet évkönyve* [Annual of the Kuno Klebersberg Historical Research Institute], IV (Budapest, 1934), 97ff.; Gyula Németh, *A honfoglaló magyarság kialakulása* [Ethnic Formation of the Hungarians of the Conquest], 2nd rev. ed., ed. *Árpád* Berta (Budapest, 1991), 46, 199, 271.
23. It is possible that the district of "Csík" had not been populated from the Kézdi region, as its inhabitants originated in a region under the deanery of Telegd - *VMH*, n. 112; by 1228, they inhabited the valley of the Maros stream - *HO*, VI, 20f.; Köpeczy, I, 291ff. and 593f.
24. *CD*, III-2, 90.
25. *CD*, III-2, 237f., and compare to *RA*, n. 438; *CD*, IV-2, 103; Köpeczy, I, 285 (in 1227).
26. Cf. K. Szabó and L. Szádecky (eds.), *Székely Oklevéltár* [Archives of Documents Pertinent to the History of the Széklers], 3 vols. (Kolozsvár, 1872-98), I, nn. 13, 20, 29; III, n. 3. See further, Zoltán Kordé, "A székelyek a XII századi elbeszélő forrásokban" [The Széklers in Twelfth Century Narrative Sources], *Acta historica Szegediensis*, 91 (1991), 17ff.
27. Köpeczy, I, 292f.
28. *CD*, IV-1, 22f.; *RA*, n. 572 recorded a Bagamér as the royal Chief Cupbearer (anno 1225).
29. Szabó-Szádecky, I, n. 10; *RA*, n. 766; *ÁUO*, VII, 171f.
30. *RA*, n. 767.
31. Hóman-Szekfű, II, 94 and 163; *RA*, n. 413; the *Andreanum*, aa. 1 and 2 stated that there will be one official in charge of the area inhabited by German settlers, will also be, at a later date, in charge of Brassó. Cf. Zimmermann-Werner, I, 34ff.; Marczali, *Enchiridion*, 146,2-9; Köpeczy, I, 335.
32. *RA*, n. 438, and Katona, V, 495 referring to this writ; on Coloman's character, see the remarks made by Thomas of Spaleto, cc. 31 and 38. See further, *RA*, n. 261 (1211); *CD*, III-1, 106f.; Zimmermann-Werner, I, 11f.; Teutsch-Firnhaber, I, 8f.
33. Bielowski, *MPH*, IV, 776ff., for the life of Salomé; Alberic on Prince Andrew - cf. *MGHSS*, XXIII, 934.
34. Hodinka, 350aff., and 356b; GVC, 31f.; a royal "serviens" named Michael, took part in this expedition - *RA*, n. 456; "Cont. Sancrucensis," *MGHSS*, IX, 627. For the writ issued "in expeditione Russiae," cf. *ÁUO*, XII, 211; *CD*, III-1, 356 (anno 1229).

35. Potthast, n. 8671; *VMH*, n. 168; *CD*, III-2, 241, and compare with the papal writ to Archbishop Robert of Esztergom, Potthast, n. 8670; *VMH*, n. 166.
36. *VMH*, n. 169 (I, 94,6-12).
37. Hodinka, 354a-356a; and his introduction, *ibid.*, 277ff.
38. Alberic, *MGHSS*, XXIII, 920; Knauz, I, 280 and 295; Potthast, n. 8153; *VMH*, n. 156.
39. Archbishop Robert had requested, and received, the jurisdiction and designation of papal legate for the Cuman mission - Potthast, n. 7984; *VMH*, n. 154; Raynaldus, *Annales*, anno 1227, par. 50.
40. Potthast, n. 8154; *VMH*, n. 157; Knauz, I, 263; "Emonis Chronicon," *MGHSS*, XXIII, 511.
41. *Székely Okmánytár*, I, n. 10; Potthast, n. 8155; *VMH*, n. 155.
42. *VMH*, n.. 156.
43. On the concept and definition of *kenéz*: "caneseo (canesios), id est, balamios (balivos?), qui iustitiam facerent;" see Rogerius, c. 35, *SSH*, II, 581,10-11; in Hungarian, he would be called *ispán* - *RA*, n. 771 (July 25, 1244), a document transcribed in the papal curia on October 31, 1375, cf. VHM, I, 297. On the position and geographic location of the "Vlachs," cf. Teutsch-Firnhaber, I, 185; also, Köpeczy, I, 301ff.; Ferenc Somogyi, *Küldetés: a magyarság története* [Destiny: A History of the Hungarians], 2nd rev. ed. (Cleveland, OH, 1978), 194; and my review of this book in *Austrian History Yearbook*, 17-18 (1981-82), 349f.
Pope Gregory IX to Archbishop Ugrin of Kalocsa in reference to establishing the Szerém bishopric - Potthast, n. 8318; *VMH*, n. 158; Raynaldus, *Annales*, anno 1229, par. 60; papal writ to Aegidius, papal legate in the area, Potthast, n. 8348; *VMH*, n. 159; Katona, V, 544.
44. The "banate" of Szerém had been established by detachment of the western portion of Cuman territory in 1228 - Köpeczy, I, 595; Ransgerd Göckenjan, *Hilfsvölker und Grenzwächter im mittelalterlichen Ungarn* (Wiesbaden, 1972), 89ff.; László Makkai, *A milkói kún püpökség* [The Cuman Bishopric of Milkó] (Debrecen, 1936), 9ff.
45. Köpeczy, I, 305ff. The conclusion may be drawn from a papal writ of October 1, 1229, Potthast, n. 8457; *VMH*, n. 162; *CD*, III-2, 216f., referring to the royal writ with a golden seal concerning the liberties and lands of the Cumans - *RA*, n. 465. One may draw a similar conclusion from the Second Cuman Law of Ladislas IV, art. 8, and articles 11-12, of August 10, 1279 - cf. Marczali, *Enchiridion*, 178ff.; *RHM*, 559ff.; and Károly Szabó, *Kún László*, in *Magyar történeti élerajzok* [Hungarian Historic Sketches] series (Budapest, 1886; repr. 1988), 83f.; compare to the writ of Ladislas IV, dated July 23, 1279, *RA*, n. 299; *VMH*, n. 556, and with the strongly worded letter of Pope Nicholas III, December 9, 1279, in Potthast, n. 21663; *VMH*, n. 557. An Austrian chronicler reported that the Hungarians began to accept the hair style and dress of the Cumans - *MGHSS*, IX, 731,2-5 and 731,29-33.
46. *RA*, nn. 766 and 767; *ÁUO*, VII, 174f.; compare to *RA*, n. 792; *CD*, IV-1, 343.
47. *RA*, n. 608; Knauz, I, 314; *Székely Oklevéltár*, I, n. 7; Teutsch-Firnhaber, I, xxxv.
48. As, e.g., *RA*, nn. 583, 584, 585, 589, 591, 592, 593, 595; Hodinka, 362aff.
49. *Ibid.*, 368a-370a; the Russian text mentioned a king, Béla, *ibid.*, 368a; compare to *ÁUO*, VII, 262ff., and VII, 282ff.; on Dénes, see *RA*, n. 608.
50. Hodinka, 3471ff.; compare to *ÁUO*, XI, 257f.
51. Alberic, in *MGHSS*, XXIII, 929,25-26; the Decree of 1222, art. 18, and King Béla IV's Laws, in Marczali, *Enchiridion*, 139f. and 168f., respectively; on royal dignity, Kantorowicz, *The King's Two Bodies*, 380, 383ff., n. 180. N. de Wailly (ed.), Jean de Joinville, *Histoire de Saint Louis* (Paris, 1874), 11 and 34; also, *MGHSS*, XXVI, 557.
52. As it may be evident from Rogerius, c. 4, *SSH*, II, 554f.; or, Marczali, *Enchiridion*, 151f.
53. *MGHSS*, XXIII, 929.

3. The Church in Hungary During the Early 1230's

> ...ut sive nos, sive filii nostri, et successores nostri hanc a nobis concessam libertatem confringere voluerint, Archiepiscopus Strigoniensis praemissa legitima admonitione nos vincula excommunicationis ... habeat potestatem.
>
> *Decretum II*, 1231, conclusion

Aegidius (Egyed), the papal legate, spent three years in the country, from 1228 to 1231, and in 1231, he dispatched a report to the curia about the wholly deteriorated condition of the realm. The report is known from a letter the Roman pontiff had addressed to the archbishop of Esztergom.[1]

Some awful matters must have been reported to him. The pontiff wrote to the archbishop telling him of the awful matters that had been reported. The matters were primarily domestic, and they prevailed contrary to divine and human laws, as Jews and Moslems were being patronized by the royal court and allowed to hold public offices to the detriment of the public good. Royal authority had been illegally used to obtain ecclesiastical property. Moslems were allowed to marry Christians, keep Christian slaves, and even entice Christians into leaving their religion. The Church was expected to pay taxes, and secular judges were permitted to handle legal matters pertinent to religious-ecclesiastical interests in courts of secular law.[2]

The curia had to call upon the archbishop to terminate these unlawful and unhealthy, immoral conditions in that country, in order to prevent non-Christians, or even Christians, from doing wrong, and to exclude the enemies of the true faith from the community of the faithful. Esztergom must severely punish those who went astray and refused to return to the Christian fold. The archbishop must rely upon secular authority, if necessary, in furthering his cause. Rome had to remind the archbishop that, after all, it was he who held the constitutional right to crown the kings of Hungary. Therefore, it was within his jurisdiction to assure that Christian ethics and ecclesiastical interests prevailed in the country.[3]

The issue, in 1231, of the Decree with the Golden Seal: King Andrew II's *Decretum II*, was the result of these papal letters.[4] The monarch, and his sons Béla and Coloman, began negotiations with members of the hierarchy in order to find solutions to persisting problems. The talks led to the issuance of the Decree in 1231, which was identical with the articles of the Decree of 1222 on essential points, although quite a few of its articles were new, or worded differently.[5]

The new Decree left out nine resolutions dealing with the privileges of the *servientes* - lesser or service nobles - denying them the privilege to move freely about the entire country. It omitted the article concerning the four head officials of the realm who had been allowed to hold several offices, or responsibilities, at the same time. It left out provisions dealing with salt tax and the annual exchange fee of "new money;" it further ignored the nobles' right to resist the monarch, were he to breach the laws of the land.[6]

The new Decree added nine new articles.[7] It specified, for example, that the *servientes* and ecclesiastics were not obligated to aid the monarch in bringing about, or actually building, public projects, in erecting fortifications for the nation's defense.[8] It further specified that the lord of a region (the King's reeve), be he a layman or a churchman, must pay compensation to peasants for damages done, or requisitions made for food and lodging in their households, - were three peasants to swear under oath that such a forceful requisition had taken place.[9]

The new Decree consented to the idea that:

(1)   Noblemen, or non-noblemen, can freely attend and take part in the debates at the annual law-day held on the feast of King St. Stephen in Székesfehérvár.[10]

(2)   Members of the hierarchy were obliged to attend the annual law-day in a body, and listen to the complaints of the poor, who were going to appear before them. They would have to find solutions to their problems, just as members of the higher clergy were expected to protect the endangered freedom of all of the country's inhabitants.[11]

(3)   The monarch cannot illegally levy and collect taxes, on his own initiative.[12]

(4)   The jurisdiction of the Palatine did not extend to ecclesiastics, marriage cases, or to any other church business; the

administration of all of these matters rested - *ratione personae materiaeque* - with the Church.[13]

(5)   Only a naturalized *hospes* of noble rank might be granted, and allowed to retain, public offices.[14]

(6)   The wife and child(ren) of a condemned criminal, thief, robber might not be punished or sold into slavery on account of her (their) husband's (father's) guilt.[15]

(7)   The king must not force the servants of a nobleman or of an ecclesiastic to perform unspecified labor for the monarch or on the royal estate.[16]

(8)   The monarch cannot collect an additional *tenth* besides the one-twentieth of the church tithe.[17]

(9)   Jews and Moslems must not hold public offices.[18]

The king and his sons confirmed these articles under oath and seal.[19] At the same time, the king authorized the archbishop of Esztergom to excommunicate him were the monarch to break any of these resolutions.[20]

Did Andrew II enact the Decree of 1231 in vain? Did he keep his promises? Did he ever intend to keep them? Did Moslems continue to occupy public offices, mainly because of the favoritism Palatine Dénes (Dioynsius) had displayed toward them, or because the Palatine had been more tolerant of them? Did the lives of the poor improve in the country? The answer had to be no - the lot of the poorer segment of the population improved not at all. For that reason, Archbishop Robert of Esztergom saw no alternative but to place the entire country under the interdict.[21]

The archbishop wanted to show some consideration for the king by only placing the royal advisors and the realm-at-large under ecclesiastic punishment, probably in the futile hope that public discontent in the country would create an outcry that would have an impact upon the attitude of the monarch and his advisors.[22]

The interdict forbade divine services to be performed, Masses to be said at the royal court, and in the country households of the nobility (probably also in churches that were under the "patronage" of a country nobleman). It forbade the administration of the sacraments, except baptism and the Eucharist, penance, and last rites. The dead would have to be buried without church blessing; the parish priests could say Mass only once a month behind closed doors and without the ringing of bells, in order to prepare the Eucharist for the sick and the dying in the parish. Archbishop Robert made every effort to clarify the position of the Holy See: the royal court had to live up to its legal enactments.[23]

The church punishment was mainly aimed at the king's advisors, as it punished Palatine Dénes, and Sámuel, Steward of the Royal Chamber; Archbishop Robert granted Nicholas, the Royal Treasurer, a stay until Maundy Thursday of that year in order to mend his ways.[24] Andrew II was not placed under the interdict, partly because the papal curia wanted to show respect for the king's position (although not for his person!),[25] and partly on the grounds that Rome justly expected him to improve his (personal) disposition.[26]

In that religious age, the interdict - forbiddance of the public celebration of the Eucharist and the cessation of public ecclesiastical functions - created a horrified reaction among the inhabitants of the realm, and Rome hoped that leading social strata in the country, and at the royal court, would, in time, acknowledge the gravity of their situation. Church interdict was not an empty phrase: every bishop had to announce it to the clergy and the faithful in his diocese and to supervise its enforcement.[27]

Indeed, the interdict was effective. Andrew II took action. He dispatched his son Béla, and several nobles, to the archbishop of Esztergom to petition him for the lifting of the punishment. The king promised to make amends and to carry out those amends. After the monarch took an oath that he had sincere intentions, Archbishop Robert temporarily suspended the interdict from the period of Ash Wednesday to the feast of King Stephen that year.[28]

Andrew II could not be trusted, however. He made use of the temporary suspension of the interdict by sending a delegation to Rome. It was headed by Palatine Dénes (whom Archbishop Robert had earlier excommunicated for divesting ecclesiastics from their prebends in favor of Moslem officials in the royal service), with the objective that he, Palatine Dénes, in the name of the king, accuse Archbishop Robert before the papal curia. The palatine had to inform Rome that the king was, and had always been, faithful to the Church. Yet what reward did he receive for his loyalty? They had closed the church doors in front of him, in his own country. They had his advisors, who had done nothing wrong, excommunicated for no valid reason. The interdict only gave him a bad name in front of the other royal houses of Europe. He now requested that his case be properly reviewed by the Holy See, and a special delegate be dispatched to Hungary to conduct the inquiry.[29]

The king's game of diplomatic chess proved successful with the Roman curia. According to a papal writ, dated July 22, 1232, addressed to Archbishop Robert of Esztergom, a papal legate had been sent to Hungary and the curia instructed the archbishop to refrain from any further action, or announcement, against the king prior to the arrival of the legate.[30] In a writ dated about a month later, the pontiff encouraged the monarch not to worry: nobody could excommunicate him (again) without the foreknowledge of the Holy See.[31]

Bishop Jacob Precorari, Cistercian monk and the Cardinal of Praeneste, was the new papal legate, authorized by the pontiff to seek out evidence concerning the status of the Teutonic Knights, who had already been expelled from the realm. The chief responsibility of the legate was, however, to examine the cause of misunderstanding between the king and the archbishop of Esztergom, and to make a decision in the case. The legate had not been authorized to excommunicate the king.[32]

In order to gain the confidence of the ranks of the Hungarian clergy, the legate had to summon a church synod in Buda for the fall of 1232. Before it, Archbishop Robert gave an account of his behavior toward the monarch and the royal court, and of his attitude toward the royal advisors.[33] The archbishop displayed little hostility toward the establishment in public, partly on the grounds that the king had, by then, returned all illegally confiscated church property to him; partly because Andrew II had exempted the archbishop's spiritual subjects (in the Esztergom archdiocese) from the jurisdiction of the palatine.[34]

The synod discussed the draft of a papal letter, dated March 3, 1231.[35] The legate forwarded to Rome a written opinion concerning the reaction of the Hungarian nobles to that papal writ, together with a letter from the archbishop of Esztergom, where he explained why he had, on account of the attitude of the king and of his advisors, announced the interdict over the kingdom. The content of both the archbishop's letter and of the written opinion of the legate are evident from the papal response to the legate.[36] The pontiff praised the tact and attitude of the legate, but warned him that were the monarch not to cooperate with him, he would have to take action against him, with the assistance of the archbishop of Esztergom.[37]

Pope Honorius III had earnestly warned the king to receive the legate in person, and to work with him; he reminded the monarch of the dreadful daily abuses that had been occurring in the country, and expressed sorrow over the fact that the king had shown no remorse at all. In fact, the ruler had done nothing to improve conditions in his realm. Papal tolerance had its limits.[38]

And yet, the king did not receive the legate in person. The delegate had to negotiate with the royal advisors instead. Negotiations went slowly. Nicholas the Treasurer, Michael, son of Aba, Master of the Stables, Bágyon the Butler, and Maurice de genere Pók, Chief Cup-bearer, conducted talks with the pope's delegate.[39]

It is known from another papal letter that Rome had instructed the legate that he must use utmost caution and tact in dealing with the Hungarian king and his sons. Were it to become necessary to rely on punishments against them, the legate was to proceed most carefully.[40]

On account of the slow progress of the negotiations with the court, the papal legate attempted to take care of other business. For instance, he intervened in the Bogomil affair in the Szerém region where, in spite of the forceful activities of Ban (Grand Reeve) Kulin, the Bogomils had been making constant headway. In 1224, the Hungarian court had placed the entire area under the spiritual jurisdiction of Archbishop Ugrin of Kalocsa, instructing him that he further make the region "safe" from all heretics. The royal court demanded that the inhabitants of the region pay attention to the constitutional rights of the Hungarian king, and pay the money due to the king.[41]

Archbishop Ugrin established order in Bosnia, fortified the territory, and turned to Rome with a request for the establishment of a bishopric in the Szerém region. The new diocese was to be located at Bán or Kolozsmonostor with the understanding that its bishop cooperate with Kalocsa in the conversion of the "heretics" in the area.[42]

The arrangement did not prove satisfactory. It was the opinion of the papal curia that only a crusade would provide a solution to the Bogomil "heresy."[43] Rome called upon Kajolan Angelos - the son of

Andrew II's sister and Isaak Angelos, who, together with his mother, had found refuge at the Hungarian court in 1222, and from his royal uncle received the "Szerém region Beyond" (i.e., the area south of the Sava river, with Belgrade, Baranch, and other fortified towns in the region) - to lead the crusade.[44]

The Szerém region he received from Andrew II had formerly belonged to the brother-in-law of Andrew II, upon whose death it reverted to the royal domain.[45] Kajolan did not live up to expectations, however. A papal writ stated that he did not fulfill his crusading vow, and the Bogomil threat continued to spread without any further hindrance. The royal official in charge of the region, Mitoslav, supported the Bogomils, sympathized with them, and encouraged them to proclaim their doctrine by word of mouth. As a matter of fact, even the bishop of Bosnia failed to take effective action against the Bogomils.[46]

It was at this stage of developments that the papal legate entered the scene. The legate deposed the bishop of Bosnia, detached the diocese from the Raguza archbishopric, and placed it under the care of the Dominican friars by naming a friar as the new bishop. The first objective of the Dominican bishop was to convert the local official - the ban[us] (Grand Reeve) - to his views. The Church slowly regained its foothold in Bosnia.[47]

It was also at this time that the legate had to investigate, with the help of a canon from Esztergom and a Dominican legal expert, the relationship between the Benedictine abbey of Pannonhalma and its servile folks. They had listened to the complaints of the latter, had accepted their statements as valid, and had redefined their rights and obligations to the abbey.[48] Were, for instance, a peasant servant of the abbey called upon to perform military service for the abbey, to fall ill and become incapacitated, could he retain his ten acre allotment? Were the servant, a simple mounted peasant of the abbey, to pay tax on his agricultural products, or on his allotment fee, would he be entitled to twenty acres of land from the abbey for his personal upkeep?[49]

The preoccupied legate[50] had to find time[51] for initiating the process of canonization for Archbishop Lukács of Esztergom,[52] and to act as a judge in the case involving the bishop in Transylvania with the monastic community Kolos, as to the status-quo of the parochial clergy in the Barca region.[53] He also had to intervene in the election of the bishop of Várad, since members of the cathedral chapter in Várad were split into two factions.[54] He had to persuade the Hungarian hierarchy to ease the burden of taxation of the parochial clergy; and, during his visits over the country, he had to call on various groups of people, and on parishes, to listen to their complaints and find solutions to their problems.[55]

Cardinal Jacob took a firm stand toward the hierarchy. For example, he suspended Bishop Bertalan of Pécs and had the suspension announced publicly, on the grounds that the bishop had visited the Iberian peninsula as a royal envoy without the permission of his ecclesiastical superior.[56] The Cardinal informed Fabian, a knight, who had unlawfully confiscated lands from the Church, to pay indemnity for the damage he had done.[57]

The legate made the clergy pay for his personal expenses as the papal envoy, and when some of the clerics rose in protest, the Cardinal, by the authority invested in him, had them punished if they were still unwilling to meet their payments.[58] The legate created quite a stir through his actions, although his stern and stubborn behavior had further undermined the powers of the Hungarian court, as exemplified by the events that occurred in the summer of 1233.

During that summer, Danilo of Halich had, once again, threatened the position of Andrew, King Andrew II's son on the Halich throne, and the king had hurried to his son's rescue.[59] He was en-route toward Halich when, on the edge of Bereg Woods, he concluded and signed an agreement with the papal envoy.[60] The domestic situation in the realm must have been as bad as the one in Halich; the Cardinal must have decided to keep an eye on both.[61] The king had earlier said that he was willing to meet with the papal envoy,[62] and the latter had authorized his chaplain that he, together with Bishop Bertlan of Veszprém and Canon Cognoscens of Esztergom, negotiate with the monarch.[63]

On August 20, 1233, the negotiating parties had reached an agreement, according to which the king promised that he would not tolerate Jews and Moslems as public office holders of the realms, or as holders of Christian slaves.[64] Secondly, salt due to, or owned by the Church would be free of toll when transported by ship or on land. In order to compensate for irregularities and/or errors in the past, the king agreed to pay ten thousand silver marks to the Church, in five installments, beginning on Easter, 1234. Third, churchmen were to be free from taxation; except in legal cases involving property, clergymen were to have free access to church courts of law. The monarch asked the envoy to inform the papal curia that, in accordance with Hungarian law, church interests in the kingdom will suffer if civil cases would only be handled by church courts of law. Fourth, the monarch promised to ask for the opinion of the clergy before levying an extraordinary tax, and for the consent of Rome - as if to prove that the Hungarian nobility at this time did not possess the prestige and influence to direct taxation, or to be free from paying taxes.[65] Fifth, the king and his sons, and the royal advisors in attendance, had to take an oath on the Book of the Gospels promising to keep the agreement. Within twenty-five days upon the completion of the Halich campaign, Andrew II would have to take another, more solemn, oath to the same effect.[66]

The legate had decided to remain in the country for the duration of King Andrew's military adventure in Halich, and to influence, if possible, both the king's behavior and the political-military developments in the realm. The monarch now ordered that the text of the treaties, sworn by himself and his two sons and by the royal advisors present, be drawn up in two copies, and authenticated with golden seals.[67]

It was ironic that Andrew II aborted his Halich campaign. Unexpected developments on the western border called for his personal attention and military presence there.[68] And yet, if it was his intention to delay, for as long as possible, the realization of the promises he had just made under oath in the Bereg Agreement, Andrew II must have fallen into his own trap. In September, he was already in Esztergom, where he, for the first time, met with the papal envoy face to face, and took his oath before him, in the presence of the Master of the Knights of St. John, promising to adhere to the articles of the agreement.[69] Interestingly, he had the document prepared in two copies, although, contrary to established custom, he had it drafted in the form of a letter addressed to the papal legate. This letter, made out in two copies, carried the full text of the Bereg treaty.[70]

On the western frontier a political and military encounter had taken place, caused by Frederick II of Austria, who almost constantly had been trouble for his neighbors along the Austro-Hungarian border.[71] The duke had occupied the town of Borostyán and the

Langeck homestead on the border of Vas county, but the Hungarians staged a counteroffensive and reoccupied both the town and the homestead.[72] In a desperate move, the duke now invaded the country with an armed force; thereupon Béla, Junior King, authorized Reeve Dénes Türje, the hero of the Halich wars and a former playmate of Béla, to initiate military action against the duke. Reeve Dénes defeated the Austrian force and invaded Austrian territory. It was part of the reeve's strategy to withdraw after a sudden (sham) attack, in order to lead the enemy astray, then turn on the duke and demolish his forces.[73]

The Austro-Hungarian political and military status-quo might have been settled peacefully, when, unexpectedly in the fall of 1233, Andrew II decided on a military maneuver against the Duke of Austria. To be successful, he needed the understanding and support of the papal envoy. The king promised the Cardinal that if he failed to carry out the articles of the Bereg Agreement by the date agreed upon, the legate would have the right to excommunicate him and place the country under the interdict.[74]

In early November, 1233, Andrew II and Béla Junior King attacked Duke Frederick, but the latter requested truce negotiations. The understanding they reached by negotiation was not a good one, nor an honest one, but Duke Frederick had no alternative. Peace once again prevailed on the western border of the country.[75]

After reaching a treaty with the Austrians, Andrew II decided not to keep his treaty with the papal legate. By the end of November, 1233, the legate had to send his chaplain, Master Albert, and the bishop of Szerém to Béla to remind him, and his father, of the promises they had made.[76] The envoy's delegates reached Béla at Fort Bács, though strangely, the report they sent back to the Cardinal made no mention of the success of their talks with the prince-junior king.[77] The outcome must have been unpleasant and discouraging because early in 1234, the papal envoy held a meeting with the Hungarian bishops, instructing them to make the monarch promise under oath that he would keep the articles of the Bereg Agreement.[78]

The text of the report sent by the Cardinal to the Roman curia might serve as a reminder that Andrew II had, partly by being sheerly irresponsible, partly by acting stubbornly, refused to honor the Bereg Agreement, on the grounds that in the king's point of view, he had to agree to it out of dire necessity. If he assiduously delayed observing it, he had delayed for one reason: to let the papal envoy know that it was the monarch who was in charge of his country's policies - not the Holy See. The monarch had assumed that the Cardinal would not use his power of excommunication in a purely political matter.[79] Earlier, through his behavior during the 1217-18 crusade, and now, on this occasion, the king wished to emphasize that he would tolerate no outside interference in his kingdom. Were he unable to thwart it, he would passively resist it.[80]

It is very likely that by assuming such an attitude, Andrew II had attempted to reassert the power he had lost in front of his nobles. His behavior certainly had an impact upon Béla, who, in a similar manner, displayed little willingness to observe the Bereg Agreement. It is utterly possible, of course, that the papal legate had also developed a different point of view. It might be concluded from the letters of the papal envoy that he simply gave up on the idea that the king would ever keep his word. The legate placed some hope upon Prince Béla who might, eventually, alter his attitude and observe the treaty, at least formally.[81]

In early March, 1234, Cardinal Jacob returned to Rome,[82] but had, before his departure, commissioned the Dominican, Bishop John of Bosnia, to pronounce excommunication over the Hungarian king were the monarch to be negligent in adhering to the provisions of the treaty by the specified date.[83] The legate also instructed the Provincial of the Franciscan Order in the country to be supportive of the bishop of Bosnia in this affair.[84]

The Cardinal was a man of foresight and wisdom, but the idea of excommunicating the king was, in itself, wrong, because the process of religious punishment was bound to go astray. The king and his court viewed with skepticism the threat of ecclesiastical-spiritual force in the field of secular diplomacy. By this time, Andrew II had different plans and political and personal interests. The king had the situation in Halich momentarily under control; he had reached an understanding with the Duke of Austria, and only very recently had he signed an agreement with the Church. Upon the death of his second wife, Andrew II decided, at the age of 58, to marry again - much to the surprise and anger of his sons.[85]

The monarch married the daughter of Alderrandin d'Este, margrave of Ancona, on May 14, 1234, assuring five thousand silver marks as dowry for the bride, and granting her all the rights and benefits due to the Hungarian Queen. As a matter of fact, he had promised to pay her a one thousand silver mark annuity out of his personal treasury for the rest of her life.[86] The chronicler might take note, as the record has it, that when Jolánta, Andrew II's daughter, had married James I of Aragon, her father had promised her twelve thousand silver marks for dowry.[87]

The king who had married for a third time had absolutely no desire to observe the terms of the Bereg Agreement. Unfortunately, the rather simple-minded and tactless Dominican bishop of Bosnia displayed no patience with the king - he excommunicated Andrew II and placed the realm under the interdict. The bishop even called upon the archbishop of Esztergom to announce, and enforce, the church punishments aimed at the king.[88]

Archbishop Robert made, as one would expect, a strong protest and refused to cooperate with the bishop of Bosnia.[89] The archbishop instructed the monarch to appeal to the curia, and Andrew II complied with his advice promptly. In turn, the bishop of Bosnia instituted charges in Rome against the Hungarian archbishop. But the royal court had been forewarned: in its appeal to Rome it argued that the monarch had, indeed, observed the articles of the Bereg Agreement. A renewed threat of excommunicating the king would have been, politically speaking, counterproductive.[89]

The attitude taken by the court was determined and guided by the counsel of the archbishop, who must have disliked the idea of a papal legate commissioning the bishop of Bosnia to take punitive action against the archbishop's king and country. Archbishop Robert and the king's court turned to Rome. In their appeal to the curia they emphasized that the monarch was willing to keep the treaty, but his nobles were not; the monarch cannot be held responsible for the rebellious behavior of his disobedient nobles.[91]

Cardinal Jacob was already in Rome, and he persuaded the curia to announce a contrary opinion in the case. Pope Gregory IX now declared that the ecclesiastical punishment - excommunication and the interdict - had been just, and reprimanded the archbishop for having displayed such lack of tact and understanding in the case. The curia wished to have a peaceful solution to this affair, and summoned the archbishop for a personal report in Rome.[92] At this time, the curia had planned another crusade against the Bogomils in Bosnia;

Rome had the crusade announced and preached in Hungary, with the request that Coloman, Andrew II's youngest son, take charge of it.[93]

The curia's change of policy, and its decision calling for another crusade, did have a two-fold outcome for Andrew II's diplomatic efforts, and for the whole affair involving Cardinal Jacob. First, it exempted Coloman and his wife from the interdict;[94] and second, by placing Coloman in command of the planned papal crusade, it excluded Bosnia from the administration of Andrew II.[95]

Papal correspondence of August 18 and 31, 1235, stated that the Hungarian monarch had, once again, illegally levied and collected taxes in his country; therefore, the bishop of Bosnia - already on the verge of lifting the interdict - had notified the king that he would have to withdraw his unlawful taxes.[96] He must further pay the money collected thus far to the papal treasury, on the grounds that he had asked for those taxes without papal approval.[97]

Andrew II was, again, most unwilling to accept the latest papal decision. He had developed a rather stubborn mental disposition in his dealings with the curia, and perceived the reasoning of church-men as another means of humiliation that would only warp his personal dignity. His royal income had shrunk considerably since he had to divide his country [*recte*: the royal domain!] between himself and his sons and nephew; he only retained one fourth of the domain for himself.[98] He had also married his daughter to the king of Aragon, and, as security for her dowry of twelve thousand silver marks, he posited the thirtieth of his royal income.[99]

The monarch now turned to Rome with the request that he receive full dispensation from the Bereg Agreement - regardless whether he had, or had not, as yet regulated his demand for taxes or his policy concerning Jews and Moslems in public offices. He requested that the curia at least allow him to collect taxes already on the books because he had to bring his domestic financial situation under control.[100]

The curia responded positively. It allowed the king to pay the ten thousand silver mark debt he owed the Church in salt dues in five annual installments.[101] As for new taxes, the curia ordered the archbishop of Kalocsa, the bishop of Nyitra, and the abbot of Pannonhalma to initiate a survey.[102] The papal writ also authorized the bishop of Vác and the abbot of Mogyoród to absolve the royal chaplains who had drafted a royal writ calling for new and unauthorized taxes.[103] The pontiff also forbade the bishop of Bosnia to announce further punishments against the monarch; excommunication of the king was out of the question.[104]

The letter of Pope Gregory IX did not reach King Andrew II. The king died unexpectedly on September 21, 1235,[105] after his daughter Elizabeth had been canonized by the Church.[106] She had been the widow of the margrave of Thuringia; during the first four days after her death many miracles had been reported to have occurred at her grave.[107]

Andrew II led an unusual life, and had an unusual burial.[108] His body had been taken to Várad to be laid to rest at the feet of King St. Ladislas,[109] when the Cistercians of Pilis abbey demanded that he be buried in their monastery, besides his first queen, Gertrud.[110] Finally, it was in Egres abbey that they buried him, next to his second wife, Jolánta.[111] May his soul find eternal rest.

NOTES

1. Cf. Potthast, n. 8761, dated March 3, 1231; *VMH*, n. 108.
2. *CD*, III-2, 241f.
3. Potthast, n. 8670; *VMH*, n. 106.
4. *RA*, n. 479; Marczali, *Enchiridion*, 134bff.; *RHM*, 428ff.
5. See the parallel edition in Marczali, *Enchiridion*, 134abff.; see further, Decree I, 1222, aa. 10-11, 20-21, 23, 25, 28, 30, and 31, in *RHM*, 412ff.
6. Cardinal Jacob of Praeneste, *VMH*, n. 187; Hóman-Szekfü, I, 507ff.
7. Decree II, 1231, aa. 5, 9-10, 18, 19, 19a, 21, 22, and 29, Marczali, *Enchiridion*, 134bff.
8. Decree II, a. 28.
9. *Ibid.*, a. 9.
10. *Ibid.*, a. 1.
11. *Ibid.*, a. 2.
12. *Ibid.*, a. 6.
13. *Ibid.*, aa. 10 and 17, and compare with Decree I, a. 8.
14. Decree II, a. 23.
15. *Ibid.*, aa. 24-25.
16. *Ibid.*, a. 12.
17. *Ibid.*, a. 29.
18. *Ibid.*, a. 31.
19. Marczali, *Enchiridion*, 142; *RHM*, 433, and the report of the legate, in *VMH*, I, 107ff., esp. 110, n. 187.
20. *Ibid.*, I, 110f.; Marczali, *Enchiridion*, 142b.
21. Cf. the report of the Cardinal sent to Rome, *VMH*, I, 108, n. 187.
22. *Ibid.*
23. On "interdict," cf. Funk and Bihlmeyer, II, 83; E.G. Krehlbiel, *The Interdict, Its History and Operation* (Washington, DC, 1909). The Roman pontiff held secular jurisdiction - see the papal bull "Per venerabilem," Potthast, n. 1794; Friedberg, II, 714ff.; the pontiff did claim the right to intervene - see the papal decretal "Novit," in Potthast, n. 2181; Friedberg, II, 242ff.
24. *Ibid.*, I, 108f.
25. Kantorowicz, *The King's Two Bodies*, 42ff.; see "Tractatus," in *LdL*, III, 673,24 and 642ff. Böhmer, 436ff.; on the authorship of the "Tractatus," *ibid.*, 177ff.
26. *VMH*, I, 109; Kantorowicz, 45ff.
27. Cf. Funk and Bihlmeyer, II, 83.
28. *VMH*, I, 109f.
29. *RA*, n. 485; *VMH*, n. 180, dated May 16, 1232.
30. Potthast, n. 8975; *VMH*, n. 181; *CD*, III-2, 302.
31. Potthast, n. 8991 (August 22, 1232); *VMH*, n. 183.
32. Potthast, n. 8993; *VMH*, n. 185; *CD*, III-2, 303.
33. It is evident from the papal reply to the archbishop - Potthast, n. 9283; *VMH*, n. 196.
34. This seems evident from a letter the Roman pontiff had sent to the Hungarian court - Potthast, n. 9282; *VMH*, n. 195, to remind the monarch of the awful abuses that plagued the realm.
35. Potthast, n. 8671; *VMH*, n. 168. Compare with Potthast,, n. 8770.
36. Potthast, n. 8671.
37. The curia had only praise for the legate's tact and behavior, though it had to instruct him to be firm in his dealings with the monarch - *VMH*, I, 116,11-12.
38. *Ibid.*, I, 114f.

39. *Ibid.*, I, 117,5-6; the names appeared on royal writs - see, e.g., *RA*, nn. 501-504; 506 and 507.

40. Potthast, n. 9274; *VMH*, n. 197, with full text in *RA*, n. 505. It was a confidential writ addressed to the legate, instructing him to show consideration toward the king's son.

41. Potthast, n. 7406; *VMH*, n. 119; Potthast, n. 7407; *VMH*, n. 118.

42. See the papal letter sent to Archbishop Ugrin of Kalocsa, dated January 20, 1229, in Potthast, n. 8318; *VMH*, n. 158; *CD*, III-2, 155; Raynaldus, *Annales*, anno 1229, par. 60.

43. Potthast, nn. 9733 and 9735 - both dated October 17, 1234; *VMH*, nn. 221 and 222.

44. On this, a papal letter, dated March 3, 1229, Potthast, n. 8348; *VMH*, n. 159; Katona, V, 544.

45. Cf. *CD*, IV-1, 447ff.

46. Potthast, n. 8155; *VMH*, n. 155. Antal Hodinka, *Egyházunk küzdelme a bogomil eretnekekkel* [Struggle of the Church with Bogomil heretics]; vol. 50 of Studies by the Students of the Budapest R.C. Major Seminary (Budapest, 1877), 88ff.; and compare to *VMH*, n. 199.

47. Potthast, n. 8154; *VMH*, n. 157.

48. See *ÁUO*, VI, 533f. and 535f., dated April 20 and June 1, 1233, respectively; the agreement of April 20 received royal sanction, *RA*, n. 513 (and, n. 514); *ÁUO*, VI, 522f.; Knauz, I, 345.

49. *ÁUO*, VI, 536ff. and 538ff.; Knauz, I, 344ff. - reconfirmed in the year after, *ÁUO*, VI, 554ff.

50. Thus, for instance, he reached an agreement in the tax-payment case of the Cistercian abbey at Pornó [Pernou] - *RA*, n. 504; *ÁUO*, VI, 517f.; or he confirmed the possession of some 20,000 cubes of salt by the abbey of Szentgotthárd, "viginti milia salia magnorum," *RA*, n. 505, with text.

51. On the Cardinal of Praeneste, see "Annales Placentenses," *MGHSS*, XVIII, 453, and the introduction to Alberic's "Chronicon," *ibid.*, XXIII, 929 and 934ff. He approved of the agreement reached between the abbey of Pannonhalma and its subject peoples, *ÁUO*, VI, 554ff. and 553f.

52. Potthast, n. 9095; *VMH*, n. 189; Katona, V, 668.

53. Potthast, nn. 9213 and n. 9211; *VMH*, nn. 192 and 193.

54. On this, the papal writs of August 25, 1236, in Potthast, nn. 10232 and 10234; *VMH*, nn. 263 and 264.

55. Potthast, nn. 9799 and 10012; *VMH*, nn. 226 and 238.

56. Potthast, n. 9985; *VMH*, n. 228.

57. Katona, V, 732.

58. Potthast, n. 9214; *VMH*, n. 194.

59. See the entries in the Halich-Volhynian Annals, Gustin MS, in Hodinka, 362aff.; on Hodinka, see István Udvari, "Antal Hodinka - Forscher der ruthenischer Geschichte," *Studia Slavica Savariensia*, 2 (1992), 66ff; on the political-military aspects, cf. M.F. Font, "Ungarische Vornehmen in der Halitsch im 13 Jahrhundert," *Specimina nova Universitatis Quinqueecclesiensis* (Pécs, 1990 [1992]), 165ff.

60. *RA*, n. 500; M.F. Font, "II András orosz politikája és hadjáratai [The Russian Policy of Andrew II and his Russian Campaigns]," *Századok*, 125 (1991), 107ff.

61. This is evident from the papal letter of August 12, 1233, in Potthast, n. 9274; *VMH*, n. 197.

62. Potthast, n. 9273; *VMH*, n. 196.

63. Potthast, n. 9272; *VMH*, n. 195.

64. Cf. *RHM*, 436ff,; *CD*, III-2, 319ff.; Knauz, I, 292ff. The Church might freely sell salt at the shipment's point of destination, from August 20 and September

8, and from December 6 to 21. A wagon load will consist of one hundred cubes of salt; one pale of salt [= a shipload] may sell for eight marks, worth one *frisaticus* [= *denarius*], the monetary unit used in the Salzburg-Frisach ecclesiastical province, cf. *RA*, n. 505, and compare with nn. 504 and 506; *ÁUO*, VI, 517f. and 519ff. On the monetary unit *frisaticus*, see Spufford, 134ff.

65. "Capitula autem sunt hec...;" *VMH*, I, 116ff., n. 198.

66. *Ibid.*, I, 118f.

67. *Ibid.*, I, 119,9-11.

68. *MGHSS*, IX, 785,43-45; on background, see *Monumenta Erphesfurtensia* saec. XII, XIII, XIV, ed. Oswald Holder-Egger, SSrg (Hannover-Leipzig, 1899), 89; *Chronica regia*, 267.

69. *RA*, n. 501.

70. *VMH*, I, 116ff.; Knauz, I, 297ff; Batthyány, *Leges*, II, 356ff.

71. Family matters must have played little or no role in this - cf. papal letters addressed to the legate, Potthast, n. 9274; *VMH*, n. 197.

72. "Continuatio Sancrucensis II," *MGHSS*, IX, 637,48-49; "Cont. Vindobonensium," *ibid.*, IX, 727,6-7; "Cont. Sancrucensis I," *ibid.*, IX, 628,1-6; *Mon. Erphesfurtensia*, 89.

73. *MGHSS*, IX, 638,11-17.

74. Archbishop Robert had previously suspended excommunication on a temporary basis, *VMH*, nn. 213 and 214 - latter under Potthast, n. 9497.

75. *MGHSS*, IX, 558,34-40; *ibid.*, IX, 628,17-21; *ibid.*, IX, 637,22-26.

76. *VMH*, n. 203.

77. "... ipsum viva voce monuimus de omnibus, que in premissis litteris continentur;" *ibid.*, I, 121.

78. *Ibid.*, n. 205. Members of the hierarchy must have been more persuasive in their efforts, because by February, 1234, the legate had met with Béla, who had promised that he would tolerate no Jew or Moslem holding public office in territories under his administration and he would persecute heretics. Cf. *RA*, n. 599, dated August 22, 1233; *VMH*, n. 208, dated February 19, 1234! Béla also promised the legate that he would force the Byzantine Church to submit to Rome - *ibid.*, n. 209.

79. "... rex expectatus ... terminum non servaverit," as it is evident from the tone of the entire letter, *VMH*, n. 213.

80. See the "self-justification" of Andrew II, in Thuróczy, *Chronica*, c. 110.

81. To be concluded from the promise made by Béla at the end of February, 1234, *RA*, n. 604; *VMH*, n. 209.

82. Potthast, n. 9460; *VMH*, n. 210.

83. Potthast, n. 9492.

84. The writ of Gregory IV to the bishop of Bosnia, Potthast, n. 9507; *VMH*, n. 215.

85. The "Chronicon rhythmicum" will, as usual, overstate the issue - *MGHSS*, XXV, 355; on the death of Queen Jolanta, cf. Albericus, *Chronicon*, *MGHSS*, XXII, 933; *CD*, III-1, 462.

86. *CD*, III-2, 376; "Rolandus Patavinus Annales s. Iustitiae," *MGHSS*, XIX, 60 and 154 (anno 1235); Katona, V, 690f.

87. *RA*, n. 537.

88. Potthast, n. 9497; *VMH*, n. 214; Katona, V, 696f.

89. As evidenced by a papal writ - cf. Potthast, n. 9492.

90. *Ibid.*, n. 9434.

91. *VMH*, I, 127.

92. Although His Holiness had reconciled himself with the archbishop, the latter had been told that the curia had disagreed with him and disapproved of his actions - Potthast, n. 9492.

93. *Ibid.*, n. 9733; *VMH*, n. 221.

94. Potthast, n. 9726; *VMH*, n. 218.
95. Potthast, n. 9735; *VMH*, n. 222.
96. Potthast, n. 9991; *VMH*, n. 231; *CD*, III-2, 431.
97. Potthast, n. 10007; Raynaldus, *Annales*, anno 1235, par. 26; Katona, V, 739f. The Dominican prior and the Franciscan provincial in Esztergom supported the position taken by the bishop of Bosnia in arguing that Andrew II had to clear himself before the curia of all charges brought against him, Potthast, n. 10009; *VMH*, n. 234.
98. Hóman-Szekfű, I, 504f.; the war with Frederick and the expedition in Halich, *MGHSS*, IX, 638,11-17, all consumed money, *VMH*, n. 214.
99. *RA*, n. 514, in reference to a papal writ, dated August 11, 1235, in Potthast, n. 9987; *VMH*, n. 230, and in connection with this, the letter sent to the bishop of Pécs, *VMH*, n. 228. See also Koller, *Historia Quinqueecclesiarum*, II, 26, note m. Albericus, "Chronicon," *MGHSS*, XXIII, 936,40-43; G. Jackson, *The Making of Medieval Spain* (New York, 1973), 81 and 83ff.
100. As it is evident from a papal writ, Potthast, n. 10009; *VMH*, n. 234; Hóman-Szekfű, I, 510ff.
101. Rome granted him a concession by allowing him to survey the activities of Moslems in his country once in three years only. Potthast, n. 10008; *VMH*, n. 237.
102. Potthast, n. 10006; *VMH*, n. 233.
103. Potthast, n. 10012; "...quatenus iniuncta ipsis penitentia," *VMH*, n. 238.
104. Potthast, n. 10013; "mandamus, quatenus sine speciali mandato nostro supra hoc nullatenus procedatis," *VMH*, n. 239. Also, the papal writ of August 18, 1235, in Potthast, n. 9991; *VMH*, n. 231; *ÁUO*, VI, 570f.
105. Cf. "Chronicon Zagrabiense," c. 18, *SSH*, I, 212,3-5; the "Chronicle" mentioned the year only, *ibid.*, I, 466,20-22; *MGHSS*, IX, 638,22. His death was unexpected; documents published in *ÁUO*, VI, 567f. and 569f.: "datum ... anno 1235o ... regni nostri tricesimo secundo;" "datum 1235o, reui [sic!] nostri 32o," must have been issued shortly before his death.
106. *Monumenta Erphesfurtensia*, 229, 762; *MGHSS*, XXIII, 937,36-39; *ibid.*, IX, 786a,15-16; IX, 786b,39-41; *CD*, III-2, 444f.; Seppelt, III, 429.
107. *Monumenta Erphesfurtensia*, 756ff.; *MGHSS*, IX, 727,8-9; *ibid.*, IX, 785,31-32; IX, 628,6-7. Pope Gregory IX had canonized her on Pentecost Sunday, 1235 - Potthast, I, 844, in ref. to Albericus, "Chronicon," *MGHSS*, XXIII, 937,36-39; Muratori, *RISS*, III-1, 580; the papal writ on canonization, Potthast, n. 9929 (June 1, 1235); Raynaldus, *Annales*, anno 1235, par. 22 and 23. See further Sándor Bálint, *Ünnepi Kalendárium* [A Calendar of Feasts], 2 vols. (Budapest, 1977), II, 475ff.; Püskely, 6ff. and 38f.; Antal Ijjas, *Szentek élete* [Lives of the Saints], 2 vols. (Budapest, 1976), II, 111ff.; E. Stein, "Életalakítás Szent Erzsébet szellemében [Developing One's Life in the Spirit of St. Elizabeth]," *Szolgálat* 32 (Munich, 1976), 41ff.; Antal Schütz (ed.), *Szentek élete* [Lives of the Saints], 4 vols. (Budapest, 1930-32), IV, 229ff.; Z.J. Kosztolnyik, "Saint Elizabeth of Hungary," in F.N. Magill (ed.), *Great Lives From History: Ancient and Medieval Series*, 5 vols. (Pasadena, CA, 1988), 655ff.
108. Because of the merits of his daughter, Saint Elizabeth, the pontiff absolved him from excommunication; cf. Potthast, n. 9998; *VMH*, nn. 231 and 232; *MGHSS*, IX, 559,1.
109. Alberic, in *MGHSS*, XXIII, 937,48-49, though the "Zagreb Chronicle" that included most of the material from the "Várad Chronicle" - cf. Macartney, 109ff. - knew nothing about a burial in Várad, *SSH*, I, 203ff., esp. 212; it named the abbey at Egres as his final resting place - *ibid.*, I, 212,4-5.
110. *MGHSS*, XXIII, 937,48-49; Hóman-Szekfű, I, 514.
111. Chronicle, c. 175, *SSH*, I, 466,22-23.

CHAPTER FOUR

THE TARTARS ARE COMING!

Tempore autem istius Bele regis....
Mangali sive Tartari cum quinquies
centenis milibus armatorum regnum
Hungarie invaserunt.

Chronicon pictum, c. 177*

When Béla IV ascended the throne at the age of twenty-nine,[1] they crowned him, for a second time, in the church of Saint Peter (the church he had built),[2] and not in the church of the Assumption that had much earlier been erected in Fehérvár.[3] The goal of his kingship was clearly set before him: to improve the deteriorated dignity of his position by restoring royal power and influence in the realm.[4] The festive act of his second coronation enhanced his prestige as the ruler; kings stood at his service - as, for instance, his brother Coloman, king of Halich, who held the ceremonial sword, and Danilo, ruler of Ladomer, who held the stirrup of his horse during the coronation ceremony.[5]

The new monarch had to take strong measures toward the nobility at the very beginning of his reign. There were personal reasons for his determined behavior. Béla IV had to show utmost strictness toward the nobles, who had earlier caused a rift between his father and himself, who had thwarted all of their efforts at diplomacy and domestic peace,[6] who had verbally, or even physically, abused him, and made at least one attempt on his life, who had tried to bring Frederick of Austria into the country to occupy his throne.[7]

When holding a field-day, or public assembly, with his barons and nobles, Béla IV had their chairs ("stools" is a more appropriate term) removed from the site of the gathering before him, and permitted only members of the hierarchy and certain nobles to remain seated during the debates and discussions held in his presence.[8] In view of the fact that far too many nobles had undeservedly received offices and landholdings from his wasteful royal father, Andrew II - thereby becoming rich and holding positions from where they could easily ignore the authority of the Crown and the summons of the king - Béla IV had given orders to repossess all grants of land and offices that had needlessly been given away.[9]

The monarch's strictness was understandable, but his timing to carry out his resolutions was bad. It was to be feared that, were a disaster to befall the country, the "barons and lords" would negate their support of the Crown - the king in trouble, a situation that had actually developed six years after the inception of his reign.[10] When the Mongolian Tartars reached the borders of the realm in the spring of 1241, the majority of the nobles rejoiced over the serious hardship of the king - without realizing that their rejoicing could easily bring about the total destruction of their country.[11] The barons were shortsighted, because they did not think ahead and act properly. In 1235, the majority of them could find little sympathy for a monarch who had become their ruler by inheritance, and who had been crowned with their consent for the second time.[12]

Therefore, Béla IV had repossessed land grants and offices that had been unworthily given away, and had his fort-district reeves assured of their position and dignity. He had toured the realm, and had himself accompanied by a large entourage whenever he visited a county seat, in order to display royal authority in front of the population.[13] He had ordered that Dénes (Gyínes) the Palatine (an office Dénes had held during the reign of his father), be blinded because he had wasted royal lands along the Drave river, and on the grounds that he had proved himself unworthy of the trust of Béla IV and of the old king. Dénes had maintained an illicit relationship with Queen Beatrice, the third wife of Andrew II.[14]

Upon the death of her husband, the queen dressed as a stable boy and escaped from the royal court with the palatine, but her identity had been discovered when she accidentally met the envoys of Emperor Frederick II en route to the Hungarian court.[15] (The emperor had sent a delegation to collect five thousand silver marks of annual tribute from the new king, Béla IV - a promise Andrew II must have made to Frederick. Outraged, Béla IV had the imperial envoys sent back empty-handed.)[16]

At about the same time, the supporters of the king had confiscated a letter written by some Hungarian barons to be handed over to the imperial envoys, in which they invited the emperor to take over the government of the realm.[17] Nicholas, son of Barch, who held the position of the palatine, was the probable author of the writ, but he fled the realm in time, and the king's men could only capture Gyula, of the clan of Kan, an accomplice of the palatine. The king had Gyula imprisoned, and confiscated the property of the escaped conspirators.[18]

Béla IV curtailed the pride of the high nobles even further. Not only did he burn the seats (*stella*) of the barons, he ordered that were any of them - in fact, were anyone - to make a complaint before him, they must not do it orally, in person, but had to present it in writing to the royal chancery. The chancellor would then investigate the petition or complaint, audit the request, and take appropriate action himself in less significant cases. Only matters considered to be important were to be submitted to the monarch's personal attention.[19]

King Béla IV had goods repossessed that had been wastefully donated by his father and predecessor. He dispatched agents to every county to audit all donations of land and office, of any privilege made during the reign of Andrew II.[20] The agents tolerated no exceptions in accordance with the royal directive.[21] They investigated the chattel and holdings of churchmen, nobles, and the people of the regional royal forts, and of office holders and lesser officials, in order to ascertain why, and how, did the individual(s) obtain the land or office they now proudly claimed as their own.[22] Were the land or office to be held without merit, the agents repossessed it.[23] These royal officials - in most instances, royal judges - were men versed in regional law and custom, who performed their task with the aid of the local bishop or other high prelate of the Church.[24]

In repossessing chattel and goods, the officials made no exception with high ecclesiastics.[25] There was an outburst of ecclesiastical reaction, of course.[26] Churchmen appealed directly to the Roman See, and the curia made a protest on their behalf. Rome reminded the king of the oath he had taken to Archbishop Jacob of Esztergom. The Holy See was surprised to hear the news, the pontiff wrote to the king, that his majesty insulting God had contemptuously defied the Church and, in apparent risk to his good name, had endangered his own spiritual salvation, by daring to repossess ecclesiastical and monastic property, despite his earlier oath that he would respect the privileges of the Church.[27] Rome had expressed concern about the king and the hierarchy because royal repossession of church lands created a bad example for the nobles to follow. The pontiff had asked and warned the monarch to return all the goods that had been taken away from the Church.[28]

Béla IV had to defend himself: he responded to Rome that he had to act in such a manner, as he had no alternative; not even ecclesiastics could claim and retain unworthily received grants or holdings. Yet the king slowly gave in to the papal demand.[29] Bishop Gregory of Győr, dispatched by the king to the Holy See, had played a role in royal diplomacy.[30] Contemporary sources depict him as a well-educated ecclesiastic of great virtue, who had previously had a part in working out arrangements among territorial proprietors in the realm. With a clear diplomatic touch, he persuaded Pope Gregory IX that the king did nothing wrong, nor would he stray from the road of law and justice.[31]

Since the issuance by Andrew II of the Decree of 1231, where the court had assured the Church of certain rights, Béla had realized that he needed the support of the Church, and returned the various goods and holdings the ecclesiastics had - without any serious justifiable reason - obtained from his father's court.[32] The king was, however, a politician, and he combined his concession with a compromise: Rome must permit him to entrust Jews and Moslems living in his country with the collection of clerical dues and income, or to farm out to them the collection of that income. The curia gave a permissive reply with the remark, though, that farming out church revenues to Jews and Moslems only lessened royal prestige (in the eye of the beholder - the Church in this case - and, the curia insisted, before the country's inhabitants), but warned Béla that, as a matter of royal policy and honor, he employ qualified Christians to function in such trusted roles.[33]

Great consternation prevailed among the Hungarian nobility. They bitterly spoke out against the king who would not grant them further gifts, who would even take away what his father had previously given them! They could no longer expect free donations or personal favors from the monarch, or from his court.[34] The king, however, went his own way in accordance with his ideas. Judged by the text of the decrees he issued, he had fairly successfully recovered royal lands, and reconstructed royal business in the realm during the first three years of his reign.[35] The Roman curia aided him greatly in this. Rome displayed leniency toward Béla IV, though such "lenient" attitude had some political-diplomatic impetus as well. The curia wanted to draw the Hungarian court into its inquisition policies in the Balkans.[36]

The Latin-Greek empire existing on the ruins of Byzantium had been declining since 1228, with the beginning of the rule of Baldwin II, whose opponent, John Vatatéz Ducas, was the brother-in-law of the Queen of Béla IV. John II Asen, ruler of Bulgaria, was also a relative, as he was married to Maria, a sister of the Hungarian king, but he was an enemy of the Latin-Greek emperor. But he had seceded from the Roman Church in order to associate himself with the Byzantine Patriarch.[37] Now, Asen II, once again, negotiated with Rome, expressing the desire of the rejoining the Church.

In the spring of 1237, the curia dispatched Bishop Salvi of Perugia as envoy to the court of John II Asen. The bishop sojourned in Hungary; at the Hungarian court he received the news that John Asen had invaded the Latin-Greek empire. Thereupon Salvi returned to Rome to await further developments. Pope Gregory IX sent him back to Hungary,[38] with instructions to preach a crusade against the ruler of Bulgaria and to publicly call upon Béla IV to join the crusade.[39] As a matter of fact, Salvi had been authorized by Rome to tell the Hungarian king that he could keep all Bulgarian territory he conquered during the campaign.[40]

The position of the legate was not a pleasant one. On the grounds that the growth of Hungarian territorial-political presence in Bulgaria could lead to political-diplomatic difficulties with the Latin-Greek empire, Bishop Salvi had to persuade Béla IV to resign all his territorial claims in Bulgaria to the care of the Holy See.[41]

Bishop Salvi, as papal legate, had visited the king at Zólyom, where Béla IV expressed interest in complying with the papal request to join the crusade, but awaited confirmation from Rome of the conditions outlined to him by the legate.[42] The legate forwarded the king's reply to Rome with a special courier.[43] The text of the king's letter calls for attention, as it throws a bright light on the personality of Béla IV, and on his diplomatic statesman-like behavior.[44] The contents of this writ may be summarized under a six-fold heading:

1. The king is related by blood and personal friendship to the ruler of Bulgaria, who obeys him, as if he were his subject, and not his relative and friend.[45]

2. Vatatéz was also a relative of the king, who had remained loyal to him and fulfilled every wish he had presented to him.[46]

3. In spite of all this, if John Asen were attacked, and a war with Vatatéz to benefit the Hungarian king's spiritual needs ensue, he would be willing, for the sake of his soul, to enter into war against the Bulgarians. However, he understood that he would retain the conquered Bulgarian lands, where he would introduce the spiritual jurisdiction of the pope.[47]

4. For the above reason, Rome may invest the Hungarian monarch with the authority of Apostolic Delegate over the to-be-conquered territories in Bulgaria, so that he may establish bishoprics there and parishes, and nominate ecclesiastics to those positions, at his own discretion. As papal delegate in Bulgaria, he would have the Apostolic double cross to be carried in front of him - a privilege that had been granted by the Holy See to his great predecessor, King St. Stephen.[48]

5. Simultaneously, Rome may order that the crusading army gathered to fight in Bulgarian territory remain under his command, and the Franciscan and Dominican friars preaching the crusade may grant the same indulgences to the participants as the ones granted to the crusaders fighting in the Holy Land. He will place himself and his country under the protection of the Holy See, and request that Rome excommunicate anyone who would dare to invade his country during his crusade in Bulgaria.[49]

6. Finally, the king requests absolution from the excommunication pronounced over him, his advisors, and his country's nobles by Archbishop Jacob of Esztergom. The legate (Bishop Salvi) was a holy man, the king wrote to Rome, but he was not familiar with the country's domestic conditions.[50]

In order to give a heavier emphasis to his requests, Béla IV had sent the bishop of Győr to Rome,[51] with the petition that the silent monks, the strict Carthusians from France or from Italian soil, be allowed to settle in Hungary. The king did this to secure favors from Rome, and to settle new religious orders in his realm.[52]

Pope Gregory IX replied quickly - without sensing the king's denial of the papal request - in a carefully phrased letter. (After all, Béla IV had argued that a Christian king, an Árpád, should not have to go to war against his own blood relatives and reliable friends!)

The pontiff was glad to hear, the papal writ read, that the king would be willing to go to war against John II Asen of Bulgaria. Imitating the examples of his great predecessors, he would offer his arms and services to God.[53] On these grounds, Rome would be willing to fulfill his requests, except one: the king cannot become an Apostolic Delegate, but he would be permitted to name a bishop who, with the consent of the curia, would, in the king's name, exercise the prerogatives and authority of an apostolic legate.[54]

As expected, the planned papal crusade did not take place.[55] When John II Asen of Bulgaria had heard about war preparations at the Hungarian court - he had been good-naturedly warned by the court, the contents of the royal writ sent to Rome were circulated - he decided not to invade the Latin-Greek empire or negotiate with Vatatéz.[56] Béla IV's carefully laid out diplomacy plan had been successful. Because of the rapidly deteriorating military situation in the East, the monarch did not have the time, nor the means, to go to war in the Balkans - where war, at this time, would have served no Hungarian interests. However, Pope Gregory IX must have been wholly ignorant about the approaching Mongol threat from the east, as he had summoned an ecumenical council to meet at Easter, 1241, and had invited the king of Hungary to attend. Béla IV could not comply with any of these papal demands, not even for the sake of his eternal salvation.[57]

At this particular time, the pontiff focused his attention on papal-German imperial politics, and paid little attention to Hungary, or to the Mongol-Tartar threat to eastern and east-central Europe.[58] On the other hand, the Holy See had realized that Emperor Frederick II had concentrated his efforts on preventing the gathering of the announced papal synod.[59] As late as October 15, 1240, the papal curia requested the Hungarian court to ignore the emperor's threats and attend the council.[60]

Béla IV could not, of course, go to the council, nor could his prelates go. He had left the third papal summons to attend (dated February 26, 1241) unanswered.[61] Indeed, one could not call it a friendly invitation.[62] The king had to refuse, even though the curia had sent a papal chaplain, John Civiella, as special envoy to the court to inform the monarch and his bishops how to avoid obstacles laid out by the German emperor for the purpose of disrupting attendance of the council.[63] Rome had further warned the Hungarian court to join a crusade against the emperor - about a month before the Tartar forces engulfed Hungary.[64]

The Tartars entered Europe from central Asia, from the region north of China and east of the Ural-Altai mountains. They were a people of Mongolian stock, who lived in tribal communities; by the end of the twelfth century, Temudsin, alias Jenghiz Khan, had united them under his command. In 1203, nine tribal chiefs had him acknowledged as their head-leader.[65] Jenghiz had them united under the standard of horse tail at the foot of the Karakorum Mountains, where a shaman pronounced to them the will of the Sky-god. Mongol-Tartar unity was born. Under Jenghiz, they had occupied China, southern Siberia, central Asia, and the region between the Aral Sea and the Indus valley.[66]

In 1222, the Tartars had crossed the Caucasus, entered Europe, and defeated the Cumans. Albericus mentioned it in his chronicle that the Christian crusaders who had been preoccupied with their siege of Damietta were among the first to have heard of them, had hurried back home, but had forgotten about the danger.[67] By 1223, the Tartars had the upper hand over the coalition of Cuman and Russian forces in the encounter at the Kalka river.[68] In 1227, when Jenghiz died, his "empire" fell apart into four territories; "Kipchak," the European area they had occupied came under the control of Batu Khan, Jenghiz's grandson.[69]

During the latter half of the 1220s, and in the early 1230s, the Bulgarians along the Kama river, the "Magyars" along the Volga, the Cumans and the Russians had to struggle with the Tartars almost continuously for their freedom, and they forced Batu to seek aid from Great Khan Ogodai.[70] With the aid of the reinforcement sent by the great khan, Batu easily broke down the rule of the Cumans and of the "Magyars" along the Volga in 1237, and turned against the Russian princes.[71] On December 21, 1237, Rjezan fell, and the khan captured Vladimir on February 14, 1238.[72]

In a manner similar to the report by the Franciscan John Plano Carpini and Ivo of Narbon, a priest, the chronicler Albericus wrote under the events of the year of 1239 that the Tartars had big heads, short necks, deep chests, huge arms, short legs, great physical strength, but lacked religion, believed in nothing, took care of nobody, and had confidence only in their leader whom they regarded as king of kings, the lord of lords.[73]

THE TARTARS ARE COMING!

During the winter of 1238, Batu had subjugated the Cumans and several Cuman chiefs had submitted to him.[74] A small segment of the Cumans led by their king, Kötény, had escaped from their captivity, however, and fled toward the west, where they requested permission from Béla IV to enter his country. Kötény had promised to become a Christian and a loyal subject of the Hungarian monarch.[75]

The Hungarian court was quite pleased with the arrival of the Cumans. The people of Kötény could aid them against the king's domestic and foreign opponents, members of the court had thought. The Cumans comprised some forty thousand men, all together some two hundred and forty to three hundred thousand souls. They became Christians: Béla IV stood godfather to Kötény. The Cumans were instructed to settle along the Tisza river, in the Tisza-Kőrös-Maros-Temes area. However, being nomads, they chose to move about with their livestock - causing damage to the crops - and created a good deal of resentment among the native (i.e., settled) population. The inhabitants of the region disliked and resented the Cumans, but Béla IV tolerated no opposition. He had need of them; they had come to stay.[76]

The court, on the other hand, had to pre-empt the expected confrontation between the newcomers and the settled population. In 1240, at Kő abbey, he had discussed the issue with his nobles, and reached the decision that the newcomers must not remain together, but that their tribal clans be broken up and re-settled in various parts of the country. Their life style, and their living standards, would thereby improve. The king charged the reeve of the particular area to deal with them, individually or in groups, and handle any misunderstanding among the newcomers and the native population.[77] Spread apart, the Cumans ought not to present a serious threat to public security, though it was feared that public resentment would delay any social fusion with them.[78]

The acceptance by the Hungarian court of the Cumans to settle in the country was the official reason rendered by Batu Khan for the planned invasion of Hungary.[79] Both the Hungarian king and the Mongol khan wished to obtain and retain the area(s) previously held by the Cumans. As early as 1227, the Hungarians had established their predominance over what was regarded as Cuman territory (outside the borders of Hungary proper - if, and where, the "border" had been clearly defined). The Cuman population there soon became Christian, and accepted the headship of the Hungarian king. However, after the battle at the Kalka river, the khan demanded surrender of that same area; the fact that the Hungarian court dared to render aid to the Cumans against the Tartars evoked the hatred of the khan.[80]

In 1238, Béla IV dispatched the Woyvoda (Grand Steward) of Transylvania to the aid of the Cumans, and the grand steward was, indeed, quite successful in his undertaking. Passing through a narrow path in the Meotis marshes, his force had surprised a Tartar division and routed it. It was on account of this Hungarian intervention on Cuman behalf that Kötény had asked for military aid from, and, if need be, submission to the government of Béla IV.[81]

Earlier, in 1236, Batu Khan had sent a letter addressed to the Hungarian king, calling upon Béla IV to surrender Kötény and his Cumans to him. The letter was delivered by Julian, a Dominican friar, who had received it from the hands of the Prince of Suzdal, who had taken it from a captured Tartar prisoner of war.[82] It was written in Mongolian, with Arabic characters,[83] and said that Szain (or Chaym, the Good and Perfect - Batu had referred to himself in such a manner), Legate of the King of Heaven, who had been granted powers to rule over the earth to elevate and to destroy, was surprised that the Hungarian *little king* [84] did not even deem it worthy of his consideration to acknowledge the arrival of thirty envoys the khan had already dispatched to him.[85]

Béla IV gave no response, neither in writing nor by sending a delegate to the khan.[86] The khan knew that the Magyars had a wealthy kingdom, a great country, and the king had large forces under his command. The king might find it difficult to submit to him, though it would be a good thing if he would. Indeed, the king had followed a path to the contrary: he had taken the Cumans, the khan's subjects, under his protection, thereby committing an act of war![87] The king ought to remember that the Cumans can (and will) easily escape: they have no permanent homes, live in tents, and do not cultivate the soil.[88]

Friar Julian had brought the letter with him.[89] Who Friar Julian was, what he was doing at the court of the Prince of Suzdal, one may find out from the report he dictated to his confrere, Friar Ricardus, a Hungarian member of the Dominican Order.[90] The friars had read the *Gesta Ungarorum*, and concluded that, when in the late ninth century the seven Magyar tribal chiefs had proceeded toward the mid-Danubian region from the Don river, not all of the Magyars had followed them.[91] If the seven chiefs had begun their journey from the area of the area of the Don, but not every tribe had left with them, then, evidently, some "pagan" Magyars must have stayed behind in the "ancient home land" - where the friars now wanted to pay a visit.[92]

Four Hungarian Dominican friars undertook the search of the *dent-maeger* - "Magyars at the Don" - in the early 1230s. They began their journey through Transylvania and went along the northern shore of the Black Sea.[93] In the third year of their sojourn, one of the friars, George by name, dressed like a merchant, had encountered a Magyar-speaking person, who notified his relatives of the event. Friar George now hurried back home with the exciting news, but had died from exhaustion upon his arrival.[94]

In 1235, another group of four Hungarian Dominican friars had left in search of the Don-Volga Magyars.[95] This time, Béla IV also supported them with money and provided a guide for them.[96] The friars took a boat to Byzantium and reached the city of Matrica in about a month. The ruler of that city - he had one hundred wives - had them entertained for fifty days, and then providing for them, sent them on their journey.[97] For a while, the friars drifted aimlessly in the desert.[98] One of them made wooden spoons to earn millet for food, lest they starve. Two of them attempted to sell themselves into slavery, without any success.[99] Did they behave like a bunch of clowns? They were fighting for their survival. Then two of them decided to go back home,[100] but Julian and Friar Bernard continued their travels.[101] Bernard died,[102] and Friar Julian, left to himself, entered the service of an Islamic ayatollah, with whom he traveled to the capital of Greater Bulgaria, where he met a Magyar woman who was married to a Bulgarian.[103] She informed the friar that, within two days distance, Magyars were living along the great Etil (Volga) river.[104]

Among the Magyars along the Etil, the "western" Hungarian friar was guided from village to village; they could speak and understand each other.[105] The "pagan" Magyars did not adore idols, Julian noted, but ate horse meat and drank mare's milk or animal blood.[106] They knew about the Magyars who had departed from their midst.[107] it was there, among these Magyars along the Etil that Friar Julian met the Tartar envoy who brought the news that the Tartar forces were camped down five days distance from there, and were preparing for an invasion of "German" lands. They were only awaiting the return of their forces sent against Persia.[108] Julian had left in a hurry with the news.[109] He arrived back at home within six months, by December 27, 1236;[110] he carefully avoided the Finnish and Russian armies during his return journey.[111]

In 1237, Friar Julian began another journey to "Great Hungary," in order to renew his search of Magyar origins.[112] He had dictated the history of his previous travels to Friar Ricardus,[113] but he recorded his second journey himself in a letter addressed to the bishop of Perugia.[114] In this letter he wrote that he had begun his latter mission with his confreres, but as soon as they had reached Suzdal, the westernmost Russian outpost,[115] he [they] heard the news that the Mongols already had devastated the area occupied by the Magyars,[116] and the Mongols had planned to invade the west.[117] In the second half of his letter, he provided an outline based on hearsay and oral information of Mongol history and of their customs.[118] It was upon his return from his interrupted mission that Julian brought with him the message of the khan to the Hungarian king.[119]

Béla IV received the letter in 1237, but did nothing for the defenses of the realm until the winter of 1240. Did he understand the Tartar danger? Did he have a serious confrontation with the unruly nobles that might have paralyzed his political-military plans?[120]

It belongs to the framework of these events, and it has been mentioned before, that the Cumans of Kötény had, together with the forces of Mistislav of Halich and Danilo of Ladomer, suffered a devastating defeat at the Kalka river, east of the Dnieper.[121] The ease with which the Tartars had defeated the combined armies of three rulers pointed toward the lack of organized resistance, and the west lay open to the forthcoming Mongol onslaught.[122] Although Jenghiz Khan died in 1237, the election held at Karakorum made Ogotai, the second son of Jenghiz, the Great Khan,[123] and it was Batu, Jenghiz's firstborn, who had been assigned the conquest of western regions - "one quarter of the Earth" - and retaining it under Tartar rule.[124]

The head command (one may refer to him as Chief of Operations) was held by Subutai Khan, who had planned and carried out the strategy for the great invasion of the west.[125] It began with the attack on the Turkish-Tartar tribes in Kovarezima, with the result that the ancient territory held by the Magyars along the Etil (that is, "Greater Hungary") had disappeared from the map, together with the other areas in that region.[126]

The Tartars! In the fall of 1240, a force of almost half a million Mongolian Tartars crossed the Dnieper and headed toward the west.[127] They captured Kiev on December 6, where they randomly murdered and devastated the surrounding country.[128] Danilo of Halich and Michael of Chernigov fled helplessly to the court of the Hungarian monarch.[129] The Tartars also occupied Vladimir on the Bug river, and had established themselves within five days of traveling distance from the Hungarian border.[130]

In early 1241, Béla IV declared a state of emergency,[131] but, because of the carnival season, nobody took the call seriously.[132] The nobles, and the lesser service nobility, *servientes*, and even personnel attached to the court - and now called to active duty - were under the impression that members of the hierarchy had only invented the danger because they did not wish to attend the church synod that had been called by the pope.[133] Worse still, the common folk looked upon the Cumans recently settled in their midst as "Russian" (that is, Tartar) spies.[134]

Canon Rogerius of Várad provided an eyewitness account about the Tartars. He had earlier visited Hungary as a member of the entourage of Jacob of Pecora - the bishop of Praeneste and papal delegate - and he had sojourned in the realm again in 1232, now himself a papal legate. In 1241, he was archdean of Várad, and had experienced in person the Tartar invasion of 1241.[135]

Rogerius gave his report the rather unusual title of *Carmen miserabile*, though he wrote it without interruption, in the form of a personal letter.[136] His use of the term *carmen* for a title, and the heading of the lead paragraph may unwillingly remind one of the first lines of Boethius' *De consolatione philosophiae*: "Carma qui quondam studio florente peregi flebilis."[137] He definitely analyzed and placed domestic conditions in Hungary prior to the Tartar invasion in a strong light, as if to find out how it was possible that the Tartars could, without any serious effort, take possession of this great and flourishing realm?[138]

The answer of Rogerius? The results of his analysis was that, in political terms, the domestic condition of the country, and the confrontation amidst its social strata in economic terms had paralyzed the activities of the monarch.[139] One may add that, in the field of foreign policy, the confrontation between the papacy and the German emperor made it impossible for Béla IV to obtain any military aid from abroad.[140] It was no small irony of the situation that Emperor Frederick II, in his letter addressed to King Henry III of England, had argued the point of view that only close Christian cooperation could bring common action against the Tartars.[141] Public opinion in the west (or, those who were guiding what would have been the equivalent of "public opinion") maintained that the entire Tartar threat was mere papal fiction,[142] while the pontiff, Gregory IX, himself lacking fiscal resources, could only console the Hungarian monarch to be determined and continue his struggle with the enemy.[143]

His thorough understanding of the domestic conditions, and of the absence of any possible foreign aid, forced Rogerius to prepare his report from the viewpoint of a wide audience, so that those who read it understood it; those who understood it believed it; those who believed it comprehended it; and those who comprehended it, had truly realized its meaning.[144]

Rogerius wrote about the day of judgment, the approaching end of the world,[145] though it is possible that by awakening Hungarian public opinion he attempted to prevent a reoccurrence of domestic quarrels of the pre-invasion period, as he wanted public opinion to have an influence upon the king and the leaders of the country: "...ut legentes intelligant et audientes non ignorent destructionis Hungarie fundamentum."[146]

In the first one-third of his "letter," therefore, Rogerius did not speak of the Mongol invasion as such, but debated events preceding it,[147] like his contemporary, Thomas of Spaleto, who had looked upon the horrible destruction caused by the Tartars in Hungary as a just punishment of God, on the grounds that the Hungarians had become greedy, sensual, and sinful.[148]

Thomas of Spaleto wrote that the mere physical appearance of the Tartars had created horror: they awful features, such short legs, though deep chests, and broad, animal-like faces. White-skinned and beardless the Mongols were, with flat noses and tiny eyes wide apart.

Their weapons included shields made out of the skin of bulls, curved swords, iron helmets, or head gear made out of leather. They carried their own bows and quivers on their backs in a military fashion.

The Mongol arrows were eight inches longer than the arrows used by the Hungarians. The tip of a Tartar bow was made out of iron or out of horn. They also carried small black and white flags, sometimes with a woolen knob on top of the flag.[149] The Mongols rode small horses that were strong and could bear thirst and hunger with ease. Excellent horsemen they were, able to pass with ease through rocks and the stony surface of the terrain. Every one of their horsemen took one stalk of forage with him to provide a three day supply for his horse.[150]

Food was not too important for them. What they regarded as important was merciless behavior toward their enemies. Bread they did not consume; they ate only animal meat. Their order-of-battle demanded that peoples whom they had subjected to their rule most recently fight in the front row in battle.[151] Were a Tartar to die during the march, or in a skirmish, or in battle, they rescued the body and buried it in an unmarked grave.[152]

Fast rivers the Mongols forded on horseback; if the water was too deep, or the river too dangerous to cross, they built wicker boats shaped like kayaks, and covered with animal skin, to get across the river. Their tents were made of animal skins or linen. The Tartars were not talkative; during a battle they remained silent, and their horses, too, stayed quiet.[153]

The warring tactics of the Tartars were described in detail by contemporaries, who recorded Tartar history according to Armenian and Mongolian sources of information, and in accordance with their own observations.[154] The Tartar mounted his horse with bow and arrow, was a skilled and almost invincible fighting man; however, he was useless on foot. They could not even walk because of the almost constant riding on horseback.[155]

The Mongols had strict military discipline, were able to fight without their leaders; they were less skilled at besieging fortifications, though. They made carefully detailed plans for besieging a fort or a town; it was part of their tactics to surprise the opponent and to outwit him. Running away from the scene of the battle was an important factor in their military strategy: they looked upon escaping from the field of military action as something necessary and not at all disgraceful. They made certain that it was they who engaged their opponent on **their** terms, and not vice versa.

In a military situation, the Mongols proved to be skilled bowmen, caused heavy damage to enemy ranks; and their bodies were armed with relatively light mail made from leather, as were their horses. This armor was effective, for arrows and weapons of the opponent slid off easily. They marched to battle in closed formation, and withdrew in formation from the scene of the engagement; they could also shoot their arrows backward at the enemy pursuing the opponents, then turn about, surprise and defeat them.[156]

Their method of warfare and military tactics were first rate, the records agree. In the case of Hungary, they applied the principle of military "strategic isolation": separate the realm from its neighbors, then invade it from four geographic directions.[157] It may be that they had assumed that the Hungarian attitude toward them would be that of disbelief. The Hungarian leading social stratum was unwilling to take the Mongols seriously; its members could not believe that the Tartars could sweep everything and everybody aside by their movements and strategy (if any). In fact, the Hungarian high nobility maintained that the entire Tartar threat was only a figment of the bishop's mind because the high churchmen did not wish to attend the council that had been scheduled by the pope to meet in Lyon, in the early spring of 1241.[158]

Were the Hungarians to expect the enemy, they had expected the arrival of the (Kievan) Russians at their border, with whom they knew how to effectively deal. The nobles regarded the Cumans settled down among them as "Russian" spies who had entered the country in order to learn of any weakness, while becoming familiar with language and customs. The Cumans' "goal," in the nobles' opinion, was to domestically prepare for its invasion.[159]

In Hungary, the monarch alone had recognized - after the fall to the Mongols of Halich and Kiev - the most serious nature of the military situation.[160] In January, 1241, in bitter cold winter, Béla IV inspected in person the Hungarian Carpathian mountain range along the Hungaro-Kievan border. He ordered the line of military defense to be fortified in the mountains and barricades to be built in the mountain passes.[161] The king had dispatched Dénes the Palatine for the defense of the "Russian Gate" (the Verecke Pass), with order to defend it from the approaching "Russians," to resist them to the very last man.[162] Béla IV now called for country-wide mobilization; he had announced that nobles, upper clergy, and all personnel assigned to the royal forts ready themselves for the approaching military threat.[163]

In mid-February, 1241, at the beginning of Lent, a royal assembly was held in Buda - the easily accessible central location of the realm[164] - where the king conducted talks with his nobles and members of the hierarchy to request that they place their military personnel at the ready.[165] The secular members of the assembly were of the opinion, however, that they (and the realm at large) had only to develop defensive tactics because the Tartars would not invade the country in a regular manner. Thieves and robbers the Tartars were, whom one could, properly readied, defeat easily and expel from the realm. Offense can be the best defensive tactic. The nobles in the king's assembly, by being irresponsibly uniformed and naive, committed a basic tactial error: they underestimated their Asian opponent.[166]

The secular nobles had also brought up the issue of the Cumans in this Lenten assembly in Buda. The Cumans had become, the nobles claimed, a serious threat to the land; what they did not say was that the Cumans had also become a thorn in the nobles' flesh because, with the organize Cuman troops supporting him, Béla IV had a large military contingent at his personal disposal that could enable him to deal with the enemy alone, without the active support of the nobility. As a matter of fact, the presence of the royal Cuman "body guard," if one may use the term, further enabled the king to keep an eye on the nobles.[167]

Could it be, this writer is tempted to ask, that in this truly critical hour of political-military decision making the Hungarian nobility, acting jealous, and in a stupid irresponsible manner (so characteristic of the physically strong, but mentally underdeveloped), wanted to divest the monarch of the opportunity of facing the enemy alone, fearlessly, and without their aid?[168] After all, had such a situation occurred, had Béla IV actually carried the upper hand over the "Russian" enemy without help from the nobles, the victorious monarch would have had to pay even less attention to them, who had previously behaved in such a selfish manner toward him.[169]

Could it be that it was the insane fear, the jealous greed of the nobles that caused the downfall of the realm in the spring of 1241?

Because the nobles, who had spoken up in the Lenten assembly, had achieved their goal: they had convinced the king that the Cumans who had entered the realm, but had, as yet, avoided establishing permanent settlements, were unreliable, and had to be kept under surveillance, and their ruler, Kötény, placed under house-arrest.[170]

Therefore, in one session of the Lenten assembly held in Buda in 1241, Béla IV had lost the only reliable segment of his armed forces. This segment was capable of fighting, if necessary, for their own survival, and was familiar with the warring methods of the Mongols. It is likely they could have taken a decisive military stand against the Asiatic warriors on the verge of invading the country.[171] The nobles, irresponsible and unable to reason on their own, had, through their rebellious attitude toward the king, dug their own grave, and the grave of their own country with it.[172]

Batu Khan divided his armies into four divisions for the invasion of Hungary. He himself stayed with the main body of the forces he had placed under the direct command of his brother Seiban, and of his sub-commanders Buruldaj and Subutaj, and approached the Verecke Pass from Ladomeria.[173] Batu's other brother, Peta Khan, together with Orda and Kajdu khans, departed to invade Silesia.[174] Batu ordered the division on the left of his army to turn southward and enter Hungary from the east, through the Borgo Pass, under the command of Kadan and Burin khans, both grandsons of Jenghiz Khan.[175]

The fourth division, commanded by Büdzsik, grandson of Ogotaj Khan, was ordered to enter Hungary through the Törzsvár Pass, and to carry out operations in the Maros valley.[176] It may be characteristic of the clever Batu that he had approached the Hungarian armed forces within a five day distance (of operations) and had, as yet, kept secret from them the deployment of his own forces.[177]

On Ash Wednesday, February 13, 1241, when the nobles had met with the king in Buda, and where the fate of the country had been decided even before the Tartars had entered the land,[178] the division on the right of Batu Khan's armies took Sandomir on the Vistula.[179] In less than six weeks, Peta Khan occupied Cracow and totally devastated Poland.[180] Henry of Silesia attempted to face the Tartars in battle, but at Liegnitz, where the decisive encounter took place on April 9, 1241, the Tartars demolished his army.[181]

In achieving victory at Liegnitz, Batu Khan had realized his first objective: to make certain that the Hungarian king receive no military help from Silesia or Poland.[182] From a military point of view, the victory on the east-northern division of Batu's armies over the assigned area was now complete. Furthermore, under the joint command of Kadan (son of Ogodej) and Toluj (grandson of Jenghiz), the left wing of Batu's armies had entered Transylvania and made certain that Hungary would be besieged from both the north and the east.[183]

Batu Khan and his main forces now came near the Verecke Pass; Siban, his brother, and Szubutej, the hero, accompanied him.[184] It was Batu's plan to break through the pass and sweep down and across the Hungarian plain, and surprise the king before he could prepare for a defensive counteraction in the field.[185] Batu's main army comprised some eighty thousand troops, of whom some forty thousand were carrying axes.[186]

On March 10, 1241 Dénes the Palatine dispatched messengers to Buda to announce that the Tartars were dismantling the barricades in the Verecke Pass.[187] On March 12, Batu's troops clashed with the small garrison of the palatine, who had with difficulty escaped from the bloodbath, though his men were cut to pieces in the encounter. Dénes hurried to Buda to make a report to awaken the nobles from their stupor: the Tartars are coming![188] Indeed, the Mongol victory at Verecke opened up the country for a full scale invasion by the enemy.[189]

The Mongolian forces must have suffered considerable losses in capturing the pass. Peta Khan withdrew his division and devastated the defenseless Moravian lands.[190] The Czechs, however, put up a fierce resistance. Their king, Wencelas, controlled a large number of troops under his command, and deployed them advantageously in the mountainous terrain of his country. The Mongols, not used to fighting in the mountains, could not defeat him. The military readiness, combined with their king's willingness to fight, and the fact that the terrain of their homeland was ideal for defensive military operations, saved the Czechs from a serious and disastrous invasion by the Tartars.[191]

The Hungarian court had realized only in mid-March, 1241, the seriousness of the military situation. The garrison of the palatine at the Verecke Pass had been totally demolished by the enemy; Dénes himself arrived at Buda with only a handful of his men.[192] In a certain way, it was the king's fault. Béla IV had purposefully played down the Tartar threat and initiated military countermeasures much too late.[193] He now interrupted the Lenten meeting in Buda, and hurriedly dispatched the upper clergy and nobles with orders to return to their homes, and bring their regional armed forces with them to the town of Pest; there they were to assemble and prepare for facing the Mongols in battle.[194]

Members of his own family Béla IV had placed under the protection of Bishop Stephen of Vác, and sent them to the western border of the realm;[195] the archdean of Arad, the archdeacon of Holy Savior at Csanád accompanied the Queen.[196] The king himself turned to Frederick of Austria for military aid,[197] and ordered his Cumans to move their military contingents to the town of Pest.[198] The king also collected royal troops from Esztergom and Fehérvár, and moved them across the Danube toward Pest, where they were to meet with the other regional military units already gathering.[199]

The record does not reveal what provisions were made for feeding the troops or the animals. The order-of-battle - if there ever existed one - and the command structure of the assembling royal forces must have been arranged only on a provisional basis.[200]

The Mongols were coming - an enemy, to be sure, still under-estimated and held in contempt by the Hungarian high command and the nobles; the latter had thought that they could easily and swiftly defeat the Tartars without any serious readiness and go home afterwards. Incredible ignorance and complete misunderstanding of the prevalent conditions characterized the public scene in Hungary by mid-March, 1241.[201]

NOTES

* *SSH*, I, 467f., rendering the date in the previous paragraph - *ibid.*, I, 477,12-14; the addition made by the Chronicler of Óbuda put the date (1241) here, *ibid.*, I, 467S,17-19, and his text further mentioned "Mangali sive Tartari."

1. See the baptismal certificate of Béla, *CD*, III-1, 155. When Béla was born, his father, Andrew II, went hunting in the Billege region around Nagyvárad; upon receiving the news, he immediately donated the village to the bishop of Veszprém, but soon changed his mind and gave it instead to his loyal Ban(us) Salamon - *CD*, IV-3, 387ff.; for a better text, see I. Nagy *et al.* (eds.), *Hazai Okmánytár* [Collection of Domestic Documents], 8 vols. (Győr-Budapest, 1865-91), cited hereafter as *HO*, IV, 44ff. The Chronicle mentioned the birth of Béla on the 18th Sunday after Pentecost, "qua cantatur Da pacem Domine;" *SSH*, I, 467,4-5.

2. *SSH*, I, 467,6-7; on St. Peter's church, cf. D. Csánki, *Magyarország történelmi földrajza a Hunyadiak korában* [The Historical Geography of Hungary in the Age of the Hunyadies], vols. 1-3 and 5 (Budapest, 1890-1913), III, 311; indirectly, Ekkehardt Eichdorff, "Einheit Europas im neuen gemeinsamen Glauben," *Die Presse-Spectrum*, Vienna, July 18, 1987, i-ii.

3. The original basilica dedicated to the Mother of God - *ibid.*, I, 322,3-4, was constructed by King St. Stephen himself, *ibid.*, I, 316,5-8; King Stephen's "Vita maior," c. 11, *ibid.*, II, 386,16-18; Hartvic, "Vita s. Stephani regis," c. 13, *ibid.*, II, 419,9-13; R.F. Kaindl, "Studien zu den ungarischen Geschichtsquellen, I-II," *Archiv für österreichische Geschichte*, 81 (1895), 323ff.; esp. 336; Keza, c. 74, drew a distinction - *ibid.*, I, 186,31, and so did the chronicler, *ibid.*, I, 443,8, by recording that Béla III had been buried there (in 1196) - *ibid.*, I, 463,3-6.

4. Cf. Rogerius, "Carmen miserabile," c. 1, *ibid.*, II, 552f.; Macartney, 88; Pintér, I, 730f. The Chronicle recorded the 18th Sunday after Pentecost, *ibid.*, I, 467,4-5, though a writ, dated 1236, mentioned the 4th Sunday of Lent, "Regis Bele coronationem in Dominica qua cantatur Laetare;" cf. *HO*, VI, 30 (a date that may belong to a previously cited document - Pauler, II, 510, n. 114).

5. *SSH*, I, 467,7-9; Mügeln, "Chronicon," c. 62, *ibid.*, II, 207,1-4; the "Chronicon rhythmicum Austriacum" made an overstatement - *MGHSS*, XXV, 355, lines 246-253.

6. Simultaneously, the king richly rewarded the officials who had remained loyal to him - to cite the case of Dénes, son of Dénes, head marshal of the stable, *RA*, n. 608; *CD*, IV-1, 21. Rogerius, cc. 4-5, reported on a conspiracy by some nobles against the king, *SSH*, II, 554ff.; the king had, in turn, confiscated their belongings - *CD*, IV-1, 33ff.

7. Rogerius, cc. 4 and 9; *HO*, VI, 106; *MGHSS*, IX, 639, anno 1235.

8. Rogerius, c. 4; Kosztolnyik, *From Coloman*, 128f.; Otto of Freising, *Chronica*, i:32; one may draw a comparison with the French king, Louis IX - cf. Jean de Joinville, *Histoire de Saint Louis*, ed. N. de Wailly (Paris, 1874), 34.

9. *SSH*, II, 555,4-13.

10. *Ibid.*, II, 559, c. 11.

11. *Ibid.*, c. 13.

12. *Ibid.*, II, 555,1-4 and 555,13-16.

13. *Ibid.*, II, 555,6-7.

14. "Annales s. Justinae Pataviensis," *MGHSS*, XIX, 154,32-36 and 155,18-22.

15. Dandalo mentioned it cautiously that Beatrice had married an elderly man in Andrew II, "iam seni nupsit," upon whose death, and because of the changed circumstances, she, dressed like a boy, had left the realm - cf. "Chronicon Venetum,"

x:15,15 and 17, in Muratori, *RISS*, XXII, 349; see also "Annales Salimbiene," iii:57, in *MPH*, IV, 707.
16. Albericus, "Chronicon," *MGHSS*, XXIII, 939,15-16.
17. *SSH*, II, 557f.
18. *Ibid.*, II, 558,4-8.
19. Rogerius, cc. 6 and 11.
20. For details, see, e.g., *ÁUO*, VII, 22f. and 23f.
21. No exceptions! - "...ut facilior (modus) universas donationes revocadi pateret, si nullam exciperet;" *ibid.*, VII, 309ff., esp. 311.
22. *Ibid.*, VII, 24.
23. "Superfluas et inutiles quorundam antecessorum nostrorum donationes de communi baronum nostrorum ac totius regni nostri consilio decrevisum revocandas;" *CD*, IV-1, 71 (anno 1237). The royal writ emphasized that it is to be done with the consent of the barons, and with the approval of the royal council, "regni concilium."
24. *ÁUO*, VII, 21f. and 22f.
25. *RA*, n. 610; *ÁUO*, VII, 9; *CD*, IV-1, 105.
26. *RA*, n. 611; *ÁUO*, VII, 31f.
27. Potthast, n. 10081; *VMH*, n. 251.
28. Potthast, n. 10082; *VMH*, n. 252 (January 16, 1236).
29. "...volumus declarare, quod cum...pater noster rex Andreas...ecclesiae sancti Michaelis de Vesprimo contuisset, et nos...eandem donationem confirmassemus;" *RA*, n. 620 (May 11, 1237).
30. Potthast, n. 10081. On Gregory, cf. Mályusz, *Egyházi társadalom*, 56ff.
31. According to the papal letter, Potthast, n. 10066; *VMH*, n. 249; *CD*, IV-1, 30f.
32. See also the two royal writs issued on October 29, 1237, concerning the goods of the abbey of Pannonhalma, *RA*, nn. 623 and 624; *ÁUO*, II, 55 and 56; Erdélyi, *Rendtörténet*, I, 755 and 754, in that order.
33. Potthast, n. 10369; *VMH*, n. 276.
34. Rogerius, c. 5.
35. As it may be evident from the royal writs issued between March, 1236 and January 29, 1238 - *RA*, nn. 610 to 637, except the writs *dubiae fidei*, as, e.g., n. 615.
36. Compare the papal writs of December 16, 1235, and of May 31, 1237, in Potthast, nn. 10066 and 10385; *VMH*, n. 277; *CD*, IV-1, 88f.
37. G. Ostrogorsky, *Geschichte des byzantinischen Staates*, 2nd ed. (Stuttgart, 1952), 346ff.; A.A. Vasliev, *History of the Byzantine State* (Madison, 1952), 441f. Earlier, the Bulgarian ruler had negotiated with the Holy See expressing his desire to join the Church - Potthast, n. 10368; *VMH*, n. 275 (May 21, 1237); Marta F. Font, "A Kievi Évkönyvek mint magyar történeti forrás" [The Kievan Annals as a Source for Hungarian History], *Történelmi Szemle*, 33 (1991), 70ff.; idem, *art. cit.*, 1988, 261f.
38. Potthast, n. 10508; *VMH*, n. 283; *CD*, IV-1, 101f.; the letter of Béla IV, *RA*, n. 308, implying that Salvi had visited Hungary twice. M.F. Font, "Ungarn, Bulgarien und das Papsttum um die Wende vom 12 zum 13 Jahrhundert," *Hungaro-Slavica*, 1988, 259ff.
39. Potthast, n. 10505; *VMH*, n. 285.
40. Potthast, n. 10508, as above, n. 38.
41. Potthast, nn. 10634 and 10631; *VMH*, nn. 297 and 193.
42. *RA*, n. 642, dated "r. a. tercio," at Zólyom.
43. "...iuxta sue legationis modum penes nos diligenter institit;" *VMH*, n. 308; *CD*, IV-1, 111ff.; Katona, *Historia critica*, V, 819ff.
44. One of the papal letters, dated August 9, 1238, referred to this royal writ - Potthast, n. 10636; *VMH*, n. 298.

45. "...et nostris iussionibus sic in omnibus est subiectus, ut notam amicus, quam subditus videatur;" *VMH*, n. 308.
46. "...existit tanta nobis devocius coniunctus, it et se et sua ad nostrum beneplacitum exibere sit paratus;" *ibid.*, I, 170f.
47. *Ibid.*, I, 171,1-5.
48. *Ibid.*, I, 171,13-24.
49. *Ibid.*, I, 171, 25-33.
50. *Ibid.*, I, 170,33-48.
51. *RA*, n. 653, dated January, 1239, and rendering a reason, why?
52. *RA*, n. 651, in connection with the papal writ of August 8, 1238, Potthast, n. 10633; *VMH*, n. 292.
53. Potthast, n. 10632; *VMH*, n. 294.
54. Potthast, n. 10637; *VMH*, n. 295; Katona, *Historia critica*, V, 824f.
55. The request of Béla IV was given a negative response in Rome - *VMH*, n. 308, but it did not prevent the king from placing the Apostolic double cross on his coat of arms - cf. Erdélyi, *Magyar történet*, I, 232.
56. By December, 1239, the idea of a mission to Bosnia had preoccupied the curia - Potthast, n. 10823; *VMH*, n. 312; see also Potthast, n. 10832; *VMH*, n. 314; *CD*, IV-1, 174.
57. Potthast, n. 10926, addressed to Béla IV; *VMH*, n. 330. The curia invited Bishop Bertalaumus of Pécs, Potthast, n. 10930; *VMH*, n. 329. See also the papal writs of October 15, 1240, addressed to the king, Potthast, n. 10952; *VMH*, n. 332, and to Archbishop Matthias of Esztergom, Potthast, n. 10945; *VMH*, n. 331. On the events leading to the Council of Lyon, 1245, see Matthew of Paris, *Chronica maiora*, ed. H.R. Luard, 7 vols., R.S. (London, 1872-83), IV, 430ff.; on the council, cf. Mansi, *Concilia*, XXIII, 633ff.; Gilbetti, "Chronicon," *MGHSS*, XXIV, 136,18-27; Patavini Roland of Padua, *ibid.*, XIX, 82, v:13-14; Vincent de Beauvais, *Speculis naturali*, liber xxiii:101, *ibid.*, XXIV, 163,5-22. On Matthew of Paris, see A. Gransden, *Historical Writing in England c. 550 to c. 1307* (Ithaca, NY, 1974), 356ff.; J.J. Saunders, "Matthew of Paris and the Mongols," in T.A. Sanquist and M.R. Powicke (eds.), *Essays in Medieval History Presented to Bertie Wilkinson* (Toronto, 1969), 116ff.
58. Karl Hampe, *Deutsche Kaisergeschichte*, 12th ed., ed. F. Baethgen (Heidelberg, 1968), 294ff.; idem, *Das Hochmittelalter*, 5th rev. ed. (Cologne-Graz, 1963), 398ff.; E. Kantorowicz, *Frederick II*, trans. E.O. Lorimer (repr. London, 1957), 457ff.; F. Baethgen, "Kaiser Friedrich II, 1194-1250," in Günther G. Wolf (ed.), *Stupor mundi: zur Geschichte Friedrichs II von Hohenstaufen* (Darmstadt, 1982), 207ff.; esp. 228.
59. Hampe, *Kaisergeschichte*, 304; Kantorowicz, 501ff.; the actual purpose of the synod was to depose Frederick II - cf. N.P. Tanner (ed.), *Decrees of the Ecumenical Councils*, 2 vols. (London-Washington, DC, 1990), I, 278ff.; Hampe, *Hochmittelalter*, 402.
60. Correspondence, as in Potthast, nn. 10945 and 10952; on March 6, the pope sent Matthias of Esztergom the pallium - cf. Potthast, n. 10851; *ÁUO*, VII, 106f.
61. Potthast, n. 10995; *VMH*, n. 333.
62. Katona, *Historia critica*, V, 900; in a writ addressed to Matthias of Esztergom, the curia requested that he "personaliter accedens" see to it that the Benedictine monasteries in Hungary adhere to the Rule - Potthast, n. 10993; *VMH*, n. 328; Katona, *Historia critica*, VI, 898.
63. Potthast, n. 10988; Huillard-Bréholles, *Historia diplomatica Friderici II*, 12 vols. (Paris, 1852-61; repr. Hildesheim, 1971), V, ii, n. 1095; *ÁUO*, II, 130 and VII, 119; *VMH*, n. 327 (dated February 12, 1241).
64. "...ut vota Crucisignatorum ipsorum in defensione, ecclesiae contra Fridericum eundem,...commutare valeas;" *VMH*, n. 327; F. Gräfe, *Die Publizistik in*

der letzten Epoche Kaiser Friedrichs II (Heidelberg, 1909), 96ff. On the 1245 Council, see Tanner, *Decrees of the Ecumenical Councils*, I, 273ff.

65. Cf. Anastasius van der Wyngaert (ed.), *Itinera et relationes Fratrum Minorum saeculi XII et XIV*, vol. I of *Sinica Franciscana* (Quaracchi-Florence, 1929), 27-130 for the text of Plano Carpini; and 164-332 for the text of William Rubruque's travels; here, cf. xlv:7; Plano Carpini, 51ff., esp. 57, and n. 2, Paul Ratchnevsky, *Genghis Khan: His Life and Legacy*, trans. and ed. Th. N. Haining (London, 1991), 89ff. and 145ff.; B. Spuler, *Die Mongolen in Iran* (Leipzig, 1939), 27ff.; F.W. Cleaver, *Secret History of the Mongols* (London, 1982), 1ff. and 205ff.; W.W. Rockhill (ed.), *The Journey of William Rubruck to the Eastern Part of the Worlds, 1253-55*, with two accounts of the earlier journeys of Plano Carpini (Hakulyt Society, 1910; repr. Liechtenstein, 1967), xiiiff.; H.H. Howorth, *History of the Mongols from the 9th to the 19th Century*, 3 vols. (London, 1876-88), I, 49ff.; B. Lewis, "The Mongols, The Turks, and The Muslim Polity," *Transactions of the Royal Historical Society*, 5th ser., 18 (1968), 49ff.; Hóman-Szekfü, I, 524ff., still a reliable interpretation; Székely, *Magyarország*, 1417ff., with limited bibliography, *ibid.*, 1713; on the other hand, László Makkay's essay in Béla Köpeczi (ed.), *Erdély története* (A History of Transylvania), 3 vols. (Budapest, 1986), I, 309ff., is more than valuable; see my review of this opus in *Austrian History Yearbook*, 22 (1991), 170ff.

66. Wyngaert, xlvff.; Carpini, v:7-18; B. Spuler, "Die Aussenpolitik der Goldenen Horde," *Jahrbücher für die Geschichte Osteuropas*, 5 (1940), 1ff., esp. 31; Ch. Dawson, *The Mongol Mission: Narratives and Letters of Franciscan Missionaries to Mongolia and China in the 13th and 14th Centuries* (New York, 1955), introduction; idem, *Religion and the Rise of Western Culture* (New York, 1958), 214ff.

67. Albericus, "Chronica," *MGHSS*, XXIII, 912,22-25; Ibn Al-Athir, *Chronicon quod perfectissimum inscribitur*, ed. K.J. Tornberg, 12 vols. (Leiden, 1851-76), XII, 233ff.

68. *Ibid.*, XII, 252ff.; Wyngaert, xlvi.

69. Wyngaert, xlvi; Carpini, v:20-21, ix:11; Rubruck, i:12, xii:6; Halich-Volhynia Annals, in Hodinka, 400aff.; *GVC*, 45f.; B. Spuler, *Die Mongolen in Iran: Politik, Verwaltung und Kultur der Ilchanzeit, 1220-1350*, 3rd ed. (Berlin, 1968); idem, *Die Goldene Horde: die Mongolen in Russland, 1223-1502*, 2nd ed. (Wiesbaden, 1965); M. v. Taube, "Russiche-litauische Fürsten an der Düna zur Zeit der deutschen Eroberung Livlands," *Jahrbücher für Kultur und Geschichte der Slawen*, n.s. 11 (1935), 367ff., esp. 443. Hóman, *Ungarisches Mittelalter*, II, 105ff.

70. Haenisch, 141 and 145ff.; Roger Bacon, *Opus maius*, ed. J.H. Bridges, 2 vols. (Oxford, 1897), I, 268; Vincent of Beauvais, *Speculi maioris...qui speculum historiale inscribitur* (Venice, 1591), 422b, c. xxix:89; Thomas of Spaleto, *MGHSS*, XXIX, 591.

71. Based on Rogerius, c. 14, *SSH*, II, 560,6-10; G. Bar Hebraeus, *Chronicon Syriacum*, ed. P. Bedjan (Paris, 1890), 460. On May 18, 1239, Béla IV had sojourned to Horon, cf. *RA*, n. 657; *ÁUO*, VII, 70, and he visited Szeged on October 27, *RA*, n. 664; *ÁUO*, VI, 72ff. On the Cumans' arrival, see "Cont. Sancrucensis II," *MGHSS*, IX, 640,8-10; the Palatine must have played a role in these negotiations, "Palatinus in nostro negotio morabatur ulta Alpes," *HO*, VI, 37.

72. Cf. Hodinka, 400aff.; *GVC*, 45f., of a letter from the Khan to Béla IV, the text of which was recorded in Friar Julian's report on his journey to Baskiria, addressed to the bishop of Perugia (anno 1237), in Bede Dudik (ed.), *Iter Romanum, Historische Forschungen*, series, II: *Der päpstliche Registerwesen*, 2 vols. (Vienna, 1855), I, 334; for a different rendering of the text, see J. Hormayr-Hortenburg (ed.), *Die Goldene Chronik von Hochenschwangau*, 2 vols. (Munich, 1842), II, 69; both texts in *ÁUO*, VII, 549ff. and 554ff., respectively. Marcartney, 86ff., and Pintér, I, 283f.

73. *MGHSS*, XXIII, 946,1-7; Matthew of Paris, IV, 275; Carpini, iii:1-11; Rubruck, 33:17-22, 34:1-3, and 11; Wyngaert, li and lii; Rubruck, 33:7-23; the Julian report, Dudik, I, 327ff.; Hormayr-Hortenburg, II, 67ff., and the papal admonition, Potthast, n. 10385; *VMH*, n. 277. The khan also sent letters to the German court - *MGHSS*, XXIII, 943,44-46. "Tartari modo interrogativo clamores loquantur, guttore rabide et horribile. Cantos mugiunt ut Thauri, vel ululant ut lupi, voces inarticulares incantando preoferunt, et hanc cantinela *Ala alali* communiter ac frequentissime canunt," - de Beauvais, *Speculi maioris*, 429a, c. xxix:71, and compare with Matthew of Paris, III, 488f (anno 1238!), and with a thirteenth century report on the Tartars, "De modis et moribus Tartarorum," *ÁUO*, VII, 546ff.

74. *MGHSS*, XXIII, 946,10-18; *SSH*, II, 560,15-22.

75. *Ibid.*, II, 553,6-18, and cc. 7 and 12; Carpini, v:11 (Wyngaert, 171, note 2); Rubruck, i:12 referred to it. Katona, *Historia pragmatica*, I, 803ff.

76. *SSH*, II, 553,18 - 554,15 and II, 557,1-16.

77. The abbey of Kő: "monasterium de Kew circa Ticiam," *ibid.*, II, 557,3-4; see further D. Fuxhoffer and M. Czinnár (eds.), *Monasteriologiae regni Hungariae libri duo* (Pest, 1858-59), I, 242f.; Pauler, II, 513. Rogerius, c. 12, agrees with the "justifiable anger" of the nobility, but leaves final judgment to the reader: "lector, si valeat, causam terminet iustitia mediante," *SSH*, II, 559,30-31.

78. *SSH*, II, 557,1-16. The writ of July 14, 1264, of Urban IV throws some light upon their arrival and settlement - see Potthast, n. 18970; *VMH*, n. 493; Knauz, I, 660f.

79. Rogerius, c. 20.

80. Cf. the khan's letter, Dudik, I, 334; Hormayr-Hortenburg, II, 69. On the spread of Christianity among the Cumans, see Albericus, *MGHSS*, XXIII, 946, 10-18; and *ÁUO*, II, 58f. M.F. Font, "Ungarn, Polen und Galizien-Wolhynien im ersten Drittel des 13 Jahrhunderts," *Acta Slavica Hungariaca*, 38 (1993), 27ff.

81. Rogerius, cc. 2 and 14; Matthew of Paris, III, 487f.

82. Dudik, I, 333; Hormayr-Hortenburg, II, 68f.

83. *Ibid.* The letter was written "litteris paganis, sed lingua Thatarica."

84. Only in the Hormayr-Hortenburg, II, 69 version: "Miror de te, Hungarorum regule, quod...;" the text by Dudik, I, 334, reads *king*: "Miror de te, Rex Ungarie, quod...."

85. "...iam tricesima vire legatos;" *ibid.* It is an overstatement; it is known from a letter of Ivo of Narbon, a priest, to the archbishop of Bordeaux that an Englishman who had become a Tartar, had, as the khan's envoy, visited the court of Béla IV on two occasions - cf., Matthew of Paris, IV, 274. The same letter, alerting Bordeaux about the Mongol threat, had served little purpose because of the hostility between the pope and the emperor - *ibid.*, IV, 270ff., 277f..; *CD*, IV-1, 275, and made mention of "heretical movements;" on the latter, see A. Borst, *Die Katharer* (Stuttgart, 1953), 180ff., and H. Grundmann, *Die religiöse Bewegungen im Mittelalter* (Berlin, 1935), 40ff. In Wienerneustadt, Ivo had stayed with the *beginae* (religious lay-women) - Matthew of Paris, IV, 272 (who also recorded the quick expansion of their movement, IV, 278); also, J. Greven, *Die Anfänge der Beginnen*, vol. 8 of *Vorreformations - geschichtliche Forschungen* (Munster i.W., 1912), 77ff., and L. Mezey, *Irodalmi anyanyelvűségünk kezdetei az Árpádkor végén: a középkori női laikus mozgalom eredetkérdése* [Beginnings of Native Hungarian Literature at the End of the Age of the Árpáds: The Origins of the Medieval Lay-women Movement] (Budapest, 1955), 5ff.

86. "...sed nec nuntios tuos, vel litteras mihi remittis," Dudik, I, 334. In Hormayr-Hortenburg, II, 69, slightly different wording.

87. "...melius tibi esset et salubrius, si te subieceres sponte mihi....Cumanos servos meos...mando tibi, et me adversarius tibi non habeas propter illos;" *ibid.*

88. "...facilius est enim eis evadere, quam tibi, quia illi sine domibus cuius tentoribus ambulantes possunt forsitan evadere;" Dudik, I 334, and compare with Hormayr-Hortenburg's reading: "...tu autem in domibus habitans, habes castra et civitates, quomodo effugies manus meas?" - II, 69.

89. *Ibid.*; Dudik, I, 333.

90. *SSH*, II, 535ff.; *RHM*, 248ff.; Macartney, 85ff.; J. Horváth, *A magyar irodalmi műveltség kezdetei* [Origins of Hungarian Literary Culture], 2nd ed. (Budapest, 1944), 50f.; Pintér, I, 283f.

91. *SSH*, II, 535,3-9. The fundamental essay by Zoltán Gombocz, "A magyar őshaza és a nemzeti hagyomány" [In Search of the Magyars' Ur-country and the National Myth], *Nyelvtudományi Közlemények*, 45 (1917-20), 129ff.; 46 (1923-27), 1ff. and 168ff.

92. *SSH*, II, 535,12 - 536,4; *VMH*, I, 151ff. (n. 271); Hóman-Szekfü, I, 533f.; the comprehensive study by Gyula Németh, *A honfoglaló magyarság kialakulása* [Development of the Magyars before the 890's], revised ed., ed. Árpád Berta (Budapest, 1991), 180f. and 182f. Further, S.L. Tóth's forthcoming opus, *A 9 századi magyar törzsszövetség szervezete és külkapcsolatai (838-896)* [Organizational Structure of the Associated Magyar Tribes in the Ninth Century and its Contacts with Foreigners, 838-896].

93. *SSH*, II, 536; Dudik, I, 337; Anonymus, c. 1, *SSH*, I, 34ff.; Thomas of Spaleto, in *Monumenta spectantia historiam Slavorum meridionalium*, ed. by members of the Southern Slavic Academy of Sciences, 43 vols. (Zagreb, 1868-1918), cited hereafter as MHSM, XXVI, 46; one may mention here the historical novel, based on solid research, by János Kodolányi, *Juliánus barát* [Friar Julian] (Budapest, 1943). On the Order of Preachers in Hungary, see H. Pfeiffer, *Die ungarische Dominikanerprovinz von ihrer Gründung 1221 bis zur Tartarenverwüstung 1241-42* (Zurich, 1913).

94. *SSH*, II, 536,6-16.

95. King Andrew II must still have been alive, "domini Bele nunc regis Ungarie;" *ibid.*, II, 536,22 and note 3.

96. *Ibid.*, II, 536,21-23.

97. *Ibid.*, II, 537,1-13.

98. *Ibid.*, II, 537,11-13.

99. *Ibid.*, II, 538,17-22.

100. "Unde necessitate coacti duo ex eis de illis partibus verus Ungariam redierunt;" *ibid.*, II, 538,22-23.

101. *Ibid.*, II, 538f.

102. *Ibid.*, II, 539,9-11.

103. *Ibid.*, II, 539,20-23.

104. *Ibid.*, II, 539,23-36.

105. "...quia omnino habent Ungaricum idioma, et intelligebant eum, et ipse eos;" *ibid.*, II, 540,5-6.

106. "...terras non colunt, carnes equinas, lupinas et huiusmodi comedunt; lac equinum et sanguinem bibunt;" *ibid.*, II, 540,6-9.

107. *Ibid.*, II, 540,10-11.

108. *Ibid.*, II, 541,5-10.

109. Although they had asked him to stay: "licet ab Ungaris invitaretur, ut meneret;" *ibid.*, II, 541,16-17.

110. *Ibid.*, II, 541,27-30.

111. *Ibid.*, II, 541,31.

112. Cf. Dudik, I, 327; Hormayr-Hortenburg, II, 67; Albericus dated it anno 1237, *MGHSS*, XXIII, 942,20-23.

113. *SSH*, II, 531.

114. Dudik, I, 327ff.; the report sent to the bishop of Perugia had been acknowledged by Rome - the bishop was a papal legate to the court of Béla IV, see Potthast, nn. 10369 and 10385; *VMH*, nn. 276 and 277 (May 27, 1237). Macartney, 86f.

115. "...cum ad ultimos fines devenissemus Russie;" Dudik, I, 327.

116. "...a Thartaris penitus sunt devastata;" *ibid.*, "Ungari pagani, et Bulgari, et regna plurima a Tartaris sunt destructa;" Hormayr-Hortenburg, II, 67.

117. Dudik, I, 333; Wyngaert, xlvif.

118. "Quid autem sint Tartari?" - Dudik, I, 327ff.; "Quod autem sint Tartari,...vobis tenore presencium enarrabo;" Hormayr-Hortenburg, II, 68f.; compare to Albericus, *MGHSS*, XXIII, 943,20-23.

119. "Praedicats litteras a Noe Duce de Sudal ad Regem Hungariorum deportavi," Dudik, I, 333; "...a Duce Sudal, et litteras Regi missas Dux ille recepit ab eis," Hormayr-Hortenburg, II, 69.

120. Did he not heed the warning of the friar? - "ego autem et socii mei videntes terram a Thartaris occupatam, et regiones munitas conspicientes etiam nullum fructum fructificandi, reversi sumus ad Hungariam;" Dudik, I, 335.

121. Cf. Hodinka, 454ab-456ab; *GVC*, 29; Wyngaert, liii; Rubruck, i:12; "Annales Pantaleonis," *MGHSS*, XXIII, 535,12-31; W. Scheck, *Geschichte Russlands*, rev. ed. (Munich, 1977), 46f. One may conclude from Rogerius, c. 14, that the Cumans had entered Hungary in 1239, *SSH*, II, 561,1-3.

122. As it may be evident from Julian's report: "Propositum enim habere dicuntur, quod veniant et expugnent et ultra Romana;" Dudik, I, 333.

123. Wyngaert, xlvif.; Carpini, v:25; "Cinggis Qahan," - cf. F.W. Cleaver (ed.), *Secret History of the Mongols* (London, 1982), 1ff. and 205f.; Spuler, *art. cit.* (1940), 6, note 12; W. Berthold, in *Enzyklopädie des Islam*, vol. I (Leipzig, 1913), 709ff.; Gebhardt, I, 377.

124. Carpini, viii:1-3, 5; ix:38-39; Matthew of Paris, III, 488.

125. Wyngaert, xlvii; Carpini, v:21; on Subutai (Sübetei) Khan, see "Sung Lien, Jüan si," in P. Pelliot, *Notes sur l'histoire de la Horde d'or* (Paris, 1949), 130ff.; also, based upon a Chinese-Mongolian historical work, *Szo-Hong-Kinlu*, c. 7, Abel Remusat has published a brief description, *Nouveaux melanges asiatiques*, II (Paris, 1829), 89ff., reprinted in *ÁUO*, VII, 560ff.

126. Rubruck, c. 7; Carpini, v:29; Kirakos Gandzakecki, "Armenian History," ed. Ödön Schütz, in *Tanulmányok az orientalisztika köréböl* [Studies Concerning the Orient] (Budapest, 1972), 255ff.; Hodinka, 400a; Albericus, *MGHSS*, XXIII, 954,1-3.

127. Wyngaert, lvi and lvii; *MGHSS*, XXIII, 943,44-46; A.M. Amnan, *Kirchenpolitische Wandlungen im Ostbaltikum bis zum Tode A. Newskirs* (Rome, 1936), 233ff.; Spuler, *art. cit.* (1940), 10f.; Matthew of Paris, IV, 109ff.

128. Carpini, v:27; "Halich Annals," in Hodinka, 404a to 406a; *GVC*, 48; B. Altaner, *Die Dominikanermissionen im 13 Jahrhundert* (Habelschwerdt, 1924), 128.

129. Hodinka, 400a-402a; *GVC*, 49.

130. *Ibid.*; *SSH*, II, 63,12-17; "Gesta Treverarum, cont. IV," *MGHSS*, XXIV, 403f.

131. *Ibid.*, XXIII, 946,10-12.

132. Béla IV dispatched the Woyvoda of Transylvania with orders to take a stand against the Mongols - *ibid.*, XXIII, 946,15; it is interesting to observe the reaction of Matthew of Paris, III, 639.

133. *SSH*, II, 560,18-22 (c. 14).

134. *Ibid.*, II, 560f.; *MGHSS*, XXIII, 946,12-15.

135. For text, cf. *SSH*, II, 551ff.; *RHM*, 255ff.; or, Schwandtner, *Scriptores*, I, 292ff.; Macartney, 88; Horváth, *Stílusproblémák*, 239; Pintér, I, 730f.; and the remarks by L. Juhász, in *SSH*, II, 545, note 1.

136. See the title, "Epistola Rogerii," *ibid.*, II, 551, or *RHM*, 255; Edward Gibbon, *Decline and Fall of the Roman Empire*, lxiv:3, Great Books, vol. 41 (Chicago, 1952), 484 and 754, note 16, remarked: "the best picture that I have ever seen of all the circumstances of a barbarian invasion." Compare to Thomas of Spaleto, cc. 37-40, cited editions, or Schwandtner, *Scriptores*, III, 601f., who did not like the Hungarians (they were too proud, overconfident), and gave a subjective report; he also mentioned three "evil" Hungarian churchmen, perhaps Benedict, bishop of Várad, Bölcs (the Learned One), bishop of Csanád, and Bishop Gregory of Győr. Also, Thuróczy's *Chronicle*, cc. 101-102.

137. See H.F. Stewart and E.K. Rand (eds.), Boethius' *Consolatio philosophiae* and *Opuscula sacra*, Loeb classics (London, 1918), i:1; E.K. Rand, "On the Composition of Boethius' Consolatio philosophiae," *Harvard Studies in Classical Philosophy*, 15 (1904), 1ff.; idem, *Founders of the Middle Ages* (Cambridge, 1928), 135ff. Friedrich Heer spoke of Boethius' constitutional concept as based upon his attitude toward the Church and background of the then prevalent monastic outlook, in his *Europäische Geistesgeschichte*, 2nd ed. (Stuttgart, 1967), 32f.

138. *SSH*, II, 551f.

139. *Ibid.*, II, 554ff., cc. 3-7, and cc. 8-12.

140. See Matthew of Paris, IV, 120ff.; Hampe, *Kaisergeschichte*, 299ff.; Kantorowicz, *The King's Two Bodies*, 97ff.

141. Matthew of Paris, IV, 112ff. and 129f.

142. *Ibid.*, IV, 119f., and compare to *CD*, IV-1, 212ff.

143. Potthast, n. 11034; *VMH*, n. 337.

144. "...examinavit, ut legates intelligent, et intelligentes credant, credentes teneant, et tenentes percipiant;" *SSH*, II, 55,12-14. E. Power, "The Opening of the Land Routes to Cathay," *Travel and Travellers of the Middle Ages*, ed. A.P. Newton (New York, 1926), 124ff.

145. "...quod prope sunt dies perditionis et tempora properant ad non esse;" *SSH*, II, 552,14-15.

146. "Quia non ad deprehensionem cuiuquam, vel derogationem, sed ad instructionem id potius examinavi;" *ibid.*, II, 552,11-12; Rogerius repeats his assertions in c. 37, *ibid.*, II, 582f.

147. *Ibid.*, II, 552ff., cc. 1-13.

148. *MGHSS*, XXIII, 589, c. 36; Schwandtner, III, 602; A. Dempf, *Die Hauptform mittelalterlichen Weltanschauung* (Munich-Berlin, 1925), 62f.

149. In MHSM, XXVI, 3-212 - for c. 40, see XXVI, 179; Schwandtner, *Scriptores*, III, 532ff., cc. 37-40; selections in *MGHSS*, XXIX, 591,11-21 (c. 38).

150. Carpini, vi:3-10 and vi:11-15; *MGHSS*, XXIX, 591,11-21 (c. 38).

151. *Ibid.*, XXIX, 591,21-26.

152. *Ibid.*, XXIX, 591,28-30.

153. *Ibid.*, XXIX, 591,31-37; Carpini, vi:12.

154. Carpini, c. 6 (Wyngaert, 75ff.); Rubruck, c. 9 (*ibid.*, 187ff.); Hóman-Szekfű, I, 530ff.; Hóman, *Ungarisches Mittelalter*, II, 127ff.; Székely, 1422f.; Erich Haenisch, *Die Geheime Geschichte der Mongolen aus einer mongolischen Niederschrift des Jahres 1240 von der Insel Kode'e im Keluren Fluss* (Leipzig, 1941, rev. ed. 1948), 99ff. and 108f.; for cross reference, see *MGHSS*, XXIX, 591,13-17; Ödön Schütz, "A mongol hódítás néhány problémája" [Questions Concerning the Mongol Onslaught], *Századok*, 93 (1959), 209ff.

155. The letter by a Hungarian bishop addressed to William of Auvergne, archbishop of Reims, *CD*, IV-1, 232ff.; Matthew of Paris, V, 75f.

156. Carpini, cc. vi and viii; *MGHSS*, XXIX, 590f.

157. *Ibid.*, XXIX, 591,1-3; Carpini, vii:3; *SSH*, II, 560,6-8.

158. *Ibid.*, II, 560,19-22; *MGHSS*, XXIX, 585,12-19.

THE TARTARS ARE COMING! 149

159. *SSH*, II, 560f.
160. *Ibid.*, II, 560,6-8; *MGHSS*, XXIX, 585,42-46; Hodinka, 454a; Toru Senga, "IV Béla külpolitikája és IV Ince pápához intézett 'Tartár levele'" [The Foreign Policy of Béla IV and his Writ Addressed to Pope Innocent IV Concerning the Tartars], *Századok*, 121 (1987), 583ff.
161. *SSH*, II, 560,8-11; *MGHSS*, XXIII, 946,15 and XXIX, 553,18-19.
162. *MGHSS*, XXIX, 553,19-21.
163. "...et fecit per totam Hungariam proclamari," *SSH*, II, 560,11-15.
164. "...versus Quadragesimam," *SSH*, II, 561,12. Rogerius described it as a village - "villa, que Buda dicitur," *ibid.*, II, 561,13; compare with *MGHSS*, XXIX, 553,40; Gerevich, *Medieval Hungarian Towns*, 38 and 43ff.; M.C. Rady, *Medieval Buda: A Study in Municipal Government and Jurisdiction in the Kingdom of Hungary*, vol. 182 of East European Monographs (New York, 1985), 3, quoting a 1232 decree of Andrew II that spoke of the "citizens of Pest" (cf. *RA*, n. 492; *CD*, VII-4, 79f.). Rady, 51, also mentioned Buda as a "New Town" development by the middle of the thirteenth century; for the 1244 Pest-Buda charter, see *ibid.*, 165ff., based on D. Csánki and A. Gárdonyi (eds.), *Monumenta diplomatica civitatis Budapest, 1148-1301* (Budapest, 1936), 41ff., that stated that after the departure of the Tartars there had existed a Christian parish, "...et salvo iure ecclesia Budensis." See further, A. Kubinyi, *Die Anfänge Ofens* (Berlin, 1972), 10, 11f., 14ff., 16f., and 25f.; idem, "Burgstadt, Vorburgstadt und Stadtburg: zur Morphologie des mittel-alterlichen Buda," *Acta archeologica Academiae Scientiarum Hungaricae*, 33 (1981), 161ff.
165. *SSH*, II, 561,15-18.
166. *MGHSS*, XXIX, 586,5-10.
167. *SSH*, II, 554, 555f., 556f., and 558 (cc. 3, 5, 8, and 10). That is why they wanted to turn the monarch against Kötény, "ut haberent de rege obloquendi," *ibid.*, II, 560,26-27 - "pugnam facere contra regem," *ibid.*, II, 561,4.
168. "Et talis opinio erat eis," remarked Rogerius rather sadly, *SSH*, II, 560,16-22.
169. *Ibid.*, II, 560,22-25.
170. That is the reason why they had persuaded Béla IV to keep Kötény and his Cumans under observation - *ibid.*, II, 561,18-22.
171. Matthew of Paris, V, 75f; *MGHSS*, XXIX, 591,39-42; Rogerius, cc. 12 and 14.
172. "...scriptor finem huius negotii imponuit; lector, si valeat, causam terminet iustitia mediante [sic!];" *SSH*, II, 559,30-31 and the whole c. 13.
173. *Ibid.*, II, 563,6-10 and 19-23; Haenisch, 145ff.; Howorth, I, 141ff. and 145f.; Spuler, *Mongols in History*, 17f.
174. Idem, *art. cit.* (1940), 12f.; *SSH*, II, 563f. Among the Prussian sources, one may mention *Cronica terrae Prussiae* and *Danziger Ordenschronik*, in H. Hirsch (ed.), *Scriptores rerum Prussicarum*, 5 vols. (Leipzig, 1861-74), I, 197f., and IV, 363ff.
175. *SSH*, II, 564,6-10; *MGHSS*, XXIX, 585,28-32; Carpini, v:20 and ix:23; Rubruck, 23:2; Köpeczi, *Erdély*, I, 309ff.
176. *SSH*, II, 564,20-26 and II, 576,25-29.
177. *Ibid.*, II, 563,18-19.
178. *Ibid.*, II, 561,11-15.
179. Hodinka, 400abff. and 454abf.; *MGHSS*, XXIX, 585 (c. 36).
180. *SSH*, II, 564,9-14; of the Polish sources, cf. *MPH*, II, 560ff.
181. *Ibid.*, II, 561; II, 804 and II, 877 (anno 1241); III, 71f., III, 489f.; IV, 56f.; *SVC*, 45ff.; *MGHSS*, XXII, 535f.; XXVI, 604f.; XXVIII, 207,33; 210,42 - 211,1. H. Aubin, *Geschichte Silesiens*, vol. I (Bresslau, 1938), 100ff.; Hirsch, IV, 363ff.

150   HUNGARY IN THE THIRTEENTH CENTURY

182. *SSH*, I, 563,15-21; Wyngaert, xlviif.; Hóman-Szekfü, I, 540; Székely, 1423ff.
183. *SSH*, II, 564,6-10; *VMH*, n. 348; *CD*, IV-1, 302.
184. *SSH*, II, 561,25-27; II, 563, note 4; *ÁUO*, VII, 560ff.
185. *SSH*, II, 654f., and compare to II, 563,11-13; II, 563,25-30.
186. Thomas of Spaleto, c. 37.
187. In "Porta Russica," *SSH*, II, 560,8-10 and 561f.; *SVC*, 68f.
188. "...et ad regem, quantum poterat, festinabat;" *SSH*, II, 561,25-30.
189. *Ibid.*, II, 561,29 - 562,6; *MGHSS*, XXIX, 585,42-46.
190. *SSH*, II, 564,2-6.
191. *ÁUO*, II, 136f.; *SVC*, 57ff; Palacky, *Geschichte*, II-1, 116ff.
192. *SSH*, II, 561,30-34.
193. *Ibid.*, II, 561,25-30, and II, 562,1-6. The name of Váncz, alias Bancsa (or Vancha de genere Vancha), chancellor from 1237 to 1240, bishop of Vác, later archbishop of Esztergom, appeared in the text, *ibid.*, II, 562,6; in March, 1240, Béla IV had referred to him as the bishop of Zagreb - *RA*, n. 608 and 674, though in a royal writ, dated September 23, 1241, he referred to him as the bishop of Vác - *RA*, n. 709. The bishop, "de genere Bancsa," alias Váncz, was also mentioned in a letter of Emperor Frederick II - cf. Matthew of Paris, IV, 114.
194. *SSH*, II, 562,6-17.
195. *Ibid.*, II, 562,7-9.
196. *Ibid.*, II, 562, 7, and compare with c. 33, *ibid.*, II, 576. C. Juhász, *A csanádi püspökség története a tatárjárásig, 1030-1242* [History of the Diocese of Csanád until the Mongol Onslaught] (Makó, 1930), 168f.
197. *SSH*, II, 562,9-10; *SVC*, 72 and n. 1.
198. *SSH*, II, 562,11-12.
199. *Ibid.*, II, 562,12-15.
200. *Ibid.*, II, 561,15-18. One may draw a similar conclusion from a remark made in (a) "Scriptum curiae Romanae," - cf. *Forschungen zur deutschen Geschichte*, XII (1872), 643ff.
201. *SSH*, II, 560,16-22.

CHAPTER FIVE

THE TARTAR INVASION

1. The Engagement at Mohi

> Anno Domini M-o CC-o XLI-o ipso
> Bela regnante Mangali sive Tartari cum
> quinquies centeni milibus armatorum
> regnum Hungarie invaserunt.
>
> *Chronicon pictum*, c. 177

On March 15, 1241, Friday of the Seven Sorrows, the Tartar force was only half a day march away from the town of Pest.[1] About ten thousand Tartars on horse must have moved about in the surroundings of the town, with the aim of trying to prevent the strategic gathering of the royal Hungarian armed force to fight them. This Tartar "vanguard" did not engage in destruction of property, nor in irrationally murdering everyone in sight, and did not burn everything to the ground in the region. It only would have delayed them.[2] The Tartars remained on the lookout, prepared to slow down the foreseen [strategic] formation of the king's forces. Orders were given to the gathering royal troops that they do not provoke fights with the Tartars must have played into the hands of the latter.[3]

Difficult it was to keep within the bounds of the royal order. Ugrin, archbishop of Kalocsa, who was the first to arrive with his contingent of troops at the designated location at Pest, felt especially insulted in his self-esteem by the king's directive.[4] Compelled to be temporarily inactive, and most probably concerned about the behavior of his unemployed troops, Ugrin could not passively stand by and watch the devastation of the countryside by the Tartars; nor did he like it that both the monarch and he were regarded as cowards by the public opinion. The archbishop, being a warrior, was not a humble man.

On March 17, he issued orders to engage the Tartar marauders in combat, and since the latter pretended to flee the area, he gave them pursuit. In the heat of the chase, he and his men failed to notice that they had entered marshy ground (that is, pretending to flee, the Tartars had purposefully led them to the area, into a lurch), where the archbishop's heavy cavalry perished, and the Tartars, in making an about face, blanketed with a hail of arrows the still unengaged segment of the archbishop's troops. With only the greatest difficulty did the archbishop and the remainder of his men escape from the bloody encounter, and deeply humiliated, return to Pest.[5]

In describing this military confrontation with enemy troops, the chronicler drew the conclusion that the archbishop and his men were militarily and psychologically unprepared for this, and any, encounter with the Tartar forces, and had breached discipline by acting contrary to direct orders from the king - regardless of the archbishop's reasoning that he had to keep his troops occupied, fed and disciplined through such a seemingly low-risk military maneuver. The entire Ugrin-related episode may point to complete lack of discipline and organization among the royal troops assembled at Pest, and creates the impression of a helpless state of unprepared-ness, and, as a matter of fact, of uncertainty on the part of the Hungarian royal high command.[6]

It must have been characteristic of the disorders of the time[7] that, on the same day, the Tartars took the town of Vác (north of Pest, on the left bank of the Danube), robbed its churches, and massacred all of its inhabitants.[8] The disorders were further increased by the attitude of Frederick of Austria, who had entered Hungary not because he wanted to aid the Hungarians against the Mongols, but for the reason that he show off his military skills and readiness in front of the Hungarians.[9]

The king's order to the contrary - unless the royal order to avoid hostilities with the enemy without provocation did not pertain to the "foreign" duke - Frederick moved against the Tartar troops, who, taken by surprise, had actually backed away from him. It must have been this "element of surprise" and the better equipment and training [discipline?] of the duke's force that had caused the Tartars to withdraw. Frederick now pursued the fleeing enemy, killed one of their leaders, cut off the arms of another (who died of his wounds shortly thereafter), and the Tartar contingent marauding in the area of Pest disappeared. Frederick had scored a victory, and the Hungarian nobles, not realizing the gravity of their situation - i.e., the seriousness of the Mongol threat - and still angry with their king, celebrated the triumph of Frederick at the expense and personal humiliation of their own monarch.[10]

Was it the victory scored by the Austrian duke? Was it the unnecessary, avoidable, and most disgraceful defeat of Archbishop Ugrin at the hands of a group of Mongol marauders? - but suddenly, there arose among the Hungarian nobles a vicious outcry of hatred toward the Cumans who had only recently been invited by the king to settle in their midst. The nobles, acting spitefully toward the king, began to identify the Cumans with the Mongols, called the Cuman "king" Kötény a Tartar collaborator who had played an active role in the devastation of their country. The Hungarian nobles still in the process of gathering their troops, without any order-of-battle, or plain military plans as how to cope with the Tartar threat, now demanded from the king that the Cumans be killed, and Béla IV, himself unready and frustrated, gave in to the nobles' demand.[11]

Béla IV probably made the mistake of his life. He gave orders that Kötény appear in front of him in person. But the Cuman leader, fearing for his life, refused to go. It may be that the king by ordering Kötény to come to him wished to save his life and retain the loyalty of the Cuman troops. But their signals were crossed and the frustrated nobles, a "mob," evidently wholly unaware of the seriousness of the Mongol threat, moved in front of Kötény's residence, besieged it, and after a short resistance had Kötény murdered, together with his bodyguard. The Cumans became a public enemy, free personal prey to be hunted down and killed by anyone.[12]

The Cumans had no alternative but to fight back. In revenge for the scandalous, unjust murder of their leader, they devastated the countryside, burning villages to the ground.[13] They also confronted Hungarian troops en route to their gathering destination near Pest - as, for instance, the troops of Bölcs, royal reeve of Csanád, and the contingent of Nicholas, son of Bárcz[14] - and carried out an awful devastation along the Danube.[15] Then they left the country toward the Bulgarian border, while the Cumans who had stayed behind submitted to Tartar rule.[16] Duke Frederick went home to Austria with his troops, while King Béla IV and his people found themselves alone in facing the immediate Tartar threat in the very heart of their country.[17]

In the beginning of April, 1241, Béla IV, urged on by Archbishop Ugrin, made his move against the Mongols.[18] The first encounter took place at Rákos, but it caused little damage; the Hungarian troops were still attempting to develop an order-of-battle formation. The complete lack of leadership was evident everywhere, in almost any step and movement that had been undertaken by the king's command.[19] Wild, undisciplined lust for war, total unappreciation of the enemy characterized the attitude of the Hungarian leaders and of their men.

The nobles simply would not comprehend the seriousness of the danger, the horrors of the Mongol invasion. When, for example, Bishop Benedict (the son of Ost) of Várad,[20] who most unwillingly complied with the king's orders to arms,[21] had heard that [the town of] Eger, northeast of Pest, had been destroyed by the Tartars, he attacked what must have seemed to him a small group of Tartar horsemen roaming about in that region. But the Mongols laid a trap for him.[22] They pretended to withdraw, placed stuffed sack dolls on their reserve horses, and awaited the Hungarian attack on the prairie. Then they withdrew from the scene for a second time, and the bishop's men came face to face with stuffed rag dolls tied to horses; the men, frightened by the number of dolls (and their horses, probably by the smell), turned and ran. The Tartars took them under pursuit and cut all of them to pieces.[23] The bishop escaped.[24]

The king's army - finally gathered together, and in some order - had made a halt at the Sajó stream, not too far from its estuary into the Tisza river, where they set up camp near a place named Mohi.[25] On the left-hand bank of the stream, Batu Khan set up his head-quarters, cleverly choosing his camp site.[26] The Sajó stream in front of him, on his right-hand side the Hernád river, on his left the Tisza river, provided him with a natural barrier of defense. Thick woods protected him from an unexpected attack in the rear.[27] Were the Hungarians to surprise his headquarters by crossing the rivers - assuming that the psychological impact of such a surprise had occurred before the attack - and were to inflict a defeat upon him, he could always escape with his men into the woods before the pursuers, who, presumably would give chase on horse and on foot. The heavily forested area further aided Batu to conceal his forces while crossing through the woods; the direction of his movements, and the positions he had taken up behind the Sajó remained wholly hidden from Béla IV and his commanders.[28]

In this regard one must, once again, blame the king for neglect, because he evidently did not have the military intelligence capability to keep abreast of the news of his opponent's movements, plans, military strength, or even strategy. Worse still, Béla IV did not seem to be too familiar with the geography (for the purpose of military deployment) of his country's terrain. Could the Hungarian high command have been so naive as to assume - an entire week after the Mongol capture of the Verecke Pass - that the Mongol armies would not pass through the mountain forests of the Carpathians?[29]

The Hungarian high command had made another serious mistake. It did not sufficiently reconnaissance the area around Mohi, nor did it undertake any of the much needed defensive preparations for an expected enemy offensive from the right-hand side of the Sajó stream. The idea conceived by the monarch and his command that they set up camp near the stream, send out scouts to observe the bridge across the stream, and the possible fording areas downstream, and to await the next move by the khan was irresponsibly naive and disastrous.

The monarch and his high command (or was it the King and his [military] advisors?) evidently could not foresee the probability that Batu Khan would invade their camp at any moment, and that his would be a sudden attack, even before the king's had made adequate preparations for fortifying their camp, and readied themselves for a countermove.[30]

If Béla IV and his staff had expected gentlemanly behavior of Batu Khan, assuming that their opponent would wait until they had rested for a few days before an encounter with them, they were gravely mistaken.[31] The Hungarians had arrived from Asia a long time before they had accepted western customs òf (military) behavior; they had become too acclimatized to western civilization during the preceding centuries, and were psychologically unprepared to face the Asiatic Mongols in a military encounter at Mohi. Dishonest and inhumanly cunning behavior, a ruthless employment of raw physical forces in the battlefield were, and would have been, the only means of effective defense against such an opponent.[32]

The number of troops encamped on both sides must have been the same in proportion; Batu Khan had some fifty thousand men under his command,[33] and the Hungarians numbered some fifty thousand men also.[34] In terms of geography, Béla IV had set up camp on the right-hand bank - that is, west of the Sajó stream, on a plain next to the village of Mohi (no longer in existence), south of the Ondó.[35]

The monarch and his advisors had made a basic mistake in their plan for the outlay of their camp: they had the tents (awnings) placed far too close to one another. The ropes holding down the tents further slowed down movements of the men, and their animals, kept secured next to them. The camp seemingly had no streets, and movement in it must have difficult in daytime and almost impossible at night. Again, the camp had no layout for streets and lights. There were no campfires lit. Worse still, they had erected a "protective fort" from wagons closely drawn together around the perimeter of the camp. Their wagons were placed closely side by side - the camp had no exits or gates - so that the "enclosed fort" concept must have hindered the movement of troops and animals in and out of the camp.[36] Carelessness characterized the entire planning process, as if to prove pointedly that the Hungarian high command, overconfident and sure of victory, had displayed only contempt for the Tartars, whom they regarded as stupid and barbaric people.[37]

The king's men now settled down in the camp and began, once again, to compare the Cumans with the Tartars.[38] Many nobles had openly expressed their hope that the monarch would suffer "some" humiliation at the hands of the Mongols because, they argued, having a minor defeat in front of the enemy would make him appreciate his own countrymen more![39] Lack of foresight had characterized the leaders and the men of the royal armed forces. They openly ridiculed the monarch when Béla IV had flags distributed to the troops, encouraged them to fight bravely in the forthcoming hard battle, to make their stand in front of the enemy.[40]

In the Mongol camp on the other bank of the Sajó stream, the Khan and his advisors were less apprehensive. Even Batu began to have doubts about the outcome of the forthcoming encounter. He was nervous and concerned about the unforeseen results of the battle. He ascended to the top of a hill near his camp to spend a day and night in meditation. Upon completing his prayers, he surveyed the Hungarian camp site across the stream; he wished to put his mind in order, to make plans. Batu was curious about the preparedness of the Hungarian forces, about their size and fighting potential. He could not believe his eyes at what he saw. All of his fears were eliminated. The Hungarians were closed in their camp like sheep in a narrow sheepfold.[41] Allah had heard his prayers and given the enemy into his hands.[42] Batu gave orders for the encounter to take place at early dawn of April 11th.[43]

The Mongol plan was simple enough: encircle the Hungarian camp, and let nobody escape. Therefore, he had, already on April 10, dispatched some of his men to capture the bridge over the Sajó, and to establish a bridgehead across, thereby to have a base on the Hungarian side of the river directly fronting the forces of the king.[44]

Another contingent - there must have been some splinter groups operating within the fifty thousand men enemy force - the Khan sent further south along the Sajó with orders to ford it and to establish another position on the right bank directly behind the camp, in the rear of the Hungarian forces. Batu had kept the main body of his forces in reserve, so that he might, at the proper moment, order a frontal attack and demolish the Hungarian camp.[45]

One must note here that the Hungarian high command - perhaps more properly, the camp headquarters - had failed to set up guard posts at the bridge, along the stream, and around the camp! The Tartar plan would have caught the Hungarians by surprise, had a Kievan - now a Tartar prisoner of war - not escaped from his captors and informed the Hungarian camp command of the immediate danger.[46]

Prince Coloman, the king's younger brother, and Archbishop Ugrin now hurried with their men to the bridge to prevent the Mongols from occupying it.[47] A segment of the Tartar force had, however, already crossed it.[48] The prince and the archbishop now attacked the enemy on the west side of the stream, surprised and defeated it. Coloman took possession of the bridgehead on the west (Hungarian) side of the stream, and posted guards to watch over it. Under the false assumption that they had won a decisive victory, and even eliminated the threat of another enemy attack, the prince and the archbishop victoriously returned to the camp with their men.[49]

In the camp, the prince and the archbishop, joined by the Master of the Knights Templar [of Hungary], stayed awake with their bodyguards, and watched over the bridge for the rest of the night.[50] (The chronicler wrote about "troops" of the three men, but he must have meant bodyguards, personal retainers, of the *comitatus* type, who stood by and fought close by their leader.) It was those three men who, together with their guards, met the second Mongol attack at early dawn on April 11th, when the Mongols easily repossessed the bridge, crossed the stream in large numbers, and nobody could stop them.[51]

Awful confusion must have prevailed in the Hungarian camp. Actually, it was this pandemonium caused by total surprise that decided the outcome of the Mongol skirmish - one could hardly call it a battle.[52] While Prince Coloman and Archbishop Ugrin had at the previous evening defeated a Tartar force and reoccupied at least a portion of the bridge - they failed to clear the bridge entirely from enemy presence and secure both of its terminals - the Mongol main force led by Batu Khan himself forded the stream southward of the bridge. At dawn, the Mongol troops drove the Hungarian garrison (guards?) from the bridge, crossed the stream in force, and began, with seven catapults, the attack on the Hungarian camp.[53]

The chronicler at this point zealously remarked that, awakened by the unusual noise, the Hungarians in the camp at first washed themselves, combed their hair carefully, slowly attached their bracelets - he must have meant body armor - when the Mongols were upon them![54] One may, of course, question the credibility of Thomas of Spaleto in recording the event. Did he interview eyewitnesses or did he rely on hearsay in collecting his intelligence?[55]

Batu's main army must have totally surprised the overconfident and carelessly relaxed Hungarians in the camp. Only Prince Coloman, Archbishop Ugrin, and the Grand Master of the Templars with their bodyguards were ready to meet with the enemy. They had encountered the Tartars - who were also confused and must have lacked a sense of direction in the dark - pushed them back to the Sajó stream, and beyond it.[56] It seemed that they had scored another victory. Batu Khan's attack at early dawn was, however, a sham. Had it succeeded, it would have decided the outcome of the Hungaro-Mongol confrontation right there. It had failed, and yet it enabled the khan to survey the area first hand, to gather intelligence on the strength of the Hungarian troops (and the Hungarian order-of-battle?), and prepare another main attack a few hours later.

In the morning, in broad daylight, when the forces of Subutai Khan had merged with the army of Batu, and the Tartars were able to surround the Hungarian compound in its entirety, they opened fire and arrayed the camp with flaming arrows.[57] The compound easily caught fire - panic broke out among the king's men, whose leadership was of no avail.[58] "In fuga" - flight from the scene was the only way out of a disaster.[59]

The Tartars had, indeed, opened up a passageway toward the south in their line of siege around the compound and let many of the king's men escape, after they had taken everything from them,[60] but they kept a lookout for the king, with orders from the khan to capture him alive.[61]

King Béla IV was surrounded by men loyal to him to the death.[62] Many of his men had sacrificed themselves for the survival of their king. Ernye, *de genere* Ákos,[63] and András, son of Ivánka, forefather of the Forgách family, both had asserted self-sacrificing behavior.[64] They had fought themselves through the Tartar ranks - that is, not through the passageway purposefully kept open by the Mongols where Batu's men were on the lookout for the king,[65] and when a small Mongol contingent had directly attacked the monarch, it was Detre, son of Mohol, who had fought them off and suffered heavy wounds in the hand-to-hand struggle.[66]

Móric (Maurus), son of Móric Pók, had killed a Tartar who had pointed his lance at the king.[67] The small group of men (royal bodyguard?) that had surrounded the king's person now fled with him toward the wooded areas of the northwest, into the Bükk Hills in Borsod county.[68] Ernye had placed his own horse under the monarch; then András, Ivánka's son, had his horse placed at the king's disposal. Prince Coloman, severely wounded, hurried toward Pest on a different route.[69]

The road leading to Pest was filled with the decomposing bodies of murdered people and animals; many had drowned in the marshes of the Tisza river.[70] Archbishop Ugrin, Archbishop Matthias of Esztergom, a brave fighting hero,[71] Gregory, bishop of Győr,[72] Ronald, bishop of Transylvania,[73] Jacob, bishop of Nyitra,[74] Eradius, bishop of Bács,[75] all had died in the encounter at Mohi, together with Albert, archdean of Esztergom,[76] and Nicholas, archdean of Nagyszeben, who was the royal vice-chancellor.[77]

The entire equipment of the Hungarian camp, much of the royal treasure, fell into the hands of the enemy.[78] The Tartars had also captured the royal tent, in which Batu Khan would later, at his headquarters on the Volga, receive foreign dignitaries and the submission of the Russian princes.[79] The royal seal had also been captured; it was found on the dead body of the royal vice-chancellor.[80]

Batu Khan knew how to exploit the unexpected victory. With the aid of some frightened clerics,[81] he had a letter written in the name of the king - he could do this as the royal seal was in his possession[82] - to warn the population to be aware of the blind anger of the Mongol dogs, and not to leave their homes.[83] Although he (that is, the king) might have lost a battle because of unforeseen misfortune, he remained hopeful that, by the grace of God, he would not give up the good fight, and would destroy the head of the enemy.[84]

It was quite a letter. Batu wanted in a such a manner to persuade the country's population to remain - not to flee. His nomad Mongols needed the agricultural population to stay in place, cultivate their fields, and feed the conquerors. It seemed to be good politics. However, the khan already had in mind the partition of the land, and had summoned into his presence the commanders of all Mongol forces operating in the country.[85]

Prince Coloman headed on changed horses toward Pest, but avoided taking the main road. He kept riding on dirt tracks in the country in order to avoid his pursuers.[86] Pest was a rather large town by this time,[87] with German inhabitants;[88] they had begged the prince to stay with them until at least their wives and children had been transferred across the Danube to safety,[89] but the severely wounded prince did not have the peace and presence of mind to stay.[90] He crossed the river, headed for Somogy county toward Següsd, where he died of his wounds.[91]

The inhabitants of Pest had hurriedly begun to fortify their town. They dug ditches, threw up earthworks, built woven reed fences, but before they had completed their projects, the Mongols appeared and put their haphazardly fortified town under siege.[92] In three days the Mongols had taken Pest and massacred the entire population.[93] Thomas of Spaleto wrote that one could hear from afar the "noise" of the killings. As if old trees in the forest were cut down with innumerable axes, the howl of crying children and shrieking women cried to heaven. There was no time for burials, nor for meals to commemorate the dead. The Tartars had massacred everyone in sight regardless of age or sex. Where was the chronicler, Thomas asked the question , who could depict in detail the misery of that most horrible day, who could report in depth on the suffering and the loss of thousands of human lives?[94]

The Mongols had devastated the town - they had to burn the remains of the thousands of unburied dead,[95] though many of the inhabitants had sought refuge behind the stone walls of the Dominican monastery near the town.[96] The Tartars did not even attack the monastery; they shot flaming arrows (matchsticks?) behind its walls, burning all the refugees to death.[97]

NOTES

1. "Venerunt versus Pestinum, quae erat maxima villa;" *MGHSS*, XXIX, 586,15-17; Rogerius, c. 21, *SSH*, II, 565,1-4; Hóman-Szekfű, I, 542f., or *MGHSS*, XXIX, 555,20-22; on Pest, see *Medieval Hungarian Towns*, 35ff., and nn. 69, 88, and 92; L. Gerevich, "A pesti és budai vár" [The Fort of Pest and Buda], *Budapest Régiségei*, 24 (1986), 43ff.; idem, "Hungary," in M.W. Barley (ed.), *European Towns* (London, 1977, 431ff.

2. *SSH*, II, 565,7-9; the Chronicle briefly mentioned the Mongol invasion, *ibid.*, I, 467f. (c. 177), by recording its date in the previous paragraph, *ibid.*, I, 467,12-14. The "Chronicler of Óbuda" recorded the date in c. 177, *ibid.*, I, 467S,17-19; both chroniclers spoke of "Mangali sive Tartari," *ibid.*, I, 467f. See further the Thuróczy *Chronicle*, c. 101, *ed. cit.*, p. 137.

3. *SSH*, I, 565,6-7.

4. Ugolinus de genere Csák, royal chancellor from 1217 to 1219 - cf. *RA*, nn. 317-353; archbishop of Kalocsa since 1219, *RA*, nn. 352, etc., who fell at Mohi, *SSH*, II, 570 (c. 28); between 1230 and 1235, he, as archbishop, also fulfilled the role of royal chancellor - *RA*, nn. 461-538; for text, see *ÁUO*, VI, 567f.; *CD*, III-2, 204; Hóman-Szekfű, I, 441.

5. *SSH*, I, 565,9-25.

6. "...quod rex non fecit aliquem in sui subsiduum properare;" *ibid.*, II, 565,24-25, compare with II, 560,22-25; Hóman, *Ungarisches Mittelalter*, II, 105ff.

7. It may not have been intentional, but the drawing in the Chronicle MS, fol. 63b, where six Tartars pursue the fleeing king Béla, who held a straight sword in his hand, but looked back upon his pursuers, has a significant title: "Adventus primus Tartarorum," *SSH*, I, 467,15-16, as if to suggest royal un-readiness for the forth-coming event.

8. *SSH*, II, 565,27-37; on the destruction of Eger, cf. *CD*, IV-3, 34f.

9. *SSH*, II, 565,2-4; Rogerius, c. 24; *MGHSS*, IX, 640.

10. *SSH*, II, 566,4-16 (c. 23).

11. *Ibid.*, II, 566,18-25.

12. *Ibid.*, II, 566f.

13. *Ibid.*, II, 567,18-26.

14. *Ibid.*, II, 567f.; "...cum Bulzu Chanadiensis episcopus et Nicholas filius Bore" [recte: Borc], *ibid.*, II, 567,29-30 - Bölcs (=Wise), or Balázs (Balasius), who will later join the forces of King Béla IV - see Spaleto, c. 39. There is a Borc "de genere Szák," *Comes curialis Reginae* (1212-13) recorded on a royal writ in 1212 - *RA*, n. 280; *CD*, III-1, 118; Katona, *Historia critica*, V, 154, and after 1222, *RA*, n. 382; *CD*, III-1, 368; also, *RA*, nn. 386,393, 394 or, in the year 1225, *RA*, n. 426; *CD*, III-2, 71; Katona, *Historia critica*, V, 480, probably identical with Nicholas the Palatine, *RA*, nn. 289 and 290. Appeared as palatine in 1219, *RA*, n. 354, as Palatine Nicholas, son of Borz, *RA*, nn. 357 and 358, though on a royal writ, dated 1221, the name was spelled Borch, *RA*, n. 362; *CD*, III-1, 316, to appear, again, as son of Borc - cf. *RA*, n. 368; *CD*, III-1, 381f.; *ÁUO*, VI, 408f.; was also known as the Reeve of the Queen's Court, and the Reeve of Sopron, *RA*, n. 382; *CD*, III-1, 368f.

15. *SSH*, II, 567f.

16. *Ibid.*, II, 568,14-15.

17. *Ibid.*, II, 567,17-19; *MGHSS*, XXIX, 556,35-37; Ebendorf, 111,13-18, a less reliable source? - *ibid.*, 111, n. 718.

18. "...instabat archiepiscopus Colocensis apud regem, ut exiret cum exercitu contra Tartaros;" *SSH*, II, 567,15-16.

19. *Ibid.*, II, 569,18-22; and Spaleto, c. 37; *MGHSS*, XXIX, 586,5.

20. Cf. *RA*, n. 471; *ÁUO*, XI, 230; in a 1243 writ, he was listed as bishop of Várad and bishop-elect of Győr, *RA*, n. 744; *ÁUO*, XII, 685f.
21. *SSH*, II, 568,18-20.
22. *Ibid.*, II, 568,26 - 569,4; compare to *CD*, IV-3, 34f.
23. *SSH*, II, 569,7-14.
24. The bishop had escaped - *ibid.*, II, 569,14-16.
25. *Ibid.*, II, 569,23-24; Spaleto, c. 37; *MGHSS*, XXIX, 586,31-34.
26. *SSH*, II, 569,27-28; *MGHSS*, XXIX, 586,34-35.
27. *SSH*, II, 569,28-30; *MGHSS*, XXIX, 586,35-36.
28. The main Mongol force - *ibid.*, XXIX, 586,16-19; *CD*, IV-1, 405f.
29. *MGHSS*, XXIX, 586,37-38; *SSH*, II, 569,30-34.
30. *MGHSS*, XXIX, 586,38-39.
31. Maybe on purpose: "volebant quidem, quod rex perderet," *SSH*, II, 569,34; the khan rejoiced, *MGHSS*, XXIX, 586,45-47.
32. "sed non sic, quia hecultima primis minime responderunt;" *SSH*, II, 570,6-7; for maps on the Tartar movements in Hungary, see Hóman-Szekfű, I, 544; Székely, 1424.
33. See the "Chronicon Posoniense," c. 68: "Tartari cum quinquies centensis milibus regnum Hungarie invaserunt;" *SSH*, II, 42,22-23; Macartney, 142f.; not to be confused with the "Annales Posonienses," *SSH*, I, 125ff.; Macartney, 84f., though Radó, *Libri liturgici*, 40, used the term "Chronicon Posoniense" when describing its contents on ff. 9-9´ of the Pray Codex, probably following the text publication of F. Toldy, *Chronicon Hungarorum Posoniense* (Buda, 1852).
34. "...fere extinguitur militia Hungarie universa;" *SSH*, II, 42,25-26, repeated by von Mügeln, "Indem streit wart erslagen die ritterschaft von Ungern nahent allzumal;" *ibid.*, II, 207,10-11; Székely, 1428ff., spoke of the battle of Mohi as a "[military] happening." Also, E. Olchváry, "A muhi csata" [The Battle of Mohi], repr. from *Századok*, 1902 (pp. 309ff., 412ff., and 505ff.).
35. "...iuxta fluvium Seo, prope villam Muhi;" *SSH*, II, 42,23-24.
36. *MGHSS*, XXIX, 586,38-42.
37. "Hungari autem habeant hec omnia in derisum de multitudine confidentes;" *SSH*, II, 569,30-33.
38. *Ibid.*, II, 570,1-6.
39. "Volebant quidem, ut rex perderet, ut ipsi chariores post modum haberentur;" *ibid.*, II, 569f.
40. "Rex suos interim hortabatur, ut ad pugnam viriliter se haberent; ...ad pugnam tamen...cor et animum non habebant;" cf. *ibid.*, II, 569,34-35.
41. "Vidi enim eos quasi gregem in quodam artissimo stabulo interclusos;" *MGHSS*, XXIX, 586,46-47.
42. "Bono animo nos esse oportet socii, quia multitudo gentis istius improvido reguntur consilio;" *ibid.*, XXIX, 586,45-46.
43. "Tunc autem nocte,...iussit aggredi pontem;" cf. *ibid.*, XXIX, 586,47-48.
44. *Ibid.*, XXIX, 586,48-49; and XXIV, 65,28-29 and 65,32-343.
45. *SSH*, II, 570,8-14.
46. *MGHSS*, XXIX, 586,49-51.
47. *Ibid.*, XXIX, 586f.
48. "...ecce iam pars quedam hostium ultra transierat;" cf. *ibid.*, XXIX, 587,3-4.
49. *Ibid.*, XXIX, 587,4-8.
50. *Ibid.*, XXIX, 587,16-19.
51. "Et ecce summo diluculo apparuit universa multitudo Tartarorum per campum diffusa;" *ibid.*, XXIX, 587,11-12. Rogerius, *SSH*, II, 570,9-11.
52. *MGHSS*, XXIX, 587,21-28; András Barosi, "A tatárjárás és Muhi csata 750 évfordulója: történetírók a tatárjárásról" [The 750th Anniversary of the Mongol

Invasion and the Battle of Mohi in the Interpretation of Historians], *Hadtörténelmi Közlemények*, 104 (1991), 3ff.
    53. *MGHSS*, XXIX, 587,8-11.
    54. *Ibid.*, XXIX, 587,12-16.
    55. See the remarks made by L. de Heinemann, *ibid.*, XXIX, 568f.; Hóman-Szekfű, I, 656; *Memoria Hungariae*, I, 43, 156 and 158.
    56. *MGHSS*, XXIX, 587,19-23.
    57. *Ibid.*, XXIX, 587,36-41; Hóman-Szekfű, I, 546f.
    58. *SSH*, II, 570,19; *MGHSS*, XXIX, 587,24-26.
    59. *SSH*, II, 570,2-26; *MGHSS*, XXIV, 65,28-29; 65,32-43; *ibid.*, XXIX, 587,46-49; *Chronica regia Coloniensis*, SSrG, 280.
    60. *MGHSS*, XXIX, 588,5-8.
    61. *SSH*, II, 571,3-4.
    62. *Ibid.*, II, 571,4-6; *ÁUO*, VI, 321.
    63. Cf. *RA*, n. 928; *CD*, IV-2, 92ff.; *RA*, n. 956; *ÁUO*, VII, 321f.
    64. *RA*, n. 885 (anno 1248); *RHM*, 498; *CD*, IV-2, 455f.
    65. *MGHSS*, XXIX, 589,12-13; on this, see also Carpini's report, vi:3 and vi:3,8.
    66. Katona, *Historia critica*, VI, 126 and *CD*, IV-2, 11, or HO, VII, 37, although it is listed as a false writ in *RA*, n. 898; however, the writ related to this matter, *RA*, n. 744; *ÁUO*, XII, 685f., *CD*, IV-1, 287ff., is valid. Woch(o)v, citizen of Pozsony, who had distinguished himself in the battle at the Sajó, and had later aided the monarch, was also rewarded, *RA*, n. 749; Knauz, I, 346.
    67. His signature appears on a royal writ of March 18, 1242: "Mauritius Pincenarum Magister in aula nostra," *RA*, nn. 715 and 716; *ÁUO*, VII, 188ff. (dated 1245!).
    68. *SSH*, II, 571,4-6, to the effect that only the monarch had fled the wooded area, "viam habuit versus silvam;" in connection with the flight of the king, see also other documents under *CD*, IV-1, 405 and IV-2, 93.
    69. *SSH*, II, 571,6-1.
    70. *Ibid.*, II, 572,23-33; *MGHSS*, XXIX, 588,10-15.
    71. *SSH*, II, 572,3-6.
    72. *Ibid.*, II, 572,10-11; *MGHSS*, XXIX, 588,19-20, and note 2.
    73. *SSH*, II, 572,11-12.
    74. *Ibid.*, II, 572,12-13.
    75. *Ibid.*, II, 572,16.
    76. *Ibid.*, II, 572,17-18.
    77. *Ibid.*, II, 572,13-16. "...ibi multa prelatorum et clericorum turba occubit;" *MGHSS*, XXIX, 588,20, and the angry outburst of the chronicler: "Heu, heu, Domine Deus!" - why does the Lord punish his priest so heavily? - cf. *ibid.*, 588,20-22.
    78. *SSH*, II, 573,16-18 and 573,24-27; *MGHSS*, XXIX, 588,8-13. "Ubi fere tota regni militia est deleta, ipso Bela coram eis...fugiatur," cf. Keza, *Gesta*, *SSH*, I, 184,14-15, and compare with "Annales Posonienses," *MGHSS*, XXIX, 440,18-22, and with the "Chronicon Posoniense," *SSH*, II, 42,21-29; the "Annales Posonienses," *ibid.*, I, 125ff. (*MGHSS*, XXIX, 502ff.), made no mention of the events of 1241. Macartney, 142f.
    79. See Carpini's report, ix:17 and Wyngaer, XLVIII.
    80. *SSH*, II, 573,36-37.
    81. *Ibid.*, II, 574,7. For comparison, see Paul Rachnevsky's study, *Genghis Khan, His Life and Legacy*, trans. Th.N. Haining (Oxford, 1993), 145ff.
    82. *SSH*, II, 573,36.
    83. *Ibid.*, II, 574,10-11.
    84. *Ibid.*, II, 574,12-16.

85. *Ibid.*, II, 574,18-23.
86. *Ibid.*, II, 571,6-8.
87. *MGHSS*, XXIX, 589,13-14, referred to Pest on the Danube as a larger village (town) - "villam magnam, que sota est super ulteriorem ripam Danubii." See also A. Kubinyi, *Die Anfänge Ofens* (Berlin, 1972), 25ff. and 30ff.; idem, "A mezőgazdaság történetéhez a Mohács elötti Magyarországon" [Some Remarks of Hungarian Agriculture Prior to 1526], repr. from *Agrártudományi Szemle* (Budapest, 1964).
88. That is, with German migrants, as evidenced by the chronicler's remark: "A burgensibus rogaretur," as in the German "Bürger;" cf. *SSH*, II, 571,10-11, and note 2.
89. *Ibid.*, II, 571,11-13.
90. *Ibid.*, II, 571,13.
91. *Ibid.*, II, 571,14-15 - *Segusd*, today called Felsősegesd, *ibid.*, II, 571, note 4; *MGHSS*, XXIX, 589,21-22; *ibid.*, XXVIII, 209,20.
92. *Ibid.*, XXIX, 589,21-26.
93. *Ibid.*, XXIX, 589,26-41.
94. *Ibid.*, XXIX, 589,42 - 590,4, and compare to *SSH*, II, 571,16-18. Strakosch-Grossman, 90f.
95. "...ignem undique posuerunt, aquam totaliter flamma consumpsit;" *MGHSS*, XXIX, 590,7-9.
96. "...addecem milia;" *ibid.*, XXIX, 590,12.
97. *Ibid.*, XXIX, 590,9-13.

2. *The Tartars Take Over the Country*

By mid-April, 1241, Batu Khan with his main force gained control of the central part of the realm.[1] The left flank of his armies led by Kadan Khan had entered Transylvania at the very end of March, on Easter Sunday;[2] their first goal was to occupy the rich Radna mines, the cleverly cultivated silver mines of German settlers. It may only prove that the Tartars broke into the country on purpose, as they must have obtained, through their military intelligence, data and precise information about the country and its resources even before their first exploratory invasion in 1241.[3]

The people of Radna fled to the nearby hills, but the Mongols, sensing that a larger military force might be stationed in the hinterland, pretended to withdraw from the area. Thereupon the people of Radna returned to their homes to celebrate what had seemed to be an easy delivery from the Tartar threat, when the latter had returned and surprised them.[4] Kadan did not disturb the town, whose inhabitants had surrendered to him, but ordered that the town mayor, Ariskald,[5] join him with six hundred men on horse, perhaps on the grounds that the khan needed knowledgeable guides for his next move into the open central Hungarian plain.[6] Kadan now led his forces through the towns of Beszterce and Kolozsvár, where he caused awful damage and killed everyone in sight.[7]

Bedsak [Büdzsik; Bochetor] Khan now entered Transylvania from the south.[8] Pozsa, the voyvoda of Transylvania (Pozsa was the son of Salom), attempted to engage him in a military encounter, but suffered defeat, and lost the greater portion of his forces.[9] Bedsak then moved in the direction of Küköllő, toward the Olt river; he occupied Küköllő, captured Nagyszeben on the same day that the engagement at Mohi had taken place, had burned Kercel abbey to the ground, and devastated Gyulafehérvár. By the end of April, he had penetrated the Hungarian plain (west of Transylvania), and took possession of the region south of the Maros and west of the Tisza rivers.[10]

About mid-April, Kadan Khan had also reached Nagyvárad, where he knew (perhaps from Ariskald from Radna) many refugees had gathered together.[11] Incredible as it may sound, the Tartar had, once again, surprised the town,[12] put it to flames, killed everyone, but refrained from attacking the fort with its wooden towers and wall protected by ditches. Kadan staged a sham withdrawal, assuming that the defenders of the fort would enter the blackened ruins of their devastated town. At early dawn on the following day, he attacked again, took the town, murdered everyone he could find, and had the cathedral burned to the ground with all the people who had sought refuge there.[13]

The forces commanded by Bedsak had devastated Csanád next;[14] Lanad Khan had joined him with his army units, and the two men moved north toward Pereg and Egres.[15] (The abbey of Egres near the Maros river was the burial place of King Andrew II.)[16] The population of some seventy villages had sought refuge at Pereg from the Mongol threat.[17] At Egres, many noble families had hoped for security, protection and survival behind the thick walls of the fortified Cistercian abbey.[18] They had "hoped" for protection; no planned defense of, or in, the realm had slowed down the Tartar threat.[19] Nobody had thought of the possibility of fighting with the Mongol forces, whose leaders, it seems quite evident, followed no definite plan in conquering the realm.[20]

Bedsak and Lanad at first ravaged the countryside around Pereg and Egres, then laid siege to Pereg. During the siege they sent, in the Mongols' military manner, the captured Hungarians first, followed by Russians, Ismaelites, Cumans - all of them fighting in the front lines. Were anyone of these unfortunate ones to turn about, they would be killed and laughed at for their lack of bravery.[21] After a week-long siege, the ditches around Egres were filled with bodies of the dead; with Egres taken the Tartars ordered the survivors of the siege to the meadow outside of what used to be the town. They made them undress, took all of their belongings, treasures, and killed them one by one with axes and sticks.[22] A similar fate had awaited Pereg. The walls of the fortified abbey were demolished by siege machinery, and the people inside surrendered out of fear and frustration (and lack of food and water supplies). With the exception of a few attractive women, the Mongols murdered them all.[23]

Peta Khan had entered the realm from the northwest, Moravia. He did not have an easy task, as his advance had been slowed down by many forts, fortified towns that blocked his route: Pozsony,[24] Nyitra,[25] Trencsén,[26] Komárom.[27] The khan avoided the fortified towns, though out of sheer anger and frustration, he totally devastated the surrounding countryside.[28] It was his strategy to invade the non-fortified settlements at early dawn, and murder in cold blood all inhabitants regardless of age or sex.[29] He made an exception with strong young men, whom he drafted into his armed forces to use them in the brutal frontal attacks at the next town or location.[30] The women he had raped on sight and then murdered. Even if he spared the lives of some very attractive women, they would fall prey to the jealousy of Tartar women, who would cut off the noses of the captured women and disfigure their faces with knives. The inhuman Tartar females placed sticks into the hands of their own children, telling them to beat every captured child to death - so the chronicler tells us.[31]

Only those who had fled in time to the woods or marshes had escaped this inhumane treatment and certain death. The Mongols had many of the escapees captured - they had to leave their hiding places to gather wood and food - but usually let them go free to inform the others that they could go home, that no harm would befall them. Therefore, the hungry "have-nots" abandoned their hiding places, returned to their villages, and resumed the daily lives.

Every village had to have a Tartar elected to serve as its mayor; the population went to till their fields, do late spring sowing and to gather the yields of their fields into barns. They had to please the Tartar mayor; the women brought him gifts. Life seemed to return to normal for several weeks; the Tartar mayors (khans) maintained law and order, even permitted the inhabitants to hold weekly markets to encourage small scale local market enterprises. After the gathering of the harvest from the fields and the holding of markets, however, the khans had all the male inhabitants gathered at one location near the village[s] and murdered them all. Next they had all of the women of the villages massacred. But they did not destroy the houses of the villagers, nor the supplies gathered in the barns, as the fall season had come and the conquerors needed food and lodging for the winter.[32]

After Mohi, King Béla IV had carefully, and very slowly, traveled toward Gömör county and reached Nyitra, where they had placed a bodyguard at his disposal, with whom he arrived in Pozsony at the realm's western border.[33] In the afternoon of day he arrived there, Duke Frederick Babenberg of Austria paid him a visit from across the border and invited him to enter his territories west of the Morava river, where he would find some luxury and personal security.[34]

Duke Babenberg, however, was not an honest person.[35] Back on his home ground, it was his first business of the day (rather, of the afternoon) to demand re-payment of the sum he had to render Andrew II (and to Béla IV, at the time still a prince).[36] The king, painfully surprised at this turn of events and totally out of money, could not meet the demand, so the Duke had confiscated Béla's gold reserves as security for the amount he had demanded from him.[37] He had also forced Béla to hand over to him Moson and Sopron counties, together with the district of Locsmánd; he had further demanded the transfer of (the fort and town of) Győr,[38] though the Hungarian garrison at Győr had set fire to the fort to thereby prevent an Austrian takeover.

Frederick had made other demands. He humiliated the king by making him sign an agreement of transfer the aforementioned areas; Béla IV, being at the mercy of the duke, was in no position to resist, and signed the document.[39] It was correctly indeed, though with strong irony, that the chronicler of the *Herimanni Altahensis Annales* recorded, *anno 1241*, that after three hundred and fifty years, Hungary had ceased to exist.[40]

Upon signing the agreement under pressure, Béla IV and his queen continued their travel toward Zagreb.[41] Totally moneyless, and without any financial reserves, Béla had to ask the abbot of Pannonhalma for a loan of eight hundred marks of silver.[42] It may be that the mention of Segesd by Rogerius was related to the crossing by the king of the Drave river toward Zagreb.[43] It was from Zagreb that the king had sent Bishop Stephen of Vác to Rome with a letter requesting aid,[44] and sent letters to Louis IX of France,[45] and to Emperor Frederick II, asking for their support.[46]

It was from Zagreb that, in May, 1241, he had dispatched, as his envoy, Stephen Banca to the papal curia. In the accompanying writ, the king greeted His Holiness in moving personal terms, requesting prayers and help. Since the Catholic faith took root on Hungarian soil through the special grace of God, Béla IV had written to the pontiff, his predecessors and his subjects always had, and since his succession to the throne, he had himself shown respect and devotion toward the Roman See, their Mother and Teacher - "ut pote matrem et magistram." Therefore, with filial affection and trust, he informs the Holy Father about the devastation that had been caused by the Mongol hordes, who had behaved like raving beasts in his country. Describing the condition of his realm, Béla IV requested that "through such support" the Christian world would be freed from the threat of total extinction. "Exurgat igitur,...vestre sancitatis provisio in adiutorium populi Christiani, et nobis ac Regno Hungarie consilium et auxilium tribuat salutare,...ne, interveniente paulum mora,...inveniri nequeat, cui valeat subveniri."[47]

On the other hand, Béla IV in his letter to the German court had promised that, in return for military aid, he would submit himself and his realm in feudal vassalage to the emperor.[48] Bishop Banca, following instructions, had further asked the Emperor to cease his anti-papal campaign, and make a military move against the Mongols instead. Frederick II was pleased to make use of the occasion; he had authorized the bishop of Vác (another envoy of Béla IV) to inform Rome that he would seriously consider such a proposal.[49]

In his answer to the monarch, the pontiff wrote that he had shed tears over Hungary,[50] and proclaimed a crusade to free the country from the Tartars.[51] It is known, though, from another source, that the pope was, by that time, most concerned about the personal safety of the prelates who had been invited to attend the synod at Lyons (summoned to meet in 1245).[52] The German emperor had those prelates persecuted who had planned to attend the synod.[53] Deeply troubled by ecclesiastical affairs, imperial politics, and the Mongol threat, Pope Gregory IX died in August, 1241.[54]

King Béla IV and his entourage now directed their travel from Zagreb to the Dalmatian seacoast.[55] Before that, while en route to Pannonhalma, the monarch gave orders to have the body of King St. Stephen transported, together with church treasures, from Székes-fehérvár to the seacoast, and placed under the care and protection of Spaleto.[56] The Queen, however, had little confidence in the people of Spaleto, wherefore the royal family moved to the Fort of Klissa, an island in the Adriatic. Numerous noble ladies, widows since Mohi, accompanied the Queen.[57]

Another disheartening irony of the king's situation was that Emperor Frederick II, who had earlier asked for the hand in marriage of (Saint) Elizabeth, Béla IV's younger sister,[58] - Elizabeth had firmly said no[59] - now had quietly ignored the Hungarian king's most difficult situation.[60] Undoubtedly, there was a tactical reason for that; Béla IV had irresponsibly neglected the country's military defenses.[61] Béla IV's position became even more difficult because of the death of his younger brother, Coloman,[62] who had fled to and died at Segesd.[63]

Leaving his family behind ("at a small court") on the island of Klissa, Béla IV now turned his attention to the defense of the realm; he hurried to the Segesd-Drave region to make preparations,[64] and await foreign help that had not arrived.[65] On account of the confrontation with the imperial court, Rome was in no position to assure international and moral support for Béla IV, nor did the Roman See possess the financial means to aid the king. Béla IV had even asked for papal intervention with the Venetian republic on his behalf for the sake of arms to wage war against the Mongols.[66]

One has to remember, on the other hand, that the papal throne remained vacant for one year and a half; therefore, it was not possible to obtain confirmation from the Holy See of the elected successors in the Hungarian hierarchy of those who had fallen at Mohi.[67] Nicholas Szügyi, the Hungarian envoy now sent to Rome,[68] had to await the outcome of the papal election in order to request from the new pontiff (Innocent IV, who had ascended the papal throne on June 25, 1243),[69] confirmation of the new archbishops of Esztergom and Kalocsa.[70] At the same time, the pope was willing to absolve the king of Norway from his vow to go on a crusade to the Holy Land were the king to spend the money he intended to use for his crusade on military aid for Hungary.[71]

Béla IV must have felt bitter indeed when he received a letter from the emperor *instructing* him to join the imperial armed forces, and, in return, Conrad, Frederick II's son, would defend him from the Tartar enemy.[72] (It ought to be pointed out, however, that Conrad had called for a crusade against the Mongols to gather at Nuremberg by July 1, 1243, but because of the lack of popular enthusiasm among the German population, the crusade did not take place.)[73]

The behavior of the emperor was rather unique, but Frederick II had not always followed coherent policies and, once again, behaved erratically. In his writ addressed to the English king, so Matthew of Paris informs us, Frederick II struck a different, although familiar, tone: he was perturbed by the demise of the Hungarians, was concerned about the future of Christianity - but blamed the Roman pontiff for every evil that had befallen mankind. Were Rome to live in peace - that is, were the Holy See to tolerate the emperor's gaining full control of the Church (in the empire and in Italy), and of the entire Italian peninsula (in breach of a promise he made to Pope Honorius III by arguing that promises made to a pope remained valid only for his pontificate) - the emperor would concentrate all his forces on a war with the Asiatic Tartars.[74]

One has also to keep in mind the various news-recording approach and the historical-ethical attitudes of the contemporary chroniclers - as, for example, a Matthew of Paris, a Thomas of Spaleto; or the source material derived from German chroniclers of the period - even to attempt to explain the erratic attitude(s) of the emperor (and his court) regarding the Mongol invasions of the East European area. One may conclude that the emperor had wholly misjudged the military-political situation by failing to recognize the ultimate aim of the Mongol threat: before the Tartars would conquer and consolidate all of their conquests in western Europe into one establishment with their own, they had at first to reconnaissance the area(s).[75]

If Frederick II placed the blame for the declining continental situation upon the shoulders of the papacy, he acted irresponsibly. The devastation by the Tartars of Poland, always loyal to Rome, of Silesia, and of the Hungarian territories had only temporarily weakened the religious-political situation for the Roman see. If, on account of this, the emperor had hoped for the loosening of papal influence in the East Central European region, so that he could establish there a more political-military position for himself, he was, or his advisors were, deadly wrong.

Every day lost in this papal-imperial controversy only aided the Mongols and undermined future possibilities of assuming a hardened and more realistic stand toward the Mongols. Had the political-military events of the day not taken a truly drastic turn, and had the Tartars not evacuated - even if only temporarily - East Central Europe, the thoughtless behavior of Frederick II might have led to an earlier lasting Mongol rule by 1242.[76]

Paul, Judge of the King's Court, was in charge of the defense of Hungarian territory on the right-hand bank of the Danube.[77] Under his command the Danube became, until Christmas, when the great river froze, the water-line of resistance.[78] By mid-December, 1241, Paul's men were constantly breaking ice on the river, as to prevent the Tartar from crossing it, from a possible Tartar invasion across the frozen river; and, for several days, they were success-ful.[79] But Kadan Khan, commander of the Tartar forces on the left bank, now staged a sham withdrawal leaving horses and other animals behind. He played the old Tartar scheme, and the men of Paul fell for it. The Hungarians crossed the frozen river to get hold of the seemingly abandoned chattel, when the Tartars suddenly reappeared, crossed the frozen river, and began to invade Trans-danubia (that is, Pannonia) in early February, 1242.[80]

There was no available organized resistance. The Tartars at first attacked Buda - more probably, the chronicler meant Ó-Buda, that is, Acquincum - burned it to the ground, and massacred all inhabitants. Then, they moved toward Esztergom.[81] (Rogerius reported that Kadan Khan had divided his forces; with the larger (main) force, he moved toward the southwest in order to capture the king in Slavonia, that is, the Drave-Save region.[82] The monarch, however, had escaped him.)[83]

Kadan had plans to destroy Esztergom quickly. The town was filled with refugees; it was protected by ditches and defense-dikes, wooden towers and palisades. Kadan placed some thirty pieces of siege machinery in position, and ordered all prisoners (of war) to build, out of reed and dirt, a wall higher than the town's defenses. From the siege machines set up behind this reed and dirt wall, he maintained a constant, by day and by night, barrage of stones upon the town's fortifications and defenders.[84] The khan had the defense ditches filled with dirt brought in in sacks, whereupon the Hungarian, German, French, and Italian burghers of Esztergom set their suburb on fire. They withdrew to the town proper. Before their withdrawal, they destroyed their property and buried their treasures - as it turned out, in vain. The Tartars took the town and murdered everyone.[85]

Three hundred well-dressed noblewomen had asked to be taken into the presence of the khan; they wished to beg him for mercy, but the khan had no change of heart. The women were robbed of their jewelry, and every one of them had her head cut off. The khan knew no mercy, was the chronicler's comment.[86] But the Fort of Esztergom the khan could not take; it was defended by Reeve Stephen (of Spanish descent) and by his archers.[87] Kadan had little choice but to move away, in the direction of Székesfehérvár.[88] Out of sheer anger and frustration he devastated the region around Esztergom, northern Pannonia,[89] and invaded Austrian territory as far as the walls of Vienna.[90] Frederick Babenberg of Austria thereupon made a counterattack, occupied Győr - the surrender of which he had earlier demanded from Béla IV[91] - but the Austrian duke only made the inhabitants of the fort-town angry. They fought with him, retook their town from him, and put its fort to flames; the Austrian garrison perished in the fire.[92]

A meeting of the delegates of various cathedral chapters and religious orders was held in Fehérvár at the end of January, 1242. They decided to send the archdean of Fehérvár to Rome with a letter from Archabbot Uriás (Oros) of Pannonhalma. The letter described the fate of the refugees at the fortified monastery of Tihany, in Zala county, and at the archabbey of Pannonhalma, and raised the argument that the Mongols could not conquer the well-fortified and rationally defended places in their country.[93] It is known from another source that the Tartars did not capture the fort of Esztergom, nor of Székesfehérvár.[94] The Tartars could not even approach Székesfehérvár because the area surrounding it was under flood waters.[95] Nor could the Tartars take Pannonhalma.[96]

Kadan Khan now moved along the Croatian military highway in the direction of Dalmatia, because he wanted to catch and take prisoner the Hungarian king.[97] It is known that Béla IV had plans to move close to the seacoast and, if need be, seek refuge in a coastal town or on the open sea.[98] Béla IV went to Spaleto, where (numerous refugees had already taken up residence,[99] but) they still received him with due respect: "dantes ei hospicis infra muros, quotquot voluit."[100]

The monarch was accompanied by Bishop Stephen of Zagreb, Stephen, bishop of Vác (who became the archbishop of Esztergom), Benedict, archdean of Székesfehérvár and royal chancellor, and elected archbishop of Kalocsa,[101] Bishop Bartholomew of Pécs, and other high clergymen.[102] But the king could obtain no sea galley from Spaleto,[103] and he had to seek refuge on the more secure island of Trau.[104] In order to express his appreciation to the town and citizens of Trau, Béla IV had reconfirmed their liberties.[105]

The khan had tried to close in on the king; everywhere he had followed the monarch's footsteps, shadowed his movements.[106] He also had murdered all of the Hungarian prisoners he had taken in the Gozd Hills.[107] But he did not besiege Spaleto; evidently, not supplying the Hungarian monarch with a sea galley had paid off politically, though one wonders whether the Spaleto town council had reached a previous agreement with the Mongol khan. Frustrated and outmaneuvered, Kadan Khan turned toward the island of Klissa.[108]

The Mongols pitted their siege machinery against the walls of the fort - causing no damage. They had made an attack on the fort itself, but the defenders had resisted with a hail of stones. As soon as he had found out that the king was not in Klissa, Kadan Khan halted the futile siege of the eagle nest,[109] and moved toward Trau island.[110]

Kadan sent messages in Croatian to the defenders and inhabitants of Trau, ordering them to hand over to him the Hungarian monarch. But, obeying the orders of their king,[111] nobody answered the khan's demand.[112] King Béla IV now had his Queen and other family members placed on a ship, and sent them out to sea.[113] He boarded a larger vessel himself to survey further developments on shore.[114] He was surprised to observe that the Mongols had, once again, disappeared from sight as quickly as they had arrived.[115] The king suspected a ploy, but, at this time, the news had turned out to be correct.[116]

What had happened was that Head-Khan Ogotai of all Mongols had died (already) in December, 1241,[117] but news of his death only arrived at Batu Khan's headquarters months later.[118] Batu decided to go back home, in order to participate in the election of the head-khan (hoping that he himself would be elected), and had ordered the withdrawal of all (of his) forces from the occupied areas.[119]

Nothing could prove more the self-confidence of the Mongols and their utter contempt for the military commanders in western Europe but the fact that they were convinced that they could afford to temporarily evacuate the east European territories they had occupied so easily, because they could just as easily reconquer them later at any given time! This point of view is supported by the remark made by Matthew of Paris, who wrote that it was common knowledge in his time that the German emperor had established direct diplomatic contacts with the Tartars on account of the confrontation the emperor had with the papacy. Consequently, the Mongols did have "inside" contacts in the Christian, west-European camp, and they could, at will, start anew, or simply continue with their "recovery" of the abandoned areas at any time of their choosing.[120]

NOTES

1. The reign of terror - *MGHSS*, XXIX, 591,13-15.
2. *Ibid.*, XXIX, 590,15-16.
3. *SSH*, II, 576,25-27; *ibid.*, II, 564,6-10; "Continuatio Sancrucensis II," *MGHSS*, IX, 640,14-18; Pauler, II, 516.
4. *SSH*, II, 564,10-20; later, the chronicler spelled the name of Ariscaldus as Aristaldus - II, 576,26.
5. "...comitem vile;" *ibid.*, II, 564,21.
6. *Ibid.*, II, 564,21-23.
7. *MGHSS*, XXIX, 590,15-17.
8. In the text stands "Bochetor;" *ibid.*, II, 564,23. *Büdzsik* can also be spelled Bedsak.
9. Cf. "Annales Frisacenses," *MGHSS*, XXIV, 65,42-43; Pauler, II, 561.
10. Hermannstadt fell on Thursday after Low Sunday, "feria quinta ante Misericordiam;" *MGHSS*, XXIV, 65,37-38. "Terra quae VII Castre dicitur totaliter vastata et disrupta est," reads a thirteenth century annotation on a codex that carries twelfth century data; cf. W. Wattenbach, "Ein Fragment über die Tartaren," *Archiv für österreichische Geschichte*, 42 (1870), 519ff., esp. 520f.; see further *Monumenta Erphesfurtensia saec. XII, XIII, XIV*, ed. O. Holder-Egger, SSrG (Hannover-Leipzig, 1899), 107 and 237; "Annales Erphordenses," anno 1242, *MGHSS*, XVI, 34,18-20. See further *MGHSS*, XXIX, 599,13; and *ibid.*, XXIV, 65, note 35.
11. *SSH*, II, 576,25-32, and II, 568,18-23.
12. *Ibid.*, II, 576,32 - 577,3.
13. *Ibid.*, II, 568,24 - 569,14; Bishop Benedict escaped and fled to Transdanubia - *ibid.*, II, 569,14-16. Bunyitay, I, 102.
14. *SSH*, II, 564,23-26.
15. *Ibid.*, II, 582,13-17; the text reads Perg.
16. Cf. Chronicle, c. 175, *ibid.*, I, 466,22-23; *MGHSS*, XXIX, 937,34-35, reads "Várad."
17. *SSH*, II, 582,15.
18. "...receperant;" *ibid.*, II, 582,16-17.
19. "Quid enim faceret populus sine principe?" - cf. "Gesta Treverorum, Cont. IV," *MGHSS*, XXIV, 404,18.
20. "Nec Tartari loca aggredi voluerunt, quousque circumcira esset terra totaliter desolata;" *SSH*, II, 582,17-19, and compare to *MGHSS*, XXIX, 599,13, as cited above, n. 10. The Woyvoda (Head Steward) of Transylvania must have been Pózsa; he held the title in 1240 - cf. *CD*, IV-3, 552f.
21. *SSH*, II, 582,21-29; on the destruction of Transylvania, see *CD*, IV-2, 147f.
22. *SSH*, II, 582,29 - 583,5; "Annales Erphordenses," *MGHSS*, XVI, 34,18-20; *CD*, V-1, 205; VII-3, 33f.
23. *SSH*, II, 583,5-11.
24. *Ibid.*, II, 563,9 and II, 564,2-6; *MGHSS*, XXIX, 599,14-17.
25. *CD*, IV-2, 456.
26. *ÁUO*, VII 135 (anno 1243), re-confirmed by Stephen V in 1272, *CD*, IV-1, 295; *CD*, IV-1, 343f, or *ÁUO*, VII, 174f.
27. *CD*, VII-3, 26.
28. The countryside surrounding Pozsony remained devastated into the late 1280's - *ÁUO*, IV, 288f. Strakosch-Grossman, 57f. and 558, n. 3.
29. *MGHSS*, XXIX, 589,2-4.
30. *Ibid.*, XXIX, 591,24-26.
31. *Ibid.*, XXIX, 588,43 - 589,2.

32. *SSH*, II, 580f.; Matthew of Paris, IV, 109ff. and 112ff. (also *CD*, IV-1, 220ff.); Matthew of Paris, IV, 210ff.; further, "Epistola Pontii de Aubon," *MGHSS*, XXVI, 604 and 605.

33. "...in confinio Austrie;" *SSH*, II, 574,30-31; II, 562,7-9, that is, where he had already sent the Queen; he fled toward Pest, Knauz, I, 346, and was accompanied by a citizen of Pozsony - *CD*, IV-1, 287ff.; *RA*, n. 744.

34. *SSH*, II, 575,1-3; Strakosch-Grossman, 102f.

35. "Dux Austrie hoc audito iniqua in corde concipiens contra eum sub nomine amicitie obvius sibi fuit;" *SSH*, II, 574,21-33.

36. *Ibid.*, II, 575,11-17; Pauler, II, 173f.; Hóman-Szekfü, I, 550.

37. *Ibid.*, II, 575,17-21.

38. *Ibid.*, II, 576,7-11, and compare with Böhmer, *Regesta*, V-1, n. 3211; see also *MGHSS*, XXIX, 638,17-24; IX, 637,48-49, and XVI, 330,33-36.

39. *SSH*, II, 575,23-30.

40. *MGHSS*, XVII, 394,1-2; IX, 508,2-3; IX, 558,41-43, etc.

41. The king's letter, addressed to the Roman pontiff, was issued from Zagreb, cf. *RA*, n. 706.

42. After he had freed himself from the duke of Austria, King Béla IV journeyed toward Lake Balaton: he had to borrow eight hundred silver marks from the abbot of the abbey of Pannonhalma - cf. Rogerius, c. 32; *CD*, IV-3, 117; P. Sörös, "Uriás pannonhalmi apát levelei a tatárjárás idejéből" [The Correspondence of Abbot Urias of Pannonhalma Abbey at the Time of the Mongol Invasion], *A pannonhalmi főapátsági Főiskola Évkönyve az 1916/17-i tanévre* [Annual of the College of the Archabbey of Pannonhalma for the Academic Year of 1916-17] (Pannonhalma, 1917), offprint.

43. *SSH*, II, 571, n. 4 and 575,29; Hóman-Szekfű, I, 551.

44. *RA*, n. 708 - based on an entry in Ricardus de s. Germano's "Chronicon," *MGHSS*, XIX, 380f., and compare to Matthew of Paris, IV, 112ff. On Ricardus de s. Germano, see Wattenbach, *Geschichtsquellen*, II, 334, and H. Herding, "Geschichtschreibung und Geschichtsdenken im Mittelalter," *Tübinger Theologische Zeitschrift*, 130 (1950), 129ff. Béla had requested help from Conrad, the German king-elect - *RA*, n. 707; *ÁUO*, II, 126f.

45. As it may be concluded from the answer of the French court addressed to the Hungarian monarch; cf. *CD*, IV-2, 220f.

46. *MGHSS*, XIX, 380,50-54; Böhmer, *Regesta*, V-1, 565f., n. 3210.

47. *RA*, n. 706; *VMH*, 335; *CD*, IV-1, 214ff.

48. In reference to *MGHSS*, XIX, 380f.; *RA*, n. 708; Rome will later declare this royal "submission" to be void - *VMH*, n. 369; *ÁUO*, I, 199.

49. *RA*, n. 706; Matthew of Paris, IV, 114; the writ by «F», a Hungarian abbot, about the Tartar devastation, *ibid.*, VI, 78ff.; for instructions given to the bishop of Vác, see Potthast. n. 11033; *VMH*, n. 338.

50. Potthast, nn. 10043 and 11034; *VMH*, nn. 342 and 337; Katona, *Historia critica*, V, 985f.

51. See the papal admonition to the bishop of Vác, Potthast, n. 11033; *VMH*, n. 338; *ÁUO*, VII, 123f. Rome also notified Coloman, king of Halich and Duke of Slavonia to the effect that those taking the cross against the Tartars will gain plenary indulgence - *ibid.*, VII, 121f. See further the papal writs to the king, and to the Hungarian bishops, Potthast, nn. 11034 and 11035; *VMH*, nn. 337 and 339.

52. Potthast, nn. 10988 and 10995; *VMH*, nn. 327 and 333; Matthew of Paris, IV, 120f.

53. Despite the fact that the synod had been summoned to deal with the Tartar threat, *ibid.*, I, 121ff., and 129f.; Potthast, n. 11015; Raynaldus, *Annales*, anno 1241, nn. 64-67. Compare to Rubruck, *ed. cit.*, i:1; Carpini, prologus, *ed. cit.*, 27f.; and Benedict the Pole, *ed. cit.*, i:1.

54. Matthew of Paris, IV, 574, commented on his death in less favorable terms: "fuit papa calculosus et valde senex, et caruit balneis, quibus solebat Viterbi confoveri"; on the other hand, Albericus spoke of him highly: "vir nobilis et religiosus et acutissime litteratus," *loc. cit.*, anno 1245; also, "Annales Senese," *MGHSS*, XIX, 230.

55. Conclusion drawn from the June 16, 1241 letter of the pope - see Potthast, n. 11032; *VMH*, n. 340.

56. *MGHSS*, XIX, 592,1-6.

57. *Ibid.*, XIX, 592,6-10; the siege of Pannonhalma must have taken place in the spring of 1242 - *SSH*, II, 585,30-33.

58. Ebendorfer, *ed. cit.*, 111,11-17. She was born of the first marriage of Andrew II - *SSH*, I, 466,16-18; Georgius Pray, *Vita s. Elizabethae viduae Landgravianae Thuringiae* (Tyrnaviae, 1780), 33ff.; *MGHSS*, XXV, 702,25-26. A. Huyskens, *Quellenstudien zur Geschichte der hl. Elisabeth, Landgräfin von Thuringien* (Marburg, 1911), 110ff.

58. Potthast, n. 9929, and I, 844; Muratori, *Scriptores*, III-1, 580; Püskely, 28; Antal Ijjas, *Szentek élete* [Lives of the Saints], 2 vols. (Budapest, 1976), II, 111ff.; Sándor Bálint, *Ünnepi Kalendárium* [A Calendar of Feasts], vol. II (Budapest, 1977), 475ff.; H. Fritzen, "Hl. Elisabeth von Ungarn," in Peter Manns (ed.), *Die Heiligen*, 3rd rev. ed. (Mainz, 1977), 400ff; Katona, *Historia critica*, V, 723.

59. Böhmer, *Regesta*, V-1, n. 3211.

60. One is to remember that Frederick II had already in December, 1241, greeted Boleslav, the new duke of Silesia and Liegnitz, as the successor of the fallen Duke Henrik - *ibid.*, n. 3249! During the winter of 1240-41, Béla IV had surveyed in person the Carpathian defense line of the country, but had made no further preparations for the country's defense - as it was made clear by Rogerius, c. 16, *SSH*, II, 561f., who also looked upon the Mongol danger as the just punishment of God - *ibid.*, II, 551f.; *MGHSS*, XXIX, 585.

61. *SSH*, II, 571,15.

62. *MGHSS*, XXIX, 592,11-14. He was buried in Cesman next to the stream Carma (that empties into the Save river), east of Zagreb; the Tartars dug up his grave and spread his bones around - *ibid.*, XXIX, 592,14-16; also, *RA*, n. 712, issued "apud Chazma" on January 19, 1242.

63. *MGHSS*, XXIX, 592,6-7.

64. *SSH*, II, 575,28-30.

65. His envoy, Bishop Stephen of Vác, *ibid.*, II, 575,27-28, had not been successful, cf. *ÁUO*, VII, 126f.; Potthast, n. 11034; *VMH*, n. 337.

66. *RA*, n. 712; the 1413 transcript of this letter is in the Vatican archives - cf. M. Huillard-Bréholles, *Historia diplomatica Frederici secundi*, vol. VI-2 (Paris, 1861), 902. Béla IV must have assumed that the pope was still alive; Gregory IX's successor, Celestine IV, ruled only for sixteen days - Muratori, *RISS*, III-1, 593; H. Kühner, *Neues Papstlexikon*, Fischer Bücherei (Zurich, 1965), 72.

67. Rogerius, c. 30; Spaleto, *MGHSS*, XXIX, 587,33-41.

68. Knauz, I, 356.

69. *MGHSS*, XVII, 190,1-2; "Annales Placentenses," *ibid.*, XVIII, 486,39-42; Matthew of Paris, IV, 604.

70. To Esztergom, Potthast, n. 11095; *VMH*, n. 347; to Kalocsa, Potthast, n. 11091; *VMH*, n. 346; Péterffy, I, 68.

71. Potthast, n. 11106.

72. Böhmer, *Regesta*, V-1, n. 3211; Matthew of Paris, IV, 298.

73. Böhmer, *Regesta*, V-1, n. 3216; Matthew of Paris, IV, 112.

74. *Ibid.*, IV, 119ff.; compare to MGEpp., I, 714, 717, 721, and 723.

75. Emma Lederer, "A tatárjárás Magyarországon és nemzetközi összefüggései" [The Mongol invasion of Hungary from an International Point of

View], *Századok*, 86 (1952), 372ff.; indirectly, see J. Spörl, "Das mittelalterliche Geschichtsdenken als Forschungsaufgabe," *Historisches Jahrbuch*, 53 (1933), 281ff.; Ödön Schütz, "A mongol hódítás néhány problémájához" [Some Questions Concerning the Mongol Conquest], *Századok*, 93 (1959), 209ff.

76. Innocent IV to the Patriarch of Aquileia, Potthast, n. 11096; *VMH*, n. 348; Hóman-Szekfü, I, 550ff.; for a different outlook, see Gebhardt, *Handbuch*, I 377f.

77. *SSH*, II, 583, note 3;Judge Paul appeared on a royal writ issued September 23, 1241, *RA*, n. 709.

78. *SSH*, II, 583,23-25; on the Christmas date, see *MGHSS*, XXIX, 565, note 1, based upon a writ, dated January 4, 1242 - *ibid.*, XXVIII, 209 (also, *CD*, IV-2, 222f.); Thomas of Spaleto spoke of a January 1242 date - *MGHSS*, XXIX, 592,18-19.

79. *SSH*, II, 583,25-27.

80. *Ibid.*, II, 53,30 -584,5, and compare to *MGHSS*, XXIX, 592,19-20.

81. *Ibid.*, XXIX, 592,2-34.

82. *SSH*, II, 584,5-7; indeed, the royal writ was issued at Chazma - *RA*, n. 712, reissued, *RA*, n. 944.

83. *SSH*, II, 584,7-8; on March 10, 1241, he had a writ issued near Trau (on the seashore), *RA*, n. 713; *CD*, IV-1, 268.

84. *MGHSS*, XXIX, 592,21-24; Hóman, *Ungarisches Mittelalter*, II, 151ff.

85. *SSH*, II, 584,14-21, though, it may seem that the defenders had, before the attack, become overconfident: "sed tanta eorum superbia, quod credebant se resistere posse toti mundo," wrote Rogerius, *SSH*, II, 584,20-21.

86. *Ibid.*, II, 585,20-26.

87. *Ibid.*, II, 585,26-28. "...cum multis balistariis...se viriliter defendebant;" cf. Carpini, vii:10, or "balistas, quam multum timent," *ibid.*, viii:7.

88. *SSH*, II, 585,28-29; Rogerius' remark on the melting snow, "in dissolutione nivis et claciei," *ibid.*, II, 585,30, may imply that the intrusion took place in February, not in December; *MGHSS*, XXIX, 592,24-25.

89. *SSH*, II, 585,33 -586,3.

90. *Ibid.*, II, 576,4-6, and 586,12-13; *MGHSS*, XXIX, 592,23-24.

91. *SSH*, II, 576,3-8.

92. *Ibid.*, II, 576,8-11.

93. *ÁUO*, II, 157f.; Pope Gregory IX to the Archpriest of Fehérvár, "B. Preposito ecclesiae Albensis, Vesprimiensis diocesis," Potthast, n. 11036; *VMH*, n. 341, for the reason that the archpriest was also the royal chancellor, *MGHSS*, XXIX, 592,41 and *RA*, nn. 709, 711, etc.; J. Deér, *Die hl. Krone Ungarns* (Vienna, 1966), 207f.; and Kosztolnyik, *From Coloman*, 249f., and 263, n. 226.

94. Towns like Esztergom, Fehérvár, and the abbey of Pannonhalma, "quod ista tria local tantum inexpugnata," the Mongols could not conquer; *SSH*, II, 585,32-33.

95. *Ibid.*, II, 585,28-30; *MGHSS*, XXIX, 592,24-28.

96. *SSH*, II, 585,30-32.

97. *Ibid.*, II, 584,5-7; *MGHSS*, XXIX, 592,28-30.

98. *Ibid.*, XXIX, 592,31-34.

99. *Ibid.* XXIX, 592,35-36.

100. *Ibid.*, XXIX, 592,37-39.

101. *RA*, nn. 709 and 711.

102. *MGHSS*, XXIX, 592,39-42.

103. *Ibid.*, XXIX, 593,5-6.

104. *Ibid.*, XXIX, 593,7-10; *SSH*, II, 584,7-10.

105. See *RA*, n. 715 (dated March 18, 1242); *CD*, IV-1, 246ff.; a briefer version, dated 1245, in *ÁUO*, VII, 188ff. Further, cf. *RA*, n. 716, on the conclusion of which, see *MGHSS*, XXIX 593, note 1.

106. *Ibid.*, XXIX, 593,12-18.

107. *Ibid.*, XXIX, 593,18-25, "ad quandam aquam" (593,19), though not the Save river, but one of the smaller creeks flowing into it.
108. *Ibid.*, XXIX, 594,10-11.
109. *Ibid.*, XXIX, 594,12-18.
110. *Ibid.*, XXIX, 594,18-26.
111. *Ibid.*, XXIX, 594,39; "mandaverat enim rex, ut nullum eis redderent verbum."
112. *Ibid.*, XXIX, 594,34-38.
113. *Ibid.*, XXIX, 594,26-28.
114. *Ibid.*, XXIX, 594,28-30.
115. *Ibid.*, XXIX, 594,38-39.
116. *Ibid.*, XXIX, 595,6-7; Ödön Schütz, *art. cit.*, 209ff., esp. 222; it formed the part of Mongol strategy to capture the ruling monarch of the region that had been invaded.
117. See Howorth, I, 158, and compare with Plano Carpini's views, as, e.g., v:6, viii:5, and ix:28; Carpini mentioned the death of Ogotai Khan as the reason for their sudden withdrawal. Ödön Schütz, *art. cit.*, 230f.
118. Spuler, *art. cit.*, 15, notes 1 and 2; idem, *Die Goldene Horde: die Mongolen im Russland, 1223-1502* (Wiesbaden, 1965). Hóman, *Ungarisches Mittelalter*, II, 105ff.; Schütz, *art. cit.*, 221ff.
119. Benedict the Pole, 3, *ed. cit.*, p. xlviii; William of Rubruck, *Itinerarium*, xxvii:9 and i:12. Thomas of Spaleto only remarked that the Mongols were forced to withdraw, and left the way they came, "tunc universa multitudo eorum inde consurgens, via, qua venerant, reversa recessit;" *MGHSS*, XXIX, 594,38-39. Schütz, *art. cit.*, 230f.
120. Matthew of Paris, IV, 119, and VI, 635, who also reported that no Hungarian bishop had arrived at the Synod of Lyons, 1245: "de Hungaria...per Tartararum vastata, nulli...;" *ibid.*, IV, 430. Lederer, *art. cit.*, 327ff.

CHAPTER SIX

THE AFTERMATH: THE 1240's

1. *Béla IV Cries to the Roman Pontiff for Help*

> "Danubius enim est aqua contradictionis."
>
> *Béla IV to Pope Innocent IV*

In his letter, addressed to Pope Innocent IV,[1] and dated November 11, the 1240's,[2] Béla IV complained to His Holiness that were the Mongols to invade his country again, this time for real, his people would not resist, but would submit to them. He asked for help in vain. He received only sympathy and words of encouragement from Rome, and the powerful rulers of the west were too pre-occupied with their own affairs. He looked upon His Holiness as the Vicar of Christ and final refuge for the Christian cause in times of dire need. And yet, although he had done everything possible for the defense of his country, he received no aid from the Holy See, nor from the German emperor, and none from the king of France.[3] He had to warn His Holiness that the defense of Hungary equaled the defense of Christian Europe. It was in the interest of his own people, and of all Christendom, that he had humbled his royal dignity in marrying two of his daughters to Ruthenian princes, and a daughter to the Polish duke, that through his son-in-laws he strengthen the diplomatic and military interests of the realm against the Tartars.[4]

He had recalled the heathen Cumans to his country - let pagan fight pagan for the Christians' sake[5] - in order to build up his country's defenses. But in order to gain the confidence of the repatriated Cumans, he had to order Stephen, his son and heir to the throne, to marry the daughter of the Cuman leader.[6] (What the king did not mention in this writ to Rome was that although he needed Cuman military knowledge and strength to fight the Mongols, he needed them even more for establishing a loyal "royal bodyguard" to enable him to negotiate effectively with his so bitterly disillusioned and disheartened nobles.) In addition, he had to take the Knights of Saint John of the Hospital in his service for the defense of his country and of the true faith. Through the efforts of the Knights, Christianity would be spread to the Sea of Constantinople, though before that accomplishment, Béla IV knew that he would have to assign them to man the fortifications along the Danube because his people knew little about fort defense. It was in the interest of all Europe that he had fortified the right bank of the Danube on the grounds that the river had become the line of military resistance: "quod esset salubrius nobis et toti Europae, ut Danubius fertaliciis muniretur. Hec enim est aqua contradictionis."[7]

The river was the "line of military defense" of European Christianity. There, Béla IV's ill-prepared forces that had suffered a tremendous defeat had, in the fall-early winter of 1241-42, opposed the Tartars for ten months - in spite of the lack of a system of fortifications and trained personnel to man them. Were the Mongols to occupy the mid-Danubian region and take possession of Hungary, all of western Europe would be accessible to them. The Huns of Attila had also moved in from the east to the west, and struck their camps on Hungarian soil - unlike the Romans, who had invaded from the west and positioned segments of their military forces within the borders of [historic] Hungary.[8]

Why does His Holiness tolerate the undisciplined behavior of the French court? Béla IV cried to the pontiff that the loss of Byzantium itself, and of the territories beyond the sea, would not cause the damage to Europe that the surrender of the Hungarian lands would.[9] Rome should send meaningful military aid; if not, the king would be forced, out of sheer necessity, to turn elsewhere for protection. Were he, in case of a renewed Mongol invasion, to receive no support from Christian Europe, he would have no alternative but to seek an agreement with the Tartars, beseeching their mercy - thereby to accept the offer the khan had previously extended to him.[10]

The question remains, of course, how greatly had the realm been devastated during the Tartar onslaught between April, 1241, and the spring of 1242? Rogerius reported that during the eight days he and his companion traveled to Fehérvár, they did not meet, nor did they see, a single living person en route. Food they had none, they lived on roots and regarded garlic and onions a luxury.[11] And yet, shortly after the retreat of the Mongols from Hungary, Béla IV was able to muster a strong military force against his neighbors.[12]

News of the death of Great Khan Ogotai, who died in mid-December, 1241, reached the Tartar field commanders conducting military operations in Hungary, in February, 1242.[13] One of the Tartar armies was at that time besieging the abbey of Pannonhalma - Abbot Uriás had repelled the attack - when the army (or army unit) was unexpectedly withdrawn, ending the siege.[14] Kadan Khan had also been notified; he, too, withdrew his men from actual military operations. But the Mongol commanders had displayed foresight in staging their pullback over areas that had been spared previous destruction; their armies had to sustain themselves with food and supplies during their retreat.[15]

Why did the Mongols depart so suddenly? Ogotai Khan had been known for being a heavy drinker, a sick man; his death must have altered Batu Khan's chance of succession.[16] But Batu had misunderstandings with both Kujuk, the son of Ogotai Khan, and Buri, Ogotai's grandson. Ogotai and Chagatai Khans did not sympathize with the father of Batu. Kujuk Khan became the heir of Ogotai.[17] He had planned to invade the west, but he died in 1252.[18]

The principle of the issue is that the onslaught caused by Batu Khan in 1241, and the ten month long devastation of the country had formed a part of a premeditated "pre-attack." This served as an intelligence gathering, reconnaissance mission aimed to give the Tartar high command information for the planned invasion that, evidently, had been carefully prepared by Kujuk Khan. Based on Plano Carpini's report, one may argue that, in accordance with Mongol military tactics, a "previous" invasion of a region had served as a preparatory reconnaissance undertaking, during which the Tartars did not steal, nor did they kill animals, but were inclined to cause great havoc and suffering among humans: "tantum homines vulnerant et mortificent."[19] The ruler of the invaded region they had sought to capture alive, or to kill if necessary, on the grounds that without taking the monarch prisoner, or murdering him, the conquest of the defeated population of the area would not have been complete.[20]

The Mongols probably had realized the importance of fortifications, but placed little emphasis on besieging them - as yet.[21] On the other hand, they had destroyed everything on the plains; "solebant esse magnae villae pro maiori parte omnes erant destructas" - in order "ut pascerent ibi Tartari" - they have ample pasture land available for their animals.[22]

One of the Mongol divisions that had invaded the country had been withdrawn in the direction of Halich.[23] What an irony of fate, in that it was the ruler of Halich who had pointed out to the Mongols, to Batu himself, the advantages of invading Hungary. At that time, Hungary's political leadership was divided, king and nobles were fighting each other; a campaign against them could easily lead to victory over the king's forces.[24]

A second Mongol division was leaving the country toward the east; wagons loaded with prey and herds of cattle and sheep were driven out of the country by the departing Tartars. They had searched every cave in the thick forests for more prisoners and spoil.[25]

Other Mongol troops moved along the northern and eastern parts of Transylvania; some departed through the central section of the country in a north to south direction, toward the Tölcsváry Pass in the southern Carpathian Mountains, destroying everything in sight, except the few forts and fortified towns they had encountered but did not conquer.[26] Batu Khan headed toward Bulgaria along the Danube (where Asen II had died a year earlier; he was succeeded by his ten year old son, Coloman, a nephew of Béla IV, as king.)[27]

Kadan Khan also withdrew his army. From the seashore toward Bosnia he went, invaded Serbian territory and Primorje, put the town and harbor of Cattaro to the torch, and destroyed the town of Drivasto. Then he crossed over Serbia from east to west, from north to south, and entered Bulgaria, in order to unite his forces with the army of Batu Khan.[28]

The Mongols had dealt with their captives, prisoners of war, in a most inhumane manner, and the captives had concluded from their treatment worsening every day that they would soon be massacred - as they were in due time. Plano Carpini made the observation about the burial places of the killed prisoners of war that they were, day after day, given less and less food to eat, and were finally killed.[29]

William of Rubruck mentioned it in his report on his mission to the court of the Great Khan of the Mongols that he had, in his journey, come across Hungarian priests administering to the needs of Hungarian slaves along the Volga river, and to German-speaking miners (from Transylvania?), who had been taken there and settled by Buri Khan in the town of Talas, west of Lake Balkas.[30]

In Hungary there was hunger. Sowing was impossible, and there was nothing to harvest. Starvation and the Tartars had caused total destruction, the sources report.[31] Law and order had disappeared. Although Michael, son of Varasd, maintained public order in the region "Beyond the Drave," and undertook strong measures against thieves and robbers, the realm at large remained in a state of lawless confusion.[32]

After the departure of the Mongols, Béla IV visited Kl(ar)issa again, accompanied by Stephko and Gregor of Brebir.[33] There, the monarch had confirmed the sons of *Comes* Stephen, *Comes* Stephko and Jákó, further the sons of *Comes* Bribina, Gregory and Daniel; furthermore, Béla IV had confirmed Obrád and his *nepotes* (nephews?), the sons of *Comes* Budyzlaus, nobleman of Brebir, for their loyal services rendered to him during the Mongol invasion.[34] The king had also recognized the counts of Veglia (the forefathers of the Zrinyi and Frangepán families) in their possessions; there, the sons of Guido and Veglia had petitioned the king to confirm them in the privileges that their father had obtained from Andrew II in the year 1223. The grant by Andrew II had survived only in a dubious transcript, but the king had confirmed it.[35]

Béla IV acknowledged that the counts of Veglia take possession of Modrus and Vinodol (in that they received thirty percent of the income of Modrus county); were the monarch to visit Croatia, one of the Veglias was to serve him, armed and equipped at his own expense. The counts were to provide the king with two galleys for the defense of the seashore, and to place three trained knights at the king's service for domestic duty; were he to go abroad, only two fully equipped knights were to serve him.[36] It is a matter of record that the counts of Veglia lived up to their agreement.[37] Béla IV had confirmed the liberties of the city of Trau,[38] and recognized the Subichok[s] family in its possession of Brebir.[39]

All of this had served the defenses of the country well. In the early 1260's, Lőrinc (Lawrence), royal Chief-cupbearer and Reeve of Sopron, was awarded the whole county of Locsmánd (*comitatus Luchman*) by the king in recognition of services Lőrinc had performed for the Crown, and with the understanding that Lőrinc would maintain law and order in that county, and participate in the

defense of the realm.[40] The stewardship (of the county of) Sempte
the monarch had imposed upon Leopold, brother of Truslef, vesting
in him the highest office in that county, "comitatum de Semptey de
nostro beneplacito duximus conferendum," so that he keep law and
order and preserve it in readiness for the defense of the whole
country.[41] Béla IV had further concluded peace with Zara. He
donated land to them, and promised them money for the reconstruction of their fortifications along the seashore.[42] In early May, 1242,
the king returned to Hungarian territory.[43]

Awful conditions prevailed in the country. The population had
decreased on account of the Mongol invasion and hunger. The
growing number of wild animals, thieves and robbers only weakened
public security.[44] Paul the Justiciar awaited the responsibility for
restoring law and order. He had, indeed, captured robbers, and given
them a choice of mending their ways or facing execution; he had
gathered and resettled the scattered population of the countryside.[45]
Reconstruction had to begin.[46] In Transylvania, where they had to
reopen the salt mines, Lőrinc, the new woyvoda (head-reeve; head-
steward), restored law and order.[47]

In Transdanubia, on the right-hand bank of the Danube, Béla
IV had gathered forces to go to war against Duke Frederick of
Austria, who had invaded Pozsony and the Hungarian border region.
The duke encountered fierce resistance;[48] Kozma and Ehellős
(Achilles), the grandsons of Thomas of Huntpázmány, defended the
fort of Pozsony. Bleeding from fifteen wounds he received in the
struggle, Kozma was captured, but Ehellős was able to retain the
frontier region for the king.[49]

Ehellős now staged a counteroffensive on the left bank of the
river: he broke into Austrian territory and approached Vienna.
Thereupon the king began his offensive countermove by re-capturing
Kőszeg (where Herbord, son of Osl, had distinguished himself), and
placed Sopron under siege.[50] By acting so, he avoided a major
military confrontation with his opponent; Frederick withdrew his
forces beyond the Lajta stream, and surrendered to Béla IV the three
Hungarian districts he had earlier taken from him by force.[51]

The determined military readiness displayed by the monarch,
Ehellős's successful drive toward the gates of Vienna, the occupation
of Kőszeg, plus the fact that Duke Frederick had left the scene and
handed over the area he had earlier so easily captured - all point to

the conclusion that, despite the terrible devastation caused by the Mongols, starvation because of lack of food, and the breaking down of law and order in the realm, that the royal court was able to muster a military force that would fight to victory and defend the interests of the country.[52]

The country-wide fear that the Mongols would return perpetuated itself.[53] The central part of the country had been totally devastated and depopulated. The harvest of 1243 had been destroyed by locusts; draught had caused intolerable problems.[54] The royal court had to request monetary loans to assure its day-to-day operations from a merchant in Pozsony,[55] and from the abbey of Güssing in Austria;[56] a certain person named Maladik, from Halich, loaned gold to the king.[57]

The previously rich bishoprics of the country had to borrow money; even the archbishopric of Esztergom was unable to repay its debts ten years after the Mongol devastation.[58] Frequently, private lands and other holdings had to be sold to assure their owners' survival.[59]

The king had to secularize ecclesiastical wealth to obtain cash,[60] regardless of the fact that during the Mongol devastation many of the episcopal centers had suffered the heaviest of damages.[61] Church treasures were lost forever in Vác,[62] Eger,[63] Nagyvárad, where the town itself had suffered heavy damage,[64] and Kolozsmonostor.[65] Street fighting in Vác and in Esztergom had caused much of the destruction.[66] Grand old families had to sell their county-sized estates: the Csáks and the Pázmánys had suffered tremendous losses in such a manner.[67]

Reconstruction of the country had to begin; the declining population had to be increased. Béla IV announced a new immigration policy, though its results were, at first, negligible. Only the famine in 1259 would bring many German settlers to Hungary;[68] guest and foreign workers, men for military service, or simple peasants were to receive landholdings and other privileges.[69] For reasons of personal security, the Germans settled on the frontier, in the hill country, in heavily wooded areas.[70] Counties like Torna,[71] Kis-Hont acquired many new settlers.[72] The town of Kassa had gained its town-charter,[73] the Saxons in Eperjes obtained specific rights,[74] together with the inhabitants of Lőcse and Késmárk;[75] it was at this time that Besztercebánya became a town, and, somewhat later, the name of Árva castle appear in the official record.[76]

The court awaited the reappearance of the Tartars every year. William of Rubruck reported that even if the depopulated Hungarian realm could muster a military force of some thirty thousand men, it would be unable to defend itself.[77] But the Mongols stayed near the Hungarian border, without actually entering the land; inhabitants of territories that used to be under the administration of the Hungarian Crown now became the tax-paying subjects of the Tartar Khan.[78] Batu Khan remained in Kipchak, ruled the area between the Dnieper, the Urals, and the Jaik river. He resided in the Sarai (near modern Astrakhan), at the estuary of the Volga into the Caspian Sea. There he received visiting foreign princes seeking his protection, or the envoys of other nations, in the tent he had captured at Mohi, that had belonged to King Béla IV.[79]

The first concern of the king was the defense of his country. In view of the fact that the Mongols did not capture fortifications at higher elevations, he had ordered the construction of new forts, and encouraged nobles to build them.[80] The agreement with Rembaldus, the *Praeceptor* of the Knights of Saint John concerning the building of fortifications and other provisions for the country's defenses[81] - constructing a fort at "Pest" (alias, on Buda Hill) after the withdrawal of the Mongols,[82] and reconstructing Fort Esztergom - all tied in with the royal objective.[83] The protection of the entire population and preservation of the country's national and economic interests were at stake.[84]

In Túróc county, Andrew, son of Ivánka, had Fort Znio constructed (where Béla IV had spent the winter of 1242-43, far away from the Great Hungarian Plain that, by that time, had turned into a complete wilderness).[85] Out of her dowry, Queen Maria had Fort Visegrád erected;[86] the abbot of Pannonhalma had Fort Szigliget (Sziget) built on Lake Balaton.[87] A new defense tower was constructed at Fort Pozsony, in whose construction Lék and Péter, two castle *iobagiones* (service nobles of the fort garrison), played a role; they were, in turn, rewarded by the king with landholdings at Nyék.[88] The abbot of Pilis Abbey had the water tower constructed at the foot of Castle Hill (in Fort Pozsony).[89]

In 1242, Béla IV laid the foundations for a chapter house for the Canons of the Zagreb cathedral chapter on Grech (Gréc) Hill, south of Zagreb; the fort on Grech Hill was built to observe and defend the region as far as the mouth of the Unna stream emptying into the Save. Béla IV provided the canons with additional territory, where they could take refuge, were the Mongols to invade again.[90]

The city of Zagreb had many Italians among its population; the Zagreb citizenry held the right to elect their judges freely, to have their own courts of law, and to appeal the decisions of their courts (judges) to the king. They possessed marketing rights, and were exempted from paying toll within the borders of the realm; they were free to dispose of their chattel and wealth even without heirs. Were they to suffer at the ands of robbers or thieves anywhere in the kingdom, the [regional land]lord was obligated to compensate them for the loss they might have suffered - probably as an indirect law and order guarantee by the royal court aimed at regional potentates.[91]

The citizens of Zagreb owed the monarch food and lodging when visiting their region, on the grounds that the Hungarian king was also the ruler of Slavonia (in this instance, Slavonia proper, the area between the Drave and Save rivers), and of the regions on the right-hand bank of the Save as far as the estuary of the Unna stream. They further owed payment of an ox, one hundred loaves of bread, and one hundred liters of wine at the inauguration of the newly appointed *ban* (*banus, bán*, Grand Reeve) of Slavonia.[92]

In 1247, the threat of a renewed Mongol invasion led to the construction of Fort Buda on the right bank of the Danube, on Buda Hill across from the town of Pest (on the left bank). In time of danger, the citizens of Pest would seek refuge in the [new] fort on Buda Hill. Pest was a free royal *villa*; Rogerius had referred to it as a large German village located *Bude opposita*.[93] Its charter had to be renewed by the king before October 15, 1244.[94] It was on the other side of the Danube that Béla IV had *Fort Pest* constructed on "New Pest Hill"[95] - thereby to distinguish the new fort from Óbuda (Old Buda; Acquincum - an ancient Roman settlement), also known by its German name as Etzelberg.[96]

The new fort and the growing settlement around it - consisting mostly of German settlers moving in from Pest - were soon to be recognized as the Town of Buda - *civitas Budensis*, a term used in the 1263 royal writ where the king extended the "liberties of Fort Buda" to the *hospites* (guest settlers of Füzitő monastery of the

Pannonhalma abbey.)[97] The [new] settlers in Buda came under the jurisdiction of the reeve of the fort, though they were allowed to retain their established privileges they had held as the inhabitants of Pest. They referred to their [new] settlement by a German name: Ofen.[98]

In September, 1239, the monarch had granted tax-exempt status everywhere in the country to the inhabitants of Esztergom;[99] he permitted them to build their own archiepiscopal town under the fort of Esztergom (*Arx*). He also donated to the archbishop of Esztergom lands with personnel in three counties.[100] Ten years later, Béla IV had the peoples of the Town of Esztergom repatriated to the fort because of the renewed threat of a Mongol invasion (of the entire country), and had bequeathed the royal palace in Esztergom to the archbishop.[101] By December, 1256, Béla IV had revoked his gift to the archbishop - probably on the grounds that the threat of a renewed Tartar attack had faded away. The citizens of Esztergom were once again free to rebuild their town.[102]

Béla IV had, presumably in 1249, the inhabitants of Székes-fehérvár transferred to the fort - "translationiem eorundem civium in dictum castrum Albense factam" - and had, at the same time, divided the landholdings between the archdean of the church in Székesfehérvár and the citizenry.[103]

Every town had to pay a determined amount of tax money and fulfill the quota of military draft; for example, a town had to place ten trained and well-equipped men in the king's military service when the monarch went to war in person.[104] Béla IV had further assumed a more tolerant attitude toward the nobility: he needed them for the country's defense and had richly endowed many of them with [new] landholdings.[105]

The king had donated, upon the request of his son Kálmán, the lands of Little John, son of George, to Dean Fila of the cathedral chapter of Zagreb, and his grant secured against any further claim by the relatives of the deceased.[106] Béla IV had confirmed the lands given by Dénes, Ban(us) of Slavonia, to Abraham *de genere* Bratila, and had erected forts to protect the realm and its inhabitants; he had established the new fort and town on Gréc Hill near Zagreb.[107] Guided by similar objectives, the monarch had reaffirmed the privileges of guest settlers at Szamobur at Fort Oclych - at the same time determining their due taxes.[108]

Two years later, Béla IV donated the land Ovwar to Reeve Mod and his son, and various *servientes* designated by name, ordering them to build a new fort at a location where, earlier, an old fort had stood.[109] Because of the aid they had rendered him during the Mongol threat, Béla IV further provided moral support, legal privileges, exemption from military draft, and commercial rights to the citizenry of Nyitra - privileges the inhabitants of Székesfehérvár already enjoyed.[110] In September, 1250, the king entrusted the Dean of Szepes with completing the construction of Fort Szepes on the Hernád stream, and obliged him to garrison it with fort personnel to be placed on active duty in case of another Mongol onslaught.[111]

The nobles formed the backbone of the nation's defense. Only after 1254 had the king cautiously reclaimed some of their lands, as he had pointed this out in his letter addressed to Pope Innocent IV.[112] He also recalled the Cumans for his service, partly to increase the fighting strength of the armed forces and partly in his own interest: with the Cuman force loyal to him, he could easily counterbalance the growing influence and arrogance of the nobles.[113]

The Cumans were given privileges and land in Bars county around Nyitra and Komárom, and in the Szitva region. The king permitted them to stay together in family (clan) groups, and to keep their pagan beliefs and way of life. Some of them misbehaved, clinging firmly to their ancient faith. But they eventually settled down in uninhabited areas of the country - uninhabited, that is, since the Mongol invasion - and caused little damage among the established population in the region. Alpra was their leader, who governed his people through clan heads, i.e., tribal chiefs.[114]

The Cumans formed a good fighting force. Since it was inadvisable to separate them and spread them all over the realm, the monarch wished to keep their loyalty by marrying Stephen, his son and heir to the throne, to Elizabeth, daughter of the Cuman leader, in 1254. Following Cuman custom, ten Cuman chiefs took their loyalty oath to the king at the wedding - over the body of a dog split in two, they promised to defend the king and the country.[115]

One may select, at random, some royal decrees from the Royal Register that deal with, or refer to, Stephen "Junior King" (since 1245; he was also Duke of Slavonia). For instance, the writ dated May 1, 1248, spoke of Reeve Osl's son, Reeve Herbord, who had earned merits during the Mongol onslaught by defending the king and his first-born, the illustrious king Stephen," "custodie karissimi primogeniti nostri Stephani regis illustris."[116] In a decree issued ten months later, a reference was made to Nicholas, reeve of Dubicha, the treasurer of Stephen Junior King.[117] Three weeks after that, Andrew, son of Ivánka, "Reeve of Royal Treasurers," had to be awarded for services he had performed for Stephen Junior King in the Fort of Turuch.[118]

The royal diploma dated July 28, 1258, carries the name of Benedict, court notary of Stephen Junior King, and of his brothers - "fratres Benedicti, Notarii aule karissimi filii nostri Regis Stephani."[119] This writ was related to a resolution issued by Stephen, Ban of Slavonia.[120] The royal diploma of 1260 dealing with the Tihany peninsula in Lake Balaton that had once belonged to Fort Zala, and now belonged to Stephen, was, with his knowledge and approval, handed over to the abbey of Pannonhalma.[121] These writs all imply that Stephen was, at a very young age, recognized as "Junior King," who, as Ban of Slavonia (and Prince of Transylvania), maintained his own court, and administered his own territories within the realm.

Béla IV attempted to expand his authority beyond the borders of his kingdom. When, for instance, Trau requested aid, the king commissioned Grand Steward Dionysius (Dénes) and Bishop Bertalan of Pécs to move to the seashore and restore law and order.[122] In 1243, the king dispatched an army to the aid of Zara. The city had its fort rebuilt, and its harbor closed off with a heavy chain, when some forty galleys of Venice, commanded by Renier Zeno, appeared before its walls. (Where were the defenders of the walls?) They strung strong ropes between the walls and the sea, thereby to thwart any attack on that part of the shore by the grand steward's cavalry unit. Dionysius was wounded in the skirmish; news quickly spread of his impending death, and Zara surrendered to Venice. The republic now gave orders for the destruction of one of the defense towers on the wall.[123]

The king, with sound diplomatic sense, concluded peace with Venice (on June 30, 1244), and had Zara surrendered officially to the republic - on condition that two-thirds of the toll collected at the city gates be handed over to the Hungarian court. In turn, the republic promised not to conclude an alliance with Beatrice d'Este, the widow of Andrew II, or with her son, Stephen, without previous consultation with the Hungarian court, nor to receive the ambassadors of Beatrice, or of her son. Béla IV promised to provide for the refugees from Zara, not permitting them to disturb Venice with their political plans in the future.[124]

The signed treaty and the policy toward Venice proved to be a success; even if Venice had retained Zara, on the grounds that the loss of Zara ended with a treaty with the republic on "equal terms," there was no victorious, nor defeated, party to the treaty.[125] Thereafter, the king was certain that no military threat would surprise him from the direction of the Dalmatian seashore at a time when he had be ready for a possible confrontation with the Mongols on the eastern border.[126] That was also the reason why he had acknowledged anew the ancient privileges of Trau.[127]

After diplomatically securing the hinterland, Béla IV enjoyed the support and cooperation of Trau. Aided by Trau, the grand steward easily secured the Hungarian control over Spaleto; he had burnt its suburbs to the grounds, and the town itself, now under Hungarian occupation, had to seek peace. Its citizens took another loyalty oath to Béla IV, and to his son and heir; they paid six hundred silver marks indemnity, and handed over six nobles in surety for preserving the peace. They even promised to elect a Hungarian noble as their count, and to surrender all the property Trau had claimed from their town. Ninoslav visited the court of Béla IV to acknowledge him as his king.[128]

THE AFTERMATH: THE 1240's

NOTES

1. See Toru Senga, "IV Béla külpolitikája és IV Ince pápához intézett 'Tatár' levele" [The Foreign Policy of Béla IV and his Writ Concerning the Tartars Addressed to Pope Innocent IV], *Századok*, 121 (1987), 584ff. Denis Sinor, *Introduction à l'étude de l'Eurasie centrale* (Wiesbaden, 1963), 314ff.; for a bibliography on Mongol history, *ibid.*, 294ff. On Canon Rogerius of Várad, who had escaped from his Tartar captors, cf. A. Turchányi, *Rogerius mester Siralmas Éneke a tatárjárásról* [Master Rogerius' "Carmen miserabile" about the Tartar Onslaught] (Budapest, 1903, 412ff. and 493ff.; Rogerius became archpriest in Sopron, then canon at the Győr cathedral chapter, *SSH*, II, 545ff.; *MGHSS*, XXIX, 547ff. (L. de Heinemann's introduction); Olcsváry, *art. cit.*, 505ff., and died as the archbishop of Spaleto in 1266, *SSH*, II, 549. He dedicated his report to the Cardinal of Palaestrina, *ibid.*, II, 551, note 1, and *MGHSS*, XXIX, 458, note 6. Archdeacon Thomas of Spaleto (who had high hopes of becoming archbishop himself), *MGHSS*, XXIX, 568ff. (Heinemann's remarks), did not like the Hungarians, but provided details about the Tartar invasion of Hungary as, e.g., c. 24, *ibid.*, XXIX, 575f. He died in 1268 - cf. his epitaph, *ibid.*, XXIX, 568,29-39. See also Gams, *Series episcoporum*, 420.
2. For text, see *VMH*, n. 440; *CD*, IV-2, 218ff.; Marczali, *Enchiridion*, 162ff.; for translations, see L. Makkay and L. Mezey (eds.), *Árpádkori és Anjoukori levelek* [Letters of the Árpád and Anjou Age, 11th-14th Centuries], vol. I (Budapest, 1960), 156ff.; Aladár Kovács, "Der «Mongolenbrief» Bélas IV an Papst Innozent IV über einem zu erwartenden zweiten Einbruch der Mongolen im 1250," *Überlieferung und Auftrag: Festschrift für M. de Ferdinándy zum 60 Geburtstag* (Wiesbaden, 1972), 495ff.; idem, "Béla levele a pápához" [The Letter of Béla IV to the Pope], *Uj Hungária Európa Évkönyve 1959* [The "Europe" Calendar for the Year 1959 of the Weekly "Uj Hungária"] (Munich, 1958), 43ff.; H. Gockenjan *et al.* (eds.), *Der Mongolensturm: Berichte von Augenzeugen und Zeitgenossen* (Graz-Cologne, 1985), 299ff.; in the translation editions the remarks made by L. Makkay and J. Gockenjan are of value and importance. See further, T. Katona (ed.), *A tatárjárás emlékezete* [In Memory of the Tartar Onslaught] (Budapest, 1981), 341ff., and J. Félegyházy, *A tatárjárás történetének s kútfőink históriája* [History of the Events and Pertinent Sources of the Tartar invasion] (Vác, 1941).
3. *VMH*, 231,21-22, though Louis IX of France heard and gave an answer to Béla IV - *CD*, IV-2, 220; *MGHLL*, II, 339 - the French monarch who, sitting under an oak tree, listened to the complaints of his people and administered justice to them; cf. Jean de Joinville, *Histoire de Saint Louis*, ed. N. de Wailly (Paris, 1874), 11 and 34.
4. *VMH*, I, 231,21-23; in 1239, Kunigunde married Boleslav of Cracow and Sandomir; about 1241, Anna married Rastiuslav Mihailovich of Chernygov, cf. Hodinka, 416a; Constance became the wife of Leo (Lev), the heir of Halich, in 1246, Hodinka, 430a and 432a; also Marczali, *Enchiridion*, 163f. and 164,5-6.
5. The sentence "per paganos hodie regnum nostrum defendimus, et per paganos infideles ecclesiae conculcamus," Marczali, *Enchiridion*, 164, reminds one of a remark by Matthew of Paris, IV, 118, quoting the letter of Frederick II to Henry III of England.
6. *VMH*, I, 231,-26-28.
7. "...quod esset salubrius nobis et toti Europae, ut Danubis fortaliter muniretur. Hec enim est aqua contradictionis," *VMH*, I, 231,41-42; Marczali, *Enchiridion*, 135; "...quod tenet salubrius nobis et toti Europae," Matthew of Paris, VI, 78ff. The Mongols crossed the Danube on Christmas Day, 1241; as long as it was possible, Paul, Justice of the King's Court and Reeve of Zala, did his best to hold the line of defense - cf. *ÁUO*, VII, 283.

8. "Quod, quod absit, si possideretur a Thartaris, esset pro ipsis apertum hostium ad alias fidei catholicae regiones....veniet qui ex parte orientis ad occidentalem veniens subiugandam;" Marczali, *Enchiridion*, 165; compare to *MGHSS*, XXIX, 592f.

9. Anastasius van den Wyngaert (ed.), *Sinica Franciscana*, vol. I: *Itinera et relationes Fratrum Minorum saeculi XIII et XIV* (Quaracchi-Florence, 1929), 331; Rubruck, epilogue, 4; Benedict the Pole's report, c. 3; and Plano Carpini, v:28, and viii:3.

10. Marczali, *Enchiridion*, 166. It is evident from a writ of Alexander IV that Béla IV had asked him for a thousand *balistarii* - Potthast, n. 17678; *VMH*, n. 454; *CD*, IV-2, 507ff.

11. *MGHSS*, XXIX, 596,45-50.

12. Already in 1243, the king had sent army units to aid Zara, *ibid.*, XXIX, 596,1-2; in 1245, Béla IV dispatched troops to Poland and Halich - Hodinka, 416a; or G.P. Perfecky (ed.), *The Hypathian Codex*, part II: *The Galician-Volhynian Chronicle* (Munich, 1973), cited hereafter as *GVC*, 52. At Mohi, Béla IV had suffered a devastating but not fateful defeat - Bartoniek, *art. cit.* (1952); Béla IV was also concerned that law and order be maintained in the devastated country - *ÁUO*, VII, 282ff., esp. 283.

13. G. Strakosch-Grossmann, *Der Einfall der Mongolen in Mitteleuropa in den Jahren 1241 und 1242* (Innsbruck, 1893), 172f.; Hodinka, 414a (anno 1242); J. Perényi, "Az orosz évkönyvek magyar vonatkozásai" [Data in the Russian Annals Related to Hungary], in G. Kemény (ed.), *Tanulmányok a magyar-orosz irodalmi kapcsolatok köréből* [Studies in Hungaro-Russian Literary Relations], vol. I (Budapest, 1961), 47ff. See further, *MGHSS*, XXIX, 594,38-39, to imply that the assertion of the Chronicle that "manserunt enim ipsi Tartari in regno Hungarie tribus annis" in incorrect; cf. *SSH*, I, 468,5-6.

14. Rogerius, c. 42.

15. *MGHSS*, XXIX, 594.

16. Jakubovsky, *Zolotai horde*, 58; *Enzyklopädie des Islam*, I, 710; Carpini, viii:4 and ix:28, 29. Batu Khan was going to participate in the election of the Great Khan - cf. *ÁUO*, VII, 560ff., esp. 563.

17. After Ogotai Khan had been poisoned, they began to withdraw, reads the report of Friar Ascellin who, in 1245, had sojourned in the court of Kujuk Khan - *CD*, IV-1, 436f.; Carpini, viii:2, ix:23, ix:32; Wyngaert, xlviii; Rubruck, 27:6.

18. The king's letter to Rome and the papal reply, dated February 4, 1247, asking Béla IV to notify the curia in the event of a new invasion, Potthast, n. 12414; *CD*, IV-1, 461f.; the envoys of Queen Maria: Jacob and Roman - *CD*, IV-1, 259f., must have arrived in Rome earlier, *ÁUO*, VII, 226, and Matthew of Paris, VI, 113. The Mongols had the region devastated as far as Wlodawa - Hodinka, 416a; *GVC*, 52; Béla IV had notified Rome, and the curia authorized the Patriarch of Aquileia to preach a crusade - *VMH*, n. 458; *CD*, IV-1, 299ff., though such an authorization must have remained rather ineffective. Cf. Ilona Pálffy, *A tatárok és a XIII századi Európa* [The Mongols and the 13th Century Europe] (Budapest, 1928), 36ff.

19. According to Tartar military strategy, the "first" onslaught always served as an intelligence gathering mission, see Carpini, viii:2, 6, 12; Benedict the Pole, c. 13, and Wyngaert, 142, n. 2.

20. The monarch of the land must be captured and murdered, cf. Carpini, vii:4 and viii:3; Schütz, *art. cit.*, 230f.

21. Lederer, *art. cit.*, 340.

22. They de-emphasized the capture of fortified places, for the reason that "...magnae villae pro maiori parte omnes erant destructae, ut pascerent ibi Tartari;" Carpini, viii:12, 13; xi:16.

THE AFTERMATH: THE 1240's

23. Hodinka, 414ab; *GVC*, 59; Strakosch-Grossman, 173; compare to *HO*, VI, 124.

24. Dimitri, commander of Danilo's armed forces, had directed Batu's attention toward Hungary - Hodinka, 406a and 414ab; *GVC*, 49; further, Hodinka, 454ab-456ab.

25. *SSH*, II, 586,6-23; *MGHSS*, XXIX, 566,9-12 and 14-15.

26. *Ibid.*, XXIX, 577,14-16.

27. *Ibid.*, XXIX, 594,47-49; *SSH*, II, 584,10-12. C. Jirecek has named the possible routes of their withdrawal, cf. his *Die Handelstrassen und Bergwerke in Serbien und Bosnien des Mittelalters* (Prague, 1879), 62ff. and 89. Also, "Annales Pragenses," *MGHSS*, IX, 169ff. and 194ff.; "Annales Otakariani," *ibid.*, IX, 181ff.; "Historia Wenceslai I," *ibid.*, IX, 167ff.; Wattenbach, II, 307 and 319ff.

28. *SSH*, II, 584,10-12; Jirecek, 74ff.; Hóman-Szekfü, I, 555.

29. Carpini, ix:39; also Rubruck, xi:2, xx:3; *SSH*, II, 586,15-20; *MGHSS*, XXIX 594,39-49 [41-47].

30. Carpini, vii:10; Rubruck, xx:3.

31. Rogerius, c. 40.

32. *RA*, n. 1101; Smiciklas, *CD*, V, 22; *ÁUO*, VII, 282ff., 283f.; IX, 64f.; XI, 323; *SSH*, II, 43,2-4 [c. 68]. Strakosch-Grossmann, 175ff.

33. *MGHSS*, XXIX, 595,6-10. During his stay in Dalmatia, two royal daughters had died - *CD*, IV-1, 270.

34. *RA*, n. 598; *ÁUO*, VII, 319ff.; *CD*, IV-2, 106ff., with different date.

35. *CD*, III-1, 403 - a forgery, *RA*, n. 401.

36. Confirmed on April 5, 1251, cf. *RA*, n. 944; *CD*, IV-2, 98ff.; and *RA*, n. 713; *HO*, VIII, 39ff.: its date, "apud Traugurium, vi id. mart. a D. 1241," but the year 1242 has been substituted, *HO*, VIII, 41, perhaps in accordance with the Florentine style of time reckoning - on this, see Grotefend, *Zeitrechnung*, I, 215.

37. *RA*, n. 715; *ÁUO*, VII, 188ff., and the king's decision between the bishop and community of Trau, *ÁUO*, VII, 130. G. Pray, *Annales regum Hungariae ab anno 997 usque ad 1614 deductae*, 5 vols. (Vindobonae, 1764-79), I, 289; Katona, *Historia critica*, VI, 153f.

38. *RA*, n. 715; *ÁUO*, VII, 188ff.

39. *RA*, n. 960; *ÁUO*, XII, 690, to confirm a writ he had issued earlier - *RA*, n. 803; *CD*, V-1, 394.

40. *RA*, n. 1327; *ÁUO*, VII, 49f.; *CD*, IV-3, 148f., and compare to *RA*, n. 1372 and *ÁUO*, VIII, 50ff.

41. *RA*, n. 1264 (the date, August 15, 1261, may be in doubt); *ÁUO*, III, 1f.

42. *RA*, n. 719, dated from Klissa (Clarissa), anno 1242; *ÁUO*, III, 143F.

43. *MGHSS*, XXIX, 595,7; Lucius, IV, 5; Katona, *Historia pragmatica*, I, 810f.

44. See *RA*, n. 779; *ÁUO*, VII, 157ff.; *MGHSS*, XXIX, 595,16-20.

45. *RA*, n. 779; *ÁUO*, VII, 282ff.

46. *Ibid.*, VII, 283f.; *HO*, VIII, 34f.; *CD*, IV-3, 323ff.

47. *RA*, nn. 733, 734, and 744; *CD*, IV-1, 275f.; *ÁUO*, VII, 131ff.; and *CD*, IV-1, 287ff., respectively. Matthias Bél, *Notitii Hungariae novae historico-geographica*, 4 vols. (Vienna, 1735-42; editio altera, 5 vols. [Budapest, 1892]), IV, 388f., and passim; on Bél, cf. C. Horváth, *A régi magyar irodalom története* [History of Early Hungarian Literature], vol. I (Budapest, 1899), 693f.

48. *SSH*, I, 468,9-15; one may note the chronicler's characterization of Duke Frederick: "dux Austrie Fridericuas vir bellicosus." Also, *CD*, IV-1, 302, and compare to Ebendorfer, 128,10-17, and note 6; *MGHSS*, IX, 643.

49. *Ibid.*, IX, 641,18-22; *RA*, n. 1091; *CD*, IV-2, 388ff.; *ÁUO*, II, 269 spoke of fifteen wounds; *RA*, n. 1092; *CD*, IV-1, 390f.

50. *RA*, n. 882; *ÁUO*, VII, 262ff., esp. 263; *CD*, IV-2, 31ff.

51. *MGHSS*, IX, 597,12-14.

52. *RA*, n. 743; *ÁUO*, VII, 135; *RA*, n. 744; *CD*, IV-1, 287f.; Bél, *Notitii*, III, 548f. Béla IV regarded the duke as his enemy, *SSH*, II, 269f.
53. Gy. Székely, "Egy elfelejtett rettegés: a második tatárdúlás a magyar történeti hagyományban és egyetemes összefüggésekben" [A Forgotten Threat: The Second Tartar Onslaught in Hungarian Historical Tradition], *Századok*, 122 (1988), 52ff.
54. *SSH*, I, 468,6-9; *MGHSS*, XXIX, 595,11-14; XXV, 360; IX, 641 and 788. Béla IV's own observation, *CD*, IV-2, 49 and 219ff.; Rogerius, c. 40; *ÁUO*, VII, 283; Knauz, I, 548; Wattenbach, *art. cit.*, (AföG), 42, and 519.
55. Knauz, I, 346.
56. *CD*, IV-2, 117f.
57. *CD*, IV-3, 59ff.
58. *Ibid.*, IV-2, 157f.
59. *ÁUO*, VIII, 119
60. *Ibid.*, II, 157f., 159f., 160.
61. *Ibid.*, II, 161ff., 163f., 171, 225f. [*VMH*, n. 356]; 354 and 355.
62. Rogerius, c. 22.
63. Idem, c. 27.
64. Idem, c. 34.
65. On the destruction of Nagyvárad, see Rogerius, c. 34; on the sufferings of Kolozsmonostor, *FRA*, Abt. 2, vol. 15, n. 76.
66. On the devastation of Hungary, cf. Rogerius, c. 39 (in Vác), c. 22 (in Esztergom), and c. 39 (in Transylvania). "Planctus destructionis," *Neues Archiv*, II, 621.
67. On this, cf. *HO*, VII, 44; *CD*, IV-2, 364f.; *ÁUO*, IX, 405f.; *CD*, IV-2, 117f.; *ÁUO*, IX, 363; Knauz, I, 343, 487, and 521; Erik Fügedi, *Castle and Society in Medieval Hungary* (Budapest, 1986), 50f., and my review of this volume in *East European Quarterly*, 22 (1988), 370ff.
68. Cf. *RA*, n. 728; Knauz, I, 548; *CD*, IV-1, 279, IV-2, 295f., IV-3, 227ff., IV-2, 157f.; *ÁUO*, III, 43f.
69. *RA*, n. 725; *RHM*, 453ff.; *CD*, IV-1, 264ff.; *MGHSS*, XVII, 344 (anno 1246); *ibid.*, IX, 789,7-21.
70. *ÁUO*, VIII, 212F.; *CD*, VI-1, 49.
71. Knauz, I, 496.
72. *ÁUO*, III, 156ff.; *HO*, VI, 42 and 157.
73. *RA*, n. 906; *ÁUO*, VII, 283f.
74. *RA*, n. 864 and n. 874; *HO*, VII, 54. Fuxhoffner-Czinár, *Monasteria*, II, 122; *CD*, VI-2, 375ff. and IV-2, 16f. Compare to *RA*, n. 742; *CD*, IV-1, 332. Katona, *Historia critica*, VI, 53, 103, 121f.
75. *RA*, n. 745; *RHM*, 460ff.; *HO*, VI, 157ff.; *RA*, n. 1059; *RHM*, 489f.; *CD*, IV-2, 296f.; *RA*, nn. 1336 and 1349 with text.
76. *RA*, n. 1551; *ÁUO*, III, 156ff., esp. 156; Fügedi, *op. cit.*, 111.
77. Rubruck, epilogue, c. 4.
78. Carpini, v:33-34; Rubruck, 1:12, 29:96, 38:17; by comparison, it may be noted that in the treaty between Stephen V and Otakar II - *RA*, n. 2094, the term *ducatus Slavonie* emerged (again) as a district under Hungarian administration - *ÁUO*, III, 247ff., esp. 248 and 253; also Potthast, nn. 18972 and 18748; *VMH*, nn. 496 and 471, respectively.
79. Carpini, ix:17; Wyngaert, xlviii
80. Carpini, v:9, vi:15-16, on the Mongols' attitude toward the siege of towns; the papal curia had warned the hierarchy to seek out and make available areas for the protection of the faithful - *RA*, n. 769, "datum apud castrum Galaas," on June 15, 1244; *ÁUO*, VII, 152ff., dated July 1, 1244.

81. *RA*, n. 853; *CD*, IV-1, 447ff.; Katona, *Historia critica*, VI, 95ff.; Zimmermann-Werner, UB, I, 73f.; Teutsch-Firnhaber, UB, I, xxxviii.
82. *RA*, n. 1043 on the construction of the fort at Pest; *RHM*, 493ff.; *CD*, IV-2, 320ff., and compare with a royal writ of 1246, *RA*, n. 841 with text, and with n. 1044; Knauz, I, 421 (abstract).
83. *RA*, n. 902 on the fortification of Esztergom; Knauz, I, 371f.
84. *CD*, IV-2, 310ff. and IV-2, 37ff.
85. On January 29, 1243, Béla IV issued a writ at Túróc, *RA*, n. 734; *ÁUO*, VII, 131ff.; esp. 133, Bél, *Notitii*, II, 349 and 361.
86. Potthast, n. 18971; *ÁUO*, III, 94ff.; *VMH*, n. 694; Knauz, I, 661, and compare with Potthast, n. 18745; *ÁUO*, VIII, 70ff., in reference to *ibid.*, VII, 501ff.; *VMH*, n. 469.
87. Pauler, II, 196, though his reference to *ÁUO*, III, 320 is misleading. Documents printed *ibid.*, III, 229f. and 230f., may, however, provide indirect data on this. *RA*, nn. 1244, 1309 [*ÁUO*, III, 18] and 1310.
88. *RA*, n. 812; *CD*, IV-1, 380f.
89. *CD*, IV-2, 218; Remig Békefi, *A pilisi apátság története* [History of the Abbey of Pilis], vol. I (Pécs, 1891), 317.
90. *RA*, n. 723; *RHM*, 451ff.; J. Tkalcic (ed.), *Monumenta historica lib. regalis civitatis Zagrabiae*, vol. I (Zagreb, 1889), 15ff.; idem (ed.), *Monumenta historica episcopatus Zagrabiensis saeculo XII et XIII*, 2 vols. (Zagreb, 1873-74), I, 88f.
91. Re-confirmed anno 1266, *RA*, n. 1493; *CD*, IV-3, 337f., and Tkalcic, *Mon. civ. Zagr.*, and compare with *RA*, n. 1504; *RHM*, 507ff.; Tkalcic, *Mon. civ. Zagr.*, I, 40ff.; *CD*, IV-3, 330ff.
92. *RA*, n. 880; *ÁUO*, VII, 255f.
93. *SSH*, II, 562,14-15; Anonymus, c. 57 wrote about the Fort of Pest, "castrum dicitur Pest," *ibid.*, I, 115,2.
94. *RA*, n. 781, dated prior to October 15, 1244; *RHM*, 466ff.; *CD*, IV-1, 326ff.; D. Csánki and D. Gárdonyi (eds.), *Monumenta diplomatica civitatis Budapest, 1148-1301* (Budapest, 1936), 41ff., and compare with *RA*, n. 841, with text. Keza, c. 13, mentioned Óbuda (Old Buda), *ibid.*, I, 156,12, also recorded in the Chronicle, c. 13, "Obudam usque hodie vocant," *ibid.*, I, 269.1. The term "vetus Buda," (*de vetere Buda*) appeared in a royal writ of July 5, 1243, *RA*, n. 747; *RHM*, 458ff.; *CD*, IV-1, 296ff.; Rady, *Medieval Buda*, 165ff.; Katona, *Historia critica*, VI, 15.
95. *RA*, n. 1043; *RHM*, 493ff., mentioning "Mons Pestiensis," and "Castrum Pestiense;" Batthyány, *Leges*, II, 390f. Katona, *Historia critica*, VI, 235.
96. *RA*, n. 1070, mentioned "Pest iuxta Danubium." A writ from 1265 spoke of "novum montem Pestiensis," Knauz, I, 521, though a writ from the Veszprém cathedral chapter referred to "Ecclesia novae Montis Budensis." Cf. *HO*, VI, 47f.
97. *RA*, n. 1375; *ÁUO*, III, 38f.; Erdélyi, *Pannonhalmi Rendtörténet*, II, 325; the settlers' *villicus* (mayor) acted as judge in their legal business, and retained, for his personal use, one-third of the fine meted out in his court; two-thirds of it went to the royal *fiscus* (treasury). The settlers could appeal to the abbot of Pannonhalma who, together with six jurors (*iurati*), had to review the case and hand down a sentence.
98. Pauler, II, 200.
99. *RA*, n. 660; Knauz, I, 328ff.
100. *Ibid.*, and *RA*, nn. 753 and 1063; Knauz, I, 424.
101. *RA*, n. 902; Knauz, I, 375.
102. *RA*, n. 1125; Knauz, I, 439f.
103. *RA*, n. 919 with text.

104. As, e.g., *RA*, n. 752; *CD*, IV-1, 332f; *RA*, n. 781; *ÁUO*, VII, 172ff.; *RA*, n. 793; *CD*, IV-1, 329f.; *RA*, n. 831; Teutsch-Firnhaber, UB, I, 66f.; Zimmermann-Werner, UB, I, 72; *CD*, IV-1, 414ff.

105. As, e.g., *RA*, n. 716 (and n. 529!); *ÁUO*, VII, 136f.; *RA*, n. 769; *ÁUO*, VII, 152ff. *RA*, n. 774; *ÁUO*, XI, 331f.; *RA*, n. 779; *ÁUO*, VII, 157ff.; *RA*, n. 1041, with text, and *RA*, n. XI, 405.

106. *RA*, n. 722; *ÁUO*, VII, 125f.

107. *RA*, n. 724; *CD*, IV-1, 255f.

108. *RA*, n. 725; *RHM*, 456ff.; *ÁUO*, XI, 323ff.

109. *RA*, nn. 723 and 725; *RA*, n. 783, on fort construction, *ÁUO*, VII, 161f. *RA*, n. 853, on Knights of the Hospital, *CD*, IV-1, 447ff.

110. *RA*, n. 885; *RHM*, 498ff.

111. *RA*, n. 933; *CD*, IV-2, 64f.

112. *RA*, n. 1031; *ÁUO*, XI, 410; *RA*, n. 1027; *ÁUO*, VII, 371; and *RA*, n. 1037 (or n. 1041, already cited above); *ÁUO*, XII, 127 with wrong date. See also I. Rákos, "IV Béla birtokrestaurációs politikája" [Béla IV's Restoration Policy Involving Land Unlawfully Given Away], *Acta historica Szegediensis* (Szeged, 1974), 3ff. as, e.g., *RA*, n. 1027; *HO*, I, 32; *RA*, n. 1082; *ÁUO*, VII, 421f.; *RA*, n. 1083; *CD*, VII-4, 117 - and yet, the king had shown consideration toward the nobles, *ÁUO*, VII, 465f.

113. "Cumanos etiam in regno nostro recepimus, et proh dolor! per paganos hodie regnum nostrum defendimus, et per paganos infideles ecclesiae conculcamus;" Marczali, *Enchiridion*, 164, and compare with *CD*, IV-3, 30ff. Pope Urban IV issued instructions concerning "pagan" Cumans - Potthast, n. 18970; *VMH*, n. 493; *ÁUO*, III, 91ff.

114. *RA*, n. 933a (anno 1250), and literature discussed; *VMH*, n. 440; Marczali, *Enchiridion*, 162ff.; *CD*, IV-2, 218ff.; on Alpra, cf. Hóman-Szekfű, I, 574 and 603; Pauler, II, 522, n. 159, in evident reference to G. Wenczel (ed.), *Magyar diplomáciai emlékek* [Writs Pertinent to Hungarian Diplomacy], 3 vols. (Budapest, 1872-76), I, 34, where Alpra became Albert.

115. "...propter defensionem fidei Christianae filio nostro primogenito Cumanam quamdam thoro coniunximus maritali;" Marczali, *Enchiridion*, 164; Knauz, I, 514; Wyngaert, lvii.

116. *RA*, n. 882; *ÁUO*, VII, 262ff., esp. 263.

117. *RA*, n. 904; *CD*, IV-2, 49.

118. *RA*, n. 907; *CD*, IV-2, 54f.

119. *RA*, n. 1188; "...fratres Magistri Benedicti, Notarii aule karissimi filii nostri Regis Stephani;" *ÁUO*, VII, 486.

120. In reference to an earlier writ, *ÁUO*, VII, 462, where Stephen's name appeared as that of the Ban(us) of Slovenia.

121. *RA*, n. 1260, that once had belonged to the Zala fort, eventually inherited by Stephen, who donated it to the abbey of Pannonhalma, Erdélyi, *Rendtörténet*, II, 309f.; abstract in *CD*, IV-3, 22.

122. *RA*, n. 788; *CD*, IV-1, 319f.; and *RA*, n. 738; *CD*, VII-4, 91ff.; Thomas of Spaleto, in *Mon. hist. Slav. merid.*, XXVI, 295ff.

123. See "De canale cronica Veneta," *Archivio storica Italiano*, VIII, 395ff., more reliable than Dandalo, in Muratori, *Scriptores*, XII, 152ff., esp. 153, and compare to Spaleto, *Mon. hist. Slav. merid.*, XXVI, 185; also, *CD*, IV-1, 444f.

124. *RA*, n. 770; *RHM*, 464ff.; *CD*, IV-1, 317ff. A few years later, many refugees from Zara would accept the offer of Venice, and return peacefully to Zara; cf. A. Theiner (ed.), *Vetera monumenta Slavorum merdionalium historiam illustrantia*, 2 vols. (Rome-Zagreb, 1863-75), I, 65 and 66 [Italian translation]; *ÁUO*, II, 155f.; Katona, *Historia critica*, VI, 39.

125. *RA*, n. 788; *CD*, VII-4, 96f., and compare with *RA*, n. 715 (anno 1242); *ÁUO*, VII, 188ff.; abridged and dated anno 1245 in *CD*, IV-1, 264ff. In the negotiations, the Town of Spaleto demanded additional territory along the border with Trau; Trau suffered defeat on the sea, and asked Grand Steward Ninoslav for help. Cf. *RA*, n. 788 (again), and compare with *RA*, n. 736 and 737; *CD*, IV-2, 307 and *CD*, VII-4, 93f., respectively.

126. *RA*, n. 881; and Theiner, *Monumenta Slavorum*, I, 217; also, Thomas of Spaleto, in *Mon. hist. Slavorum merid.*, XXVI, 206f.

127. *RA*, n. 780; *CD*, IV-1, 319f.; *RA*, n. 738; *CD*, VII-4, 91ff.; *Mon. Slav. merid.*, XXVI, 295f.

128. *RA*, n. 770; *RHM*, 464ff.; Katona, *Historia critica*, VI, 36.

2. Béla IV Caught in a Political Web Between Halich and Vienna

> Post hec autem rex Bela reversus est de maritimis partibus; et ducem Austrie Fredericum virum bellicosum ante Novam Civitatem gens occidit in prelio Hungarorum; et transfixit per maxillam. Licet tamen idem dux occiderit in hoc bello, Bela rex prefatus triumphum cum Hungaris perdidit.
>
> *Chronicon pictum*, c. 177*

By dispatching army troops for the support of his son-in-laws in Halich and in Poland, Béla IV actually aided Boleslav against Conrad of Mesovia.[1] Earlier, when Rostislav Mihalovich, son of the prince of Chernigov, had fled before the Mongols to the court of Béla IV, he received the hand in marriage of Anna, one of the king's daughters. It was this marriage the monarch had referred to in one of his writs addressed to the papal curia, and some royal letters made mention of Rostislav (Rastislaus) by name, as the king's son-in-law.[2] Pope Urban IV cited, in fact, a royal writ that bespoke the estates of Rostislav and his wife Anna.[3]

The king had lost many of his troops as prisoners of war in his campaign at Kiev, among them Grand Steward Füle (Filja), who during the 1219 Russian expedition of Andrew II had fought bravely at Kiev;[4] now, he had been tortured to death by Danilo (Danyii), prince of Halich.[5] Béla IV supported Rostislav in an attempt at reoccupying Halich.[6] In 1245, the prince had tried to subdue Przemysl with the aid of his Hungarian father-in-law, but could accomplish little against Danilo. The Russian annals report that Rostislav had to flee back to the court of Béla IV before the approaching army of Danilo - and of Prince Vasilko.[7]

The Romanovich family of Danilo had toyed with the idea of establishing an alliance with the Holy See in face of the renewed Mongol attack(s); at the same time, however, he conducted negotiations with Batu Khan, perhaps out of the realistic fear for the future of Halich. Danilo went in person to visit Batu Khan by late October, 1245.[8] He spent twenty-five days with the khan, whom he had to acknowledge as the overlord of the Halich region; in return, Batu did allow Danilo to govern Halich in *his* name.[9]

When Danilo had returned from Batu Khan's headquarters, Béla IV sent envoys to him with the request that Leo (Lev), son of Danilo, marry Constance, Béla's other daughter.[10] Although the Hungarian court had, in the past, relied on the court of (Kiev-)Halich for intelligence data about the Mongols, it seems likely that the king was concerned about the visit of Danilo to Batu Khan's headquarters.[11] Nicholas, son of Obrich, was now sent to Kiev to prepare a report on the Mongols.[12] By this time, Béla IV had realized that he needed to play a justifiable game of diplomatic chess with the court of Halich; the king gave up his plan to restore Rostislav as the ruler of Halich, and recognized Danilo as the one who held that position. In order to compensate Rostislav, Béla IV gave him the grand stewardship(s) of Slovenia and of Macho.[13]

In late spring, 1246, Béla IV took firm military action against Frederick of Austria. The duke, to whom Emperor Frederick II had promised to grant the title of king, had constantly harassed his neighbors, the Czechs, Bavarians, and, in 1246, he invaded Hungary.[14] Béla IV grew furious over this "unprovoked" invasion, and so he mobilized his armed forces and marched toward Németújvár at the border.[15]

In the morning of June 15, 1246, the Hungarian troops crossed the Lajta stream and approached the camp of the duke. Some Cuman units also supported the king,[16] even though Béla IV only recently had taken them back to his service,[17] and so did some Kievan units under the command of Danilo.[18] Early in the ensuing battle a spear hit Duke Frederick in the face, who fell dead from his horse.[19] The Austrians had, however, won the engagement; they had taken many Hungarian prisoners, among them Paul, Justice of the Realm, Reeve Simon, the hero of Esztergom, and many others.[20]

The matter of fact tone of the Chronicle that upon the return of Béla IV from the Adriatic seashore, the Hungarians (*gens Hungarorum*) had killed Frederick of Austria in the engagement at Wienerneustadt ("ante Novam Civitatem"); that they had the duke, a belligerent man, knifed through his front jaw ("transfixit per maxillam"); and, although the duke had died, *ceciderit*, in the confrontation, the Hungarians could not score a victory - only provided confirmation on this battle, without rendering specific details.[21]

In relation to the battle at the Lajta, one may view the report of the Russian chroniclers for additional data. The Gustin Annals reported, for example, that Danilo went to Hungary to aid Béla IV, and it was he who had the Austrian duke killed in the engagement.[22] The Hypathius manuscript, on the other hand, stated that the duke was by then already dead.[23] According to a German source, Duke Frederick had warred with the Russian king, *rex Ruscie*, whom he had killed, but from whom he also received a deadly blow.[24] The Halich-Volhynia Annals, on the other hand, record that the duke of Austria had been killed by one of his own men.[25]

A writ issued by Béla IV for Andrew, son of Tamás, rewarding him for the heroic role he played in the engagement at the Lajta stream, may throw some light upon the statement of the Kievan-Halich source, because it must have been through the information he had received from the prince of Kiev-Halich that Béla IV knew of Andrew's heroism.[26] Accordingly, the "rex Ruscie," alias Prince of Halich, could also have been Rostislav, the son-in-law of Béla IV; Leo, Danilo's son, had only married later the other daughter of the king.[27]

Béla IV made a statement that he regarded Frederick of Austria as his most dangerous enemy (personal opponent; a threatening person),[28] whose death ended the war.[29] Still, the king had the border kept under surveillance after the battle, as it is witnessed by an agreement he had reached with the Knights of St. John - an understanding so characteristic of the relationship Hungary had with its neighbors[30] - and approved by the Holy See.[31]

The situation with Austria remained unsettled. As early as 1250, the king led another expedition against Austria; a chronicler recorded that in June, 1250, Hungarians devastated Mariazell.[32] A Russian source reveals that Danilo, after he had met with King Béla IV at Pozsony, gave a helping hand in this latest campaign - though, one must add, the chronicler being notoriously wrong on chronology, identified this military undertaking with the events of 1246.[33] Hostilities only ended because of the intervention of the Czech monarch, Otakar II.[34]

The Hungarian court faced a rather difficult and complicated diplomatic situation. It had to have peace in the east, and had to seek allies against the Mongols. By relying upon family ties, the king used, or attempted to rely upon Danilo as a permanent military and political ally, but the clever prince - whose hands were tied by the agreement he had reached with Batu Khan - had requested that negotiations continue. Danilo might even have sought further concessions from Béla IV.[35]

It is a matter of record that Danilo had dispatched Patriarch Cyrill to the court of Béla IV with some intelligence (transmitted in a letter the patriarch carried with him) about the Mongols; incidentally, the letter can be regarded as written proof of the existing understanding between Halich and Batu Khan at that time.[36]

The Russian chronicler says that Danilo had ordered the patriarch to travel through Hungary to Nicea, where he had to discuss the establishment of a metropolitan see for Russia. Maria, the queen of Béla IV, was a daughter of Theodore Lascaris, ruler of Nicea, and good relations had existed between the Hungarian monarch and his Greek father-in-law. Danilo must have wanted to exploit the family relationship, in order to assure political success for the mission of his patriarch. Béla IV had promised the patriarch that, were Danilo to conclude an agreement with him, he would provide an escort for Patriarch Cyrill to make certain of his arrival in Nicea (and, probably, to intercede with his father-in-law on behalf of the patriarch).[37]

So it came about that a wedding took place between Leo, son of Danilo, and Constance, daughter of Béla IV, attended by Danilo in person. The king and Danilo met at Zólyom (Izvolin),[38] where they reached an understanding over the fate of the Hungarian prisoners of war who had been captured in the battle of Jaroslav; they were allowed to return home.[39]

Were one to accept as valid the incorrect dates in the Russian chronicles, the time of the Zólyom meeting could be set in the year 1250.[40] And yet, the meeting and negotiations held in Zólyom ought to be placed four years earlier, on the basis of the writs that had been issued at the Hungarian court. According to the royal register, in 1246, there were two,[41] and four documents in 1247, that were issued at Zólyom;[42] between 1248 and 1253, no royal writs, dated from Zólyom, were logged in the register.[43] Consequently, one may argue that it was during the documented stay of the monarch at Zólyom that the talks between him and Danilo took place. At the same time, a royal writ dated in April, 1247, mentioned the release of a certain Bheled (Bwled) from war captivity, as if to refer to the discharge of prisoners of war negotiated in the talks held at Zólyom.[44]

The letter of the monarch, dated November 15, 1246, addressed to the papal curia might be of further interest in that the king had asked for the curia's approval of appropriating Austrian lands for himself.[45] But the papal reply did not refer to the essence of the royal request;[46] instead, the curia instructed the papal envoy in Hungary to conduct an inquiry into the affair. Rome did not say no, but it remained cautious, without taking sides, as is evident from the papal writ sent to Henry Raspe, the German anti-king.[47]

One ought to note, regarding the issue involving the Austrian lands, that upon the unexpected death of Frederick in 1246, the Babenberg male line had died out, thereby causing a good deal of conflict as to its inheritance.[48] On the female line, Margaret, aunt of the deceased duke, had made a strong claim; she was the widow of Henry, son of Emperor Frederick II; and Gertrud, daughter of Henry, the younger brother of the fallen duke, had also held a claim. Neither of the heirs of the female line had the right of inheritance, however, on the grounds that, without a male heir, the land(s) were to revert to the emperor. Frederick II himself had designs on the hand in marriage of Gertrud - were her father to die prematurely, the emperor might claim the inheritance for himself.[49] But Duke Frederick of Austria had earlier promised the hand of Gertrud to Vladislas, son of the Czech Vencel, who, in fact, had married Gertrud after the untimely death of Frederick Babenberg.[50]

The emperor was at war with the Roman pontiff at this time. Innocent IV had excommunicated Frederick II, and openly supported the election of a German anti-king. The papal curia did not wish for the emperor to gain control of Austria[51] (it must have been in exploitation of the circumstances that Béla IV wanted to occupy the Babenberg inheritance, and to obtain papal approval of it), nor would the curia tolerate Hungarian intrusion in the former Babenberg regions. Such an intrusion could easily have led to a conflict with the Czech court.[52] On these grounds, Pope Innocent IV decided to support Gertrud's second husband, Hermann of Baden (her first husband had died in 1247) in acquiring the inheritance.

The Hungarian court had no desire to challenge the papal verdict, and Béla IV abandoned his plan.[53]

In about 1250, when the Austrian and Styrian nobles gained power and devastated the frontier along Hungary, Béla IV called for an insurrection of the Hungarian nobility (at a bad time, though; the men were at work in the fields), to halt the harassment. The chronicler reported that the Hungarians had "misbehaved" during the military operation: they murdered many people, burned churches to the ground, destroyed fortifications as well as peasant villages between Vienna and the Semmering. It was only upon the deaths of Hermann and of Emperor Frederick II that Béla IV ordered his forces to return.[54]

In the fall of 1250, the Czech Otakar made an attempt to take the Babenberg inheritance; a majority of Austrian nobles invited Otakar, who at that time was the margrave of Moravia, to become duke of Austria. In order to gain legal confirmation of his new title, the nineteen year old Otakar married the forty-six year old Margaret, sister of the fallen Frederick Babenberg. Béla IV could not permit a Czech takeover of the Austrian lands without a papal, or imperial, sanction; the king took military action against Otakar, on the grounds that the widow of the last Austrian duke, Hermann of Baden, had requested help from him.[55]

When Otakar "invaded" Austria, the Hungarians, "invited" by Gertrud, devastated the surroundings of Vienna, while the Cumans, by now members of the Hungarian forces, caused some havoc in Moravia.[56] Gertrud had summoned Hungarian military help, and Béla IV had persuaded Gertrud to marry the son of the duke of Halich - "accepit maritum regem Ruscie," the chronicler recorded - though the marriage must have been of a brief duration: in the words of the chronicler, "rex Ruscie relicta uxore rediit ad terram suam."[57]

The senseless war, in which so many human lives were lost, churches and buildings damaged, and treasures destroyed, must have disturbed Pope Innocent IV, who dispatched the Spaniard Velasco, an Apostolic Confessor at St. Peter's basilica in Rome, to the Hungarian court with orders to establish peace between Béla IV and his opponents.[58]

Although the king previously had serious problems with the papal curia over the occupancy of the archiepiscopal see of

Esztergom, he complied with the papal wish. He withdrew his forces from Olmütz, and was prepared to accept a papal verdict. And yet, when Rome had sent another envoy, Bishop Bernard Rubeus Caraccioli of Naples, to the Czech and Hungarian courts,[59] Béla IV had authorized Bishop Fülöp of Zagreb, and a Franciscan friar, to represent him at the papal curia. The king let Rome know that he was willing to restore the towns and fortifications he had occupied in Moravia, but he expected Otakar to act in a similar manner.[60]

In the meantime, Otakar (the margrave of Moravia) became King Otakar II of Bohemia. He wished to remain on good terms with Rome, and had, without much hesitation, accepted the peace proposals of the previous papal legate Velasco.[61]

Under papal pressure (so judged by the tone and contents of the writs sent by the curia to both the Czech and Hungarian courts), peace had, therefore, been restored between Béla IV and Otakar II. The chronicler who recorded, under the year 1254, on the Peace of Pozsony, and on one of the treaty's articles, that Otakar II allowed Béla IV to retain Styria (of the Babenberg inheritance), made, however, further mention of an expedition by Otakar II to Prussia,[62] as if to confirm the report by Thomas Ebendorfer who wrote that Otakar II had, after his successful venture to Prussian territory, met with the king of Hungary on the Semmering to negotiate with him the question of the Babenberg inheritance.[63] Alfons Lhotsky, editor of the Ebendorfer text, has pointed out, however, that the "meeting" did not take place on the Semmering, but in Buda, in the year 1253, in which case Otakar's Prussian venture had to take place a year earlier.[64] Entries in the Hungarian royal register record that Béla IV named Stephen of Gútkeled, grand steward of Slavonia, as royal Captain (Reeve) of Styria.[65]

As long as he was alive, the emperor had caused trouble for both the Babenberg heirs and Béla IV; from the latter he demanded payment of an earlier "unsettled" debt.[66] The king appealed to Rome, and obtained a dispensation from Innocent IV to the effect that he owed the emperor no debt. In 1241, when the king, out of fear of the Mongols, had promised to submit to the emperor in return for armed assistance, Frederick II ought to have had the moral obligation to aid a Christian monarch facing the Mongol threat out of a sense of Christian solidarity, but he did not. Béla IV had neither moral nor fiscal obligation toward the German court, the papal writ said.[67]

From Béla's point of view, the tragic aspect of the situation was that he entrusted his son and heir, Stephen, Junior King,[68] with the government of Styria, and authorized Stephen of Gútkeled to act as royal reeve (Captain) of Styria.[69] Because the Styrian nobles were unhappy with the Hungarian rule, and turned to Otakar II, Stephen had no alternative but to flee Styria. In order to compensate his son, Béla IV made him Prince of Transylvania, and appointed him Lord of the Cumans.[70] Unexpected and rapid advancement in the ranks whetted Stephen's appetite for power: he now demanded that, as Junior King, he obtain co-regency with his father over the entire Hungarian realm. When Béla IV refused, Stephen turned against him, and against the supporters of his father, by devastating their estates countrywide.[71]

The case - rivalry between father and son - reminds one of the incident recorded in the Second Book of Samuel, where Absalom, the third son of King David, had organized a revolt against his own father. By imitating a "foreign" example, Absalom had demanded more powers for himself.[72] In Hungary, the confrontation between king and prince (Junior King) had not only endangered the position of the king, who had done so much for the reconstruction of his country after the Mongol onslaught of the early 1240's, but had threatened the interests of the entire kingdom. As if during his brief stint as governor of Styria - where his subjects had despised him, as they revolted against the misrule of his reeve-captain, Stephen of Gútkeled[73] - Stephen had tasted too deeply the feudal values (already on the decline) of the west, and demanded from his father the establishment of an autonomous area for himself.[74]

Stephen, Junior King, looked upon his royal father as someone "first among the equals," the chronicler Simon de Keza recorded, as if it had been the custom of the land.[75] It was characteristic of domestic conditions in Hungary in the 1260's that a chronicler and a prince (also crowned Junior King) could dream about establishing feudal conditions in the realm at a time when feudalism had entered its decline in cultured western countries.[76]

The royal father and the princely son met at Pozsony for a military encounter in the field, but departed the scene without actual military engagement. They negotiated a truce instead, dividing the kingdom among themselves. Areas east of the Danube - including Transylvania - were acquired by the prince with full constitutional rights and court privileges (though the king retained one half of the income of the Transylvania salt mines); the western part of the country - including the area north of the Danube - remained under the actual control of the king.[77]

The truce between father and son had not been taken too seriously by the papal curia. Pope Urban IV, again, commissioned Velasco as envoy to find out whether the "Agreement of Pozsony" had been observed by both parties. Velasco had, however, encountered lively opposition from both sides during his investigation; the parties concerned were opposed to what they regarded as foreign interference in their domestic affairs, and had openly scorned the legate's proposal to re-negotiate the treaty. Such talks, the royal party contended, would lead nowhere, and would only cause an endless delay.

Therefore, in a writ dated from Lipcse, "aput Lypcha," on August 3, 1263, Béla IV informed His Holiness that, because of the cooperation of the Hungarian bishops, he and his son had reached an understanding, and he had to question the value of the proposal the legate had made to re-open negotiations and plan a new agreement. He, the king, in the presence of the papal envoy (*penitentiarius*) and of dignitaries of the realm, herewith confirmed the agreement he and his son had previously reached. He promised not to embarrass Stephen, or harm Stephen's wife, nor harass their subordinates, their chattel and other belongings, nor take military action against him. Béla IV had confirmed the early (Pozsony) agreement under oath - and under the threat of papal excommunication.[78]

In 1260, personal hostilities between Béla IV and Otakar II led to war that ended in Hungarian defeat.[79] Although the Czech monarch had toyed with the idea of conquering Hungary, he decided against it because he realized that it was beyond his means to occupy the "magnum Hungariae regnum," and the renewed Mongol threat presented a real danger to both Bohemia and Hungary.[80]

In the Treaty of Vienna, 1261, Béla IV renounced his claim to Styria - territory he had already lost[81] - and Otakar II agreed to marry Constance, a granddaughter of Béla IV.[82] Also, Kunigunde of Brandenburg, a niece of Otakar II, was to be engaged to Béla, Béla IV's young son. (The marriage took place in 1264).[83] In such a manner, Béla IV had changed course in his foreign policy. He had turned the previous Hungaro-Czech hostility into a family affair - most probably under the influence of his Byzantine-born queen, Maria Lascaris, to whom, in 1259, he donated the fort of Visegrád, and the queen had the fort restored out of her own money.[84] Béla IV had warned his sons that Fort Visegrád could become, in case of a renewed Mongol invasion, an important segment of the country's line of military defense along the Danube, and reminded the spiteful Stephen of his duty to defend the interests of the entire kingdom.[85]

Prince Béla received, as a gift for his wedding in Pottenburg, the forts of Moson, Pozsony, and Nyitra, together with Vas, Zala, Somogy and Baranya counties in the southern half of Trans- danubia.[86] But his elder brother, Stephen the Junior King, had occupied the lands of their mother in the (his) eastern part of the realm, and, because of this breach of good faith, war broke out anew between father and son. Worse still, the nobles had encouraged both parties to fight. The Cumans supported the king, but the forces of Stephen had the upper hand in the battle at Déva.[87] Peter of the clan of Csák led the troops of Stephen. However, after the engagement, the king's forces turned north, occupied Patak, where they placed Elizabeth the Cuman, Stephen's wife, and their children under house arrest: they became royal captives. Next, the royal forces reached the Carpathians, and strongly decimated the forces fighting for Stephen. And yet, Stephen's adherents had fought for him at Feketehalom, and pushed the royal troops southward, to the Danube. In 1265, at the battle of Isaszeg, Stephen had captured Henry of Kőszeg and his brothers, all commanding officers of the king's forces.[88]

It took the two Hungarian archbishops prolonged negotiations to arrange for a truce between father and son. Beside the grave of Blessed Margaret on Rabbits' Island in the Danube, Béla IV and Stephen renewed their treaty of 1266. The re-negotiated treaty had an interesting provision in that it stressed the idea that Stephen was as much the lord in his own territories in the country as his father was in his own territories. In order to prevent a full-scale separation of the realm, however, the prince had acknowledged that his father held an honorable superior position: he was King of the Kingdom.[89]

The re-negotiated treaty had another curious resolution: Stephen had only permitted free peasants to move freely about in his areas of the realm, but denied free movements to the nobles and lesser nobles living there. It may further be worth noting that in the same document, the lesser nobles, Cumans, and barons were mentioned "side by side," at the same social level, not in a hierarchical order. Finally, Béla IV and Stephen agreed that they would conduct court hearings (proceedings in legal matters) in "both countries," in mid-Lent, on September 8, and on the Feast of St. Nicholas; and judges of "both countries" shall hand down sentences in their courts of law on those specific days.[90]

The "Austrian question" in the west had not been settled as yet, when Béla IV had to concentrate his efforts at facing political and military developments in the east. The Tartars had announced the invasion of Europe.[91] Now, it may be that the Hungarian court had realized that the sudden withdrawal by the Mongols from the country in 1242 could only have been a termination of their large scale maneuver for a future full-scale invasion - an invasion following afterwards, within a few years, culminating in a full-scale occupation of the west.[92] Béla IV had expected the Tartars to return because they had not taken him, and his court, captive.[93]

The king sent a message to Rome about the renewed Mongol threat through his uncle, the Patriarch of Aquileia, who had been authorized by the Holy See to preach against the Mongols.[94] Matthew of Paris must have referred to this papal authorization when he mentioned the Tartars, who had turned around, heading toward Hungary again.[95]

Béla IV had fortifications erected along the Danube, and commissioned the Knights of St. John of the Hospital to garrison the line of defense along the river. It was in this spirit of resistance that he had earlier signed an agreement with Rembaldus, *Praeceptor* of the Knights.[96] The Knights were to receive the Szerém (Zeurin) region, and the area controlled by the Vlach *kenéz* (ethnic reeve[s] for the Vlachs settled in the region) named John and Farkas, with the exception of the area that came under the jurisdiction of the Voyvoda (Grand Reeve; Grand Steward) Lynioy, from the southern Carpathians to the Danube. The monarch had that particular area retained for his personal use and supervision.[97]

The king had ordered that the Vlach population of the region aid the Knights in their administration efforts over the area, and gave the Knights the right of free transportation of salt - that included one-half of the income derived from the sale of salt. He had also assigned to the Knights the "Cuman lands" located east of the Olt river, except the area under the administration of Seneslaus, reeve (*kenéz!*) of the Vlachs, with the understanding that the Knights receive the whole income from the area for the first twenty-five years of their administration, and one-half after that.

The Knights obtained four hundred acres of specific land - including the Pezath estate and the Woyola estates that had been taken from Fort Krassó. In return, the Grandmaster of the Order promised specific military services to and for the king, took the oath of loyalty to the king, and stated his intention to re-populate the territories his Order was given by the monarch. The Knights agreed to provide one hundred trained and equipped men (knights) for fighting the pagan, and consented to defending one of the towers in the border forts of Pozsony, Moson, and Sopron; in case of a renewed Mongol attack, they would provide an additional sixty knights for the concentrated defense of the aforementioned towers.[98]

It is clear from the text of the treaty that the Knights would also aid the king in campaigns against enemies in the Bulgarian, Cuman, and Greek territories, to defend the interests of the realm, and the cause of Christianity, from the heathen and heretics - be they the "pagan" Mongols. Prelate Ehellős (Achilles) of Székesfehérvár, royal vice-chancellor, signed the agreement with the *Praeceptor* - Grandmaster of the Order. Archbishop Benedict of Kalocsa, royal chancellor, issued it, with signatures affixed to it by the nobles for authenticity.[99]

During all this time, when the king had kept a watchful eye on the borders of the realm, and made preparations for the defense of the southeast and in the east, he now had to take precautions toward the northeast against the Mongols. It was known that John Plano Carpini, the Franciscan friar who began his journey to the Far East from Lyon in April, 1245, as the papal envoy to the court of the Mongol Khan,[100] had, after a brief visit with Batu Khan in the Kipchak in May, 1247, returned and rested in Kiev,[101] where he was entertained for eight days in early June by the Romanovich family: Danilo and Vasilko.[102]

Through the efforts of Plano Carpini, the Romanovich family acknowledged the spiritual primacy of Rome over, and in, Kiev.[103] The fascinating, and to be expected, outcome of this Rome-Halich-Kiev connection might have been that its realization had perturbed the peace of mind of the ruler of Nicea. One might suspect that it was the reason why Danilo had dispatched Patriarch Cyrill to Asia Minor, to explain the new political-religious situation to the ruler in Nicea.[104]

It is evident from a papal letter, dated August 27, 1247, that negotiations were going on between Danilo of Halich and Pope Innocent IV, and Rome had made some concessions: the curia allowed the Russian (Kievan) hierarchy and clergy to retain their liturgy - as long as it did not disturb established customs of the Roman rite.[105] The curia also permitted the "Russian King" Danilo and (King) Vasilko of Ladomer to rely upon military force if needed to recover territory that justly belonged to them: "...recuperandi possessiones, terras, et alia bona ad vos herditario."[106]

In another letter, dated on the same day, Innocent IV had agreed that crusaders, or churchmen (*cruciferorum vel aliorum religiosum*) active in the territories under the two rulers' control, obtain no property without the rulers' explicit permission.[107] In two letters, dated the following day, Rome gave permission - through its envoy, the Archbishop of the Prussian, Estonians, and Latvians[108] - that individuals born out of wedlock, "dummodo non sint ad adulterino, vel incestuso coitu procreati," may obtain dispensation to take holy orders in the Church, and/or receive ecclesiastical benefices.[109] (As if by coincidence, the curia further granted Vasilko an annulment of his marriage on the grounds of consanguinity).)[110]

Pope Innocent IV specifically instructed his envoy how to behave toward Danilo of Halich, who only recently had converted to Christianity; in essence, the pontiff stated that the Russian clergy and nobles had to cease living in schism with the Roman See, and to take an oath of loyalty to the (Roman) Church.[111] In order to ease the burden of the legate, and to ensure a smooth transition, the curia allowed the "Russian," that is, Galician, Halichian, and Lubician (Lubiciensis) bishops to continue wearing the archiepiscopal pallium.[112] Rome further extended special protection to the ruler of Ladomer, "volumus prosequi prerogativa favoris et gratiae specialis,"[113] and recognized in particular the clergyman Hezelo de Vilstorf, who meritoriously distinguished himself in negotiating the church union between Rome and Halich-Kiev.[114]

It may be concluded that Rome, by receiving Halich-Kiev into the Church, had established an intelligence-gathering watchpost at the easternmost border of Christian Europe, as regards the Mongol threat.[115] Danilo maintained direct communication with Batu Khan (even though the threat of another Mongol invasion did not originate with Batu, but with Kujuk Khan, the rival of Batu.)[116] The pontiff's last known letter addressed to Danilo "Regi Russie illustri," dated January 22, 1249, ought to be referred to, where the curia had requested the prince, "Rex," that he report on, *intimare procures*, and provide information he might gain about the renewed Mongol threat, "quod Tartarorum exercitus versus Christianitatem dirigat gressus suos," to the German Knights (in Prussia).[117] In a writ dated two days later, the curia informed the Knights in Prussia about the contents of this letter.[118]

The Rome-Halich-Kiev "union" had its own problems, of course. Danilo had to explain to Rome that since the Roman See had provided no actual aid against the Mongols (the question may be raised, though, how, through what agency could the curia have sent such aid?), Danilo refused to accept the crown the pontiff had sent him.[119] The ruler of Halich must have been concerned about Batu Khan, for he had reasons for concern. He also had to sever his relations with Patriarch Cyrill;[120] however, judged by the tone and text of the papal writ of May 14, 1253, diplomatic ties between Rome and Halich remained intact (or were restored after Danilo's refusal of the crown), because Danilo had forwarded some intelligence data to Rome about the approaching Mongol threat.[121]

Friar Plano Carpini visited Béla IV to inform him about the renewed Mongol danger.[122] The king received Carpini at his court in Zólyom, where he had earlier reached the agreement with Danilo of Halich.[123]

The Luxemberg manuscript of the Carpini report carries a thirteenth century annotation to the effect that the Hungarian court had envoys sent to the court of the Khan - after Carpini had departed on *his mission* to the Khan - and the envoys returned with the report that the Mongols were making war preparations, as if to support Carpini's remark that the Mongols would, after three winters, invade Polish and Hungarian territories again.[124] Still, the question must be asked, was this entry on the manuscript made in 1247, or was it added, as an afterthought, in 1254?

The circumstances surrounding the development of political and religious synthesis between Danilo of Halich-Kiev and the

Roman See call for an additional observation. Béla IV, in his attempt to distinguish between the claims of Boleslav and/or Rostislav, and Danilo Romanichov, had decided for the latter on the grounds that the Romanichovs wanted to expand their religious-diplomatic ties with the papal curia, thereby creating an avenue for an ecclesiastical and diplomatic relationship with the Roman See.

Béla IV must have been guided by a twofold concept in reaching his decision. Partly, it was his loyalty to Rome that predominated his diplomatic and foreign policy; when Rome opposed his request for the Austrian Babenberg inheritance on the grounds that it threatened relations between Rome and Prague, Béla IV accepted the curia's decision and withdrew his request. Partly also, the monarch acknowledged the advantages of the political and diplomatic game of chess Danilo had played with Batu Khan; Halich now had to serve as an intelligence-gathering outpost for the Hungarian court on events developing in eastern Europe.

There remain a few unanswered questions, however. Did Danilo initiate the diplomatic process with Rome, or did the curia encourage the prince of Halich to take the initiative? What role, if any, had Cyrill, the Patriarch, to play in this diplomatic more? - or Friar Plano Carpini for that matter, the curia's legate extraordinary to the court of the Mongol Khan?

The ruler of Kiev must have taken the first step by sending Patriarch Cyrill to the court of Béla IV with late intelligence data on the Mongol threat. Evidently, he wanted to prove to Béla IV that he had obtained valuable news about the plans of the Mongols, because he had been in personal contact with the khan. He wanted to explain to Theodore Lascaris his need for diplomatic and religious ties with the Roman See because the patriarch had visited Nicea. Yet, was it really from Nicea that Danilo had hoped to receive ecclesiastical recognition of himself - and of the status-quo of the Church in Kiev?

The idea of spiritual conversion of Kiev to Roman Catholicism might have emerged as secondary in importance before the eyes of the papal court, as it is quite evident from the (texts of the) dispensation(s) that were granted by the curia to high churchmen and nobles in Kiev. Rome must have viewed the recently converted ruler of Halich-Kiev as a diplomatic-military intelligence-gathering source - a role the prince might, incidentally, have already fulfilled - as important as establishing a religious base in a Russian capital.[125]

Therefore, in referring to the letter Béla IV had addressed to Pope Innocent IV, and cited at some length at the beginning of this chapter, one might reach the startling conclusion that it was written after the meeting of the king with Carpini at Zólyom: "...cogeremur nontamquam filii sed privigini necessitate compulsi, quasi extra gregem patris expulsi, suffragiis mendicare."[126] Plano Carpini was present at the election of the new Great Khan;[127] and he brought with him the latest news on the Tartar readiness to invade and permanently occupy western Europe.[128]

Béla IV's letter did, incidentally, mention Bishop Bertalan of Pécs[129] (who would have resigned his episcopal see by the year 1251,[130] and would be addressed by a papal writ as "Episcopus *quondam* [italics mine!] Quinqueecclesiensis")[131] it did speak of a war with heretics,[132] as if referring to the papal letter of late January, 1247, where the pontiff had issued a call for military action to be undertaken against "heretics" in Bosnia.[133]

The writ of Béla IV that, because of its imprecise date had caused a good deal of controversy, must have been drafted and published in the late 1240's. It was probably issued on November 11, 1248, from Sárospatak. The place of issue could not have been more coincidental. It was from Sárospatak that one could keep under steady observation the military highway leading toward Halich,[134] just as it was another military road, the one leading toward Fehérvár, that had been mentioned in the text of the Charter for the Abbey of Tihany, issued by King Andrew I, in 1055.[135]

NOTES

* Cf. c. 177, in *SSH*, I, 468,9-17.
1. See Hodinka, 414a and 416a [for date]; *GVC*, 55ff.; *MPH*, II, 838 and III, 13; Font, *art. cit.* (1990), 18. On the name of Rostislav, Ractislaus, Raziclaus, Rozyslaus, see, e.g., *RA*, n. 853, where he is being referred to as Prince of Halich and Grand Steward (Ban[us]) of Slavonia, *VMH*, n. 393; *CD*, IV-1, 447ff.; also, *RA*, n. 946, as Prince of Halich, *ÁUO*, XI, 373f.
2. *RA*, n. 1011, as Prince of Halich and Lord of Macho, Békefi, *Pilisi apátság*, I, 316: facsimile; *CD*, IV-2, 214f.; Prince of Halich and the king's son-in-law in *RA*, n. 1226; *HO*, VI, 97f.
3. *RA*, n. 1406; Potthast, n. 18975; *VMH*, n. 500; F. Palacky, *Literarische Reise nach Italien in 1837* (Prague, 1838), n. 302.
4. Hodinka, 432a, 344a; *GVC*, 57; *RA*, n. 939; *CD*, IV-2, 65.
5. Hodinka, 416b and 428a; Katona, *Historia critica*, VI, 139.
6. Hodinka, 416a, 418a; *GVC*, 52; also, *RA*, n. 853 (June 2, 1247), as cited above.
7. Hodinka, 418a, 420a, 426a, 428a-430a; *GVC*, 57; the writ of May 10, 1251, referred to a landgrant for Rostislav - *RA*, n. 946, as cited above. It may seem that Rostislav fled to the court of Béla IV after a second defeat his forces had suffered at the hands of Danilo, though it is possible that, after the previous defeat, he again invaded Halich, but was halted by Danilo's forces. The writ that named him Prince of Halich and Lord of Macho, etc., was dated June 28, 1254, *RA*, n. 1011, as *supra*.
8. Hodinka, 430a; *GVC*, 56; *ÁUO*, VII, 163ff., esp. 164; compare with Carpini, ix:2, 3, 48 and 49.
9. Hodinka, 4301; B. Szcsesinak, "The Mission of Giovanni de Plano Carpini and Benedict the Pole of Vratislava," *Journal of Ecclesiastical History*, 7 (1957), 12ff.
10. Indeed, the king promoted Germanus, son of Wysobor and a *servilis* from Ujvár, to a royal *iobagio*, or the role he played in the delegation sent to Danilo, cf. *RA*, n. 955, with text.
11. Hodinka, 430a; *GVC*, 59.
12. Cf. *ÁUO*, VI, 163ff., though according to *RA*, n. 763, it could be a spurious document; compare with *ÁUO*, X, 242ff. (anno 1296), esp. 243; Knauz, I, 446f.; *HO*, IV, 28ff.
13. Hodinka, 428a, 430a; *RA*, n. 853; Zimmermann-Werner, I, 73f.; further, *RA*, nn. 946 and 1226; Marta F. Font, "Ungarische Vornehmen in der Halitsch im 13 Jahrhundert," *Specimina nova Universitatis Quinqueecclesiensis* (Pécs, 1990 [1992]), 165ff.
14. Cf. Thomas Ebendorfer, *Chronica Austriae*, ed. Alfons Lhotsky (Berlin-Zurich, 1967), 120,1-20; also, in Pez, SSRA, II, 689ff., esp. 738f.; "Herrimanni Annales Altahanses," *MGHSS*, XVII, 393,10-12; also *ibid.*, IX, 598 and 789.
15. Ebendorfer, 120,4-6; A. Huber, *Geschichte Österreichs*, vol. I (Gotha, 1885), 477f.; H. Dienst, *Die Schlacht an der Leitha, 1246* (Vienna, 1971).
16. Ebendorfer, 120,33; *MGHSS*, IX, 598,4-11; Lhotsky, *Quellenkunde*, 23ff.; K. Uhlirz, "Das Lokal der Leithaschlacht, 1246 und das Testament Herzog Friedrichs II," *MIÖG* , 21 (1990), 155ff., and the arguments of J. Lampel, in *Monatsblatt des Altertumvereins zu Wien*, 6 (1900), 17ff.; Erna Patzelt, *Österreich bis zum Ausgang der Babenbergerzeit* (Vienna, 1947), 167f., saw it differently: "im Jahre 1246 sah sich Friedrich von Österreich in Nord und Ost von Feind bedrängt." She wrote that it was Béla IV who had attacked first because he wanted to regain the counties he had earlier lost; most probably, she based her argument on Ebendorfer, 120,1-4 (Pez, II, 724), but the "Herrimani Annales" recorded that the counties had already been recovered

by Béla IV - *MGHSS*, XVII, 393,10-12; *ibid.*, IX, 789; in fact, the counties lost to Frederick had been recovered as early as 1242 - *CD*, IV-1, 286; *CD*, IV-2, 288ff.
    17. Ebendorfer, 120,6-8, and note 2; *MGHSS*, IX, 559; Hóman-Szekfű, I, 564f.; György Györffy, *Einwohnerzahl und Bevölkerungsdichte in Ungarn bis zum Anfang des XIV Jahrhunderts* (Budapest, 1960), 23.
    18. Hodinka, 434ab; *GVC*, 61f.
    19. Ebendorfer, 120,13-23; Keza, *Gesta*, c. 72; *SSH*, I, 184,15-18; did his own men murder him? - *MGHSS*, XVII, 394,16-17; *ibid.*, IX, 559,27-30.
    20. *SSH*, I, 468,15-17; compare with *ÁUO*, VII, 282ff., esp. 283f.; *RA*, n. 901; Ebendorfer, 120,10-13; *MGHSS*, IX, 598,4-11: the Hungarians had suffered heavy defeat; further, *ibid.*, IX, 789.
    21. *SSH*, I, 468,9-17.
    22. Hodinka, 434b; *GVC*, 64.
    23. Hodinka, 436a; *GVC*, 64.
    24. *MGHSS*, XXII, 541,15-19.
    25. Hodinka, 436a [anno 1250!]; *GVC*, 64.
    26. *Ibid.*; *RA*, n. 1055 (December 20, 1255); *CD*, IV-2, 313ff.
    27. *MGHSS*, IX, 642,1; *ibid.*, IX, 655,17-20; IX, 559,28, spoke of "rex Gomanorum." *RA*, n. 1406; Hodinka, 436a; *GVC*, 59; Danilo's son Leo [Lev] was married to Constance, sister of Anna, both daughters of Béla IV; however, Leo's marriage took place later - cf. Hodinka, 416a, 430a; *GVC*, 59.
    28. *ÁUO*, II, 269f.
    29. Cf. Ebendorfer, 120,15-16.
    30. As it may be concluded from *RA*, n. 853; *CD*, IV-1, 447ff.; *VMH*, n. 393; Katona, *Historia critica*, VI, 95f.
    31. Potthast, n. 14016; E. Reiszig, *A jeruzsálemi Szent János Lovagrend Magyarországon* [The Knights of St. John of the Hospital in Hungary], 2 vols. (Budapest, 1925-26), I, 58ff.
    32. There Erne, Master of Horse, and Reeve of Varasd, had distinguished himself; cf. *RA*, n. 928 (July 7, 1250); *CD*, IV-2, 92f., dated it 1251. Compare with *RA*, n. 856; *ÁUO*, VII, 321ff.; Mór Werthner, *IV Béla története* [The History of Béla IV] (Temesvár, 1893), 112; for the Austrian point of view, see "Auctarium Maria-cellense," *MGHSS*, IX, 647, anno 1250; further, *ibid.*, IX, 642,46 - 643,38.
    33. Hodinka, 434b; *GVC*, 61f.; *CD*, IV-2, 65; earlier, in June, 1249, Béla IV issued a writ in Pozsony, *RA*, n. 909; *ÁUO*, VII, 285, and had it confirmed on October 7, 1249 - *RA*, n. 911; *ÁUO*, VII, 285.
    34. *MGHSS*, IX, 642f., anno 1250, that, if correct, may state that the Austrians had invaded in 1249, and the Hungarian court had called for countermeasures in 1250! See Ebendorfer, 123,3-6; Huber, *Geschichte*, I, 523. Hermann, husband of Gertrud, the sister of Frederick Babenberg, had designs on the territory and had hope to obtain it with papal help - *MGHSS*, IX, 642; F. Hausmann, "Kaiser Friedrich II und Österreich," *Probleme um Friedrich II*, ed. J. Fleckenstein (Sigmaringen, 1974), 300.
    35. Hodinka, 430a and 438; again, the reward of *servilis* Germanus, son of Wysobor, for his "in legationibus nostris ad dilectum cognatum nostrum Danilam illustrem, ducem Ruthenorum;" *ÁUO*, VII, 505f.; *RA*, n. 955, and n. 1227; L. Gyármány, *Tardy: Slawenhandel in der Tartarei* (Szeged, 1983), 14.
    36. Hodinka, 432a; *GVC*, 59; Carpini, ix:2.
    37. Hodinka, 432ab; *GVC*, 59; Gy. Moravcsik, *Byzantium and the Magyars* (Amsterdam-Budapest, 1970), 96f.; and a more realistic interpretation in Hóman-Szekfű, I, 565; Mór Werthner, *Az Árpádok családi története* [Family History of the Árpáds] (Nagybecskerek, 1892), 485 and 488.
    38. Hodinka, 432a; *GVC*, 59; on Zólyom, cf. Fügedi, *Castle and Society*, 55; a royal writ spoke of its construction - cf. *RA*, n.1051 with text. The royal domain:

218   HUNGARY IN THE THIRTEENTH CENTURY

praedium, at Zólyom included the later counties of Túróc, Liptó and Árva - see Elemér Mályusz, *Túróc megye kialakulása* [Formation of Túróc County] (Budapest, 1922), 5f.
      39. Hodinka, 432a; *GVC*, 59.
      40. If Duke Conrad of Mesovia had died in 1247 - cf. Rocznik Krakowski, *MPH*, II, 838; Rocznik Wielpolski, *ibid.*, III, 13 - his talks with Danilo must have taken place in, or before 1247; cf. Hodinka, 432a (anno 1251, in reference to 1247!). On the mission of Cyrill to Nicea, cf. G. Stöckl, "Kanzler und Metropolit," *Wiener Archiv für Geschichte des Slawentums und Osteuropas*, 5 (1966), 163ff., esp. 167.
      41. *RA*, nn. 836 and 837; *ÁUO*, II, 189f. and VII, 195 (dated 1245!); the writs were dated from *Zolum* "sub castro Polona," and "in Zolim."
      42. *RA*, n. 857; further, nn. 858, 861 and 862; *ÁUO*, II, 193, VII, 225f., XI, 348 and 346 - all dated "in Zolum."
      43. In *RA*, n. 1015, probably on September 16, 1254, the entry reads "in Zoulum" (sic!), its being the first writ issued since the one logged as n. 872; cf. *VMH*, n. 435. E. Sebestyén, *A magyar királyok tartózkodási helyei* [Places of Residence of the Hungarian Monarchs] (Budapest, 1938), 19ff.
      44. *RA*, n. 850; *ÁUO*, VII, 223f.; for Egyed, son of Thomas of Ulosz(i), who "indesinenter et indefesse seruisset" the king; see *supra*, n. 35.
      45. *RA*, n. 839; *ÁUO*, VII, 226f., dated 1247!
      46. As it may be evident from *RA*, n. 846; *VMH*, n. 387; Huber, *Geschichte*, I, 516.
      47. Potthast, n. 12409.
      48. Ebendorfer, 124,3 - 125, 8 and 125ff.
      49. Hausmann, *art. cit.*, in Fleckenstein, 286.
      50. Zöllner, *Geschichte*, 111ff.; Hantsch, *Geschichte*, I, 101ff.
      51. Potthast, n. 11722; *VMH*, n. 353; Haller, IV, 182ff.; Jedin, *Handbuch*, IV, 173ff. and 416f.; Th. C. VanCleve, *The Emperor Frederick II of Hohenstaufen* (Oxford, 1972), 473ff.
      52. *RA*, n. 846, in reference to a papal writ; *CD*, IV-1, 458ff.; *VMH*, n. 378. Potthast, nn. 15313, 15318, 15322; *VMH*, nn. 431, 432, and 433; Fraknói, I, 69f.
      53. Potthast, n. 10533*; *VMH*, n. 423; *RA*, n. 991, and compare with *CD*, IV-1, 459f. and IV-2, 27; Ebendorfer, 124,11-21 and 129,15-17.
      54. Ebendorfer, 135,1-10; Hermann of Baden wanted to inherit the Babenberg lands, but had scored no success - *MGHSS*, IX, 642,5-8; upon his death, anno 1250, Béla IV *devastaret* the territory - *ibid.*, IX, 642,46-56, and the Czech monarch intervened, leading to Hungarian withdrawal, *ibid.*, IX, 643,32-38.
      55. Cf. J. Lampel, "Die Landesgrenze von 1254 und das steirische Ennstal," *Archiv für österreichische Geschichte*, 71 (1887), 297ff., esp. 318f. and 342; F. Pesty, *A magyarországi várispánságok története különösen a XIII században* [History of County Fort Stewardships in Hungary Especially During the 13th Century] (Budapest, 1882), 315; Huber, *Geschichte*, I, 524, n. 2, and compare with *CD*, IV-3, 199 and IV-2, 314ff. On June 8, 1249, Béla IV had issued a writ in Pozsony, *RA*, n. 909; *ÁUO*, VII, 285; in his writ of July 7, 1250, the king rewarded Master Erne, reeve of Várad (Woros), *RA*, n. 928; *CD*, IV-2, 92 (anno 1252), and *RA*, n. 956 (November 17, 1251); *ÁUO*, VII, 321ff., esp. 322: "eciam in conflictu belli, quod commisimus contra ducem Austrie." Or, the royal recognition of Oltumanus, son of Petrus *de genere* Gurka, a royal reeve: "...cum exercitu valido intrassemus in Austriam contra Teutonicos in vastro Walterstorph;" *ibid.*, VII, 338ff., esp. 339; *RA*, n. 968; also, Werthner, *Árpádok*, 112.
      56. *MGHSS*, IX, 643,4-14.
      57. *Ibid.*, IX, 643,14-15, though he added that "rex Ruscie relicta uxore rediit at terram suam;" *ibid.*, IX, 643,16.

THE AFTERMATH: THE 1240's

219

58. This may be evident from the July 1, 1253, writ of the pope, Potthast, n. 15034; Rome further instructed Velasco to bring the marriage of Otakar and Margaret in order: blood relationship between them to the fourth degree, and being brother-in-laws at the third level formed marriage impediments; cf. *VMH*, n. 423; Lucas Wadding, *Annales Minorum seu trium Ordinum a s. Francisco institutorum*, 17 vols. (Quaracci, 1931-35), III, 589; *Bullarium Franciscanum Romanorum Pontificum constitutiones, epistolae ac diplomata contines, tribus Ordinibus Minorum...a s. Francisco istitutis concessa*, 4 vols. (Rome, 1759-1904), I, 663 and 664; F. Monay, *A római magyar gyóntatók* [Hungarian Confessors at St. Peter's] (Rome, 1956), 10ff.
59. Papal writs of April 2, 4, and 6, 1254, see Potthast, nn. 15313, 15318, 15322; *VMH*, nn. 431, 432 and 433.
60. *CD*, IV-2, 249; *VMH*, n. 435 (June 24, 1254), Wadding, III, 589.
61. *MGHSS*, IX, 183f.; Balics, II, 351f.; Palacky, *Geschichte*, II-1, 196 and n. 265; Loserth, *op. cit.*, 136ff.
62. Innocent IV on July 13, 1254, Potthast, n. 15460; *VMH*, n. 435; Palacky, *Reise*, n. 241.
63. *CD*, IV-2, 53.
64. Ebendorfer, 135,1-10, and note 3 to the effect, Lhotsky says, that the "meeting" took place in Buda; Otakar went to Prussia in 1252; Ebendorfer, admittedly, provided a rather uncertain date - Lampel, *art. cit.*
65. *RA*, nn. 1057 and 1058; *ÁUO*, VII, 484; *RA*, n. 1089.
66. Most probably in reference to the promise Béla IV had, in 1241, made to the emperor that, were Frederick II to help him against the Tartars, he would submit himself and his country to him - *RA*, n. 708; *MGHSS*, XIX, 380,49-53; and his letter on behalf of the emperor to the papal curia, *RA*, n. 622.
67. Potthast, n. 11821; *CD*, IV-1, 372, and *RA*, n. 839; *ÁUO*, VII, 226f. [anno 1247!]; *CD*, IV-1, 458ff. [anno 1246!].
68. Stephen was born in 1239 - *RA*, n. 828; *CD*, IV-1, 404.
69. *MGHSS*, IX, 642,12-15. A letter, dated 1259, referred to Stephen as "Captain" of Styria - *HO*, VIII, 74.
70. *RA*, n. 1199; *ÁUO*, VII, 484f. In a writ, dated July 27, 1260, Stephen was mentioned as "Dominus Cymanorum," and as "Prince of Styria" - *ÁUO*, VII, 524f.; in a 1257 writ, he appeared as "Dux Transylvaniae" - *ibid.*, XI, 440. On Stephen's territorial claims, cf. *ibid.*, II, 321, 322; and *ibid.*, V, 66, XI, 461f.; *HO*, VI, 104.
71. *MGHSS*, IX, 644,10-11 and 644,21-22; on Stephen's first encounter with his father, cf. *ibid.*, IX, 645,21-22, for reasons revealed by Stephen himself - *CD*, V-1, 103; Knauz, I, 477, presents another angle!
72. Samuel, II, 13-14.
73. Zöllner, 112f.; Hantsch, I, 104f.
74. Keza, c. 73, *SSH*, I, 184.
75. *Ibid.*, Anonymus, cc. 5-6 and 57, *ibid.*, I, 39ff., and I, 114,13-16.
76. Heer, *Geistesgeschichte*, 163ff.; Marc Bloch, *Feudal Society*, trans. L.A. Manyon (Chicago, 1961), 421ff.; Hampe, *Hochmittelalter*, 386ff.
77. As it may be evident from a later writ - *RA*, n. 1303; *CD*, IV-3, 71. Stephen acted independently in his part of the realm - *ÁUO*, VIII, 5ff., 8f., and 9ff., as Duke of Transylvania. He had issued a writ at Pata, *ibid.*, III, 24, at Kassa - *CD*, IV-3, 50, and in Heves [county], *ibid.*, IV-3, 204f.
78. *RA*, n. 1346, "aput Lypcha," in Knauz, I, 630ff.; *ÁUO*, III, 34ff.; *VMH*, n. 459.
79. *MGHSS*, IX, 177a,43-49; IX, 177b,43-51; also, *ibid.*, IX, 559f., 560,13-18, 644,19-30, 655,41-48; further, *ibid.*, XIX, 180f.; XXV, 362,6 and 9-28; also, *ibid.*, XVII, 401,46-54 (Kroissenbrunn). In the Chronicle, MS, fol. 63´a, there is a picture in a simple frame depicting the cavalry attack at Hainburg; in the middle of the drawing is Béla IV on a white horse, in body armor, and a crown on his head: "Pugnat rex

220 HUNGARY IN THE THIRTEENTH CENTURY

cum Othocaro." Cf. Dercsényi, *Chronicon pictum*, fol. 63v; for text, *SSH*, I, 468f. (c. 178).

80. *Ibid.*, IX, 184ff. - doubted by Katona, *Historia critica*, VI, 312; Pray, *Annales*, I, 30; *MGHSS*, XXX-1, 400f., 401,8-9, caused by an unexpected Hungarian counterattack? - *CD*, IV-1, 112. On the mission of Panyi, see *ÁUO*, XII, 7f.

81. *RA*, n. 1335; *CD*, IV-3, 100f.; Palacky, *Geschichte*, II-1, 184f.; Katona, *Historia critica*, VI, 377f.

82. After he had obtained separation from his former wife, formerly a religious sister (Dominican), Otakar II asked for the hand in marriage of Margaret, the older daughter of Béla IV, who was a Dominican sister since the age of three; she turned him down. Cf. "Vita b. Margarithae Hungaricae" auctore P. Ranzano, *Acta Sanctorum*, Ian. II, 900ff., c. 2; *Acta Sanctorum Hungaricae*, I, 77ff., c. 14: "Nuptiae repudiatae...;" see also Ranzano, *Epithoma*, 129, ind. xvi; "Vita b. Margarithae Hungarica (Legenda Neopolitana)," in Ferdinánd Knauz (ed.), *A nápolyi Margit-legenda* [The Margaret Legend of Naples] (Esztergom, 1868), 30ff., i:2 and i:25; Palacky, *Geschichte*, II-1, 184f.

83. On Kunigunde and Otakar II, see Böhmer-Ficker-Winkelman, *Regesta imperii*, n. 1183; *MGHSS*, IX, 186f.; H. Krabbo, *Regesten der Markgrafen von Brandenburg* (Leipzig, 1910), nn. 900 and 901, and 868; Palacky, *Geschichte*, II-1, 189ff.; *MGHSS*, IX, 178; XVII, 402,42-44.

84. *RA*, n. 1223; *ÁUO*, VII, 501ff.

85. *Ibid.*, VII, 502f.

86. Potthast, n. 18972; *VMH*, n. 496, and compare to Potthast, nn. 18971, 18973, 18974; *VMH*, nn. 494, 497, 498, respectively; further, *ÁUO*, III, 96f., 94ff., 98, and 97f., respectively.

87. Potthast, nn. 18970 and 18972; *VMH*, nn. 493 and 496; *ÁUO*, III, 91 and 96. Or, the papal warning to Stephen not to disturb Anna in the possession of her holdings - Potthast, n. 18981; *ÁUO*, III, 101f.

88. Innocent IV confirmed the donation of Béla IV for his daughter Anna, widow of Rostislav, and their sons, - cf. Potthast, n. 18975; *VMH*, n. 500 - and warned Stephen not to threaten Anna in her holdings, Potthast, n. 18981; Knauz, I, 664; *ÁUO*, III, 100f.; *VMH*, n. 506.

89. Cf. *RA*, n. 1481; *VMH*, n. 517; *ÁUO*, III, 128ff. and 136ff., in accordance with the papal confirmation, *ibid.*, III, 144f.; Potthast, n. 19702; Knauz, I, 695ff.

90. Again, Potthast, n. 19702; *VMH*, n. 518 (n. 517); *CD*, IV-3, 364ff.

91. See the Synod of Lyon, 1245, in Mansi, *Concilia*, XXIII, 605ff., art. 16; also, *VMH*, n. 366; *ÁUO*, VII, 197ff.; VanCleve, 480ff.; excommunication of the emperor, Mansi, XXIII, 613ff.

92. Cf. Ödön Schütz, "A mongol hódítás néhány problémája" [Some Questions Concerning the Mongol Conquest], *Századok*, 93 (1959), 209ff.

93. Hodinka, 430a; *GVC*, 57; Carpini, ix:48. Béla IV had notified Rome - see the papal reply, Potthast, n. 12414; *CD*, IV-1, 461f. Hodinka, 414a and 416a; *GVC*, 51 and 55ff.

94. For the papal writ addressed to Berthold, cf. Potthast, n. 11096; *VMH*, n. 348; the question remains, however, was the authorization based on false hopes? Cf. Ilona Pálfyy, *A tatárok és a XIII századvégi Európa* [The Mongols and Late 13th Century Europe] (Budapest, 1928), 36ff.; Matthew of Paris, IV, 410ff., and further papal instructions sent to the archbishops of Esztergom and of Kalocsa, Potthast, n. 12414; *CD*, IV-1, 462.

95. Carpini, viii:9-15; Matthew of Paris, VI, 133.

96. *VMH*, I, 208ff.

97. In that the Hungarian court continued to receive one half of the income derived from it.

98. The Knights further agreed to provide one hundred trained and equipped men to defend a tower each at Pozsony, Moson, and Sopron; they would send sixty additional knights, if needed; Reiszig, I, 58ff.
99. *RA*, n. 853; *VMH*, n. 393; *CD*, IV-1, 447ff. Innocent IV had it transcribed on July 19, 1250 - Potthast, n. 14016; Katona, *Historia critica*, VI, 95f.
100. Carpini, prologus, 1-4; Benedictus Polonus, cc. 1-2; Potthast, n. 11607; *VMH*, n. 362; J. de Rachewiltz, *Papal Envoys to the Great Khan* (London, 1971), 41ff.
101. Carpini, ix:47; Polonus, c. 12.
102. Carpini, ix:46-48.
103. Carpini, ix:48; Hodinka, 432a; *GVC*, 59; Potthast, n. 12813; *ÁUO*, VII, 236f.; B. Altaner, *Die Dominikanermissionen des 13 Jahrhunderts* (Habelschwert, 1924), 16ff.; G. Markovic, *Gli Slavi ed i Papi*, 2 vols. (Zagreb, 1897), I, 363ff., and II, 220ff.
104. Potthast, n. 12686, 12687, 12688; *ÁUO*, VII, 236f., 237, and 238; Moravcsik, *Byzantium*, 96f.; Werthner, *Árpádok*, 485 and 488.
105. Potthast, n. 12669; *ÁUO*, VII, 232f.
106. Potthast, n. 12668; *ÁUO*, VII, 233f.; Carpini, ix:3 and 48; Polonus, c. 2; Wyngaert, lxi.
107. Potthast, n. 12670; *ÁUO*, VII, 234.
108. *ÁUO*, VI, 235.
109. Potthast, nn. 12671 and 12672; *ÁUO*, VII, 235 and 235f.
110. Potthast, n. 12775; *ÁUO*, VII, 240.
111. Potthast, n. 12686; *ÁUO*, VII, 236f.
112. Potthast, n. 12687; *ÁUO*, VII, 237.
113. Potthast, n. 12688; *ÁUO*, VII, 238.
114. Who "...clarissimi in Chriso filii Danielis regis Ruscie nuntiorum, cum quibus idem clericus pro Sedis Apostolicae negotiis fideliter, ut accepimus, laboravit;" Potthast, n. 12689; *ÁUO*, VII, 239f.
115. Béla IV had acted as an intercessor on behalf of Danilo in front of the papal curia, recommending resumption of relations - cf. *RA*, n. 991; *VMH*, n. 452 [anno 1254!]; Knauz, I, 406ff. and 408, note. Also, Potthast, n. 14769, addressed to Cardinal Stephen of Praeneste, *ÁUO*, II, 227.
116. Carpini, ix:2, 3, 48, and 49.
117. Potthast, n. 12810; *ÁUO*, VII, 267, dated January 19, 1248 - a repeat of Potthast, n. 11339, dated April 20, 1244?
118. Potthast, n. 12813.
119. Hodinka, 440a and 442a; *GVC*, 67.
120. G. Soranzo, *Il papato, l'Europa cristiana e i tartari: un secolo dei penetrazione occidentale in Asia* (Milan, 1930); P. Pelliot, "Les Mongols et la papauté," *Revue de l'Orient chrétien*, 23 (1922), 3ff.; 24 (1924), 225ff.; 28 (1931), 3ff.; A.N. Nasanov, *Mongoli i Rus* (Moscow-Leningrad, 1940), 33 and 38f.; G. Vernadsky, *The Mongols and Russia* (New Haven, 1953), 147.
121. Danilo had Rome notified - Potthast, n. 14972; Carpini, ix:49.
122. The thirteenth century entry on the manuscript of Plano Carpini's *Itinerarium* may refer to this - cf. G. Itsványi, "XIII századi feljegyzés IV Bélának a tatárokhoz küldött követségéről" [A Thirteenth Century Annotation on the Embassy Sent by Béla IV to the Mongols], *Századok*, 72 (1938), 270ff. The manuscript dated Carpini's departure anno 1246 (1245!), and his visit at the court of Béla IV may have occurred in 1247 - cf. D. Sinor, "John of Monte Corvino's Return from the Mongols," repr. from the *Journal of the Royal Asiatic Society*, 1957. Still, the exact date of the annotation remains unknown. G.A. Bezzola, *Die Mongolen in abendländisches Sicht, 1220-1270* (Bern-Munich, 1974), 123; K.E. Lupprian, *Die*

Beziehungen der Päpste zu islamischen und mongolischen Herrschern im 13 Jahrhundert (Vatican City, 1981), 53.

123. Hodinka, 432a; *GVC*, 59; Carpini, ix:47. J. Bequet and L. Hambis, *Jean de Plan Carpin, Histoire de Mongols* (Paris, 1965), 102f.

124. Carpini, viii:2, 4-5; ix:38, Itsványi, *art. cit.*, 270; D. Sinor, "The Mongols in Western Europe," in R.J. Wolf and H.W. Hazard (eds.), *The Later Crusades*, vol. III of *History of the Crusades*, ed. J.R. Strayer (Philadelphia, 1962, etc.), 513ff.

125. Potthast, n. 14972.

126. Marczali, *Enchiridion*, 164.

127. Carpini, v:18, ix:28 and 31; Polonus, c. 8.

128. Carpini, viii:2, 5; ix:38-39.

129. Cf. *RA*, n. 933b; *CD*, IV-1, 298 (dated 1243!)

130. To be succeeded by Achilles (Ehellős), the former royal chancellor - *RA*, n. 933; *CD*, IV-2, 64; Achilles appears as the bishop-elect on a writ of July 23, 1251 - *RA*, n. 949; *CD*, IV-2, 95.

131. Potthast, n. 14966; *VMH*, n. 418; in October, 1253, Béla IV dispatched an envoy to the papal curia - *RA*, n. 1000; *VMH*, n. 230; Knauz, I, 411 (though *CD*, IV-2, 145, dated it 1252).

132. "...contra paganos et scismaticos [sic!] ad defensionem regni nostri et fidei Christiani;" Marczali, *Enchiridion*, 164.

133. Potthast, n. 12407; *VMH*, n. 376; and, Potthast, n. 12664; *VMH*, n. 382; *CD*, IV-1, 467f.; John V.A. Fine, Jr., "Was the Bosnian Banate Subjugated to Hungary in the Second Half of the Thirteenth Century?" *East European Quarterly*, 3 (1969), 167ff.

134. *RA*, n. 933a; Hóman-Szekfü, I, 578.

135. Cf. Marczali, *Enchiridion*, 81ff.; Hóman-Szekfű, I, 283; Kosztolnyik, *Five Kings*, 77 and 178, note 52.

CHAPTER SEVEN

BÉLA IV'S LAW OF 1251, AND THE PROBABLE IMPACT UPON IT BY AURELIUS AUGUSTINUS' CONCEPT OF "QUI IMPERANT,... NEQUE IMPERANT... PRINCIPANDI SUPERBIA, SED PROVIDENDI MISERICORDIA"
(*DE CIVITATE DEI*, XIX, 14)

> Imperant autem qui consulunt; sicut uir uxori, parentes filiis, domini seruis....
>
> Augustine, *De civitate Dei*, XIX, 14*

Aurelius Augustinus established the Christian philosophy of history.[1] The ancient world regarded history as nature's perpetual rhythm of decline and rebirth. To Augustine, history had a beginning, a meaning, and a purpose.[2] The history of man was constituted by man's search of the supernatural deity. The beginning of history was supernatural revelation that led man to the notion of God. The purpose of history was to make clear God's perfect manifestation to man. The meaning of history was God revealing Himself to man, and man becoming one with God. Therefore, history was man's acceptance of God, or rejection of Him.[3]

Those who turned away from God constituted the citizenry of the *civitas terrena [diaboli]*, the earthly city.[4] Those who accepted God, those who held the opinion that only those events through which God enters the world have a meaning, constituted the citizenry of the *civitas Dei*, the heavenly city. The community of the chosen was not, however, permanent. At the end of time, it would submerge in the kingdom of God.[5]

The government of Béla IV had been served by many individuals who held university degrees. Suffice it here to refer to

Archbishop Benedict of Kalocsa, "magister" and royal chancellor, who had signed and authenticated with the royal seal the Law of 1251.[6] Vice-chancellor Smaragdus, archpriest of Székesfehérvár, was known as *magister*.[7] Archdean Albertus of Esztergom, a member of the king's royal council, who had died at Mohi, was referred to as *magister* by Rogerius.[8]

In the 1220's, Paulus Hungarus (Pál Magyar), a Dominican friar, had taught law at the University of Bologna. Friar Paulus had played an important role in establishing the Hungarian Dominican province, and had been murdered by the Mongols at the altar of the Dominican church in Pest in 1241.[9]

The cathedral school in Veszprém, so savagely destroyed in 1276, did have a law faculty. A royal writ mentioned the learned members of the faculty, whose libraries were burnt in the fire caused during the destruction.[10] The royal letter referred to the burned down school as the equivalent of the one in Paris - undoubtedly a strong overstatement, though an indication that other subjects, including theology, were taught besides law, at the cathedral school of Veszprém.[11]

Many of the king's advisors and officials at the court held advanced university degrees, and were trained in both theology and law. A good number of them, mostly monks and clergymen, were educated theologians - even though Rome had to warn them not to neglect the study of theology in favor of law.[12] Thirteenth century theology included the teaching of Saint Augustine, the study of *De Civitate Dei*, in its curriculum.[13] The clerical advisors serving the Hungarian king's court made use of their education in the performance of their duties.

After the 1241-42 Mongol invasion that had not only caused terrible destruction in Hungary, but had also heavily decimated the population, the main concern of the Hungarian king, Béla IV, was to re-populate the country in as short an interval as possible.[14] It is known from his letters, and from data derived from the chronicles, that Béla IV had to invite foreign settlers to live in his country, and had to richly endow them with property and legal privileges. He had also taken the Jews under his protection. He had accepted them as legal inhabitants of the realm because of their solid economic contacts with other countries' governments and peoples. Béla IV needed them on account of the poverty of his kingdom and his people.

In the country so heavily devastated by the Tartars, continued domestic warfare wrought additional destruction, and had consumed significant amounts of money. The royal court was deeply in debt. Its strained financial situation could, in part, be improved only through international financial contacts of the Jews. That was the reason why Béla IV had, in 1251, promulgated his *Iura Iudaeorum*: Laws for the Jews.[15]

Earlier Hungarian legislation had already dealt with Jews living in the country. Articles 10 and 27 of what is known today as King Ladislas I's *Decretum I*, anno 1092, had, for instance, forbidden marriages between Jews and Christians, and did not permit Jews to keep Christian servants. At the same time, the law obligated Jews to refrain from physical, manual work on Christian holy days. Were a Jew not to obey the law, the tool(s) he had been working with would be taken from him: "ne scandalisetur christianitas, cum quibus instrumentis laboraverit, illa amittat."[16]

Articles 74 and 75 of King Coloman the Learned's *Decretum* (the king had died in 1116), compiled by the cleric named Albericus, ordered that Jews may not do business with Christian slaves, nor could they keep Christian maid servants. Jews might retain their land(holding)s - cultivated by non-Christian labor - but had to reside at a bishop's residence or in an episcopal town.[17] Article 60 of the First Synod of Esztergom, held during King Coloman's reign, stated that Jew could not keep Christian maids, servants, or paid mercenaries or mercenary private armies.[18] These legal resolutions had further been confirmed by King Coloman's *Lex pro Iudaeis data*.[19]

In the beginning of the thirteenth century, the rather unfavorable public disposition toward Jews did not really change in Hungary, but the realization of legal, judicial enactments concerning Jews did. For example, article 24 of the 1222 *Decretum I* of King Andrew II (Hungarian Golden Bull) stated that no Jew might hold the position of county treasurer - rather, tax collector - "comites camere...Iudaei fieri non possint" - but the court did not enforce the resolution.[20]

Article 31 of the 1231 *Decretum II* of Andrew II (a revised version of the Golden Bull of 1222) repeated the enactment concerning Jewish and other non-Christian officials in a firmer tone

- "monetae et salibus, ac aliis publicis officiis, Iudaei et Saraceni non praeficientur" - but the article of the law had not been enforced.[21]

It was in the middle of the two decades between 1231 and 1251 that the notorious Mongol invasion had occurred, and it brought forth important changes in this respect. The Hungarian monarch, who was anxious to reconstruct his country after the disaster, had farmed out the collection of royal taxes and other revenues to the Jews; in his hardship he could borrow money only from them. In turn, he had to protect their status-quo and their interests.[22]

The basic idea of the Jewish Law of Béla IV was that Jews were guests in the realm and they had to be treated as guests. Because the Christian population had behaved with hatred toward the Jewish social element, the king had to take legal action to defend them, to prove that he was on their side. Like King Coloman in his Jewish laws, Béla IV, too, had to legislate as regards to collateral loans obtained from Jews. Since he could not do this in accordance with Hungarian laws, he had to follow foreign examples, as, for example, the "Letter of the Jews" issued in 1244 by Duke Frederick Babenberg of Austria.[23]

Béla IV had essentially assured the Jews in Hungary of their rights and privileges, be it financial loans, commercial business transactions, acquisition of property, or ownership of land. He had placed them on the same social level as the *hospes* (migrants) and guests in Hungarian society. He had the Jewish faith and their synagogues and schools placed under royal protection.[24]

The king's protective legal policy of the Jewish stratum in society had its price, however, Contrary to any precedent in Hungarian law, a foreign social element unexpectedly needed judicial public protection and recognition. In Hungary, only royal power could protect the Jew. Consequently, the Jew was suddenly looked upon as royal [or, treasury] "property" - a legal concept very similar to the ones prevalent in western royal courts.[25]

The Jew was allowed to speculate, and "strike it rich," but whatever riches he had accumulated for himself were not really his, but belonged to the king [or, the treasury], on the grounds that all Jewish property and the Jew's personal security depended upon the good will of the ruler. "Si Iudaeus recipere poterit nomina pignoris omnia, que sibi fecerint obligata, quorumque nomine vocentura nulla de hiis requiscione facta...quas nullatenus acceptabit."[26]

The *Iura Iudaeorum* established judicial guidelines in Hungary as regards mortgages and criminal cases between Jews and Christians. It stated that in a case before a court of law that concerned the person of Jew, his financial and property rights and claims, a Christian might not present testimony by himself; a Jew[ish] witness must also testify: "nullus Christianus contra Iudaeum, nisi cum Christiano et Iudaeo in testimonium admittatur."[27]

If a Jew had denied that he had acted as a mortgagee to a Christian, or if the amount of the loan were higher than the amount claimed by the Christian debtor, the oath taken by the Jew decided the issue.[28] A Jew might accept anything for mortgage, except bloody or wet cloth, or clothing, or church vestments. Were a Jew to loan money to a nobleman on the noble's goods serving as security, or against a writ signed by the nobleman, the property or goods received by the Jew in security became his in accordance with the law, as long as the [noble] Christian debtor did not repay the borrowed amount in full. The Jew could not, however, assert administrative jurisdiction over the Christians living on the property in the areas mortgaged to him under these conditions, now in his possession.[29]

If the mortgaged goods were stolen goods, but the Jew did not know the goods were stolen, so stating under oath, he was not obliged to release them unless the debt had been paid in full. If the mortgaged goods were stolen from the Jew, or were destroyed by fire, he was not to be held responsible for them. Interest had to be paid within one month on mortgaged goods released without a payment of interest. One could not pay, or gain release from, mortgage on a holiday. If someone were to force a Jew to take payment on a holiday, he would be persecuted by law as one who had caused damage to the treasury.[30]

Anyone who struck, wounded, or beat a Jew was to pay a court fee to the king and compensation (pain money) to the Jew: "reus nobis solus penam secundum consuetudinem regni, uuelnerato duodecim marcas argenti et expensas, quas pro suimet curacione expenderit medicine."[31]

If the accused individual (who had been found guilty) had no money to pay the fine, they punished him. If a Christian murdered a Jew, all property of the former had to be confiscated by the monarch, and the culprit given additional punishment. Were it not possible to identify the murderer, the suspect had to fight a judicial combat.[32]

The royal tax collector was not permitted (under pain of death) to collect toll from the dead body of a Jew that had to be carried from one location to another during the Jewish funeral. If anyone threw objects at a synagogue - school? *schola Iudaeorum* - he had to pay a fine of one silver mark to the Judge of the Jews (*Iudex Iudaeorum*). The law regarded it as a felony to lead Jewish children astray.[33]

The Jew pays the same amount of the toll as the burgess of the town where he had, in transit, concluded business deals, and sold his goods - but not necessarily where he lived. Serious trouble or controversy among Jews was not to be handled by the Judge of the Town, but through the royal treasurer or by the monarch. In less important cases, it was the Judge of the Jews who handed down the sentence. The Judge of the Jews was a Christian, who had to fill the role of mediator between the Jews and the king. On his travel rounds in the realm, the monarch would not stay with a Jew, nor would he spend the night at a house of a Jew; nor was a Jew obligated to provide lodging and guest privileges for the monarch.[34]

Important is the final, the thirty-first, article of the Law that says that the Judge of the Town had to be held responsible for keeping the provisions of the law, under the threat of removal from office.[35]

The Law for the Jews was dated December 5, 1251, and authenticated with a double seal: "duplicibus sigillis nostri munimine roboratur."[36] It came down to posterity in transcripts. It had been transcribed several times. The St. L. Endlicher edition of the text is based on a 1464 transcript of the age of King Matthias Corvinus (*ob.* 1490).[37] In the text printed by both Endlicher and Henrik Marczali - Marczali reprinted Endlicher's text, while the latter based his edition on the mentioned transcript - the name of the official - the Royal Chancellor - who had signed and issued it is missing. Therefore, it is from the writs that had been entered into the Royal Register, and from the names of officials who had signed and issued those writs, that one might conclude that the person who had signed and issued the Law for the Jews was Archbishop Benedict of Kalocsa, the royal chancellor.

The name of the archbishop appeared on documents dated November 23 and 24, 1251, that had been issued prior to the Law for the Jews, and so recorded in the register. The archbishop had been issuing royal writs since April 21, 1244; his name appeared on the charter for the Canons of Prémontré, and on the charter for the Cistercian abbey at Pilis, as late as 1252 and 1254, respectively.[38]

The fact that Béla IV's *Iura Iudaeorum* fairly closely followed the text of the "Letter for the Jews" promulgated by Frederick Babenberg of Austria, does not minimize its importance. In a case, for instance, where an accusation had been made against a Jew, and the court of law needed to hear a Jewish witness besides the Christian one, the court did not base the need for a Jewish witness on a precedent in Hungarian law - "que tangit personam aut res Iudaei, nullus Christianus contra Iudaeum, nisi cum, Christiano et Iudaeo in testimonium admittatur" - but followed proceedings that had a resemblance to Frederick Babenberg's "Letter."[39]

Otakar II of Bohemia had also borrowed from the Austrian directive for his laws concerning Jews in Bohemia.[40] It might have been from this particular circumstance that certain Austrian historians had arrived at the conclusion that there had, already in 1254, existed the first known Austro-Czech-Hungarian code of law.[41]

One ought to regard the entire "Law for the Jews" of Béla IV as an example of the independent jurisdiction of the Hungarian monarch serving his people's interests, as well as his own. As Bálint Hóman had remarked, in accordance with King Béla IV's Letter for the Jews (Hóman wrote "Letter," not "Law'), Jews living in the country came under the personal protection of the ruler. Their legal status in various instances was quite close to that of the *hospes* element in Hungarian society. One has to be reminded that Frederick Babenberg in his "Letter for the Burgesses of Wienerneustadt," dated 1239, had authorized the latter not to employ Jewish officials in their midst.[42]

In view of the fact that the issuer of royal documents between 1244 and 1252, Archbishop Benedict of Kalocsa, was a well educated, highly qualified man (as was his successor, Vice-Chancellor Smaragdus, bishop-elect and archpriest of Székes-fehérvár), one may conclude that the leading Hungarian clergymen who held high ecclesiastical and secular positions in that age, all possessed solid educational backgrounds, including knowledge of canon law.[43]

It was, in fact, the spirit of the age that caused ambitious clergymen to seek higher education at the universities so much that Pope Gregory IX had to forbid bishops from granting spiritual jurisdiction over the faithful to clerics in the cathedral chapters who held master's degrees.[44]

In this time period, common law prevailed in the Hungarian law courts, and it made the teaching and studying of Roman law unnecessary. In a letter addressed to the clergy, dated 1254, Pope Innocent IV had recommended against the study of Roman law, and had, in fact, expelled clerics from their prebends who had studied Roman law.[45] (The Cistercians, under pain of excommunication, were forbidden to read Roman law; nor were they allowed to read Gratian's *Decretum*, the synthesis of Canon law.)[46]

And yet, there were a handful of individuals in the country who had been trained in law and jurisprudence during the 1240's and 1250's, while the record knows of a Hungarian student-nation at the University of Bologna in the year 1265. Students were sent to Bologna, an Italian notation says, in order to acquire learning and knowledge, love and divine grace, and to drink from the font of wisdom. (It must have made them feel honorable.)[47]

The papal writ addressed to the Hungarian clergy emphasized the necessity of their receiving a thorough grounding in theology.[48]

The leading Hungarian clergymen of the age had thus obtained educational foundations in divine science that included the knowledge of the doctrine of Aurelius Augustinus - one of the four Great Latin fathers of the Church.[49] In his writ of November 17, 1276, Ladislas IV had emphasized that the so savagely destroyed cathedral school at Veszprém with its faculty of law had been equal to the school in Paris, an overstatement that may not correspond to reality, but may lead to the assumption that, for instance, in the Veszprém cathedral school they had provided advanced education at the west European level.[50]

The list of books of the 1240's in the library of the cathedral chapter at Veszprém recorded a volume of forty sermons of Pope Gregory the Great, the last of the Great Latin fathers (d. 604),[51] together with a separate volume of select sermons by Aurelius Augustinus (d. 430), Leo the Great (d. 461), and Fulgentius for the

Sundays of the ecclesiastical year.[52] The doctrine of Aurelius Augustinus had, on the other hand, contained the Christian idea of history. In his opus, *De civitate Dei*, Augustine, as a philosopher of history, had said there were "two cities:' the one, a community of god-fearing people, the city of saints, and the other, the commonwealth of the godless social element.[53] The righteous Jews belonged to the "heavenly city," he said.[54]

Augustine had argued that man was neither a servant, nor a creature of time, but rather its master, one who would turn history into a creative process, an organic whole, turning the past into the present and, in accordance with human understanding, assuring mankind's spiritual, intellectual, and social advancement. As Augustine saw it, the heavenly state was the maintainer of justice - it made certain of law and order. Faith ruled over the state, because the Church had dominated the moral order, as it had enjoyed the protection of temporal power. In such a manner those who ruled had to serve the needs of their subjects, on the grounds that they did not rule out of greed for power, but out of the sense of responsibility toward their subordinates.[55]

In Augustine's point of view, the ruler could not become conceited because of his authority, for the reason that he had to be merciful: "neque imperat principandi superbia, sed providendi misericordia." The ruler maintained the law, "iustitia civilis," and the Church the moral order, as reason played a decisive role in an earthly society motivated by heavenly values. Man on his own may, however, be unwilling to assert the idea that he could decide his own fate, reasoned Augustine. The entire nineteenth book of *De civitate Dei* radiates the desire for peace, the concept of rational human behavior and of divine theology.

The City of God, Augustine pointed out, was not a thousand year old kingdom, nor was it the church of the hierarchy; it was reality that stood over time and space, a social structure, in which Justice was king, and Love was law.[56]

Augustine's ideal Christian ruler had the well-being of his subjects before him: "imperant, qui consulunt,...neque principandi superbia, sed providendi misericordia."[57] The Hungarian monarch legislated on behalf of his people(s). His attitude might have been evident in the prefatory note of his Law of 1251 - a law that had some similarity with, and yet was so much contrary to, the "Letter for the Jews" of Frederick Babenberg.

The influence of Aurelius Augustinus upon the Jewish laws of Béla IV is remarkably evident in several respects. The bishop of Hippo wrote his work at the time when the barbarians had invaded the Roman empire, only a few years after the sack of Rome by the Visigoths.[58] The Hungarian monarch had issued his laws during the years of his country's reconstruction following the withdrawal of the Mongols from his country.

Augustine reacted as a theologian and as a Christian philosopher of history to the barbarians' challenge. Béla IV had turned as a legislator to the problems that evolved in his country's rebuilding. In the eleventh book of his *City of God*, Augustine analyzed the principle of the "two cities," bearing in mind that, on this earth, both diverge - in time and in space.[59] The Hungarian king wanted to rebuild, on a legal foundation, the relationship between his Christian people(s) and the non-Christian element living in their midst - as if the Augustinian concept of *republica Christiana* had echoed in the introductory words of the Jewish laws of the Hungarian monarch.[60]

Incidentally, that prefatory note may further clearly reflect the mental disposition of the royal advisors, and educated churchmen, who were responsible for drafting that law, in fact, for preparing all the laws of his reign. Béla IV could rightly expect his subjects to loyally obey the laws he had enacted. "Quum uniuscuiusque nostre percipienciam inuenire,...hec iura ordinauimus ipsis inuiolabiliter obseruanda."[61]

A similar attitude might be evident in the resolutions reached at the 1252 church synod held by Archbishop Stephen Vancsai of Esztergom in 1252.[62] In accordance with the documentation available in two source collections, one can hypothesize that the archbishop had a synod held at his archiepiscopal see in late October, 1252.[63] In another edition of the text of the resolutions, there is a different date attached to the text: "anno gratiae MCCLVI," as if referring to the year when the synod was actually held, even though the editor recorded Vancsai as the Esztergom archbishop in that year.[64] In another edition of the text - it is rather a résumé of the resolutions to which the editor added a list of names of those participating in the synod - the gathering was listed as a "national" church assembly held in Esztergom in 1256, under the presidency of Archbishop Benedict.[65]

One can argue that the 1252 Synod of Esztergom had been summoned with a given purpose: during the first two days of its meetings, the participants discussed church business and disciplinary matters.[66] On the third day, the assembly debated arguments involving tithe payments between Bishop Zeland of Veszprém and Abbot Balasius at the Benedictine house in Zalavár.[67] During the debate ten parish priests of Zala county testified that, by ancient custom, the tithe was due to the abbey.[68]

In other words, on the third day of its gathering, the synod, as a provincial meeting, might have constituted an ecclesiastical judicial tribunal, in which the bishop handed down the sentence through the cooperation of those gathered together.[69] (This could hardly have been a singular instance at the time. It is known, for instance, from a writ of Pope Honorius III that, in 1224, Archbishop Thomas of Esztergom had taken similar action - not in person, but through a representative - in a like case.)[70] The synod of Esztergom gathered in October, 1252, had realized its goal, as stated by the archbishop: it had successfully upheld church discipline according to the religious and secular law - in the spirit of Saint Augustine.[71]

NOTES

* Aurelius Augustinus, *De civitate Dei*, written between 413 and 426, is available in several editions, as, for instance, B. Dombart and A. Kalb (eds.), *Sancti Avrelii Avgvstini De civitate Dei libri XXII*, 2 vols., 5h ed., ed. J. Divjak (Stuttgart, 1931; repr. 1981); E. Hoffmann, in *Corpus scriptorum ecclesiasticorum Latinorum* (Vienna, 1866, etc.), vol. XL, esp. XL-2, 397ff.; or in J.P. Migne (ed.), *Patrologiae cursus completus, series latina*, 221 vols., cited as *MPL*, 41, cols. 13ff., esp. 642f. E. Portalié's essay is perhaps the best introduction to St. Augustine, in *Dictionnaire de théologie catholique*, ed. A. Vacant *et al.*, 15 vols. (Paris, 1903-50), I, cols. 2268-2472 - in English translation by R.J. Bastian, *A Guide to the Thought of St. Augustine* (London-Chicago, 1960); important also is P. de Labriolle, *Histoire de la litterature latine chrétienne* (Paris, 1920), 519ff., esp. 546ff.; its English translation by H. Wilson, *The History and Literature of Christianity* (London, 1924; repr. New York, 1968), 389ff., esp. 408ff.

See further E. Gilson, *History of Christian Philosophy in the Middle Ages* (London, 1955), 70ff., an annotated translation of his classic, *Histoire de la philosophie médiévale*, 2nd ed. (Paris, 1943). Paul Simon, *Aurelius Augustinus: sein geistiges Profil* (Paderborn, 1954), 116ff. and 152ff.; E. Norden, "Die lateinische Literatur im Übergang vom Altertum zum Mittelalter," in P. Hinneberg (ed.), *Die Kultur der Gegenwart* (Berlin-Leipzig, 1907), esp. 422f., where he looks upon Augustine's *City of God* as the first historical-philosophical opus of the medieval period. Norden also regarded Augustine as the great(est) poet of the early Church - *ibid.*, 419. On the other hand, H. Scholz, *Glaube und Unglaube in der Weltgeschichte* (Leipzig, 1911), 150f., argued that one cannot speak of a philosophy of history on the grounds that the foresight of Divine Providence forestalls any historical development! Compare with the learned article by R. Lorenz, "Wissenschaftslehre Augustins," *Zeitschrift für Kirchengeschichte*, 67 (1955-56), 29ff. and 213ff.

Augustine's philosophy of history was discussed by A. Dempf, *Sacrum imperium: Geschichts- und Staatsphilosophie des Mittelalters und der politischen Renaissance*, 4th ed. (Stuttgart, 1963), 116ff. and 129f. For background, one is to read O. Bardenhewer, *Geschichte der altchristlichen Literatur*, 4 vols. (repr. Darmstadt, 1962), IV, 434ff., esp. 456ff.; Ch. Dawson, "The *City of God*," in M.C. D'Arcy (ed.), *St. Augustine* (New York, 1957), 43ff. - a reprint of *A Monument to St. Augustine* (London, 1930); H. Pope, *Saint Augustine of Hippo* (Westminster, MD, 1949), 26ff. and 195ff.; the comments of Friedrich Heer, *Europäische Geistesgeschichte*, 2nd ed. (Stuttgart, 1965), 91f.; idem, *Die Tragödie des Heiligen Reiches* (Stuttgart, 1952), 141ff.

1. Cf. Augustine, *De civitate Dei*, i:1.
2. *Ibid.*, xiv:1 and 28; xv:2; F.E. Franz, "De Civitate Dei, xv, 2, and Augustine's Idea of Christian Society," *Speculum*, 25 (1950), 215ff.
3. *De civitate Dei*, xi:1; xv:1.
4. *Ibid.*, xv:1; xix:17.
5. *Ibid.*, xxii:30.
6. Cf. *RA*, nn. 958, 960, 962, 976. Elemér Mályusz, *Egyházi társadalom a középkori Magyarországon* [The Ecclesiastics' Stratum in Medieval Hungary] (Budapest, 1971), 35ff. and 55.
7. *RA*, nn. 1023 and 1041.
8. *SSH*, II, 572,17; on the canons of episcopal chapters in Hungary, cf. Mályusz, 59ff.
9. Cf. Life of St. Dominic, cc. 202 and 210-211, in *ASS*, Aug. I, 558ff.; Pintér, I, 291, 246, and 247; Horváth, *Irodalmi kezdetek*, 50f.
10. *RA*, n. 2723, with text; *RA*, n. 2747; Katona, VIII, preface; *CD*, V-2, 347; also, *RA*, n. 2789; *CD*, IX-7, 692f.

11. *RA*, nn. 2641 [and 3272, *ÁUO*, IV, 255f.].
12. Cf. Potthast, n. 15570; *CD*, IV-2, 254ff.
13. David Knowles, *The Evolution of Medieval Thought*, 2nd ed. (London-New York, 1988), 202, 265f., and 271f.; Jaroslav Pelikan, *The Growth of Medieval Theology (660-1300)* (Chicago-London, 1978), 270ff.; P.R.L. Brown, "Augustine: Political Society," in Beryl Smalley (ed.), *Trends in Medieval Political Thought* (Oxford, 1965), 1ff.
14. On the Mongol invasion, see the brief entry in the Chronicle, "Tempore autem istius Bele regis anno Domini millesimo CCXL primo Mangali sive Tartari regnum Hungarie invaserunt." *SSH*, I, 467f.; on fol. 63b of the Chronicle MS, there is a drawing that shows, in a simple frame, six Tartars in Cuman dress with drawn swords pursuing the fleeing King Béla and his men - cf. Dercsényi, *Chronicon pictum*, I [facsimile]. The "Leutschau Chronicle" (Szepesszombat: "Georgenberg Chronicon"), *SSH*, II, 282,9-14, reported that in the vanquished country children were being devoured by their starving mothers; on the chronicle, see Macartney, 147 and I.W. Nagl and J. Zeidler, *Deutsch-österreichische Literaturgeschichte*, vol. I (Vienna, 1899), 331f. See also "Continuatio Sacracrucensis II," *MGHSS*, IX, 640f.; the "Plancus destructionis Hungariae," *ibid.*, XXIX, 604 and/or *SSH*, II, 593,2-6; Rogerius, "Carmen," cc. 21, etc., esp. c. 35, *ibid.*, II, 581,5-10 or *MGHSS*, XXIX, 563; Macartney, 88 and 89. Thomas Spalatensis "Historia Spalatina usque ad 1266," cc. 37-40, *MGHSS*, XXIX, 570ff.; or, Schwandtner, III, 352ff.; Johannes de Thurocz, *Chronica Hungarorum*, ed. E. Galánta and J. Kristó (Budapest, 1985), c. 101; in Schwandtner, I, 39ff., ii:101.

Source material on the invasion, collected and translated, with good introduction by György Györffy, *A tatárjárás emlékezete* [In Remembrance of the Tartar Invasion] (Budapest, 1987); a major portion of the material was previously published by Györffy in his *A Napkelet felfedezése* [In Search of the Orient] (Budapest, 1965); Hóman-Szekfü, I, 539ff.; Székely, 1417ff. On the comments of King Béla IV concerning the invasion, see *CD*, IV-2, 49, 65f., and 219ff.; Knauz, I, 548.

15. Text of the *Iura Iudaeorum*, published according to a 1464 transcript, in *RHM*, 473ff.; in Marczali, *Enchiridion*, 158ff., selections; Hóman, *Ungarisches Mittelalter*, II, 162; compare to W. Ch. Jordan, *The French Monarchy and the Jews* (Philadelphia, 1989), 142ff., concerning the evolution of Capetian policy toward the Jews in France.

16. For previous legislation concerning Jews in Hungary, cf. Ladislas I's *Decretum I*, anno 1092, in *RHM*, 325ff.; Kosztolnyik, *Five Kings*, 105ff. and 193f., n. 2; idem, *From Coloman*, 1ff. and 13, n. 7.

17. King Coloman the Learned's *Decretum*, *RHM*, 358ff.; Kosztolnyik, *From Coloman*, 46ff.

18. Decrees of the First Synod of Esztergom, *RHM*, 349ff.; Kosztolnyik, *From Coloman*, 58ff.

19. Coloman the Learned's Law for the Jews, *RHM*, 371f.; Kosztolnyik, *From Coloman*, 65 and 76, n. 105; B. Hirsch-Reich, "Joachim von Fiore und das Judentum," in P. Wilpert (ed.), *Judentum im Mittelalter* (Berlin, 1966), 228ff. One may mention the remark of the ninth century Agobard de Lyon (*ob.*, 840) on meat, deemed unsuitable for Jewish diet, being sold to Christians - in his "De insolentia Judaeorum," c. 3 - cf. *MPL*, 104, col. 73; also, *ibid.*, 104, 147ff.; S. Grayzel, *The Church and the Jews in the 13th Century* (Philadelphia, 1955), 72.

20. Cf. Marczali, *Enchiridion*, 134aff.; *RHM*, 412ff.

21. Cf. *ibid.*, 428ff.; Marczali, *Enchiridion*, 134bff.; Hóman-Szekfü, I, 491ff.; Székely, 1320ff.

22. In his writ, dated December 9, 1239, the Roman pontiff gave permission to the Hungarian monarch and to the king of Portugal to farm out collection of revenues to Jews, cf. Potthast, n. 10829; *VMH*, n. 313.

23. Cf. A. Rauch (ed.), *Rerum Austricarum Scriptores*, 3 vols. (Vienna, 1793-94), cited hereafter as *RASS*, II, 201ff. - republished by A. v. Meiller, "Österreichische Stadtrechte und Satzungen aus der Zeit der Babenberger," *Archiv für österreichischen Geschichtsquellen*, 10 (1853), 87ff., with text, 146-48.

24. Cf. "Iura Iudaeorum," *RHM*, 473ff., aa. 10, 12, 13, 14.

25. Cf. Jean de Joinville, *Histoire de Saint Louis*, ed. N. de Wailly (Paris, 1874), 31; compare with *RHM*, 473ff., aa. 1 and 2, 28-30.

26. *Ibid.*, a. 5. For nearly three decades after the Mongol invasion, it was the same royal appointees who had carried on with the business of Béla IV's government - see Hóman-Szekfű, I, 558f.; I. Hajnal, "IV Béla király kancelláriájáról" [Remarks on the Chancery of Béla IV], *Turul*, 32 (1914), 1ff.

27. *RHM*, 473ff., a. 11.

28. *Ibid.*, a. 2.

29. *Ibid.*, a. 24.

30. *Ibid.*, aa. 27 and 28.

31. *Ibid.*, a. 9.

32. *Ibid.*, a. 10.

33. *Ibid.*, art. 13, 14, 25.

34. *Ibid.*, art. 12, 21, 23.

35. *Ibid.*, a. 31; in Marczali, *Enchiridion*, 160.

36. Cf. *RA*, n. 962; RMH, 477; Marczali, *Enchiridion*, 160.

37. *RHM*, 473.

38. Archbishop Benedict's signature on royal writs, - see *RA*, nn. 958 and 960; *ÁUO*, VII, 319ff., and XII, 690f. Text of writ, dated April 21, 1244, *ibid.*, XI, 333; *RA*, n. 762. The writ for the Canons of Prémontré, *RA*, n. 979; *CD*, IV-5, 294. Charter for Pilis abbey, dated June 28, 1254, *RA*, n. 1011; *CD*, IV-2, 214f., and its facsimile in Remig Békefi, *A pilisi apátság története* [History of the Abbey of Pilis], vol. I (Pécs, 1891), 316. Documents signed and issued by Smaragdus, in *RA*, nn. 1023 and 1041. On Archpriest Albertus, see Rogerius, "Carmen," in *SSH*, II, 572,17.

39. *RHM*, 473ff., art. 1.

40. H. Jirecek (ed.), *Codex Iuris Bohemici*, vol. I (Prague, 1867), 134ff., did, in parallel columns, publish the text of Austrian, Czech, and Hungarian Jewish laws.

41. Erna Patzelt, *Österreich bis zum Ausgang der Babenbergerzeit* (Vienna, 1946), 160, argued that Frederick's law issued in 1234 (!) that stated that in case of a serious anti-Jewish charge in a court of law a Jewish witness must also testify, had been taken over by both Béla IV and Otakar II; therefore, one might speak of the first Austro-Czech-Hungarian code of law.

42. Hóman-Szekfű, I, 563; Hóman, *Ungarisches Mittelalter*, II, 161f.; Meiller, *art. cit.*, 127 and 128f., further discussed the social standing of the Jews in Vienna and the anti-Jewish tendencies of the town of Wienerneustadt; Patzelt, *Österreich*, 159; Kohn, *Zsidók története*, I, 102ff.

43. The Third Lateran Synod, 1179, art. 18, and the Fourth Lateran Synod, 1215, art. 11, cf. Mansi, *Concilia*, XXII, 227f. and 999, respectively, spoke on the education of the clergy; see also J. Alberigus (ed.), *Conciliorum oecumenicorum decreta*, 2nd ed. (Freiburg, 1962), 193 and 215; on schools and education in medieval Hungary, cf. Remig Békefi, *A káptalani iskolák története Magyarországon 1540-ig* [History of the Cathedral Schools in Hungary Prior to 1540] (Budapest, 1910), 160ff. and 344ff.; P. Ransanus, *Epithoma rerum Hungarorum*, ed. P. Kulcsár (Budapest, 1977), ind. ii; my review in *Austrian History Yearbook*, 17-18 (1981-82), 361f.; J. Gutheil, "Veszprém árpádkori jogi főiskolája" [The Law Faculty at Veszprém in the Árpád Age], *Vigilia*, 26 (1961), 459ff. St. Katona, *Historia regum Hungariae stirpis mixtae*, 12 vols. (Budae, 1787-92), I, preface, ord. viii, described the destruction of the school in 1276; on this, the royal writs in *RA*, nn. 2720, 2747, 2789,

BÉLA IV'S LAW OF 1251   237

and 3273; Károly Szabó, *Kún László* [Ladislas the Cuman] (Budapest, 1886; repr. 1988), 36f.

44. Cf. Potthast, n. 9213; *VMH*, n. 193.

45. Canon law was taught at the universities - see H. Denifle, *Die Entstehung der Universitäten des Mittelalters*, vol. I (repr. of the 1895 ed., Graz, 1956), 698; Matthew of Paris, *Chronica maiora*, vol. VI; Addimenta, R.S. (London, 1883), 190f. The papal legate sent to Hungary and Poland had recommend (in 1279) that archdeacons possess a knowledge of Canon law - C. Péterffy (ed.), *Sacra concilia ecclesiae Romano-Catholicae in regno Hungariae celebrata*, 2 vols. (Vienna, 1742), I, 114, cap. 38.

46. J.T. Noonan, "Gratian Slept Here: The Changing Identity of the Father of the Systematic Study of Canon Law," *Traditio*, 35 (1979), 145ff.; on Gratian, see also J.A. Brundage, *Law, Sex and Church in Society in Medieval Europe* (Chicago-London, 1987), 229ff. Regular clergy were forbidden to read law - cf. the Synod of Tours, 1163, in L. Duchesne (ed.), *Liber pontificalis*, 3 vols., rev. ed. (Paris, 1957), II, 408ff.; nor were the Cistercians allowed to read Gratian's *Decretum* - see L.J. Lekai, *The While Monks* (Okauchee, WI, 1953), 160; Békefi, *Pilis*, 89; see also G. LeBras, "Canon Law," in C.G. Crump and E.F. Jacob (eds.), *Legacy of the Middle Ages* (Oxford, 1926; repr. 1951), 321ff.

47. H.D. Sedwick, *Italy in the Thirteenth Century*, vol. I (Boston-New York, 1912), quoting Brunetto Latini; compare to J. Koch, *Artes liberales* (Leiden-Cologne, 1959), 84ff.; K. Flasch, *Das philosophische Denken im Mittelalter, von Augustin zu Machiavelli* (Stuttgart, 1986), 246ff.

48. Innocent IV on December 9, 1254, Potthast, n. 15570; *CD*, IV-2, 254ff. György Bónis, *A jogtudó értelmiség a Mohács előtti Magyarországon* [Hungarian Intelligentsia Trained in Law Prior to 1526] (Budapest, 1971), 21ff., to the effect that Hungary had a trained clerical stratum in the 1200's; also, E. Veress, *Olasz egyetemeken járt magyarországi tanulók anyakönyve és iratai, 1221-1864* [Matriculation Entries of Hungarian Students in Italian Universities, 1221-1864] (Budapest, 1941), xxxiif., recorded nearly eighty students prior to 1301. P. Kibre, *The Nations in the Medieval Universities* (Cambridge, 1948), 9, mentioned a (the) Hungarian student nation at Bologna. On Hungarian scholars in Bologna, as, e.g., the Dominican Paulus Hungarus, cf. "Vita s. Dominici," by Theodore Appoldia, *ASS*, Aug. I, 558ff., cc. 210-211; E. Várady, *Docenti e scolari ungheresi nell'antico studio bolognese* (Bologna, 1951), 6ff.; Horváth, *Irodalom kezdetei*, 50f.

49. Cf. H. v. Campenhausen, *Lateinische Kirchenväter*, (Stuttgart, 1960), 151ff.

50. Cf. *RA*, n. 2747.

51. The catalogue of books in the library of the cathedral chapter in Veszprém - cf. H. Hurter (ed.), *Nomenclator literarium theologiae catholicae theologos exhibens aetate, natione, disciplinis distinctos*, 5 vols. (Oeniponte, 1903-13), II, 72. On Gregory the Great, cf. Funk-Bihlmeyer, I, 228ff.; Hans Kühner, *Neues Papstlexikon*, Fischer Bücherei (Frankfurt-Hamburg, 1965), 34f.

52. On Leo the Great, *ibid.*, 28; Funk-Bihlmeyer, I, 224ff. On Fulgentius, presumably bishop of Ruspe in the late eighth century, see M.L.W. Laistner, *Thought and Letters in Western Europe*, rev. ed. (London, 1957), 42.

53. See V. Stagemann, *Augustins Gottesstaat* (Tübingen, 1928), 49ff.; E. Lewalter, "Eschatologie und Weltgeschichte in der Gedankenwelt Augustins," *Zeitschrift für Kirchengeschichte*, 55 (1934), 12ff.; H.I. Marraou, *St. Augustin et la fin de la culture antique* (Paris, 1938), 39ff., analyzed the writer in St. Augustine against the literary backdrop of his age. Arno Borst, *Der Turmbau von Babel: Geschichte der Meinungen über Ursprung und Vielfalt der Sprachen und Völker*, 4 vols. in 6 (Stuttgart, 1957-63), II, 391ff., esp. 398ff., took a similar approach; on the thirteenth century, *ibid.*, II, 730ff.; P.R.L. Brown, "Political Society," in Beryl Smalley (ed.), *Trends in Medieval Political Thought* (Oxford, 1965), 1ff.; N.H. Bayness, "The

Political Ideas of St. Augustine's De civitate Dei," in his *Byzantine Studies* (London, 1955), 288ff.
    54. Augustine, *De civitate Dei*, iv:34.
    55. Book XIX of the *City of God* was cleverly discussed by H.J. Diesner, "Die Ambivalenz des Friedensgedanken und die Friedenspolitik bei Augustin," in his *Kirche und Staat im spätrömischen Reich* (Berlin, 1963), 46ff. Augustine explained the purpose of his book in his *Retractiones libri II*, ii:34, in *MPL*, 32, cols. 583ff., esp. 647. He had borrowed the title from Ps. 87,3 (Vulgate, 86,3); Ps. 48,1 or Ps. 46,4 (in the Vulgate, 47,2 and 45,5) - cf. *De civitate Dei*, xi:1.
    56. Cf. Sermon 138, iii:7, in *MPL*, 33, cols. 532ff., esp. cols. 532bc, 533ab, and 525f. There is a brief, but thorough annotation on the *City of God* in an old college text - cf. Jeremiah F. O'Sullivan and J.F. Burns, *Medieval Europe* (New York, 1943), 104ff.
    57. Sermon 138, ii:19 and v:24.
    58. See Augustine's Epistle 130, in *MPL*, 33, cols. 494ff, esp. 494bc, and compare with his *Confessions*, ed. J. Bernhart, 3rd ed. (Munich, 1955), 502ff., x:8. On Augustine's view of Man considering his fate, see his Sermon 302, *MPL*, 33, cols. 1385ff., esp. cols. 1386bc and 1388b. On Augustine's sermons, see Labriol, 561ff.; in English translation, 419ff.
    59. *De civitate Dei*, xi:1 and xiv:28.
    60. *Ibid.*, xv:4 and xxii:30.
    61. See the Law of 1251, introductory part, in *RHM*, 473; Marczali, *Enchiridion*, 158.
    62. Cf. Knauz, I, 394ff.; on Archbishop Stephen Vancsai, Potthast, n. 11081; *VMH*, n. 343; Cardinal, Potthast, n. 14769; *VMH*, n. 398 - also a *magister*, Rogerius, "Carmen," *SSH*, II, 562,6; see Z.J. Kosztolnyik, "In the European Mainstream: Hungarian Churchmen and Thirteenth-Century Synods," *Catholic Historical Review*, 79 (1993), 413ff.
    63. Knauz, I, 394ff.; *CD*, IV-2 153ff.; C. Eubel (ed.), *Hierarchia catholica medii aevi*, 3 vols. (Monasterii, 1910-14 [vol. III in 1910!]; repr. 1960), I, 523; Henrik Marczali, *Ungarische Verfassungsgeschichte* (Tübingen, 1910), 3f.; A. Szentirmai, "Die ungarische Diözesansynod im Spätmittelalter," *Zeitschrift der Savigny Stiftung für Rechtsgeschichte*, kan. Abt., 47 (1961), 266ff.; G. Adriányi, "Die ungarischen Synoden," *Annuarium historiae conciliorum*, 8 (1976), 541ff.
    64. Batthyány, *Leges*, II, 391f.; in *CD*, IV-2, 153ff., dated it anno 1252: "Nos Stephanus...archiepiscopus Strigoniensis significamus,...in synodali nostra congregatione, in die festi s. Lucae evangelistae universis abbatibus, praepositis, et clero nostrae diocesis solemniter celebrata." In 1256, Cardinal Vancsai lived in Rome - *ibid.*, IV-2, 396.
    65. Péterffy, *Concilia*, I, 86f.; one is to remember, though, that Péterffy did make mistakes: for instance, he listed Paulus, instead of Zelandus, as bishop of Veszprém, spoke of Nicholas of Nyitra instead of Vincent (named in a contemporary writ, cf. *CD*, IV-2, 328), and wrote Paulus, instead of Jób, for the bishop of Pécs; H. Szovrényi, *Synopsis critico-historica decretorum pro Ecclesia Hungariae Catholica editorum* (Vesprimi, 1807), 23ff.; see further P.B. Gams, *Series episcoporum Ecclesiae Catholicae* (Regensburg, 1873), 376; Batthyány, *Leges*, II, 392 accused Péterffy of "manufacturing evidence."
    66. Knauz, I, 394ff.
    67. *CD*, IV-2, 154f.; Knauz, I, 395.
    68. *Ibid.*
    69. The synod had to function as a judiciary tribunal - Szentirmai, *art. cit.*, 288; provincial church synods had met in such a capacity before - Potthast, n. 7466; *VMH*, n. 89; *CD*, III-2, 48f.
    70. Potthast, n. 7159; *ÁUO*, I, 198.
    71. *CD*, IV-2, 153.

CHAPTER EIGHT

THE END OF BÉLA IV'S REIGN: THE LAW OF 1267

> Ordinauiumus, ut quod singulis annis in festo sancti Regis unus ex nobis Albam venire debeat, et de quolibet comitatu due uel tres nobiles debeant conuenire, ur in eorum presencia de omnibus damnis et iniuriis per quoscunque datis et illatis omnibus querelantibus satisfiat.
>
> *Law of 1267*, art. 8

Béla IV, by the grace of God, King of Hungary; Stephen, the country's Junior King and Prince of Transylvania; Béla, junior Prince of the whole of Slovenia, acting in compliance with the advice and consent of the barons, herewith confirm the nobles of the realm, members of the service nobility, "nobiles Hungarie uniuersi qui seruientes regales dicuntur," in the liberties they had obtained from King Saint Stephen: "ipsos in libertate a s. Stephano rege statuta at obtenta dignaremur conseruare."[1]

The monarch upon the withdrawal of the Mongols had attempted reconstruction of this country by issuing legal decrees of particular regional interest[s], and through general legislation in the Royal Council. When the immediate Mongol threat ceased to exist, and the bloody confrontation with his elder son ebbed, Béla IV concluded, in Pozsony, an agreement with Prince Stephen, Junior King, and confirmed it by the pacification at Poroszló,[2] and in Szakoly[3] - although he only ratified it as a treaty that ended the warring between them, on Rabbits' Island (in the Danube) on March 26, 1266.[4] The treaty had been reaffirmed by Pope Clement IV on June 22, 1266, after the pontiff had heard the royal promises made by both parties under oath.[5] Only then had the time come for the enactments of the laws on the large scale, in adherence to the Laws of 1222 - the "Golden Bull" of Andrew II. Thus, the Law of 1267 by Béla IV and his two sons may be looked upon as a continuation of a legislative process that dated back to 1222, or as a modified version of it, reflecting the country's changed condition.

The Law of 1267, to wit, is to be distinguished from the Bull of 1222 by various changes. First of all, in 1267, it was not the monarch, but the lower (service) nobility, who had gathered together without royal summons: "quod nobiles...ad nos accedentes, pecierunt a nobis humiliter et devote, ut ipsos in libertate...dignaremur conseruare."[6] The monarch, indeed, with the advice and consent of his barons, only acquiesced to their demands. It is significant that the monarch had assented to the demands of the lesser nobility not on his own powers, but through the consensus of the higher nobility.

Evidently, by this time, there had existed a social order of barons: higher nobility who had acted as the king's council.[7] And the lower nobility, in order to counterbalance the influence of the barons as royal councilors, began to organize themselves by counties. According to article eight of the Law of 1267, it had happened for the first time that such an organization had taken place in the realm. On the annual law-day held on the feast of King Saint Stephen at Székesfehérvár, two to three (lesser) nobles had arrived from the counties to take part in the meetings: "Albam venire...et de quolibet comitatus due vel tres nobles conuenire debeant."[8]

Another difference occurred in 1267. Béla IV, following the example of King Saint Stephen, asked for the opinion of the royal council, and acted with its consent, in contrast to the Bull of 1222 where Andrew II made laws by himself, on his own powers.[9] (One is to remember, though, that the structure and membership of the royal council in King Saint Stephen's day had differed from the council of Béla IV during the late 1260's.)

In the early eleventh century, it was the bishops and high nobles; in the 1260's, it was the barons who constituted the council. The difference from the Bull of 1222 was further underlined by the fact that, in 1267, the country had been *de facto* divided between Béla IV and his son; Prince Stephen had exercised nearly full sovereign rights in his territories.[10] Yet, in the field of legislation, the unity of the country had suffered no damage.[11] The two to three lower nobles of each county who attended the annual law-day had demanded that the monarch validate the decrees he had issued, and he had sanctioned them. Béla IV had, "baronum habito nostrorum consilio et assensu," identified himself with the petitions of the service nobility.[12]

St.L. Endlicher, who had published the text of those resolutions "e membrana tabularii regi," divided them into ten articles, with a special conclusion;[13] Henrik Marczali, in his edition of the text, based "on the original manuscript," printed it without dividing it into articles, but with an identical text.[14] However, the text and directives of the Law of 1267, where the monarch handed down his resolutions in answer to the request of the barons, fall far behind the tone of the forceful, and where needed, personal decisions enacted by King Saint Stephen.

King Stephen had, for instance, decided on his own, "regali nostra potencia," on questions of private property, and its inheritance;[15] in another case, he took action after hearing his *Senatus*, "secundum senatus nostri decretum,"[16] or reached his decision in the royal council, "in hoc regali concilio."[17] Only on one occasion was he willing to involve the whole Senate in reaching a decision: "consensimus igitur petitioni totius senatus."[18] In 1267, when it was the lesser nobles, and not the monarch who had summoned the meeting, Béla IV, partly to counterbalance the possible impact made by the service nobility, and partly because he had to be cautious, asked for the opinion - in fact, for the assent - of the barons before formulating his decision.[19]

The usage of the term "baron" is also significant. In its Hungarian context, it was article eight of the 1231 Decree of Andrew II that had applied the expression *baro* for the first time, depicting a social element right after mentioning the archbishops and bishops, but before the social stratum of the service nobility.[20] One ought to bear in mind, however, that mainly article thirty-one of the Bull of 1222 referred to a social hierarchy of bishops, *iobagiones*, and nobles - "tam episcopi, quam alii iobagiones ac nobles regni nostri," as if to state that the 1231 use of the term *barones* had replaced and became a new expression for *iobagiones* in Hungarian society,[21] probably following the English usage of barons.[22]

On the other hand, the fact that the fourth article of King Saint Stephen's *Admonitiones*, as transcribed in the sixteenth century Ilosvay codex, made mention of barons: *baronum* - in contrast with an earlier transcript of the Admonitions, where the term "baronum" simply fell out - may prove that the expression "baron," as a social designation in Hungary had already been in use during the early 1200's.[23]

In the Law of 1267, the king and his sons established the tax-exempt status of the service nobility and the peoples living on their lands, and granted them exemption from forced lodging in their homes.[24] They ordered the return of the lands that were at the disposal of the county fort[s] and lands designated for the usufruct by the fort personnel: *ministeriales*.[25] They announced that (service) nobles must properly be tried in royal courts of law,[26] and royal *servientes* may [also] part company with their original lords (who had given them status-quo) for the service of another high lord.[27] The service nobles also regained their landholdings that had previously been occupied by peoples of the royal domain [villages], by towns, fort personnel, or by the military assigned to a (district) fort.[28]

The royal (service) noble who had no living heir to inherit his holdings was free to make arrangements for the inheritance of his chattel.[29] The law modified earlier provisions concerning the military obligations of nobles.[30] The monarch and his sons solemnly promised to keep the annual law-day on the feast of King Saint Stephen.[31]

The law stated that the holdings of a noble who had died in the line of duty be inherited by his "clan," while his *acquired* chattel (goods) may go to whom he had previously designated as heir(s).[32] The monarch and his sons promised to take immediate care of any legal grievance referred to them by a lesser noble, without a previous written petition.[33]

King Béla IV, Stephen, Junior King, and Prince Béla swore an oath to keep these royal promises, by now articles of law, under the threat of excommunication by the Archbishop of Esztergom: "sic nos Deus adiuvet et sancti Dei ecclesia."[34] (In the Marczali edition, the text reads *evangelia* instead of *ecclesia*, and he printed "vivificum dominice crucis lignum," instead of "et unificum crucis signum.")[35]

In the decrees of 1267 they left out four articles of the Golden Bull of 1222 related to the royal *servientes* [service nobility], but retained regulations on their service(s) due, forced lodging, military responsibilities in wars abroad, and a paragraph regulating their free movements countrywide.[36] They also renewed four articles with major changes:

1. A noble [royal *serviens*] could only be tried by barons in a court of law, and taken into custody after the sentence had been

handed down by the court: "presentibus baronibus, sine ira, odio uel
fauore iudicetur, iuris ordine obseruato."[37]

    2. Every fort district [county] was obligated to send two to
three lesser nobles to the annual law-day at Fehérvár. Grievances
against the barons had to be discussed only in their presence: "et de
quolibet comitatu due uel tres nobiles debeant conuenire, ut in eorum
presencia de omnibus damnis et iniuriis per quoscunque datis et
illatis omnibus satisfiat."[38]

    3. The will of a *serviens* [lesser noble] who had fallen in the
line of duty, but who had no male heir, was only valid for his
"acquired" goods; his other goods or holdings would be inherited by
his relatives: *aviticitas*! (The wording of the text is significant: "ad
manus regias non deuoluantur.")[39]

    4. If the childless noble had not died in the line of duty, his
holdings would be reclaimed by the royal treasury - "possessiones
eius...ad presenciam nostram euocentur" - and the monarch would
give them away: "et ipsis ac baronibus nostris presentibus." That is,
before giving his goods away, the monarch was obligated to grant a
hearing to the relatives of the party concerned (the childless nobleman) in the presence of his barons.[40]

    The Law of 1267 also contained three new decrees:

    1. Appeals and grievances of the service nobility would be
directly handled by the monarch, without a previous written petition
to be made by the noble requesting that the king hear the case in
person: "ad quemcumque nostrum se transferre uoluerint" - thereby
ending a previously introduced custom of requesting writs before
starting procedures: "cause noblium sine peticionibus debeant
expediri."[41]

    2. Two of the barons, who possessed the trust and confidence
of both the monarch and the service nobility, "quibus nos et ipsi
nobiles idem duximus adhibendam," would reclaim from the fort
personnel ("seu uduarnoci, seu castranses") the previously, for
whatever reason, confiscated lands of the service nobility:
"quacunque occasione occupauerunt et detinent."[42]

    3. The monarch must return the holdings to the forts, and to
the fort personnel, and the latter - who were mainly foreign settlers -
would enjoy their privileges as freemen. "...et ipsi illi gaudere
debeant priuilegiato nomine hospitum liberorum."[43]

The eighth article of the Law of 1267 that stated that two to three nobles from each fort district [county] appear on the annual law-day in Fehérvár, so that matters of public interest, every grievance ("de omnibus damnis et iniuriis"), be discussed in their presence, "ut in eorum presencia"[44] bears witness to English, or Iberian Argonese influence.[45]

In 1213, John of England had asked the *vicecomes* of Oxford, and directed the shires to send four discreet individuals to his announced *Concilum magnum* - "...et quattuor discretos homines de comitatu tuo" - so that he could discuss with them matters of public concern at the meeting(s) of the Great Council - "ad loquendum nobiscum de negotiis regni nostri."[46] A later example occurred when Henry III of England, in sending out summons for his 1265 parliament, had asked that two knights from each shire appear: "venire faciat duos milites de legalioribus...singulorum comitatum ad regem."[47] (Here, the use of the term *legaliores* is reminiscent of an earlier document, the 1166 Assize of Clarendon by Henry II,[48] as if to underline the observation made by Bryce Lyon that the development of the English parliament in the thirteenth century was not an unexpected event, but the outcome of a process that originated in the twelfth century.[49] The assumptions of Lyon are supported by the far earlier arguments of C. Ilbert.)[50]

The term "baron" - in Hungarian *báró* - is, therefore, the Hungarian version of the English baron, *barones*; in its Hungarian context, it first appeared in the 1220's and 1230's,[51] as the modified variant of *iobagio* used in the Bull of 1222.[52] In referring to its English origins, may it suffice here to cite the 1215 Articles of the Barons ("capitula quae Barones petunt et dominus Rex concedit"),[53] or, the 1215 Magna Carta - regardless whether the 1215 version had been declared null and void by Pope Innocent III in August, 1215;[54] and the classic definition by F.W. Maitland of the distinction between the *baro maior* and *baro minor*.[55] On Iberian soil, the barons had taken an active part in the *cortes*, together with members of the hierarchy, high nobility, and town representatives since the late twelfth century.[56]

In Hungary of the late 1260's, the county existed under the administration of the [lesser] nobles, to be differentiated from the former "royal" fort district, the administrative organization of which had progressed strongly since 1231, as witnessed by the eighth article

of the Law of 1267.[57] Because of the legalization of the nobles'
landholdings - property rights assured to them by law - the lesser
nobles (royal service nobility in the counties) had gained representation next to the barons, and had assumed an even firmer role in
public life.[58] Their *iudex nobilium* [*szolgabíró* in Hungarian], that is,
"Judge of the service nobility," gained a predominant position in
public. In 1269, the lesser nobles in Zala county had, for example,
reported in compliance with a royal summons, and investigated a
murder case in their particular area. The "County under the nobles,"
in other words, the organized status-quo of the lesser nobility
countywide, had become an administrative political reality in the
Hungarian west and northwest - that is, Transdanubia and the area
north of the Danube - by the third quarter of the century.[59]

King Béla IV had increased membership of the *servientes*
(royal service nobility) by emancipating numerous common "free"
knights (*milites*) to the rank of mounted royal *servientes*, and by
granting noble status to many free men serving as royal troops.[60] To
cite but two examples, Béla IV had emancipated Vejte, a fort guard
and fisherman in Hont, who had served in the royal cavalry unit
surrounding the king's person during the Mongol onslaught, from
the status of fort guard-fisherman to the rank of royal service noble,
and provided him with five plough shares: 600 acres of land for
sustenance.[61] The king had also elevated Milasz (Miloz) of Nógrád-
Dejter, a minor royal official in charge of royal drinks (*pintér*),
together with his two sons, to the rank of royal service noble,[62] on
the grounds that the sons had promised that they would, fully
equipped and trained on horse, serve in the king's armed forces. The
sons fulfilled their promise by taking part in the wars of Béla IV
with Otakar II.[63]

These, and many royal writs alike granting noble status to
mere freemen in servile strata, stressed the fact that the newly
emancipated royal *servientes* (service nobles) would henceforth
perform active military duty under the king's standard - thereby
fulfilling their requirements for social emancipation: "sub vexillo
regio debeant militare;...in expeditionibus nostris expresso modo
nobis seruient."[64] This later definition has a special ring to it, as if
the recently emancipated royal service nobles, on active duty under
the royal standard, had formed the core of the kings' army; they had

fought for him, whenever and wherever he had sent them, and protected him from any of his enemies.

In the late 1260's Béla IV withdrew from public life. When the Serb Grand Reeve Uros attacked the region of Macho, it was Prince Stephen, who had captured Uros; the latter, being held captive in Stephen's court, had asked for the hand in marriage of Stephen's younger daughter for his son Dragutin.[65] When, in 1269, Abbot Bernard of Montecassino, the envoy of Charles the First of Anjou, king of Naples-Sicily, visited Hungary to ask for the hand of marriage of Maria, Stephen's elder daughter, for his son and heir to the Sicilian throne, Charles (the Lame), the old monarch took no part in these dynastic marriage negotiations. The envoy had further arranged for the engagement of Isabella of Naples to Ladislas, the son of Stephen.[66]

Béla IV must have realized that since the last Byzantine emperor had made Charles I of Anjou - brother of Louis IX of France - heir to the Byzantine throne, the court of Naples-Sicily had an increasing diplomatic need in the Balkans for a dynastic marriage alliance with Hungary. The wise old monarch had no desire to play a part in this complicated game of diplomatic chess.[67]

Probably Béla IV had serious doubts about the long-term outcome of such dynastic negotiations. Had not Abbot Bernard reported to his royal master in Naples that the Hungarian monarch was a most powerful one, that he had many weapons, and nobody would dare attack him from the north or from the east? Were he to invade someone else's territory, his princely opponent would have to acknowledge his might by either submitting to him or by establishing blood ties with his dynasty.[68]

One has to know about the background of the marriage agreement of the Anjous, that the brother of Louis IX of France had ended German rule in Italy in August, 1268, and established the realm of Naples-Sicily.[69] Charles of Anjou was a papal vassal, a mighty prince on Italian soil, and the exiled Latin-Byzantine emperor had also named him [his] heir of the Latin-Byzantine throne. Therefore, Charles, as the Italian heir of the German-Roman emperors, had, in fact, decided to restore the ancient Roman empire - in the east and in the west.[70]

He included Hungary in his plan. Upon the death of his Queen, Charles I of Anjou had asked for the hand in marriage of Margaret, a daughter of Béla IV; Margaret said no to the proposal.[71] Charles of Anjou now made a new arrangement to bring about a marriage between his son, Charles (the Lame), prince of Salerno, and Maria, daughter of Stephen, the son of Béla IV. At the same time, Isabella (in Hungarian, Erzsébet), daughter of Charles, was to marry Stephen's son, Ladislas.[72]

These marriages actually led to the formation of an anti-German alliance, though nobody could have realized their historic importance at the time. To wit, the dynastic claim of the Anjous to the Hungarian Crown in 1290 was based on the marriage of Charles of Salerno and Maria, and so were the Anjou policies in the fourteenth century in building up a great Hungarian kingdom in east central Europe.[73]

In 1269, these marriage alliances had greatly elevated the prestige of the Árpád dynasty. Two grandchildren of Béla IV had married into the French royal family; a third became the wife of the Czech king, who himself was a powerful German imperial prince and an imperial elector. These circumstances could not have escaped the attention of the Anjou monarch of Naples-Sicily, who reminded his ambassador to the Hungarian court that *Lord* Stephen was king of Hungary, prince of Transylvania and Slovenia, master of the Cumans, and an offspring of great and saintly kings.[74]

It was in the year of marriage alliances concluded with the Anjous - even though it was not Béla IV, but his son and heir, Stephen (Junior King), who had signed the treaties - that Prince Béla had died;[75] and, in 1270, King Béla IV followed his younger son to the grave.[76] They dying monarch expressed his last wish that his "beloved son," Otakar II of Bohemia, protect his Queen, Anna, and her adherents (from the wrath of his own son, Prince Stephen).[77]

In 1271, Margaret died, the daughter of Béla IV, who had earlier refused the marriage proposal of Charles I of Naples-Sicily.[78] Her saintly life, and miracles that had been associated with her, were presented by 110 witness to the papal commission for her beatification that consisted of the Archbishop of Esztergom, the Bishop of Veszprém, and the Cistercian Abbot of Zirc.[79] The eyewitness accounts given during the hearings conducted between 1271 and 1273, were recorded by John of Vercelli (Iohannes Vercellensis), general of the Dominican order, who, based on that record, wrote in 1276, *A Life of Margaret of Hungary*.[80]

The life and the reign of Béla IV might be characterized by a series of lost battles and wars; and yet, he had reconstructed the country. Not only did he leave his realm and its old provinces intact, but had built their administration, political ties, and the economy. He had strengthened Hungarian government in Croatia, on the Dalmatian seashore; had Bosnia, Halich, and Macho closely allied with his realm, and had wholly reorganized the Szerém region. He established strong blood ties with both Halich and Serbia, and made it clear that northern Bulgaria recognized him as feudal overlord.[81]

Béla IV had rebuilt the country, reconstructed old cities, established new townships.[82] He wholly reorganized the administration of the realm, with new districts [counties] created.[83] He had settled foreign immigrants in the land, in order to repopulate parts of the kingdom that had been devastated by the Mongols. He created order out of chaos in the country's fiscal policy and reorganized its administration.[84] The king knew how to select his advisors and head officials, who had served him well; he placed qualified individuals in leading positions everywhere. His cabinet (*curia regis*) stayed in office for a period of twenty-five years.[85]

Some foreign chronicles have referred to him as "bloodthirsty;"[86] but, from the Hungarian chroniclers' point of view, he was a whole person, a *decent* ruler.[87] His faithful Queen, Maria, the proud offspring of the Byzantine throne, had lived long enough to witness the coronation of her son, Stephen V, and of Stephen's wife, Isabella (Erzsébet).[88] Shortly thereafter, she, too, followed her husband to the grave. Her body was laid to rest next to her husband, and their younger son, Béla[89] in a crypt of the Franciscan Minorites in Esztergom.[90]

NOTES

1. Cf. *RA*, n. 1547; text in *RHM*, 512ff.; Marczali, *Enchiridion*, 168f.; *CD*, IV-3, 391ff.; excerpts in Teutsch-Firnhaber, I, xlvii.
2. *RA*, n. 1791; Knauz, I, 476ff.; *CD*, IV-3, 69f.; excerpt in Teutsch-Firnhaber, I, xlviii; Zimmermann-Werner, I, 87; further, Bél, *Notitiae Hungariae*, I, 118f.; Pray, *Annales*, I, 311; Katona, VI, 360f.
3. *RA*, n. 1801; Knauz, I, 485f.; *CD*, IV-3, 160ff.; Bél, I, 122f.; Pray, *Annales*, I, 314f.; Katona, VI, 370f.
4. On Rabbits' Island, today St. Margaret's Island, see *RA*, nn. 1481 and 1488; *ÁUO*, III, 128ff. and 136ff.
5. After the pontiff had listened to the arguments of both parties involved - Potthast, n. 19711; *VMH*, n. 518; *ÁUO*, III, 144f.
6. *RHM*, 512f.; Marczali, *Enchiridion*, 168; one is to note the wording: the nobles had "pecierunt a nobis humiliter et devote;" was it respect shown by the nobles toward the king [his person, his office], or was it the careful wording of the chancellor who drew up the document? "Et in aliis libertatibus...ipsos nobiles manutenebimus." The royal writ was issued on September 7, 1267, at Buda - *RA*, n. 1521, might refer to the wording of art. 5 of this document! See *ÁUO*, VIII, 19f.
7. "...habito baronum nostrorum consilio et assensu;" *RHM*, 513; Marczali, *Enchiridion*, 168.
8. *Ibid.*, 169; *RHM*, 514, and compare with the Bull of 1222, art. 1, *ibid.*, 413; Marczali, *Enchiridion*, 134a.
9. *Ibid.*, the prefatory introduction to the Bull of 1222; see further King St. Stephen's Laws, art. i:22, *ibid.*, 69ff.; *RHM*, 310ff., or, the king's *Admonitiones*, art. 7, *SSH*, II, 619ff., or, Marczali, *Enchiridion*, 63ff.
10. As evidenced by the two writs cited above, *RA*, nn. 1481 and 1484, in note 4; Hóman-Szekfű, I, 576f.; Hóman, *Ungarisches Mittelalter*, II, 179ff.
11. To be concluded from the wording of the writ, "Nos Bela Dei gratia rex Hungarie, *et* [italics mine] Stephanus per eundem iunior rex Hungarie, et dux Transylvanie *et* [italics mine] Bela iunior dux totius Sclavonie;" *RHM*, 512; one may note, though, that instead of "per eundem," one should read "per eandem," that is, Stephen became Junior King by the grace of God, and not by the good will of his royal father! See Pauler, II, 538, note 206, referring to his reading of the text, as preserved in the Hungarian National Archives, DL 622. Jenő Szűcs, "Az 1267-évi dekrétum és háttere," [The Decree of 1267 and its Background], in É.H. Balázs *et al.* (eds.), *Mályusz Elemér emlékkönyv* [Memorial Volume in Honor of Elemér Mályusz] (Budapest, 1984), 341ff.
12. "...ut in eorum presentia de omnibus damnis et iniuriis per quoscunque datis et illatis omnibus satisfiat;" art. 8, *RHM*, 513. E.S. Kiss, "A király generális kongregáció kialakulásának történetéhez" [Comments on the History of the Development of the Royal Convention], *Acta historica Szegediensis*, 39 (1971), 3ff., esp. 15ff. On the role of the nobles as such, see the Laws of King St. Ladislas I, as, e.g., his *Decretum I*, art. 42; his *Decretum II*, art. 10, and *Decretum III*, art. 2; *RHM*, 325ff.; Marczali, *Enchiridion*, 87ff.; Kosztolnyik, *From Coloman*, 7ff., and 15, n. 68.
13. *RHM*, 512.
14. Marczali, *Enchiridion*, 167ff.
15. See Stephen's Laws, art. i:16, *ibid.*, 69ff.; *RHM*, 310ff.; Emma Bartoniek, *Szent István törvényeinek XII századi kézirata: az admonti kódex* [The 12th Century MS of King St. Stephen's Laws, the Admont Codex], with a reduced facsimile of Cod. med. aevi 433 of the Széchenyi Library (Budapest, 1935), 15ff.; Kosztolnyik, *Five*

Kings, 110ff. The text in *MPL*, 151, 1243ff., follows a different numbering system of the articles.
16. Stephen's Laws, art. i:14.
17. Stephen's Laws, art. i:29.
18. Stephen's Laws, art. ii:2 (art. 35 in *MPL*, 151, 1251f.).
19. "...quorum peticiones...considerantes fore iustus,...habito baronum... consilio et assensu duximus admittendas;" *RHM*, 513, Marczali, *Enchiridion*, 168 - introductory part; Elemér Mályusz, "A magyar köznemesség kialakulása" [The Formation of the Hungarian Service Nobility], *Századok*, 74 (1942), 272ff. and 407ff., esp. 414f.
20. *RHM*, 428ff.; Marczali, *Enchiridion*, 139b.
21. *Ibid.*, 142a.
22. On this, see *ibid.*, 168, note 1; on the English usage, cf. F.W. Maitland, *The Constitutional History of England* (Cambridge, 1911), 64ff.; Lyon, 142ff.; G.B. Adams, *Constitutional History of England* (New York, 1931), 55ff., 64.
23. King St. Stephen's Admonitions, art. 4, *SSH*, II, 619ff., here 623,24; the *MPL*, 151, 1235ff., here 1239c, version has a different wording - Kosztolnyik, *From Coloman*, 265, n. 257; and, on the Ilosvay codex, see *ibid.*, 15, n. 68.
24. The Law of 1267, art. 1; compare to the Bull of 1222, art. 3, Marczali, *Enchiridion*, 135a; Heinrich Fichtenau, "Spätantike und Mittelalter im Spiegel von Urkundenformeln," *MIÖG*, Erg. Band 18 (1957), 84.
25. Law of 1267, art. 2; one may note that "et ipsi illi" is bad reading of the text; on DL 622, Hungarian National Archives, it reads "ne ipsae villae gaudere." Cf. Pauler, II, 538, note 206, to wit, that the villages be returned to the fort personnel, without forcing them to a lower social level - that of the "free" foreign settlers. See also E. Ladányi, "Libera villa, civitas, oppidum; terminologische Fragen des 13 Jahrhunderts," *MIÖG*, 70 (1962), 336ff.
26. Law of 1267, art. 3; compare to Bull of 1222, art. 2.
27. Law of 1267, art. 4; compare to Bull of 1222, art. 18.
28. Law of 1267, art. 5; in the text, *nobiles*: "terre nobilium...restituantur ipsis nobilibus;" therefore, the rewarded service nobles serve the monarch with great effort, proving their worthiness - cf. Peter Váczy, *A szimbólikus álamszemlélet kora Magyarországon* [The Age of Symbolic State Concept in Hungary] (Budapest, 1932), 23ff.
29. Law of 1267, art. 6.
30. Law of 1267, art. 7; compare to Bull of 1222, art. 7.
31. Law of 1267, art. 8; compare to Bull of 1222, art. 1.
32. Law of 1267, art. 9; compare to Bull of 1222, art. 10.
33. Law of 1267, art. 10.
34. See conclusion, second paragraph: "Si quis autem nostrum imposterum presentis statuti et libertatis a s. Stephano constitute transgressor erit, quod absit...," and compare it to the conclusion of the Bull of 1231, Marczali, *Enchiridion*, 142b; A. Kurcz, "Aregna und Narratio ungarischer Urkunden des 13 Jahrhunderts," *MIÖG*, 60 (1962), 336ff.
35. See conclusion, first paragraph, *RHM*, 514; on the *staurotheka* (reliquary of the True Cross), upon which the king and his sons swore the oath, see A. Somogyi, "La staurotheque byzantine d'Esztergom," *Balkan Studies*, 9 (1968), 139ff.; and, the arguments of Deér, *Hl. Krone*, 215ff., on "lypsanotheka": living wood of the Holy Cross! also, E.M. Kovács, "Signum crucis: a magyar kettőskereszt ábrázolásai" [Depictions of the Hungarian Double Cross], in György Székely (ed.), *Eszmetörténeti tanulmányok a magyar középkorról* [Ideological Essays on the Hungarian Middle Ages] (Budapest, n.d.), offprint.

36. Compare with the Bull of 1222, aa. 10b, 14, 17, 18, in Marczali, *Enchiridion*, 134ff.
37. Law of 1267, art. 3, *ibid.*, 168f.
38. *Ibid.*, art. 8.
39. *Ibid.*, art. 9.
40. *Ibid.*, art. 6.
41. *Ibid.*, art. 5, and, mainly, art. 10.
42. *Ibid.*, art. 5.
43. *Ibid.*, art. 2; and, *supra*, note 25.
44. Marczali, *Enchiridion*, 168f., art. 8.
45. Cf. H. Mitteis, *Der Stat des hohen Mittelalters*, 8th ed. (Weimar, 1968), 322, note 1; 416 and 419. E. Mályusz, "Die Entstehung der Stände in Ungarn," *L'organisation corporative du moyen age: Études présentés a la Commission internationale pour l'histoire des assemblées d'États* (Paris, 1939), 15ff., and compare with Mitteis' remarks in *Historische Zeitschrift*, 161 (1940), 572ff., esp. 576f.; F. Eckhart, "La diete corporative hongroise," in *L'organisation corporative du moyen age*, 215ff.; E. Hantos, *The Magna Carta and the Hungarian Constitution* (London, 1904), 151; R.B. Merriman, "The Cortes of the Spanish Kingdoms," *American Historical Review*, 16 (1911), 485ff.; Ch. E. Chapman, *A History of Spain* (New York, 1918), 89ff. and 99f.; G. Jackson, *The Making of Medieval Spain* (New York, 1972), 92f. and 98f.
46. Stubbs, *Charters*, 287; cf. Adams, 176: in 1220, two knights were chosen in the county court to assess and collect a carucage for the county.
47. Stubbs, *Charters*, 415.
48. Stubbs, *Charters*, 143; or, Edward I's parliament of 1295, when the monarch "praecipimus firmiter iniungentes quod de comitatu praedicto duos milites et de qualibet civitate...duos cives" to appear in parliament, *ibid.*, 486; F. Palgrave (ed.), *Parliamentary Writs*, vol. I (London, 1827), 28ff.
49. Lyon, 413ff.; Geoffrey Templeman, "The Historiography of Parliament to 1400 in the Light of Modern Research," *University of Birmingham Historical Journal*, 1 (1948), 203ff.
50. Cf. Courtney Ilbert, *Parliament, Its History, Constitution, and Practice* (London, 1917), 7ff.
51. See art. 8, Marczali, *Enchiridion*, 139b; *RHM*, 430; in the text of King St. Stephen's Admonitions, based on a later transcript, and printed in *MPL*, 151, 1239c, art. 4, the term *barones* appears, while in an earlier transcript, it does not - *SSH*, II, 623,24, see above, note 12. On the transcript, Kosztolnyik, *From Coloman*, 15, n. 68. The first appearance of *baro* in the previous function of an *iobagio*, was dated 1228 by E.S. Kiss, *art. cit.* (1971), 12; Gy. Bónis, *Hűbériség és rendiség a középkori magyar jogban* [Feudalism and the Nobles' Estate in Medieval Hungarian Law] (Kolozsvár, 1947), 128ff.
52. As, e.g., aa. 10, 19, 30 of the Bull of 1222, Marczali, *Enchiridion*, 138a, 140a, and 142a; *RHM*, 414, 415, and 416 - in contrast with *nobiles*, cf. *ibid.*, aa. 1 and 31 of the Bull of 1222; and, earlier, the Laws of Ladislas I, *Decretum I*, art. 42; *Decretum II*, art. 10, and *Decretum III*, art. 2; Kosztolnyik, *Five Kings*, 105ff. and 193, note 2; idem, *From Coloman*, 2ff.; Elemér Mályusz, *A magyar köznemesség kialakulása* [Formation of the Hungarian Lesser Nobility as Social Class] (Szeged, 1942), 422ff.: out of the ranks of the royal *nobilis serviens*, and of the stratum of royal landholders obligated to fort duty, *iobagiones castris*.
53. Stubbs, *Charters*, 290 and 296ff.
54. The papal writ, "Etsi carissimus," in Potthast, n. 4990; text in *Bullarium magnum Romanum*, vol. III (Rome, 1733 etc.; repr. Graz, 1963), 172ff.; or, C.R. Cheney and W.H. Semple (eds.), *Selected Letters of Pope Innocent III Concerning*

England (London-New York, 1953), 212ff., esp. 216; C.R. Cheney, "King John and the Papal Interdict," *Bulletin of the John Rylands Library*, 31 (1948), 295ff.; McIlwain, 231f.; J.C. Holt, "The Barons and the Great Charter," *English Historical Review*, 70 (1955), 1ff.
    55. Cf. Maitland, *Constitutional History*, 64ff.; Lyon, 142ff.
    56. R.B. Merriman, *The Rise of the Spanish Empire*, vol. I: *The Middle Ages* (New York, 1918; repr. 1962), 98ff. and 217ff.; T.N. Bisson, "Prelude to Power: Kingship and Constitution in the Realm of Aragon, 1175-1250," in R.I. Burns (ed.), *The Worlds of Alfonso the Learned and James the Conqueror* (Princeton, 1985), 23ff.
    57. Marczali, *Enchiridion*, 134b and 169; *RHM*, 428f. and 514. Mályusz, *Köznemesség*, 414f.
    58. In the county of Győr, the *iudex nobilium* [szolgabíró] had to oblige the local legal customs; "iuxta mores patrie" had he handed down his sentence. The testimony of the invited witnesses had to be taken "coram nobilibus;" cf. Erdélyi, *Rendtörténet*, I, 747.
    59. *RA*, n. 1652; *ÁUO*, VIII, 269, Szűcs, *art. cit.*, 357f. and 361.
    60. Mályusz, *Köznemesség*, 415; J. Holub, *Zala vármegye története* [History of Zala County] (Pécs, 1929), 97ff.
    61. "In collegium et numerum regalium seruiencium nostrorum, et ad nostram recepimus,...eximentes ipsum ab officio et condicione piscacionis;...ut terram cuiusdam seruientis nostri Iwan uocati de uilla Pyrwusi quinque aratorum sufficientem, sine herede decendentis, sibi conferre dignaremur;" *RA*, n. 894; *ÁUO*, VII, 256f.
    62. "...quod quibusdam buchariis nostris, uidelicet Miloz et duobus filiis eius...et de cetero ab officio buchariorum exempti...;" *RA*, n. 973; *ÁUO*, VII, 342f.
    63. To be concluded from the fact that the writ had been issued "in castris iuxta Viennam...contra ducem predictum;" *ibid.*, VII, 343.
    64. *Ibid.*
    65. *RA*, nn. 1604, 1605, and 2225; text[s], in *HO*, VIII, 96f.; *CD*, IV-3, 490, and V-1, 238f.; also, Zimmermann-Werner, I, 120; compare with some of the writs issued by Uros, King of Serbia, in *ÁUO*, III, 283ff.
    66. See the writ by the Abbot of Montecassino addressed to the Hungarian barons, dated mid-September, 1269 - Wenczel, *Anjoukori diplomácia*, I, 21ff. Compare with G. del Guidice (ed.), *Codice diplomatico del regno di Carlo Ie II d'Angio*, vol. III (Naples, 1902), 136ff.; *ÁUO*, VIII, 316ff.; Potthast, n. 23384; *VMH*, n. 588.
    67. The fact that Kunigunde of Cracow had complained to her niece, Kunigunde of Prague, about her concern for both Bélas - cf. Palacky, *Formelbücher*, 279; furthermore, that the dying king had asked his son-in-law to look after Queen Anna and her adherents after his death, may be looked upon as characteristic of Béla IV's mental-spiritual disposition before he died. Cf. *RA*, n. 1664; *ÁUO*, III, 204; Palacky, *Formelbücher*, 268f., and compare to the message sent by Elizabeth, daughter of Béla IV, and Duchess of Bavaria, to the Czech Kunigunde, *ibid.*, 280; *ÁUO*, III, 205.
    68. *Ibid.*, VIII, 316f.: "Domus Hungariae;" Guidice, *Codice*, III, 136ff.; one is tempted to compare his expressions to the remarks made in Helmoldi Bozoviensis, *Chronica Slavorum*, ed. B. Schmiedler, SSrG, 3rd. ed. (Hannover, 1937), 6,27-28: "Ungarica gens validissima quondam in armis strenus, ipsi etiam Romano imperio formidolosa." Although Russian historians did not look favorably on this opus, *ibid.*, xif., their dislike did not weaken the validity of this assertion; see Wattenbach, *Geschichtsquellen*, II, 338ff.
    69. Cf. Iohannes Victoriensis, *Liber certarum historiarum*, ed. F. Schnieder, SSrG, 2 vols. (Hannover-Leipzig, 1909-10), I, 136f. and 205. Lhotsky, *Quellenkunde*,

292ff., referred to Johann von Viktring's work as a "grosse Geschichtsdarstellung," most valuable, "sehr hoch eingeschätzt," *ibid.*, 298. Also, G.M. Monti, *Da Carlo I a Roberto di Angio* (Milan, 1936); A. Wachtel, "Die sizillienische Thronkandidatur des Prinzen Edmund von England," *Deutsches Archiv*, 4 (1941), 98ff.; Loserth, *Geschichte*, 143f.

70. See Giovanni Villani, "Istorie Florentine," vii:1, in Muratori, *RISS*, XIII, 225f.; on popes Alexander IV and Urban IV, see Michael of Aragon, "Vitae pontificum Romanorum," *ibid.*, III, 592ff. and 593f. E. Dade, "Versuche zur Wiederrichtung der lateinischen Herrschaft in Konstantinople im Rahmen der abendländischen Politik, 1261-1310," Dissertation, Jena, 1937, on Balkan politics - still worth reading! F.R. Lewis, "Otakar II of Bohemia and the Double Election of 1257," *Speculum*, 12 (1937), 512ff., discussed background politics at some length.

71. Margaret took the vow of chastity as a member of the Order of Preachers - cf. P. Ransanus, "Vitae b. Margarithae Hungariae," iii:14-17, in *Acta Sanctorum*, Ian. II, 906f.; idem, *Epithoma rerum Hungararum*, ed. P. Kulcsár (Budapest, 1977), 128f., ind. xvi.

72. *RA*, n. 1894; *ÁUO*, VIII, 315 and 315f.; Wenczel, *Anjoukori diplomácia*, I, 22f.; Guidice, *Codice*, III, 136f.; Palacky, *Formelbücher*, 279. For the family tree of Charles, see *SSH*, I, 478,3-7.

73. "...scilicet centra omnes Teutonicos, et Thetoniae adherentes;" *ÁUO*, VIII, 312f.; Hóman-Szekfű, I, 580f.; Hóman, *Ungarisches Mittelalter*, II, 174ff.; F.M. Mayer, Raimund Kaindl, and Hans Pirchegger, *Geschichte und Kulturleben Öster-reichs bis 1493*, 5th rev. ed. (Vienna-Stuttgart, 1958), 63ff.

74. *ÁUO*, VIII, 316f.; *VMH*, n. 588.

75. *MGHSS*, IX, 797,30-32; Béla had issued a writ before his death, cf. *ÁUO*, VIII, 203f.

76. *SSH*, I, 469,9-11 (c. 179); *Monumenta Erphurtensis*, ed. O. Holder-Egger, SSrG (Hannover-Leipzig, 1899), 260,26-28; 458,5-6; 681,1-6. Wattenbach, *Geschichtsquellen*, II, 198ff.; also, Victoriensis *Liber*, 208; *MPH*, II, 840ff.; Katona, IV, 509.

77. *RA*, n. 1664; *ÁUO*, III, 204; Palacky, *Formelbücher*, 268. Anna, daughter of Béla IV, fled to the Czech court, taking with her the coronation treasures - *MGHSS*, IX, 708,41-48; IX, 730,31-33 and *ÁUO*, III, 254; the Remichronik, c. 88, stated that the old king himself gave the treasures to Anna. On the frustrated anger of Stephen V, see *ÁUO*, III, 247ff and 249f.

78. Ransanus, *Epithoma*, 130.

79. Upon the request of King Stephen V, brother of the deceased Margaret - cf. *RA*, n. 1918; *ÁUO*, VIII, 296f.; Hováth, *Irodalmunk kezdetei*, 225 and 319f.; Pintér, I, 555f.; Ransanus, *Epithoma*, 206; Kornél Böle, *Árpádházi boldog Margit szenttéavatási ügye és a legősibb Margit legenda* [The Canonization Process of Blessed Margaret and the Earliest Margaret Legend] (Budapest, 1937), 17ff.

80. Elemér Lovass, *Árpádházi Boldog Margit élete* [Life of Blessed Margaret of the House of Árpád] (Budapest, 1939), and in his essay on Blessed Margaret, in *Pannonhalmi főapátsági Szent Gellért Főiskola évkönyve 1940-41* [Annual of Saint Gerard College of the Archabbey of Pannonhalma, 1940-41] (Pannonhalma, 1941), 21ff., had argued that Friar Marcellus, confessor of Margaret, wrote a Life of Margaret, presented it to Iohannes Vercellenisis, head of the Dominican Order, who accepted it as his own - to give it more credibility. In 1276, Rome ordered another canonization inquiry; two papal canons and a public notary conducted the hearings, and, based upon the testimonies of the cited witnesses, Friar Garinus de Giaco wrote, in 1340, another Life of Blessed Margaret - cf. *Acta Sanctorum*, Ian. II, 90ff.; compare with the so-called *Legenda Neopolitana b. Margarithae: A nápolyi Margit Legenda*, ed. N. Knauz (Esztergom, 1868), 30ff.

81. Cf. Thuróczy, *Chronica*, c. 103; Hóman-Szekfű, I, 566f.; Hóman, *Ungarisches Mittelalter*, II, 182ff.

82. Hóman-Szekfű, I, 562f.; Gerevich, *Medieval Hungarian Towns*, 34f.

83. Kristó, *Vármegyék*, 428f. and 459ff.

84. Cf. Bálint Hóman, *Magyar pénztörténet 1000-1325* [Hungarian Monetary History, 1000-1325] (Budapest, 1916), 443ff.

85. Hóman-Szekfű, I, 558.

86. "...quia vir sanguinuus fuit;" *MGHSS*, IX, 651,28; and, Victoriensis *Liber*, 194ff. and 200ff.

87. *SSH*, I, 469f., I, 470,6-10, and 470, 24; Ransanus, *Epithoma*, 123f. and 139f.

88. On the coronation of Stephen V, cf. *CD*, V-1, 237; he was in Buda on May 13, 1270 - *RA*, n. 1919; had confirmed an earlier privilege on May 21 - *RA*, n. 1921. On the nobles supporting Stephen V, see *RA*, n. 1963; *ÁUO*, VIII, 237ff. and 281f.

89. *SSH*, I, 469,11-14 and 469,44-45; Wadding, *Annales Fratrum Minorum*, IV, 418; *CD*, IV-3, 266.

90. *SSH*, I, 470,1-10.

CHAPTER NINE

LADISLAS IV THE CUMAN

1. *Struggle for the Throne*

Upon the death of Stephen V on August 6, 1272, his ten year old son, Ladislas IV, succeeded to the throne,[1] at a time when rivalry for power among the great lords, and the attempts of Otakar II of Bohemia at territorial expansion, were threatening the realm.[2] In his writ addressed to the hierarchy and the secular nobles of the realm, Pope Gregory IX had correctly summarized the situation. He warned them about what Scripture had to say of a country where peace would not prevail. He asked them to uproot any misunderstanding among themselves, and, together, in common agreement with and mutual respect for each other, they stand by their king, and aid him with their advice and deed, thus fulfilling an obligation toward his position. But the pontiff had also warned the Czech monarch to conscientiously observe the articles of the agreement he had earlier signed with King Stephen V.[3]

The warnings of the pope remained unheeded. The hostilities of the warring great noble families in the countryside had reached an even wider proportion in the country. Hatred and political greed turned the realm into war-zones of physical confrontation. Grand Steward Joachim of Slavonia had captured, then released the young heir to the throne, Ladislas, so that he would be crowned in the year 1272.[4] The mother of Ladislas (of Cuman descent) went in person to formally receive Joachim and her son,[5] but the populace misunderstood the meaning of this visit, and besieged the house of the widow of Stephen V.[6] The Queen had created the impression that, by meeting with them, she approved of the capture by Joachim and of the temporary imprisonment of her son, the heir to the throne.[7] The misdeed had caused the early death of her husband, the father of Ladislas, and the populace reacted accordingly. For five years after the coronation, Ladislas IV had remained the ward of his mother;[8] the regency of that weak woman, untrained in the art of government, proved to be a disaster for the country, as it mirrored the lack of self-esteem and unhappiness of the country's inhabitants.[9]

That was why Henry of Kőszeg had returned from his exile abroad, the former grand steward and staunch supporter of Béla IV;[10] however, his arrival led to a vehement confrontation at the meeting with Béla, Duke of Macho on Rabbits' Island in the Danube. Béla was the son of Rastislav of Halich (afterwards duke of Macho), and the brother of Anna, the wife of the Czech king, Otakar II. (One may recall that Béla could easily have been in line for succeeding to the throne!) Béla was murdered at their personal encounter, and the nuns of the monastery on Rabbits' Island had to collect the remains of the brutally murdered Béla, in order to bury him with decency.[11]

The duchy of Macho was now divided among four great noble families into several ducal territories known as Só, Ozóra, Bosnia, and Kucho. It was as if the parties in power were vying for predominance around the Queen. It meant confrontation between Joachim and Henry of Kőszeg on the one hand, and the group of Csák and Aba clans on the other - between interests related to the German blood and the Magyar values.[12]

The Hungaro-Austrian military clash in the spring of 1273 may be cited as an example characteristic of some of the major difficulties that had plagued the early months of the reign of Ladislas V. The Austrian forces captured Győr, placed its bishop in chains,[13] though Aegidius, grand steward of Bosnia and Slavonia successfully defended Pozsony.[14] One may also refer to the confrontation with the Czechs, who occupied Nyitra in May, 1273;[15] Grand Steward Andrew, son of Ivánka, easily defended Gyímeskő during their sudden attack,[16] and Henry of Németújvár crossed the Morava to catch by surprise the invading Czech king at Laa.[17] Otakar II transferred his theatre of military operations to Hungarian areas by occupying Magyaróvár;[18] however, when her received the news of the election of Rudolf of Habsburg as German king, Otakar II broke off his military operations in Hungary.[19]

The fact that the royal writs shed light on all of these events - the young king being present in person at the recapture by his forces of Szombathely;[20] his presence when his men had retaken Nagyszombat;[21] and some royal letters provide detailed evidence of his personal presence at the siege of Fort Detrekő, which, incidentally, ended in Hungarian victory - only lead to the conclusion that the young king, still a minor, took his royal obligations seriously.[22]

The question is, did his mother, the Queen-regent, maintain a weak, disorganized "cabinet" (a *curia regis*) of royal advisors? At the court, nobles had vied with one another for power. Before 1276, the office of the palatine had changed hands six times.[23] When the king and his Mother-regent ended their personal feud,[24] and the Czech forces were withdrawn from Hungarian territory, it was the oligarchs of the realm who turned against the king, causing bloody wars between the monarch, the Mother-regent, and members of the various parties, some who supported, some who opposed, the king.[25]

In the fall of 1273, it was the "party" (political interest group) of the Gútkeled-Kőszeg families who strove for dynastic prominence in the country; in summer of 1274, Joachim and Henry of Kőszeg gained personal control of both the king (still a minor) and the Mother-regent, and had carried on, in the name of the king (!), with the government of the realm.[26] It was also they who had prevented Nicholas, archpriest of Székesfehérvár, from gaining nomination and papal appointment to the archiepiscopal see of Esztergom.[27]

The old families supported the monarch and his mother, but they must have observed the scandalous behavior of the widowed queen toward her clerical favorite, Nicholas the archpriest, and her preference for the political support of German interest groups in the country led by the Gútkeled-Kőszeg clan. Máté Csák, a loyal supporter of the king, a learned and balanced individual, who had belonged to the adherents of Stephen V, eventually took charge of the upbringing and education of young Ladislas IV;[28] Péter Csák, his brother, a most vehement and thoughtless man, was a determined opponent of the Kőszeg clan;[29] István Csák, the other brother, was less wild than his brother Péter, and yet a difficult person.[30] Ugrin Csák, Master of the Horse (Master of Stables), was a distant scion of the Csák family.[31]

It was at this time that Péter Csák had, as Palatine, entered the political scene; he guarded the king and took military action against the Kőszeg clan. In the ensuing battle of Fövény, near Fehérvár, Henry of Kőszeg was killed; his sons fled the country.[34] From the fall of 1274, for the next ten years, the Csák family had control of the administration of the realm - except for three months in 1275, when Joachim, once again, held the palatine's position; and in 1276, or in 1281, when the sons of the fallen Henry of Kőszeg, and Joachim, held the country's government under their supervision.[35] In the early 1280's, the Csáks and the Abas together watched over the destiny of the country. Although both of their "parties" (family interest groups) committed their share of bloody atrocities in the land, their misdeeds remained unnoticed and unpunished.[36]

The fact that the archiepiscopal see of Esztergom - the seat of the Hungarian Primate - remained vacant, as difficulties surrounded its occupancy, had remained an administrative problem for the king. The queen's favorite - one is to remember that she was still the king's official guardian! - Nicholas, now archpriest of Transylvania, had tried to persuade the canons of the Esztergom cathedral to elect him as their archbishop;[37] with threats and promises he gained the support of some of the canons, but the chapter voted instead for Benedict, the archpriest of Arad,[38] who was also the royal vice-chancellor.[39]

Benedict won the election and Nicholas resorted to physical force to occupy the archbishop's seat, and the canons of Esztergom had no alternative but to appeal to Rome. The curia now cited Nicholas to appear before it, but the archpriest refused.[40] Therefore, it became the nobles' responsibility to find a solution. The nobles, unhappy with the administration of the queen, made certain that her favorite, Nicholas, lose his archiepiscopal prebend, whereupon Ladislas IV recognized Benedict as the rightful archbishop of Esztergom. Benedict requested papal confirmation.[41] His envoys sent to Rome, both canons from Esztergom, could not appear before the curia, however: Nicholas, playing malicious politics, had them detained in Dalmatia.[42]

It may be the irony of history that Pope Innocent IV, who had charged Cardinal Hadrian with investigating the Esztergom affair, had died within six months. The pontiff was a firm supporter of Charles of Anjou. Hadrian succeeded him on the papal throne, but he followed his predecessor to the grave during the first month of his papal reign.[43] The new pontiff, John XXI, who again asked Archpriest Nicholas to appear before him,[44] also died in the early months of his pontificate.[45] Now, Archbishop Benedict had died,[46] and his death only increased the irony of circumstances (of the affair of Esztergom) because Ladislas IV, still acting under the guardianship of his mother, now recognized Nicholas as the archbishop of Esztergom [47]

The royal recognition of Nicholas as the archbishop made the canons of the Esztergom cathedral chapter angry on the grounds that it was made under pressure from the queen. The canons declared the archiepiscopal see vacant, and chose Peter, bishop of Veszprém, to occupy it. Archbishop-elect Peter dispatched archpriest Paul of

Veszprém to Rome for the pallium. Nicholas also sent envoys to the curia. The case went before Pope Nicholas III, who set the date of January 27, 1278, for a hearing.[48]

Archpriest Paul raised damaging charges against Nicholas before the curia. He described his immoral behavior, and cited his lack of qualifications for the high church office. The envoys of Nicholas had to request a delay for the papal hearing, on the grounds that Archpriest Nicholas needed time to prepare for it. But the archpriest failed to appear on the re-scheduled date of April 25, 1278, saying that important state affairs kept him preoccupied at home. He had also felt alarmed by a long journey to Rome; he had received death threats.[49] He sent an envoy instead with instructions and a writ to certify his election to the see of Esztergom as valid.

Nicholas III wasted not time; he heard the case on June 1, 1278, and handed down a sentence against archpriest Nicholas, declaring him unqualified for the high office. Nor did the pontiff confirm Bishop Peter as the new archbishop of Esztergom. The curia cited political circumstances for its decision: it did not turn Peter down on personal grounds. Rome reserved the right to fill the archiepiscopal see.[50] Pope Nicholas III dispatched a papal legate in the person of Philip of Fermo to Hungary, and placed him in temporary administrative charge of the see of Esztergom.[51]

During all this controversy involving Esztergom, Máté Csák exploited the deteriorating domestic conditions of the country by invading Bohemia; thereupon, Otakar II led an attack on Hungary. The Czechs occupied Nagyszombat, Nyitra, Győr, and Sopron; their success increased their self-confidence and strengthened the self-assurance of their king. When, for instance, the German estates had elected Rudolf of Habsburg, Otakar II ignored the outcome of the election and refused to take the oath of homage to the new German ruler.[52] But Rudolf fought back: he declared the feudal estates of his "faithless" Czech vassal forfeit and entered into a military alliance with the Hungarian court against Bohemia.[53]

It was Ladislas IV's turn to surprise Otakar II, who withdrew his forces from Hungary, returned the occupied areas, and simultaneously submitted to Rudolf as King of Germany; thereupon the German monarch reinstated the Czech ruler in his Moravian and Czech possessions.[54] The clever Czech prince went one diplomatic step further: he renounced the territory he had earlier purchased in

Austria, promised to donate it as dowry for his daughter, were she to marry the son of Rudolf, and to pay four thousand silver marks to subsidize the expenditures of the German royal court.[55]

Conditions in Hungary had not improved, however. Head Steward Joachim, who had recently been removed from office, was replaced by Péter Csák,[56] the one who, after the battle of Polgárdi, had devastated the estates of the Kőszeg clan, and had savagely destroyed the cathedral and sacristy-treasury of the Veszprém cathedral, together with its well-known cathedral school - merely because the bishop of Veszprém happened to be a member of the Kőszeg family.[57] It must have been characteristic of the chaotic public conditions in the country that, while earlier the government had brought forth no charges against the murderer of Duke Béla of Macho (the royal court did not even dare to think of persecuting the attacker), now the utterly merciless and bloody destruction of the Veszprém cathedral and cathedral school likewise failed to excite the royal conscience to order an inquiry into the causes and nature of the savage attack. In the Veszprém cathedral, divine services had to be suspended for over a year on account of the savagery of the destruction.[58]

It was no mitigating circumstance that the palatine, Péter Csák, had been very angry with a member of the Kőszeg family: Péter of Németújvár-Kőszeg, the ordinary of Veszprém. It is quite evident from later pertinent royal writs that Péter Csák had been seeking revenge against the clerics of Veszprém, wanting to rob them of their possessions and to steal the treasures of the cathedral. That is the reason why Csák had collected a private armed force - mostly from the ranks of his personal servants - and assured himself the support of a few disgruntled nobles, so that he might steal the treasures of the cathedral. He wanted to overturn the altars, tear up and burn documents and writs that had been preserved for centuries in the sacristy, murder in cold blood as many individuals as he could, or capture and imprison them.[59] In spite of the pious tone and promise of full restitution that had been made in several royal documents, this evil deed remained unpunished, even though no such evil had ever befallen the country in human memory.[60]

The cathedral suffered in stolen or demolished treasures and rich liturgical vestments a loss of at least fifty thousand silver marks. In the sacristy, three thousand silver marks worth of books were destroyed, together with priceless royal gifts that had been donated to the cathedral. Archpriest Paul suffered a personal loss of three thousand silver marks, and his entire library collection valued at least at one thousand silver marks. The royal payment of compensation amounting to ten thousand silver marks to be distributed to me fifteen members of the school's law faculty formed but a small restitution of their losses.[61]

The king's letter, dated November 18, 1276, mentioned that in Veszprém the cathedral school that had flourished since the days of King Saint Stephen (*ob*. 1038), and had attained a reputation "similar to that of the school(s) of Paris," was burned to the ground during the raid. The royal writ that survived only in a fragment, spoke of "liberalium artium studia" in Veszprém that was similar to the one in Paris, without mentioning the Veszprém's school faculty of law.[62] On these grounds, the expression *studia, studium* being used in the writ may bear witness to the fact that the school did not have a law faculty, and it was not a "university," regardless whether, as an institution of learning, it was being referred to as "studium."[63]

The use of the term *studia* in the royal writ may have implied that the destroyed cathedral school was not a university, but the king wished to rebuild it, and to reconstruct its curriculum that included the study of law: "ut ibidem studium,...reformetur et cultus iustitiae divinaeque laudis organa...restaurentur." That is, *reformetur*: to reorganize there the study of law; *restaurentur*: next to the renewed studies in divine science(s).[64]

Simultaneously, the phrase used in the king's letter that the donation made by the monarch was intended for the cathedral in Veszprém ("Wesprimensi ecclesiae") and *not* for the cathedral school leads to the conclusion that the royal gift encouraged the restoration of the school "in suae desolationis ruinae," where they also could, in the future, teach the basic (introductory) subjects in law (pre-law), as it had long been the custom within the liberal arts curricula all over Europe at the time. The remark made by Ladislas IV in his letter of November 28, 1283, may further point to the fact that the destruction of Veszprém had been carried out by the country's tyrants during the years of the king's minority.[65] This, in connection with the king's other remark that the thievery and evil deed were carried out by the Palatine, Péter Csák, "in vastu et spolio Petri Palatini inter alia bona eiusdem Ecclesiae Wesprimensis amisissent," may excuse the young king of any responsibility for the misdeed.[66]

It was ironic that, at the time, the "Saxons" in Transylvania had been seeking revenge against the bishop of Gyulafehérvár by burning his cathedral to the ground.[67] During this time, the country had become so downtrodden on account of the almost constant domestic warring that people had to slaughter their draft animals - so the chronicler reported, although one has reasons to suspect the sincerity of the chronicler's remarks on the grounds that he was so hostile toward the monarch - and they had to replace animal strength by pulling two-wheeled carts by sheer manpower; in fact, common folk began to nickname the two-wheeled wagon of the time as "the cart of Ladislas the Cuman."[68]

Rudolf, the new German king, decided to support the Czech nobles, who were opposed to the reign of their king, Otakar II. To give credibility to his support of the Czech nobles, Rudolf drew the Hungarian court into his plans.[69] Rudolf and Ladislas IV met at Hainburg to discuss plans for an anti-Otakar II alliance.[70] In the summer of 1278, some forty thousand Hungarian troops - the number rendered by the chronicler seems to be very high indeed - had gathered at Győr, crossed the Danube at Pozsony, and were prepared to aid the two thousand armed knights of the German king.[71]

The Czechs commanded some thirty thousand troops (again, the number seems to be far too high),[72] and were holding the fort near Laa under siege. The Hungarian troops were still crossing the Danube when George, the son of Simon of the clan of Baksa (the forefather of the Sós family in Sóvár), had surprised the Czech forces with some eight thousand cavalry aided by Austrian auxiliaries.[73] Otakar II made the attempt to withdraw to the Morava river, but the Hungarian main force by then had crossed the river, taking up positions north of Stillfried.[74] The decisive encounter with Otakar II took place northeast of Dürnkrutt on Friday, August 26, 1278.[75]

At nine o'clock in the morning, after the Cumans had "softened up" the enemy ranks with their hail of arrows, Máté Csák led the attack with the main body of the Hungarian troops. Csák fell from his horse, but his men rescued him.[76] István Gútkeled, Justice of the King's Court, led another attack with the right wing of the

Hungarian forces against the enemy's left wing, and overthrew it. At the same time, however, the Czech left wing pushed back the Austrians, and King Rudolf fell off his horse into a creek, though his men helped him back on the horse.[77] György Simon Baksa and the Cuman troops now put to flight the Polish auxiliaries of the Czech king, whereupon Otakar II himself led an attack on Rudolf, seeking a personal encounter with him. But Otakar's horse fell, and Ulrik Kapeller savagely attacked him with fifty men; the king, bleeding from sixteen wounds, died. Kapeller stripped the body.[78] Approaching Hungarian troops expelled the Czechs from the scene of the encounter, and the battle was over. Later, the Hungarians would decorate the church at Székesfehérvár with the captured standards and shields collected from the battlefield.[79]

King Rudolf wrote a letter - a very neatly phrased letter - to express his thanks to King Ladislas IV,[80] to whom he owed the victory, then granted overlordship of Austrian Styria and of the former inheritance of the Babenbergs to his son Albert.[81]

This Hungarian victory, fought for foreign interests on foreign soil, failed to calm down the revolutionary action against Ladislas IV. After the papal curia had received news of the latest insurrection in Hungary, the Roman pontiff wanted to intervene in person between the monarch and his opponents, but decided to send a legate, Philip of Fermo, instead. The curia had frequently been informed about domestic troubles in Hungary, and it realized that party strife and domestic violence undermined royal power and devastated the realm, as well as the harvest which assured the population's food supply. Church rights became a booty for thieves and other common criminals who had gained the upper hand in many parts of the country. The pontiff had wished to pay a private visit to the country, but he was unable to do so. That is why he dispatched an envoy who would punish and restore, weed out and plant, all in the name of the Lord. Let the king become a role model for men of high ecclesiastical and secular rank; may he worship God and observe the laws of the Church, so that the will to live and prosperity return to the realm's peoples, and normalcy to the land.[82]

At first, Ladislas IV was not very happy with the envoy's mission to his country;[83] he had to be persuaded to receive and treat the papal envoy with respect.[84] Philip of Fermo also had to make a decision concerning the controversy surrounding the election of the bishop in Trau,[85] and had asked the king to take an oath promising to cooperate with him. In order to substantiate the promise, Ladislas IV was expected to summon a synod to gather in Buda on July 23, 1279.[86] The king took an oath to observe every decision the papal legate was going to make in the synod;[87] as a descendant and successor of King Saint Stephen, he would have to force the Cumans to submit to the law and order of [the Church and] the land.

Legate Fermo also took an oath before the high clergy and high nobles of the realm to preserve the Catholic faith in the country, protect the libraries of the realm, and to assure that the Cumans were converted to the faith and to a civilized way of life. They might, however, adhere to (some of) their ancient customs, and derive their income from their cattle and booty gathered in the war.[88]

A month later, when he "came of age" on the Feast of James, "anno Domini 1279 in aetate legitima constitutus," Ladislas IV convoked the diet at Tétény.[89] It was this legislative assembly that enumerated in its resolutions the three recognized estates of the realm - *praelati*, *barones*, and *nobiles*,[90] - without mentioning the lesser [service] nobility or other social strata of the realm. On the other hand, the text did speak of the Cuman nobles who had attended the diet, "cum universis praelatis ecclesiarum, barronibus (sic!) nobilium regni nostri et Cumanis omnibus congregationem generalem fecissemus celebrari."[91] This assembly was, as yet, not the diet of the estates, because it lacked the representative element of the country's interests in the lesser nobility (who were not invited to attend), and it had little similarity with the representatives of towns in the Castilian and Aragonese *cortes*, or with the English parliament, where the knights of the shire spoke for the interests of their districts.[92]

At Tétény, the king had promised to re-examine his previous and irresponsibly made grants of land or office, and retake them, if necessary.[93] He had warned the Cumans to cease behaving like nomads and pagans in the (civilized and Christian) land, dress properly and to wear their beards in a less offensive manner (although he had to make concessions concerning the wearing of beards). He told the Cumans to return all Christians they had taken prisoner in previous encounters (within the country), and ordered them to build permanent settlements on both banks of the Tisza river. The Cuman leaders, Alpár, Uzúr, and Charnial [Chamiai] were told to submit to the teaching of the Church, and to identify with the behavioral rules of Christian society.[94]

The papal legate attending the diet had further rendered an agreement that land grants given to the Cumans border on the land-holdings of the nobles and of the Church for the reason that the Cuman settlers and the inhabitants of the other estates meet one another, intermingle, and intermarry.[95] The Cumans were given some autonomy in judicial matters: their own tribal laws and tribal judges to administer the law to them. But, they understood that the king's palatine was their chief justice, and, if need be, they could appeal to the king.[96] In token of their promises, the Cumans gave hostages: "prout sunt septem obsides, quae nos ad tempus faciemus obtineri."[97]

NOTES

1. Cf. "Annales Austricae," *MGHSS*, IX, 704. He was born in 1263 - see *RA*, n. 1809; *ÁUO*, VIII, 68f.; *CD*, IV-3, 152 (excerpt).

2. Finta, son of David of the Aba clan, a former palatine of Béla IV; Aegidius (Egyed), treasurer, and reeve of Pozsony; Gregory, reeve of Vas county - all revolutionaries who secretly sympathized with Otakar II of Bohemia, Stephen V's arch-opponent - had broken into the house of Queen Elizabeth, Stephen V's widow. Domokos, son of Péter Csák, had defended the Queen during the break-in; cf. the letter of the Queen, *CD*, V-2, 231f. Grand Steward Nicholas of Transylvania, loyal to the Queen, had freed young Ladislas from his captors - on this, Ladislas himself, *ibid.*, V-2, 425, though it appears to be a forgery, *RA*, n. 2846. But a royal writ of January 23, 1274, mentioned that the king, his mother and the great lords of the realm made peace, *RA*, n. 2446; *CD*, VII-5, 391f.

3. Potthast, n. 20540; *VMH*, nn. 529 and 530.

4. *RA*, n. 2301; *CD*, V-2, 37f.; Katona, *Historia critica*, VII, 618, referring to himself as "Ladislas tercius;" *ÁUO*, IV, 341f.; Szabó, 97 and 192. The only mention in the Chronicle: "Ladizlaus filius eius et coronatus est eodem anno;" *SSH*, I, 471,10-11.

5. On Joachim, see Szabó, 7, and note; *RA*, nn. 2952 and 2947; *ÁUO*, IV, 177f. and 178ff., though Szabó, 188, had made a correction.

6. On this, the writ of the Queen, *CD*, V-2, 231f.; Szabó, 4ff., mentions a palace revolt that must (also) have endangered the position of the archbishop of Esztergom; cf., *RA*, n. 3376; Knauz, II, 204.

7. Szabó, 7, and note, based on a royal writ, *RA*, n. 2947; *ÁUO*, IV, 177ff., esp. 178.

8. In an agreement signed September 12, 1277, Otakar II of Bohemia still refused to acknowledge Ladislas IV as "a man of age;" *CD*, V-2, 65ff.; *MGHLL*, II, 419; also, *MGHSS*, IX, 709, and Palacky, II-1, 256f. On the other hand, the German monarch Rudolf talked to Ladislas IV as an equal: "Indue mente virum, fili ac socie praedilecte!" *ÁUO*, IV, 87, and signed a treaty with him, *MGHSS*, IV, 709; and, Rudolf was able to assure the support of Charles of Sicily of the treaty - Wenczel, *Dipl. eml.*, I, 41ff.

9. Henry of Németújvár joined the supporters of Ladislas IV; by December 2, 1272, he became grand steward of Uzora and Só - *RA*, nn. 2328-2332; *HO*, VIII, 148, 149; *ÁUO*, IX, 4f.

10. In May, 1273, Henry also became grand steward of Slovenia, *RA*, n. 2362; *ÁUO*, IX, 4f.

11. Cf. Szabó, 9, n.3; however, an Austrian source remarked that it was his own countrymen who had killed him - *MGHSS*, IX, 704; "...quidam comites Ungariae" had him assassinated, *ibid.*, IX, 799.

12. Hóman-Szekfű, I, 608, providing a roster of court officials under Ladislas IV, See further *Diplomata historiam domini Matthaei de genere Csák illustrantia*, eds. Béla Karácsonyi and Gyula Kristó (Szeged, 1971), nn. 1, 2, and 4, the latter in reference to *RA*, n. 2672.

13. *MGHSS*, IX, 704, 729, 744; Szabó, 18f.

14. On the role of Egyed, grand steward of Bosnia, in defending Pozsony, see *RA*, n. 2362; the king rewarded two fort *iobagiones* who were wounded during the siege - *RA*, n. 2382. In the following counter-attack, the Hungarian forces recaptured Győr.

15. *MGHSS*, IX, 704, 711, 744.

16. Andrew, son of Ivánka, had defended Gyímeskő, *RA*, n. 2660 with text, dated December 10, 1275.

17. On the Czech defeat near Laa, see *MGHSS*, IX, 705, 745: the "surprise attack" was led by Henry of Németújvár - *RA*, n. 2729; *ÁUO*, IX, 147f.

18. *MGHSS*, IX, 705, 744.

19. *Ibid.*, IX, 510, 713; Szabó, 14.

20. *RA*, n. 2662.

21. *RA*, n. 3241; *ÁUO*, XII, 386f.

22. It is known from royal writs that the siege of Detrekő ended in victory - *RA*, nn. 2455, 2488, and 2521; *ÁUO*, IX, 51ff. and 25ff., and 63ff.

23. Szabó, 18f., and note; 19, and note 3 and 4.

24. *RA*, n. 2415 with text.

25. As evidenced by his writ of October 9, 1273, where the king donated confiscated property to Master John, archpriest of Gömör, *RA*, n. 2417; on October 17, 1273, he gave the goods of a traitor to Justice Walter of Buda, *RA*, n. 2418. But the magnates had caused a bloody confrontation between the monarch, his mother and party adherents - *RA*, n. 2446.

26. Bloody party strife recorded in *CD*, V-2, 425f., but it may be a forgery, *RA*, n. 2846; Szabó, 21, n. 2; the king's adherents held the queen captive - *ÁUO*, IV, 100 and 175, and *RA*, n. 2513 with text. G. Pray, *Vita s Elisabeth viduae necnon b. Margarithae virginis* (Tyrnaviae, 1780), 33ff.; 345f. recorded that the king had become very ill, but the prayers of Margaret helped his recovery. The monarch did reward his physician for his services, *RA*, n. 2529; *ÁUO*, XII, 113.

27. Gregory X to bishops Jób of Pécs and Timót of Zagreb, ordering them to conduct an investigation - Potthast, n. 20685; *VMH*, n. 528. On March 10, the king had written to Rome about Bishop Lampert of Eger, who had taken possession of a parish in Hatvan that belonged to the Canons of Prémontré - *RA*, n. 2353; Katona, *Historia critica*, VII, 641. Compare to *RA*, n. 2355 with text, signed by Bishop Benedict of Várad and royal vice-chancellor, and Nicholas, archbishop-elect of Esztergom, or to *RA*, n. 2376 with text; however, on *RA*, n. 2378, the archiepiscopal see is listed as vacant, while on *RA*, n. 2449 with text, it was Benedict who signed as archpriest of Buda and royal vice-chancellor, with the see of Esztergom being vacant. On *RA*, n. 2457, Benedict's name appears as that of archbishop-elect of Esztergom, archpriest of Buda, and royal vice-chancellor.

28. Máté Csák, head steward [Voyvoda] of Transylvania, later Palatine (on various occasions), was the brother of Péter Csák, who became the father of the dreaded and notorious Máté Csák of Trencsén - Szabó, 25, n. 2.

29. *RA*, n. 2364; *ÁUO*, IV, 23ff.; IX, 12ff.; see also *RA*, n. 2477; *ÁUO*, IX, 71ff.

30. *RA*, n. 3068; *ÁUO*, XII, 288.

31. *RA*, n. 3309; *ÁUO*, IX, 388.

32. *RA*, n. 2558; *ÁUO*, IV, 39. Also, *RA*, nn. 2564 and 3560; for the latter, *ÁUO*, VII, 111.

33. *RA*, n. 2571, and n. 2803 with text.

34. *RA*, n. 2569; *ÁUO*, IV, 37ff. and IX, 73ff. Also, *RA*, n. 2559; *ÁUO*, XII, 88.

35. Hóman-Szekfű, I, 608, insert.

36. *Ibid.*, I, 593ff. and 608.

37. Szabó, 23f.; Fraknói, I, 80f.

38. *RA*, nn. 2351, 2354, 2355, and 2356.

39. On *RA*, n. 2444, Benedict still signed as archpriest of Buda; on *RA*, n. 2445, however, his signature is that of the archbishop-elect of Esztergom; compare to *RA*, nn. 2449 and 2457.

40. *RA*, nn. 2445, 2457-80, etc.; Potthast, nn. 21232 and 21233, *VMH*, n. 540 and *CD*, V-2, 423, respectively.

41. Potthast, nn. 20613 and 20614; *VMH*, nn. 532 and 533. Péterffy, *Concilia*, I, 91.

42. See the writ, dated April 11, 1276, of Charles of Sicily, in Wenczel, *Dipl. eml.*, I, 38.

43. Potthast, II, 1709f.; *MGHSS*, XVIII, 563,11-14 and 685,47-49.

44. Potthast, n. 21232.

45. *MGHSS*, XVIII, 568,1-3 and 285,1-23; Kühner, 76f.; Seppelt, III, 542f. The numbering is incorrect - Potthast, II, 1710, note; "einen Papst Johann XX hatte es nicht gegeben," Seppelt, III, 539.

46. *RA*, n. 2749 - the last writ signed by Archbishop Benedict; n. 2750 was signed by Nicholas, Archpriest of Transylvania and royal vice-chancellor.

47. *RA*, n. 2752, and note to n. 2751; Potthast, n. 21328; *VMH*, n. 542.

48. Cf. A. Theiner (ed.), *Monumenta spectantia historiam Slavorum meridionalium*, 6 vols. (Zagreb, 1870-82), cited hereafter as *Mon. Slavorum*, I, 96 [as of January 27, 1278]; Potthast, n. 21266.

49. Potthast, n. 21328; *VMH*, n. 542.

50. See *ÁUO*, IV, 103ff.; *VMH*, I, 326f.; the king did mention Nicholas as the archpriest-elect of Fehérvár and vice-chancellor, *RA*, n. 2917; *ÁUO*, IV, 98f., but in his writ of January 30, 1279, he had referred to the vacancy in Esztergom - *RA*, n. 2942; Zimmermann-Werner, I, 135.

51. Potthast, n. 21412; *VMH*, n. 544. Potthast, n. 21420; *VMH*, n. 548. The curia requested cooperation from the Hungarian court, Potthast, nn. 21414 and 21415, by the high clergy, Potthast, n. 21418, and the nobles, Potthast, n. 21419.

52. *MGHSS*, IV, 399; on Otakar II, cf. Palacky, II-1, 236, n. 306, based on a Vatican MS. On the presumed attitude of the Hungarian court, see Palacky, II-1, 242, supported by Szabó, 33. An Austrian source spoke of a "temporary" Hungaro-Czech treaty - cf. *MGHSS*, IX, 801, anno 1275!

53. Arnold Busson, "Der Krieg von 1278 und die Schlacht bei Dürnkrut. Eine kritische Untersuchung," *Archiv für österreichische Geschichte*, 62 (1881), 3ff., a 143 page essay, esp. 67ff. and 78ff.; Szabó, 38f.; Palacky, II-1, 249f., on the meeting between Rudolf and Otakar II; Ladislas' mother hated the Czech ruler - *CD*, V-2, 320f. and 322. See also the writ of Ladislas IV addressed to Catherine, wife of Dragutin, Prince of Serbia, *CD*, V-2, 315ff.

54. *MGHLL*, II, 407; *CD*, VII-5, 418ff.; Palacky, II-1, 250ff.; Szabó, 44. Otakar II promised Ladislas to return the treasures Anna had previously taken with her to Prague - *MGHSS*, IX, 708.

55. Palacky, II-1, 250ff. It was about this time that Ladislas IV had declared himself to be of age: "...cum Domino concedente in etatem legitimam pervenisse-mus;" *HO*, VII, 164; *RA*, n. 2824. Or, in a writ, *ibid.*, n. 2823: "ad regni gubernacula feliciter pervenimus."

56. After November 10, 1277, Péter Csák became the palatine - *RA*, n. 2823; Knauz, II, 76.

57. *RA*, n. 2747; *CD*, V-2, 347ff.; Szabó, 36f.

58. As mentioned in a royal letter of August 3, 1276, *RA*, n. 2720.

59. By the end of July, 1277, the monarch had visited the destroyed cathedral of Veszprém - *RA*, n. 2789; *CD*, IX-7, 692ff., esp. 692; Remig Békefi, *A káptalani iskolák története Magyarországon 1540-ig* [History of Cathedral Schools in Hungary Prior to 1540] (Budapest, 1910), 160ff. and 369; idem, "Az árpádkori közoktatásügy" [Public Schooling in the Árpádian Age], *Századok*, 30 (1896), 207ff., 310ff., and 413ff.

60. On the royal promise of restitution, see *RA*, n. 2750; *CD*, VII-2, 464ff.,; also, Békefi, *Káptalani iskolák*, 369.

61. *Ibid.*, VII-2, 464.
62. *RA*, n. 2747, as cited above, n. 57.
63. Cf. H. Denifle, *Die Universitäten des Mittelalters bis 1400*, vol. I: *Die Entstehung der Universitäten* (Berlin, 1885), 9f. and 45ff.
64. *CD*, V-2, 34.
65. *RA*, n. 3272; *ÁUO*, IV, 255f.
66. *RA*, n. 3109; *ÁUO*, IX, 299.
67. See *CD*, VII-4, 173ff. The "Saxons" wanted to have separate jurisdiction under the archpriest in Szeben - independent of the bishop! - *RA*, n. 2857; Teutsch-Firnhaber, I, 113; Zimmermann-Werner, I, 133, thereupon the Hungarian bishops had the "Saxons" excommunicated, cf. *CD*, VII-4, 219ff.; Teutsch-Firnhaber, I, 115; Zimmermann-Werner, I, 132. On this, also a royal writ, *RA*, n. 3151; *ÁUO*, IX, 330f. The cathedral in Gyulafehérvár remained in ruins for the next decade; only in 1287 had Bishop Peter begun rebuilding it at his own expense - Teutsch-Firnhaber, I, 139f. and 170; see further, *RA*, n. 2858 [cited before]. In order to compensate the bishop, the king gave him the salt mine at Torda and various land grants, *RA*, n. 2858.
68. On this, *MGHSS*, IX, 805,49-50; "...biga scilicet, duarum rotarum vehiculum,...currus regis Ladislai dicebatur," *SSH*, I, 474,10-14. Of course, one must raise doubts about the objectivity of the chronicler responsible for this portion of the record. See Kristó, *art. cit.*, *Memoria Hungariae*, I, 229ff.; Elemér Mályusz, *A Thuróczy Krónika és forrásai* [The Thuróczy Chronicle and its Sources] (Budapest, 1967), 57ff.
69. Prince Andrew to marry Rudolf's daughter, *CD*, V-2, 388ff., and, in connection with it, an anonymous letter from a bishop sent to Rome, *ÁUO*, IV, 89 (anno 1276). H.R. von Zeissberg, "Über das Rechtsverfahren Rudolfs von Habsburg gegen Ottokar von Böhmen," *Archiv für österreichische Geschichte*, 66 (1885), 1ff. and 69 (1887), 1ff.
70. *MGHLL*, II, 419; *CD*, V-2, 65f.
71. *Ibid.*, V-2, 454f.; *MGHSS*, IX, 709; he had gained the support of Charles of Sicily, *RA*, n. 2779; Wenczel, *Dipl. elm.*, I, 41f.; Szabó, 64ff.; *RA*, n. 2887; *CD*, V-2, 501f.: Ladislas IV sojourned in Pozsony on August 6, 1278.
72. Cf. Busson, *art. cit.*, *AföG* (1881), 84ff.; *Reimchronik*, c. 152; *MGHSS*, XVII, 534; IX, 249, 708, 730; Szabó, 47ff.; Otakar II was encouraged by his wife - *MGHSS*, IX, 709, 710: "Continuatio Cosmae Pragensis," *ibid.*, IX, 191.
73. Some 10,000 Czech troops to face some 40,000 Hungarian and 16,000 German troops - *ÁUO*, IV, 170f., the numbers are far too high, even if a non-Hungarian source spoke of some 30,000 men strong Hungaro-German force, *MGHSS*, XVII, 249.
74. Rudolf at Marchegg, on August 14 - *ibid.*, IX, 745.
75. *Ibid.*, IX, 709; IX, 731; Keza, c. 74, *SSH*, I, 186,4-15; *Reimchronik*, lines 16112-17279 [c. 141]. Busson, in *AföG* (1881), 93ff., expressed limited appreciation of Keza's "Gesta Ungarorum," *ibid.*, 98, though admitted that Hungarian help was a necessity; he spoke of "die Notwendigkeit der ungarischen Hilfe." His arguments can be supported by the chroniclers, as, for instance, in *MGHSS*, XVII, 123. The Czechs' battle cry sounded like "Prague, Prague!" - the Hungarians called "Christ, Christ!"
The picture reproduced in Szabó, 67, from the Chronicle, fol. 63´a, has the wrong caption and faulty application. It depicts the encounter between King Béla IV and Otakar II, in the year 1260: "Pugnat rex cum Othocaro." Cf. *SSH*, I, 468 (c. 178).
76. See *RA*, n. 3005; *ÁUO*, IX, 223ff.; Omodé, later palatine, had lost the pointing finger on his right hand in the engagement, *RA*, n. 3668; *ÁUO*, XII, 496ff., and V, 2ff.

77. They killed the horse from under Rudolf; *Reimchronik*, cc. 151 and 159; Palatine Máté Csák was also in danger, but was rescued by Dénes, son of Peter of the clan of Osl - *RA*, n.3005 (as above). Busson, *loc. cit.*, 88ff.; Johann Huemer, "Rhythmus über die Schlacht auf dem Marchfelde (1278)," *Archiv für österreichische Geschichte*, 67 (1886), 183ff.; the "Chronicon rhythmicum Austricum" made no mention of Ladislas IV. (For text, cf. *MGHSS*, XV.)

78. See *Reimchronik*, cc. 160-63; the chronicler mentioned possible treason on the Czech side, c. 160. It was some "ignobiles" who had captured the exhausted Czech king - "Historia annorum 1264-1279," *MGHSS*, IX, 653. Busson, *art. cit.*, *AföG* (1881), 54ff. and 141ff.; Berthold Schenck v. Emmerberg and Sigfried Märenberg were *not* the ones who had killed the wounded Otakar II - *ibid.*, 145. There were some 14,000 dead, many of whom had died while being shoved into the Morava river - Chronicle, c. 181, *SSH*, I, 471,14-17; "Cont. Vindobonesis," *MGHSS*, IX, 708, 709, 710; "Annales Salisburgenses," *ibid.*, IX, 803, 804; "Chronicon Sanpetrinum," *ibid.*, IX, 116; "Chronicon Colmar.," *ibid.*, XVII, 250, 251; further, a writ from the Hungarian king, *RA*, n. 2953; *CD*, V-2, 500f. On July 27, 1279, Rudolf had notified the Doge of Venice of his victory - achieved with Hungarian aid (!), *ÁUO*, IV, 165f.; also, *MGHSS*, IX, 745, 804.

79. Cf. Keza, c. 74, *SSH*, I, 186,28-32.

80. *Ibid.*, I, 186,19-21.

81. Szabó, 68, argued that Ladislas IV did not know how to exploit the victory, even though he had a good opportunity to do so - see *CD*, V-2, 457. After the battle, the Hungarian (and Cuman) troops of Ladislas IV became, frankly, burdensome to the German king - *MGHSS*, IX, 802. Rudolf had also supported in Rome the king's request for the canonization of Margaret, the younger sister of Ladislas IV; cf. *ÁUO*, IV, 166f.

82. Potthast, n. 21469, dated October 7, 1278; *VMH*, n. 552, and compare to the report by the bishop of Olmütz on conditions in Hungary, *MGHLL*, IV, 591ff.; *ÁUO*, IV, 10ff.; *VMH*, n. 535. The bishop's report was subjective, because he supported King Otakar II - Hefele, VI, 128; nor was he a friend of Rudolf, or of Ladislas IV - Palacky, II-1, 225f.; also, Raynaldus, xiv, anno 1273 (!).

83. *ÁUO*, IV, 191ff.; Potthast, n. 21661: Ladislas received the legate with respect; *VMH*, n. 560.

84. *CD*, IV-4, 205.

85. See the papal writ of December 9, 1279, Potthast, n. 21660; *VMH*, n. 559; or, the letter of February 28, 1278, where the legate did comply with the request of the Szeben chapter for [added] canonical positions (*stallums*) in the chapter - Knauz, II, 92. The legate was also able to persuade the counts of Németújvár to submit to him, cf. *ÁUO*, IX, 185f.; *HO*, I, 73, and compare to *RA*, n. 2945 and Balics, II-1, 420, although at the expense of the bishop of Veszprém, who had suffered damages, *ÁUO*, IV, 53; the king, however, compensated him, *CD*, V-2, 265f.

86. *RA*, n. 2962.

87. The resolutions were recorded in Marczali, *Enchiridion*, 175ff.; *RHM*, 554ff.; see further, comments by Pray, *Annales*, I, 342ff., and P. Horváth, *Commentatio de initiis ac maioribus Jazygum et Cumanorum eorumque constitutionibus* (Pest, 1801), 66ff.; I. Gyárfás, *A jázkúnok története* [History of the Jaz(y)go Cumans], 2 vols. (Kecskemét, 1870-73), II, 432ff.; Pray, *Dissertationes*, I, 115ff.

88. See Keza's remark: "ex fructu animalium et preda sola habebant vitam suam, ut Cumani," *SSH*, I, 192,28-29, and, almost in connection with it, the firmly worded writ by Pope Nicholas III, dated December 9, 1279, Potthast, n. 21663* in eundem modem; *VMH*, n. 557; *CD*, V-2, 572ff.

89. The writ by Palatine Máté, dated July 25, 1279, *ÁUO*, IX, 250, and IV, 213f. For the record of the Tétény assembly, see *RHM*, 559ff.; Marczali, *Enchiridion*,

178ff., though, according to *RA*, n. 3000, the version we have access today has to be an interpolated document! See also *VMH*, n. 556.

90. The king, who "came of age," had summoned the meeting - *RA*, n. 2999; *ÁUO*, IV, 176f.

91. Cf. *RA*, n. 2999, and n. 2997, where the king had confirmed Demeter, reeve of Sáros, in his possessions "coram omnibus baronibus regni nostri, qui ad congregationem nostram convenerant;" *ÁUO*, IV, 181f. Further, *RA*, n. 2998, where the king let Benedict, archdeacon of Fehérvár, and his brother retain their possession of Csősz (Chuuz); and, *RA*, n. 2784. The letter from Palatine Csák, dated July 25, 1279, from "circa Thetin" (Tétény), *ÁUO*, IV, 250; Nicholas, Grand Steward of Slovenia, signed a writ issued by the king "in Tetun, in generali congregatione tocius regni Hungarie;" *CD*, VII-5, 593f. The writ concerning a sentence handed down by Palatine Csák in the case of Simon Fuki and his brothers was issued after the diet - "fatum super Veterm Budam sexto die termini prenotati;" *ÁUO*, IV, 203.

92. See G.O. Sayles, *The Medieval Foundations of England*, rev. repr. (London, 1966), 448ff.; idem, *The King's Parliament of England* (New York, 1974), 35ff.; on the Spanish *cortes*, see remarks by Mitteis, 379ff. and 414f.

93. As, e.g., *RA*, n. 2998.

94. *RHM*, 559ff.; Marczali, *Enchiridion*, 178ff., though the text may be "dubiae fidei!" - *RA*, n. 3000; Szabó, 82ff.; Katona, *Historia critica*, VII, 796ff.

95. Diet of Tétény, art. 5 (in Marczali, a. 7).

96. *Ibid.*, aa. 6 and 12.

97. *Ibid.*, prefatory note; the Tétény resolutions received papal approval, Potthast, n. 21663; *VMH*, n. 558; Z.J. Kosztolnyik, "Rome and the Church in Hungary in 1279: The Synod of Buda," *Annuarium historiae conciliorum*, 22 (1990), 68ff., esp. 75f.; Szabó, 85f., remarked that the king was in no condition to enforce his will, or to support the resolutions of the synod - a conclusion drawn from the writ of Pope Nicholas IV, Potthast, n. 22764; *VMH*, n. 577 - a "re-draft" of a letter by Honorius IV, Potthast, n. 22585; *VMH*, n. 573; see also *MGHSS*, XVII, 207,35-36.

2. The Synod of Buda, 1279

In the month of September, 1279, the papal legate had a church synod held in the Castle of Buda.[1] The one hundred and twenty-nine resolutions of this ecclesiastical assembly were, surprisingly, not preserved for posterity in their entirety in Hungary, but only in the synodical collection(s) of the Polish church province of Gnesen, where many of the articles relate to the Church and conditions in Hungary.[2]

According to the resolutions of the Synod of Buda, the Church (parishes, monasteries) must have tax-exempt status; a secular person may only make a gift or a grant of land to the Church with the approval of higher church authority - in order to prevent the donor from the realization of any false of selfish motives.[3] The cleric who held a church prebend (benefice) must not have another cleric substitute for him; he must stay in place and perform his religious functions.[4] Jewish renters must obtain no land grants, land lease, or any other income from the Church.[5]

The archpriest may receive no money for the burial of someone accidentally killed, but who died remorsefully - as if to point to the personal responsibility of the prelate, in this instance, the archpriest, in both his spiritual and temporal capacity, for investigating any murder, that had been committed in his area of jurisdiction.[6] Anyone who would dare to take illegal possession of a church, or of a monastic building (or, of a monastery), and turn it into a den of thieves, or stable for horses, would be excommunicated and properly persecuted in accordance with secular laws.[7] Anyone who would dare to turn to a secular court of law in matters pertinent to the Church (thus, to canon law) would be excommunicated.[8]

Were the King, or the Queen, to hinder any judicial proceedings in church courts of law, they would be denied entry of a church and barred from attending church services. Anyone who assaulted a clergyman, or willfully maintained contact with an excommunicated person; or a cleric, who had an excommunicated individual admitted to church service, administering the sacraments to him, would be excommunicated and suffer full loss of official and personal prestige (in the community).[9] Any individual, who spoke disparagingly of honest work, of agricultural activity, or work in the vineyard; anyone who falsified a papal writ or decree; anyone who dared to use or rely upon the sacraments for false prophecy or magic; anyone who practiced abortion, had taken false oaths, had borne false witness in marriage cases before a church court of law; anyone who had caused a fire or had broken into a church; anyone who had committed willful murder, or practiced simony; anyone who had taken clerical orders under false pretenses - all would suffer the punishment of excommunication.[10]

Jews must wear a piece of red cloth and Moslems a piece of yellow cloth on their outer garment(s) in order to be distinguished from "ordinary" people.[11] The papal legate also took a further position concerning non-Christians: Greek schismatic priests may build a church or a chapel or perform religious services, but only with the consent of the regional Roman ordinary.[12] Jews and Moslems could not be appointed as public tax- or toll-collectors in the realm.[13]

High clergymen must also wear tonsure as a reminder that they were ranked higher than ordinary monks. When riding on horseback, the bishop must wear a surplice (laced white shirt: *camisia*) under the *cappa* (cloak), over which he was to wear a hood for protection from the rain.[14] A bishop, or any clergyman, must not wear clothing with colorful lining; only bishops can wear silk and expensive ornaments, woven gloves; secular clerics may wear them only if permitted by a higher authority.[15] In transit, a clergyman may take meals in an inn, but he may not engage in any kind of business there, nor take part in any entertainment there; he may play no game of dice! A clergyman must be a role model for anyone leading a decent, moral life.[16]

A married cleric could not be named vice-chaplain to a church or parish; the priest must not marry. Had he been married before ordination to the priesthood, he may not keep his children born in that marriage living with him. Nor may he have a woman live in his house.[17] An ordained clergyman would not take part in handing down a death sentence (in a trial by a court of law), nor will he perform medical surgery. Nor will he give blessing at ordeals.[18]

A priest will not wear or carry a sword or halberd (battle ax), except in self-defense, and then only with the approval of his ecclesiastical superior.[19] The cleric who received a church prebend will preserve it intact.[20] If a cleric wanted to become an archpriest, he must study canon law at a university for three years.[21]

Every parish priest must possess a book of liturgy, a breviary, and a catechism; he will wear shoes when attending common prayers in choir.[22] The papal legate gave further instructions on how the parish clergy ought to teach the faithful in their parishes the elements of faiths and how to administer the sacraments to them.[23]

A monk who became a bishop would keep wearing the habit of his order. He must keep law, order, and silence in the monastery - in this case, the bishop's household - as well as in the refectory and sleeping quarters (dormitory).[24] A (regular, ordinary) monk may not leave the premises of the monastery without the superior's permission; he may not become a student or attend lectures at a university without the superior's permission; he will not study Roman law.[25] A monk will not receive church prebend(s). He may only help out in a parish.[26]

A secular person (be he a noble or a merchant) must not take, confiscate, or appropriate church income or property.[27] The legate had to enact a series of decrees to support this resolution; in fact, he had to obligate the monarch, the barons, and all the faithful to defend the Church, its property and buildings, in the realm, and to ascertain that the Church retained its tax-exempt status.[28]

A layman will take a bow before the altar, the crucifix, and the statue or icon depicting the Mother of God. A layman may baptize an infant, but only a priest can give the infant a name. The infant may not have more than three godparents[29] Marriage may take place without a priest, but it must be announced a month earlier in the church, on a Holy Day, and the exchange of marriage vows must be held publicly. Mistresses and/or courtesans will not be tolerated publicly - or privately.[30] People will not dance in a cemetery, nor will people carry their trash to a cemetery and dump it there.[31] The (parish) priest does not live in the church, nor does he keep his private belongings there - except in time of war, or if his place of residence had suffered fire damage.[32]

In order to summarize what has been said before, one may observe that six of the resolutions dealt with specific abuse(s) in the Church in the country - as, for example, articles that forbade laymen to make ecclesiastical appointments.[33] There is an article that determined the amount of the burial fee to be charged for a person who had killed himself, or who had been killed.[34] Further resolutions dealt with established church abuses in the country, or with the destruction of church goods by theft or through confiscation. A person who had purposefully damaged church property, or occupied a church for personal use, would be excommunicated.[35]

Interestingly, article 67 repeats this ordinance, as if to signify that the clerics in Hungary were not taking threats of church punishments seriously - or that the punishments could not be enforced.[36] Furthermore, one article threw light on a common Hungaro-Polish problem: the archpriest's position to be held by someone who had studied canon law (at a university) for three years.[37] (The resolution does not state whether the "studiosus" had to take and successfully pass his examination.)

There are other articles that dealt with clerical problems and repeated what had already been stated, as, for instance, by the First Synod of Esztergom in the early twelfth century.[38] Examples include the prohibition on the Hungarian cleric (from the text it is not clear whether he was an ordained priest or a student in minor orders) against frequenting taverns;[39] and the article that forbade clergymen to attend an ordeal - clerical presence still permitted by the First Synod of Esztergom but forbidden by the Fourth Lateran Synod in 1215.[40] Article 13 forbade a cleric to carry a weapon, be it a sword or a knife (bord).[41]

Various entries cited resolutions that had been enacted into law by previous synods,[42] and by the Constitutions of Pope Innocent IV.[43] One may also note here that the numbering of articles by Hube is different from the numbering provided by Endlicher. Further, the 1209 Synod of Avignon, the 1231 Synod of Rouen, and some of the resolutions of the 1267 church gathering held in Vienna did have an impact upon the resolutions of the 1279 Synod of Buda.[44] To cite but one example, various enactments of Buda treated the celibacy issue in Hungary in accordance with the articles agreed upon in Vienna, 1267. A priest must not tolerate a woman to live in his house; did he beget a child after his ordination to the priesthood, he had to give up the child, as he could not raise him.[45]

The vicar, who was the archpriest's right-hand man, had to be unmarried.[46] On the other hand, a lay person had to be married to the woman he lived with.[47] Valid marriages enjoyed the blessing of the Church[48] - an article from which one may conclude that a married man could not be ordained to the priesthood.[49]

Five additional articles dealt with the organization of the legislative proceedings of the synod.[50] For example, article 129 stated that, in order to avoid further abuse, the resolutions of the synod had to be made public within two months after its cessation, had to be written down in large letters on tables that were to be bound together into a book that was to be kept chained in a church, so that anyone could have free access to them.[51] (One may ask the question, though, how many people could read, or had the educational background to comprehend what they were reading?) Various decrees dealt with church doctrine, of course, or with church discipline, order of the Mass in the divine liturgy, the administration of sacraments, and the list of approved holidays of obligation.[52]

Every cathedral chapter in the realm was obligated to have the synodical resolution copied down within two months of the conclusion of the synod, have them bound into a book that was to be kept in the sacristy of the cathedral.[53] The articles had to be read and explained in front of the members of the chapter, or before a monastic chapter, four times a year; they had to be read and commented on at the annual diocesan synods.[54]

The legate had prepared in advance details to be discussed at the synod of Buda, though, it seems, the proposed articles were not debated in their entirety during the assembly, because the resolutions published in the Hungarian source - that is, the manuscript that carries the resolutions - abruptly ended with article 69.[55] It must have been only at the synod he held in Gnesen that the Cardinal Legate had the whole agenda debated at length, with the discussions resulting in 129 resolutions, and he must have regarded the synodical articles debated and approved as binding upon clerics and their faithful in territories under his spiritual jurisdiction as the pope's delegate.[56]

Ladislas IV, who had not enforced the earlier agreement he had made in the "Laws for the Cumans" - thereby breaching his oath, as the legate, under pressure from the Hungarian barons, had to warn him[57] - felt threatened by the resolutions that had been reached at the synod, the more so because the legate had the king excommunicated and had named, without any regard for royal privileges, ecclesiastics to vacant church prebends in the realm.[58] The king in his anger called upon the citizens of Buda to exclude the participants of the synod from attending the assembly by refusing them food and drink.[59] The legate had no alternative but to suspend the meetings of the synod, but insisted that its resolutions (that had been reached thus far) be made public.[60]

The king's erratic behavior, and the papal envoy's resolution to suspend the meetings may explain the fewer number of articles, 69 out of 129, attributed to the 1279 Buda synod. It may also provide the reason why the legate had the (a) synod soon thereafter (re)assembled in Gnesen on Polish soil, and (b) had his proposed synodical agenda discussed there in its entirety.

In September, 1279, the legate moved his residence to the border town in Pozsony in order to be more secure from the ever more threatening attitude of the king.[61] One may note, however, that the Queen did not approve of her husband's behavior and angry outbursts against the papal envoy, nor did she support his church policy.[62]

In the town of Pozsony, on the border of the realm, the legate decided to use his ultimate spiritual weapon: he had the monarch excommunicated together with his evil advisors, and placed the population of the country under the interdict; he had hoped that the people would grow impatient with the king and cause him to enter a path of inner renewal.[63]

The writ of Pope Nicholas III, where he praised the steadfast spiritual strength of the Hungarian queen; or the report by the Austrian chronicler that the king, now depressed and without friends, had, out of a sense of sheer frustration, rejoined the ranks of his Cumans, only bear witness to the desperate situation of King Ladislas IV. The queen withdrew her support from him; the Roman pontiff in a separate writ, again, praised the attitude of the queen, and expressed confidence in and support for the actions of his envoy - the curia stood behind him. Nicholas III sent letters to the nobles, the German Rudolf, and to Charles of Sicily requesting that they all try to persuade Ladislas IV to change his mind and his attitude toward Philip of Fermo.[64]

The letters from the curia were not written in vain. Ladislas IV decided not to follow the advice of his Cuman mistress - to have the legate killed. Instead, he met with the legate to confess to him that he done wrong, and suffered rightly the punishment of the Church. Once more, he took an oath upon the Gospels that he mend his ways, and, "in a Hungarian manner," shook hands with the envoy to assure him that he would honor his earlier promises.[65]

At this point, one may also pay attention to an observation made by Károly Szabó that there is no available evidence that the king at this stage of events had led an immoral life, or that he had been unfaithful to his queen before his personal clash with the papal legate. Queen Izabella had been living at the Hungarian court since 1270. She and Ladislas were married in 1277, and even the papal writ, dated December 9, 1279, where the curia relied upon language couched in the strongest of terms with the monarch, made no mention of any moral misbehavior on his part.

It is known how strongly the curia had looked upon royal marriages, and the pontiff would certainly have mentioned moral lapses on the part of Ladislas had there been any. Therefore, Szabó's conclusion that one cannot really speak of the marital infidelity of Ladislas IV before the events of late 1279, may stand as correct.[66] Taken from a purely personal point of view, one may understand, however, why the king had visited the trans-Tisza region - "Cuman country" - after his famous handshake with the papal legate; he might have visited there to seek a safe haven from his personal (baronial, oligarchic) domestic enemies. He might have done this on purely psychological grounds, seeking solace among friends after being personally humiliated by the papal envoy, and abandoned, probably for the first time, by his queen.[67]

The legate, after all, had completely ignored the monarch in summoning, without royal consent, a "national" synod in Buda, at the seat of the royal government, and he did this in spite of the concessions Ladislas IV had already made to the papal curia. The young king, who only two years earlier had come of age, and whose father, King Stephen V had, for a brief reign of two and a half years, full control of the realms' domestic and diplomatic activities, including appointments to ecclesiastic prebends, felt justly outraged by the curia's policy to undermine everything he did, to ruin his personal prestige before his people. Didn't the legate know anything about human psychology?[68]

In a strongly worded writ, Rome bitterly complained about the plague having caused drastic damages in Hungary, where secular potentates could confiscate church property under false pretenses; where the Church had to assume certain temporal obligations; where royal legislation concerning churchmen had accused them of crimes against public order under false pretenses; where faithless Greek schismatics were being permitted by the royal court to exercise their religion freely; and where Jews and Moslems were allowed to function as official tax- and toll-collectors of the government - as if attempting to establish a legal base for the papal curia to formally take charge of the realm's domestic affairs.[69]

Or, did the papal court unwillingly admit defeat in handling the situation, because Rome had created a situation Ladislas IV could not possibly accept? Even Louis IX of France, a saintly monarch, would not tolerate papal intervention in the *ecclesiastical affairs* of his kingdom![70] That is why deposed archbishop Nicholas (of Esztergom) and Archpriest Gregory of Esztergom, both loyal to Ladislas IV, had advised him to issue a proclamation deploring the unfair and tyrannical attitude of the papal legate, and to make an appeal to Rome.[71]

It might have been sheer coincidence, or the irony of fate, that shortly after the issue of this royal writ, Nicholas fell ill and died, and archpriest Gregory was found murdered in his bed. The legate gave permission - he had placed the country under the interdict - to bury the deposed archbishop in consecrated ground; but for some reason the news also spread that the legate had further granted an indulgence to anyone who threw stones upon Nicholas' coffin at the burial site, and a heap of stones arose over the casket of the archbishop.[72] Could it have been an enemy of the king with close ties to the royal court who had spread this rumor on purpose - to widen the rift between the king and the papal legate? Because Ladislas IV reacted swiftly, in anger: he looked upon the incident as desecration of his friend's burial, and breaching all diplomatic custom, had the legate arrested and placed under guard by the Cuman detachment of his bodyguard.[73]

One may fear, though, that the king had acted thoughtlessly. The person of the legate was untouchable; by ignoring his diplomatic status, Ladislas IV had to fear a reaction. The Hungarian nobles, some not necessarily his friends and some his outright opponents, led by Palatine Finta, son of David of the Aba clan, captured the king and placed him under house arrest; they had also notified Rome on their personal disposition in this case.[74] The legate advised the curia to dethrone Ladislas IV, but Charles of Sicily intervened on his behalf and the pontiff decided against it.[75]

One ought to note that, although foreign sources placed these events in the year of 1281, following the Hungarian royal register entries, the year of 1280 would be the correct date. No royal writ was entered in the register between June 27 and August 1, 1280.[76] Nor could it have been a coincidence that, when Rudolf of Germany and Charles of Sicily had signed an agreement on May 10, 1280, they promised to aid the Hungarian monarch.[77]

Common sense had finally prevailed. Master Paschasius, archpriest of Pozsony, had convinced the king to seek reconciliation with the legate, and Ladislas IV had persuaded the Cuman detachment of his bodyguard to free the legate; at the same time, the king also regained his freedom. On August 9, 1280, he issued a writ in Esztergom, and on August 18, two more letters.[78] In one of those writs he personally thanked Archpriest Paschasius for his services. In the other, he extended his apology to the legate for having persuaded the "cives" of Buda to interrupt the meetings of the synod at Buda in the previous September.

Ladislas IV had confessed his guilt, and expressed willingness to make amendments; it was on account of his youth and the ill advice he received that he had acted in such a deplorable manner. He begged for forgiveness and, as penance, he offered one hundred silver marks for the construction of a hospital, whose location the legate would designate. He promised that by following in the footsteps of his saintly predecessors, he would take military action against heretics in Bosnia, and in other neighboring territories, to assure that the teaching and law of the Church would prevail there.[79]

NOTES

1. *RA*, n. 3066; Katona, *Historia critica*, VII, 835; Hóman, *Ungarisches Mittelalter*, II, 208ff.; Szabó, 86ff.; Waldmüller, 188ff.; Kosztolnyik, in *AHC* (1990), esp.. 76ff.

2. See Romualdus Hube (ed.), *Antiquissimae constitutiones synodales provinciae Gneznensis* (Petropolis, 1865), 72-130; Hefele, V, 190ff. Péterffy, I, 92f.; *RHM*, 565ff.; Mansi, *Concilia*, XXIV, 269ff., carry incomplete and modified versions, only 69 articles. Sámuel Kohn, "AZ 1279-es budai zsint összes végzései" [A List of All the Resolutions of the 1279 Synod of Buda], *Történelmi Tár* (Budapest, 1881), 543ff.

3. Synod of Buda, 1279, art. 29-30, 36, 37, and 49-50; compare with the ecclesiastical Council of Vienna, 1267, a. 10, Mansi, XXIII, 1167ff.; and Buda, a. 59, to be compared to the 1209 Synod of Avignon, a. 17, Mansi, XXII, 783ff.

4. Buda, aa. 16 and 23.

5. Buda (Gnesen), art. 125 (in Hube and Kohn, 548; as a matter of fact, aa. 125-127); compare to Avignon, a. 2.

6. Buda (Gnesen), aa. 76, 80, 81; compare to the Council of Rouen, 1231, a. 21, Mansi, XXIII, 213ff.

7. Buda, a. 52, following Vienna, 1267, a. 11.

8. Buda, aa., 24-25, following Rouen, 1231, a. 26; and, Buda, a. 59, following Avignon.

9. Buda, aa. 15, 29-30, 37, and 77 (Hube), and aa. 24-25.

10. Buda, aa. 17, 25, 30, 32, 39, 47, 54, etc.

11. Buda (Gnesen), aa. 125-127; compare to Avignon, 1209, a. 2.

12. Buda (Gnesen), aa. 4 and 126, closely following I Esztergom, c. 61; text in *RHM*, 349ff.; Kosztolnyik, *From Coloman*, 58ff.

13. Buda (Gnesen), a. 127.

14. Buda, a. 1.

15. Buda, aa. 2, 3; Avignon, 1209, a. 18; Hefele, V, 843ff.

16. Buda, aa. 5, 8; I Esztergom, c. 61. Buda, a. 46, compare to Avignon, a. 17.

17. Buda, aa. 8, 12, 14, 32, and compare to the Synod of Szabolcs, 1092, c. 3, and I Esztergom, c. 31 [in part] and II Esztergom, cc. 9-10; Kosztolnyik, *From Coloman*, 7ff. and 64f.; Rouen, 1231, a. 35.

18. Buda, aa. 8-9; IVth Lateran Synod, 1215, c. 18, Mansi, XXII, 1006-07; summarized by Potthast, I, 437f.; Funk-Bihlmeyer, II, 181 and 186. A. Garcia y Garcia, *Constitutiones Concilii quarti Lateranensis una cum commentariis gloassatorum* (Vatican, 1981); Helene Tillmann, *Papst Innocenz III* (Bonn, 1954), 186ff.; S.R. Packard, *Europe and the Church Under Innocent III* (repr. New York, 1986), 91ff.

19. Buda, aa. 6, 7, and 11; Rouen, 1231, a. 20; also, Council of Meaux (Paris), anno 846 (845), c. 50, in Mansi, XIV, 830; Hefele, IV, 115. Indirectly, cf. S.N. Troianos, "Die Wirkungsgeschichte des Trullaneum (Quinisextum) in der byzantinischen Gesetzgebung," *Annuarium historiae conciliorum*, 24 (1992), 95ff.

20. Buda, aa. 36, 37, 49-50; Vienna, 1267, c. 10, *AUO*, IV, 118. Buda, a. 58; G. Bónis, "Die Entwicklung der geistlichen Gerichtsbarkeit in Ungarn vor 1526," *Zeitschrift der Savigny Stiftung für Rechtsgeschichte*, kan. Abt., 49 (1963), 174ff., esp. 195.

21. Buda, a. 38.

22. Buda, aa. 14, 28, 42-44, 83 (Gnesen).

23. Buda, aa. 14 and 28; also, a. 73.

24. Buda, a. 5.

25. Buda, aa. 64 and 66: "ad scholas ire, vel aliud quam grammaticam, theologiam, aut logicam in scholiis audire praesumant."

26. Buda, a. 66.

27. Buda, aa. 24, 49, 53-53; Vienna, 1267, c. 10; also, "Concilium apud Pontem Audomari," anno 1279, c. 10, in Mansi, XXIII, 223c; or, Rouen, 1231, cc. 14-15; Avignon, 1209, c. 17.

28. Buda, aa. 15, 29-30.

29. Buda, a. 13.

30. Buda, aa. 12, 14, 32; Rouen, 1231, c. 35; I Esztergom, c. 31; Szabolcs, 1092, a. 3 - and more firmly enforced by II Esztergom, cc. 9-10. See further, Rouen, 1231, c. 25.

31. Buda, aa. 44, 46; Audemer, 1279, c. 10; Rouen, 1231, c. 14-15; Avignon, 1209, c. 17.

32. Buda, a. 41.

33. Buda, a. 24, and compare to a. 50.

34. Buda, a. 46.

35. Buda, aa. 50, 51, 57.

36. Buda, a. 67 (Gnesen).

37. Buda, a. 38.

38. Buda, aa. 4 and 6; compare to I Esztergom, cc. 48-52 and 61 (cf. *RHM*, 349ff).

39. Buda, a. 4; "quod nulla persona ecclesiastica,...clerici et tabernas prorsus euitent." Compare to IV Lateran, c. 16.

40. Buda, a. 8; I Esztergom, c. 45; IV Lateran, c. 18.

41. Buda, a. 11: "gladium uel cultum, quod uulgaliter dicitur boret, portent;" *RHM*, 570. See further, Ch. du Cange, *Glossarium ad scriptores medie et infime Latinitatis*, ed. L. Favre, 10 vols. (Niort, 1883-88), I, 704.

42. As, e.g., aa. 21 and 23; compare to Lyon (Lugdunense), 1274, cc. 13-14 (Mansi, XXIV, 90f); and a. 40 (a. 43 in Hube!), aa. 97 and 123 (*Történelmi Tár*); IV Lateran, 1215, cc. 19, 22, 66 (Mansi, XXII, 1007, 1010f., 1054); Kosztolnyik, *AHC*, 22 (1990), 79f.

43. Cf. *Corpus Iuris Canonici*, ed. Ae. Friedberg, 2 vols. (Leipzig, 1879-81; repr. Graz, 1959), II, 1007, tit. xiv: De sententia et re iudicata.

44. Adriányi, *art. cit.*, *AHC*, 8 (1976), 246; Kosztolnyik, *ibid.*, 22 (1990), notes 90-99.

45. Buda, aa. 12 and 117 (*Történelmi Tár*); compare to Vienna, 1267, c. 10. Further, Buda, aa. 14, 19, 32, and 53.

46. Buda, aa. 10.

37. Buda, aa. 47, 48, 118 (Hube).

48. Buda, aa. 119, 120, 122-23 (in Hube, and in *Történelmi Tár*!).

49. Buda, a. 121.

50. Buda, aa. 18-22, 82, 129.

51. Buda, aa. 129 (in Hube, 163f.; *Történelmi Tár*, 549); Vienna, 1267, c. 19 (Mansi, XXIII, 1175f.); C.H. Hubertus, "The Codex," *Proceedings of the British Academy*, 40 (1954), 169ff.; Waldmüller, 195f.

52. Buda, aa. 21, 42-44, 83; also, aa. 32 and 126.

53. Kosztolnyik, *art. cit.*, *AHC*, 22 (1990), 79, n. 83.

54. Buda, a. 129.

55. *RHM*, 568ff., art. 69 (a. 67 in Hube).

56. Hube, 72f.; *RHM*, 565f.; Mansi, XXIV, 272. On the Gnesen synod, see the Polish annals, as, e.g., "Annales Grissowienses," *MGHSS*, XIX, 541,21; "Annales Cisterciensium in Heinrichow," anno 1281 (!), *ibid.*, XIX, 545,20-22; also, *ibid.*, XIX, 605,23-24, and note 49. The legate sojourned there until the end of August, 1282 - see *ibid.*, XIX, 646,3; or, in A. Bielowski (ed.), *Monumenta Poloniae historica*, 6 vols. (Lvov-Cracow, 1864-93; repr. Warsaw, 1960-61), cited hereafter as *MPH*, II, 847.

57. Potthast, n. 21663; "Annales Salisburgenses," *MGHSS*, IX, 805f.; Odoricus Raynaldus, *Annales ecclesiastici*, vol. XIV (Rome, 1648), anno. 1279.

58. Eubel, I, 464; Knauz, I, 102; *VMH*, n. 553; Potthast, nn. 21412-16, and 21610-11, that is, the curia approved, as it may be evident from the writ of Martin IV, August 28, 1282 - *ÁUO*, IV, 242; see further the papal writ of September 30, 1282, Potthast, n. 21933; *VMH*, n. 570.

59. Cf. *RA*, n. 3066; *CD*, V-3, 28f. Raynaldus, *Annales*, III, 509; Pray, *Annales rerum Hungaricarum*, 349.

60. *RHM*, 565f.

61. Potthast, n. 21660; *VMH*, n. 559, provide information on this. The legate remained bitter: "sed nichil in rege proficiens repatriavit," recorded in the Chronicle, *SSH*, I, 473,9-16. Also, *MGHSS*, IX, 805,24-29, and evidenced by a papal writ, Potthast, n. 21661; *VMH*, n. 560. Note the contrast between his departure from, and the previously recorded arrival in Hungary; he arrived in a Cardinal's dress on a white horse, accompanied by a Hungarian knight in green dress riding a brown horse - Dercsényi, *Chronicon pictum*, I, fol. 65a, "H" initial. The record by Keza, cc. 74-75, on Ladislas' victory over his enemies may be applicable here - *SSH*, I, 185ff.

62. As pointed out by Nicholas III, Potthast, n. 21663; *VMH*, n. 557; *ÁUO*, IV, 201. Queen Izabella had been living in Hungary since 1270 - Wenczel, *Dipl. eml.*, I, 27, 29; Szabó, 90.

63. Once again, from a papal writ, Potthast, n. 21660.

64. The curia tried, through Rudolf of Germany and Charles of Sicily, to persuade Ladislas IV to comply with the legate's demands, cf. Potthast, n. 21663; *ÁUO*, IV 191ff. and 198ff.

65. Over "ligno crucis altari, primo et iterum regia fide data Ungarico more iurasti...;" *VMH*, n. 564; Katona, *Historia pragmatica*, I, 883.

66. Cf. Szabó, 103f., and note 5; Potthast, n. 21662; *VMH*, n. 561.

67. *MGHSS*, IX, 805f.; *RA*, n. 3014, at Somlyó, east of the Tisza river, *ÁUO*, IX, 264.

68. The report from the convent appears in the royal writ, dated April 11, 1280, *RA*, n. 3048; *CD*, V-33, 85; Szabó, 91, n. 3.

69. Potthast, n. 21663.

70. On Saint Louis IX of France, see E.M. Hallam, *Capetian France*, 3rd ed. (London-New York, 1986), 204ff.; Jean, Sire of Joinville, *Vie de Saint Louis*, trans. M.R.B. Shaw, in Penguin edition of *The Chronicles of the Crusades* (New York, 1963), 161ff., esp. 167ff.; Ch. Petit-Dutaillis, *Feudal Monarchy in France and England*, trans. E.D. Hunt (London, 1936; repr. New York, 1964), 259ff.; Hampe, *Hochmittelalter*, 407.

71. Potthast, n. 21663; *VMH*, nn. 557 and 564.

72. One, written by Gregory is known - Knauz, II, 115; on Nicholas, see *ibid.*, II, 97; on the background, see the "Annales Salisburgenses," *MGHSS*, IX, 806,2-14, and the negative views expressed by Katona, *Historia critica*, VII, 776ff.; Szabó, 92 f. Also, *MGHSS*, XVII, 207,35-36; *Reimchronik*, lines 24732-24764.

73. *MGHSS*, IX, 806,35-38.

74. *Ibid.*, XIX, 616,2-7.

75. On the intervention of Charles of Sicily, see "Chronicon Austrie Germanicum," in Pez, I, 1098.

76. Szabó, 96f., noted that no royal writs had been issued between June 27 and August 1, 1280; still, a writ dated May 30, 1280, *RA*, n. 3054 with text; a letter, of July 16, 1280, *RA*, n. 3055; and a writ dated July 19, 1280, were entered in the Register, although the writ may be a forgery, as it was re-written twice and (re-)dated August 1, 1280 - cf. *RA*, n. 3057; *ÁUO*, IX 274f.

77. *CD*, VII-5, 449f.

78. *RA*, n. 3057; *HO*, VI, 257.

79. *RA*, nn. 3065 and 3066; *ÁUO*, IV, 214f.; *CD*, V-3, 28f.; Katona, VII, 835f.

3. *The Assassination of Ladislas IV*

When they heard of the reconciliation between the king and the papal legate, the Cumans staged a revolt against Ladislas IV, giving the king no alternative but to take military action against them.[1] He could do this with ease because the Cumans suddenly invaded the fortified monastery of Hoy-Szentlőrinc. Although the invasion had failed because of the resistance by Nicholas, son of Péter, and Nicholas, son of Imre, reeves of royal horse grooms and royal table-servers ("baccinifer comes"), the latter had lost thirty-seven men in the engagement, thus providing Ladislas IV with a convenient cause for a military showdown with the Cumans.[2]

In the battle near Lake Hód, the king led his troops in person against the Cuman forces; the latter had put up a hard fight, but Ladislas IV had the upper-hand in the situation.[3] After it was over, Queen Izabella made a donation to commemorate the victory. The wording of her deed, "in conflictu, quemidem dominus noster Rex habuit contra perfidiam Cumanorum," may further prove that the queen did have a loving marital relationship with her royal husband.[4]

The report by the chronicler provided some interesting data on this engagement. In 1282, Oldamér (Oldamir) and his Cuman forces invaded the country near Lake Hód because he wanted to gain control of the country's government, "volens hostiliter regnum invadere Hungarorum, ut suo dominio subiugaret," the chronicler said.[5] King Ladislas IV had entered the battle like King Joshua, "ut fortis Iosue," of the Old Testament,[6] and in the heat of the battle a sudden rainstorm occurred that, by the grace of God, aided the king to gain victory: "victoriam obtinuit divino fretus auxilio."[7]

The chronicler spoke of the leader of Cuman territories ("*dux Cumanie*") who had gathered armed Cuman forces, "congregato exercitu Cumanorum," for the purpose of breaking into the Hungarian realm. The chronicler maintained that, as far as one could tell, Oldamér, "dux Cumanie," had penetrated Hungary "from abroad," because he wanted to aid the Cumans inside the country in their planned insurrection against the monarch. However, by the grace of God, "ex divina clementia," he lost his gamble.[8]

The circumstantial evidence that "foreign" outside interference played a role in the battle at Lake Hód may explain the vehement nature of the military encounter with the Cumans, where the monarch - rather, the Hungarian cause represented by him - had to win, "divino fretus auxilio," the encounter at Hód. The chronicler's report throws some light on the question why the fleeing Cumans had sought and found refuge with the Mongols - located outside of, and close to, Hungarian territories - to provide a cause for another Tartar invasion of Hungary.

The Cumans, especially their leader "from abroad," must have assumed that Ladislas IV would encounter serious domestic opposition under any circumstances, and the realm, where a previous Hungaro-Cuman military confrontation had caused heavy losses in life and property, would be easy prey for a renewed Mongol attack. The specific remark made in the record that the Mongols had again invaded Hungary because of the encouragement of the Cumans, "quorum instinctu," meant that the Cumans of Oldamér had not accomplished their particular task in their attempt to humiliate the hated Hungarians, and it was the Mongols' turn to invade and totally annihilate that country.[9]

The Hungarian chronicler emphasized that only a very few of the fleeing Cumans had arrived in Tartar territory, but those who had escaped had not been defeated ("pauci de ipsis Cumanis, qui evaserant ad Tartaros fugientes"),[10] meaning that Oldamér departed with the remains of his demolished army to Wallachia. Ladislas IV had followed them to the very border of Mongol territory.[11] A royal writ of 1286 referred to this segment of the campaign without, however, providing an exact date for the expedition.[12]

In pursuing closely the fleeing Cumans, the Hungarian king had reached the region of the Lower-Danube. In other words, the Cumans who had been defeated at Lake Hód had fled across the Transylvanian Alps to the Mongols in (the) Nogaj (region).[13] By the spring of 1285, the Mongols invaded Hungary. One of the Mongol armies had penetrated the country as far as the town of Pest; another devastated the Great Plains as far as the Carpathian mountains.[14] During the month of July, 1285, the monarch had promoted several of his lesser officials who had distinguished themselves in the defensive battle(s) with the Mongols; "...et specialiter eo tempore, quo Tartari, capitales regni nostri inimici, tyrannica feritate adierant regnum nostrum."[15]

It was mainly the Austrian chroniclers who provided details about the renewed Mongol onslaught of Hungary. They must have gained their information from Hungarian sources, as if to confirm the brief record of it in the Chronicle. The Austrian chroniclers spoke of a large number of invading Tartars; the chronicler of Salzburg recorded that the Mongol military camp covered an area of ten miles in width and six miles in depth.[16] (The question remains, however, where, if ever, was such a camp erected, and who were the eyewitnesses who had so exactly observed the outlay and size of the Tartar camp?)

The population took to flight, of course, mainly toward Transdanubia (the area south and west of the Danube); a royal writ recorded ferrymen at Buda exploiting the situation by overcharging refugees, whom they were to ferry across from the left bank to the right of the Danube.[17] The appearance of the Mongols at Pest was unexpected, and caused panic among the inhabitants - as it is more than likely that Pest, located on the left bank of the river, was unprotected from and undefended against any military invasion. Queen Izabella remained without any military protection; she had to barricade herself in Fort Buda, and had to observer how court personnel, including officials and pages, ran out of the fort and fell upon the approaching Tartars.

Serious military resistance on the plains was not possible. Only in the hills could the Mongols be slowed in their advance and be brought to a halt. It was in the hills of western Transylvania that suddenly summoned royal troops had met the Mongols head-on and defeated them. The Transylvanian Széklers were slow to realize the magnitude of the threat of a renewed Tartar onslaught, but when they did, they fought strenuously against them.[18]

A colorful drawing in the Chronicle manuscript, fol. 64´a, the initial "C," depicts Ladislas IV in Cuman dress carrying the orb in his right hand and in his left, the scepter; on fol. 64´b, under a caption (in red): "Secunda vice intrant Tartari," there is a drawing with a simple red frame, and on a gold base, recording the battle(s) between the Hungarians and the Tartars. In the background of the drawing there are brownish rocks; on the left, two women among the Cumans, and a woman in red dress among the knights on the Hungarian side, seeking refuge. (Could they have been the three mistresses of the king?)

In spite of the caption, the drawing preserved a scene in a Hungaro-Cuman, and not a Hungaro-Mongol, encounter! In the drawing, a Cuman takes a bow-shot at the king, but he is being shielded by a Hungarian knight with drawn sword.[19] The chronicle text is brief: the Mongols had entered Hungary for a second time, had mercilessly devastated the country, had burnt everything as far as the town of Pest - "et usque Pesth universa miserabiliter combusserunt."[20]

There is a rapture in the text - or, the chronicler changed his narrative by recording that the king hated his queen (she was the daughter of the king of Sicily), and spitefully took many Cuman and other mistresses.[21] The concubines poisoned the heart of the king, and the barons and nobles of the realm began to detest him: "et a suis baronibus et regni nobilibus odio habebatur."[22]

It was as if the chronicler passed moral judgment on the monarch by looking upon the renewed Tartar invasion as the just punishment of God; he almost verbatim repeated the firmly worded letter of Pope Honorius IV, dated March 12, 1287. He had been informed by various [oral?] reports, and even by hearsay, the pontiff wrote, that the king had departed from the just path of his predecessors, and was leading a sinful life, endangering his own spiritual destiny. He neglected God and religion, kept pagan Cuman company (and even associated himself with the Mongols), dissolved his marriage by sending his queen to prison - thereby causing a public scandal - and earned the contempt of man and God.[23]

One may suspect that the contributor of this portion of the Chronicle had gained access to official records for information, and knew about the reply the king received from the papal curia. His record will not be downgraded by the fact that no papal writ had been received in Hungary; "littera et registrata fuit remissa...et postea mutata," the curial annotation reads, on the grounds, perhaps, that its contents evidently became public. The text of the writ appeared, with some alterations, in the letter of Pope Nicholas III, dated August 8, 1288, and delivered at the Hungarian court.[24]

The historian searching for straight evidence in the case has to turn to Keza's *Gesta Ungarorum*; Keza, the loyal cleric of "the invincible and powerful King Ladislas (IV)," had complied with his master's wish and expanded his narrative to include the history of the Huns - as he knew it and could interpret it. Keza described Attila the

Hun (*ob.* 453) as a (Hungarian) national hero - though he had to enrich Attila with some of the personal characteristics of Ladislas IV. Keza had identified his royal master with the ruler of the Huns.[25]

"His Lord Ladislas," Keza had argued, wished to imitate, or even realize, the immense political and military might and ferocious pagan example of Attila, because the political interests of the monarch had been immensely served by the latest Mongol threat, and actual invasion, and that on the grounds that the high nobility of the realm - the oligarchs (the Aba, Baksa, Borsa, and other clans) so preoccupied with confronting each other and intriguing against their king - now had to form a united front against the "common" enemy, the Tartars, in their midst.[26] But Keza failed to mention that, during the late 1280's, his king had fallen into a stupor of personal fear and political madness, as he had invited Cumans, Moslems, and even some Tartars to serve in his armies, and named Moslems and "pagans" to high public offices. This is not to omit the fact that the king had, at one time and for a brief period, led an un-Christian "pagan" life himself.[27]

Cardinal Philip of Fermo, the papal legate, had spent another year in Hungary because he wanted to lessen the bad influence of evil advisors upon the king and wished to keep observing him. Furthermore, he had worked hard to restore peace, law and order in the realm, as he cooperated with everyone who had turned to him or had supported him.[28] In 1281, he traveled to Poland, where he also held Apostolic jurisdiction as papal legate.[29] By September, 1281, he had returned to Hungary - the last official writ he had issued from Hungarian soil is dated September 8, 1281 - and from there he went back to Rome.[30] An Austrian source reports that before his departure from Hungary he had made the remark that under no circumstances would he accept another papal mission to that country; his activities there had been a failure.[31]

Ladislas IV had, indeed, informed the new pontiff, Martin IV, about the harsh attitude of the departed papal legate, and the pope, in his letter of August 28, 1282, had authorized the king to name (appoint) his country's leading churchmen![32] In another writ, dated the end of September, 1282, the pontiff had expressed support for the monarch, though gently warned him that it was only through the grace of God that he had escaped recent political and military mishaps, and he ought to stay on the rightful path - one that was pleasing to God. He came from a family of saints; therefore, he must remain loyal to the Church, propagate the faith, neither subscribe to, nor tolerate, un-Christian religious customs by wearing "foreign" dress, which was so unbecoming of a Christian king. Pope Martin IV had assured the king that the curia would not curtail the rights of his crown. If he behaved with the dignity worthy of a Christian king, the pontiff would treat him like a father.[33]

In the next five years, a hiatus appears in Hungaro-papal relations. Papal writs sent to the Hungarian court, and letters dispatched to the curia by the king or the bishops fail to appear logged in the papal register.

The military victory he had scored over the Cumans at Hód(mező) temporarily freed Ladislas IV from pressures by his opponents at home, although the oligarchs continued in their irresponsible attitude. The Németújvár clan stand as an example: Bishop Timót of Zagreb had the family excommunicated because of the moral misbehavior of its members.[34] Finta, son of David of the clan of Aba, whom the king had earlier regarded as a favorite, "quod dilecto et fideli nostro Finta palatino," and had made him, the former Head Steward (Voyvoda) of Transylvania, royal Palatine, turned out to be an unreliable high official.[35]

By 1281, the king had to replace him as palatine with Iván of Németújvár;[36] the same royal writ made mention of a military expedition aimed at Finta, "cum contra Fintam infidelem nostrum exercitum habuimus" - an indication of the fact that the former palatine did not take his deposition lightly.[37] However, Palatine Iván, known as "Palatine John," also proved unworthy of the trust placed in him, and on August 20, 1282 - the Feast of King St. Stephen, time of the annual field-day of the country's nobles - Ladislas IV had to replace Iván by Máté Csák, the archenemy of the Németújvár clan.[38] The king regarded himself as "one who had come of age,"[39] and requested church support; he referred to the church in Esztergom as his spiritual mother, and made a donation to Archbishop Ladomér of Esztergom, with whom he maintained good personal and working relations.[40] Things appeared to return to normal, when, with tragic suddenness, Máté Csák, the palatine, had died in April, 1282.[41]

The king now demanded that the Németújvár clan return all of the fortifications its members had illegally confiscated from the crown, or had occupied by use of military means in the recent past. In order to enforce his order, Ladislas IV had authorized military action to be taken against them.[42] He must have made a hurried decision, however, because the authorized military operation had been quite in vain. This is evident from the fact that several of his writs were dated from his camp, "sub castro Paristian," Fort Borostyánkö he was besieging during the months of January and February, 1284.[43] He had to abandon the siege of the fort, and moved toward the Tisza river region in June of that year.

In a writ he signed in that area, "in villa Chegue [Csege]," the monarch had permitted Nicholas, son of Nicholas, to build a fort on his estate in support of the military defenses of that region, though with the understanding that Nicholas would not carry out personal raids of the surrounding countryside.[44] It may seem that the king had little confidence even in the peaceful attitudes of his supporters.

Simultaneously, the royal court had to issue letters to confirm the legal rights and interests of the Church; one of these writs was dated from Buda,[45] several documents from the Tisza region "next to the ferry at Xsege [sic];"[46] two writs were issued at Dada ("in Doda"), and at Kürü ("prope Kevrew"), both located in the same area.[47]

In a letter addressed to his mother, and presumably dated August 4, 1284, Ladislas IV created the impression of an intellectually and emotionally mature and responsible young monarch, who displayed a strong sense for law and justice among his peoples. The letter bears witness to his noble manner of thinking and thoughtful behavior towards others.[48]

The royal writ, dated 1289, and issued by Bishop Gregory of Csanád, royal vice-chancellor at the time, refers to an uprising in the Szepes region, where the insurgents had besieged the royal fort at Szepes.[49] The king had moved to oppress the revolt with his army of Hungarians, Cumans and (forcefully drafted!) Mongols under the personal command of Nicholas Grendi.[50] This Hungaro-Cuman-Mongol military "cooperation" on the side of the monarch did have a mean side-effect, however; during the siege of Szepes, the Cuman and Mongol troops in the royal army also raided and burnt down the house of the canons of the Szepes chapter.[51] During their raid, the seal of the founding charter, dated 1248, of the canon's chapter was broken; in 1290, Andrew III would have to confirm the existence of the charter.[52]

The king did not feel personally responsible for this misbehavior of the troops - most probably, the Cuman and Mongol troops involved in the incident were drunk because of their victory over the besiegers of Fort Szepes - but the event did not increase public confidence in the political leadership of the young monarch. To clear his name, Ladislas IV had disclaimed any responsibility for the affair in his letter, dated August 22, 1285, to the archbishop of Esztergom (and, for the Church in Hungary), where he "had been baptized, blessed, anointed and crowned" - the Church that had been like a Mother to him. He could bear only affection and good will toward the Church in Esztergom.[53]

After he had the Tartars expelled from his country, the king visited northern Hungary to meet with his fugitive relative, Leszko the Black, Prince of Cracow, the adopted son and heir of Boleslav and Kunigunde; she was a daughter of Béla IV. (Leszko's mother, Griffina, the wife of Ladislas the Prudent, was the daughter of Rastislav of Macho and Ann, a grandaughter of Béla IV.)[54] Conrad, Prince of Mazur, had Leszko expelled from his land, stripped of his inheritance, and Leszko, after he had placed his wife under the protection of the burghers of Cracow, fled to Hungary. Ladislas IV responded to Leszko's needs; the royal Cuman and Hungarian (in that order!) army units under the command of György of Sóvár, had engaged in a battle with the troops of Conrad on the Rába stream and destroyed them. Leszko was free to go home under the protection of a Hungarian royal army detachment, commanded by György Sóvár.[55]

When Charles of Sicily died in Naples, Ladislas IV placed his queen, who was the daughter of Charles, in a monastery, as if welcoming the opportunity to dissolve his marriage with the loving, but forceful - even predominant - wife. So the record has it.[56] The validity of this report requires closer investigation. Did the king act soberly, on his personal initiative, or did he momentarily succumb to an evil advisor's irresponsible suggestion? It is a matter of record that when Archbishop Ladomér of Esztergom - the church that had crowned him! - had, upon authorization he received from the curia, freed Queen Izabella from her confinement, Ladislas IV made peace with her at once, begged her forgiveness, and expressed his horror over his thoughtless misdeed.[57]

In June, 1286, Ladislas IV had a diet held at Rákos; its resolutions failed to survive, but the king had made a mention of it in his writs.[58] It was at the diet of Rákos that he had, with his new seal, confirmed a deed he had granted earlier;[59] he acted in conformity with the diet, "habito super hoc in generali congregatione tocius regni nostri in rakus celebrata, omnium prelatorum et baronum nostrorum consilio et consensu."[60] The use of his "new" seal is mentioned in a writ issued "before" September 3, 1288: "concessimus litteras dupplicis sigilli nostri novi, quod...de prelatorum et baronum nostrorum consilio fecimus innovari."[61] In late June, 1286, the king had issued a writ at Buda, and four documents in Rákos - proof of his whereabouts during that time.[62]

The Chronicle reported that the barons once again revolted against the king, including the Németújvár-Kőszeg clan, and, exploiting the situation, Albert of Austria invaded the country, occupying some thirty-six forts.[63] It was at this junction of events that Andrew "of Venice," grandson of Andrew II by his third marriage, had made his appearance as "Lord of Slovenia" on the chessboard of Hungarian domestic politics.[64] In order to master the rapidly deteriorating situation, Ladislas IV now summoned another diet at Fövény, and attempted to reach a truce with members of the oligarchy, and with the country's barons.

Once again, it is the royal writs that describe the events. The letter, dated June 23, 1289, "prope Fuen" (Fövény), granted, in accordance with the resolutions of the diet [assembled there], a gift for the "Archbishop and perpetual Reeve" Ladomér of Esztergom.[65] In a similar manner, the king made donations and granted privileges at the diet of Fövény,[66] and ordered that, with the approval of his bishops, barons and nobles in the diet, and for the benefit of his soul, the Cistercian monastery at Háromkút attain compensation for damages it had suffered during the previous confrontations among members of the oligarchy.[67]

The letter of gift Queen Izabella had made to the Sisters of Rabbit Island may even determine the date of this diet; "quod cum post generalem congregationem tocius regni nostri in Fuen, a.D. 1289, circa festum b. Johannis Baptistae celebratam."[68] The Queen made peace with her husband, referred to him as her beloved man,

Hungary's sublime king.[69] She had also referred to the diet of Fövény in taking possession of properties that had illegally been taken from her; "et post congregationem generalem regni Hungariae prehabitam circa Fuen."[70]

The diet at Fövény did have a politically unifying effect; although two palatines had control over the realm - Nicholas, son of Herrik, in Transdanubia, and Rénald of Básztély in an area east of the Danube - they restored political unity in the country, and caused Albert of Austria to leave Hungary in peace.[71]

By 1290, Ladislas IV had to face another uprising at home; previously, he had defeated the Németújvár clan, and for a short period peace prevailed in the land.[72] But the monarch was forced, for reasons of his personal security, to live in a military camp: he feared assassination. In November, 1289, he was in Somogy (county),[73] a month later, he visited Bakony,[74] moved to the Csanád region;[75] he spent Christmas in Kőrösszeg.[76] The Queen remained under the personal protection of Archbishop Ladomér.[77]

In early March, 1290, the king sojourned near Cegléd;[78] he was at Mezősomlyó by mid-March,[79] and in Karánsebes by the end of April.[80] He had moved from the southwestern portion of the country to the southeast, Transylvania. In May, he was at Cheenk,[81] and issued four writs from Zekes (Székes).[82] On June 18, he gave order for the nobles in Ugocsa county.[83] On June 24, he established headquarters at Szarvashalom (Zorvoshalom), where he issued his last known writ.[84] The king moved to Cuman territory in his realm, and had, in fact, named Mize (Misze), a convert from Islam to the Catholic faith, as his palatine. (Gossip, the chronicler says, has it that Mize had, afterwards, abandoned his new religion.)[85]

Ladislas IV looked with confidence toward ending the war effort with the oligarchy, as he was able to conclude alliances against them with Prince Henry Boroslav and Vencel, son of the Czech king.[86] However, members of the oligarchy had by then decided to assassinate the monarch. The question may be raised, of course, whether the oligarchs had thought of obtaining the approval of the Roman curia for their plan to "dethrone" the king?

Regarding the letter of Pope Nicholas IV, dated May 20, 1290, where the pontiff had firmly admonished the king to improve his manner of living, and to return to the Christian fold; had the pontiff assumed that King Ladislas became a pagan by seeking personal safety among the Cumans, and leaving his queen behind under the protection of the archbishop of Esztergom?[87] And did this play a role in the decision-making process of the oligarchy? Did the oligarchs, who looked upon the monarch as an outcast because he had "abandoned" the Christian fold in seeking refuge among the Cumans, decide to dethrone, or even murder him?

Rome had named a[nother] legate to Hungary, Bishop Benvenuto of Eugubinus, with specific instructions to persuade Ladislas IV to return to the Christian path, and, in lieu of public penance, to organize and lead a holy crusade for the Church![88] (Clearly, the Holy See had no notion of, or it had been misinformed about domestic conditions in Hungary. For the king to leave the safety of the Cuman camp would have been suicidal; had he left the country on a crusade, he would not have returned to it alive.)

In order to stress the serious nature of the legate's mission in Hungary, the curia sent letters to Rudolf of Germany, Albert of Austria,[89] Vencel II of Bohemia, and to the Polish princes.[90] The pontiff appealed to the "generous" nature of the Hungarian and non-Hungarian nobility, asking them to aid the legate in his mission.[91] On July 23, 1290, the curia also sent letters to John, Nicholas, and Henry, "Grand Stewards" in Slovenia, [92] and notified Radoslav and Stephen in Slavonia, informing them about his concern for the Hungarian king.[93]

The pontiff even dispatched letters to Roland, the Voyvoda (Grand Steward) of Transylvania, and the latter's brother, arguing that Ladislas had sunk to an unacceptable level of personal behavior through his cultivation of Moslems, Tartars, and pagans, and through his barbaric treatment of the queen.[94] The curia sent letters of complaint to everyone, and had lodged a complaint to the Hungarian nobles about their monarch's personal behavior.[95] And, as a last resort, the curia sent a writ to the king himself to warn and admonish him. Pope Nicholas IV had organized a conspiracy against the king's vicious and incompetent advisors with the purpose to free him from their vicious circle. "Sane, fili carissime, nuper ad audientiam nostram aliqua de tuis actibus pervenerunt, que si veritati deserviant, si opere compleantur, tue saluti et fame preiudicabant."[96]

The reader of these papal letters is under the impression that either the curia had not been fully informed about politics in Hungary, or individuals provided the curia with some information about the monarch, his private life, and his public policies. One may further conclude that, judged by the tone and almost identical content of these writs, certain members of the Hungarian oligarchy had assumed that Rome had thought that the time had come to have a moral reckoning with the faithless, fickle monarch, who would not be regarded as a Christian king any longer. That is why Rome had sent an envoy to Hungary.[97]

The scenario for dethronement, or even regicide, is evident from the letter sent to Roland, Voyvoda of Transylvania.[98] The oligarchs had to make their move quickly if they wished to carry out *their own* punitive action toward the beleaguered monarch, *before* the papal envoy could undertake any preemptive steps, invading, thereby, the field of Hungarian politics.

Ladislas IV was en route to Kőrösszeg in Bihar county in an attempt to reestablish contacts with his followers. He was getting ready for a final military encounter with the Kőszeg clan. Then, unexpectedly, three hired assassins - Arbóc, Törtel, and Kemens - murdered the twenty-eight year old monarch when he was asleep in his royal tent.[99]

Where were the bodyguards? Did the king feel so secure in the camp that he saw no need for his personal security? Were the guards his assassins? The record is far from clear on this. On fol. 65b of the Chronicle manuscript, in the "P" initial, with the inscription above it: "The murdered King Ladislas and his murderers," the royal tent with the coat of arms is depicted. In the tent, the king is lying on a bed. On the left of the drawing, two of the assassins carrying a lance are leaving the scene of the crime.[100] This drawing, of course, only represents a mid-fourteenth century view of the assassination. A sentence that had been added to the text states that Kapóz (Jacob; James) of the clan of Barsa had arranged for the murder.[101]

The chronicler next recorded that the king was buried at Csanád.[102] Questions raised regarding the murder - whether the oligarchs had played a role in the royal murder, or only wished to frighten him into submission, or to force him to resign his throne - remain unanswered. The accomplished fact remains that a duly elected and crowned monarch had been brutally assassinated by three known individuals.[103]

It was murder: regicide, pure and simple. It will not be lessened by a probable error on the part of the conspirators who did not want to murder him. An added passage appearing in some chronicle manuscripts, "...in quo rege qui sine herede decessit, defecit semen masculinum sanctorum regum," may imply that the conspirators - not the actual assassins! - fearing renewed intervention from the papal curia, wanted to name their own candidate to the Hungarian throne by removing, though not necessarily murdering, Ladislas IV from power.[104]

A later report in the Chronicle supports such an assumption. Upon the murder of Ladislas IV, the barons of the realm made Andrew ("of Venice"), a nephew of Ladislas IV, king. "Cum autem rex Ladislas fuisset occisus, baronibus regni Andreas dux feliciter coronatur."[105] One may note here that the chronicler (of this portion of the record) merely noted the barons' desire to *have* a king; he did not find it appropriate, or necessary, to observe that, although the barons could elect a king, only the archbishop of Esztergom had the right to anoint and crown him.[106]

Queen Izabella remained in Hungary for nine more years before returning to Naples, where she took the veil. She died as a member of the Order of Saint Dominic in the year 1304.[107]

NOTES

1. Keza, c. 75, though without a date or place, *SSH*, I, 187,1-7.

2. *RA*, n. 3284; "...in ecclesia sancti Laurencii de Hoy cum lesione et morte xxxvii servicium suorum...pro defensione...contra Cumanos;" *ÁUO*, IX, 380f. Further royal correspondence in *RA*, nn. 3341 with text, 3342; *ÁUO*, IX, 383f. and 384ff., though the text printed there may be "dubiae fidei," *RA*, n. 3342; further, *RA*, n. 3237 with text.

3. Members of the Aba clan - *RA*, n. 3686; *ÁUO*, XII, 496f.; members of the Rátold clan - even though the diploma is a forgery, *RA*, nn. 3238, 3239; and, a nobleman named Rofoyon (Rafain!), *RA*, n. 3348; Szabó, 102, n. 6. It was Reeve Rafain who led the attack, *RA*, n. 3348; Teutsch-Firnhaber, I, 134; on Reeve Simon, *RA*, n. 3332.

4. The queen made a donation upon receiving the good news, "in conflictu, quem idem dominus noster rex habuit contra perfidiam Cumanorum;" the writ may serve as proof that the queen and the king were on good terms. Cf. *ÁUO*, IV, 264ff.

5. *SSH*, I, 471,18-20.

6. *Ibid.* I, 471,21.

7. *Ibid.*, I, 472,8.

8. *Ibid.*, I, 472,3-8, and Keza, c. 75, *ibid.*, I, 187,9-13. On the source(s) of information of the chronicler, see S. Domanovszky, "A magyar király-krónika XIV századi folytatása" [The 14th Century Continuation of the Hungarian Royal Chronicle], *Berzeviczy Emlékkönyv* (Budapest, 1934), 25ff.; E. Mályusz, "Krónika problémák" [Questions Concerning the Chronicle], *Századok* (1967), 457ff., esp. 467f.; J. Horváth, "Die ungarischen Chronisten aus der Angiovozeit," *Acta linguistica Academiae Scientiarum Hungariae*, 21 (1971), 324ff.

9. *SSH*, II, 44,14-18.

10. *Ibid.*, I, 472,9-10; II, 44,14-18.

11. Mentioned in a writ in 1286, *RA*, n. 3410: *HO*, VI, 315.

12. *RA*, n. 3079, and n. 3978; the writ cited in support of this as a forgery - *RA*, n. 3070.

13. *SSH*, II, 44,19-20, repeated in the Chronicle, *ibid.*, I, 472,9-10.

14. *Ibid.*, I, 472,10-16; II, 44,20-22; Polish Annals, *MPH*, II, 850. For the Russian (Kievan) point of view, cf. Hodinka, *Orosz évkönyvek*, "Halich-Volodimer Annals," 448Af. and 450Bf., anno 6790 (1282-83); on the differentiation of dates in the Russian sources, see Marta F. Font, "Ungarische Vornehmen in der Halitisch im 13 Jahrhundert," *Specimina nova Universitatis de Iano Pannonio nominatae* (Pécs, 1990), 165ff.; idem, "A Kijevi Évkönyv mint magyar történeti forrás" [The Kiev Annals as Hungarian Historical Source], *Történelmi Szemle*, 34 (1991), 70ff. Further, the letter of Archpriest Benedict of Esztergom, Knauz, II, 419, 452; Teutsch-Firnhaber, I, 173ff.

15. *RA*, n. 3368; *ÁUO*, IV, 276ff.; also V, 20ff., and IX, 465ff., 518ff; X, 180ff., and XII, 497; Keza, c. 75; Knauz, II, 196 and 199.

16. *MGHSS*, IX, 657, 713, 809.

17. *RA*, n. 3367; Batthyány, *Leges*, II, 481f.

18. *CD*, VII-2, 109. *RA*, n. 3534 - a writ for the Széklers in Aranyos, cf. Teutsch-Firnhaber, I, 147; *CD*, V-3, 452ff.; *Székely levéltár*, I, 21f.; Szabó, 118ff. Z. Kordé, "A székelyek a XII századi elbeszélő forrásokban" [The Széklers in 12th Century Narrative Historical Sources], *Acta historica Szegediensis*, 92 (1991), 17ff.

19. The Chronicle depicted the king in Cuman dress, with royal scepter in his right hand, and the orb in his left, fol. 64´a, "C" initial; on fol. 64´b, there is a drawing of two young women among the Cumans, and one among the Hungarian knights seeking (their) protection; were they the king's Cuman mistresses, Edua,

Köpcsecs, and Mandula? Cf. *SSH*, I, 473,2-3. Above the drawing, with a red frame and a gold base, there is a caption in red: "Secunda vice intrant Tartari." György Székely, "Egy elfelejtett rettegés: a második tatárjárás a magyar történeti hagyományban" [The Forgotten Fear: The Second Tartar Invasion in Hungarian Historical Tradition], *Századok*, 122 (1988), 52ff.

20. *SSH*, I, 472,11-16.
21. *Ibid.*, I, 472,17-18, and 472f.
22. *Ibid.*, I, 473,5. At the same time, the writ, addressed to his Mother, bears witness to the monarch's noble manner of thinking, and to his mature sense of political justice - *RA*, n. 3155.
23. Potthast, n. 22585; *VMH*, n. 573; *ÁUO*, IX, 330f.; *MGHSS*, XVII, 35-36.
24. Potthast, n. 22764; *VMH*, n. 577. Szabó, 120, argued to the contrary: Ladislas IV had led a moral life and defended the interests of the country. He cited various documents to prove this, as, e.g., *RA*, n. 3360; *ÁUO*, IX, 425; *RA*, n. 3361; Teutsch-Firnhaber, I, 137, and *HO*, VIII, 237f. Also, *RA*, n. 3392; Knauz, II, 204, and *RA*, nn. 3391 and 3392 with text.
25. Keza, cc. 1 and 2-23; *SSH*, I, 141ff. István Bóna, *Der Anbruch des Mittelalters: Gepiden und Longobarden im Karpathenbecken* (Budapest, 1976), 67ff., 86ff., and 102ff.; idem, *A húnok és nagykirályaik* [The Huns and Their Great Kings] (Budapest, 1993), 63ff., and 74ff.
26. *Ibid.*, c. 75; Mályusz, *Thúróczy Krónika*, 51ff.
27. Pauler, II, 378ff.; Ladislas IV did make ecclesiastical appointments, see *ÁUO*, IV, 242 - upon authorization he received from Rome - cf. Potthast, n. 21933; *VMH*, n. 570.
28. As, e.g., in *ÁUO*, XII, 315; *HO*, VI, 261; FRA, XV, 142.
29. Potthast, n. 21666; on the Polish synod, see Hube, 72ff.; Hefele, VI, 188ff.; Fraknói, I, 80f.; Hóman-Szekfű, I, 603f.
30. *HO*, VI, 247, dated 1279! In *CD*, VII-2, 45f., the date is 1273; see Kosztolnyik, *art. cit.*, *AHC*, 22 (1990), 83 and n. 120, where the date of "June, 1281," is a printer's error! I. Ipoly *et al.* (eds.), *Codex diplomaticus patrius Hungaricus*, vol. IV (Budapest, 1876), 247; *MPH*, II, 120.
31. Potthast, n. 21663, *note 2: "in eundem modum regi Ungarie." *SSH*, I, 473,9-16.
32. Potthast, n. 22764.
33. Potthast, n. 21933.
34. *ÁUO*, XII, 336.
35. *RA*, n. 3086 and n. 3056. On the document entered as n. 3113, Finta still signed as the Palatine.
36. *ÁUO*, IX, 312f.
37. *RA*, n. 3126, mentioned an expedition against the faithless Finta; *ÁUO*, IX, 297.
38. *ÁUO*, IV, 243, dated "in crastino s. Bartholomei a.D. MCCLXXXIII."
39. *RA*, n. 3312.
40. Potthast, n. 21933.
41. Last will and testament of Máté Csák, *ÁUO*, IX, 360f.
42. *MGHSS*, IX, 712.
43. *RA*, nn. 3288, 3292 (dated between January 9 and February 16, 1284).
44. *RA*, n. 3317; *HO*, VI, 350, no date.
45. *RA*, n. 3319 with text.
46. *RA*, n. 3318, and n. 3230.
47. *RA*, n. 3331, at Dada, *ÁUO*, IX, 389f.; *RA*, n. 3322, near Kürü, *ÁUO*, IV, 263f.; *RA*, n. 3326; *HO*, VI, 304.

48. *CD*, V-3, 245f., dated August 5, 1284, though *RA*, n. 3155 placed the events in the year 1282, even if some cited events may related to 1284 - see Katona, VII, 895 (anno 1284). The edition in *ÁUO* is dated 1275. The monarch had been traveling; for example, his writ of September 15, 1284, was issued at Esztergom, *RA*, n. 3336; later, it was from Szarvas that he sent a writ, *RA*, n. 3340. Szabó, 120, maintains that he monarch served the country's interest by maintaining an ambulatory court; see, e.g., his writ, dated May 28, 1285, from Gyulafehérvár, *RA*, n. 3361; *HÓ*, VIII, 237; Teutsch-Firnhaber, I, 137. In mid-August, he was in Sáros (county), *RA*, n. 3360; also, *RA*, n.3375; Knauz, II, 204; by the end of September in Liptó, *RA*, n. 3391 (could this writ be of a later date?); further, *RA*, n. 3392 with text.
49. *ÁUO*, IV, 336f.; Teutsch-Firnhaber, I, 146 - a forgery? Cf. *RA*, n. 3529; was Gregory of Csanád the royal vice-chancellor at the time?
50. *RA*, n. 3545, and compare to n. 3534; Katona, VII, 997.
51. *RA*, n. 890.
52. *RA*, n. 3684.
53. *RA*, n. 3376; Knauz, II, 204.
54. Leszko the Black was the adopted son of Boleslav of Cracow and Kunigunde, daughter of Béla IV - *MPH*, I, 837ff.
55. *RA*, n. 3499, n. 3502; Katona, VII, 953.
56. See letter by Queen Izabella, *CD*, VII-2, 127, and Szabó, 123, n. 3. The canons of the Veszprém chapter did try to help, *ÁUO*, IV, 341f. The Queen did thank them, *HO*, VI, 343.
57. Honorius IV addressed three letters to the king and to the archbishop of Esztergom, all dated March 12, 1287 - Potthast, n. 22585; *VMH*, n. 573; and yet, the writ had not been forwarded to the king. A re-draft, "toned down," was sent to the court at a later date, Potthast, n. 22764; *VMH*, n. 577.
58. He promised to pay serious attention to the affairs of the realm - *RA*, n. 3406 (June 18, 1286); *ÁUO*, IX, 443.
59. *RA*, n. 3413.
60. *RA*, n. 3415; *ÁUO*, IV, 282f.
61. *RA*, n. 3497 with text; compare to *RA*, n. 3498 with text.
62. *RA*, n. 3405, issued "iuxta Rakus," June 17, 1286; *RA*, n. 3408, "datum in Rakus," June 16, 1286; Szabó, 126. *RA*, n. 3047 with text, "datum Bude," before June 24, 1286; *RA*, n. 3411 with text, "datum in Rakus," June 30, 1286. *RA*, n. 3412, "datum in Rakus." *ÁUO*, IV, 284, printed a writ issued at Ercsi, although with a wrong date - *RA*, n. 3600.
63. See the writ of Andrew III, in 1294, *RA*, n. 3983; *ÁUO*, V, 96f., in ref. to *RA*, n. 3420. On the background, see *MGHSS*, IX, 714, 862. The "rebels" and the "loyalists" [to the king] were murdering each other, *RA*, nn. 3532, 3533; *ÁUO*, IX, 556f. and 557. Gy. Kristó, "Uj adatok és régi vélekedések Csák Mátéról" [New Data and Old Fashioned Opinions About Máté Csák], *Acta historica Szegediensis*, 75 (1983), 29ff.
64. *SSH*, I, 477,5; *Reimchronik*, lines 39972-39973 and 40125-40205; also, *MGHSS*, IX, 716,19-22, and XVII, 78,37-38; *ibid.*, IX, 749,27-29. On the Czech background, see Palacky, II-1, 318f. and 329ff., and refer to the Bohemian "Chronicon curiae regiae," a work he described in his *Würdigung der alten böhmischen Geschichtsschreiber* (Prague, 1830), 137. A letter printed in *CD*, VII-2, 120, spoke of Arnoldus of Strigau: Arnold of Strido, a turncoat. In the spring of 1289, the king was in Csepel, *RA*, n. 3517, and compare to nn. 3536 and 3538; on May 26, 1289, he issued a writ at Rákos, to state that he had oppressed the revolt, *RA*, n. 3518; *ÁUO*, IX, 495.
65. *RA*, n. 3522; Knauz, II, 250, though the contents of the letter may apply to 1279, cf. *ÁUO*, VI, 778f. The gift for Archbishop Ladomér was confirmed by Andrew III on September 1, 1290, *RA*, n. 3656; Knauz, II, 267; *CD*, VI-1, 74f.,

"corrected" the place name from Fuen to Wien (Vienna!) *CD*, VII-5, has the same writ with a 1289 date.

66. *RA*, nn. 3523 and 3524, "datum in Hawen" (Foewen?); *HO*, VIII, 266.
67. *RA*, n. 3525.
68. *ÁUO*, IX, 527ff.
69. *Ibid.*, XII, 470.
70. *Ibid.*, IV, 341f.: "et post congregationem generalem regni Hungariae prehabitam circa Fuen." See Note C, on page v.
71. Nicholas of Némétújvár was still palatine on September 8, 1289, *CD*, V-3, 481, though on a royal writ of September 9, Renoldus had signed as palatine, *RA*, n. 3530. The *Reimchronik* celebrated Albert's victories; Magyaróvár surrendered to him, lines 30679-30700. It was at the siege of Magyaróvár that Bicsó Óvári had lost his title to the fort, a title King Stephen V granted him - cf. *RA*, n. 3786 and n. 3784 with text.
72. *Reimchronik*, lines 31273-31360. Bishop Peter of Veszprém had been murdered in 1289, *MGHSS*, IX, 715; a writ from the Queen made mention of Benedek (Benedict) as the new bishop of Veszprém, *ÁUO*, IX, 525ff., esp. 528. Albert returned the captured forts, *Reimchronik*, lines 30801-30832; lines 30931-31120 on the invasion by Iván, though the king refused to help him, Szabó, 165ff., esp. 168.
Rózsa Zsőtér, "Megjegyzések IV László itineráriumához" [Some Remarks on the Itinerary of King Ladislas IV', *Acta historica Szegediensis*, 92 (1991), 37ff.
73. *RA*, n. 3537.
74. *ÁUO*, IX, 496, a forged writ, or, it ought to be dated 1287! See *RA*, n. 3462.
75. *RA*, n. 3538.
76. In Kőrösszeg, *RA*, n. 3539; Szabó, 171.
77. The queen had remained under the protection of Archbishop Ladomér, *ÁUO*, IX, 343 (dated October 17, 1289).
78. *RA*, nn. 3551 (*ÁUO*, IX, 523) and 3552; Teutsch-Firnhaber, I, 155.
79. According to *CD*, VII-3, 93, though the date should read March 30, 1278 - *RA*, nn. 2850 and 2851.
80. *RA*, nn. 3553, and 3554; Katona, *Historia critica*, VII, 1004.
81. *RA*, n. 3555; Zimmermann-Werner, I, 164.
82. *RA*, n. 3557, Szabó, 172f.; *RA*, n. 3558, *ÁUO*, IX, 549; *RA*, n. 3559, *ÁUO*, IX, 561f.; *RA*, n. 3560, Szabó, 173.
83. Dated from Csanád - *RA*, n. 3561; *ÁUO*, IX, 564; Szabó, 173.
84. Dated from Zorvosholm, *RA*, n. 3562; *ÁUO*, IX, 521f. Further, *RA*, nn. 3563 and 3565 (*ÁUO*, IX, 519ff.) refer to him, though the writs were logged in the Register under the wrong year.
85. "...olim Saracenus, tunc tamen gratiam baptizmatis consecutus," *SSH*, I, 474,21-22. "Mize quondam palatinus" - a quote from the letter of the king's mother, Lady Tomasina, no date, *ÁUO*, X, 184ff., esp. 185; also, Wenczel, *Anjoukori dipl.*, I, 481 and 518. Eyze (Lyze) was Mize's brother - *SSH*, I, 474,24, known as a "wild" individual, "vir maxime violentiae;" cf. Imre Nagy (ed.), *Codex diplomaticus Hungariae Andegavensis*, 6 vols. (Budapest, 1879-91), I, 35 and 481.
86. Cf. Palacky, II-1, 324ff., who based his information on the "Chronica aulae regiae" (of the Czech court), in Dobner, *Monumenta historica Bohemarum*, V, 63 - "die Hauptquelle der böhmischen Geschichte für die Jahre 1283 bis 1338," Palacky, II-1, 331f. Idem, *Würdigung*, 137. Duke Henry IV of Bohemia had died on June 23, 1290 - Palacky, *Geschichte*, II-1, 333, and notes 328 and 429. Gyula Kristó, *Az árpádkor háborúi* [The Wars of the Árpádian Age] (Budapest, 1986), 132ff. and 178ff.
87. Potthast, n. 23284; *VMH*, n. 583; *ÁUO*, IV, 357ff.

88. Potthast, n. 23283; *ÁUO*, IV, 354ff., with note on margin: "Legatio ista non habiit effectum." Also, Potthast, n. 23339; *CD*, VII-5, 484.
89. Potthast, nn. 23285-86; *VMH*, n. 584 [for both]; *ÁUO*, IX, 361; further, Potthast, n. 23386; Katona, VI, 1001.
90. Potthast, n. *23338 (addressed to Vencel and to the bishops of Prague and Olmütz); cf. J. Erben and F. Embler (eds.), *Regesta diplomatica necnon epistolaria Bohemiae et Moraviae*, 2 vols. (Prague, 1855-74), II, 649. In *VMH*, it is still under n. 584!
91. Potthast, n. 23328; *ÁUO*, IV, 361ff. and 375f.
92. Potthast, n. 23329; *VMH*, n. 585; *ÁUO*, IV, 363ff.
93. Potthast, n. 2330; *ÁUO*, IV, 365f. The pontiff wrote, again, to Nicholas, grand steward of Slovenia, and Master Paul, son of Stephen, grand steward of Slavonia, as if to record his concern for King Ladislas IV! - Potthast, n. 23331; *ÁUO*, IV, 367; the pontiff had even contacted Gregory, a former grand steward of Slavonia, "nato quondam Gregorii Bani Sclavoniae," Potthast, n. 23332; *ÁUO*, IV, 367.
94. Potthast, n. 23333; *ÁUO*, IV, 368f. Letters were sent by the papal curia to Stephen and Brisde, grand stewards of Bosnia - Potthast, n. 23334; *ÁUO*, IV, 369ff., to John and Leonard of Vegla - Potthast, n. 2335; *ÁUO*, VI, 371ff.; and to the counts of Almissa: "comitibus Almassi" - Potthast, n. 2336; *ÁUO*, IV, 373f.
95. Potthast, n. 23337, "in eundem modum;"*ÁUO*, IV, 375f.
96. Potthast, n. 23342; *ÁUO*, IV, 377f.
97. This may be concluded from the already cited papal writ of May 20, 1290, Potthast, n. 23284: "te tamquam filium predilectum a via mala pravisque retrahere studiis, ad actus revocare laudabiles et ad semitam salutarem sategit hactenus,...ut...proveniret;" *ÁUO*, IV, 357.
98. Potthast, n. 23333.
99. "Et specialiter ab Arbuz, Turtule et Kemenche, ac eorum cognatis et complilibus...;" *SSH*, I, 474,1-2 and 474,15-18. In connection with names and persons, see *RA*, n. 3444; *ÁUO*, IV, 368f.; and *RA*, n. 3509; Zimmermann-Werner, I, 152 and 159.
100. Dercsényi, *Chronicon pictum*, I, fol. 65b.
101. They had also assassinated a certain Nicholas, brother of a certain Aydus, *SSH*, I, 474,24-25 and 474,49-50. *RA*, n. 3509; Teutsch-Firnhaber, I, 145; Zimmermann-Werner, I, 159.
102. *SSH*, I, 474,34 and 474,51-52.
103. *SSH*, I, 474,15-16; Szabó, 180; on Nicholas, son of Öböl, see *HO*, VI, 225; *CD*, VII-5, 170f.
104. *SSH*, I, 474,19-20.
105. *Ibid.*, I, 476f.
106. "Andreas dux feliciter coronatur," *ibid.*, I, 477,2-3; on Esztergom's crowning the kings of Hungary, see Kosztolnyik, *From Coloman*, 244 and 260, n. 134; 279 and 289, n. 24.
107. Szabó, 184f. Potthast, nn. 23387-88; *VMH*, nn. 590 and 591; and, Potthast, nn. 23503 and 23502; *VMH*, nn. 597 and 596.

CHAPTER TEN

THE CULTURAL BACKGROUND

1. *Literary Remains and Chronicles*

The conquering Magyars of the late ninth century did not leave written literary remains behind, although they undoubtedly had traditional orally-transmitted literature (sagas), as some remarks by Anonymus - the unanimous author of the *Gesta Ungarorum* - bear witness to.[1] Anonymus based his Hungarian *gesta* on an earlier Hungarian history that had probably been composed and edited during the 1090's, since then lost,[2] and on the basis of written data, even though he ignored the "false tales of peasants," and the verbose folksongs of the bards.[3] And yet, Anonymus depended upon those despised "peasant stories" that had been preserved in the folk poetry of the bards. He narrated, for example, the Hungarian conquest of Transylvania by pursuing oral folk tradition (sagas), and stated that Duke Tétény, who had planned, and whose men had carried out the campaign, had, by their conquest assured a good name for themselves.[4]

Anonymus had recorded folk poetry by writing about the "all kind of songs" by the bards, and his reports were verified by the monk Eckehard of the monastery of Saint Gall in the tenth century, who described the "awful cries, wild dances and songs" (prayers?) of the marauding Magyars, who had invaded the monastic community[5]; or, by the recorded "Symphonia Ungarorum" sung by a peasant girl Bishop Gerard of Csánad had heard during one of his missionary journeys in the Hungarian countryside.[6]

The conquering Magyars and the peoples they had conquered in the mid-Danubian region during the 890's all shared in the European culture of the tenth century. They became participants of the Latin ecclesiastic civilization evolving in all of western Europe at the turn of the millennium.[7] The formation of early Hungarian Christian culture was connected with the Benedictine reform movement of Cluny.[8] The Cluniac missionaries brought with them their religious books, outline(s) of church law, and, frequently, their collections of lives of the saints. By the 1080's, the Benedictine abbey of Pannonhalma had some eighty books in their library.[9]

The Christianization of Hungary was begun by Albert, the "Apostle of the Czechs;" it was the Czech Benedictines who settled down at Pannonhalma.[10] In the abbey's founding charter King St. Stephen of Hungary (*ob.* 1038) donated large tracts of land for the maintenance of the monks and of the abbey.[11] Soon thereafter, Benedictine houses flourished in Bakonybél,[12] Pécsvárad,[13] Zobor Hill,[14] and Fort Zala (Zalavár).[15] The abbey of Tihany, established by King Andrew I in 1055, also became famous,[16] and fame surrounded the abbey in Somogyvár (Fort Somogy), founded by King Saint Ladislas I in 1091.[17] Several smaller monastic communities were established that played an important role in spreading the written word everywhere in the country. All of the monastic houses maintained schools, libraries and scriptoria to copy books and manuscripts.[18]

Latin was the language of instruction in schools and of the early literary fragments that have survived the ravages of time, although in the earliest officials writs composed in Latin, Hungarian expressions and place names had already appeared, perhaps as a reminder of the force of the spoken native language: the Magyar tongue of the time.[19] Legal texts and enactments were written down at first,[20] and the eleventh century historical narratives provided a picture of the then-recent Magyar (Hungarian) past.[21] By the end of the eleventh century, King Stephen I, his son Emery, and Emery's tutor, Bishop Gerard of Csánad, were canonized, and the lives of the first Hungarian saints were written accordingly,[22] together with the codes of law, as for example, the Laws of King St. Stephen,[23] and the resolutions of church synods held under the reign of King Ladislas I.[24] The "Admonitions" of King St. Stephen addressed to his son and heirs[25] of the throne that, like the Frankish royal mirrors of the ninth century, announced the principles of Christian kingship, were further regarded as laws (of the land).[26] The "Admonitions" carried the characteristics of the spirit of (the age of) King St. Stephen I.[27]

The first "legend" recorded in Hungarian literature dealt with the lives of Saints Zoerard and Benedict of Zobor Hill, authored by Maurus, a monk, abbot of Pannonhalma abbey, who became the bishop of Pécs.[28] Then there were three lives that discussed the reign and person of King St. Stephen, his *Vita minor*, the *Vita maior*, and Bishop Hartvic's *Vita* of King St. Stephen, composed in the reign of

King Coloman the Learned in the early twelfth century.[29] The authors were clerics educated in Benedictine schools, who were acquainted with regional tradition(s).[30] Two lives narrated the activities of Bishop Gerard of Csánad; the authors further depicted the historical backdrop of the age of Gerard in colorful terms.[31] Bishop Gerard had further authored the *Deliberatio supra cantum trium puerorum* of the Book of Daniel, where he described in detail the background of the early Christianization of the realm.[32]

The folklorist narrative of the Life of Saint Ladislas (*ob.* 1095) composed at a later date, was heavily mixed with written ecclesiastical records.[33] Ladislas' canonization took place in the reign of Béla III (*ob.* 1196),[34] and it was Béla III who had introduced the usage of writs in making petitions to him or to the royal court - be they property transactions or legal court cases. Reliance on writs drafted in Latin gave a strong impetus to reliance upon the written Latin word in the country.[35]

The late twelfth century *Sermon and Prayer at the Tomb* could be regarded as an early example of Hungarian [language] sermon literature;[36] the text of the prayer was in Hungarian, as if to prove that the monks who were pursuing their education and wrote their compositions in Latin also cared a good deal for the cultivation and usage of Hungarian. The sermon was a transliteration (not a translation) into Hungarian of a more lengthy funeral talk (homily?) in Latin. The Hungarian text carried clearly written sentences, and it was not a mere "copy" of the Latin - as if to emphasize that Hungarian of the age was a clearly spoken language. It even provided a sound Hungarian translation of certain Latin phrases, as, for example, of *morte moriatur*, rendering as one's dying a death's death.[37]

Hungarian historiography did not imitate the German chronicles, but followed the form of the *gesta* in use in Latin Europe, which had more secular characteristics. This form better served the ideals of the ruling dynasty, and was written with literary style and artistic goals. The scribes were actually secular, well-educated clerics who lived at the court, and had traveled widely in the world. These scribe-chroniclers had approached the information at their disposal with critical awareness. Clerical courtiers they were with university degrees, and knew how to draft a chronicle of histories based upon oral history and written documents.[38]

The first known Hungarian *gesta*, the *Gesta Ungarorum*, dated back to the 1090's (the reign of Ladislas I, *ob.* 1095), the text of which had been lost, and whose contents were (can be) only traceable from later *gesta* compositions. Its author(s) strongly supported the royal dynasty and the people against the political-military adversaries of the age.[39]

The first *gesta* that survived was the *Gesta Ungarorum* by Anonymus "P. dictus magister," the notary, by the name of Paul or Peter (probably referring to himself: *predictus*, on the previous, by now lost, leaf of the text manuscript), of King Béla III (*ob.* 1196).[40] Anonymus was proud of his educational background and of the fact that he could put together a history of his people in a book.[41] It was Anonymus who spoke with a scholar's contempt of the empty twitter of folk bards and the false tales of peasants, and tried to avoid - without much success - their data while writing.[42]

Anonymus included two pagan legends - that of "The White Horse" and of "The Dream of Emese" - into his narrative, and transformed them, so that they would not offend Christian beliefs.[43] He further regarded the dynasty of the Árpáds as the descendant of Attila (the Hun); he most probably took his information from the "inner circle" of family tradition of the royal court. He must have had his reasons for connecting the ferocious pagan Attila with the Christian Árpád kings; he even assigned to the pagan ancestors of the Árpáds the spiritual gifts of the Holy Ghost.[44]

Anonymus narrated Hungarian history from the Magyars early settlement in Lebedia (plain between the rivers) to the end of the reign of Duke Géza, the year of 997.[45] Although he had to consider the prevalent ideas of his own age, Anonymus had preserved a treasury of many good historic data for posterity. He possessed a self-assured style, and wrote his narrative in rhythmic prose.[46] He stated that Scythia was the ur-country of the Magyars, a fortunate region where even shepherds wore colorful clothing everyday.[47] Álmos was the first elected leader of the Magyars,[48] whose son, Árpád, had carried out in fiercely fought battles the [Hungarian] conquest of the mid-Danubian region during the 890's.[49]

Writing of the [national] *gesta* (or of the chronicles) bore witness to the European cultural and political orientation of the Magyars (Hungarians) and awakened their ethnic consciousness early; in Anonymus' *gesta*, the twelfth century Magyars reached self-identity as a people, in that Hungarian histories written in Latin became the originators of ethnic national Hungarian literature.[50]

The prefatory note by Anonymus to his *Gesta Ungarorum* was a striking example of the personal pride of a writer who could claim to possess a strong "European" background. His opus documented the existence of ethnic folklore and poetry, even though he unsuccessfully tried to distance himself from it, with the contemptuous attitude of a scholar who only relied upon authentic source material (oral or written) for the composition of his historical narrative.[51] If his readers were unwilling to believe the written word concerning wars and heroic deeds, he wrote, let them turn to the empty chatter of the bards, or the tall tales of peasants, who would not let the memory of heroic deeds disappear into oblivion. Anonymus even named Roman Acquincum in Pannonia as the headquarters of Attila (the Hun), and presented the Hun leader's image and accomplishments versus the socio-political backdrop of his own age, the Hungary of the late twelfth century, in describing social strata, court [of law] proceedings, or even table manners - basing his evidence upon the material found in the songs of the national bards.[52]

Simon de Kéza, cleric at the court of Ladislas IV (the Cuman)[53], used colorful imagination to continue the traditional genealogy of Attila with Hungarian history. Attila and Árpád came from the same stock of people, Kéza wrote, because, in his interpretation, Huns and Magyars were the same people.[54] Árpád only carried out the second conquest of the country (the mid-Danubian basin) because Attila before him had once already occupied the land.[55] The outline of his work showed the origins and early settlement of the Hun-Magyars in the mid-Danubian region; narrated the deeds of the Huns, together with the "second conquest" - the *return* to the country by Árpád in the late ninth century.[56] Kéza's main narrative dealt with Hun history based on a Hun *ur-gesta* rich in details borrowed from western historical sources; he even enriched Hun history with early events pertinent to Magyar history.

Kéza remained loyal to his king, though he could not help but notice that, in order to overcome European hostility toward Hungarian history, he had to identify the Magyars with the threatening Huns - depicting the former as descendants of world conquerors.[57] Therefore, he provided a biblical pedigree and origin for the early Magyars, including stories of the miraculous doe and wife capture (rape of the wives as means of their capture), as traditional folk narratives.[58] In writing this he reflected the more liberal outlook of the royal court of his age, the late thirteenth century.

The first half of Kéza's work deals with the Huns; in the latter half, he discussed the Magyars.[59] In the appendix of his work, he characterized the nobles of foreign descent, and the non-noble social strata that lived in the country by the late 1200's.[60] His main objective, though, was to identify the Huns with the Magyars; for instance, he spoke of the Tower of Babel, Menrot (Nimrod) of Persia, Hunor and Magor in the Meotis (Lake Azov) region; he narrated the incident of the miraculous doe, the move to Scythia, the captains (leaders) of the Huns, and the conquest by the Huns of Pannonia. He characterized Etele (Attila) as a person, a leader of men, and depicted the court of Attila in some detail; Kéza reported on the battle of Chalons (451), on the siege and capture by the Huns of Aquileia, on the marriage of Ildiko (a Byzantine princess) to Attila (in 453), and recorded Attila's death - to be followed by the rapid disintegration of his empire.[61]

In recording Hungarian history, Kéza described the "return" of the Huns - that is, of the Magyars - led by Árpád, their captain, into the mid-Danubian region; he reported on the Hungarian captains (tribal leaders), on their marauding ventures in the west and southeast; he mentioned the battle of Lechfeld. Kéza briefly spoke of the eleventh century Hungarian kings, of Bishop Gerard of Csanád; he discussed King Coloman the Learned of the twelfth century, kings Andrew II and Béla IV of the thirteenth century; he recorded the reigns of Stephen V and Ladislas IV, who aided Rudolf of Habsburg against the Czechs. Kéza accomplished all of this by providing an outline of events, not a narrative. The brevity of his treatment of Béla IV's reign is quite remarkable; he devoted a good deal more attention to Ladislas IV, referring to him as a loyal son of the Church, the faithful ally of the German king, Rudolf of Habsburg, against Otakar II of Bohemia.[62]

The fourteenth century *Chronicon pictum* by Mark de Kálta closely followed Kéza's outline of events, though Kálta added a good deal more information to his narrative.[63] Kálta composed his work upon orders from Louis the Great of Hungary (*ob.* 1382), and attempted to write a national chronicle by using other sources of information and historical works.[64] He further added information on the early fourteenth century rulers of the country.[65]

During the eleventh through thirteenth centuries, the Hungarians had experienced all aspects of European cultural changes. In the beginning of the eleventh century, Italian, Slavic, German and Frankish Benedictines were spreading religion and spirituality that originated from the abbey of Cluny,[66] though the religious-cultural influence of Byzantium had also been quite strong in the country.[67] The churches constructed in Hungary in this age showed the influence of the early Christian basilica style: rectangular in plan, with a central nave terminating in an apse, as exemplified by the churches built at Székesfehérvár, Pécs, and Esztergom.[68]

In the twelfth century, French influence began to predominate in the realm through the activities of Cistercian monks and the Canons of Prémontré, who were aided by Hungarian clerics who had pursued their studies in Paris.[69] In the field of architecture, the Romanesque style played an increasing role, with its principle of the stone vault: stone or brick roof constructed on the arch; the barrel vault was semi-cylindrical in shape, while the groin vault resulted from two barrels intersecting at right angles. Churches built in Romanesque style at Apátfalva, Ják, Lébény and Véresszentkereszt may serve as good examples.[70] It was under the influence of Romanesque style that Hungarian historiography had made a start.[71]

In the latter half of the thirteenth century, after the Mongol onslaught, a religious revival had spread in the country, mainly through the activities of Franciscan and Dominican friars, who were supported by the Cistercian monks and the Hungarian Paulists.[72] Through the influence of German settlers (civilian population), German spirit and influence had gained the upper-hand in the realm leading to the development of Gothic style in Hungary, with its ribbed vaulting - the one in which a framework of ribs was supported by light masonry - and its pointed arch and flying buttress, as exemplified by the cathedrals in Kassa and the Church of the Great Mother of Hungary on Castle Hill of Buda.[73]

Toward the end of the century, the Church in Hungary undertook a missionary role in the Balkans, where "Catholic" and "Hungarian" became synonymous.[74] Italian and French cultural input gained deeper inroads in the realm, as evidenced by the illuminations of the already referred to Chronicle by Kálta, the *Chronicon pictum*.[75]

Besides the (fairly comprehensive) national *gesta*, there was another *Gesta Ungarorum* written in about 1235 - a work that had been referred to by Friar Ricardus in his report on the Dominican mission to, and in search of the Magyars who had stayed behind in the area east of the Sea of Azov in the ninth century.[76] The *Gesta Ungarorum* of 1235 dealt with the ur-history of the Magyars, provided questions concerning the fate and whereabouts of the Magyars who had remained behind - as if to support the plan of King Béla IV to convert the "pagan" Magyars to the Christian faith. The king's idea of missionary work must have coincided with the missionary policies of the Holy See at that time.[77]

Besides the reports of the Dominican friar Julian and his associates on their journey in search of the ur-country of the Magyars east of the Azov Sea, and on the approaching Mongol threat in the 1230's,[78] there were two descriptive histories that preserved for posterity the horrors of the Mongol invasion in the early 1240's. One was the *Epistola*, or, as it is known, *Carmen*, by the archpriest Rogerius of Várad, on the devastation of Hungary by the Tartars;[79] Rogerius had been named by the Holy See to a canon's benefice in the cathedral chapter of Nagyvárad; he had been captured by the Tartars with other members of his chapter, but had escaped from his captors.[80] His *Epistola* is truly a report by an eyewitness about the destruction of the country by the Mongols.

The other historical work is the writing by Thomas of Spaleto, an archpriest, who wrote about the high churchmen in Dalmatia of the thirteenth century, and on the account of his personal connections with the Church and ecclesiastics in Hungary; he also had much to say about the Mongol devastation of the country.[81] One may further mention the anonymous cleric-poet who wrote, perhaps during the winter of 1241-42, an elegy (*Planctus*) on the Mongol devastation of Hungary; he compared the country's previously existing conditions with the hardships that were caused by the Mongolian onslaught.[82]

The "Magyar" (Hungarian) linguistic remains date back to the eleventh-thirteenth centuries. They include: (1) the Founding Charter of Tihany Abbey, dated 1055, by King Andrew I (*ob.* 1060), a royal writ in Latin that also contains fifty-eight Hungarian words, including one sentence in Hungarian and nine suffices.[83] It must have been rather difficult to write and spell Hungarian words in a Latin text, the more so because in early Hungarian, suffices formed separate words. The founding charter was written in Roman *minuta erecta* script, and it may be looked upon as the first authentic document drafted and written in Hungarian. It is the oldest Magyar linguistic remain that has survived in the original.[84]

(2) The oldest coherent Magyar linguistic remains is the previously referred to "Sermon Over the Tomb," from around the year 1200, found in a Benedictine sacramentary called the Pray codex.[85] This *Sermo super sepulchrum* (caption in red) was a Hungarian burial homily recited at the site of the burial.[86] Next, a longer text of meditation [on death] followed, which was, because of its subject matter and trend of thought, in tune with the Hungarian homily, as if to explain it. The text of the Hungarian text comprised 26 lines, and six lines contained the Hungarian translation of the Prayer at the Tomb. The homily consisted of 227 words, the prayer of 47 words - a total of 274 Hungarian words that corresponded to 190 words of the dictionary.[87] The homily was well written. There must have been a reason for its appearance in one of the two liturgical sacramentaries of the period, only two of which had remained of the liturgical books in use in Árpádian Hungary prior to the Mongol invasion.[88]

(3) An Old-Magyar translation of a *Planctus Mariae*, an elegy on the Sorrows of the Mother of God, dated about 1300, and preserved in a codex at Louvain, would be another Hungarian linguistic document of the age. It was a Hungarian versification of the "Planctus Mariae" by Godefriedus de Sancto Victor [Godfrey, sub-prior at St. Victor's, *ob.* 1196]. It was an example of folk mysticism that offered a flavor of the flagellant movement of the time.[89] The Hungarian text of the elegy is, in part, a causal transliteration of the first half of the Planctus text that had been copied into the codex; and, in part, it is a paraphrase of the text, a total of 37 lines. The leaf of the codex that (must have) contained the Hungarian version [transliteration?] of the second half of the elegy had been torn from the codex. The Hungarian version of the elegy provided a promising beginning to Hungarian poetry and literature for ages to come.[90] The codex of Louvain was turned over to the National Széchenyi Library in Budapest in 1982.[91]

NOTES

1. Cf. J. Horváth, *A magyar irodalmi műveltség kezdetei* [The Beginnings of Hungarian Literary Culture], 2nd ed. (Budapest, 1944), 5ff.; Cyril Horváth, *A régi magyar irodalom története* [History of Early Hungarian Literature] (Budapest, 1899), 10ff.; Jenő Pintér, *Magyar irodalomtörténet* [History of Hungarian Literature: A Synthesis], 8 vols. (Budapest, 1930-410, I, 32ff. and 46ff.; Anonymus, *Gesta Ungarorum*, prologue, *SSH*, I, 33ff.; Macartney, 59ff.

2. L.J. Csóka, *A latin nyelvű történeti irodalom kialakulása Magyarországon a XI-XIV században* [Development of Latin Language Historical Literature in Hungary during the Eleventh-Fourteenth Centuries] (Budapest, 1967), 668f., discussed a sentence in the Chronicle, c. 82: "Est autem scriptum in antiquis libris de gestis Hungarorum;" *SSH*, I, 338,11-12, as a reference to an earlier historical source. Gy. Györffy, *Krónikáink és a magyar őstörténet* [Hungarian Chronicles on Early Hungarian History] (Budapest, 1948), 54, 69f.; J. Győry, *Gesta regum - gesta nobilium* (Budapest, 1948), 55, 92f. 95.

3. Cf. the references made by Anonymus: "ex falsis fabulis rusticorum, vel a garrulo cantu ioculatorum;" *SSH*, I, 33f., and compare with "...ut dicunt nostri ioculatores;" *ibid.*, I, 65,19; or "credite garrulis cantibus ioculatorum, ex falsis fabulis rusticorum," *ibid.*, I, 87,9-10, etc.; J. Horváth, *Műveltség*, 76ff. Friar Ricardus reporting to the Holy See on his mission to the Volga-Magyars, had referred to an early historical source - "scripta antiquorum" (*SSH*, II, 536,4-5) - as a [his] source of information on the early ["pagan"] Magyars, who had not entered Hungary in the 890's; Gyula Kristó, "Egy 1235 körüli Gesta Ungarorum körvonalairól" [On the Outline of a Gesta Ungarorum of around 1235], *Középkori kútfőink kritikus kérdései* [Critical Questions Concerning Medieval Hungarian Historical Sources], vol. 1 of *Memoria saeculorum Hungariae*, eds. J. Horváth and Gy. Székely (Budapest, 1974), 229ff.

4. Anonymus, cc. 24 and 25-27, especially: "...ut dicunt nostri ioculatores; omnes loca sibi aquirebant et nomen bonum accipiebant;" *SSH*, I, 65,19-20.

5. Cf. Ekkehardus, "Annales Sangallenis maiores," *MGHSS*, I, 77 (anno 913); "Annales Alemannici," anno 913, *ibid.*, I, 76; Regionis abbatis Prumiensis *Chronicon*, ed. F. Kurze, SSrG (Hannover, 1890), anno 917; and the Chronicle, c. 61, *SSH*, I, 309.

6. *Ibid.*, II, 497f. and note on 498; II, 475; Pintér, I, 117 and 170f.; on Gerard, see Kosztolnyik, *Five Kings*, 36ff. and 157f., nn. 9-24.

7. *Ibid.*, 14ff. and 135ff.; idem, *From Coloman*, 248ff. and 262ff.; Hóman-Szekfű, I, 181ff.; Hóman, *Ungarisches Mittelalter*, I, 173ff.; Péter Váczy, *A középkor története* [Medieval History], vol. 2 of *Egyetemes történet*, ed. B. Hóman *et al.*, 4 vols. (Budapest, 1936-38), 373ff.; Hampe, *Hochmittelalter*, 42f.; idem, "Kaiser Otto III und Rom," *HZ*, 140 (1929), 513ff.

8. A. Brackmann, "Die Anfänge der abendländischen Kulturbewegung in Osteuropa und deren Träger," in his *Gesammelte Aufsätze*, 2nd rev. ed. (Cologne-Graz, 1967); H. Hoffmann, "Von Cluny zum Investiturstreit," *Archiv für Kulturgeschichte*, 45 (1963), 165ff.

9. Cf. Csaba Csapodi, *A legrégibb magyar könyvtár benső rendje* [The Oldest Hungarian Library] (Budapest, 1957), on the book collection at the abbey of Pannonhalma. See further, P. Hilsch, "Der Bischof von Prag und das Reich in sächsischer Zeit," *Deutsches Archiv*, 28 (1972), 1ff.; Pintér, I, 124ff.

10. *SSH*, I, 188,6-12, and compare with "legenda maior," c. 4, *ibid.*, II, 380,7-20; Hartvic, "Life of King St. Stephen," c. 3, *ibid.*, II, 405,9-28; further, the

Chronicle, c. 38, *ibid.*, I, 295,17-26, and c. 205, *ibid.*, I, 492,25-31 (in reference only!) Bruno of Querfurt, "Vita s. Adalberti ep. et mart.," *MGHSS*, IV, 596ff., though Christianity struck roots only slowly - Kosztolnyik, *Five Kings*, 40 and 158f., n. 35; idem, "The negative results of the enforced missionary policy of King Saint Stephen of Hungary: The Uprising of 1046," *Catholic Historical Review*, 59 (1973-74), 569ff.; A.S. Czermann, *Die Staatsidee des hl. Stephan* (Klagenfurt, 1953); F. Pelsőczy, "Szent István, pap és király" [Saint Stephen: Priest and King], *Vigilia*, 36 (1971), 513ff.

11. *SSH*, I, 100,1-6; text of the founding charter in László Erdélyi (ed.), *A Pannonhalmi Szent Benedekrend története* [History of the Benedictines of Pannonhalma], 12 vols. (Budapest, 1902-07), I, 589f., with a facsimile, *ibid.*, I, 56; also, *MPL*, 151, 1253ff. (abbreviated!); *RA*, n. 2: it is an interpolated version of the authentic original! R.F. Kaindl, "Studien zur ungarischen Geschichte, iii-iv," *Archiv für österreichische Geschichtsforschung*, 82 (1895), 587ff., esp. 625ff.

12. Its charter (Batthyány, *Leges*, I, 385f.) is a falsification, cf. *RA*, n. 9, but there are references to it - see *RA*, n. 57, *ÁUO*, I, 38 (anno 1092); *RA*, n. 484, *ÁUO*, I, 292f.; further, *RA*, n.1131.

13. It is a falsification, cf. *RA*, n. 6; Péterffy, *Sacra concilia*, I, 4f.; J. Stilting, "Vita sancti Stephani regis Hungariae," *Acta Sanctorum*, Sept. I, 562ff.; it was a falsified writ based upon the charters of Pannonhalma and of the bishopric of Pécs; cf. *RA*, n. 93 (Batthyány, *Leges*, II, 249f.), transcribed by Andrew II in 1228, cf. *RA*, n. 446; *CD*, III-2, 118ff.

14. *RA*, n. 136, and nn. 43 and 46; *CD*, VII-4, 57f., and V-1, 311f.; Katona, *Historia critica*, III, 212f.

15. Falsification, *RA*, n. 8; Batthyány, *Leges*, I, 383f.

16. Erdélyi, *Rendtörténet*, X, 487ff., but the character of Tihany is authentic - *RA*, n. 12; Marczali, *Enchiridion*, 81ff.; further, *RA*, n. 23; Erdélyi, X, 496; Kosztolnyik, *Five Kings*, 179, n. 58; Pintér, I, 111ff. [and I, 136]; Horváth, *Műveltség*, 25.

17. *RA*, n. 24; Marczali, *Enchiridion*, 100ff., even though it may not be an authentic version in its present form. Pintér, I, 96ff.; Remig Békefi, *A káptalani iskolák története Magyarországon* [History of the Cathedral Schools in Hungary] (Budapest, 1910), 44ff.; for documentation, *SSH*, II, 494 (Gerard's "Vita maior," c. 10); Knauz, I, 42; L. Fejérpataky, *Kálmán király oklevelei* [Diplomas Issued by King Coloman the Learned], Értekezések a tört. tud. köréből, XV-5 (Budapest, 1892), 43; Kosztolnyik, *Five Kings*, 24ff. and 147, nn. 22-24; on the school at Pannonhalma, cf. Erdélyi, *Rendtörténet*, I, 590; Csóka, 619ff.

18. Horváth, *Irodalmi műveltség*, 13ff.;

19. The Tihany Charter, *RA*, n. 12; Marczali, *Enchiridion*, 81ff.; Emil Jakubovich and Dezső Pais (eds.), *Ó-Magyar Olvasókönyv* [Old Hungarian Reader: Introduction to and Collection of Early Historic and Literary Documents in Hungary] (Pécs, 1929), 18ff.

20. Cf. "Leges s. Stephani regis," in Emma Bartoniek, *Szent István törvényeinek XII századi kézirata, az admonti kódex* [The Admont Codex of the Laws of King St. Stephen] (Budapest, 1935), 15ff., with facsimile; text also in *RHM*, 319ff.; Kosztolnyik, *Five Kings*, 110ff.

21. Cf. J. Félegyházy, "Történeti irodalmunk kezdetei" [The Beginnings of Hungarian Historical Literature], *Vigilia*, 34 (1969), 329ff.; Pintér, I, 172ff.

22. Cf. Hartvic's "Life of King St. Stephen," c. 24, *SSH*, II, 342ff.; *Acta Sanctorum*, Sept. I, 562ff.; "Life of St. Emeric," c. 7, *ibid.*, Nov. II-1, 487ff.; *SSH*, II, 458ff.; Berthold's "Chronicon," *MGHSS*, VI, 438f.; *CD*, I, 460ff.; J. Karácsonyi, *Szent Gellért élete és müvei* [Life and Works of St. Gerard] (Budapest, 1887); further,

SSH, II, 478f. and 504f.; Kosztolnyik, *Five Kings*, 94, 97, and 200. Gy. Balanyi, "Magyar szentek, szentéletű magyarok" [Hungarian Saints, Saintly Hungarians], *Katolikus Szemle*, 15 (Rome, 1963), 100ff.
23. See *RHM*, 310ff.; Marczali, *Enchiridion*, 69ff.; Felix Schiller, "Das erste ungarische Gesetzbuch und das deutsche Recht," *Festschrift Heinrich Brunner* (Weimar, 1910), 379ff.; J. v. Sawicki, "Zur Textkritik und Entstehungsgeschichte der Gesetze König Stefan des Heiligen," *Ungarische Jahrbücher*, 9 (1929), 395ff.; J. Madzsar, "Szent István törvényei és az u.n. symachusi hamisitványok" [King St. Stephen's Laws and the So-called Pseudo-Symachus], *SIE*, II, 204ff. F. Banfi, "Vita di s. Gerardo de Venezia nel codice 1622 della Bibliotheca universitarie de Padova," *Benedictina*, 2 (1948), 262ff., with text following 288ff.
24. *RHM*, 325ff.; Marczali, *Enchiridion*, 88ff.; Kosztolnyik, *From Coloman*, 3ff.; L. Mezey (ed.), *Athleta patriae. Tanulmányok Szent László történetéhez* [Studies on the History of King St. Ladislas] (Budapest, 1980), and my review of this volume in *Catholic Historical Review*, 68 (1982), 130f.; idem, "Ungarn und Europa im 12 Jahrhundert," *Vorträge und Forschungen*, 12 (1968), 255ff.
25. *SSH*, II, 619ff.; *RHM*, 299ff.; Marczali, *Enchiridion*, 63ff.
26. On background, see M.L.W. Laistner, *Thought and Letters in Western Europe, AD 500-900*, 2nd ed. (London, 1957), 315ff.; R. McKitterick (ed.), *The Carolingians and the Written Word* (Cambridge, 1989), 37ff., 60ff.; Hincmar of Rheims, "De regis persona et regio ministerio," *MPL*, 125, 833ff., written for Charles the Bald; idem, *De ordine palatii. MGH Fontes iuris Germanici antiqui*, iii, ed. Th. Gross and R. Schieffer (Hannover, 1980), 32ff.; on Hincmar, Heinz Löwe (ed.), Wattenbach-Levison, *Deutschlands Geschichtsquellen im Mittelalter*, segment 5 (Weimar, 1973), 516ff. Also, Jonas of Orleans, "De institutione regia," *MPL*, 106, 279ff.; Sedulius Scotus, *De rectoribus Christianis*, ed. S. Hellmann (Munich, 1906), 19ff.
27. Unlike Jonas' report on Louis the Pious' unhappy quarrel with his sons, and his abdication - in order to avoid misgovernment! - *MPL*, 106, 283ad, but in the spirit of Sedulius Scotus: a wise ruler summons wise men to his council and does nothing without their advice - Hellmann, 38,16-18; (also, *ibid.*, 86,5-10, that the king is the vicar of God in the government of the Church [in his realm!]). Also, Hincmar, *De ordine palatii*, 44,113-125, on the monarch. His ideas were borrowed from Adalhard of Corby's "De ordine palatii" - Laistner, 317.
28. Cf. *SSH*, II, 347ff., text 357ff.; Pintér, I, 159ff. The name of Bishop Mór (Maurus) appeared on the founding charter of Tihany abbey (a. 1055), cf. *RA*, n. 12; Marczali, *Enchiridion*, 81ff., 85; D. Vargha (ed.), *Szent Mór emlékkönyv* [Memorial Volume in Honor of St. Maurus] (Pannonhalma, 1936), 363ff.
29. *SSH*, II, 363ff.; *MGHSS*, XI, 222ff.; L. Hain, *Repertorium bibilographicum*, 2 vols. in 4 (Stuttgart-Tübingen, 1826-38; repr. Milan, 1948), II-1, nn. 9996-98; Macartney, 161ff.; Kosztolnyik, *Five Kings*, 200. Gy. Kristó, "A nagyobbik és a Hartvic legenda szövegkapcsolataihoz" [Textual similarities Between King St. Stephen's "Vita maior" and the Hartvic "Life of King St. Stephen"], *Acta historica Szegediensis*, 90 (1990), 43ff.; Horváth, *Stílusproblémák*, 136ff.
30. Csóka, 105ff. and 154ff.
31. *SSH*, II, 463ff.; *Acta Sanctorum*, Sept. VI; Karácsonyi, *Szent Gellért*, passim; J. Balogh, "Szent Gellért és a «Symphonia Ungarorum»" [St. Gerard and the «Symphonia Ungarorum»], *Magyar Nyelv* (Budapest, 1926), offprint; Pintér, I, 269ff.; Kosztolnyik, *Five Kings*, 16ff and 135, nn. 2-34.
32. *Ibid.*, 46ff. and 161ff., nn. 2-45; "Deliberatio supra hymnum trium puerorum," -cf. G. Silagi, Untersuchung *zur «Deliberatio» des Gerhard von Csanád*, Münchener Beiträge zur Mediävistik und Renaissance Forschung (Munich, 1967); Irén Zoltvány, "A magyarországi bencés irodalom a tatárjárás előtt" [Benedictine

Literature in Hungary Prior to the Tartar Invasion], Erdélyi, *Rendtörténet*, I, 337ff.; Gy. Györffy, "A magyar egyházszervezés kezdeteiről az újabb forráskritikai vizsgálatok alapján" [The Origins of Ecclesiastical Organization in Hungary According to the Results of Latest Research], *A Magyar Tudományos Akadémia* II osztályának *Közleményei*, 18 (1969), 199ff.

33. Cf. *SSH*, II, 509ff., text 515ff.; *Acta Sanctorum*, Iun. VII, 286ff.; Macartney, 171ff.; Csóka, 226ff. and 526f.; Horváth, Stílusproblémák, 188ff.; Pintér, I, 272ff.

34. Kosztolnyik, *From Coloman*, 267ff. and 284, nn. 2-17; J. Török, "Szent László a középkori magyarországi liturgiában" [St. Ladislas in the Medieval Hungarian Liturgy], in Mezey, *Athleta patriae*, 135ff.

35. Kosztolnyik, *From Coloman*, 269f. and 285, nn. 23-30; Hóman-Szekfű, I, 395ff.; Horváth, *Irodalom kezdetei*, 24ff.; Gy. Györffy, "A magyar krónikák adata a III Béla-kori peticióról" [Entries in the Hungarian Chronicles on Written Petitions at the Court of Béla III], *Memoria Hungariae*, 1, 333ff.

36. Pintér, I, 251ff.; Horváth, *Irodalom kezdetei*, 80f. and 83ff.

37. See Jakubovich-Pais, 65ff., based upon a reading of the text persevered in the Pray Codex; on the latter, see Polycarp Radó, *Libri liturgici manuscripti bibliothecarum Hungariae* (Budapest, 1947), 31ff., esp. 58 (in reference to the codex, fol. 136).

38. Hóman-Szekfű, I, 390ff.; Csóka, 453ff. and 495ff.; Friedrich Heer, *Europäische Geistesgeschichte*, 2nd ed. (Stuttgart, 1965), 96ff.; Alfons Lhotsky, "Otto von Freising: seine Weltanaschauung," in his *Aufsätze und Vorträge*, vol. 1 (Vienna, 1970), 64ff.; Dempf, *Sacrum imperium*, 229ff.; J.J. Baldwin, *The Government of Philip Augustus* (Berkeley-Oxford, 1986), 362ff.; Antonia Gransden, *Historical Writing in England, 550-1307* (Ithaca, NY, 1974), 356ff.; Kosztolnyik, *From Coloman*, 166ff.

39. Csóka, 660ff., esp. 668, Györffy, *Krónikáink*, 69f., in reference to *SSH*, II, 535f.; "...est autem scriptum in antiquis libris de gestis Hungarorum," *ibid.*, I, 338,11-12; A. Tarnai, "A Képes Krónika forrásaihoz" [Some Remarks on the Source Material for the Chronicle], *Memoria Hungariae*, 1, 203ff.

40. Cf. Kornél Szlovák, "Wer war der Anonyme Notar? Zur Bestimmung des Verfassers der Gesta Ungarorum," *Ungarn Jahrbuch*, 19 (1991), 1ff.

41. *SSH*, I, 33,5-25.

42. *Ibid.*, I, 33f.; Kosztolnyik, art. cit., in *Vorlesungen* (1986); Győry, *Gesta regum*, 64f.; J. Leclercq, "L'humanisme Bénédictine du VIIIe eu XIIe siècle," *Studia Anselmiana*, 20 (1948), 1ff.; Csóka, 499ff.

43. The «Dream of Emese» in Anonymus, c. 3, *SSH*, I, 38,51-2; the «Legend of the White Horse» in Anonymus, c. 14, *ibid.*, I, 53f.

44. *Ibid.*, I, 35,6-15 [c. 1]; I, 53f. [c. 14]; I, 101,15-19 [c. 50]; his referring to sources, *ibid.*, I, 87,7-11 and 87,14-16. On Attila, see also Bóna, *Húnok*, 57ff., and 62.

45. *Ibid.*, I, 116f. [c. 57].

46. Horváth, *Stílusproblémák*, 196ff.

47. Anonymus, c. 1, *SSH*, I, 34,14-19.

48. *Ibid.*, I, 39f., c. 5.

49. *Ibid.*, I, 50ff., cc. 12-14.

50. Horváth, *Irodalom kezdetei*, 35ff.

51. *SSH*, I, 33f., 65,19, 87,8-16.

52. *Ibid.*, I, 94,6-23; Szlovák, in *Ungarn Jahrbuch* (1991), 1ff.; P. Váczy, "Anonymus és kora" [Anonymus and his Age], *Memoria Hungariae*, 1, 13ff., dated Anonymus early thirteenth century.

53. Cf. Simon de Kéza, *Gesta Ungarorum*, c. 1, in *SSH*, I, 141; Macartney, 89ff.; Pintér, I, 275ff.

54. Kéza, c. 2, *SSH*, I, 141f.
55. Kéza, cc. 27 and 21, *ibid.*, I, 165f. and 612f.; Bóna, *Húnok*, 63ff.
56. Kéza, cc. 7-23.
57. Kéza, c. 24, *ibid.*, I, 164.
58. Kéza, cc. 4-5 and cc. 24-94; Kosztolnyik, *Five Kings*, ixf.; A. Bartha, *Hungarian Society in the 9th and 10th Centuries* (Budapest, 1975), 47ff., and my review in *American Historical Review*, 83 (1978), 1243f.
59. Kéza, cc. 3-23, and cc. 24-94; Horváth, *Stílusproblémák*, 350ff.
60. Kéza, cc. 95-99.
61. H. Homeyer, *Attila* (Berlin, 1951), 161ff. and 174ff. Bóna, *Húnok*, 92 and 187ff.; Adolph Bachmann, "Die Völker an der Donau nach Attilas Tode," *AföG*, 61 (1880), 189ff.
62. Szűcs, in *Memoria Hungariae*, 1, 187ff.
63. *SSH*, I, 239ff.; D. Dercsényi, *Chronicon pictum: Képes Krónika*, 2 vols. (Budapest, 1963), vol. 1: facsimile; Macartney, 133ff.
64. *SSH*, I, 239, c. 1; D. Dercsényi, *Nagy Lajos kora* [Louis the Great of Hungary and his Age] (Budapest, n.d. [1941]), 61ff.
65. *SSH*, I, 479ff., cc. 188, etc.
66. Hóman, *Ungarisches Mittelalter*, I, 307f.; P.v. Váczy, *Die erste Epoche des ungarischen Königtums* (Pécs, 1935), 50ff and 92ff.; A. Brackmann, "Die politische Wirkung der kluniazenischen Bewegung," in his *Gesammelte Aufsätze*, 2nd rev. ed. (Cologne-Graz, 1967), 290ff.; idem, "Die Anfänge der abendländischen Bewegung in Osteuropa und deren Träger," *ibid.*, 76ff.; J. Deér, "Szent István politikai és egyházi orientációja" [King St. Stephen's Political and Ecclesiastical Orientation], *Katolikus Szemle*, 1 (Rome, 1949), 27ff.
67. Cf. Jakubovich-Pais, 14ff.; F. Dölger, "Die mittelalterliche Kultur auf dem Balkan als byzantinische Erbe," in his *Byzanz und die europäische Staatenwelt*, rev. ed. (Darmstadt, 1964); Czermann, 10, 24, 44; Gy. Moravcsik, "Die archaisierenden Namen der Ungarn in Byzanz," *Byzantinische Zeitschrift*, 20 (1929-30), 247ff., reprinted in his *Studia Byzantina* (Budapest, 1967), 320ff.
68. See Ernst Adam, *Baukunst des Mittelalters*, 2 vols. vols. ix-x of *Ullstein Kunstgeschichte* (Frankfurt am Main-Berlin, 1963), I, 38ff. and 66ff.; Th. v. Bogyay, "L'iconographie de la «Porta speciosa» d'Esztergom et ses sources d'inspiration," *Revue des études byzantines*, 8 (1950), 85ff.; A. Kralovánszky, "The Settlement History of Veszprém and Székesfehérvár in the Middle Ages," in L. Gerevich (ed.), *Towns in Medieval Hungary* (Budapest, 1990), 51ff.
69. Archbishop Lukács of Esztergom was a former student in Paris; "vidi Parisius Lucam Hungarum in schola magistri Girardi Puellae, virum honestum et bene literatum." Cf. Th. Wright (ed.), Gualteri Mapes, *De nugis curialium distinctiones quinque* (London, 1850), 73, dist. ii:7; on Walter Map, see G.O. Sayles, *The Medieval Foundations of England* (London, 1948), 369 and A.L. Poole, *From Domesday Book to Magna Carta*, 2nd ed. (Oxford, 1955), 239. On the archbishop, cf. Z.J. Kosztolnyik, "The Church and Béla III of Hungary, 1172-96: The Role of Archbishop Lukács of Esztergom," *Church History*, 49 (1988), 375ff.; A. Gábriel, "Angol-magyar kultúrkapcsolatok a párizsi egyetemen" [Anglo-Hungarian Cultural Ties at the University of Paris], *Uj Hungária Évkönyv,1959* (Munich, 1958), 73ff.
70. Adams, *Baukunst*, II, 38ff.; I, 101ff., Hans Jantzen, *Kunst der Gothik* (Hamburg, 1957), 147ff.; K. Bosl et al., *Eastern and Western Europe in the Middle Ages* (London, 1970), 85ff., 175ff., and 189f.
71. Hóman, *Ungarisches Mittelalter*, I, 407ff.
72. Hóman-Szekfű, I, 556ff.; F. Hervay, "A Pálos Rend elterjedése a középkori Magyarországon" [The Expansion of the Paulist Order in Medieval Hungary], *Mályusz Elemér emlékkönyv*, 159ff.; G. Gyöngyösi, *Vitae Fratrum*

316   HUNGARY IN THE THIRTEENTH CENTURY

eremitarum ordinis sancti Pauli primi eremitae, ed. F.L. Hervay (Budapest, 1988), and my review in *Catholic Historical Review*, 76 (1990), 125f.; Andor Tarnai, "A magyar nyelvet írni kezdék" [They Began to Write in Hungarian], in *Irodalmi gondolkodás a középkori Magyarországon* [Literary Thinking in Medieval Hungary] (Budapest, 1984), 103ff.

73. Adams, II, 25ff.; H.R. Hahnloser, *Villard de Honnecourt* (Vienna, 1935); Erwin Panofsky, *Gothic* (Meridian repr. 1985); L. Gerevich, "The Rise of Hungarian Towns Along the Danube," in his *Towns in Medieval Hungary*, 26ff., esp. 38ff.; J. Csemegi, *A budavári főtemplom középkori építéstörténete* [Architectural History of the Main Church in Buda in the Middle Ages] (Budapest, 1955), 54ff.; M.M. Takács, *A budavári Mátyás templom* [The Matthias Church in Buda Castle] (Budapest, 1940).

74. Cf. *supra*, 283, n. 79; Kosztolnyik, *art. cit.*, *AHC* (1990).

75. Dercsényi, *Nagy Lajos*, 141ff.; E. Mályusz, "A Képes Krónika kiadásia" [The Editions of the Chronicle], *Memoria Hungariae*, 1, 167ff.; Dercsényi, *Chronicon pictum*, II, 7ff.

76. "Inventum fuit in Gestis Ungarorum Christianorum...;" Ricardus, preface, *SSH*, II, 535,3; Kristó, in *Memoria*, 1, 229ff.; Katona, *Tatárjárás*, 7ff. Further, "in Gestis Ungarorum inventis," *SSH*, II, 536,1; "sciebant per scripta antiquarum, quod...;" *ibid.*, II, 536,4-5; Ricardus spoke of "Ungaria maior," *ibid.*, II, 535,4, where the Magyars, "sicut et hodie sunt pagani;" *ibid.*, II, 535,12. Csóka, 668, had suggested two different sources; he regarded the expression "scripta antiquorum" in connection with the sentence in the Chronicle, c. 82: "est autem scriptum in antiquis libris de gestis Hungarorum," *SSH*, I, 338,11-12; on this, also Györffy, *Krónikáink*, 54, 69f.

77. Ricardus, *SSH*, I, 535ff.; letter of Pope Gregory IX, in Potthast, n. 11033; *ÁUO*, VII,123f.; *VMH*, n. 338; also, Potthast, n. 11025; *ÁUO*, VII, 131; *VMH*, n. 336. It is the learned opinion of Kristó that the "Gesta Ungarorum Christianorum" mentioned by Ricardus was a new opus of about 1235, a work that dealt with the problem(s) of the early Magyars. Kristó in supporting his theory refers to Regionis abbatis Prumiensis *Chronicon*, ed. F. Kurze, SSrG (Hannover, 1890), 131f., who spoke of the early Magyars "in oriente;" or, Gottfried of Viterbo, *Pantheon*, spoke of two countries of the Magyars, with the remark that they migrated from their "primo regno" to Pannonia, *MGHSS*, XXI, 103f. and 133, when Gottfried, speaking of the Scythian Avars (he meant pre-Magyars), observed that their country was located above [north of?] the meadows of the Meotis; in other words, Gottfried had no knowledge of the Magyars living eastward in the twelfth century. One may mention here the writ of Gregory IX to Béla IV (July 1, 1241), words of consolation; Potthast, n. 11042; *VMH*, n. 342; *CD*, IV-1, 228f.

78. See *SSH*, II, 535ff.

79. *SSH*, II, 551ff.

80. *SSH*, II, 545ff.; Horváth, *Stílusproblémák*, 239ff.; Pintér, I, 730f.

81. Cf. *Mon. hist. Slav. merid.*, XXVI, 3ff.; *MGHSS*, XXIX, 570ff.; Schwandtner, III, 532ff.; Pintér, I, 731.

82. *SSH*, II, 593ff.; Pintér, I, 288f.

83. *RA*, n. 12; Jakubovich-Pais, 19ff.; Erdélyi, *Rendtörténet*, X, 487ff.; and *SSH*, I, 345,17-19.

84. István Hajnal, "Kézmüvesség, írásbeliség és európai fejlődés" [Handicrafts, Literacy, and Cultural Progress], *Századok*, 123 (1989), 407ff. - scheduled for publication in 1948! Further, Pintér, I, 111ff.; Kosztolnyik, *Five Kings*, 77f., 178f., nn. 55, 57-58; Horváth, *Irod. müv.*, 50.

85. Discovered by Austin Canon Xystus Schier (d. 1772), before the Jesuit George Pray - cf. Jakubovich-Pais, 65ff.; in the Pray codex, according to latest numbering of the leaves, on fol. 136 - Radó, *Libri*, 36ff., here 58; Pintér, I, 263ff.; C.

Horváth, *Regi irodalom*, 48ff.; F. Kühár, "A Pray-kódex rendeltetése, sorsa, szellemtörténeti értéke" [Purpose and Ideological Value of the Pray Codex], *MKSz*, 63 (1939), 213ff.
86. Thirty-two lines of Hungarian text, including six lines of prayer.
87. Jakubovich-Pais, 67f.
88. Márián R. Prikkel, "A Pray kódex," in Erdélyi, *Rendtörténet*, I, 439ff. On codices containing sermons, cf. R. Szentiványi, *Catalogus concinnus librorum manuscriptorum Bibliothecae Batthyanianae Albae in Transylvania* (Szeged, 1958), 229f., n. 412).
89. Cf. *SSH*, I, 469f.; Jakubovich-Pais, 123ff. On summarizing the results of recent research, cf. András Vízkeleti, *"Világ világa, virágnak virágja..."* (*Ó-magyar Mária Siralom*) [Planctus: An Old-Hungarian Marian Poem] (Budapest, 1986), passim; idem, "Die altungarische Marienklage und die mit ihr überlieferten Texte," *Acta Litteraria*, 1986, 3ff. - a 24 page reprint.
90. László Mezey, *Irodalmi anyanyelvűségünk kezdetei az árpádkor végén* [Beginnings of Hungarian Literature at the End of the Árpád Age] (Budapest, 1955), 18ff. On Godfrey, cf. F.J.E. Raby, *A History of Secular Latin Poetry*, 2 vols., 2nd ed. (Oxford, 1957), II, 13f.; idem, *A History of Christian Latin Poetry*, 2nd ed. (Oxford, 1953), 297, note 3. Text in G.M. Dreves and C. Blume, *Ein Jahrtausend lateinischer Dichtung* (Leipzig, 1909), 281f.; and J. Kehrein, *Lateinische Sequenzen des Mittelalters aus Handschriften und Drucken* (Mainz, 1873), 177f.; Ede Petrovich, "A pécsi egyetemi beszédgyüjtemény (a müncheni kódex)" [The Sermon Collection at the University of Pécs (The Munich Codex)], *Jubileumi tanulmányok a pécsi egyetem történetéböl* [Studies on the Jubilee of the University of Pécs], ed. A. Csizmadia, vol. I (Pécs, 1967), 163ff
91. See report in *Magyar Hírek* (Budapest), May 29, 1982; F. Pusztai, "Ami van, mibőllett?" [Anything About The Background?], *Élet és irodalom*, November 7, 1986, 12.

2. *Towns and Townships*

One cannot seriously discuss royal policy for establishing towns in Hungary before the reign of Béla IV.[1] (The royal writs attributed to Andrew II granting tax-exempt status to locations named Dés and Garmszentbenedek were forgeries.)[2] One may summarize, however, from the available sources that towns like Esztergom, Székesfehérvár, Győr, Sopron, or Pest and Zagreb, were of earlier origin, and had, as ecclesiastical or trading centers, served a defensive military purpose also.[3]

Esztergom, Székesfehérvár, Győr, and Zagreb were settlements dating back to the tenth and eleventh centuries. Built on Roman foundations, their Latin population formed Roman folk remnant, much like the Latin population of some villages (hamlets) in Transdanubia [the area south and west of the Danube] - Pleidell noted in his already cited essay.[4] Rogerius recorded in the 1240's that, for example, the predominant social stratum in Esztergom comprised, next to the Magyar population, Franks and Lombards; most probably, he was referring to the social structure and conditions of Várad (where he was archpriest until the arrival of the Mongols, and where Franks and Lombards had been living [together] for a long period of time).[5]

The basis for town developments in medieval Hungary had thus been formed in Roman times.[6] Esztergom, Fehérvár, Győr, Sopron all date back to earlier beginnings, though one may question the regional tradition, "local color," and patriotism of their inhabitants. That is to say, those old "town" settlements had no hinterland to speak of for further development, had no "town limits;" the royal court expanded their territorial limits - to include some smaller populated areas in the surroundings of those towns, whereby the early town core had formed the nucleus of a new growing township. For instance, Béla IV had, in 1269, donated the lands of the Sopron fort personnel (*ministeriales*) to the town of Sopron, thereby increasing the town's territory;[7] and, Ladislas IV had acted in a similar manner in 1277.[8]

Although the towns of Roman origin had in such a fashion formed the roots [foundations] of town settlement and institutions in Hungary, the merchants of the towns remained unperturbed about changes in the political leadership of their communities. The merchant paid attention to his own business interests, and displayed little curiosity about political affairs of the country at large. He only became concerned with politics when the political leaders at the local (or higher) level seemed to be less than willing to assure him of the basic conditions needed for carrying out his activities in trade, or in commerce. He had not heard of "country values," nor had he even realized their proper meaning. The social welfare of his "fellow citizens" - other social groups living in the town, probably at a lower social level - and the freedom and work opportunities of the town's lower social strata barely concerned him.[9]

Even with the opportunity, the merchant would not think of speaking about, or demanding "political rights" before the monarch, or his regional potentate, because he depended on the good will and protection of the king, or the king's regional reeve, and the local bishop. Even the Frank merchant named Samo who, tradition has it, had organized the Czech lands into a political unit, had established contact with his "subjects" (business partners), as a businessman, and it was commercial-business interests, not patriotism, that guided his attitude toward them.[10] Regarding it from this point of view, one may recall that the early Magyars, living under Khazar rule in the mid-ninth century, had entered into the world of international trade (though, to maintain that it was the Magyars who had founded Kiev would be absurd.)[11] It remains a historic record that Kievan fur merchants paid regular visits, made regular business trips to Esztergom during the twelfth and thirteenth centuries.[12]

In his description of Hungary during the second crusade, Odo de Deogilo spoke of the Danube as one of the arteries of international trade, where numerous ships had carried the goods and riches of various districts to the known city of Esztergom; "et multarum regionum divitias nobili civitati Estrigim navigio convehit."[13] The region, Odo remarked, was rich in the production of agricultural goods.[14]

Odo's statements are supported by the earlier annotations made by Cosmas of Prague, who had referred to Esztergom as the capital of Hungary, the see of the archbishop, and the center of the country's trade. It was in Esztergom where merchants - Germans, Poles, Kievans, and Italians - came to sell their linen, fabrics, hides, and domestic utensils. The Hungarian sold corn, wheat, wines, hides, animals, iron ore, and metals in Esztergom.[15] In other words, commercial routes in medieval Europe went through Hungary. The country's social strata active in commerce and trade held interest in developing town life - partly before the Mongol invasion, and definitely after the 1240's when the Hungarian court had seriously implemented town policy by involving the merchant stratum, be it Hungarian or "foreign" (Jewish and Moslem) men of trade and commerce. Towns played a role in the military defense plans of the realm. Fortified towns had resisted the Mongol onslaught in 1241-42 and had slowed it down.[16] There arose a need for new fortified towns during the thirteenth century, when the royal court had real fear of the Mongols' striking again, as they did, on a much smaller scale, in the 1280's.[17]

The early German hypothesis that Hungarian town life had developed under German influence, on the grounds that the Magyars were not town builders, and Roman towns in Pannonia had been swept away by the barbarian invasions, is unacceptable.[18] On the other hand, the viewpoint that towns had developed next to a fort, or a bishop's seat, as if to benefit from their protection, is also applicable in Hungarian context - as evidenced by the already cited examples of Esztergom, Sopron, and even Székesfehérvár.[19]

Sopron was of Celtic origin, surrounded by six to eight meter high ramparts of burned hard clay that were not destroyed by the Romans, who used them as an insert in the two meter thick walls they had built.[20] The location itself was a bishop's residence in the late sixth century, and by the mid-ninth century, it was a flourishing church center, even though Einhard had referred to it as "...locu site desertus - deserta civitas;" probably the [a former] Fort of King Odo (Ödenburg, or Pusztavár in Hungarian) meaning "Fort Wasteland."[21]

The town [*civitas?*] of Esztergom also had pre-Magyar beginnings in that a "civitas Latinorum" stood there in the early Middle Ages; Roman foundation(s) served as a base for Hungarian town development. The merchant class was not disturbed by the emergence of a new political stratum in its already established business circle.[22] It was in Esztergom that Prince Géza had held his court in the second half of the tenth century; public opinion regarded the town as the headquarters of Attila the Hun, and a Frank chronicler made a distinction between the royal fort and town, separating the "Latin" episcopal segment of the settlement from e area inhabited by the "foreigners."[23]

The territorial and public rights of the various social strata had not even changed much after 1242. Also Székesfehérvár was of Roman origin, a *claustrum* [*curta?*], as witnessed by recent excavations. Marshes surrounded it from all sides; in times of troubles the inhabitants of the countryside had fled behind its walls for protection since ancient memory.[24]

The first instance of Béla IV's deliberate town-building policy could have been his town privileges issued for Nagyszombat in 1238; mainly, it was a charter of freedom. In this charter, the monarch determined the legal, judicial, military rights and obligations of the Nagyszombat *cives*. These responsibilities included the right for the *cives* to elect their own judges, to enjoy the same privileges "like the citizens" of Fehérvár in paying toll, exchanging money, electing the parish priest(s), to move freely in or out of the community, and the necessarily related judicial regulations.[25] In reading the text of the royal writ, especially the first two paragraphs - "ut ad regiam coronam specialiter pertineant" - and the ninth paragraph, one gains the impression that the monarch had the writ issued to protect himself and the Crown from the high nobility, as if to stress the need for the existing relationship between himself and the *cives*, and among the citizenry; "...uillicus omnes inter eos uel extraneos eis exortas iudicandi in quacunque lite ciuli uel criminali habeat facultatem."[26]

The letter Béla IV had sent to Pope Gregory IX requesting aid against the Tartars was dated from Zagreb,[27] where the bishop's see had been established by Ladislas I.[28] In 1242, Béla IV had determined the various rights of the *hospites* of the town to be founded on Grech Hill in Zagreb ("in Zagrabia in monte Grech"), and their obligations to fortify the hill.[29] "Et illam partem regni ad securitatem confinii et alia commode munire et firmare," to support his concept that the "foundations" of the town, that is, establishing a fortified township adjacent to the already existing town-core, the bishop's see, served a defensive military purpose.[30]

The writ for Zagreb did not mention that a town had existed there before; the "Latin town" in Zagreb - that is, the bishop's town - and the "royal town" established by Béla IV did not form one unified township. Its jurors [town council] and judges had acted and existed separately during the medieval period.[31] The earlier writ by King Emery, dated 1198, only confirmed the privileges and immunities of the episcopal town of Zagreb, granted by his predecessors. [32] A letter, dated 1266, by Béla IV rewarded the *cives* of the *royal town* ("fideles nostri ciues eisdem castri") with tax exemptions and other privileges, including the obligation the constructing the walls of (the town of) Zagreb.[33]

In the case of the town of Zólyom, the monarch in a writ confirmed their charter of privileges that had been lost during the Mongol onslaught, and recognized the existence of earlier town settlement there.[34]

Pest as a place-name had appeared in a royal writ of 1148, concerning the tax tariffs of the harbor of Pest on the Danube.[35] Béla IV had further issued a writ in Pest on February 7, 1240, and one on March 13 in Buda.[36] In Pest after the Mongol invasion one could speak of a town transfer from the left- to the right-hand bank of the Danube.[37] The right bank ferry terminal on the river had been under the administration of Pest, on the left bank of the river. The deed of transfer of the town from the left bank of the Danube to the right bank lacks direct written documentation; the Law Code of Buda mentioned that one-third of the taxes due to Buda were payable by (the inhabitants of) Pest.[38] The judiciary position of the Judge of Buda was held by a member of the town council of Buda, and Buda had the right to inspect and tax goods entering its harbor - a right the town of Pest had previously obtained from Béla IV. The monarch had further confirmed the possessions the citizens of Buda - now, New Pest - had received from him after the Mongol invasion.[39]

Pest, like Székesfehérvár and Esztergom, had always been granted tax-exempt status by King St. Stephen; such a conclusion can be based upon a writ by Béla IV, where he confirmed anew the privileges and obligations of the "hospites nostri de Pesth," asserting that "cum esset notaria, duximus renouandum et presentibus annotandum."[40] The newcomers had been referred to as Ismaelites by the chronicler. The Hungarian chronicler observed that in Pest, "castrum, quod dicitur Pest," Volga Bulgarians had settled down earlier;[41] the name of Pest had also appeared in other historical sources dealing with events of the eleventh century, as, for instance, the reference to "portus, qui vulgo dicitur Pesth."[42]

The migrant inhabitants (*hospites*) of Beregszász (Luprechtzaz) obtained royal recognition of their privileges and duties in 1247,[43] and in the following year, the *cives* of Nyitra, who already held certain liberties, were granted privileges like those held by the citizens (*cives*) of Székesfehérvár; "licet ipsi fuissent prius libertatis utique commendandae...."[44] One ought to note that while earlier royal writs stressed the rights and obligations of migrants (*hospites*) as town dwellers, this royal writ spoke of the king's citizens of Fort Nyitra, "fideles nostri ciues castri Nitriensis," who had heroically defended their fort from the Tartars.[45] Nyitra was already mentioned in 836 by the bishop of Salzburg;[46] the settlement had functioned as an episcopal see in the 880's.[47]

In 1253, Vágújhely gained royal letters of privileges,[48] as did the migrants (*hospites*) of Besztercebánya in 1255.[49] The migrants of Füzitő were granted liberties similar to the *civitas* Buda in judicial court proceedings in the year 1263.[50] Béla IV likewise assured privileges similar to those held by the settlers in Buda for the foreign settlers in Komárom in 1265 - thereby establishing their town.[51] (Prince Coloman, younger brother of Béla IV, had issued, in 1231, a letter of liberties for the German, Saxon, Hungarian, and Slovene settlers in Vukovar in Croatia - it was the town's founding charter - so as to underline his support for the town policies of his royal brother.)[52] The foreigners of Késmárk in Sepes [northern Hungary] received their royal charter in 1269; "supplicationibus hospitum nostrorum de Kesmark in Scepis inclitani, hanc eis libertatem duximus condendam," thereby bringing to a conclusion the town establishment policy of Béla IV. The court started to develop a town dweller *civis* class among the population of the country.[53]

By means of settling down foreigners, the monarch had carried out an economic and military home defense policy. By granting privileges and determining obligations, the king and his court had expected and actually built upon the loyalty of the settlers by providing them with the opportunity to take up permanent residence in the realm, and to grow peacefully in population. It did not mean, however, that the monarch had expected the settlers - who did not even know the country's language, nor did they know its customs - to seek active participation in the government of the realm.[54]

King Béla IV not only had to care for the country's reconstruction after the Mongol invasion, especially increasing its heavily decimated population, but he also had to be concerned about establishing a reliable political base for himself among the town people of newcomers. These were formidable tasks, especially against the powerful domestic political and military opponents.[55] The Hungarian monarch had performed a basic task by carrying out the reconstruction of the country in a real sense of the term. The new settlers (*cives*), alias town dwellers, loyal to king and country, stood by the monarch, who, with the support of the hierarchy, certain members of the high nobility and of the lesser (service) nobility, had attempted to place his throne and the country's future on solid popular support of the high clergy, certain nobles, *and* the emerging town dwellers.[56]

Béla IV's new town policy was continued by his son and heir, Stephen V, who in 1271 exempted the *cives* of Fort Győr from the jurisdiction of the regional royal reeve, and let them retain their freedom(s) similar to those of the citizens of Fehérvár.[57] The backbone of the population in Győr were the *hospites* (foreign settlers, migrants) who had transferred their residence from the town to the fort of Győr, while retaining their privileges similar to those held by the *cives* of Székesfehérvár. Among the migrant settlers of Győr - "inter ipsos hospites nostros," and here one is to note that the royal writ referred to them as *hospites nostros*, that is the king's foreign settlers - lived servants, dependents of the fort personnel [*ministeriales?*], regional tax collectors, and other supply personnel, who had become citizens of the "royal town" of Győr.[58] The king had granted them full privileges like those of the episcopal quarter of the town (be they members of the bishop's household or that of the cathedral chapter), on the grounds that they already had established residence among the town's other citizens, and under the condition that they pay their *terrarium* (tax to the bishop).[59] This "census per terragium" tax due to the local ordinary had to be collected by the Citizens' Judge of the episcopal quarter of the town. The citizens of the royal quarter of the town paid their *census*, or *terragium*, tax on, or services owed for the use land to the royal treasury.[60]

Earlier, in 1260, Béla IV forbade the reeve of Győr region, the tax-collectors of Győr, and the territories of other places, to charge higher taxes than the legally fixed amount.[61] Béla III had, in 1185, elevated the fort personnel [*ministeriales?*] of Győr to the ranks of *iobagiones* (lesser or service nobles),[62] and a writ issued by Andrew II referred to the service personnel (nobility) of Győr.[63] It is of interest to note that in 1009, it was in Győr where King St. Stephen I had issued the founding charter of the bishopric of Pécs (Quinqueecclesiae).[64]

In Esztergom, a similar situation had developed, where the monarch granted tax exempt status in trade all over the realm for the town quarter that had been established by the archbishop, so that he and the inhabitants - *cives* and *hospites* - defend it from enemy attacks.[65] The town of Esztergom also had a far earlier beginning, but only the settlement in the southern quarter had formed the "royal town."[66] The archbishop's town (the quarter of the cathedral chapter) had made up the "upper" segment of the town - a circumstance that had caused much friction between them.[67]

Andrew III had attempted to ease the situation in his writs of 1290 by expanding town limits;[68] but controversies erupted and continued between the two segments for some time.[69] As late as 1296, Andrew III had to intervene in the struggle between the archbishop of Esztergom and the town dweller "cives et hospites."[70] Royal residence had been established in Esztergom in the year 1000. In the royal palace, Béla II had entertained Emperor Frederick I Barbarossa for four days in 1189, and gave a formal reception in his honor in the fort itself.[71] In 1203, after the coronation of his infant son (Ladislas III), King Emery had his brother Andrew (later Andrew II) held captive in the royal palace.[72]

The royal writs dealing with towns almost always refer to the privileges of the *hospites*, the foreign newcomers (foreign-born town dwellers) - in Székesfehérvár, had held from King St. Stephen, in spite the fact that no such writ can be found in the royal register.[73] Only a writ, issued by Béla IV on May 6, 1237, referred to it.[74] On the other hand, Béla IV had confirmed all of the ancient liberties of the "cives" of Székesfehérvár.[75] The tradition attributed to St. Stephen must, however, have been firmly entrenched in the popular mind because Béla IV granted similar privileges to the *cives* of Nyitra and to the *hospites* of Saxon, Magyar, Slovak, and other descent establishing residence in the territorial possessions of the abbey of Garamszentbenedek - privileges similar to those held by the foreign settlers in Pest, Fehérvár, and Buda.[76]

The royal writ issued in the year 1002 and registered at the very beginning of the royal register placed, among others, Székes-fehérvár (Alba) under the jurisdiction of Bishop István (Stephen) of

Veszprém;[77] a royal document dated 1221 mentioned the Latin inhabitants of Fehérvár and the population of the episcopal town of Veszprém,[78] while a letter of Andrew II spoke of the Latin "hospites" living in Fehérvár.[79] According to a writ of 1181, Székesfehérvár had lost a legal case in a court of law battle versus the chapter of canons of Zagreb.[80] After the Mongol onslaught, it was in Fehérvár that Béla IV had, in 1243, issued a letter confirming the archpriest of Buda in his court jurisdiction over the citizens of Óbuda.[81] In 1249, the monarch had issued orders for transfer of the *cives* of Székesfehérvár to the fort for their own protection.[82]

The cited royal documents call attention first, to Székesfehérvár, where one could speak of a settlement that had existed before the Magyar conquest of the 890's; its inhabitants were, in part, the descendants of the ancient peoples that had formed the population of the "episcopal town:" the bishop's quarter in the later developing town. In part, they were foreign settlers who lived outside of the bishop's quarter, but began, in due time, to fuse with the inhabitants, and their quarter eventually united with the bishop's quarter of the town.[83] Second, the citizen stratum that lived in Székesfehérvár depended entirely upon the good will of the monarch; although the king had provided them with given privileges - privileges he had not withdrawn from them - the latter would not even think of demanding political rights from the king or from the royal court.[84]

NOTES

1. Cf. Ambrus Pleidell, "A magyar városfejlődés néhány fejezete" [Some Chapters on the Development of Towns in Hungary], I-III, *Századok*, 68 (1934), 1ff., 158ff., and 276ff., here esp. 13; Bálint Hóman, *A magyar városok az Árpádok korában* [Hungarian Towns in the Reign of the Árpáds] (Budapest, 1908), 68; Emma Lederer, "A legrégibb magyar iparososztály kialakulása" [Formation of the Oldest Segment of the Hungarian Industrial Working Class], *Századok*, 62 (1928), 494ff. Compare to Alfons Dopsch, *Die Wirtschaftsentwicklung der Karolingerzeit*, 2 vols., 3rd ed., ed. Erna Patzelt (Cologne-Graz, 1962), I, 955ff.: «Das Städtewesen».
2. On the status of Dés and Garamszentbenedek, cf. *RA*, nn. 346 and 618.
3. Pleidell, 284f.; Thomas of Spaleto spoke of the "cives" of Fehérvár as "Latins;" cf. *Mon. Slav. merid.*, XXVI, 172, also 118 and 203; Elemér Mályusz, "Geschichte des Bürgertums in Ungarn," *Vierteljahrschrift für Sozial- und Wirstschaftsgeschichte*, 29 (1927-28), 365ff.
4. Pleidell, 279f.
5. Rogerius, "Carmen," c. 39, *SSH*, II, 584, but spoke of the town of Pest as a German village, c. 16, *ibid.*, II, 562; and of Várad, c. 34, *ibid.*, II, 576ff.
6. Pleidell, 292ff., 294; J. Szalay, *Városaink a XIII században* [Hungarian Towns in the 13th Century] (Budapest, 1878); L. Gerevich, "The Rise of Hungarian Towns Along the Danube," in his *Towns in Medieval Hungary*, 26ff.; E. Fügedi, "Das mittelalterliche Ungarn als Gastland," *Die deutsche Ostsiedlung des Mittelalters als Problem der europäischen Geschichte*, ed. W. Schlesinger (Sigmaringen, 1975), 471ff.; G. Bárczi, "A középkori vallon-magyar érintkezések" [Valoon-Hungarian Contacts in the Middle Ages], *Századok*, 71 (1937), 399ff.
7. G. v. Below, *Der Ursprung der deutschen Stadtverfassung* (Düsseldorf, 1854), 15ff.; *RA*, n. 1642; *CD*, IV-3, 513ff.; Imre Nagy, *Sopron város története* [History of the Town of Sopron] (Sopron, 1889), 33.
8. *CD*, V-2, 375f. and V-2, 397ff., lands held by the Sopron fort personnel to be handed over to the town; compare with *ÁUO*, V, 171f.; *RA*, n. 4133 (anno 1297).
9. Cf. Henri Pirenne, *Economic and Social History of Medieval Europe* (New York, n.d.), 49ff.; idem, *Medieval Cities* (Garden City, NJ, 1956), 75ff.; Erna Patzelt, *Die fränkische Kultur und der Islam* (Baden-Brünn, 1932), 211ff.
10. Cf. *MGHSS rerum Merovingicarum*, II, 144f.; *MGHSS*, IX, 388,1; 396,65 and 563,27-28; IX, 768, anno 655; Patzelt, 217ff.; F. Palacky, *Geschichte von Böhmen*, vol. I (2nd repr. Prague, 1844), 55ff., 80f.
11. Hodinka, 27f., 24aff.; the Kievan "Hungarian Gate," *ibid.*, 158aff.; Kosztolnyik, *Five Kings*, ixf.
12. Knauz, II, 238; Patzelt, 190ff.; Pleidell, 304.
13. Cf. Odo de Deuil, *De profectione Ludovici VII in orientem*, ed. V.G. Berry (Latin-English) (New York, 1948), 30; excerpts in *MGHSS*, XXVI, 59ff.; text also in *MPL*, 185, 1202ff.
14. Berry, de Deuil, 30.
15. Cf. Cosmas of Prague, "Chronica Bohemorum," *MGHSS*, IX, 64,13-14, 96,2-3, and 105,29-33.
16. Samuel Kohn, *A zsidók története Magyarországon* [History of the Jews in Hungary], vol. I (Budapest, 1884), 57ff. and 405ff.; idem, "Héber források és adatok Magyarország történetéhez" [Hebrew Sources and Data on Hungarian History], *Történeti Tár*, 1880, 99ff.; see further the three legalistic comments made by Jehuda-ha-Cohen, d. 1070, in Mainz, concerning Hungary, in *ÁUO*, VI, 573ff. - based on the collection of Meir v. Rothenburg (Prague, 1608), nn. 903, 904, and 935. If authentic, the letter of Ibn Sáprút de Cházda, court physician of Caliph Abdurrahmán III of Cordova to Joseph, King of the Khazars, ca. 950 AD, though the date would be closer

to 1150! - mentioned Jews living in Hungary, cf. Kohn, *Zsidók*, I, 28; for a counter-argument concerning the authenticity of the letter, see J. Mandel, *József kazár király válaszlevelének hitelessége* [The Authenticity of the Reply of King Joseph of the Khazars] (Pécs, 1929), 18.

17. *SSH*, I, 472f.; Rogerius, c. 40, *ibid.*, II, 585ff., and royal writs, *RA*, nn. 647, 723, 885, and 919. On the other hand, Pleidell had argued that Moslem Bulgarians from the Volga had settled in Hungary in great numbers during the 900's; in fact, the name of Pest was of Bulgarian origin - compare with Anonymus, c. 57, *SSH*, I, 114f., and the Chronicle, c. 83, *ibid.*, I, 339,10-12. According the Laws of King Ladislas I, Jewish and Arab merchants had lived in Hungary in large numbers - *RHM*, 327f., "Leges," i:9-10. See further, Zs. P. Pach, "Egy évszázados történészvitáról: áthaladt-e a levantei kereskedelem útja a középkori Magyarországon?" [On a Century Old Historical Debate: Did Levantine Trade Move Through Medieval Hungary?], *Századok*, 95 (1972), 849ff., and in his "Levantine Trade and Hungary in the Middle Ages," *Études historiques hongroises*, 1975, ed. D. Nemes, *et al.* (Budapest, 1975), 283ff.

18. Cf. K. Schünemann, *Die Entstehung des Städtwesens in Südosteuropa* (Bresslau-Opeln, n.d.), 7f, 17ff., and 32ff.; Mályusz, *art. cit.*, in *Vierteljahrschrift*, 365ff.

19. *RA*, n. 1642; Béla IV gave the landholdings of the fort personnel to the "cives" of Sopron; *CD*, IV-2, 513f.; Gerevich, *Hungarian Towns*, 28ff.; Pleidell, 159ff.; Siegfrid Rietschel, "Die Stadtpolitik Heinrichs des Löwen," *HZ*, 102 (1909), 237ff., esp. 254ff.; Dopsch, II, 95ff., 101, and 105f.

20. Imre Holl, "The Development and Topography of Sopron in the Middle Ages," in Gerevich, *op. cit.*, 96ff.; D. Dercsényi, *Sopron és környéke műemlékei* [Artifacts, Monuments in Sopron and its Surroundings], 2nd ed. (Budapest, 1956); I. Holl, "Sopron im Mittelalter," *Acta archaeologica Hungarica*, 31 (1979), 105ff.

21. Cf. Einhardi *Vita Caroli Magni*, ed. Oswald Holder-Egger, SSrG (Hannover, 1911), c. 13; it was a bishop's see in the 590's, noted Pleidell, 289; Th. v. Bogyay, "Die Kirchenorte der Conversio Bagoariorum et Carantenorum: Methoden und Möglichkeiten ihrer Lokalisierung," *Südostforschungen*, 19 (1960), 52ff.; L. Bella, "Scarabantiai emlékek" [Memories of Ancient Sopron], *Archaelógiai Értesítő*, 19 (1894), 74ff.; idem, "Scarabantia sánca" [Fortifications of Ancient Sopron], *ibid.*, 16 (1896), 223f.; E. Klebel, "Die Ostgrenze des karolingischen Reiches," *Jahrbuch für Landeskunde von Niederösterreich*, neue Folge, 21 (1928), 348ff., repr. in *Die Entstehung des deutschen Reiches. Wege der Forschung, Sammelband* (Darmstadt, 1955), 1ff.; Franz Zagiba, *Die altbayerische Kirchenprovinz Salzburg und die hll. Slawenlehrer Cyrill und Method* (Salzburg, 1963); Karl Oberleitner, "Die Stadt Enns im Mittelalter. Ein Beitrag zur Geschichte der deutschen Städte," *Archiv für österreichische Geschichte*, 27 (1861), 1ff.

22. Cf. "Life of Archbishop Conrad of Salzburg," *MGHSS*, XI, 63ff.; Patzelt, *Fränkische Kultur*, 211.

23. Arnold, *Chronica*, iv:8; for a counterargument, that Attila's *ordu* (headquarters) were located east of the Tisza river, see Bóna, *Húnok*, 59ff.

24. Gerevich, *Hungarian Towns*, 74ff.; H. Göckenjan, "Stuhlweissenburg, eine ungarische Königsresidenz von 11-13 Jahrhundert," in F. Zernack (ed.), *Beiträge zur Stadt- und Regionalgeschichte Ost- und Nordeuropas* (Wiesbaden, 1971), 135ff.; Josef Deér, "Aachen und die Herrschersitze der Árpáden," *MIÖG*, 79 (1971), 1ff.

25. *RA*, n. 647; *RHM*, 444ff.; *CD*, IV-1, 132ff.; Nyitra would be mentioned as an ecclesiastic center in the ninth century, cf. "Conversio," c. 11, *MGHSS*, XI, 12. Also, *ibid.*, IX, 64,13-14.

26. *RHM*, 445, c. 5.

27. *RA*, n. 706 (May 18, 1241).

28. On a royal writ issued by Coloman the Learned, *RA*, n. 43, Manases signed as the bishop "Zagoriensis;" *CD*, VII-4, 57ff.; L. Fejérpataky, *Kálmán király oklevelei* [The Royal Writs of King Coloman], vol. XV-5 of *Értekezések a történettudományok köréből* (Budapest, 1892), 40ff.; and, King Emery had confirmed the church of Zagreb in its possession of lands it received from King Ladislas I, *RA*, n. 188; and, compare with *RA*, n. 178; J. Tkalcic (ed.), *Monumenta historica episcopatus Zagrabiensis saec. XII-XIII*, 2 vols. (Zagreb, 1873-74), I, 9; *ÁUO*, XI, 72f. King Béla IV made mention of a [judicial] testimony given before the bishop of Zagreb, *RA*, n. 1692; in 1207, King Andrew II had mentioned, next to Bishop Gottardus of Zagreb the ban(us) Cheffanus [Chepan?] as "comes Sagurensis." Cf. *RA*, n. 229; *ÁUO*, VI, 313ff.

29. *RA*, n. 723; *RHM*, 451ff.

30. Cf. J. Tkalcic (ed.), *Monumenta historica lib. reg. civitatis Zagrabie*, vol. 1 (Zagreb, 1889), 15ff.; Smiciklas, IV, 172ff.

31. The May 11, 1198 letter of Prince Coloman, in *Mon. civ. Zagrabie*, 1, 1f., and *Monumenta historica Zagrabie*, I, 189f, 252f., 323; II, 219.

32. *RA*, n. 188, as cited above, n. 27.

33. A new royal privilege, *RA*, n. 1504; *RHM*, 507ff.

34. *RA*, n. 752; *CD*, IV-1, 332ff.

35. *RA*, n. 77; Batthyány, *Leges*, II, 381f., under the date of 1149, *ibid.*, I, 243f.

36. *RA*, nn. 672 and 673.

37. *RA*, n. 781; *RHM*, 466ff.; *ÁUO*, VII, 172ff.

38. Cf. A Michnay and P. Lichner, *Ofner Stadtrecht* (Pozsony, 1845), 32, 45, and 125.

39. *Ibid.*, 62 and 239f.; *RA*, n. 781; it would be mentioned in a judicial decision handed down by the Palatine in 1496 - a decision based on a writ dating back to the times of Béla IV.

40. *ÁUO*, XI, 11ff.; G. Wenczel, "Buda regeszták" [The Buda Registers], *Történeti Tár*, 1 (1855), 83f.; Gy. Györffy, "A székesfehérvári latinok betelepülésének kérdése" [The Question Concerning the Latin Settlement in Székesfehérvár], in A. Kralovánszky (ed.), *Székesfehérvár Évszázadai*, 2 vols. (Székesfehérvár, 1972), II, 37ff.; Fügedi, *art. cit.*, in Schlesinger, *Deutsche Ostsiedlung*, 471ff.

41. Anonymus, c. 57, *SSH*, I, 114f., and Chronicle, C. 83, *ibid.*, I, 339,12 - as confirmed by a writ of Béla IV, *RA*, n. 781; *RHM*, 466f.; and *ÁUO*, VII, 172ff.

42. *SSH*, I, 339,12. "Pest magna et ditissima" [German merchant town], *SSH*, II, 562; Odo de Deogilo, *De profectione*, 30 [or, *MGHSS*, XXVI, 62, 20] and the references by H. Marczali, "Árpádkori emlékek külföldi könyvtárakban" [Heritage of the Árpád Age in Western Libraries], *Történeti Tár*, 1878, 167ff. On "Ofen," cf. L. Gerevich, "Hungary," in M.W. Barley (ed.), *European Towns: Their Archaeology and Early History* (London, 1977), 431ff.

43. Luprechtzaz - see *RA*, n. 867, spelled Luprechthaza ("hospites nostri...de Luprechthaza"), in *RHM*, 471f.

44. *RA*, n. 885.

45. *RHM*, 498f. (anno 1258!); *SSH*, II, 357.

46. Cf. "Conversio," anno 836, *MGHSS*, XI, 12,5-8.

47. *CD*, I, 215f. (if authentic!); E. Dümmler, *Geschichte des oströmischen Reiches*, 2nd ed., 3 vols. (Leipzig, 1887-88), II, 174ff., esp. 177f.; Z.J. Kosztolnyik, "Nagy Károly dunavölgyi politikájának előre nem látott következményei" [The Unforeseen Consequences of the Mid-Danubian Policy of Charlemagne], *Proceedings of the Árpád Academy and of the 20th Annual Meeting of the Cleveland Hungarian Association, 1980* (Cleveland, Ohio, 1981), 175ff.

48. *CD*, IV-2, 174.

49. *RA*, n. 1059; *RHM*, 489ff.; Knauz, I, 426f.

50. *RA*, n. 1375; *ÁUO*, III, 38f.

51. *RA*, n. 439; Knauz, I, 520f.; *CD*, IV-3, 282ff. - seemingly contradicted by a royal writ of 1268, Knauz, I, 550.

52. Smiciklas, III, 346.

53. *RA*, n. 1636; *RHM*, 517f.; *HO*, VI, 157f.

54. This is evident from royal diplomas, as, e.g., *RA*, nn. 747, 619, 885.

55. That is why, for instance, the king had confirmed the archpriest of Buda in his [secular] jurisdiction over the citizens of Óbuda - *RA*, n. 747; *RHM*, 458f., or confirmed the "cives" of Székesfehérvár in their liberties - *RA*, n. 619; on the same grounds, he granted privileges to the citizens of Nyitra, privileges identical with those of the citizens of Fehérvár, *RA*, n. 885; *RHM*, 498f.; on Nyitra as a church center, cf. *MGHSS*, IX, 64,13-14, and 96,2-3.

56. Cf. Odo de Deogilo, *De profectione*, 30; the charter issued for Pest, *RA*, n. 781; *RHM*, 466ff., and compare it with the privileges of Késmárk, *RA*, n. 1636; *RHM*, 517f.

57. *RA*, n. 2132; *RHM*, 526ff.; compare to *RA*, n. 2077; *CD*, V-1, 146ff., esp. 149.

58. On the grounds of military defense - Pleidell, 25.

59. In Győr, the "census" was collected by the Judge of the Citizens of the Chapter of Canons (of the cathedral), on behalf of the bishop and of the canons, *RA*, n.2132.

60. Hóman, *Magyar városok*, 109f.; Rietschel, *Markt und Stadt*, 133ff.; G. v. Below, "Zur Entstehung der deutschen Stadtverfassung," *HZ*, 58 (1887), 193ff., esp. 201ff.; A. Eckhardt, "Das Ungarnbild in Europa," *Ungarische Jahrbücher*, 22 (1942), 152ff.

61. *RA*, n. 1237; *RHM*, 491ff. (anno 1251! - cf. *RA*, n. 1040).

62. *RA*, n. 139; *ÁUO*, I, 78.

63. Anno 1210 - *RA*, n. 255; *ÁUO*, VI, 341ff.

64. *RA*, n. 5; Batthyány, *Leges*, I 373f.; Koller, I, 62f. Gy. Balanyi, "Szent István király mint a magyar keresztény egyház megalapítója" [King St. Stephen, Founder of the Church in Hungary], *SIE*, I, 346ff. The corpse of the rebel leader Koppány was hanged from the gate(s) of Ft. Győr in the first year of Stephen's reign - *SSH*, I, 313f.

65. *RA*, n. 660; Knauz, I, 328f.

66. *RA*, n. 753: citizens and guests; *RA*, n. 1063: citizens. Prince Géza (d. 997), held court in Esztergom - cf. King Stephen's "Vita minor," *SSH*, II, 394,11-12 and note 2. Arnold of Lübeck, *Chronica*, iv:8, made a distinction between the royal fort and the [more recent] town. In the "Niebelungenlied," it is Attila's town; Max Buchner, "Um das Niebelungenlied. Ein Beitrag - keine Lösung," *Ungarische Jahrbücher*, 9 (1929), 196ff.; K. Storck, *Deutsche Literaturgeschichte*, 10th rev. ed., ed. M. Rockenbach (Stuttgart, 1926), 90ff.; H. de Boor, *Die höfische Literatur*, 7th ed. (Munich, 1966), 155ff.

67. Pleidell, 30ff.; Gerevich, *Hungarian Towns*, 31f.; E. Nagy, "Rapport préliminaire des fouilles d'Esztergom, 1964-69," *Acta archaeologica Hungarica*, 23 (1971), 181ff.

68. *RA*, nn. 3668-69.

69. *MGHSS*, IX, 590,16-22.

70. *RA*, n. 3986; *ÁUO*, X, 137ff.

71. Arnold of Lübeck, *Chronica*, iv:8 (anno 1189), in the country's "metropolis" - cf. also "Vita Archiepiscopi Conradi" of Salzburg, *MGHSS*, XI, 74,3-15 (anno 1131).

72. Cf. Thomas of Spaleto, Chronicle, c. 24, in *MHSM*, XXVI, 81f.; Schwandtner, III, 569.
73. See *ÁUO*, XI, 11ff.
74. *RA*, n. 885; *RHM*, 498f., anno 1248; *CD*, IV-2, 455ff., anno 1258; in VIII-2, 436f., Fejér referred to the year 1248.
75. *Ibid.*
76. *RA*, n. 368; *CD*, III-2, 476ff.
77. Cf. *RA*, n. 3; Batthyány, *Leges*, I, 371f.
78. In a 1496 transcript, prepared (and signed) by Palatine István Zápolyi - *RA*, n. 619.
79. *RA*, n. 429; *ÁUO*, VI, 431f.
80. *RA*, n. 131; *ÁUO*, XI, 45f.; Smiciklas, II, 176f.
81. *RA*, n. 747; *RHM*, 458f.; Batthyány, *Leges*, II, 365f.
82. *RA*, n. 919, with text!
83. See, e.g., *ÁUO*, VI, 431f.; A. Kralovánszky, "Székesfehérvár X-XI századi településtörténeti kérdései" [Problems Concerning the Settlement of Székesfehérvár in the Tenth-Eleventh Centuries], in his *Székesfehérvár*, I, 36f.; L. Nagy, "Székesfehérvár középkori topográfiája," *ibid.*, II, 199ff.; E. Fügedi, "Der Stadtplan von Stuhlweissenburg und die Anfänge des Bürgertums in Ungarn," *Acta historica Academiae Scientiarum Hungaricae*, 15 (1969), 103ff.; Gy. Györffy, *Az Árpád-kori Magyarország történeti földrajza* [Historical Geography of Árpádian Hungary], vol. II, 3rd ed. (Budapest, 1987), 363ff.
84. As it is clearly evident from a writ of Andrew III, dated 1294, concerning the legal controversy between Archbishop Ladomér and the "cives" of Esztergom - *RA*, n. 3986; Katona, *Historia critica*, VII, 1114f.

3. *Cultural Conditions in Hungary in the Reports of Western Chronicles*

In debates on twelfth century history, domestic troubles and foreign wars characterize the Hungarian condition. The surviving Hungarian records depict a merciless world, where only in monasteries, or in the protective quiet of cathedral chapters, could one pursue intellectual activity and cultivate writing. Even a writer had to be an individual with noble instincts and will power: he had to have strong faith, iron will, and nerves to begin writing, especially about history, so that he might fearlessly tell nothing but the truth, without seeking the benevolence of the king or the regional secular potentate. It was no easy task for the contemporary chronicler to report events "sine ira et studio," even though he was a celibate cleric, a monk, who did not have to worry about his family for reporting with a truthful pen.[1]

In discussing the early years of the reign of Frederick Barbarossa, the German chronicler Otto of Freising wrote about Hungary, the land, its conditions and people in his *Gesta Friderici Imperatoris*.[2] He admired the richness of the landscape, and described it as God's earthly paradise, like ancient Egypt, rich in forest and wood, filled with numerous kinds of birds and animals. But he mostly admired divine tolerance that so barbaric a folk could have such a wonderful country of their own! The Magyars were a morose people, observed the Cistercian monk and abbot. He later became bishop, the uncle of the German emperor, and the scion of a powerful and overly rich family, and considered the Magyars with the condescending contempt characteristic of his clan.[3] He found the Magyars' behavior wild, their language barbaric. Because their country was frequently devastated by barbarians, the inhabitants displayed crude behavior, and lacked cultured habits and civilized manner of speech. The Huns had invaded their territories before; then came the Avars who ate raw putrid meat; and then the Magyars arrived from Scythia.[4]

And yet, as if jealousy would mingle between those lines, when, for instance, Otto noted that the Hungarian monarch held great prestige among his people, even though he shared the cares of the country's government with them. Otto must have meant the nobility, although in his text every Magyar attended the assemblies summoned by the king, where every headman took his seat (*stella*) with him to sit down during the discussion(s). The ruler thoroughly debated everything with his nobles, and the latter continued the debate amongst themselves. They held assemblies during the summer, even in winter.[5] As if the idea, realized by Andrew III, had originated here, in that the monarch, together with his service nobles and high clergy, carried on the business of his people in the diet serving his own interests, and the future of his country![6]

The Magyars respected their ruler; nobody could utter a sound in his presence, and if a high noble dared to insult the king by speaking ill of him, anyone, even a lesser noble or official, had the right to arrest the individual and to bring him to justice. Only the king could issue money, and in judicial cases brought before his court, only he could hand down the sentence. Interesting is the remark of Otto that, for the purpose of administration, the country was divided into seventy-plus counties.[7] According to him, the administration and government of the country functioned fairly smoothly even in that bloodthirsty age.

One could not, however, speak of town life. The Magyars' towns/villages consisted of miserable structures made of reed, Otto of Freising wrote; only rarely could one come across a wall, or house structure. There were some wooden homes, a few built of stone. The Magyars despised the comforts of a home; in summer, they lived under tents; only in winter did they move into their reed huts.[8] But, when the ruler summoned them to arms, they answered his call without a murmur or a question. In a village, nine peasants, or seven, had to provide for the training and equipment of one warrior for the king's army. The Magyars' order of battle created a very bad impression: their weapons were old, except the equipment of the nobles of foreign birth (*hospites*), who had surrounded the king [in battle], and of the paid mercenaries (*solidarios*). Brave they were not, though they knew how to fight; they had learned it from "foreigners" - they imitated the Germans' method of fighting and order of battle.[9]

The brief remarks made by Otto of Freising concerning life and towns in Hungary were supported by the Czech chronicler, Cosmas of Prague, who, contrary to Otto, mentioned Pozsony as a (the) Hungarian [fort]town,[10] and spoke of Esztergom as *urbs*[11] that is, a developing town, the capital of the realm. Cosmas remarked good-naturedly,[12] that there were only a few settlements in the country that might be regarded as town[ships]. He was fond of Esztergom, having been ordained a priest there by the archbishop of Esztergom.[13] Esztergom he described, however, as the country's center of administration, an archiepiscopal see (and the religious center of the realm),[14] and as an economic junction visited by foreign merchants (German, Polish, Russian, and Italian) who had brought with them linen, cloth, wool, hides, home utensils, while the Magyars were trading in corn, wines, hides, live animal stock, and iron ore.[15] Odo de Deogilo, who visited Hungary accompanying his king, Louis VII of France on the Second Crusade, also referred to Esztergom, the "noble city," as the capital of the country, the seat of the archbishop, and as a commercial-trading junction in international trade, confirming the report of Cosmas of Prague.[16]

In 1189, Emperor Frederick I Barbarossa had journeyed through the land during the Third Crusade.[17] His crusaders, and perhaps even the emperor himself, were amazed at the wealth of the country. Ship-and wagon-loads of bread and wine were brought before them, fodder for their horses, and meat animals to feed the troops.[18] Arnold of Lübeck reported on this by saying that the emperor and Béla III had met in Esztergom.[19] On the occasion, the Hungarian queen, the sister of Philip II Augustus of France, had donated a large tent to the emperor, a tent that could be divided into four compartments and was decorated with scarlet tapestry. Thereupon the king made a gift of two silos filled with fine flour to the crusaders.[20]

Everywhere the emperor and his men were greeted very hospitably. Béla III had organized a four-day royal hunt in honor of his imperial guest and gave a fabulous dinner party in Aquincum: "Etzilburg," *urbs Adtile dicta*, where Attila had had his headquarters.[21] When the emperor and his crusaders left the country, the king gave five thousand sacks of flour to them work five thousand silver marks. He also made additional donations, including a camel loaded with gifts. The chronicler further recorded that beyond the Hungarian border, in the Balkans, the emperor and his army were given a far less friendly reception.[22]

It is an interesting characteristic of the chronicler's narrative that he referred to Esztergom as "civitas," "metropolis," or as *centrum* of the realm, and Otto of s. Blasius, another chronicler, mentioned once again only Pozsony as a town in Hungary, without any reference to Esztergom. Otto of s. Blasius recorded that in 1189, King Béla III had richly entertained Emperor Frederick Barbarossa and his army as they traveled through Hungary.[23]

It is known that Béla III, on several occasions, sat under an oak tree with his nobles, and listened to the complaints and requests of all those who appeared in front of him, and handed down sentences in court cases that had been appealed to him.[24] The monarch had a huge private domain in the country. In peacetime, he traveled all over the realm with a large entourage collecting moneys due to him, looking after the economy of his estates, listening to the grievances of his service nobles, and making inquiries about the behavior and attitudes of his public officials in the kingdom.[25] But his journeying in the countryside had caused problems; for a royal dinner expected to be given by the regional host - and to which the king's entire entourage had to be invited - they had to slaughter twelve oxen, bake one thousand loaves of bread, and serve four barrels of wine.[26] The nobles made a protest against the royal visits; it is evident from art. 3 of the Golden Bull of 1222, and from art. 8 of the Decree of 1231, that the king must, hereafter, seek no hospitality from the villages of his freemen (nobles), or their hamlets, without an explicit invitation to do so.[27]

Under such circumstances - even though public administration had been functioning fairly well, as is evident from the royal writs issued in the period, and from the correspondence of the bishops[28] - town life, orderly planned economy had existed only in a very crude form in the country, and cultural standards were at a low level. The nobles possessed a military type of "culture," a kind of army training based upon war experience; the clergy's educational standards were not very high either, except those of the clerics who had attended western universities, and were employed in the royal curia and pontifical offices, or in the administrative positions of the realm.[29]

The early decades of the thirteenth century, the irresponsible reign of Andrew II, were not the time of positive accomplishments. The upper clergy and the lesser nobility began to demand the right to participate in government,[30] and when the son of Andrew II, Béla IV had tried to restore order in the administration of the country and among the nobility, and had attempted to end the havoc caused by his father's thoughtless office and landgrants policy, the furious upper nobility revolted against him and refused to support the king when the Mongols invaded the country.[31]

Out of the deviations, caused by the Tartars, grew with frightening force that of the arrogant predominance of the oligarchy during the latter half of the century. Everyone in the country suffered within their social stratum.[32] The reconstruction of the realm that had made great strides under the reign of Béla IV, from whom the Church received abundant holdings,[33] artistic churches were built in flourishing Gothic style and the new religious orders occupied an important position in the formation of religion and culture, setting high ethical and esthetic standards, came to an abrupt end.[34]

Hungarian clerics who had studied in Paris, Bologna, or Pavia emerged head and shoulders above their contemporaries. It was they who occupied positions at the court or in the administration of the country during the 1200's, and were sent or selected to act as envoys by the court of high churchmen abroad.[35] As it has been mentioned above, the cathedral school of Veszprém occupied a position of preeminence in teaching, learning, and the cultivation of liberal arts in the country.[36] It was a sign of the times, however, that this center of learning and education fell prey to the wrath of angry oligarchs who were jealous of each other.[37]

It was characteristic of the age that the people of the kingdom lacked culture; an educated social stratum did not exist in the land. When preparations were made for the canonization of Margaret, sister of Ladislas IV, Italian clerics conducting the official inquiry (required for her canonization) had heard one hundred witnesses, and prepared a written record of the hearings. It soon became evident from this record that the upper social strata - the nobles - had only a shallow education, if any. They could not properly answer questions, such as "how old is your child?" They did not know their own ages, and were unable to provide precise chronological data; "it had happened on a rainy day," "mid-winter," "in deep snow," etc., were their answers, hardly a reliable data base. Only one nobleman, Alexander Kadarkalászi, gave intelligent answers, and he answered the questions in Latin.[38]

Or, there was the case of the Guthkeled Bible. In 1263, Vid Guthkeled had compensated the Benedictine abbey at Csatár with his estates in the Mura region and Somogy county for the two volume bible set he had borrowed from, but failed to return to, the abbey. Guthkeled had, as a matter of fact, taken out a loan of twenty-seven and a half silver marks, pledging the bible as security to the financier at Vasvár. Later, he even asked for more credit, pawning the bible as security. Finally, he exhausted his credit and went bankrupt - he was unable to meet even the interest payments on the loan, and the two volumes were retained by his creditor in Vasvár. The Csatár, now Guthkeled, Bible eventually came into the possession of the abbey of Admont.[39]

It may suffice to enumerate three characteristic data to depict the hopeless public conditions in Hungary during the last three decades of the century. First was the barbaric assassination of Béla, possible heir to the throne, that remained completely unpunished. There was no strong judicial system in the country to punish the person who did it, and whose involvement in the affair had been common knowledge, and to sentence him to the fullest extent of the law, thereby setting an exemplary punishment for the crime that had been committed.[40]

Secondly, Peter Csák was the archenemy of Péter of Németújvár, bishop of Veszprém, and because Csák wished to possess the treasures of the cathedral, had burned the church to the ground together with the cathedral school in a mad frenzy. The king, Ladislas IV, had later partially compensated the bishop, the church, and the school for damages, but the court did not have the moral stamina and military strength to hunt down and punish the culprit, who happened to be one of the most powerful magnates of the realm.[41]

Lastly, in 1277, the German settlers [Saxons] in Transylvania invaded and ruined the town of Gyulafehérvár on the grounds, they claimed, that the bishop had been responsible for the death of one German settler. They had to seek revenge. They burned down the church with all the people seeking refuge there, murdered the arch-priest and several clerics, some laymen, including Hungarians. The king had not taken any action to punish their deed.[42]

Nor did it serve the good name of the court that, in 1269, King Béla IV and his nobles wanted to deny the bishopric of Zagreb to Timothy, the bishop-elect, on the grounds that Timothy came from a very poor family. Pope Clement IX had to intervene in the defense of the bishop-elect to receive the royal sanction.[43] In 1285, the second Mongol invasion of the country occurred; after the Mongols left, renewed Cuman insurrections devastated the land. The chronicler recording the events of the reign of Ladislas IV was telling the truth when he provided a rather unflattering report on the reign of the "Cuman" king. "Illo tempore biga, scilicet duarum rotarum vehiculum a regni incolis currus regis Ladislai dicebatur, quia... homines more pecorum bigis iuncti vices animalium inpendebant."[44] Modern historians, as, for example, Károly Szabó, painted a more positive and human picture of him.[45]

marriage.[5] In time, Stephen had returned to Italy, had been elected *podestà* in Ravenna,[6] but had to flee to Venice (for reasons not mentioned by the chronicler), where a rich Venetian citizen, after he had convinced himself that Stephen was truly the son of the Hungarian monarch, gave him the hand in marriage of his daughter, and named him his heir.[7] In Venice, a son was born to him, whom he named Andrew after his grandfather. Upon advice received from his fabulously rich maternal uncles, Andrew went to Hungary during the reign of Ladislas IV. As prince of the House of Árpád he had claimed, as inheritance through his grandfather, a portion of the realm's territory: "quod esset dux, qui deberet habere portionem in regno regis Andree titulos avi sui."[8] Upon the assassination of King Ladislas IV, the barons of the country had crowned him king; "cum autem rex Ladislas fuisset occisus, a baronibus regni Andreas dux feliciter coronatur."[9]

The chronicler failed to mention that Arnold of the clan of Buzád, Lord of Fort Strido in Muraköz (plain between the Mura and Drave streams), had captured the prince and taken him to Vienna, where he became the guest of Albert, Duke of Austria. But when Andrew dared to criticize the family of his host, the latter had assumed a less than friendly attitude toward him,[10] and Archbishop Ladomér of Esztergom came to the rescue of Andrew. The archbishop relied upon the cooperation of the Vilhelmites in Vienna to help smuggle the prince, disguised as a monk, out of Vienna on a boat in the Danube.[11] Hungarian nobles boarded the ship en-route, accompanied Andrew to Buda, and crowned him in Fehérvár.[12]

The *Reimchronik* reports that Archbishop Ladomér had anointed the king; it was he who put the cloak of King St. Stephen on his shoulders, placed the sacred Crown upon his head, and the orb and scepter into his hands.[13] Then, King Andrew III took his oath of office "before the country," and the bishops took their loyalty oath "before the king." The monarch swore to guard justice, maintain peace, protect the Church; to defend widows, orphans, and helpless people; to safeguard the privileges of the Crown, and to recover territories of the realm that had been lost.[14]

The Hungarian chronicler(s) did not provide details of events leading to the coronation, and the Chronicle left out particular description of the royal coronation itself. The chronicler(s) only recorded that Andrew had been crowned by the barons of the realm, who had made him their king[15] - as if to confirm thereby the report of the Styrian chronicler. The Hungarian chroniclers' assertions are the more interesting because they had emphasized the coronation by the barons of Andrew - "a baronibus regni Andreas dux *feliciter* coronatur," and that they did it "feliciter," with satisfaction. The chroniclers ignored thereby the constitutional public role of the archbishop of Esztergom in performing the royal coronation. It was the Styrian chronicler instead who provided the details on the coronation, as well as on the contents of the coronation oath taken by Andrew III.

The style of the Chronicle text changes with c. 181; the reign of Ladislas IV, and that of Andrew III (1290-1301), the succession by the Anjous to the Árpádian throne, and the rule of Charles I of Anjou in Hungary (1308-42) were narrated by a chronicler of the Anjou age (in Hungary, in this instance, the early fourteenth century).[16] Judged by the style of the text, it was this early four-teenth century chronicler who provided a report on the flagellant movement in Hungary toward the end of the reign of Béla IV,[17] and it was he who wrote the previous segment of the Chronicle that recorded the murder, in 1213, of Queen Gertrud, Andrew II's first wife.[18]

This chronicler looked upon the past from the point of glorification of his king, Charles I of Anjou, and changed the narrative of the previous chronicler(s) by drawing a picture of his own age instead. In order to support the claims of the Anjous, this chronicler had revised what contemporary characterization chronicler Simon de Kéza had created of the reign of his king, Ladislas IV the Cuman.[19] The Anjou-age chronicler hardly paid any attention to the battles that had been fought and won by King Ladislas, but painted a more vividly colored picture of the socio-political and economic deterioration of the realm.[20] The reign of Andrew III was of interest to him only as long as it aided the Anjous' succession to power. That is why he purposefully provided a long genealogical narrative of the family descent of Andrew III.[21]

The chronicler (of the Anjou age) paid attention to spiritual-religious developments. Although he did not express any opinion on the flagellation movement - no early fourteenth century Minorite could know when his views were to become heretical![22] - he depicted the functions of papal legate Fermo,[23] the politicking of

Cardinal Gentilis in Hungary,[24] and recorded how "false" clergymen had dared to excommunicate the Pope![25] The chronicler simultaneously stressed the positive outcome of the Franciscan Gentile's mission in Buda,[26] in sharp contrast with the failed diplomatic undertaking, unsuccessful function as a papal legate of the Dominican Boccassini.[27] (The chronicler also recorded that Andrew III was buried in the church of the Franciscan Minorites in Buda.)[28] In identifying this chronicler, one has in mind Friar John as the author, a Minorite, and provincial of his Order in Hungary,[29] and it is known that the Anjous had looked very favorably upon the Franciscans. Charles Robert had a monastery built for them in Lippa, in honor of the Blessed Lays (Layws), a then recently recognized friar with a saintly reputation.[30]

Within a month of his coronation, Andrew III had a Diet held in Óbuda.[31] Several royal writs referred to this "Congregatio generalis."[32] The Diet had renewed the articles of the (Hungarian) Golden Bull of 1222, the *Decretum I* of Andrew II, concerning the liberties of the lesser nobility.[33] Henceforth, the nobles were not obligated to go to war with the barons (of their particular region), but only with the king, and with him only when he went to war in defense of the country.[34] Nor could high royal officials - the Voyvoda, Ban(us), Grand Steward - request forced lodging (for themselves and for their entourage) from a lesser nobleman.[35] Grants made by Ladislas IV to the sons and brothers of those who died in the line of duty were confirmed by the Diet, and barons who had no male offspring were allowed to make their will as they pleased over their chattel and landholdings.[36]

The nobles were obligated together with the barons and members of the hierarchy to hear complaints in the annual law-day at Fehérvár, and to address them.[37] In lieu of paying the tithe, a nobleman paid one-fourth of a silver mark after one furrow (of land), and his serfs paid a measure after one *kepe*, that is, the nobles paid twelve measures after 120 acres of land; his serfs paid one measure after 52 sheaves of wheat.[38]

New money (currency) issued annually was to be introduced separately in each county (district) by the county reeve, who was accompanied by four nobles: "four elected honest men."[39] The sentence handed down by the reeve and the four nobles who handled court of law cases involving theft, tithe, new money, larceny, etc., might be appealed to the king.[40] Foreigners, non-nobles, county reeves who had abused their offices in the past, could not become public officials, nor could they be elevated to the rank of royal counselor.[41]

The Diet of 1290 enacted articles in support of the nobility: the Palatine, Treasurer, Vice-Chancellor, and the Count of the King's Court could only be noblemen;[42] the sub-reeve of a county could only be a noble; the county reeve and four nobles would accompany the palatine when holding court (of law) in the district, and they could appeal his sentence to the monarch.[43] They cannot hand down a sentence over a justice of the archbishop's court, or over the nobles of a village, or over the servants of a nobleman.[44] The noble and his servants pay no toll;[45] only merchants coming home, or going abroad had to pay it.[46] The relatives of a noble could, after a proper appraisal, reclaim the "filial quarter," which was one fourth of the noble's lands given to his daughter. It was also possible to claim the widow's dowry, and even the confiscated goods that had been taken from him in punishment.[47]

The Diet curtailed the unjustified prerogatives held by barons. Nobody could possess, or inherit for life the office of a county reeve.[48] No baron could defend a condemned criminal at his court.[49] The Diet declared void the unlawful donations and illegal confiscation of goods (that had been) ordered by Ladislas IV.[50] It authorized the king to order the destruction of fortifications that had served as bases of operations for robbers and common criminals, and voided recently established tolls. It forbade farming out for money of official titles for public office(s).[51]

The articles concerning ecclesiastics declared that nobody may be cited to appear before a court of law without a writ issued by a cathedral chapter or a monastic chapter.[52] The Diet declared that the Church possessed inalienable rights, and stated that all unlawfully taken privileges be returned.[53] Only the king might pass judgment on ecclesiastical privileges.[54] The king follows regular court procedures in judging a case. In case of royal pardon, he grants compensation to the plaintiff.[55]

The Diet ordered that the Church receive a fee of forty *denarii* (worth one *pensa*) for administering the oath of compurgation for (one hundred) accused individuals before a court of law presiding over an ordeal.[56] The Diet further acknowledged the claim of the church in Fehérvár to reserve the right to appoint its prelate (the archpriest) to the office of the royal Vice-Chancellor.[57] The Diet also decreed that the height of the walls and towers of a noble's castle might not exceed that of a nearby church steeple.[58]

The royal chancery set its fees for issuing writs: one gold mark, or ten silver marks, for a writ with a wax pendant affixed to it; two measures for a letter of patent, and one measure for a closed writ with no seal affixed to it.[59]

It is very important to note that the Saxons also attended the Diet through their representatives.[60] The Diet had assured them of their status quo among the ranks of the nobility and exempted them from taxation or obligatory hospitality for royal officials (in transit) or military personnel (in time of war). It defined their military obligations anew in making them to accompany the king in time of war, when the monarch had to defend the realm against invading enemies. Were the king to go on a military expedition beyond the borders of the country, they would accompany him solely for a payment of a fixed fee. The Diet had assured every Saxon noble who had died without an heir that his family had the right to inherit his holdings, which would not be confiscated by the royal treasury.[61]

The Diet of 1290 accomplished its major goal by realizing Simon de Keza's utopian views of a common political and social front with the lesser (service) nobility to resist the barons' continued political influence in the political and administrative affairs of the realm. It established an advisory committee of churchmen and nobles, who were to examine and approve, or disapprove, of the donations made by Ladislas IV. It supported the nobles' control of county governments by keeping the county reeve, who was a royal nominee, from handling court of law cases without the presence of four noblemen (of the county).

It forced the palatine to accept the presence of four nobles (of the county; and that of the reeve) while making his tour of the county, administering justice. It ordered four "honest elected" men to supervise the annual exchange of the new currency in the district. The fact that a county reeve could handle a court of law case without written summons issued by a cathedral chapter, or a monastic community, strengthened the position of ecclesiastics and that of the lesser nobility.

The resolutions of the 1290 Diet in Óbuda actually support the statement Andrew III had made in his writ addressed to his relative, King James II of Aragon; namely, that he hoped that this country, torn for so long by constant controversy and punitive partisan wars, would reach a peaceful understanding with all parties concerned through his succession to the throne and his coronation. Petty particular controversies would cease, as would the bestial hostility and irrational behavior, and everyone would find personal liberty and peace of mind: "...in assumptione et coronatione nostra in pacem et concordiam covenerunt universi deposita feritate hostili,...salva civiliter, sicut res exigit singulis actione."[62]

The fact that the royal coronation of Andrew III had, indeed, been performed by Archbishop Ladomér of Esztergom, is evident from the annotations of the *Reimchronik*, and from the correspondence of the monarch, as for, example, from his cited writ to the court of Aragon-Sicily; from his letter, dated September 1, at Óbuda;[63] and from his letter, dated September 22, at Zólyom, in which he gave directives concerning the extraordinary status held by the archdiocese of Esztergom.[64] (One is to recall that, from the papal point of view, only the archbishop of Esztergom had the right to crown the kings of Hungary.)[65] Andrew III strongly needed the coronation act to be performed by the rightful archbishop, because the assassination of his predecessor had created a most difficult personal situation for him, as questions arose regarding his rightful inheritance of the throne.[66] He was not the son and heir of the murdered monarch; he had claimed the crown through his paternal grandfather - reaching back through two generations.[67]

After enduring the stubborn hostility of Ladislas IV toward the Church,[68] it was the Church that stood by the new monarch, Andrew III,[69] and its leaders requested to share in the power that the king had granted to the nobles in government.[70] As if a new governmental structure had emerged in the country of Andrew III, the example of which, recent research informs us, could have been taken from the area under the spiritual jurisdiction of the titular archbishop of Aquileia, and especially from western, Spanish, German, English, or even Italian ideas of government.[71] The Hungarian diets of the 1290's, and the council of Andrew III that consisted of elected members, showed similarities with the representative estates in the north Italian Friaul (Aquileia), and with the *cortes* of Aragon and Leon, the German court's call for representatives of the merchant class at the meeting of its "curia," and, to a certain extent, with the English parliaments of Edward I. Its politico-intellectual basis was prepared by clerical lawyers - doctors of law educated in western schools, now active in the court of Andrew III.[72]

What were the foreign examples the court of Andrew III wished to follow? On the Iberian peninsula, Alfonso IX had announced a gathering to meet at his court in Leon, so that he may, together with members of the hierarchy, high nobility (*magnates*), and representatives of every town in his realm, "regni mei," to talk about common business.[73] In front of the elected representatives the monarch declared that he would start no war, conclude no peace, nor make resolutions without their consent; only with their cooperation would he rule.[74]

Alfonso IX had another *cortes* held in 1208, to make laws, together with members of the hierarchy, the nobility, the barons - he separated the nobles from the barons (actually, they met separately since 1188) - and with the elected representatives of the towns of his kingdom; "destinatorum a singulis civitatibus, de universorum consensu," so that he might, together with them, legislate on his own behalf and on behalf of his people.[75] Alfonso X the Learned of Leon and Castile had, in 1258, held a *cortes* in Valladolid with his high clergy and the great men of the country ("ricos ommes)" and with the town representatives, in order to legislate and to state that he would sanction laws they all together had legislated on, so that everyone, including himself, was obliged to observe them.[76] He looked upon himself as the vicar of God in front of his people, and it was his obligation to protect the common good and just cause of his people in the temporal world.[77]

A word of explanation will be in order here. The queen of Emery of Hungary (*ob.* 1204) was Constance of Aragon, who, upon the death of her husband and advice received from the Roman pontiff became the wife of Emperor Frederick II.[78] In her entourage an Aragonese nobleman named Simon had entered Hungary. He became a royal reeve, and was mentioned in several official writs.[79] Also included was Tota, the lady-in-waiting of Queen Constance (afterwards, a lady-in-waiting of Queen Gertrud, Andrew II's first wife), who was spoken of in at least two royal letters.[80]

On German soil, it was Rudolf Habsburg who, in 1274, had asked the archbishop of Salzburg and the bishops of Passau and Regensburg that they invite to the assembly they would summon the citizens of towns besides the imperial lords and barons; "et communitatibus civitatum...colloquientur." In the same manner Rudolf had summoned a meeting of the "Curia generalis," "quia non est in rerum natura possibile quod substantia corporis universi capite sine membrorum subvencione evocare."[81] This is reminiscent of the arguments of John of Salisbury, who stated that the kingdom was like the human body, where the head without members of the body, and the "body" without its "head" did not exist. Political might itself included the basic principles of rational behavior: reason governed "rem publicam!" The English monarch, Edward I, summoned in 1290 and 1294, the lesser nobles [*milites*] of the shires to appear in front of him, and to comment on everything he and the lords had already discussed in their meeting.[82]

Would it have been too early to experiment with the Hungarian estates in the government of the realm during the reign of Andrew III? Did the monarch have the power and authority to enforce legislative enactments of the Diet of 1290? According to evidence derived from the royal registers, the king had to confirm every grant, donation of land or office, his predecessor had made - including that of the county of Ung - and he did with the cooperation of the lesser nobility.[83]

The writs logged in the register frequently mention unsafe county roads, thievery, and other troubles in an age that knew no domestic peace. Frequently, royal writs speak of gross corruption, senseless destruction everywhere, that heavily damaged the whole country.[84] Numerous outside interferences in the affairs of the realm, the appearance of various pretenders to the royal throne did not make the monarch's position any easier, nor did the continued rebellion led by the Kőszeg clan cement the king's public image and position.

Rudolf of Habsburg gave credibility to the hearsay that Andrew III was not an Árpád descendant, and gave the country away as a fief to his son, Albert of Austria.[85] Albert, the godson of Emperor Frederick II, had witnessed the visit of the envoy(s) of Béla IV at the imperial court in the year 1241, when Béla IV had promised that, were he to receive aid from the emperor against the

Tartars, he would submit himself and his country to him in fiefdom. The Holy See, however, held the point of view that because of the receipt of the Hungarian Crown from the hands of the pope, Hungary could only be, and remain a fief of the Roman See. Therefore, the curia raised a strong protest against the realization of the plans of both Rudolf and Albert concerning Hungary;[86] and yet, the curia supported the quest by Queen Maria of Naples - a sister of the deceased Ladislas IV - to the Hungarian throne versus the claim of Andrew III.[87] It meant that the papal court had wholly misunderstood the right of inheritance of Andrew "of Venice." Nor did it help the monarch's case that pretenders had arrived in Hungary from Poland, one of whom claimed to be Prince Andrew, younger brother of the deceased Ladislas IV.[88]

King Andrew III took action against the false brother of his predecessor at first; George, son of Simon of the clan of Baksa had the false prince expelled from Sáros county, and his men had the claimant drowned in a stream (the Sajó stream).[89] The pretender did not receive aid from Poland because Andrew III's first wife, Fenana, was Polish, the orphaned daughter of the duke of Kujava.[90] The king, however, had to go to war against Duke Albert.[91] The king took some eighty thousand men (so the chronicler reports) to lay a siege to Vienna, and in less than a month, he concluded a peace treaty in Hainburg with his Austrian opponent. In the treaty, the duke had surrendered his territorial conquests in Hungary, together with his territorial demands, and resigned his claim to the Hungarian throne. Albert "only" asked that King Andrew destroy all forts along the Hungaro-Austrian border.[92]

The Peace of Hainburg did concern mostly the forts and possessions of the Kőszeg clan, and by destroying their castles Albert wished to secure his own border zone. But he could also have acted out of a political calculation - he knew that any royal order that weakened the power of the Kőszeg clan would turn them against their king. In such a manner, he had not only freed himself of a dangerous neighbor, but had burdened the Hungarian king with a most unwelcome opponent - increasing the chances of domestic war in Hungary. Albert had hoped that King Andrew would turn to him for military aid, and they would, together, fight their "common" enemy!

Indeed, by destroying the border fortifications the king had earned the hostility of the Kőszegs.[93] Under the leadership of Ivan, son of Herrik, they had joined the party of Queen Maria, that is, of her son, Charles Martel, and recognized his right to succeed to the Hungarian Crown.[94] Neither Maria nor her son remained idle, nor did they wish to appear thankless toward the Kőszegs. Ivan had obtained from the Italian pretender the counties of Sopron and Vas in fiefdom,[95] and the Brebir family had been rewarded with the stewardship of the Adriatic seashore.[96]

Charles Martel now began to dress in a Hungarian fur coat, adopted as his coat of arms a shield with silver stripes on a red background, married Constance, daughter of Rudolf of Habsburg,[97] and named his relative, Stephen Dragutin, Duke of Slavonia.[98]

King Andrew III had to make a countermove. He went to Zagreb, placed Ivan of Kőszeg under arrest (although Ivan had been - or pretended to be - seeking peace), took from him the territory and title(s) he received from Queen Maria, and let him go free.[99] From Dragutin, the king reclaimed the territory and title Duke of Slavonia, and placed the region, together with the county of Pozsega, under the administrative supervision of his militarily-minded and strong-willed mother, Tomasina Marosini.[100]

It was now the Anjou sympathizers of the Kőszeg clan that began domestic violence by occupying Pozsony - even though the fort was recaptured by Matthew Csák (son of Péter Csák, who had played an important role in the country's politics during the 1270's).[101] But during the counterattack, the king himself was captured by the Kőszeg clan and held prisoner for several weeks.[102] In order to counterbalance the growing political might of his opponents, King Andrew made his mother governor of all the territory from Transdanubia to the Adriatic.[103]

The king's opponents did not remain inactive. As is evident from the record, it must have been at this time in his reign - "in cuius imperio quiddam nobiles regni" - certain nobles, that is, *scilicet* - the sons of Herrik (of the Kőszeg clan), John and Ban(us) Henry, Ugrin, son of Pócs of Ujlak, and many others, "aliique quamplures" - guided by their antipathy toward the monarch - "in preiudicium Andree regis" - had turned to the pope, Boniface VIII, with their request for a king.[104]

The pontiff looked favorably upon their plea, and sent the eleven year old Charles to Hungary in 1299, when Andrew III had still occupied the Árpád throne (in the text: "aduc Andrea rege vivente").[105] Purposefully, too, the chronicler remarked that when Charles had reached the age of maturity, "ut autem, iste Carolus regnare valeret," the pontiff had dispatched legates to Hungary to support him "contra regem Andream." The papal envoys, however, accomplished nothing, and returned to Rome.[106]

In this manner, a division of the realm along dynastic lines had, once again, become a reality.[107] In 1295, Charles Martel and Queen Fenana had died.[108] Palatine Mize in the Tolna region,[109] Matthew Csák in the Vág river valley,[110] George Baksa in Sáros county,[111] and the Barsa family in Bihar county had gained power.[112] The king's mother, Tomasina, had suppressed the revolt of the Palatine, and she had defeated the uprising of the Babonik clan.[113]

In 1296, the king occupied Kőszeg.[114] It was in this military operation that he received military aid from Albert of Austria, whose political instincts had proven to be correct; Andrew III, a widower since the death of Fenana, now married Agnes, the daughter of Albert,[115] rendered his father-in-law military aid in his quest for the German imperial crown. In the battle of Göllheim beyond the Rhine, three hundred bearded Hungarians with braided hair fought on the side of Albert, and defeated Adolf of Nassau (who had been killed in action), and Albert gained the German imperial throne.[116]

Andrew III's daughter from his marriage to Fenana, the six year old Elizabeth, was now engaged to the nine year old Vencel of Bohemia, and she remained in Vienna.[117] It may have been the formation of this twofold family marriage tie with western dynasties that made Matthew (Máté) Csák, who until now had remained loyal to the royal family, jealous; he turned away from the king in the year 1298.[118]

Andrew III took the disloyalty of Matthew (Máté) Csák very seriously, and established powerful alliances with nobles of the realm, whose interests could be served by a humiliating defeat of Csák and his clan. The king's mother, Tomasina Marosini, curtailed the influence of the Anjous and of the four Babonik brothers in the "Region Beyond the Drave," that is, the area south of the Drave, and on both banks of the Save streams. (The father of the Baboniks was the former head steward of the region called Slovenia.)[119]

In the valley of the Vág river, Demeter, the reeve of Pozsony and Zólyom, held back the forces of Matthew Csák, thereby to prevent the consolidation in the north of Transdanubia of the Babonik brothers' forces serving the Anjous with the army of Matthew Csák.[120] Andrew III had further undermined Anjou interests by taking away the archiepiscopal see of Esztergom from archbishop-elect Gregory, who had turned pro-Anjou after his election to that see (and after Andrew III had confirmed him in his position as archbishop), by January, 1300.[121]

During this development of political and military events, the administration of the country broke in two. Two palatines divided the country: Apor of the clan of Pác in Transdanubia (that is, the area south and west of the Danube), while Roland of the clan of Rátold took control of the areas east of the Danube river.[122] Simultaneously, the king had to reach a defensive-friendship treaty with Demeter, the reeve of Pozsony and Zólyom.[123]

In 1290, during the Diet, Andrew III had hoped to overcome his opponents with the sincere support he expected to receive from his nobles.[124] He had hoped in vain. The overbearing greed of the barons had threatened to fatefully undermine the authority of the monarch and eliminate the liberties of the nobility.[125] In 1298, led by the hierarchy, the king and his nobles had met for the purpose that they, "with the approval of the barons," reach a decision concerning immediate reconstruction of the country.[126]

In the Diet of 1298, *congregatio generalis*, the high clergy and lesser nobility had, therefore, stayed together. The latter group also included the Cuman, Saxon, and Székler nobles.[127] The barons, however, *pout moris est*, met separately, and affixed their own seal to the resolutions reached at the meetings of the gathering.[128] Many of the barons had been living like independent regional kings, very much like the German princes after 1250, during the "interregnum," until the assassination of Adolf of Nassau - and wished to assert their opinion and use their influence over the development of public affairs.[129]

Many nobles had also served in the armed troops - *banderia* - under the standards of various barons, since many nobles had little choice but to fight, live, and die under the banner of the regional potentate for no cause of their own.[130] From the text of the dietary resolutions one may conclude, however, that the selfish grouping of the barons did not evolve into an upper house of the high aristocracy.[131]

The Diet brought forth resolutions in support of the monarch, the nobles, and the Church; for instance, articles supportive of the nobles declared that only one son in the family was obligated to serve under the king's banner in times of war (fought in defense of the realm);[132] nobles may, of their own free will, serve in baronial forces, but they could not be forced to do so.[133] The palatine on his circuit of the country could not hold his court of law within the confines of a hamlet or village, but on the common meadow, and preferably, not hold a court (of law) in winter.[134]

The annual issuance of money was to be overseen by the country reeve and four nobles of the county, who made certain that the bronze content of the silver coins remained one-fifth of its value for two years, and one-tenth after that.[135] Issued new money ("denars") in circulation were the legal tender at regional (and local) county fairs. (In the text, the fair director must accept issued money as legal tender; were he not to, he would lose his right to hold the fair.) The "owner" or "keeper" of the fair was designated as the person who had the right to hold the fair at a certain location, at a given time, by paying a special fee for the privilege to the royal court.[136] The Diet ordered that a house-owner [head of household] pay one-twelfth of a silver coin in lieu of the exchange fee for the new money.[137] Anyone who coined, or issued "false" money, or issued it illegally, would lose his chattel, his entire household.[138]

Ecclesiastical goods, such as bishop's belongings, could not be confiscated upon his death; if someone had taken them unlawfully, he must return them with payment of interest.[139] The people of ecclesiastical estates pay no taxes, or other dues, and only provide over-night accommodation for the local (land)lord of the parish - or of the religious community.[140]

The Diet had further upheld the king's (official and personal) prestige. It recognized Andrew III anew as the natural lord of the kingdom.[141] It ordered that the royal lands - that may include large sections of the country - and holdings that belonged to the queen, but had been unlawfully taken from her, be returned (to the king and queen), and the monarch had the power to reconquer them by force if necessary.[142] Evidently, the monarch had to rely upon military force to exectue with vigor the decrees of the Diet.[143]

The assembly further increased the number of royal counselors by sending representatives to the royal council besides the barons: eight bishops and eight *knights* [lesser nobles] would be elected to serve in the King's Council, who, by taking turns every three months, form each time, a team of two men, would always accompany the monarch - who would have to pay them. Without their advice and consent, the monarch could not grant office, or land, to anyone; if he did, it would be void.[144] The queen also must select her Judge (of the Queen's Court) from among the ranks of the lesser nobility, and not from among nobles of foreign birth.[145] Tolls payable to the king and queen, and recently established tolls would be regarded as illegal, and would be discontinued.[146]

The Diet declared that the hierarchy would serve advance notice on excommunicating anyone who would not return illegally confiscated goods to the rightful owners. The king would strip them of their goods and, if need be, of their noble status, and could use military force to carry out the punishment.[147] Castles and fortifications that had been constructed without royal permission would be demolished.[148] Goods unlawfully held would be investigated under oath by four nobles in every county, and by an appointee of the court.[149]

Monks and friars would not administer the sacraments to those who had been excommunicated by church authorities.[150] The person who had given a grant, or gift to a monk, or friar to allow an excommunicated person to receive the sacraments would be excommunicated.[151] The individual who dared to collect pawns on abolished tolls would also be excommunicated.[152]

The 1290 laws of Andrew III proposed the creation of a domestic front against the growing influence of the barons - in the royal council; in the country - perhaps to realize the idea formulated by the chronicler Simon de Kéza, and he proposed this with the support of the hierarchy.[153]

The 1290 laws went beyond the 1222 decree of Andrew II (the Golden Bull) in two essential points: (1) the king let it be known that he would name his chief officers of the realm with the consent of the nobility, "ex consilio nobilium regni nostri, ex antiqua consuetudine regni nostri," thereby assuring a place for the nobility and the knights [lesser nobles] in the government of the country; (2) when the palatine made his annual circuit holding courts of law in the realm, four nobles in each county stayed with him, observing and reporting on him to the king, in order to assure the nobles' actual participation in the administration of the legal system of the realm.[154]

Upon the death of Ladislas IV - no friend of the Church - the high churchmen helped Andrew III in the exercise of his royal duties. As elected members of the King's Council, the bishops had, together with members of the nobility, assured for themselves an active role, approved by law, in the country's government. In such a manner, a government by the estates (of high churchmen and lesser nobles) had emerged in Hungary during the reign of the last Árpád king. It was a government based on Spanish, English, German, and French patterns, and it shared the burden of governing the country.[155] His constitutional development resulted from the family blood ties formed by the Árpád marriage alliances with the Aragonese[156] and French royal dynasties,[157] and German princely families.[158]

The diets held by the estates in Friaul, northern Italy, may well have influenced dietary developments in the realm of Andrew III.[159] It most probably was in Friaul, a region under the spiritual jurisdiction of the Patriarch of Aquileia, that the first constitutionally structured government based upon representative estates was developed in "central Europe." Hungarian clerics schooled in law (obtaining their university education in that particular region of Italy), and active at the court of Andrew III, might have prepared an ideological base for this innovation in their own country's government.[160]

The question is whether the constitutional experiment with the estates had remained a mere experiment - on the grounds that it was restricted to a small social circle of the king and his advisors - or, had the Diet of 1290 followed the main outline of the Decree (Golden Bull) of 1222, where Andrew II had announced that he: (1) would name the realm's head officials in accordance with the expressed wish of his nobles,[161] and (2) promised that the palatine holding courts of law countrywide would be accompanied, in addition to the county reeve, by four knights [service nobles] of the particular county?[162]

One may cast doubts upon the resolutions of the 1290 Diet. Did Andrew III possess the might to enforce those enactments at a time when he had no alternative but to confirm the land- and office grants his predecessors had made - including the landgrant of the entire county of Ung to Amadé Aba?[163] The royal diplomas of these years made almost constant reference to the insecurity of roads and travel countrywide, and to the continued destruction of public and private properties everywhere - revealing a most discouraging picture of the public condition.[164]

The monarch also had his problems with foreign policy. It is recorded in the Chronicle that during the second year of his reign he had defeated the duke of Austria.[165] As explained above, Albert was unwilling to return the forts he had occupied and kept in western Hungary during the 1280's, and caused King Andrew to take to arms to regain them.[166] Andrew III had been successful; he marched on Vienna,[167] defeated Albert. However, the duke in the following Treaty of Hainburg was able to secure possession of some of his territorial conquest in Hungary. He had arranged for the return of only a few fortifications - in that he requested that the others be demolished in the mutual interest of peace and security on the Hungaro-Austrian border.[168]

Did Andrew III naively subscribe to the agreement, without realizing that the duke had played a crude political-diplomatic trick on him? Albert had not only returned all of the occupied forts, but by insisting that the forts be destroyed - he knew that they had belonged to the Kőszeg clan, who had been until this time loyal supporters of the king - he also wished to turn the Kőszeg clan (whose forts were now being destroyed) against the king.[169]

Albert of Habsburg originated the policy that forced the Kőszeg clan to work for the enthronement of Charles of Anjou as the king of Hungary, already during the reign of Andrew III.[170] The purposeful remark of the chronicler may point toward such a policy. Certain nobles, the chronicler reported - the sons of Henry, alias Kőszeg, John and Grand Reeve [Ban(us)] Henry, Ugrin, sons of Pócs of Ujlak, and "many others" - had turned to the Roman Pontiff out of prejudice toward Andrew III to ask him for a king, as if King Andrew had not been their reigning monarch during the last three and a half or so years.[171] At this stage of events, the Kőszeg clan had also pressured the lords of the Dalmatian seashore to join the cause

of the Anjous in their quest for the Hungarian Crown, and urged the
royal court in Naples to prepare for military action, if needed,
against the legitimate monarch of the country.[172]

The policy, therefore, of Albert of Habsburg to drive a wedge
between the ruling Hungarian monarch and the Kőszeg family had
been successful. The Kőszegs led an insurrection against their king,
occupied Pozsony (although only temporarily), and had even
imprisoned the monarch for a brief period of time.[173]

Andrew III, cornered in this serious game of politico-
diplomatic chess, had no alternative but to place his mother,
Tomasina Marosini, in charge of the government in the region
between the Danube and the Adriatic - wholly realizing the danger
that, in such a fashion, he might cause, once again, a dynastic
division of the realm. The Borsa family east of the Tisza river rose
against the king, but Marosini was able to suppress their insubordi-
nation (led by a former palatine named Mize) by reclaiming from
him the fort of Szekcső in Baranya county. She had also restored
order in the area south of the Save river.[174]

In order to take serious counteraction against members of the
Kőszeg clan, and to reclaim [repossess] their fortified castle at
Kőszeg, Andrew III had to rely upon the military support of Albert
of Austria, whose daughter, Agnes, he had married after the death of
his first wife.[175] Albert must have seen the fulfillment of his dream
in the hope of gaining direct access to the Hungarian Crown.

It must have been the reason why Máté [Matthew] Csák, until
then a loyal supporter of the king,[176] became his worst enemy in the
year 1288.[177] King Andrew III now had to seek the support of those
nobles and noble families whose interests and political ambitions
were served by the anticipated oppression of Máté Csák. However,
the king's powers and influence were weakened by the fact that, once
more, two palatines had gained control of the realm's administration.[178]

The Diet of 1298,[179] in which the *universitas nobilium* of
Hungarian, Székler, Saxon, and Cuman nobles had played a role next
to the realm's bishops and barons,[180] had elevated Albertino
Marosini, the king's uncle, to the ranks of the Hungarian nobility[181]
- as if to render a legal recognition of the rights and privileges of the
barons and (high) nobility,[182] thereby to determine anew the
"doctrine of equality" among all - higher and lesser nobles [service

nobles; knights] - as it had been formulated by the chronicler of the age, Simon de Kéza.[183]

The existence of the nobles' *estates* as an institution can be ascertained by the fact that the Diet's resolutions were determined by the *estates* of bishops and abbots, and of the nobility[184] - excluding the barons[185] - with the full consent of the monarch, but without his active participation.[186]

The constitutional status held by members of the (higher and lesser) nobility was further supported by the circumstantial evidence that an article of this diet repeated a decree of the 1290 dietary resolutions that said that the monarch must steadily be accompanied by two bishops and two nobles - *elected* to serve, by rotation, for three months a year. The latter were the elected *representatives* of the country's knights [lesser nobility].[187] And yet, the situation had not improved dramatically; the Diet enacted laws, but it was up to the king and the barons [still!] to sanction and carry out those laws.[188]

Sanctioning of the new legislation was necessary, since the resolutions of the 1298 Diet made the monarch responsible for the deteriorating conditions in the country - as if to emphasize the then prevalent public opinion that the enactments of the Diet of 1290 were not, and had not been, implemented.[189] However, the legislators had recognized the fact that the barons and other potentates in the realm were responsible for the decline of public order, when and where nobody could feel safe in his own home, or in the country at large.

The king's powers were strengthened by at least four articles in 1298. Those resolutions stressed the argument that the monarch was the natural lord of the country, who could, by the use of force if necessary, restore and maintain law and order, and reclaim territories that had been unlawfully taken from the royal domain or from the queen. The king could even request foreign aid, were an insurrection to break out in the realm.[190]

The Diet of 1298 paid attention to the Church and the demands of the knights [lesser nobility]. This was understandable because it was the estates of the members of the higher clergy, and of the nobles, who had prepared and had the resolutions enacted in the assemblies.

The 1298 Diet assured full freedom to the Church.[191] The Church (the hierarchy) supported the monarch, and it rightfully expected the latter to sanction laws that guaranteed public law and order in the realm.[192] Andrew III had also restored the wealth that had been illegally confiscated from ecclesiastics; nor did he claim possession of a bishop left behind upon his death.[193] The Diet obligated the monarch that he reconquer portions of the territories that had been conquered by foreigners, and restore the judicial unity of the whole country, "quasi quoddam ius totem."[194]

The resolutions of 1298 remained ineffective.[195] The great nobles of the land did not take the king seriously.[196] As late as 1299, Andrew III had to fight a war with Matthew (Máté) Csák.[197] Perhaps it was on those grounds that the king had summoned another national diet in the year 1300: he wanted to prove that he was in charge of the government of the kingdom.[198]

It was truly a crude irony of history that, when he - the last ruler of the Árpád dynasty - was able to successfully parry the maneuvers of his opponents in front of the papal curia in Rome, early death claimed him in the prime of life.[199]

Tomasina Marosini, the mother of Andrew III, had died in 1300.[200] The king had departed from this earthly life on January 14,1301, and was buried in the church of the Franciscan Minorites in Buda.[201] Stephen, the Justice of the Realm, the son of Head Reeve Ernyey, and a good a friend of the king, commemorated the deceased ruler by saying that with his death the last golden twig had fallen from the family tree of the Árpáds (who had ruled the country for centuries). All inhabitants of the land, regardless of their social stratum, knew that they had lost their natural lord, and were truly sorry for his death.[202]

There is no historical evidence to support the suspicious remark made by the Austrian chronicler that Andrew III had been poisoned.[203] The unexpected death of the Hungarian king would not have aided even the ambitious plans of Albert of Habsburg who, by then, occupied the German imperial throne.[204]

NOTES

1. Cf. *Reimchronik*, cc. 381-406: the barons grew tired of Ladislas IV, "odiosus fit," and called upon Andrew of Venice, lines 39795-39973; Archbishop Ladomér supported them, lines 33995-40064; J. Kaufmann, *Eine Studie über die Beziehungen der Habsburger zum Königtum Ungarn in den Jahren 1278 bis 1366* (Eisenstadt, 1970), 45ff.

2. Cf. Dercsényi, *Chronicon pictum*, I [facsimile], fol. 65´; Z.J. Kosztolnyik, "III András és a pápai udvar" [Andrew III of Hungary and the Papal Court],*Századok*, 126 (1992), 646ff.

3. Cf. Dercsényi, I, fol. 66b; *SSH*, I, 477,15-19. Charles' family tree, *ibid.*, I, 478,3-13, and the papal writ of May 31, 1303, Potthast, n. 25252;*VMH*, I, 379ff. (n. 635); *CD*, VIII-1, 121ff. Also "Chronicon Posoniense," *ibid.*, II, 45,1-28.

4. *Reimchronik*, lines 39962-39973; *SSH*, I, 475f.; II, 45,11-28.

5. *SSH*, I, 466,16-18, and I, 476,3-8; II, 45f.; O'Callaghan, 346f.; F.O. Brachfeld, *Dona Violante de Hungria, reina de Aragón* (Madrid, 1942); one of their daughters, also named Jolán(ta), became the queen of Alfonso X the Learned - R.I. Burns, *The Worlds of Alfonso the Learned and James the Conqueror* (Princeton, 1985), 211ff.

6. *SSH*, I, 476,8-10; II, 46,3-4; H.D. Sedgwick, *Italy in the Thirteenth Century* (Boston-New York, 1913), 162ff.; Daniel Waley, *The Italian City Republics* (New York-Toronto, 1969), 56ff.

7. *SSH*, I, 476,10-14; II, 46,4-8.

8. *Ibid.*, I, 476,14-19; II, 46,8-13.

9. *Ibid.*, I, 476,19 - 477,3; "...a baronibus coronatur," *ibid.*, II, 46,13-14; on the date, *ibid.*, I, 473f., and the "Várad Chronicle," *ibid.*, I, 213,20-23; also, P. Ransanus, *Epithoma rerum Hungararum*, ed. P. Kulcsár (Budapest, 1977), 132, ind. xvii; my review of this volume in *Austrian History Yearbook*, 17-18 (1981-82), 361f. The Pozsony Chronicle named those who had turned against Andrew III: "videlicet Ugrinus filius magni Pous [Porch, *SSH*, II, 46,38] de genere Kak [Chak, *ibid.*, II, 46,39], Iohannes, Nicolaus et Heinrici banus, filii Heinrici, magister Laurencius dictus Chete cum filio suo magistro Zleukus ac plures...;" *ibid.*, II, 46,15-20. On the son of Pócs, cf. *HO*, IV, 65; *ÁUO*, IX, 107.

10. *Reimchronik*, lines 40001-40057; and, 40083-40205; Huber, *art. cit.*, in *AföG*, 218ff.; further, "Cont. Vindob.," *MGHSS*, IX, 716,19-22; the "short" Annals of Worms, *ibid.*, XVII, 78,37-38. On the Vilhelmites, see Knauz, II, 184.

11. *Reimchronik*, lines 40933-41007.

12. See his letter addressed to James of Aragon-Sicily, *RA*, n. 3662 with text, dated September 8, 1290; and *Reimchronik*, lines 41089-41213.

13. *Ibid.*, lines 41214-41262.

14. *Ibid.*, lines 41262-41291, and compare with *RA*, n. 3651 - his Charter of Coronation; the coronation took place on a Sunday - cf. *Reimchronik*, line 41216; according to the Várad Chronicle, on the 13th day after the death of Ladislas IV, cf. *SSH*, I, 213Wf.; the Chronicle has the 18th day, *ibid.*, I, 475,4-5. Ladislas IV was murdered on the Monday before the Feast of St. Margaret (July 10), *ibid.*, I, 473f. Queen Fenana spoke of the merits of Archbishop Ladomér - cf. Knauz, II, 308; *CD*, VI-1, 90, and she stated further that it was Tivadar [Theodore], archpriest of Fehérvár, who had taken her from Poland to Hungary, cf. *ÁUO*, X, 36f.; judged by her remarks, the time schedule provided by the *Reimchronik* is out of order.

15. *SSH*, I, 436f., and I, 213Wf.; *ibid.*, II, 45,8-9.

16. Chronicle, cc. 181-212, *ibid.*, I, 227ff.; see Domanovszky's introduction, *ibid.*, I, 22ff.; Horváth, *Stílusproblémák*, 256f.; Csóka, 602f. and 604ff., who wrote

that the segment of the text may have been written by a contemporary author; Hóman, *Szt. László korabeli*, 63f.

17. Chronicle, c. 179, *SSH*, I, 469f.; L. Mezey, *Irodalmi anyanyelvűségünk kezdetei az Árpád-kor végén* [Beginnings of the Hungarian Vernacular at the End of the Árpádian Age] (Budapest, 1955), 20f. Bishop Bruno of Olmütz reported to Rome on the status of heretics in Hungary - *VMH*, I, 307ff., recording that every homeless heretic received a warm reception in Hungary; on this, see also "Cont. Praed. Vindob.," *MGHSS*, IX, 731, and "Cont. Zwettlensis III," anno, 1261, *ibid.*, IX, 656. The same source also recorded a fragment of a flagellant song, *ibid.*, IX, 728. The spread of heresy in the Balkans must have occurred through Hungary as, for example, through merchants traveling to Byzantium - as it may be evident from the Cuman Laws of Ladislas IV - cf. Marczali, *Enchiridion*, 176.

18. Chronicle, c. 174, *SSH*, I, 464.; *ibid.*, II, 41f. (c. 65); the Zagreb Chronicle said nothing on this - *ibid.*, I, 211f. (c. 18).

19. Kéza, "Gesta," cc. 1 and 74-75, *SSH*, I, 141, and 185ff.; Szűcs, *art. cit.* (Kézai problémák), *Memoria Hungariae*, 1, 187ff.; Pintér, I, 275ff.; Horváth, *Stílusproblémák*, 371f.

20. *SSH*, I 474 (c. 185).

21. *Ibid.*, I, 475f.; II, 45f. (c. 76).

22. See Anno Borst, *Die Katharer. Schriften der MGH*, vol. XII (Stuttgart, 1953), 180ff.; Heribert Grundmann, *Die religiösen Bewegungen im Mittelalter. Historische Studien*, vol. 267 (Berlin, 1935), 40ff.; K. Schünemann, *Die Entstehung des Städtewesens in Südosteuropa*, Südosteuropäische Bibliothek, vol. 1 (Breslau, n.d.), 129ff.; I. Sinka, *Magyarország árpádkori fő-és székvárosa* (Szeged, 1936). The Chronicle made one simple statement: "...plebs flagellis seferiendo universaliter discurrebat," *SSH*, I, 469,9, and concluded its report with the text of a song, *ibid.*, I, 470,7-10.

23. *Ibid.*, I, 473 (c. 183). H. Holzapfel, *Handbuch der Geschichte des Franziskanerordens* (Freiburg i.Br., 1909), 50f.

24. *SSH*, I, 485ff. (c. 194).

25. *Ibid.*, I, 481f. (c. 190).

26. *Ibid.*, I, 478,24-26.

27. *Ibid.*, I, 478,13-15.

27. *Ibid.*, I 473,13-15, though added he was elected pope upon the death of Boniface VIII: "et sibi mortuo Bonifacio VIIIo in summum pontificem eligitur et creatur," *ibid.*, I, 482,8-10; Fraknói, I, 117; F. Ehrle, "Die Spiritualen, ihr Verhältnis zum Franziskanerorden und zu den Fratricellen," *Archiv für Literatur- und Kirchengeschichte des Mittelalters*, 3 (1887), 554ff.

28. *SSH*, I, 482,4-8, and 482,10-22.

29. Cf. A. Domanovszky, "A magyar királykrónika xiv századi folytatása" [The Continuation of the Hungarian Royal Chronicle in the 14th Century], *Berzeviczy Emlékkönyv* (Budapest, 1934), 21ff., esp. 31ff.; see also Elemér Mályusz, *A Thúróczy Krónika és forrásai* [The Thúróczy Chronicle and Its Sources] (Budapest, 1967), 57ff.

30. Charles Robert had established the Franciscan monastery at Lippa, "dominus rex Fratribus Minoribus edificare ecclesiam in Lyppa," *SSH*, I, 491,4-5, and note 3; also, *ibid.*, I 499; J. Karácsonyi, *Szent Ferenc Rendjének története Magyarországon 1711-ig* [History of the Franciscan Order in Hungary until 1711], 2 vols. (Budapest, 1922-24), I, 34ff. On the mission to Avignon, cf. *VMH*, I, 544f. (anno 1331).

31. Cf. *RA*, n. 3656; Knauz, II, 267; *RA*, n. 3663; *ÁUO*, V, 1f.; compare to *RA*, nn. 2657-58.

32. *RA*, n. 3672 with text; and n. 3668; Knauz, II, 271; *CD*, VI-1, 55f.

33. *RA*, n. 3705 (February 22, 1291); *RHM*, 615ff.; Marczali, *Enchiridion*, 186ff.; further, Teutsch-Firnhaber, *Urkundenbuch*, I, 159ff.; Zimmermann-Werner, *Urkundenbuch*, I, 173ff.; cf. art. 25.

34. *Ibid.*, art. 10.

35. *Ibid.*, art. 35.

36. *Ibid.*, aa. 7, 8, and 26.

37. *Ibid.*, art. 25.

38. *Ibid.*, art. 21, determining the collection of the tithe of wheat and wine products, "...quo quolibet aratro unum fertorem pro decimis solvat;" the term "aratrum" must have meant one ploughland; the term "ferto" must have meant ("ein Viertel"), one fourth of a silver mark; further, "...populi autem ipsorum nobilium et Saxonum de singulis capeciis [capecium?] solvant unum pondus," with "capecium" meaning one [portion of] plough(land) [one day's work?], and "pondus" one twelfth of "ferto."

39. Marczali, *Enchiridion*, 186ff., art. 12.

40. *Ibid.*, art. 14.

41. *Ibid.*, art. 4.

42. *Ibid.*, art. 9.

43. *Ibid.*, art. 14.

44. *Ibid.*, art. 15.

45. *Ibid.*, art. 18.

46. *Ibid.*, art. 16, and art. 18; "impignorationes" meaning "repressalis," that is, the right of any free person [royal subject?] who had been harmed, whose property had been damaged by a "foreigner," that is, someone in transit, not in permanent residence in the country, to make reprisals on, demands from the latter, regardless where he came from; cf. J. Holub, *Századok*, 55 (1921), 133f.

47. Marczali, *Enchiridion*, 186ff., art. 30.

48. *Ibid.*, art. 2.

49. *Ibid.*, art. 31.

50. *Ibid.*, art. 8.

51. *Ibid.*, art. 8b and art. 19.

52. *Ibid.*, art. 5.

53. *Ibid.*, art. 1.

54. *Ibid.*, art. 2.

55. *Ibid.*, aa. 27-29.

56. *Ibid.*, art. 32. Articles 26 through 34 are not numbered in Marczali! See *RHM*, 619f.

57. Marczali, *Enchiridion*, 186ff., art. 9b.

58. *Ibid.*, art. 19a.

59. *Ibid.*, art. 22.

60. *Ibid.*, aa. 10, 11, 21, 26, 30. Three royal writs directly refer to the Diet of 1290; *RA*, n. 3656, Knauz, II, 267; *RA*, n. 3663, *ÁUO*, V, 1f., mentioning resolutions of the Diet, and *RA*, n. 3672 with text, "...in congregatione nobilium generali supra veterm Budam."

61. *RA*, n. 3662, with text.

62. *Reimchronik*, lines 411263-41292.

63. *RA*, n. 3656,

64. *RA*, n. 3668, Knauz, II, 271; *CD*, VI-1, 55f.

65. Cf. Caspar, *Register Gregors VII*, ii:13, ii:68, iv:25, vi:69; Kosztolnyik, *From Coloman*, 244 and 260, nn. 134-135; idem, *art. cit.*, *Church History*, 1980, 380.

66. *SSH*, I, 477,4-13, and 477f. (c. 187).

67. *Ibid.*, I, 475f. (c. 186); "Chronicon Posoniense" also named nobles who had asked the pope for another king, *ibid.*, II, 46,15-20; on the death of Andrew III, his burial in the church of the Franciscan Minorites in Buda, *ibid.*, II, 47,1-3.

68. See, e.g., the resolutions of the 1279 Synod of Buda, *RHM*, 265ff.; Hefele, *Conziliengeschichte*, V, 188f.; Waldmüller, *Synoden*, 188ff.; Z.J. Kosztolnyik, "Rome and the Church in Hungary in 1279: The Synod of Buda," *Annuarium historiae conciliorum*, 22 (1990), 68ff.; *RA*, n. 2962; Potthast, nn. 21600 and 21601; *RHM*, 554ff.

69. Papal writ, March 12, 1299, Potthast, n. 24791, *VMH*, n. 618, providing clear evidence on this; for background, cf. P. Caramello (ed.), S. Thomas Acquinatis *Summa Theologiae*, 4 vols. (Turin-Rome, 1950), vol. II, IIaIIae, qu. 90, art. 1.

70. See the resolutions of 1290, aa. 11, 5, 15, or the resolutions of 1298, prefatory note, and aa. 26-28.

71. Thus, e.g., it was Andrew III who had summoned the diet of 1298: "...dominus Andreas Spiritu Santo suggerente...et fidelibus consiliis acquiescens, congregationem indixit generalem," the resolutions of which were placed into writing by members of the (attending) hierarchy - Marczali, *Enchiridion*, 191f.; *RHM*, 630f.

72. Mályusz, *Egyházi társadalom*, 35ff.; Gy. Bónis, *A jogtudó értelmiség a Mohács előtti Magyarországon* [Der Juristendstand in Ungarn vor Mohács, 1526] (Budapest, 1971), 21ff.

73. "...cum celebrarem curiam apud Legionem cum archiepiscopis et episcopis et magnatibus regni mei, et cum electis civibus ex singulis civitatibus...;" cf. M. Colmeiro (ed.), *Cortes de los antiquos reinos de Leon y de Castilla*, 5 vols. (Madrid, 1861-1906), I, n. VII, i, 39-42, aa. 1-15 (and compare with *ibid.*, I, n. I, i-xi, aa. 1-48); Mitteis, 414f., noted that the cortes in Aragon was an institution of secular origin; it did not evolve from ecclesiastical synods, as in Castile. See further, R.B. Merriman, "Cortes of the Spanish Kingdoms in the Late Middle Ages," *American Historical Review*, 16 (1911), 476ff.; and J.F. O'Callaghan, "The Beginnings of the Cortes in Leon-Castile," *ibid.*, 74 (1969), 1503ff.

74. "Promisi etiam, quod non faciam guerram vel pacem vel placitum, nisi cum concilio episcoporum, nobilium, et bonorum hominum per quorum consilium debeo regi;" *ibid.*, n. VII:3, i:40; "...apud Beneventum et presentibus episcopis et vassalis meis, et multis de qualiobet villa regni mei in plena curia;" *ibid.*, n. VIII, 1.

75. "...una nobiscum venerabilium episcoporum cetu reverendo, et totius regni primatum et baronum glorioso colegio, civium multitudine destinatorum a singulis civitatibus considente,...;" *ibid.*, n. X, i, 46f., aa. 1-6.

76. "...de universorum consensu hanc legem edidi mihi et a meis posteris omnibus observandam;" *ibid.*, n. X, i, 47, and n. XIII, i, 54f.; compares with Alfonso the Learned's encyclopaedia of laws, *Las Siete partidas del rey Don Alfonso el Sabio el Nono*, ed. G. Lopez, Spanish with Latin, 3 vols. (Madrid, 1555; repr. 1972) I, i:11, 18-19, and i:2, 6, etc. This "lexicon of laws" includes almost 2700 essays on legal topics, cf. R.I. Burns, *The Worlds of Alfonso the Wise and James the Conqueror* (Princeton, 1985), 12; J.F. O'Callaghan, *A History of Spain* (Ithaca-London, 1975), 358ff.; Mitteis, 416f. The king and queen legislate with the cooperation of the realm's spiritual and secular lords, the barons - by now separated from the nobles - *and* the representatives of the towns - "convenientibus...una...et totius regni primatum et baronum glorioso colegio, civium multitudine destinatorum a singulis civitatibus considente." Cf. Colmeiro, *Cortes*, I, 46ff., n. X. Mitteis, 416f., argued that James I had been able to overcome the opposition of the high nobles, who wished to control him.

77. Cf. Colmeiro, *Cortes*, I, n. XIII (p. 54ff.); he regarded himself as the Lord's vicar, who had to serve the right and the good of his people in the temporal sphere - cf. *Siete partidas*, II, i:5, as it was his special duty to observe the laws, *ibid.*, I, i:9, R.I. Burns (ed.), *Alfonso X the Learned of Castile and his Thirteenth Century Renaissance* (Philadelphia, 1990).

78. Constance of Aragon - *SSH*, I, 463 (c. 172). On her second marriage - upon papal command - see *Chronica regia Coloniensis*, ed. G. Waitz, SSrG (Hannover, 1878), 184; Zurita, I, 84 and 103.

79. *RA*, nn. 393, 433, 495, 731, 732, and 746; Heinrich Finke (ed.), *Acta Aragonensia: Quellen zur deutschen, italienischen, französischen, spanischen, zur Kirchen- und Kulturgeschichte*, vol. III (Berlin, 1922; repr. Aalen, 1966), note to number IX, on p. 16.

80. On Tota, see *RA*, nn. 198 and 362. Andrew III's aunt (daughter of Andrew II from his second marriage) was the (second) queen of James I of Aragon - Chronicle, c. 186, *SSH*, I, 475ff.; she must have been a very determined woman - cf. O'Callaghan, *op. cit.*, 346f. As Mitteis, 416f., noted, James I did his best to keep his nobles at bay, and he succeeded.

81. Cf. *MGHLL*, Const. III, 67, and 58; Rudolf of Habsburg had ordered that, in 1274, the town citizens also attend the assembly he had summoned to debate matters of public concern: "quantenus cum baronibus, comitibus, liberis ministerialibus, militibus, civibus et communitatibus civitatum," *MGHLL*, sect. IV, iii:67 *and* 56. Gebhardt, I, 398ff.; H. Mitteis, *Die Rechtsidee in der Geschichte*, ed. Leiva Petersen (Weimar, 1957), 269ff. and 697ff.

82. Cf. Iohannes Saresberiensis *Policraticus, sive de nugis curialium et vestigiis philosophorum libri octo*, ed. C.C.I. Webb, 2 vols. (Oxford, 1909), v:2, D. Knowles, *The Evolution of Medieval Thought*, 2nd ed. (London-New York, 1988), 124ff.; McIlwain, 320f.; Walter Ullman, "John of Salisbury's Policraticus in the Later Middle Ages," in K. Hauck (ed.), *Geschichtsschreibung und geistiges Leben im Mittelalter: Festschrift für Heinz Löwe zum 65 Geburtstag* (Cologne-Vienna, 1978), 519ff. A similar situation had emerged in England under Edward I during the wars with Wales - cf. Stubbs, *Charters*, 465, 477f., and 481f.; Bryce Lyon, *A Constitutional and Legal History of Medieval England* (New York-London, 1960), 346ff. and 418ff.

83. *RA*, n. 3686 (County of Ung); *ÁUO*, XII, 496; or *RA*, nn. 3688 (Knauz, II, 274); 3690 with text; 3696, *ÁUO*, X, 25; 3699, *ÁUO*, V, 20; *RA*, n. 3704 with text (a gift by Stephen V); 3737 with text; 3706; *CD*, VI-1, 88; Katona, *Historia critica*, VII, 1059; *RA*, n. 3758 with text.

84. *RA*, n. 3752, *ÁUO*, V, 24; n. 3757 with text; n. 3767 with text, etc.; also, *RA*, nn. 3768 with text, 3784 with text, 3841 with text, etc.

85. See the papal writ to the papal legate Benevenutus instructing him also to report on conditions in Hungary - Potthast, n. 23384; *VMH*, n. 588.

86. On this, cf. an earlier letter to Rudolf, Potthast, nn. 23386 and 23385 [in that order]; *VMH*, nn. 689 and 588.

87. The Holy See made a firm protest to both Rudolf and Albert - Potthast, nn. 23543 and 23544, *VMH*, nn. 598 and 599; Katona, IV, 1052, with references to the writs of Gregory VII, in Caspar, *Register*, ii:133, iv:63, and iv:25, dated October 28, 1074, April 23, 1078, and June 5, 1078.

88. *RA*, n. 37822, *CD*, VI-1, 135; Katona, *Historia critica*, VII, 1079; also, Potthast, nn. 23515 (*CD*, VI-1, 81) and 244791 (*VMH*, n. 618); on the occupation of Ft. Kőszeg, cf. *RA*, n. 4088 [October 19, 1296]; *CD*, VI-2, 195ff.

89. Cf. "Cont. Vindob.," *MGHSS*, IX, 716; the writ issued by the "false" Andrew [Andrew the Pretender], for George, son of Simon, *CD*, VI-1, 23; further, "Annales Polonienses," in *MPH*, II, 879, and III, 184; "Vita Kyngae ducissa," *ibid.*, IV, 704, 726, commented on by Katona, VII, 1026; G. Wenczel (ed.), *Anjoukori diplomáciai emlékek* [Diplomatic Correspondence of the Anjou Age], 3 vols. (Budapest, 1874-76), I , 208, that the court of Naples was concerned about the Pretender, the (a) False Andrew, as late as 1317!

90. *RA*, n. 3804, *CD*, VI-1, 123; *RA*, n. 2782, *CD*, VI-1, 135; Katona, VII, 1073 and 1079; *RA*, n. 3820; *SSH*, I, 476f., and I, 213f.; *Reimchronik*, lines 41080-

41150, and 41240-41; archpriest Theodore went for her to bring her home from Poland, *ÁUO*, X, 36f.; Queen Fenana made mention of Archbishop Ladomér, Knauz, II, 308; on a writ dated 1290, Fenana appears as queen - *HO*, VIII, 289 and VI, 369.
    91. *SSH*, I, 477,3-4, II, 46,14-15; also, e.g., *RA*, n. 3820, *CD*, VI-1, 138. "Cont. Vindobonensis," *MGHSS*, IX, 716,29-45 and 717,34-36 (anno 1293!). Before the actual military strike, a Hungarian envoy had visited Vienna - Wenczel, *Anjoukori diplomácia*, I, 77.
    92. Cf. "Cont. Floracenses," *MGHSS*, IX, 749,29-39; "Cont. Vindobonensis," *ibid.*, IX, 716,45 - 717,7; "Annales Mellicenses," *ibid.*, IX, 510,39-40; *RA*, n. 3960 with text; a different version in *ÁUO*, X, 135ff.; *RA*, n. 3817, *HO*, IV, 791; *RA*, n. 3818 with text; n. 3822, *CD*, VI-1, 128; n. 3831, *HO*, VIII, 302. The monarch had compensated the citizens of Pozsony for the damages they had suffered from Albert - *RA*, n. 3937, *RHM*, 623ff., and n. 3838, *HO*, II, 21f.
    93. Cf. Wenczel, *Anjoukori diplomácia*, I, 98; *HO*, VI, 388; VIII, 319; VII, 230f. For a brief duration, they had even captured the king and held him captive - "Annales Mellicenses," *MGHSS*, IX, 510,42. Károly Szabó, "III Endre fogsága" [The Captivity of Andrew III], repr. from *Századok*, 1884, 97ff.; Huber, *art. cit.*, *AföG*, 22, n. 3.
    94. According to the letter, dated March 13, 1299, of Pope Boniface VIII, in *VMH*, I, 385; *SSH*, I, 477,4-13; the "Pozsony Chronicle" also named the conspirators, *ibid.*, II, 46,15-20, and referred to the "positive" papal reply, *ibid.*, 46,21-23, and II, 46f.; Potthast, n. 24791.
    95. Wenczel, *Anjoukori diplomácia*, I, 81ff., 85, 94ff.; Huber, *art. cit.*, 220f.; *Monumenta spectantia historiam Slavorum meridionalium illustrata*, 48 vols. (Zagreb, 1868-1918), I, 125, 139, 192; Huber, *art. cit.*, 220f.
    96. Wenczel, *Anjoukori diplomácia*, I, 94ff.
    97. *SSH*, I, 478,7-13; Pozsony Chronicle, *ibid.*, II, 46,29-31.
    98. *VMH*, I, 377.
    99. *RA*, n. 3878 (June 22, 1292), rewarding him for services with his war with Ivan, *ÁUO*, V, 66ff., and compare with *RA*, nn. 388 (*ÁUO*, XII, 530f.) and 3892 (*ÁUO*, XII, 525).
    100. The evidence for this, printed in *CD*, VII-4, 225ff., and dated 1293, is false - see *RA*, n. 3954. In her correspondence in the year 1295, Marosini referred to herself as "Ducissa tocius Slavonie et gubernatrix citra-Danubialium partium usque mare [maritima?] Sclauonie a Danobio [sic!] usque mare," cf. *ÁUO*, X, 183f.; in another writ, *ibid.*, X, 184ff., Marosini says that her dear son, King Andrew, the successor of King Ladislas, was betrayed by the Herrik boy, who had turned traitor "contra regem Andream, dominum suum naturalem." She also mentioned Mize by name ("quondam Palatinus"). She had issued writs, *ibid.*, X, 213f., dated at Pozsega, or the one addressed to the chapter of canons at Pozsega, dated 1300, *ibid.*, X, 375.
    101. *RA*, n. 4121; Mark Csák was the son of Péter Csák, the former palatine, cf. *ÁUO*, X, 150f.; Mark was "Magister agasonum" (Master of the [Royal] Stable) in the year 1294. See further, *RA*, n. 3983, *ÁUO*, V, 96f., and RA, n. 4088, *CD*, VII-2, 195ff. On the behavior of the Herrik boys, see the writ of Boniface VIII sent to the archbishop of Esztergom, *ÁUO*, X, 273f., dated July 11, 1297.
    102. Cf. "Annales Mellicenses," *MGHSS*, IX, 510,42, and compare with *RA*, n. 3878, *ÁUO*, V, 66ff.
    103. *Ibid.*, X, 183f., 186f.
    104. *SSH*, 477,4-13; II, 46,15-20.
    105. *Ibid.*, I, 477f.; II, 46,21-23.
    106. *Ibid.*, I, 478,14-22; II, 46,21-23.
    107. *ÁUO*, V, 150 (dated October 6, 1296, cf.), *RA*, n. 4085; also, *ÁUO*, X, 184ff, esp. 185; *ibid.*, X, 122f., *RA*, n. 4035; n. 4067, *ÁUO*, V, 147; *RA*, n. 3997,

ÁUO, X, 149f., and X, 295ff., as referred to in RA, n. 4205; Katona, Historia critica, VII, 1188f., RA, n. 4316, ÁUO, X, 368f.

108. Wenczel, Anjoukori diplomácia, I, 87f. On May 1, 1295, Queen Agnes issued a writ, ÁUO, X, 180ff.; and there is a writ, signed by Queen Fenana, dated September 8, 1295 - HO, VII, 242; according to the Chronicle, Fenana died during the Advent of 1296, SSH, I, 477,22-24. RA, n. 4145 recorded a writ by Andrew III in favor of his new Queen - Katona, VII, 1177. The daughter born to Andrew III and Fenana was (Blessed) Elizabeth of Hungary, who had died as a religious sister in Töss in 1338; cf. Mária Püskely, Árpádházi Boldog Erzsébet és a 14 századi misztika [Blessed Elizabeth of the House of Árpád and 14th Century Mysticism] (Rome, 1980), 48ff.; and my review, "Blessed Elizabeth of Hungary: The Dominican Sisters at Töss and 14th Century Mysticism," East European Quarterly, 21 (1987), 135f. See further, Acta Sanctorum, Maii II, 123ff.; W. Migg, "Heinrich Seuse und Elisabeth Stagel," Neue Zürcher Zeitung, January 22, 1966, 20; K. Gránicz, "Az utolsó árpád-házi királyleány emléke a tössi címerben" [Memory of the Last Royal Daughter of the House of Árpád in the Töss Coat-of-Arms], Vigilia, 44 (1979), 319ff.

109. RA, n. 4085, ÁUO, V, 150, and X, 184ff.

110. Who became Magister agasonum in 1294 - ibid., X, 150f. See further, ibid., V, 242f., X, 273f. (ecclesiastical excommunication: Knauz, II, 365ff.!), and ÁUO, X, 406f.

111. RA, n. 3982 (HO, V, 77f.), and n. 3804, Katona, Historia critica, VII, 1073.

112. ÁUO, X, 368f., esp. 369.

113. Reimchronik, c. 717; Wenczel, Anjoukori diplomácia, I, 136.

114. "Cont. Vindobonensis," MGHSS, IX, 719; Andrew III's writ, dated October 6, 1296, was issued at Kőszeg, RA, n. 4085, ÁUO, V, 150; a writ by Arch-bishop Ladomér was issued at ("under") Ságsomlyó, ibid., V, 155f.; see further RA, n. 4211 (of January 18, 1299), ÁUO, V, 204ff.: "...in expugnatione castri Kwzeg [sic], quod per magistrum Johannem filium Henrici bani, tunc nostrorum et regni nostri infidelem, detineabatur...." Compare to CD, VI-2, 263: "...ivissemus sub castro Kőszeg;" ÁUO, X, 252ff., esp. 252: "...qui in expugnatione castri Johannis filii Henrici bani Kozik vocati...," though it may be a false document, RA, n. 4125. RA, n. 4316: "...cum contra filios Henrici bani infideles nostros et regni nostri exercitum duxissemus, et castrum Simegiense, quod contra nostram detinebat maiestatem, fecissemus preliari...;" ÁUO, X, 368f., esp. 369.

115. "Cont. Vindobonensis," MGHSS, IX, 719; also, IX, 750; XVII, 718. Queen Agnes, RA, n. 4145, Katona, VII, 1177; n. 4185, HO, VI, 431; the letter of Agnes where she had referred to her father as King of the Romans, HO, VI, 353, may be dated ca 1299, though its date cannot be determined by the fact that Agnes (had) received Pozsony county at the end of the year 1297 - RA, n. 4145 (as cited above).

116. Reimchronik, cc. 666 and 681; "Cont. Vindobonensis," MGHSS, IX, 720; also, ibid., XVII, 69, 140, and 264; or, the rewards granted by the king - RA, nn. 4187 with text, 4186 and 4188, ÁUO, XII, 191, and V, 183f., respectively. In connec-tion with the Hungarian participation, cf. HO, I, 93ff.; Gebhardt, I, 408f.

117. MGHSS, IX, 720 and 721.

118. RA, nn. 4115, 4121, 4122, ÁUO, X, 258ff.; and RA, n. 4169. See the list of Andrew III's head officials, in Hóman-Szekfű, I, 616, as, e.g., Amadeus Aba from 1293 to 1296; in 1297 it was Matthew Csák; from 1298 to 1299, Lóránt Rátót held the position, together with Apor Pécz.

119. Reimchronik, lines 77880-78020; on its date, Wenczel, Anjoukori diplomácia, I, 136; on August 28, 1300, Andrew III issued directives from Zagreb - RA, n. 4325; J.B. Tkalcic (ed.), Monumenta historica liberae regiae civitatis Zagrabiae metropolis regni Dalmatiae, Croatiae et Slavoniae, vol. I (Zagreb, 1889),

77; T. Smiciklas (ed.), *Codex diplomaticus regni Croatiae, Dalmatiae et Slavoniae*, vols. VI, VII, and XV (Zagreb, 1909, 1934), VII, 396.

120. Cf. Imre Nagy (ed.), *Anjoukori Okmánytár: Codex diplomaticus Hungaricus Andegavensis*, 6 vols. (Budapest, 1879-91), I, 52; Pauler, II, 583f., n. 374, dated it late August-early September, 1299.

121. *RA*, nn. 4173 and 4174, where Gregory appears as the archbishop-elect of Esztergom; on *RA*, n. 4167 (*ÁUO*, X, 294f.), and nn. 4167-69, as the archpriest of Fehérvár and vice-chancellor; on *RA*, n. 4204 (*ÁUO*, X, 300f.), again as archpriest, though it is, or seems to be, a false writ! *RA*, nn. 4173 (Katona, *Historia critica*, VII, 1184f.) and *RA*, n. 4174 (*ÁUO*, V, 186). In early 1298, Archbishop-elect Gregory was still loyal to Andrew III, as he cooperated with other members of the hierarchy - cf. *HO*, VIII, 372. In a certain manner, though, the pontiff sympathized with the Anjous; see his writ of May 1, 1298, in *VMH*, I, 381.

122. On "this" side of the Danube, Palatine Lóránt Rátót - *ÁUO*, V, 236ff., and XII, 383f.; on the "other" side of the Danube, Palatine Apor Pécz - *HO*, VI, 430f., VIII, 380f. and 385f. Lóránt had a brother called Dénes - Nagy, *Codex diplomaticus Hungaricus Andegavensis*, I, 45; in the summer of 1297, Matthew was still palatine - *CD*, VI-2, 82f., regardless of the contents of the papal writ published in *ÁUO*, X, 273f., dated June 27, 1297.

123. *HO*, VI, 441f.

124. See prefatory note, Marczali, *Enchiridion*, 186, a portion missing in *RHM*, 615; *RA*, n. 3705, dated February 22, 1291. See also Teutsch-Firnhaber, *UB*, I, 1559ff.; Zimmermann-Werner, *UB*, I, 173ff.

125. Cf. *RA*, n. 4132, *ÁUO*, V, 172f., on unsafe roads in the country; *RA*, n. 4133, *ÁUO*, V, 171f., on run-down conditions of towns (as, e.g., Sopron) and villages in 1297; *RA*, n. 4142, *CD*, VII-5, 535f., in Pozsony, where confusing conditions had prevailed.

126. *RA*, n. 4209 - where the high clergy "in unum convenientes, accepta auctoritate ex consensu domini regis et baronum totius regni, prouti et aliorum,...tractare coepimus de his, quae regiae magnificentiae et statui regni totius ac etiam ipsarum ecclesiasticarum personarum et ordinum aliorum consuletur;" Marczali, *Enchiridion*, 192, prefatory note, part two; *RHM*, 631.

127. "...cum omnibus nobilibus Hungariae, singulis Saxonibus, Comanis in unum convenientes...;" Marczali, *Enchiridion*, 192; *RHM*, 631.

128. In the text: "et baronum totius regni, prouti et aliorum...;" *ibid*. Pauler, II, 581, n. 357, argued in reference to "prout moris est," that it was not customary for the high clergy and [high] nobility to meet and debate separately from the barons, therefore the reference to the barons must be a later addition [to the text]. And yet, it was very much a custom (usage), as it is evident from the summons of Edward I of England to his parliaments - cf. Stubbs, 479ff., parliamentary writs, anno 1294, or earlier, the 1290 Summons of Knights of the Shire, *ibid.*, 477f.: "...duos vel tres de discretioribus...militibus de comitatu,...cum plena potestate pro se et tota communitate comitatus praedicti, ad consulendum et consentiendum pro se et communitate illa hiis quae comites, barones et proceres praedicti tunc dixerint concordanda."

129. Gebhardt, I, 385ff.; Loserth, *Spätes Mittelalter*, 183ff.; W. Stubbs, *Germany in the Later Middle Ages* (1908; repr. New York, 1969), 60ff. Hóman-Szekfű, I, 622f.

130. *RHM*, 638, art. 27.

131. As it is evident from the preface; their resolutions "de legali consensu domini regis et baronum processerunt;" *RHM*, 631 and 639. In Marczali, 192 and 197, the latter portion is missing, and the numbering of the articles is different.

132. The Diet of 1298, art. 19, only in *RHM*, 635f.

133. *Ibid.*, a. 27.

134. *Ibid.*, a. 29.
135. *Ibid.*, a. 30.
136. *Ibid.*, a. 31.
137. *Ibid.*, a. 31, second half.
138. *Ibid.*, a. 32.
139. *Ibid.*, aa. 3 and 5.
140. *Ibid.*, aa. 23 and 25 (in Marczali, aa. 26, 27, 28); art. 30 forms the first half of art. 25 in *RHM*.
141. Diet of 1298, art. 1.
142. *Ibid.*, a. 5.
143. *Ibid.*, a. 6, the latter half, that forms art. 7 in Marczali; compare to *RA*, n. 4189, almost forcing the monarch to take a firm stand against his opponents.
144. Diet of 1298, a. 20 (in Marczali, a. 23!).
145. *Ibid.*, a. 21, upper half (in Marczali, a. 24).
146. *Ibid.*, aa. 18 and 21, lower half.
147. *Ibid.*, aa. 23 and 25, and latter half of a. 22.
148. *Ibid.*, a. 9 (in Marczali, a. 10!).
149. *Ibid.*, a. 12.
150. *Ibid.*, a. 14.
151. *Ibid.*, a. 14, second half.
152. *Ibid.*, aa. 17-18.
153. Kéza, c. 97, in *SSH*, I, 193.
154. See articles 9 and 14 of the 1290 Diet, *RHM*, 617, and Marczali, *Enchiridion*, 188. *RA*, n. 3705 [dated February 22, 1291!].
155. "...et consensu venerabilium patrum archiepiscoporum, episcoporum, baronum, procerum, et omnium nobilium regni;" prefatory note, lower half, in Marczali, 186; the "upper half" of the prefatory introduction is printed in *RHM*, 615. On Ladislas IV and the Church, cf. Kosztolnyik, *art. cit.*, *AHC* (1990), 74.
156. Kosztolnyik, *From Coloman*, 213f., and 230, nn. 170 and 174-75; Heer, *Geistesgeschichte*, 172f.
157. Béla III's first wife was Agnes (Maria), daughter of Raynold Chatillon of Antioch - Kosztolnyik, *From Coloman*, 203, and 224, nn. 43-48 and 51; also, *ibid.*, 212f., and 229, nn. 156-63.
158. The second wife of Andrew III was the daughter of Albrecht, Duke of Austria - cf. Chronicle, c. 186, *SSH*, I, 477,24-27. "Cont. Vindobonensis," *MGHSS*, IX, 719; Huber, in *AföG*, 65 (1884), 224, and note.
159. This is based on the arguments of József Gerics, "Krónikáink és a III András-kori rendi intézmények friauli-aquileiai kapcsolatairól" [Essay on the Relationship Between the Hungarian Chronicles and the Connection of Friaul-Aquileia with the Hungarian Estates in the Time of Andrew III], *Filológiai Közlöny*, 21 (1975), 309ff., a well-documented, thorough study; Simon de Kéza, the chronicler of Ladislas IV, had studied in northern Italy, and it is possible that the representative institutions of Friaul under the jurisdiction of the Archbishop of Aquileia had had an impact upon the chronicler Kéza, and had influenced the thinking of King Andrew III.
160. Cf. E. Mályusz, *Egyházi társadalom a középkori Magyarországon* [The Ecclesiastical Social Stratum in Medieval Hungary] (Budapest, 1971), 35ff.
161. Marczali, *Enchiridion*, 188, a. 9: "conscriptis libertatibus nobilium regni Hungarie antiquis insertis etiam quibusdam articulis de novo concessis eisdem nobilibus privilegium concessit;" *RHM*, 617 does not carry this portion of the text.
162. *Ibid.*, 617., a. 14; *RA*, n. 3752, *ÁUO*, V, 24, referred to Andrew III's coronation, while *RA*, n. 3674 stated that the two archbishops and the bishops of Eger and Nyitra had participated in his coronation. See further, *RA*, n. 3960 with text, on the defense of Pozsony by Máté Csák.

163. *RA*, n. 3800, *ÁUO*, XII, 507f.; *RA*, n. 3897, *ÁUO*, X, 81f.; *RA*, nn. 3838, 3834 with text, 3820, 3822, 3823, 3818 with text, etc.; further, *RA*, nn. 3678 with text, 3676 with text.

164. It happened in Leon, in 1020: "...in present domini Adefonsi et uxoris eius...convenimus apud Legionem,...et issu ipsius regis talia decreta decrevimus;" Colmeiro, I, n. I (p. 1ff.).

165. "Ego Fredenandus rex et Sanctia regina ad restorationem nostrae Christianitatis, fecimus concilium in castro Cojanca,...cum episcopis et abbatibus et totius nostri regni optimatibus;" *ibid.*, I, n. III (p. 21ff.).

166. "...quod nec faciam guerram vel pacem, vel placitum, nisi cum concilio episcoporum, nobilium, et bonorum per quorum consilium debeo regi;" *ibid.*, I, n. VII:3 (p. 40), and compare with n. VII (*ibid.*, I, 39ff.).

167. *RA*, nn. 3737 and 3796; Huber, *art. cit.*, *AföG* (1884), 206; before the campaign, Andrew III's envoy had visited Vienna, *HO*, VIII, 195, and Wenczel, *Anjoukori diplomácia*, I, 77. Otto Brunner, *Structures of Government in Medieval Austria*, tr. H. Kaminsky, et al. (Philadelphia, 1992).

168. Cf. *MGHSS*, IX, 716,45 - 717,7; *ibid.*, IX, 716,29-45, and 717,34-36 (anno 1293!); IX, 510,37-40; IX, 749,29-39; *ibid.*, IX, 658,14-15; Andrew III's writ of January 18, 1294, *RA*, n. 3961, *ÁUO*, X, 135f., with text. Also, *RA*, n. 3962, *CD*, VI-1, 299f.

169. See in this context, *ibid.*, VI-1, 232d., and the royal writ of March 17, 1293, *RA*, n. 3908, *CD*, VI-1, 242f.; *RA*, nn. 3909 and 3910, the latter with text; the texts of these letters also refer frequently to the unruly behavior of the oligarchs.

170. Wenczel, *Anjoukori diplomácia*, I, 78ff.

171. *SSH*, I, 477,4-13; II, 46,15-20.

172. Wenczel, *Anjoukori diplomácia*, I, 81ff., 87f., 90 and 96.

173. "Annales Mellicenses," *MGHSS*, IX, 510,42; Huber, *art. cit.*, *AföG* (1884), 222 and n. 3; Károly Szabó, "III Endre fogsága, 1292" [The Captivity of Andrew III in 1292], repr. from *Századok* (1884), 97ff., still a useful study. See further, *RA*, nn. 3888 and 3892, *ÁUO*, XII, 525f. and 530f.

174. Tomasina - "Princess of the Slavs?" *CD*, VII-4, 225ff., though false - cf. *RA*, n. 3954; *ÁUO*, X, 183ff., 213f., and 375. See also *RA*, n. 3935 (July 11, 1293); *ÁUO*, X, 175; *RA*, nn. 4016 and 4073.

175. *MGHSS*, IX, 719; 750,24-25; XVII, 718,19-21; *SSH*, I, 477,22-25. Andrew III visited Vienna in early 1296 - *HO*, II, 25; the letter of his new queen, Agnes, where she had referred to her father as King of the Romans, could be dated in the late 1290's - *HO*, VI, 353. *ÁUO*, X, 36f., carries a letter by Queen Fenana, dated 1291, and *HO*, VII, 242, published a writ by her, dated September 8, 1295, a date contradicted by the writ, dated May 1, 1295 of Queen Agnes, *ÁUO*, X, 180ff. The Chronicle set the date of 1296 as the year of Fenana's death, *SSH*, I, 477,22-24. The German chroniclers report that Andrew III had not been a faithful husband to his second wife - *MGHSS*, XVII, 78,37-38; or, the *Reimchronik*, lines 74456-74514, Queen Agnes had inherited (as her dowry) the county of Pozsony, *RA*, n. 4145, and n. 4185, Knauz, II, 456; Katona, *Historia critica*, VII, 1177.

176. In 1294, he was still the reeve of Pozsony and master of the [royal] stable (magister agasonum), *RA*, n. 3959, *ÁUO*, X, 150f.; also, *RA*, n. 4121.

177. This is evident from the writ dated October 29, 1299, *RA*, n. 4275; "Unde nos cum baronibus et nobilibus regni nobiscum iniudiciae assidentibus," *RA*, n. 4168 with text; and from the prefatory note of the 1298 Diet, *RHM*, 630f., and 632.

178. Cf. Hóman-Szekfű, I, 608: Rénold Básztély in the area "this side of the Danube;" Miklós Kőszegi in Transdanubia in 1288-89; in 1290, Mize took over from Básztély. Mize was known as the reeve of Bodrog and Tolna, *RA*, n. 3741.

Rolandus, son of Baas, was mentioned in *RA*, n. 4192 and n. 4211, *ÁUO*, V, 185 and 204ff.

179. *RHM*, 630ff.; only a royal writ refers to it, *RA*, n. 4189, quoting from art. 7 of the Diet's resolutions! Huber, *art. cit.*, *AföG* (1884), 225f. Also, Batthyány, *Leges*, II, 506ff.; Marczali, *Enchiridion*, 191ff.; Hóman-Szekfű, I, 622f.

180. In such a manner, every social stratum participated in the affairs of the country! - diet, "congregatio generalis;" *RHM*, 631; the text enumerated the participating members of the hierarchy. Now, it was the high clergy that set the tone, and aided the monarch. Batthyány, *Leges*, II, 507, spoke of a "concilium mixtum," while Palazzini, III, 398, wrote about an "assemblea conciliare mixta."

181. As indicated by art. 6 of its resolutions - were the king unable to deal with his opponents, he may ask for armed support for his cause; "licitum sit illi auxilium aliunde implorare, per quod convinci possit feritas delinquentium." Marczali, 193, a. 6; *RHM*, 633, a. 6 - its upper half! Albert(inus), the uncle of Andrew III - *RA*, n. 3752, had appeared here as "frater noster karissimus," *ÁUO*, V, 24f.; at the diet, he appeared as prince of Slavonia, *RA*, n. 4259, and as the perpetual reeve of Pozsega county, *RA*, n. 4260, *CD*, VII-5, 545ff. - assuming that it is not a forgery.

182. Diet of 1298, art. 23 (in Marczali, 194); it is art. 20 in *RHM*, 636.

183. Cf. Kéza, c. 97, *SSH*, I, 193 (and c. 95, *ibid.*, I, 192f.).

184. "Nos itaque, Iohannes dei gratia archiepiscopus..., tractare coepimus de his, quae regiae magnificientiae et statui regni totius et ipsarum ecclesiasticarum," etc., *RHM*, 631; Marczali, *Enchiridion*,192.

185. "...ex potentia baronum et aliorum potentum provenientes," though in the interest of public peace, "consensu domini regis et baronum totius regni," resolutions were enacted, *ibid.*

186. Andrew III only summoned the diet: "Andreas Spiritu Sancto suggerente...congregationem dixit generalem...," *ibid.*, 191; *RHM*, 631.

187. Diet of 1298, a. 23 (a. 20 in *RHM*), in reference to the Diet of 1290, aa. 9, 14, 25.

188. "...accepta auctoritate ex consensu domini regis et baronum totius regni," preface, Marczali, *Enchiridion*, 192; *RHM*, 631.

189. Diet of 1298, aa. 1 and 2, 5, 6 (second, or lower, half, *RHM*, 632), a. 7 in Marczali, *Enchiridion*,193, in reference to *RA*, n. 4189.

190. Diet of 1298, aa. 1-2, 7, 23 in Marczali; aa. 1-2, 6, and 20 in *RHM*.

191. *Ibid.*, aa. 22-24; in Marczali, aa. 26-28.

192. *Ibid.*, a. 1.

193. *RA*, n. 4189, as above, n. 189.

194. Diet of 1298, a. 21.

195. That may have been the reason for the Diet of 1299 - Batthyány, *Leges*, II, 512ff.: "Synodus regia Rakossiensis," as referred to by *RA*, n. 4252 and n. 4258 (dated July 28, 1299); *ÁUO*, X, 329ff.: "In congregatione regni nostri generali," and 330: "una cum prefatis venerabilibus patribus, baronibus ac nobilibus regni nostri sentencialiter decrevimus;" one is to note the emphasis (even here) on the lesser nobility: *ac nobilibus!* It had to convene because of art. 34 of the resolutions of the Diet of 1298, Marczali, *Enchiridion*, 195.

196. That was the reason for the horrible punishment, cf. *RA*, n. 4252, a writ that, incidentally, spoke of the 1299 diet. Cf. Nagy, Codex *diplomaticus Hungaricus Andegavensis*, II, 30f. It [= syn. reg. Rakossiensis] did have firm anti-Rome tendencies, and archbishop(-elect) Gregory had failed to appear in [or before] it; as a matter of fact, he had threatened anyone with excommunication who would dare to attend - a most remarkable attitude, since as late as 1298, Gregory had co-existed peacefully with other members of the Hungarian hierarchy. Cf. *HO*, VIII, 372.

197. *RA*, n. 4275.

198. Perhaps, a royal writ, printed in *ÁUO*, X, 458, and dated June 11, on the Feast of Barnabbas, 1300: "datum...in generali congregatione domini regis, quam in Pest cum baronibus, Cumanis et aliis nobilibus regni celebravit;" also referred to by Knauz, II, 479, may be regarded as the record of the last diet held by Andrew III in the year 1300.

199. On January 13, 1301, the day before he died, Andrew III had issued a writ - *RA*, n. 4342, *ÁUO*, V, 267; he had died on January 14, 1301 - *SSH*, I, 478,22-24; "Várad Chronicle," *ibid.*, I, 214,5-10.

200. *SSH*, I, 478.

201. Andrew III had died on the Feast of St. Felix: January 14 (1301); cf. *SSH*, I, 478. On the feast, see *Missale Romanum*, and H. Grotefend, *Zeitrechnung des deutschen Mittelalters und der Neuzeit*, 2 vols. (Hannover, 1891-92; repr. Aalen, 1984), I, Tafel xxix. The Pray codex does not carry the feast, and it placed the Feast of Bishop Hilarius on January 13th - cf. Radó, *Libri liturgici*, 37.

202. Hóman-Szekfű, I, 625. Upon his death, the papal curia decided to take action in Hungarian succession politics, see Potthast, n. 25081 and 25252, *VMH*, n. 635; Kosztolnyik, *art. cit.*, *Századok* (1992), 653 and n. 104.

203. *MGHSS*, IX, 721,40-48; *Reimchronik*, lines 78299-78356; on the sorrow of the Queen, *ibid.*, lines 78356-78400.

204. Cf. Gebhardt, I, 412ff. Charles Anjou (Caroberto) was crowned by Archbishop(-elect) Gregory of Esztergom with "a" crown, as it may be evident from a writ addressed to Benedict Geszthi, in Nagy, *Codex diplomaticus*, I, 80f.

CHAPTER TWELVE

ANDREW III:
THE FIRST CONSTITUTIONAL MONARCH

1. *Constitutional Developments*

> Ut dominum Andream ex regali stirpe descendentem reveramur tamquam dominum naturalem.
>
> *Diet of 1298, Article 1*

In the light of the resolutions of the Diet of 1298, the conclusion can be drawn that the barons meeting aside from members of the hierarchy and nobility - independently of the monarch - had, at the turn of the century, asserted their influence upon the government because they wielded private military might greater than the military powers of the king.[1] It was their aim to limit royal power in legislative, judicial, and administrative matters, or to share those powers with him.[2]

A similar struggle had occurred in England between the issuance of the Magna Carta,[3] and the time of Simon de Montfort's conspiracy against the king,[4] which had only been neutralized through the Dictum of Kenilworth and the Statute of Marlborough passed by the Great Council (*concilium magnum*, later parliament), in favor of the monarch, Henry III.[5] In France, Philip II Augustus could only assert himself against the greed for power of the great nobles by leaning on the increasing support of the professional, merchant, and artisan "middle class" strata.[6]

Earlier, the perpetual royal domain (*dominium*) had formed the power base of the Árpád kings. As soon as the great nobles had gained more territory and military strength, however, they demanded a share for themselves in the royal legislative, judicial, and administrative powers of government. Any attempt to curtail royal power depended upon the outcome of the confrontation between those two power factions, the nobles and the king.[7] In western Europe the conflict was carried out by private means;[8] in the country of Andrew II, public principles derived from the nature

of constitutional developments asserted themselves. The realm of the
Árpáds knew no pure feudalism. Although the political, social, and
economic structures of the Árpád era had been, to some extent,
influenced by western feudal ideas in government and in the administration of landholdings, the royal patrimony remained the king's
power base, even though he had followed given feudal ideas in his
exercise of political-diplomatic and military leadership.[9]

Otto of Freising bears witness that the dignity of Christian
kingship had prevented the Árpáds from exercising their powers like
tyrants.[10] When the monarch began to lose power on account of his
declining prestige and dignity, the feudal system in the west already
drew toward a close; it was replaced by the nobles' *estate* - guided by
common law and by mutual socio-political family interests.[11]

The late twelfth century Hungarian chronicler, Anonymus *P.
dictus magister*, defended the king's dignity, and the people's
traditional right to elect the monarch, from the attempts of the
potentates who were supported by their private *dominium* - and the
common law of the realm. Anonymus wrote that the Árpáds held
power they had gained from their ancestors, who had been elected by
the heads of the [seven] tribes that had taken part in the conquest of
the land during the 890's. They had asserted themselves as the
descendants of the conquerors, insisting that it was their forefathers
who had Árpád elected. They wanted to share their powers with the
successors of Árpád.[12] On the other hand, Simon de Kéza, the
chronicler of the late thirteenth century, attributed political rights to
all - higher and lesser nobles - because it was the nobles' *estate* that -
whose members - elected the country's military and political leaders
and judges.[13]

The Hungarian *Holy Crown*, that according to tradition had
been received by King Saint Stephen from Pope Sylvester II in the
year 1000,[14] became the public symbol of royal power in that its use
(as, for instance, at the coronation of Andrew II,[15] and later, of
Charles I of Anjou).[16] was the prerequisite of constitutional exercise
of kingship.[17] In time, this constitutional concept developed into the
"Doctrine of the Hungarian Crown."[18] Andrew III had taken, like
his grandfather, Andrew II, who swore to preserve the rights of the
Church (and Rome had to remind him, many a time, of that
promise),[19] the oath of coronation to assure the security of his
kingship, and of the inhabitants of his kingdom.[20] During the reign

of the Árpáds, the *corona sacra* became synonymous with *regia dignitas, regimen, regnum* - that is, kingship (but not kingdom!) - that gained a carefully defined meaning in István Werbőczy's *Tripartitum*, a collection of medieval Hungarian customary laws, to the effect that the king would not exercise powers alone, but together with the nobles' *estate*.[21]

This assumption was mirrored in the Laws of 1351 by Louis the Great of Hungary (1342-82), where the king, acting upon petitions from the higher clergy, barons, the country's great men, and nobles, had confirmed the articles of the Golden Bull of 1222 that constitutionally limited the exercise of royal powers.[22] Interestingly, King Louis himself could not see any limitation of his own authority in approving the resolutions of 1222, because he regarded them only as guidelines for thwarting the personal abuse of royal might.[23]

The constitutional limitations placed on the assertion of the king's powers were related to developing changes in the structure of Hungarian society, and to the organizational activities of the barons and nobles, who strove for similar privileges. The nobles' *estate*, still in formation, demanded political rights for the [lesser] nobility vs. the exercise of unlimited royal power,[24] as if Anonymus had not already emphasized the constitutional rights claimed by the descendants of the conquerors.[25]

Therefore, during the reign of Andrew II, the nobility, and the service nobility, following the example of Spain,[26] and because of the growing influence in the country of nobles of foreign birth (*hospites*),[27] wished to assert their demands for political rights.[28] The royal court had attempted to slow down their reactionary attempt. In 1231 (under Andrew II), and in 1267 (under Béla IV), members of the nobility who came fully armed to attend the diet were only allowed to appear as petitioners, not as constitutional partners of the monarch in government! At his own initiative, Béla IV had issued a personal writ of privileges for them, only to confirm their ancient rights by his royal power.[29]

Anonymus, with his twelfth century upbringing, still depicted Árpád as a ruler with unlimited powers.[30] Kéza, however, followed the prevalent late thirteenth century concept, and spoke of the seven armies led by tribal leaders in the conquest of the land (the mid-Danubian region) in the 890's, with Árpád, the son of Álmos, being the most noble and powerful among them. It was the family of Árpád, Kéza wrote, that headed the [migrating] Magyars during their forward move, and provided the rear guard protection, when passing through unknown territory during their migrations, before arriving in their present-day country.[31]

As late as the time of Prince Géza (972-97), every Magyar was expected to appear armed in the field-day assembly (*communitas*), and hear its resolutions.[32] On the annual field-day, one could remove any high official unworthy of his position; relieve a judge of his function, if he was found unworthy, thereby voiding his unjust decisions.[33] In Kéza's report, the barons vying with the monarch for power, the service nobility aiming at self-governance and asserting its will in the *communitas* of the county, already mirrored the age of Ladislas IV, when the baronial oligarchy had, for the first time, appeared as a rival of the king, and the service nobles, in their standing by the king, saw an opportunity for the realization of their constitutional rights.[34]

Until 1270, the Hungarian monarch alone held legislative powers. In 1222, the high nobles,[35] and the higher clergy in 1231, had attempted to place limitations on the exercise of royal power.[36] The resolutions of the diet of 1267 were initiated by the lesser nobility, but only gained approval through the personal recognizance by the monarch.[37]

The Royal Council, consisting of high functionaries held a role in both the legislative and administrative spheres of government, but it was not a constitutional body, because the king himself had selected its members.[38] The situation had changed during the reign of Ladislas IV, when the Royal Council had transformed itself into an organ of oligarchic government. This was done in order to limit the assertion of kingship, for the monarch was a minor at that time.

As early, or as late as 1267, the Hungarian barons had fully separated themselves from members of the higher clergy and higher nobility. The Decree of 1267 - in a certain way, the third version of the "Golden Bull" of 1222[39] - revealed that the barons held a firm foothold in the Royal Council (*Curia regis*) between the King and the nobles.[40] Although the monarch could not act without the collaboration of the barons (this obligation had been inflicted upon him in the Royal Council), a coalition, first, of the high clergy loyal to the king, and second, of the nobles who had socially and rightfully asserted themselves by their participation in public business, had necessarily encountered the forced collaboration between the king and the barons.

In 1267, Béla IV had recognized, "habito baronum consilio et assensu," the nobles and service (lesser) nobles (the Knights) as the nobles' *estate*; "nobiles regni Ungarie, qui universi, qui servientes dicuntur," and confirmed them in their liberties that dated back to the age of King St. Stephen (*ob.* 1038).[41] The cause of the nobility had been greatly aided by the fact that the social and constitutional developments in the realm since the 1250's led to the unification of the lesser nobles (*servientes regis*) with the nobles of the realm (*nobiles regni*) into the nobles' *estate*. The Resolutions of 1267 spoke of "universi nobiles regni nostri seu seruientes regales."[42] Many in servile status were elevated, for service performed, to the ranks of the royal (service) nobles, and consequently, to that of the nobility (*nobilium*).[43]

The oligarchical (royal) council wholly shared the king's legislative and administrative powers.[44] Its constituents were, *de iure*, named by the monarch, although, *de facto*, controlled by the oligarchy - contrary to the king's desire and interests.[45] The oligarchical Council did not reflect the royal will, nor did it secure the future of the kingdom.[46]

In this struggle for power, the great lords frequently fought with each other,[47] while the king relied upon the support of the hierarchy and of the lesser (service) nobility; therefore, he had to promote the constitutional rights and political advancement of the latter.[48] In such a manner, the nobles, who had been organizing themselves in the counties into a nobles' *estate*, had entered the political arena, thus becoming a social factor in the politics of the realm.[49]

As of 1267, the *Congregatio generalis*, legislative diet had established itself, although it still followed ancient customs: the lesser nobles might have appeared armed before it, with the consent of the monarch and the barons, to debate issues on the agenda. The bishops and the (non-service) nobles did attend without royal summons.[50] In 1267, and in the 1290's, the barons still asserted their constitutional rights in the Council. However, they shared governmental powers with the monarch before the diet.[51] The king and the barons had to sanction the resolutions the bishops and nobles had reached in the diet.[52]

Ladislas IV would not accept the prevalent condition and attempted to break up the predominance of the *estates*.[53] Only his successor had gained a realistic estimation of the situation: in 1290, Andrew III had summoned a regular diet. The barons of the country and the nobles, by custom, regularly met every year on the Feast of King St. Stephen in Székesfehérvár to discuss publicly conditions of the realm, to supervise the function and activities of the barons (in the Council; did they behave themselves in office? Did they protect the well-being of the country?), further to punish, or to reward them, etc. [54] However, beside the customary and regular annual law-day assembly, Andrew III had summoned separate diets. Therefore, the monarch had made it clear that although he still named, "by ancient custom," the country's head officials, such as the Palatine, Treasurer, Judge of the Realm, and the Vice-Chancellor, he made those appointments after he had listened to the advice of his nobles.[55]

In 1298, the scenario had changed. Andrew III had applied the direct influence of the members of the higher clergy and of the nobility - *nobilium regni mei* - to the realm's governmental affairs by placing the government beyond the supervision of the barons and of the Royal Council. They king had ordered the *estates* of the higher clergy and of the Knights (lesser nobility) each to delegate two *representative* members to the King's Council, in order to assure a reliable representative government for the entire country.

The episcopal representative advisors were from the Esztergom and Kalocsa ecclesiastical provinces, and had to serve alternating three month terms in the King's Council. The delegates of the service nobles' *estate* were to be *elected* by the diet, and paid by the royal treasury.[56]

The diet passed resolutions concerning a "more correct government" of the wealth of the Queen to the effect that she should select her advisors from among the service nobles, and from the ranks of foreigners or foreign born nobles (*hospites*), while the King should appoint barons to serve with them to protect the interests of the Queen.[57] It may merit notice that although the monarch had, in 1290, issued his resolutions in the manner of an old-fashioned royal privilege,[58] years later, in the Diet of 1298, it was the assembled bishops and nobles who had placed in writing the resolutions they had reached, and had *their* seals affixed to those resolutions, forwarding them to the king and the barons for their approval and sanction.[59]

In such a manner, the constitutional movement that began with the issue of the *Decretum I*, that of the (Hungarian) Golden Bull issued by Andrew II in 1222, came full circle. The constitutional rights of the lesser nobility had gained lawful regulation in the favor of the royal *servientes*, who were the factor of the nobles' *estate* that expressed the popular will and represented the people's interest in managing the fate of the country. Through the legislative activities of Andrew III, the nobles had gained public recognition of their constitutional rights; the service nobles' *estate* - due to the legislation of the 1250's and 1280's, the *nobles' estate* - had gained the right to pass legislation in the diet, and to be consulted in the annual law-day at Székesfehérvár. The constitutional responsibility of members of the hierarchy and of the lesser, by now all nobles, serving as representative advisors in the King's Council had, thereby, been established.[60]

Recognition granted to the land-holding greater nobility of their right to legislate with the king, and to take part in the diet, had, in turn, made possible the legal confirmation of the nobles' rights. The nobles had claimed the ancient privilege of participating in the government of public affairs on the grounds that they were the descendants of the conquerors of the land in the 890's. This remained an unwritten right until it had been acknowledged anew in the thirteenth century, for as long as the Árpáds held control over all legislation.

During the 1290's, the knights (lesser or service nobility) had also gained a role in legislative-political action: the royal directives of 1222, 1231, and 1267 - decrees that had been issued as royal privileges - had improved the social status-quo and political status of the segment of the lesser nobility that found itself on the lower fringe of the nobles' *estate*. In the 1290's, it was the diet of the nobles that confirmed the (lesser) nobles' ancient rights of liberty in articles of constitutional law.[61]

The observation made by Bálint Hóman that it was the common consensus of the country that elevated Andrew III to kingship, even though his reign was only made possible through the coordination of interests by various socio-political groups [parties?]

of the land, that had previously opposed each other, is correct. It also supports the explained point of view.[62]

Andrew III must have gained important experience from his Aragonese royal relatives;[63] namely, that the monarch legislate together with the great men of his country, and the representatives of towns[64] (because without them the king and queen could not reign and rule).[65] Coupled with the atmosphere of the Italian republics where Andrew III grew into manhood, this must have made him realize that, in his country, it was the nobles' *estate* that expressed and represented public opinion, and had the right to participate in its governmental affairs.[66] It was personal impressions in his early years, and the education Andrew had gained on Italian soil that had prepared him to become the country's first constitutional monarch.[67]

The public spirit of the Italian city states, where the government, in spite of its dictatorial tendencies, served the common good, if for no other reason than to keep the public peace, caught the attention of young Andrew, and made him decide that a ruler, and a country's ruling social stratum, had the responsibility to serve the common interests of the land.

The chronicler remarked that Andrew had previously visited Hungary. During his earlier entry, most probably carried incognito, he must have observed the confrontation between his uncle, the king, and the oligarchy - a confrontation that not only undermined the dignity of kingship and weakened the monarch's ability to govern, but further endangered the well-being of the people. The peasantry, the industrial craftsmen class, or the merchants, who were still at the very beginning of their social formation as a stratum, had suffered because of the political vacuum and personal insecurity created by that confrontation. In a country torn by war, no regular productivity could occur in the fields or in industry; business would strike no serious roots as war tore up the fields and held back other activities of civilized life.

With his clear analytical mind and youthful enthusiasm, young Andrew knew that one had to rapidly improve the realm's conditions. But the king would not have been able to make improvements alone - he needed supportive allies. With their aid and cooperation, he would begin reconstruction of the land.

The monarch found his allies among members of the lesser nobility because at that time - one has in mind Andrew's first impressions gained during his visit in the 1280's - the country did not have an established stratum of industrial craftsmen and merchants that would have counterbalanced the irresponsible and wasteful actions of the oligarchy in politics and in government.

Next to the quoted chroniclers, it is the letter Andrew III wrote to his relative, James II of (Aragon-)Sicily, that provides evidence of Iberian influence on constitutional representative developments in the Hungarian diets of the 1290's. In this writ, Andrew III, first, *announced* that he had been crowned constitutionally: "successimus...in totius regni Hungariae gubernaculum, solium et coronam iure et ordine geniturae." As evident by the introductory lines of the resolutions of 1290, he had obtained the crown from the hands of the Archbishop of Esztergom in Székesfehérvár, "apud Albam, in loco nostro cathedrali, annuente domino fuissemus coronati."

Second, he *rationalized* that he had obtained the throne because of the support of the higher clergy, higher nobility, barons, especially the service nobility - and other prelates of the Church: "*ac* universis nobilibus, *necnon* ecclesiarum prelatis" [italics mine]. Consequently, third, he *promised* that he would fulfill his obligations in accordance with the oath of coronation he took,[68] by maintaining law and order in the realm and by serving the common interests of his people; "ut regnum...in assumptione et coronatione nostra in pacem et concordiam...cupimus...conformari."[69] He literally echoed the words of the dietary resolutions of Alfonso X the Learned, "per quorum consilio debeo regi."[70]

The Hungarian Crown was the symbol of constitutional royal power: its use at the coronation of Andrew III - and later at the coronation of Charles I Anjou of Hungary - had been the prerequisite of the constitutional exercise of that power.[71]

Therefore, in the writ to James II, Andrew III emphasized that, first, it was the higher clergy, higher nobility, barons *and* the knights (service nobility)[72] who supported his rights to the crown by acknowledging him as the natural, or constitutional, lord of the kingdom: "in dominium et ut dominum naturalem."[73] His argument, incidentally, can be supported by the writ of Pope Boniface VIII, dated May 31, 1303, where the pontiff, perhaps unwillingly, spoke highly of the family tree of the Árpáds,[74] as if to provide evidence of the diplomatic success of Andrew III at the papal curia.[75]

Second, the monarch argued that since it was the members of the hierarchy, high nobility, and service nobility who had made him king, he performed his duties through the cooperation of the *estates* of the hierarchy, aristocracy, and the knights (service nobles), whose members represented the realm's common interests before him, before the diet, and in society.[76]

Town life in Hungary was, according to the remarks made by the Hungarian chronicler, still stagnating in the thirteenth century.[77] It was only Béla IV who had begun a serious attempt at establishing towns in the kingdom.[78] By inviting foreign settlers, Italian craftsmen and merchants, Béla IV supported the development of town life.[79] Towns, aided by the increase of trade, commerce, and industrial activities, also began to play a role in the defenses of the realm.[80]

The merchant social stratum in Hungary, if and where it had existed at all, had been far too preoccupied with its own affairs.[81] Its members did not have the time, nor the desire, to care for public common interests.[82] May if suffice here to refer to the rather uncivil confrontation between the archbishop of Esztergom and the merchants in Esztergom over taxes, business and financial matters.[83] Therefore, Andrew III had no alternative but to turn to the knights (the service nobility) of the country, instead of the non-existent "middle class" town dweller social stratum.[84] The knights by their county to county organization - the county *estate* - spoke for the interests of the entire country before the king in the Royal Council and before the diet that had been summoned by the king.[85]

The circumstances surrounding the succession of Andrew III to the throne, the real political forces that guided the future of the kingdom, made the king understand that he owed his Crown to the resolutions that had been reached by the barons, high clergy, and lesser nobility of the country[86] - the chronicler's remark, "qua ratione meruerit coronam regni Hungarie accipere," might be applicable here. Under these conditions, the monarch had to accept limitations on his power; however, he had to keep up his guard to ascertain that, to counterbalance the influence of the barons in the Royal Council, he assure the position of the nobility in his country's government. "...quod cum dominus Andreas Dei gratia rex Hungarie, conscriptis libertatibus nobilium regni Hungarie...eiusdem nobilibus privilegium concessit."[87]

It is an interesting coincidence that this particular portion of the dietary resolutions is missing in the 1849 text edition by St. L. Endlicher of those dietary enactments.[88]

The mentality of the lesser nobility and the esteem held by courts of law in Andrew III's reign might be characterized by the case of the lesser noble Benedict of Borsod county, who had murdered his wife. The woman's father, Váró, and her brother, Peter, took their grievance before the county court of law, but had reached an out-of-court settlement before the reeve of Fort Boldvakő on October 31, 1300. According to the agreement, Benedict had to bury his wife in consecrated ground at his own expense, pay two silver marks - one to Váró and one to Peter - and to promise to go on a pilgrimage to Rome not later than Septuagesima Sunday, 1302. Were he not to keep his promises, he would be regarded as someone who had fallen in a judicial duel.[89]

Andrew III had to be confident that the King's Council would maintain constitutional responsibility and that the immediate influence of the bishops and nobles upon the government would protect his kingship. His unexpected death in January, 1301, did not prevent him from fighting to the end or from fully realizing his resolutions.[90]

NOTES

1. "...exclusis quibuscunque baronibus, prout moris est;" cf. *RHM*, 631f.; Marczali, *Enchiridion*, 191f., preface; for text, *ibid.*, 191ff.; *RHM*, 630ff.; Batthyány, *Leges*, II, 506ff.

2. The lesser nobility, churchmen, and the inhabitants ("regnicolae") could also protest - cf. *ibid.*, esp. Marczali, *Enchiridion*, 191; *RHM*, 631, prefatory note.

3. Cf. Stubbs, *Charters*, 296ff.; Lyon, 314ff.; J.C. Holt, *Magna Carta* (Cambridge, 1969), 63ff. and 201ff.

4. Stubbs, 411ff.; Maurice Powicke, *The Thirteenth Century*, 2nd ed. (Oxford, 1962), 151ff.; Lyon, 343ff.

5. Stubbs, 419ff.; Lyon, 344 and 433; H. Mitteis, *Der Staat des hohen Mittelalters*, 8th ed. (Weimar, 1968), 379ff.; Powicke, 216ff.

6. See E.M. Hallam, *Capetian France* (London-New York, 1980), 156ff.; Achille Luchaire, *Social France in the Time of Philip Augustus*, ed. and trans. B. Krehbiel (New York, 1912; repr. 1967), 306ff.

7. See the Golden Bull of 1222 of Andrew II in Marczali, *Enchiridion*, 134aff.; *RHM*, 412ff., and its "re-issue" in a modified version of 1231 - *ibid.*, 428ff.; Marczali, *Enchiridion*, 134bff.; Hóman-Szekfű, I, 491ff. and 507ff.; Z.J. Kosztolnyik, "Triumphs of Ecclesiastical Politics in the 1231 Decretum of Andrew II of Hungary," in *Studiosorum speculum*, eds. F.R. Swietek and J.R. Sommerfeldt (Kalamazoo, MI, 1993), 155ff.

8. Hampe, *Hochmittelalter*, 386ff.; Heer, *Geistesgeschichte*, 157f.; Péter Váczy, *A középkor története* [Medieval History], vol. 2 of *Egyetemes történet* [Universal History], ed. Bálint Hóman et al., 4 vols. (Budapest, 1936-38), 516ff.; J.R. Strayer, "Feudalism in Western Europe," in *Feudalism in History*, ed. Rushton Coulborn (Princeton, 1956), 15ff.

9. Compare the introduction of the Golden Bull of 1222 - cf. Marczali, *Enchiridion*, 134a, with the introductory remarks of Béla IV's Decree of 1267, *ibid.*, 168, and with the prefatory note of Andrew III's Laws of 1290, *ibid.*, 186; *RHM*, 615; *RA*, n. 3705; Jenő Szűcs, "Az 1267-évi dekrétum és háttere. Szempontok a köznmesség kialakulásához" [The Decree of 1267: Some Comments on the Formation of the (Hungarian) Lesser Nobility], *Mályusz Elemér emlékkönyv* [Memorial Volume in Honor of Elemér Mályusz], ed. Éva H. Balázs (Budapest, 1984), 341ff, esp. 349.

10. Cf. Ottonis et Rahewini *Gesta Friderici I. Imperatoris*, SSrG, ed. G. Waitz (Hannover-Leipzig, 1912; repr. 1978), i:32; H. Simonsfeld, *Jahrbücher der deutschen Geschichte unter Friedrich I* (1908; repr. Berlin, 1967), 650ff.; Kosztolnyik, *From Coloman*, 177.

11. Cf. Andrew III's Laws of 1298, preface, Marczali, *Enchiridion*, 191f.; Hóman-Szekfű, II, 37ff., and the rather interesting observations made by Ferenc Eckhart, *Magyarország története* [An Interpretative History of Hungary] (repr. Buenos Aires, 1952), 99ff.; Gerics, *art. cit.*, *Fil. Közl.*, 309ff.

12. See Anonymus, *Gesta*, cc. 5, 6, *SSH*, I, 39ff.; Macartney, 67ff.; Z.J. Kosztolnyik, "A View of History in the Writings of Gerhoch of Reichersberg and the Medieval Hungarian Chronicles," *Die ungarische Sprache und Kultur im Donauraum: Vorlesungen des II International Kongresses für Hungarologie*, Wien, 1986 (Vienna-Budapest, 1989), 513ff.

13. Cf. Kéza, *Gesta*, cc. 74 and 76, *SSH*, I, 175ff., and cc. 24-26, *ibid.*, I, 164ff.; Macartney, 89ff., esp. 108f., Szűcs, *art. cit.*, as *supra*, note 9, 390ff.

14. Cf. Hartvic, "Vita sancti Stephani regis," cc. 9-10, *SSH*, II, 412ff., esp. 414,19-24; Kosztolnyik, *Five Kings*, 8f. and 132, nn. 47-52.

15. Chronicle, c. 174, *SSH*, I, 464,6-11.

16. Cf. Marczali, *Enchiridion*, 205ff.; Hóman-Szekfű, II, 52f.; Chronicle, cc. 192 and 194, *SSH*, I, 484f., and 485f., esp. 486,14-20; also, *CD*, VIII-1, 391ff.; *VMH*, I, 374f.

17. Kantorowicz, *The King's Two Bodies*, 354f., and n. 144; J. Deér, *Die hl. Krone Ungarns* (Vienna, 1966), 183ff.; A. Timon, *Ungarische Verfassungs- und Rechtsgeschichte*, 2nd ed., trans. F. Schiller (Berlin, 1904), 509ff.; Kosztolnyik, *From Coloman*, 274ff.

18. Hóman-Szekfű, II, 417ff. and 618f.; see further, István Werbőczy, *Tripartitum opus iuris consuetudinarii incliti regni Hungariae*, anno 1517, ed. S. Kolozsváry and K. Óvári, *Werbőczy István Hármaskönyve* (Budapest, 1892), I, iii-iv, ix; in Marczali, *Enchiridion*, 347ff., esp. 351ff., pars. I, tit. iii-iv, ix; Hóman-Szekfű, II, 588ff. On Werbőczy, cf. János Horváth, *Az irodalmi müveltség megoszlása* [Differentiation of Hungarian Literary Culture], rev. ed. (Budapest, 1944), 213ff.; Tíbor Kardos, *A magyarság antík hagyományai* [The Hungarians' Ancient Traditions] (Budapest, 1942), 28.

19. Potthast, n. 6318; "qui quum teneantur et in sua coronatione iuraverit regni sui et honorem corone illibata servare," - Friedberg, II, 373.

20. *RA*, n. 3651; *Reimchronik*, lines 41263-41292; Timon, 339 and 520ff. The monarch knew that his *regiminis potestas* depended upon the Crown - cf. *RA*, n. 3900 (dated prior to January 10, 1293); *CD*, VI-1, 237ff., dated January 10, 1292. Deér, *Hl. Krone*, 216f.; *RA*, n. 3880, *CD*, VI-1, 196f.; J.B. Tkalcic, *Monumenta historica episcopatus Zagrabiensis saec. XII et XIII*, vol. I (Zagreb, 1873), 228f.

21. The germ of the idea may be traced back to Kéza, cc. 44, *SSH*, I, 172f.; György Bónis, *Középkori jogunk elemei, rómani jog, kánon jog, szokásjog* [Elements of Medieval Hungarian Law, Roman Law, Canon Law, Customary Law] (Budapest, 1972), 141ff., and 235ff.

22. Cf. Marczali, *Enchiridion*, 216ff.; F. Dőry, *Decreta regni Hungariae* (Budapest, 1976), 124ff., esp. the wording of art. ix; Ferenc Somogyi, "The Constitutional Guarantee of 1351: The Decree of Louis the Great," in S.B. Várdy et al., eds., *Louis the Great, King of Hungary and Poland* (New York, 1986), 429ff.

23. Marczali, *Enchiridion*, 218ff., cc. i, iv, v, vi, etc.; Hóman-Szekfű, II, 200ff., Dezső Dercsényi, *Nagy Lajos kora* [The Age of Louis the Great of Hungary] (Budapest, n.d. [1941]), 61ff.

24. Cf. Kéza, c. 97, *SSH*, I, 193; Kristó, *A vármegyék kialakulása*, 100ff.

25. Cf. Anonymus, cc. 40-41, *SSH*, I, 83ff., and cc. 46 and 57, *ibid.*, I, 94 and 114ff.; Kosztolnyik, *art. cit.*, Wien, 1986.

26. Andrew II's older brother, King Emery, married Constance, daughter of the king of Aragon - Chronicle, c. 172, *SSH*, I, 463,8-11. H. Svrita (J. Zurita), *Indices rerum ab Aragoniae regibus gestarum ab initiis regni ad annum MCDX* (Caesaraugustae, 1578), I, 84. Iohannis Victoriensis *Libri certarum historiarum*, ed. F. Schneider, SSrG (Hannover-Leipzig, 1909), 299, 312, 332f., and 367. Jolán, Andrew II's daughter of his second marriage, was married to James I of Aragon - *SSH*, I, 476,5-8; J.F. O'Callaghan, *A History of Medieval Spain* (Ithaca-London, 1976), 346f., characterized her as a very determined woman; also, F.O. Brachfeld, *Dona Violante de Hungria reina de Aragon* (Madrid, 1942).

27. Simon, who became a Hungarian royal reeve, came from Aragon, and he was mentioned in several royal writs - cf. *RA*, nn. 393, 443, 495, 731-32, and 746. The royal register also shows one record on Tota (from Aragon), the Lady-in-waiting to Queen Constance, Emery's wife - *ibid.*, nn. 198 and 362. Kéza, c. 91, dealt with Simon of Aragon, *SSH*, I, 190f.

28. See the Diet of 1290, aa. 3 and 4, and the Diet of 1298, a. 24, in Marczali, *Enchiridion*, 187 and 194. For "Spanish examples," cf. Alfonso X the Learned's *Las Siete partidas*, ed. G. Lopez, 3 vols. (Salamanca, 1555; repr. Madrid, 1972), i:1,18-19 and i:2,11; R.I. Burns, *The Worlds of Alfonso the Learned and James the Conqueror*

(Princeton, 1985), 12; T.N. Bisson, "Prelude to Power: Kingship and Constitution in the Realm of Aragon," *ibid.*, 23ff.; R.B. Merriman, "Cortes of the Spanish Kingdoms in the Later Middle Ages," *American Historical Review*, 16 (1911), 476ff.

29. Cf. prefatory note, Golden Bull, 1231, Marczali, *Enchiridion*, 134b; and prefatory note to the Laws of Béla IV in 1267, *ibid.*, 168; also, *RHM*, 428f., and 512f., respectively.

30. Anonymus, c. 40, *SSH*, I, 83,10-19. Szlovák, *art. cit.*, *Ung. JB* (1991); Gyula Kristó, "Szempontok az Anonymus Gesta megvilágosításához" [Some Remarks on Anonymus' Gesta Ungarorum], *Acta historica Szegendiensis*, 66 (1979), 45ff.; Péter Váczy, "Anonymus és kora" [Anonymus and His Age], *Középkori kútfőink kritikus kérdései* [Critical Questions Concerning Medieval Hungarian Sources], vol. 1 of *Memoria saeculorum Hungariae*, eds. J. Horváth and Gy. Székely (Budapest, 1974), 13ff., L.J. Csóka, *A latinnyelvű történeti irodalom kialakulása Magyarországon a XI-XIV században* [Development of Latin Language Historical Literature in Hungary During the Eleventh-Fourteenth Centuries] (Budapest, 1967), 453ff.

31. Kéza, cc. 27,28-33, *SSH*, I, 165ff.; Jenő Szűcs, "Kézai problémák" [Questions Concerning Kéza], *Memoria Hungariae*, I, 187ff.; idem, *art. cit.*, as cited above, note 9, 390ff.; Csóka, 599ff.

32. Anonymus, c. 57, *SSH*, I, 113ff.; Kéza, c. 42, *ibid.*, I, 172,3-8.

33. Kéza, cc. 95 and 96.

34. Kéza, c. 97; János Horváth, *Árpádkori latinnyelvű irodalmunk stílusproblémái* [Stylistic Questions Concerning the Latin Language Literature in the Árpád Age] (Budapest, 1954), 372ff., esp. 377ff.

35. Cf. Marczali, *Enchiridion*, 134a and 142af. - preface and art. 31.

36. See Conclusion to Bull of 1231, *ibid.*, 142b.

37. "...quod nobiles regni Hungariae universi qui seruientes regales dicuntur ad nos accedentes, pecierunt a nobis..., ut ipsos in libertate...dignaremur conseruare...;" *ibid.*, 168.

38. See, e.g., the different names of officials appearing as signatories on royal writs - *RA*, nn. 378, 381, 383, 395, etc.; or, art. 30 of the Bull of 1222, Marczali, *Enchiridion*, 142a.

39. *RA*, n. 1547; Hóman-Szekfű, I, 578ff.

40. "Quorum petitiones et instantias..., habito Baronum nostrorum consilio et assensu duximus admitendas;" prefatory note, Marczali, *Enchiridion*, 168.

41. *Ibid.*

42. *Ibid.*, and compare to *RA*, n. 1531; *ÁUO*, VIII, 19f.: "una cum baronibus regni." Also, *RA*, n. 1859, with text; n. 1864, with text; n. 1873, with text; n. 1824, with text, and n. 1901, with text. Hóman-Szekfű, I, 574ff., St. L. Katona, *Historia pragmatica Hungariae*, 3 vols. (Budae, 1782, etc.), I, 834ff.

43. *RA*, n. 955, with text; n. 1155, *ÁUO*, VII, 452f.; *RA*, n. 1157; also, *RA*, nn. 2104 and 2605. *RA*, n. 2598, and n. 2635, with text: "in cetum et numerum servientum regalium...duximus transferendos." *RA*, n. 2635; n. 2104: "in numerum, cetum [sic] et collegium nobilium regni nostri duximus transferendos." *RA*, n. 2609, *ÁUO*, VIII, 26ff.

44. Kéza, c. 75; see further the signatures on documents issued during his reign - *ÁUO*, IX, 1f., 2f., 4f., 49ff., 51ff., etc.

45. On this, see the pertinent sentence in the "Constitutions" (Diet) of 1298: "...dominus Andreas...congregationem indixit generalem: ad hec...nec non et nobis huius regni, exclusis quibuscunque baronibus, prout moris est,...subveniretur." *RHM*, 631; Marczali, *Enchiridion*, 191ff., supported by art. 3-7, *ibid.*

46. This may be sensed from the opening sentence of the same document: "Tempore coronationis domini Andreae...omne conditiones seu libertates regni Hungariae ab antiquo observatae...fuerint declaratae;" *RHM*, 630f.

47. Certain nobles had appealed to the pope for another king! *SSH*, I, 477,4-13.

48. See the Diet of 1298, art. 12 (*RHM*, 634), and compare to art. 20 (art. 23 in Marczali, *Enchiridion*!)

49. See 1267, art. 8, and compare to Golden Bull of 1222, art. 7.

50. On the annual law-day [diet?] of 1267, "nobiles regni Hungariae universi qui servientes regales dicuntur, ad nos accedentes, pecierunt a nobis...;" *RHM*, 512; Marczali, *Enchiridion*, 168.

51. See the conclusion of the Decree of 1231.

52. "...accepta auctoritate ex consensu domini regis et baronum totius regni...;" *ibid.*, 192; *RHM*, 631, preface.

53. As, for instance, the wording in the "Libertas hospitum de villa latina in Scepus" asserting that "regalis sublimitatis immensitas, cuius est in multitudine subiectorum gloriari, quantum tenetur quoslibet incolas regni sui in suis iuribus conservare...;" *ibid.*, 535.

54. See preface to the decrees of 1290, *ibid.*, 615f.; and *RA*, n. 3705 (dated in February 22, 1291!)

55. Decree of 1290, art. 9, *RHM*, 617.

56. Decrees of 1298, art. 20, *ibid.*, 636; art. 23 in Marczali.

57. *Ibid.*, art. 5 and 21 (art. 24 in Marczali, *Enchiridion*, 194).

58. "Ut igitur hec nostra ordinatio...robor obtineat perpetuae firmitatis,...concessimus litteras duplicis sigilli nostri munimine roboratas;" *ibid.*

59. ...who had sanctioned them by affixing their seals to them; cf. second half of prefatory note, and the last paragraph of the document, *RHM*, 631 and 639; the latter half of the preface in Marczali only, p. 192. Art. 35 in Marczali has a different wording. Articles listed after art. 45 might have been "borrowed" from the dietary acts of 1299 - Batthyány, *Leges*, II, 515ff. A possible reference to this diet could be *RA*, n. 4209, dated October 28, 1299, though its wording calls for caution - *CD*, VII-4, 253f.

60. "...in unum convenientes,...ex consensu domini regis et baronum totius regni, prouti et aliorum,...tractare coepimus de his quae...et statui regni...consularetur;" preface, Decrees of 1298.

61. Details published only in Marczali, 195ff., such as aa. 67-69, 75, and, to a certain extent, aa. 70 and 72-73 - following Batthyány, *Leges*, II, 515; Hóman-Szekfű, I, 658.

62. *Ibid.*, I, 615; Fritz Kern, *Kingship and Law in the Middle Ages*, trans. S.B. Chrimes (Oxford, 1939), 188f.

63. *SSH*, I, 476,5-8.

64. Cf. *Siete partidas*, i:1,18-19; i:2,11, and *Espaculo*, introduction, in *Opusculos regales del rey Alfonso el Sabio* (Madrid, 1866); and O'Callaghan, *op. cit.*, 346f., and *art. cit.*, *AMR* (1969), 1503ff.

65. Mitteis, 416; M. Colmeiro, *Cortes de los antiguos reinos de León y de Castilla*, 5 vols. (Madrid, 1896-1922).

66. *SSH*, I, 476,2-5; on the Italian background, see the classic by Daniel Waley, *The Italian City Republics* (New York-Toronto, 1969), esp. 56ff., and 110ff. Also, D.R. Resnick, *Preaching in Medieval Florence* (Athens, GA, 1989), 86ff., and 96ff.; F. Schevill, *History of Florence* (new York, 1936; repr. 1970), 87ff., and 119ff.; J. Larner, *Italy in the Age of Dante and Petrarch* (London-New York, 1980), 38ff.; J. Morris, "Venice, the Triumphant City," in W.L. Langer (ed.), *Perspectives in Western Civilization*, 2 vols. (New York-London, 1979), I, 167ff.

67. Cf. his letter addressed to James II of Sicily, *RA*, n. 3662, with text. The wording in *RHM*, 615, preface; Marczali, *Enchiridion*, 186f., is very similar.

68. See *RA*, n. 3662, with text; *Reimchronik*, lines 41263-41292; Helene Wierunowski, *Vom Imperium zum nationalen Königtum* (Munich-Berlin, 1930), 141ff.; the papal writs in Potthast, nn. 7443, 9080; the oath taken by Andrew II - *RA*, n. 224, was re-written by Innocent III, in Potthast, n. 3712; *CD*, III-1, 90f.

69. *RA*, n. 3662; and, n. 3651.
70. Cf. *Cortes*, I, n. VII, a. 3; the ruler had issued the law with the consensus of all concerned - *ibid.*, I, n. VIII, a. 1.
71. Marczali, *Enchiridion*, 205ff.; Hóman-Szekfű,, II, 52f.; Kantorowicz, 339 and 355, note 144; compare with Friedrich Heer's idea on "Weihe und Krönung," in his *Die Tragödie des Heiligen Reiches* (Stuttgart, 1952), 216f.
72. On the western concept of the "lesser," or service nobility, "serf knights," see A.L. Poole, *Obligations of Society in the XII and XIII Centuries* (Oxford, 1946), 35ff.; on class distinctions among the nobility - sergeants and serf-knights - see Marc Bloch, *Feudal Society*, trans. L.A. Manyon (Chicago, 1961), 320ff., esp. 332ff.
73. *RA*, n. 3662.
74. Potthast, n. 25254; *CD*, VIII-7, 29ff.
75. See *ÁUO*, V, 260ff.; Fraknói, *Veszprémi püspökség levéltára*, II, xlii.
76. Diet of 1298, art. 23 - art. 23 in *RHM*!
77. *RA*, nn. 3841, 4133; *ÁUO*, V, 171f.; L. Gerevich, "The Rise of Hungarian Towns Along the Danube," in his *Towns in Medieval Hungary* (Budapest, 1990), 26ff.
78. Cf. Ambrus Pleidell, "A magyar városfejlödés néhány fejezete" [Chapters on the Development of Town Life in Hungary], *Századok*, 68 (1934), 1ff., 158ff., and 276ff. - still a fundamental work.
79. *Ibid.*, 13.
80. Béla IV donated the lands of the fort personnel to the citizens of Sopron - *RA*, n. 1642; *CD*, IV-3, 513f.; Gerevich, *Hungarian Towns*, 28ff.
81. *RA*, nn. 3659, 3660.
82. "...quo cum cives seu hospites nostri de Suprunio" be tax-exempt, "sicut cives Albenses et Budenses, per totius regni nostri climata;" *RA*, n. 4132; *ÁUO*, V, 172f.
83. *RA*, n. 3699; *ÁUO*, V, 20ff.; Knauz, II, 354ff.
84. As, for instance, *RA*, nn. 3852, 3857, 3869, 3908, 3910, 3939, 4008, 4015; Jenő Szűcs, "Nationalität und Nationalbewusstsein im Mittelalter," *Acta historica Academiae Scientiarum Hungaricae*, 18 (1972), 1ff., and 245ff.
85. Idem, "Theoretische Elemente in Meister Simon de Kézas Gesta Ungarorum, 1282-85," in his *Nation und Geschichte: Studien* (Vienna, 1981), 263ff., esp. 274ff.
86. "...et consensu...patrum archiepiscoporum, episcoporum, baronum, procerum et omnium nobilium regni nostri apud Albam,...fuissemus coronati...;" Marczali, *Enchiridion*, 186.
87. *SSH*, I, 475,6-8.
88. "...et in regni gubernaculum successimus iure et ordine geniturae, habita congregatione generali" - as if to call attention to the fact that after his coronation the Diet recognize his rights of inheritance, "ordine geniturae." In his recognition the hierarchy did play an important role - in order to neutralize the aims and policies of the Roman curia.
89. *HO*, VII, 300f.
90. "...virilem stirpem Arpadianam, ultra IV secula Hungarie dominatam, in tumulum secum traxit, variisque morte sua turbis ac aemulorum studiis regnum obiecit," - remarks made by Katona, *Historia critica*, VI, 1249; compare with *RA*, n. 4093, with text, on Stephen, son of Ban[us] Erney, former Justice of the Realm, *RA*, n. 4185 (dated July 23, 1298). The last letter issued by King Andrew III was dated January 14, 1301, *RA*, n. 4344; *ÁUO*, V, 267; Gy. Kristó (ed.), *Anjoukori Oklevéltár* [Documents of the Anjou Age] (Budapest-Szeged, 1990), n. 4; Queen Agnes, in her writ dated January 15, 1301 (3 die Oct. Epiph.), referred to the death of her husband - cf. Kristó, *Oklevéltár*, n. 7; *CD*, VI-2, 326.

2. *The Anjou Claim to the Árpád Throne*

> Quorum instantiam papa admittens quendam puerum XI annorum nomine Karolum anno MoCCoXCoIXo vivente adhuc Andrea rege in Hungariam destinavit.
>
> *Chronicon pictum*, c. 187

The claim of the Anjous of Naples to the Hungarian Crown reaches back to the 1260's. During the *interregnum* following the death of Emperor Frederick II, Rome had authorized the brother of Louis IX of France to occupy the throne of Naples-Sicily, south of the papal states. The pontiff was Clement IV,[1] and the invited papal candidate for the south Italian throne was Charles of Anjou, Count of Provence, who had occupied Naples, captured and executed Conrad IV, the son (though still a minor) of Frederick II, who represented the anti-papal Hohenstaufen interests on southern Italian soil.[2] Charles I of Naples-Sicily was an outstanding monarch, who had plans for the possession of all Italy, for building a new eastern [Roman] state on the ruins of the declining Byzantine empire.[3]

It must have been for this purpose that he allied himself with the Árpád family. In the fall of 1269, Charles I of Naples-Sicily had concluded a marriage contract with the Hungarian court. It was in accordance with this agreement that Charles' youngest daughter was to marry Ladislas (later Ladislas IV of Hungary), son of Stephen V, while the daughter of Stephen V, Maria, was sent to the court of Naples to become queen of Charles' I son, [the future] Charles II the Lame, with whom she ascended to the throne of Naples in 1285.[4]

Upon the assassination, in 1290, of her brother, Ladislas IV, Queen Maria claimed the Hungarian Crown, and requested the help of Pope Nicholas IV to obtain it.[5] The Holy See remained hesitant and asked the archbishop of Esztergom for a report. When Esztergom did not respond, the papal curia sent, as legate, the bishop of Gubbio to Hungary with instructions to gain first-hand information on political conditions in the realm. The bishop of Gubbio did not enter Hungary, however; John Ugoccione, the bishop of Aesi, became the papal envoy instead.[6]

During this time, the German court had announced its claim to Hungary - regardless of the fact that the Hungarian *estates* had already acknowledged the succession of Andrew III, the last scion of the Árpád dynasty that had ruled the country since the 890's, to the Crown.[7] The German king, Rudolf of Habsburg, gave Hungary as a fief to his son Albert, and notified Rome to that effect. Pope Nicholas IV, who viewed Rudolf's policies with suspicion, made a protest, and instructed the bishop of Aesi to express papal objections to both Rudolf and his son, were he to meet with them during his journey as a papal envoy.[8]

In his letter of January 31, 1291, the pontiff simultaneously stressed his argument that Hungary was, as it had been for a long period of time, subject to the authority of the Holy See; nobody should dare to attack, occupy, or claim possession of its territory. The curia formulated the idea anew that the Roman pontiff alone could decide the question of succession to and occupancy of the Hungarian throne. The papal writ did not refer to King Andrew III by name; earlier, the pontiff had instructed his legate that he protect the widow of the deceased Ladislas IV - she was the daughter of the King of Naples! - as if to inform the bishop of Aesi that the curia was prepared to defend and support the Anjou interests in Hungary.[9]

Under these circumstances the papal legate arriving in Hungary did not recognize Andrew III as king, though he had been told to persuade Andrew to submit his claim to the throne for arbitration by the papal curia - as a time when Andrew III had already been crowned king.[10] Andrew's enemy, Iván of Németújvár, had, at the same time, taken an oath in front of the pope's envoy to the effect that he would only acknowledge as king the one who had been designated by the Roman curia.[11] The king's loyal supporters, including members of the hierarchy, were unwilling even to hear about the papal intervention in what they regarded as their own domestic affair. They looked upon the papal confirmation attempt as unnecessary, and had threatened to excommunicate anyone who dared to oppose them.[12] On the other hand, the bishops had emphasized their point of view that they recognized the papal envoy as the official spokesman of the curia.[13]

Upon the death of Nicholas IV, the papal throne remained vacant for two years, and the king of Naples had to visit Rome to urge the cardinals at the conclave to hurry up with the election of a new pope.[14] Celestine V was, indeed, loyal to Charles I of Naples, but he did not interfere in the Hungarian succession question.[15] After he had resigned his high office, the royal house of Naples attempted to draw the new pontiff, Boniface VIII, into the controversy. At the dinner following the coronation of Pope Boniface VIII, Charles II the Lame, and his son, Charles Martel, the "kings of Naples and of Hungary," served at his table, the chronicler reported.[16]

A word of explanation will be in order here. Boniface VIII in his bull *Unam sanctam* elaborated on the idea already expressed by Pope Gelasius in the fifth century that the Church held two-fold authority; "sed quidem pro ecclesia, ille vero ab ecclesia exercendus. Ille sacerdotis, in manu regum et militum, sed ad nutum et patientiam sacerdotis."[17] The pontiff re-emphasized the view held by Bernard of Clairvaux, and repeated the statement Gregory IX had made in a writ addressed to Germanus, the Byzantine Patriarch, to the effect that spiritual authority was over all; above it, no secular power held jurisdiction.[18]

Odofriedus, imperial civil servant in about the mid-thirteenth century, wrote in his *Commentary on the Digest* that the emperor had power over everyone, and nobody dared to contradict him in temporal matters. And yet, in his *Commentary on the Code*, Odofriedus concluded that next to spiritual authority temporal power, too, had its jurisdiction. Rome, however, played a predominant role in both the spiritual and the secular scene, on the grounds that were a temporal power to commit a "sin," the spiritual authority had the right to intervene *ratione materiae*, because of its claim to spiritual jurisdiction.[19]

Iohannes of Viterbo, author of *De regimine civitatum* during the pontificate of Urban IV, observed that in society one had to deal with man and God. Man consisted, however, of body and soul, so it was necessary that he lived under a two-fold jurisdiction. God ruled over man through the services of the *sacerdotium* in religious-spiritual matters, and in human affairs, through those of the *imperium*. The two swords representing the two-fold jurisdiction were to be handled by various magistrates; still, all authority and power came from God.[20]

One can, therefore, understand that when members of the Hungarian nobility had turned to Rome with the request for a[nother] king, Boniface VIII must have looked upon their petition as an opportunity to test his ideas through papal diplomacy; "quomodo in preiudicium regis Andree, Karolus puerum papa in Hungariam mittitur pro rege."[21]

The pontiff did not necessarily follow Anjou politics, however. For example, he called upon the counts of Németújvár, adherents of the Anjou pretender(s) to the Árpád throne, to return church goods they had earlier confiscated to their rightful owner(s).[22] The papal curia only changed course in its diplomacy upon the death of Archbishop Ladomér of Esztergom. The chapter of canons in Esztergom had elected Gregory Bodoli, prelate at Székesfehérvár and royal vice-chancellor, as successor, and Andrew III had approved of the election. But Bodoli had second thoughts and had reversed his position after receiving royal approval of his election to the see of Esztergom; he had joined the Anjou party in the field of secular politics. The king, Andrew III, had no alternative but to withdraw his approval of Archbishop-elect Gregory, and declare the archiepiscopal see vacant. The Esztergom chapter of canons now requested the papal curia not to recognize Gregory as [the new] archbishop of Esztergom.[23]

Rome, indeed, left the confirmation of Gregory of archbishop pending, and named him "Procurator pro tempore" to administer the Esztergom church province.[24] The curia failed to notify either Charles of Anjou, or King Andrew III, of its decision, however. Furthermore, the papal writ issued on the occasion differed from the usual form letters issued by the papal court. In his writ, the pontiff strongly bemoaned the miserable condition of the country; he decried the fact that the kingdom had fallen so low: evil threatened the country, he wrote, because its population had rapidly declined in the recent past. Towns and villages became uninhabited. Heretics, schismatics, and pagans surrounded the realm and penetrated its territory. Only Archbishop-elect Gregory, now archiepiscopal procurator in Esztergom by the will of the Holy See, could find solutions to these problems. Gregory had been instructed to organize the inquisition in Hungary, with the help of the Dominicans, against heretics and schismatics. Gregory would punish everyone who dared to disturb the common peace of the land, and display anti-ecclesiastic tendencies, privately or publicly.[25] (As if Boniface VIII had wholly disregarded the future of Hungary - he was mainly concerned with organizing the inquisition.)

The letter of Pope Boniface VIII carefully avoided mention of the competition for the Hungarian Crown. He did not openly support Charles Martel's candidacy for the Árpád throne, though he left no doubt that he knew that Gregory supported the Anjous' claim to the Crown.[26] Although Archbishop-elect Gregory had made no appearance at the diet of Rákos, meeting in May, 1299,[27] he had sent a personal representative to bring public charges against Andrew III, accusing the monarch of harassing the church in Esztergom, and had called for a church assembly to gather in Veszprém soon.[28]

Members of the Hungarian hierarchy reacted with displeasure against the "summons" issued by Archbishop-elect Gregory by asserting that they had not seen, and had not been aware of the papal authorization of Gregory as administrator of the Esztergom church province; on those grounds, they disobeyed his call for a church synod to gather in Veszprém. The bishops had made it clear, however, that they were loyal to the Holy See, and requested anew that the archbishop-elect appear in person at the diet, and personally inform them of his appointment as the papal delegate.[29]

Archbishop-elect Bodoli did not attend the diet at Rákos held in 1299, nor did he submit a [the] writ to clarify his position; as a matter of fact, he had threatened with excommunication anyone who dared not cooperate with him.[30]

It must have occurred at this occasion that Andrew III decided to take matters into his own hands: with the support of the diet, he made an appeal to Rome. The king instructed the bishop of Várad to draft an official writ of appeal to the papal curia, even though there is no evidence that the king's letter had ever arrived in Rome. It had not been logged in the papal Register.[31] But it is known that Archbishop-elect Gregory suddenly found himself isolated in his politics, and he could not carry out his threats; indeed, he had to seek political and personal refuge with the Németújvár family. Gregory had also tried to arrange with Charles II of Naples to dispatch troops to Hungary for the support of Charles Martel's claim to the throne - and presumably, he did this with the tacit understanding of the Holy See.[32]

In the spring of 1300, the archbishop-elect of Esztergom dispatched, "in the name of the higher clergy and higher nobility in Hungary," a delegation of Dalmatian friars to the court of Naples with the request that it send Caroberto, alias Charles Martel, to

Hungary.[33] The court of Naples turned to the curia for advice, but the envoys of Andrew III, active in Rome at this time, parried the plan. When in August, 1300, Caroberto landed at Spaleto for the purpose of reaching Hungarian territory to claim the Crown, King Andrew III, who, incidentally, was not overly concerned about the ambitions of Caroberto,[34] had staged a diplomatic counter-offensive.[35]

Andrew III did not permit the pretender to enter the realm in the company of the papal legate. He had Peter Bonzano of Trevisoi acting as envoy, stationed in Rome, to make certain that the papal curia did not support Caroberto. As evident from the letters of Bonzano, his mission was not fruitless. Pope Boniface VIII had assumed a neutral position in the matter, and did not encourage the pretender (or the court of Naples) to undertake further action. "Quod nepos regis Caroli contra consilium et voluntatem domini papae et cardinalium amicorum suorum missus fuit per dominum regem [i.e., Charles Martel] in partem illas, et quod dominus papa (ei non dedit) aliquod auxilium." Indeed, were Andrew III to take captive the "boy" ("quod si haberitis puerum in manibus vestris"), he was to hand him over to the Roman pontiff: "quod mitteritis eum ad dominum papam."[36]

It is quite evident from the report of Bonzano that he also held another commission. He had to ascertain that the curia void the appointment of Archbishop-elect Gregory to the see of Esztergom, and elevate Bishop Antal of Csanád, a loyal supporter of Andrew III, to the archiepiscopal see. However, one must conclude from the letter of Bonzano, dated from Venice, on September 18, 1300, and addressed to Michael Marosini,[37] and from his report of October 25, 1300, dispatched to the Hungarian court, that he had to entertain certain doubts about the outcome of his secondary mission. He could only hope that negotiations between the curia and the bishops of Csanád would be successful, he wrote. "Sed spero, quod cito a domino papa negocium vestrum et domini episcopi feliciter expedietur."[38] It becomes clear from Bonzano's third letter, dated early November, 1300, that talks with the Holy See were broken off - "et quod si eius negocium non possit expediri;"[39] the curia did not divest Archbishop-elect Gregory of his see, or of his status.[40]

The Chronicle reported that the papal envoys sent to Hungary to negotiate on behalf of Charles Robert for the Hungarian Crown had accomplished little; they had returned to Rome by the time King Andrew III died unexpectedly on the Feast of St. Felix, 1301, in Buda Castle.[41] But even his death did not solve the problem of succession, because the pretender (by that time, he had departed toward Pest in the company of a few Hungarian nobles who had joined him)[42] was crowned by Archbishop-elect Gregory with *a* crown (on the grounds that *the* Crown had been retained by its guardian, the Archpriest of Székesfehérvár).[43] Iván of Kőszeg, however, had decided to move against the [crowned] pretender, take him prisoner, and occupy Esztergom with his forces. Caroberto had no alternative but to flee to the nearby Cistercian abbey at Bélakút.[44]

It is evident from the record that upon the death of Andrew III, the barons of the realm were soon divided into two groups over the issue of royal succession and coronation. Matthew (Máté), Amade, and Ugrin, "potentissimi principes in regno," and many nobles supported Charles Robert, and named him [their] king, "by word, not by deed" - *verbo, sed non facto.*[45]

Another group of many great lords of the country, "viri valde magnifici," led by Domonkos, the former treasurer of the deceased monarch, and Archbishop János (John) of Kalocsa, had, together with certain members of the hierarchy, offered the Crown to King Vencel of Bohemia, because of his blood ties with the Árpád family.[46] King Vencel, in turn, named his son, also known as Vencel, to the Hungarian throne. The high lords of the kingdom and members of the hierarchy accepted young Vencel as their king. They took a written oath to him and the archbishop of Kalocsa crowned him with the Crown in Székesfehérvár.[47]

And yet, King Vencel - the Hungarians called him Ladislas the Czech - did not actually possess royal powers, nor did Charles Robert; the Chronicle reported that in one part of the country people looked upon Ladislas the Czech, in other parts of the realm regarded Charles Robert, as their king.[48]

King Vencel of Bohemia, father of Ladislas the Czech, had sensed the awkward nature of the future-less situation. Rome made a vehement protest about the coronation of Ladislas by the archbishop of Kalocsa,[49] on the grounds that it was the archbishop of Esztergom who alone had the right to crown the kings of Hungary[50] - and this in spite of the chronicler's report that, at the time of Ladislas' coronation in Székesfehérvár, the see of Esztergom had been vacant.[51] King Vencel decided to take his son home, and to take the Hungarian Crown with him to Prague.[52]

It was at this time that the diplomats of the royal court of Naples entered the political scene. Benedict Geszthi persuaded the papal curia to undertake a move that would secure the position of Charles Robert on the Árpádian throne.[53] The Roman See complied with the request, and dispatched the Dominican Nicholas Boccassino, Cardinal-bishop and seasoned diplomat, as papal legate to Buda. Boccassino had been instructed to work for furthering the cause of Charles Robert in Hungary, even though his writ of commission made no mention of the royal succession to the Hungarian Crown.[54]

The attitude of the papal curia toward the candidacy of Charles Robert to the throne, and, in general terms, the views of Pope Boniface VIII of the Hungarian court, may be traced back to Pope Gregory VII in the eleventh century. He had stated that Hungary was, as it had been since the times of King Stephen I, a fief of the Holy See. It is known, the pontiff wrote, that King Stephen received his crown from, and had offered his kingdom to the Holy See.[55]

The ideas of Gregory VII were accepted by Pope Innocent III,[56] who had further emphasized that only the archbishop of Esztergom crown the kings of Hungary; the archbishop of Kalocsa could perform the coronation only if the see of Esztergom were vacant.[57] In his letters addressed to the Hungarian court, Pope Boniface VIII identified himself with these points of view.[58] As he explained it in his bull *Unam sanctam*, the Roman pontiff had the right to decide who the next monarch would be,[59] even though Charles Robert had not properly been crowned with the Crown, nor had his coronation been properly performed at Székesfehérvár (by Archbishop-elect Gregory, whose status had not yet been ruled on by the papal curia).[60]

Cardinal-legate Boccassino spent several days in Buda - he even had time to summon a synod - but accomplished little, and returned to Rome. He wrote a report on his unsuccessful mission, as did Simon, an archpriest of Pozsony, in a detailed letter sent to the bishop of Veszprém.[61] It is known, however, from the papal correspondence that His Holiness had cited both [crowned] pretenders to the Hungarian throne to appear before him, so that he may adjudge their claims.[62]

On May 31, 1303, Pope Boniface VIII handed down his sentence in favor of Charles Robert.[63]

••••

During the thirteenth century, the savage might of the Cumans had disappeared from the stage of Árpád history, and so did the threatening power, greed for conquest and expansion of the Mongols that devoured the Cumans and kept only the regions east of the Carpathian Mountains under its control.[64] In the south, Byzantium had receded to the southern edge of the Balkan peninsula. Along the Danube, the Bulgarian realm of Kajolan grew divided against itself - though, simultaneously, Serbia became stronger, for no other reason than that the Árpád kings, Andrew II, Béla IV, and Ladislas IV, had been preoccupied with other matters and pursued no real policy in the Balkans.[65] In the west, the glorious days of the medieval empire came to an end. The universal (Roman) empire of the German nation had ceased to exist with the fall of the Hohenstaufen.[66]

Hungary under the Árpáds (896-1301) survived all the difficult times.[67] It remained Hungarian, a national Hungarian kingdom. People from many ethnic groups had entered and settled down in the land, as if to bear witness to the correctness of the views held by the founder king, Saint Stephen (ob. 1038), who said that fragile and weak was the country where only one language and one code of ethics prevailed. He had warned his successors to show good will and respect toward guests and foreign settlers in their midst, thereby to increase the country's strength. "Nam unius lingue uniusque moris regnum imbecille et fragile est."[68]

After the Mongol onslaught(s), mostly German immigrants, but also Cumans, Széklers, Serbs and Vlachs (Romanians) - "Valhen, Zockel, Syrfen, Vlachen" - lived within the borders of the realm.[69] The Germans had been critical of the Hungarians for being inconsiderate of others, and unwilling to yield on any issue (though they stayed and did not emigrate back to their homeland).[70]

The character of the kingdom had remained Hungarian even after the death of Andrew III. The Czech Venceslas, the son of Hungarian mother, Queen Kunigunde, did not want to become king because, he said, he did not learn Hungarian, and how could one become king without being able to listen to the people's complaints and pass judgment among them?[71]

At Charles Robert's first coronation in Buda Castle in 1309, great families, like the Csáks, the Türjéks, and families of foreign origin that became Hungarian,[72] such as the Rátolds, the French Zsámbors, the German Herders, were present, and so were the archbishop of Spaleto, the sons of Baboniks, the great counts of Slovenia.[73] The coronation oath taken in Latin was explained in Hungarian, "in Ungarico exposita."[74]

Hungary of the Árpáds was not a polyglot, federal "country." It had remained Hungarian and kept its national values, because Árpáds' descendants had the country established on the border of western Europe, and followed a policy of cooperation with eastern peoples. The Árpáds had learned from them, had accepted them as settlers in their country. The dynasty had retained the people's integrity, while simultaneously learning how to gain the trust of the newcomers.[75]

The Árpáds loved peace, but were ready for war, and did not seek compromises to avoid hardships. When an enemy attacked the land, the Árpáds fought back hard in self-defense. They fought the good fight for the interests and the survival of their country.

NOTES

1. Cf. J. Loserth, *Geschichte des spätern Mittelalters*, Abt. II of *Handbuch der mittelalterlichen und neueren Geschichte*, ed. G. v. Below and F. Meinecke (Munich-Berlin, 1903), 124ff.; Gebhardt, I, 382ff.

2. Funk-Bihlmeyer, II, 193; Loserth, 143ff.; Kühner, *Papstlexikon*, 74f.

3. See John Lerner, *Italy in the Age of Dante and Petrarch* (London-New York, 1980), 38ff.

4. *Ibid.*, 42f.

5. Cf. G. Wenczel (ed.), *Anjoukori diplomácia emlékek* [Documents of Diplomacy During the Reign of the Anjous], 3 vols. (Budapest, 1874-76), I, 21ff. (September 13-15, 1269). Compare with *SSH*, I, 478,3-10.

6. See Potthast, nn. 23384-23385; *VMH*, n. 588; Funk-Bihlmeyer, II, 194; Fraknói, I, 98.

7. *SSH*, I, 476f.; *Reimchronik*, lines 39972-73; Katona, *Historia critica*, VI, 1052. The pontiff had little respect for Rudolf - Hefele, VI, 212.

8. Potthast, nn. 23543-23544; *VMH*, nn. 598-599.

9. Potthast, nn. 23510, 23547; *VMH*, nn. 593 and 600.

10. Cf. Potthast, n. 23384.

11. Potthast, n. 23791; *VMH*, n. 618.

12. Of March 13, 1299; Potthast, n. 24773.

13. *SSH*, I, 475,7-8; Potthast, n. 23773.

14. See Teutsch-Firnhaber, *Urkundenbuch*, *FRA*, Abt. 2, XV (1857), 179.

15. *SSH*, I, 478,14-22; on the death of the pontiff, *Annales Jacobi Aurie*, *MGHSS*, XVIII, 340,25-28; Potthast, II, 1214; Hefele, VI, 269.

16. *Ibid.*, VI, 272.

17. Haller, V, 132f; Hefele, VI, 284.

18. Spiritual authority judges all and is judged by none; cf. the papal bull *Unam sanctam*, Potthast, n. 25189; Ae. Friedberg (ed.), *Corpus Iuris Canonici*, 2 vols. (Leipzig, 1879; repr. Graz, 1959), II, 1245ff.; A. Dempf, *Sacrum imperium*, 4th rev. ed. (Munich-Vienna, 1973), 314f.; C.H. McIlwain, *The Growth of Political Thought in the West* (New York, 1932), 245f.

19. Bernard of Clairvaux, "De consideratione," iv:3,7, in J. Leclercq and H. Rochair (eds.), *S. Bernardi opera*, vol. 3 (Rome, 1963), 435ff.; Dempf, 220f.; Pope Gregory to Germanus, in Matthew of Paris, *Chronica maiora*, 7 vols., RS. (London, 1872-83), III, 467.

20. Odofriedus, *Commentary on the Digest* (Lyon, 1550), intr. i:1; *Commentary on the Code* (Lyon, 1550), i:1.

21. *De regimine civitatum*, ed. G. Salvemini, in *Bibliotheca iuridica medii aevi*, III, 127f.; McIlwain, 264; *Siete partidas*, I:1,18-19; II:1,19.

22. Chronicle, c. 187.

23. *ÁUO*, X, 273f.

24. Potthast, n. 24773; Knauz, II, 433ff.; Fraknói, I, 103.

25. *VMH*, n. 615.

26. Potthast, n. 24773; on Boniface VIII, see Funk-Bihlmeyer, II, 248ff., esp. 250f.; T.S.R. Boase, *Boniface the Eighth* (London, 1933), 73f.; A.C. Shannon, *The Popes and Heresy in the Thirteenth Century* (Villanova, PA, 1949), 27ff., and 48ff.

27. Cf. *CD*, VI-2, 201ff.; royal writs issued July 1, 1299, and July 17, referred to the diet, *RA*, nn. 4251 and 4252, and so did a writ of July 28, 1299, *RA*, n. 4258; *ÁUO*, X, 329f. The curia had recognized Maria as Queen; cf. Boase, 263f., in ref. to *CD*, VI-2, 150.

28. Cf. Z.J. Kosztolnyik, "In the European Mainstream: Hungarian Churchmen and Thirteenth Century Synods," *Catholic Historical Review*, 79 (1993), 413ff., esp. 430.

29. Potthast, n. 24773.

30. *VMH*, n. 616; Hóman-Szekfű, II, 32ff.; Hóman, *Ungarisches Mittelalter*, II, 263ff.

31. Cf. Z.J. Kosztolnyik, "III András és a pápai udvar" [Andrew III of Hungary and the Papal Court], *Századok*, 126 (1992), 646ff., 651, and n. 80.

32. Fraknói, I, 107.

33. Wenczel, *Anjoukori diplomácia*, I, 143; Hóman-Szekfű, I, 617f.; Hóman, *Ungarisches Mittelalter*, II, 225f.

34. Wenczel, *Anjoukori diplomácia*, I, 143.

35. *ÁUO*, V, 260.

36. *Ibid.*, the supporters of Andrew III in Rome included Bishop Antal of Csanád and Benedict, bishop of Vác - Vilmos Fraknói, *A veszprémi püspökség római levéltára* [The Roman Archives of the Veszprém Bishopric], 2 vols. (Budapest, 1896-99), II, p. xliii.

37. *ÁUO*, V, 262; see further, Potthast, nn. 25080 and 25045; *VMH*, nn. 622 and 619; *CD*, VI-2, 313ff., and 308ff.

38. Of the letters sent by Peter Bonzano, three remained: one, of September 18, 1300, sent from Venice to the address of Michael Marosini in Zara, *ÁUO*, V, 260f., to record that the monarch was sending money to the archbishop of Esztergom for Friar Antal, with instructions that "si factum domini Antonii non posset expediri," the amount be applied for payment of the royal debt. In another writ, Bonzano described himself before the king as "eius devotus procurator et serviens." Cf. *ibid.*, V, 262f.

39. Bonzano had expressed hope that negotiations between the curia and the bishops would be successful - *ibid.*, V, 262; Huber, *art. cit.*, 299, n. 5.

40. *ÁUO*, V, 263f.; finances had something to do with the [proposed] appointment of Bishop Antal to the see of Esztergom; it was Bishop Emery of Várad who made the appeal.

41. *Ibid.*, X, 329ff.; and yet, from the king's point of view, Gregory had no longer held his see: "sedes Strigoniensis vacabit;" *SSH*, I, 480,21-22, and 47-48. On royal documents, dated January 9, February 13, and March 18, 1298, Gregory had signed as archpriest of Fehérvár and royal vice-chancellor - see *RA*, nn. 4167 (*ÁUO*, X, 294f.), 4168 with text, and 4169 with text; on royal writs dated February 17 and 24, 1298, Gregory had signed as archbishop-elect of Esztergom - *RA*, nn. 4173 and 4174; *CD*, VI-2, 122f., and *ÁUO*, V, 186, respectively. On a writ, dated 1298, and logged under *RA*, n. 4204, he had signed, once again, as archpriest of Fehérvár and royal vice-chancellor, *ÁUO*, X, 300f., although this could be a false document. On March 29, 1298, it was the Franciscan Antal, bishop of Csanád, who had signed as royal vice-chancellor - see *RA*, n. 4176; *CD*, VI-2, 124f. On Boniface VIII, see B. Ptolemaeus, in Muratori, *RISS*, XIII, 9ff.; and A. Augerit, *ibid.*, III, 10ff.; Kühner, *Papstlexikon*, 79ff.

42. *SSH*, I, 478,14-26; the Várad Chronicle, *ibid.*, I, 214,5-10; on the date, cf. H. Grotefend, *Zeitrechnung des deutschen Mittelalters und der Neuzeit*, 2 vols. (Hannover, 1891; repr. Aalen, 1984), I, Tafel xxix; the Pray codex (a twelfth century sacramentary) recorded the Feast of St. Hilarius (January 14) on January 13; cf. Polycarp Radó, *Libri liturgici manu scripti bibliothecarum Hungariae* (Budapest, 1947), 37. F. Kühár, "A Pray kódex rendeltetése, sorsa, szellemtörténeti értéke" [Purpose, Fate, and Intellectual Value of the Pray Codex], *Magyar Könyvszemle*, 63 (1939), 213ff. Further, a writ of Queen Agnes, dated 1314, in *FRASS*, VI, 257. See

also *Cont. Vindob.*, in *MGHSS*, IX, 721,40-48; *Reimchronik*, lines 78299-78356; Huber, *art. cit.*, 230; Hóman-Szekfű, I, 625.

43. *SSH*, I, 479,4-10. An addition to the Chronicle reported that upon the death of Andrew III, Vencel, son of the Czech king, had entered Hungary and was crowned king in Fehérvár - *SSH*, I, 479,17-19, also *ibid.*, I, 479,20; Knauz, II, 444, that is, the coronation took place in Esztergom.

44. Compare with the papal writ of May 31, 1303 - Potthast, n. 25252; *VMH*, n. 635 (I, 397ff.). The chronicler also explained that when Archbishop John of Kalocsa had crowned the Czech Vencel king, the see of Esztergom had been vacant - *SSH*, I, 480,21-22, although, the chronicler noted, "electus ipsius ecclesie erat Gregorius, filius Wotend [Botond], custos tunc Albensis ecclesie;" *ibid.*, I, 479,47-48.

45. *Ibid.*, I, 479,10. The chronicler only remarked that he belonged to a group of nobles who wanted to have Vencel as king - *ibid.*, I, 479,10-13.

46. Cf. *SSH*, I, 479,4-10; "verbo, sed non facto" - it was a diplomat's manner of saying that Charles was not properly crowned. "Proper" or "correct" coronation would have involved acclamation, anointment, and coronation with the Hungarian "Holy Crown;" cf. Timon, 114ff.; Hóman-Szekfű, II, 42f.; Kosztolnyik, *Five Kings*, 9f., and 132, nn. 53-54.

47. *SSH*, I, 479f., and rendered the reason, why? - *ibid.*, I, 480,4-9.

48. *Ibid.*, I, 480,14-21; Knauz, II, 414, that is, in Esztergom; Palacky, *Geschichte*, II-1, 350ff.

49. *SSH*, I, 481,6-13.

50. *Ibid.*, I, 481,13-21; Potthast, n. 25088; *VMH*, n. 627; Palacky, II-1, 353ff. The argument of Boase that Vencel of Bohemia had sought at once to realize his son's claim goes contrary to the chronicler's report. See also the papal writ of October 17, 1301, in Potthast, n. 25067.

51. Pope Innocent III, in *MPL*, 215, 413, and 463; also, 216, 50c and 51c; Z.J. Kosztolnyik, "The Church and Béla III of Hungary: The Role of Archbishop Lukács of Esztergom," *Church History*, 49 (1980), 375ff.; esp. 380; idem, *From Coloman*, 244; Timon, 318f., 509ff., 543, and 536.

52. *SSH*, I, 480,21-22; *Chronicon Posoniense*, *ibid.*, II, 447,25-26; Potthast, n. 25090; *VMH*, n. 625.

53. *SSH*, I, 481,13-21.

54. See I. Nagy (ed.), *Anjoukori Okmánytár* [Documents of the Angevin Age in Hungary], 6 vols. (Budapest, 1878-91), I, 80.

55. Potthast, n. 25045; *VMH*, n. 619.

56. *Ibid.*, n. 622 (Potthast, n. 25080); *CD*, VI-2, 313ff., and compare with the writs of Gregory VII addressed to the monarchs of Hungary, in Erich Caspar (ed.), *Das Register Gregors VII (MGH Epistolae selectae)*, 2 vols. (Berlin, 1920-23; repr. Munich, 1990), ii:13 (October 28, 1074) and vi:29 (March 21, 1079), *inter alia*; Kosztolnyik, *Five Hungarian Kings*, 92ff., and 187ff.

57. Caspar, *Register*, i:5 (March 17, 1074), and ii:63 (March 23, 1075); also ii:70 (April 17, 1075), and compare with the letter of Innocent III, *MPL*, 463bc; Kosztolnyik, *From Coloman*, 234ff., and 244.

58. Helene Tillman, *Papst Innocenz III* (Bonn, 1954), 74f., and n. 57; Boase, 262ff., and 328ff.; Kosztolnyik, *From Coloman*, 244 and 262, n. 193.

59. Potthast, n. 25080, as cited above.

60. *Ibid.*, n. 25189; Friedberg, II, 1245ff.

61. Potthast, n. 25090.

62. As it may be evident from the papal writ, Potthast, n. 25088; *VMH*, n. 627, and compare with the papal writ of June 10, 1302, Potthast, n. 25159; *VMH*, n. 628. Also, *ibid.*, n. 626 (Potthast, n. 25086); Fraknói, I, 369, note 336; the letters of Boccassino, in Knauz, II, 499f.; *CD*, VIII-7, 25ff.

63. Potthast, n. 25085; *VMH*, n. 626 (it contains both papal writs, Potthast, nn. 25085 and 25086).
64. Potthast, n. 25252; *VMH*, n. 635; *CD*, VIII-1, 121ff.; also, Palacky, *Reise*, n. 416.
65. Hóman-Szekfű, I, 574ff.
66. Hampe, *Kaisergeschichte*, 233, and 321f.
67. *SSH*, I, 478,13-22.
68. King St. Stephen's *Admonitiones*, art. vi, cf. *ibid.*, II, 625,5-6.
69. "Valben, Sirven, Zokel, Wallach," *Reimchronik*, lines 80282-80390.
70. *Ibid.*, lines 80410-80417.
71. *Ibid.*, lines 80427-80434.
72. Cf. *VMH*, I, 820f., n. 1256. On the papal commission of Cardinal Gentile, *ibid.*, n. 664, and n. 669.
73. Cf. Kéza, cc. 76-94, *SSH*, I, 187ff.; Hóman-Szekfű, II, 52ff.; on the "first" coronation of Charles I Anjou, cf. *SSH*, I, 486,16-20.
74. Cf. *VMH*, I, 823ff., n. 1259; also, *FRASS*, VIII, 365.
75. St. Stephen's *Admonitiones*, aa. i, iii, and vi, *SSH*, II, 619ff.; St. Stephen's *Leges*, preface, in Marczali, *Enchiridion*, 69f.; and Emma Bartoniek (ed.), *Szent István törvényeinek XII századi kézirata* [The Twelfth Century MS of the Laws of King St. Stephen] (Budapest, 1935), 18f.; compare to Friedrich Heer, *Die Tragödie des Heiligen Reiches* (Stuttgart, 1952), 141ff.

APPENDIX I

A THIRTEENTH CENTURY WOMAN: SAINT ELIZABETH OF HUNGARY*

Elizabeth of Hungary was born in Sárospatak in 1207 to King Andrew II of Hungary and Gertrud of Andechs-Meran. Her mother met a tragic death in 1213, when Hungarian conspirators had her murdered. Elizabeth's two maternal uncles, Berthold, titular Patriarch of Aquileia, and Bishop Eckbert of Bamberg, who had played a role in the assassination of Philip of Swabia and sought refuge at the Hungarian court, were high ecclesiastics. In 1211, Hermann I, Landgrave of Thuringia, sent a delegation led by Knight Walter of Vargila to Pozsony to request the hand of Elizabeth in marriage for his son, Hermann. The landgrave probably wanted to restore his weakened social and financial resources through this marriage with the Hungarian royal family. He may also have hoped to rely on the support of the Eastern monarch in the deadly struggle between Otto of Brunswick and Frederick, the new papal protégé for the German throne. Bishop Eckbert may have suggested the plan, though it is possible that Otakar of Bohemia may have also tried to establish a triple alliance by including the King of Hungary. From another point of view, family ties between one of the leading noble families in the empire and the Hungarian court might have enhanced the diplomatic position of Andrew II against some German princes, who still looked upon Hungary as a country to be invaded and plundered. Knight Vargila successfully concluded a marriage agreement, and the four-year-old bride, richly endowed, was dispatched to the Thuringian court at the castle of Wartburg, near Eisenach. A bathtub of pure silver and a thousand pieces of gold formed only a portion of her dowry. It is known from her husband, Louis, that the Thuringian court had never before seen such riches. They also expressed surprise at Elizabeth's large personal entourage of servants and nurses.

Hermann I maintained an elaborate court and provided for poets and artists of the age. It may be that Walther von der Vogelweide or Wolfram von Eschenbach (while working on his

* Appendix I appeared as a separate entry in *Great Lives From History, Ancient and Medieval Series* (Pasadena, CA, 1988), 655ff., published here with the permission of Salem Press.

Parzifal, c. 1200-1210; English translation, 1894) spent some time at the castle at Wartburg. Elizabeth was educated at the Thuringian court; the curriculum included the study of contemporary poetry and writers, the history of leading families in the empire, art appreciation, Latin, and religion. As a child, Elizabeth liked to play, ride horses, and participate in games as well as pray in the chapel. Even as a child she displayed empathy and compassion toward the poor. Concerned with Elizabeth's appearance as a lady of society, however, her mother-in-law cautioned her about being too loud and exuberant.

In 1213, when her mother was murdered, the six-year-old Elizabeth saw her bloody, mutilated body in a dream. After that, she spent more time in prayer before the crucifix and began to dress more simply. She began to pray for the murderers of her mother. Elizabeth was nine when she lost her fiancé, Hermann, and one year later her father-in-law died. It was at this time that Louis, her fiancé's younger brother, became Elizabeth's protector and good friend. After discussing Elizabeth's uncertain future, Louis decided that she would be his wife. They were married in 1221 in the presence of the nobles of Thuringia and of other German regions. Knight Vargila led Elizabeth to the altar, and her father sent additional gifts. At the end of September, 1222, the young couple visited King Andrew at Pozsony. Traveling by horse, they were horrified at the destruction and decline of the country. It was the year of the Hungarian Golden Bull, by which the Hungarian nobles, discouraged by the nearly total disintegration of law and order in the realm, had forced the king to share his government with them.

Life's Work

Under the guidance of her confessor, Father Rodinger, a Franciscan friar, Elizabeth began to lead a deeper spiritual life, carried out charity work, and established an orphanage (the first in Central Europe). She cared for lepers, of whom she was not afraid, and constructed a twenty-eight bed hospital for them. She then came under the spiritual directorship of Master Conrad of Marburg, the noted mystic, Franciscan preacher, and ascetic.

In 1225, Louis embarked on a military campaign summed by the emperor, and in his absence, Elizabeth governed Thuringia. She healed the wounds caused by natural disasters and was concerned about social discrimination among the disadvantaged; she fed nine hundred poor people daily, provided tools and obtained work for the able-bodied unemployed men, and taught the women to spin. At the same time, she represented her husband in high society, received distinguished guests at the court, and participated in hunting parties.

In 1227, Louis was again summed by the emperor and joined a Crusade; Elizabeth was expecting their third child. By the time Gertrud was born, Louis was already dead, having fallen ill at Otranto. Elizabeth's brothers-in-law, uneasy about her spending habits, forbade her to handle her own financial affairs, prompting her to leave Wartburg in October, 1227, with her three small children. Nobody in Eisenach, however, would accommodate them. After placing the children in foster homes, Elizabeth, accompanied by two of her royal servants, Guda and Isentrud, finally found shelter in an innkeeper's stable. She spun cloth for a living until Mechtild, Abbess of Kitzingen, provided for her in the abbey. Her uncle, the Bishop of Bamberg, placed his castle at Pottstein at her disposal. The bishop tried to persuade her to marry Emperor Frederick II, but Elizabeth firmly declined the proposal. Only the future of her children concerned her; for herself, she desired to live in poverty. She had her husband's remains buried in the monastery which he had founded at Reingardsbrunn. After the burial, and with Knight Vargila's support, she regained her right to manage the estates she had inherited as a widow. Making a vow in the Franciscan church in Eisenach to renounce all earthly love and free will, she retained her property for the sake of her children, Hermann, Sophia, and Gertrud, and for making provision for the poor. She did not live in the castle at Wartburg but in nearby Wehrda, in a primitive house built of blocks of dirt. She spun to earn her living and assisted in the hospital she had founded.

In order to deepen Elizabeth's humility, Conrad used crude methods such as flagellation and beatings, the dismissal of her two servants, forbidding her to distribute large sums of money to the poor, and allowing her to give only one slice of bread each to the hungry. Elizabeth used her own bed to care for a young boy sick with dysentery; when he died, she put a girl with leprosy in her bed. Augmenting the abuse and humiliation suffered at the hands of Conrad, gossip now began to undermine Elizabeth's reputation. She was ridiculed for her loud laughter, her refusal to dress in black, and the apparent ease with which she forgot her deceased husband. There were even rumors that she was happily engaged in an affair with the friar, about which she was confronted by Knight Vargila. In response, Elizabeth showed the marks of the flagellations and beatings received from Conrad.

Knowing that she was weak and would die soon, Elizabeth stayed in bed for the last two weeks of her life, finalizing the arrangements for the distribution of her wealth and her children's future. Three days before she died, she sent everyone away from her except Conrad, who remained at her bedside. She died in the early hours of November 17, 1231. Her body lay in state for four days in the Franciscan church at Eisenach, dressed in clothing of the poor. During this time, the inhabitants of Thuringia came to her coffin not to pray for her but to ask for her intercession on their behalf. It is reported that during the following days and weeks, numerous miracles occurred at her grave.

Conrad informed Pope Gregory IX of the death of Elizabeth, and the pontiff authorized the friar to make preparations for her canonization. When Conrad was murdered in July, 1233, the Bishop of Hildesheim carried on with the canonization process. It was then that the *Libellus de dictis IV ancillarum* (Depositions of Saint Elizabeth's four handmaidens - Isentrud, Guda, Iremngard, and Elisabeth) was recorded in writing, followed by a strict ecclesiastical investigation. On May 26, 1235, in Perugia on the Feast of the Pentecost, Pope Gregory IX entered Elizabeth's name in the canon of saints (cf. the papal bull "Gloriosus in maiestate"). The first church erected in her honor was built by her brother-in-law Conrad, who was grand master of the German Order, at Marburg. On May 1, 1236, her coffin was elevated upon the altar in the presence of her children, brothers-in-law, four archbishops, eight bishops, and a multitude of German, Hungarian, Czech, and French pilgrims.

Saint Elizabeth of Hungary lived according to the Christian ideal, fusing it with the pastoral concept of the mendicant orders in teaching and practicing humility and social equality. She did not believe that social stabilization could occur by suddenly elevating the lower strata; rather, she believed that the upper classes should willingly descend to the aid of the poor. In addition to building a hospital and establishing an asylum for homeless children, Elizabeth demonstrated an attitude toward the poor that was realistic as well as humane. Thus, although she developed a plan for feeding the poor, she abhorred idleness, quoting from Saint Paul that one who did not work would not eat.

Bibliographical Note

Nesta de Robeck, *St. Elizabeth of Hungary* (Milwaukee, 1953); Anne Seeholtz, *St. Elizabeth* (New York, 1948); articles in *Catholic Encyclopaedia*, 5 (New York, 1913), 389ff., and in *New Catholic Encyclopaedia* 5 (New York, 1965), 282; H. Fritzen, "Hl. Elisabeth von Ungarn," in Peter Manns (ed.), *Die Heiligen*, 3rd rev. ed. (Mainz, 1977), 400ff., on her background and life, render reliable information.

See Albert Huyskens, *Quellenstudien zur Geschichte der hl. Elisabeth, Landgräfin von Thüringen* (Marburg, 1911), 110-268; Dietrich v. Apolda, "Vita s. Elisabeth libri VIII," with an appendix of the record of 49 officially approved miracles, in Georgius Pray, *Vita s. Elisabethae viduae langravinae Thuringiae* (Tyrnaviae, 1780), 33-218, for historical sources and background material.

Further, Maria Maresch, *Elisabeth, Landgräfin von Thüringen* (M. Gladbach, 1918); Gisbert Kranz, *Elisabeth von Thüringen* (Augsburg, 1957); Walter Nigg and Helmut Nils Loose, *Die hl. Elisabeth: das Leben der Landgräfin von Thüringien* (Freiburg i. Br., 1979); Ansgar Volmer, *Die hl. Elisabeth, Landgräfin von Thüringen und Hessen* (Hildesheim, 1931); Mária Püskely, *Árpádházi Szent Erzsébet* [St. Elizabeth of the House of Árpád] (Rome, 1981); Ilona Sz. Jónás, *Árpád-házi Szent Erzsébet* (Budapest, 1986) provide valuable interpretation of the sources and informative reading. Martin Ohst named Pozsony (Pressburg) as St. Elizabeth's birth place; cf. his "Elisabeth von Thüringen in ihrem kirchengeschichtlichen Kontext," *Zeitschrift für Tehologie*, 91 (1994), 424ff.

APPENDIX II

MEDIEVAL HUNGARIAN THEOLOGIANS*

> Et Pelbartus plebians: artus nomine
> miles docuit plebem, vicit et hostem,
> obtinet nomen,...tu nostrae decus
> gentis, tu gloria nobis iam credita
> cernis, et caelum te patria tenet et
> Deum cum patre Seraphico nobis ora.
>
> *Inscription on the tomb
> of Pelbárt of Temesvár*

In the latter half of the fifteenth century, during the reign of Matthias Corvinus (1458-90), and in the early sixteenth century, some Hungarian churchmen enhanced religious scholarship in their own country and abroad by their preaching and writing. The writings of these men exemplify the development in Hungary of support for the doctrine of Immaculate Conception. These men also spoke out against the moral and spiritual deficiencies of the court. The activities and writings of these theologians pose a challenge to the chronicler of literature and of intellectual and religious history.[1]

The Dominican friar Michael of Hungary may be mentioned first. The author of thirteen sermons dealing with the cycle of the church year, he based his sermons on scripture, the writings of the Fathers, and some non-Christian ancient writers. His writings concern eternal salvation. He encouraged the educated clergy to prepare homilies on their own. Michael's sermons appeared in print by 1482 and were published in various subsequent editions.[2]

Michael of Hungary should not be confused with a second theologian, Michael the Hungarian (Michael of Pannonia), a member of the Order of Hungarian Paulists (an order established by Canon Özséb [Eusebius] of Esztergom [ob. 1264]), and a fearless debater in theology at the royal court of Buda.[3] Michael the Hungarian, in the presence of King Matthias, publicly debated with, and successfully defended against, the Dominican Anthony of Zara the doctrine of "Virgo Purissima," the Immaculate Conception of the Blessed Mother of God. He wrote books on Mariology; he wrote a book on the lives of hermits in which he defined the essence and rules of cenobitic life; and he wrote on procedures to be followed and topics to be discussed at the regional and local chapter meetings of his order.[4]

Although his books are lost, his wit and intelligence gained him access to Matthias' court and to members of the hierarchy. Yet his order's chronicler records that Michael became overconfident and set his mind to seek the highest office of his order. The "mob," both the humble faithful who listened to his homilies and the underpaid and uneducated lower clergy who, as usual, claimed to have a deep-set faith and a greater love of God, prevented him from realizing his objective. They told him that he had no faith in God because he had forgotten about love of the Creator, and they accused him of pride and arrogance, and of neglect of his priestly vocation. Defeated at home, he went to study Hebrew in Paris, where he disappeared without a trace. "Miserabile proprietatis vitium" (an appropriate award for his sins), commented the order's chronicler about his fall, cursing his memory.[5]

Andrew of Pannonia, a former officer in the army of János Hunyadi (Hungarian regent, 1446-52, and father of King Matthias), studied theology in Venice and entered the Carthusian order at Ferrara. In 1467 he published his *Libellus de virtutibus*, which was written for the personal use of Matthias Corvinus. He wrote another book of a similar nature for Prince Ércole d'Este, and also books on meditation on life and death. A list of his publications is recorded in the necrology of the Carthusian monastery in Bologna.[6]

Nicholas de Mirabilibus of Kolozsvár (*Ex septem castris* [from the land of seven castles], in Transylvania) was a Dominican friar of great learning who won fame as a preacher. He lived in Florence and preached about conscience. He also reported on a debate (which he lost) with George Salvatius on whether or not the sin of Adam was the greatest sin ever committed. In 1493 he obtained permission to hold public lectures - or disputations - at the court of Vladislas II of Hungary. He lectured publicly from his published opus, *De prae-destinatione*.[7]

Another theologian, Johan of Késmárk, published a *Summa theologiae* in the 1470's.[8] Yet another, Adalbert of Csanád, a Hungarian Paulist and poet-humanist, published a book of poetry on the Immaculate Conception; Adalbert's confreres, who knew little about poetry, dismissed his poems as nonsense.[9]

The writings of Gregory Bánffy (Caelius Pannonius), prior of the Hungarian Paulists at Monte Caelio in Rome, made a strong impression upon Professor Ince (Innocent) Dám, O.F.M., who devoted years of study and research to the development of the doctrine of the Immaculate Conception in Hungary. Bánffy (*ob.* 1545) was, it seems, the first person to prepare a Hungarian translation of the Rule of Saint Augustine.[10] As a biblical scholar, Bánffy wrote commentaries on the Book of Revelation of John, applying its message to his own times. For instance, in that context he commented on the battle of Mohács (August, 1526), where Louis II of Hungary lost his life and kingdom fighting Suleiman the Magnificent. He described the approach of the Ottoman Turks to the gates of Vienna (in 1529). In colorful terms he depicted the fall of Buda to the Turks (in 1541).[11] And in his comments on the twelfth chapter, he pointed to the Immaculate Conception as the sole hope for the world.[12] Bánffy expressed similar views in his *Commentary on the Song of Songs*. The world lived in sin, he wrote, and only a repentant sinner could hope to become one with the Creator.[13]

The activities and writings of the theologians mentioned thus far may serve as an introduction to the works of the two great Franciscan scholars of the times: Oswald (Osvát) de Laska and Pelbárt of Temesvár.[14] The name of Pelbárt of Temesvár was first recorded in the matriculation list of the University of Cracow in 1458.[15] At that time at Cracow grammar was taught according to a Franciscan master, Aristotle's logic served as a major field of concentration in the study of philosophy, classics were debated endlessly, and religious studies emphasized scripture as interpreted by the Franciscan Nicolaus Lyranus, and dogma followed the interpretation of John Duns Scotus.[16]

Pelbárt obtained a solid educational background at the university, yet he kept an open mind. He recognized the importance of the views of Bernard of Clairvaux and of Thomas Aquinas as over the ideas of Duns Scotus.[17] Pelbárt received his bachelor's degree at Cracow in 1463, finishing in the top quarter of his graduating class.[18]

It is of interest to note in light of political and cultural conditions in Hungary at this particular time, that the works of Oswald de Laska and Pelbárt of Temesvár had to be published outside of Hungary. Even during the reign of the renaissance monarch, Matthias Corvinus, a stimulating intellectual atmosphere simply did not exist in the realm, and there were no printing houses in the country at that time.[19] The life span of the Andreas Hess press in Buda in the early 1470's probably was very short. However, in Poland, for example, available printers and the clientele of the intelligentsia did make the publication of the Latin works of the Hungarian Franciscan theologians profitable.[20]

Oswald de Laska (Osvát Laskai) wrote two major works, *Biga salutis* [Wagon of Salvation] in three volumes, and *Gemma fidei* [Jewel of Faith], which have come down to us.[21] His *Biga salutis*, a collection of homilies for Sundays and holy days written for the educated clergy, has appeared in four editions, though possibly two additional editions were printed. The *Gemma fidei* is a collection of dogmatic homilies written for the less well educated clerics who possessed neither the scholarly background, nor the intellectual curiosity to prepare sermons independently.[22] Friar Oswald also co-authored a third volume, and completed the fourth of Pelbárt of Temesvár's major four-volume work.[23]

Pelbárt of Temesvár completes the list of important theologians of the age in Hungary. In 1483, Pelbárt was professor of theology at the house of studies of the Franciscan order in Buda, according to the house chronicler at Buda.[24] The house of studies, together with the Franciscan monastery in Esztergom, the see of the Hungarian primate, formed the intellectual center of the Franciscan order in the realm.[25] A document of 1495 refers to Pelbárt as guardian of the house at Esztergom, adding that, in fact, the head of a house of religious studies in the order was a position of responsibility.[26]

From Esztergom Pelbárt must have returned to the house in Buda, in order to devote himself to writing. He died there on January 22, 1504, falling asleep with a smile on his lips.[27] The order's martyrology records his feast as May 27.[28]

Pelbárt wrote books and collected sermons because, he said, he wanted to aid his fellow clerics in their pastoral work and to help his students.[29] He explained scripture by taking a rational approach toward exegesis, and he composed sermons for particular feasts of the ecclesiastical year.[30] He aimed to reach out to the emerging Hungarian lay intelligentsia as an audience.[31] In his summer sermons, he inserted tales taken from folklore to keep his listeners awake in the heat or to illustrate a point to be made in his homily.[32]

Pelbárt Szalóczi recently asserted that Pelbárt of Temesvár's homilies on truth and falsehood were based on folklore.[33] As a matter of fact, his sermon for Easter Monday became the first piece of a Hungarian folk-tale to be published, and it was published in Latin.[34] Pelbárt also dealt with the Hungarian saints; he may have written his version of the life of Elizabeth of Hungary directly from the official record of her canonization.[35]

Pelbárt is the author of four major works that have made him well known. The first is the *Stellarium coronae benedictae Mariae Virginis in Laudem eius pro singulis praedicationibus elegantissime coaptatum*.[36] He wrote this work, he stated, because of a promise he made to the Mother of God: in 1479 and 1481, he had been struck by the plague, but owing to her intercession, he claimed, he recovered.[37] The work itself is a semi-poetic and semi-scholarly piece of theological literature.[38] It may be regarded as the most poetic of his writing and, perhaps, his best. It is an outstanding example of the religious literature of the age.[39]

Pelbárt used the scholastic method in developing his ideas. For example, his *Stellarium* comprises twelve books (*libri*); a book consists of parts (*partes*), and a part of sections (*articuli*). He uses marginal notation (*distinctiones*) to help determine and explain points of meditation and argument. In his work he discusses two major theses: (a) the Mother of God was assumed bodily into heaven; (b) She is, in her heavenly glory, an intermediary of divine grace for all humankind.[40]

He believed firmly in these two theses, and he wrote about them with conviction.[41] He uses supportive arguments to prove a point. For instance, in the fourth book he explains the Immaculate Conception and relies on rational arguments to silence the opponents of the doctrine; in the fifth book he discusses the birth of the Mother of God, and the perfection of her body. In the ninth book he argues her love for her Son by claiming that her love for God formed a treasure of her motherly affection for humankind. In the last three books he describes the nature of her love, records her assumption into heaven, and urges the reader to respect her.[42]

The second major work is the *Pomerium* [Garden of Fruit Trees], a collection in three volumes of sermons written over the course of eighteen years. It consists of about five hundred homilies, divided into three parts: (a) *Sermones pomerii de sanctis* [...about the saints]; (b) *Sermones de tempore* [...for the season: Sundays of the ecclesiastical year]; and (c) *Sermones quadragesimales* [Sermons for Lent].

Pelbárt believed that just as there were different kinds of trees in a garden, so there ought to be various sermons in the possession of a good preacher. These three volumes contain the essence of Pelbárt's ideas and teaching. He sees no need for the "pagan" classics, accuses Aristotle, Cicero, and Virgil of "heresy," and looks upon astronomy as a "sinful" science.[43] However, he speaks out on behalf of the weak and the oppressed, and criticizes the tyrant.[44]

Do not search for, but get hold an opportunity - any opportunity - he says, and do not be afraid of man's anger.[45]

In his homily on the resurrection of Christ, Pelbárt proclaims that God may glorify those who have been humbled because of Him, because human wickedness cannot prevail over divine justice.[46] Justice shall overcome evil even if it suffers temporal defeat and oppression. The wicked shall perish in their wickedness, while the just shall prevail in the end.[47] Pelbárt answers a question concerning law by claiming that it is the guide to an honorable way of life. And yet, he says, one ought not to be jealous of those who do not adhere to the law of God.[48]

Pelbárt does not justify the political glory and literary fame of the court of King Matthias from the ethical-spiritual point of view.[49] He sees the wasteful pomp and loose morals of the court, and the misery of the poor set against it. He observes with open eyes the selfish and proud monarch and his greedy lords. He flagellates in his sermons the soft living and earthly riches of the clergy, referring mostly to the hierarchy.[50]

Pelbárt points out the laws passed by the first Hungarian monarch, King St. Stephen (*ob.* 1038), and draws a comparison between the times of the early eleventh century and the age of the renaissance king. Pelbárt cries aloud: if only the monarch and powerful lords would keep the laws of the land - that is, the laws of the first Hungarian king! But no, the lords are common thieves, he says, who rob the Church of God and the poor people.[51]

It is no surprise that both the *Stellarium* and *Pomerium* were published abroad, and appeared in some twenty editions each.[52]

The third work is the *Expositio Psalmarum*, Pelbárt's commentary on the Books of Psalms. This work was published abroad in two known editions; in it he deals seriously with Catholic dogma.[53] It seems, however, that Pelbárt was not able to complete his opus magnum: the fourth work, the *Aureum Rosarium theologiae ad Sententiarum libros IV...quadropartitum*. Professor Dám maintained that he had discovered the stylistic handiwork of Oswald de Laska, Pelbárt's pupil and later good friend, in the third book of the *Rosarium*. Dám looked upon Oswald as the co-author of the fourth book, completed, no doubt, upon the death of Pelbárt, and printed, all four books together, in five known editions.[54]

The authors of the *Rosarium* schematize Catholic dogma in accordance with Peter Lombard's *Sententiarum libri IV* of the twelfth century. Pelbárt and Oswald wrote on: (a) the Trinity and divine qualities; (b) Creatures - creation and fall; (c) Divine grace - restoration of relations between the Creator and his creatures; (d) Sacraments and final judgment.[55]

The authors' basic idea centers around God's love for humanity and humanity's love for the Creator. They summarize their observations in alphabetical order. It may be of great interest to note that the authors deny nominalism and instead rely upon philosophy to explain theology. They follow Thomas Aquinas, and agree with Richardus of Mediavilla, of the Franciscan school, on the doctrine of the Immaculate Conception.[56]

In his *Stellarium* Pelbárt states that Mary was born without original sin, and that the Church celebrates not the sanctification but the conception of the Mother of God.[57] The papal bull of February 27, 1477, announcing that Mary was free from original sin had added an octave, solemn vespers, and indulgences to the Feast of the Immaculate Conception.[58] Pelbárt wrote that if Thomas Aquinas, Alexander of Hales, or Bonaventure were alive today, they too would approve of the doctrine of the Immaculate Conception, and announce it publicly.[59]

Pelbárt attempted to place various interpretations of the doctrine on a common denominator. For example, Duns Scotus, though he spoke of Mary's sanctification - "B. Virginem sanctificatam fuisse ante antivitatem ex utero" [the Blessed Virgin who had been sanctified before her birth] - later had asserted that Mary was free from original sin.[60]

Aquinas reasoned about the sanctification of Mary: "rationaliter creditur quod beata Virgo sanctificata fuerit antequam ex utero nascetur" [it can be rationally believed that the Blessed Virgin had been sanctified before her birth].[61] But in his commentary - actually, his university lecture notes - on Peter Lombard's *Sentences*, he recognized the validity of the doctrine of the Immaculata. "Talis fuit puritas Beatae Virginis, quae a peccato originali et actuali immunis fuit" [Such was the purity of the Blessed Virgin that she had been immune to original sin and to actual sin].[62] Pelbárt (and Oswald) therefore accepted the arguments of Thomas on the Immaculata, even though Thomas had confirmed his views only in his lecture notes on Peter Lombard's book of theology.

Pelbárt must have been aware of the fact that not even the bull of Sixtus IV made the doctrine of the Immaculata obligatory. But if the pontiff had not approved of, neither had he forbidden arguments about it.[63] Although the papal constitution *Greve nimis*, dated September 5, 1483, declared that those who do not subscribe to the view that the Blessed Mother was free of original sin have sinned gravely, and condemned those who were accusing believers in the Immaculata with heresy, it also stated that the Roman See had not as yet reached a final verdict on this doctrinal question.[64] The sixteenth century manuscript, Ott. lat. 857, in the Vatican Library, carries an abstract of the *Rosarium*.[65]

The fact that eight codices carry detailed portions of Pelbárt's writings in Hungarian translation shows the popularity of his works during the sixteenth century.[66] His works appear in the following: the *Tihany*, *Kazinczy*, and the *Nagyszombat* codices, the latter being the work of an unknown scribe; the *Érsekújvár* codex, copied in part by Mária Sövényházi, another Dominican; the *Teleki* volume, of whose numerous scribes one, Ferenc Sepsiszentgyörgyi, a Franciscan, is known. The *Cornides* manuscript, formerly a large codex, now divided into five parts in the University of Budapest Library; and the *Érdy* codex, authored by an anonymous Carthusian monk regarded by library historians as a grand master of Hungarian - in both language and style - in the early sixteenth century.[67]

These codices all were transcribed in Hungary, and all of them contain portions, or detailed selections in Hungarian, of the writings of Pelbárt.[68] During the reign of Matthias Corvinus and of his immediate successors, Hungarian sermon literature must have been in great demand in the realm.[69]

Pelbárt had finished his studies abroad, and it was during the two decades he spent outside of Hungary that he became a scholar. He may have been a well-known author abroad even before he began to teach at the order's house of studies at Buda in 1483. Pelbárt probably attempted to stay in touch with the currents of religious thought and philosophy in the West through his publishers outside of the realm.

Intellectual life could still be dangerous in Hungary, as the personal tragedies of Bishop János Vitéz of Várad and Janus Pannonius, the scholar of Italian renaissance reputation, might indicate. These two intellectuals and former protégés, turned political opponents of the monarch Matthias, were both accused by the king of treason toward the state.[70] Although convicted of treason, neither Vitéz nor Pannonius were executed. Vitéz fell from grace and Pannonius fled the country, dying during his flight. Hungarian society of the age was not yet mature enough to support, not was it capable of assuring a permanent foundation for, the activities of an intellectual circle in the realm.[71]

Pelbárt admitted that conditions at home failed to impress him. He compared the laws and the life of the first Hungarian king, St. Stephen I, with Matthias Corvinus' humanism, which so sadly lacked the basic element of civilized behavior. (Matthias Corvinus may be looked upon as the Hungarian equivalent of the twelfth century English monarch, Henry II.)[72] The friar drew his conclusions to the detriment of King Matthias and the latter's immediate successors.[73]

A debate was held before Matthias Corvinus at the royal court in Buda between Michael of Pannonia and Anthony of Zara on the merits and the doctrine of the Immaculate Conception. But the mere occurrence of the theological debate does not prove the sincere interest of the monarch in, or his readiness for, a stimulating intellectual discussion of an important theological question. It proves only that Matthias, a renaissance king not of royal descent but supported, in the manner of his contemporary Italian despots, by the intelligentsia and writers of the people, wanted to merit their trust and respect, and to earn for himself the appreciation of posterity.[74]

It was, however, Pelbárt of Temesvár who earned the respect of posterity. He preached convincingly on the Immaculate

Conception, a doctrine defined, but not made obligatory, by the Roman See, and publicly discussed by Thomas Aquinas in his university lectures. Not only did Pelbárt bear witness to his love for the Mother of Christ, but he, as a theologian of the Quattrocento with a European reputation, and an authority on the life and laws of King St. Stephen I of Hungary, preserved his country's place in the continental mainstream.

NOTES

* This is a slightly revised version of my article in *Church History*, 57 (1988). It is published here with the permission of the Editor of *Church History*.
1. For background, cf. Antonius de Bonfinis, *Rerum Ungaricarum decades IV*, ed. Joseph Fógel, 4 vols. (Leipzig-Budapest, 1936-41), III, 218ff., and IV, 1ff., though "unkritisch, nur für die Zeit Matthias glaubwürdig;" see August Potthast, *Bibliotheca historica medii aevi*, rev. ed., 2 vols. (Berlin, 1896), I, 163. Ransanus, *Epithoma*, ind. 29-37; text also in Schwandtner, *Scriptores*, I, 322ff.; Thurócz, *Chronica*, iv:63-67, *ibid.*, I, 39ff., or in Galántai-Kristó, cc. 258-262. On Thurócz, cf. L. Hain, *Repertorium bibliographicum*, 2 vols. (Stuttgart-Tübingen, 1826-38; repr., 2 vols. in 4, Milan, 1948), I-2, 414, nn. 15516-18; Mályusz, *Thuróczy Krónika*, 124ff., and 145ff. Mátyás Zsilinszky, "Mátyás legrégibb történészei" [King Matthias' Earliest Chroniclers], in Sándor Márki (ed.), *Mátyás király emlékkönyv* [Memorial Volume in Honor of King Matthias] (Budapest, 1902), 241ff.; Tíbor Kardos, "Mátyás király és a humanizmus" [King Matthias and Humanism], in Imre Lukinich et al. (eds.), *Mátyás király emlékkönyv születésének ötszázéves fordulójára* [Memorial Volume on the 500th Anniversary of the Birth of King Matthias], 2 vols. (Budapest, n.d. [1940]), II, 9ff.

Karl Nehring, "Quellen zur ungarischen Äussenpolitik der zweiten Hälfte des 15 Jahrhunderts," *Levéltári Közlemények*, 47, (1976), 87ff.; Tíbor Klaniczay, "Galeatto Marzio és Mátyás," *Világosság*, 18 (1977), 32ff.; Béla Stoll (ed.), *A magyar irodalomtörténet bibliográfiája* [Bibliography of Hungarian Literature] (Budapest, 1972), 238f.; Csaba Csapodi, *Bibliotheca Corviniana* (New York, 1969); Gábriel Adriányi, "Die Kirchenpolitik des Matthias Corvinus," *Ungarn Jahrbuch*, 10 (1979), 83ff.

János Horváth, *Az irodalmi műveltség megoszlása* [Differentiation Between Religion and the Secular Aspects of Hungarian Literary Culture], 2nd ed. (Budapest, 1944), 147ff.; Pintér, I, 453ff.; Hóman-Szekfű, II, 467ff., and 516ff.; Lajos Elekes (ed.), *Magyarország története 1526-ig* [History of Hungary Prior to 1526] (Budapest, 1961), 302ff.; Vilmos Fraknói, *Hunyadi Mátyás király* [King Matthias Hunyadi] (Budapest, 1890), 139ff.; Dezső Csánki, "Matthias König der Ungarn," *Ungarische Rundschau*, 2 (1913), 85ff., and 316.

2. Cf. Cyrill Horváth, "Michael de Hungaria XIII beszéde" [Thirteen Sermons by Michael of Hungary], *Irodalomtörténeti Közlemények*, 5 (1895), 129ff.; Hain, *Repertorium*, I, 113ff., nn. 9043-9050; Tíbor Klaniczay, *A magyar irodalom története 1660-ig* [History of Hungarian Literature to 1660] (Budapest, 1964), 139; Mályusz, *Egyházi társadalom*, 351ff.; Cyrill Horváth, *A régi magyar irodalom története* [History of Early Hungarian Literature] (Budapest, 1899), 64ff.; for an analysis of his sermons by a theologian, see Ince Dám, *A Szeplőtelen Fogantatás védelme Magyarországon a Hunyadiak és a Jagiellók korában* [Defense of the Immaculate Conception in Hungary of the Hunyadis and of the Jagiellos] (Rome, 1955), 18ff., and 93ff.

3. Cf. L.N. [sic!], *Radix et origo coenobitarum religionis s. Pauli primi eremiti cum brevissima monasterii s. Crucis in Pilisio territori Strigoniensis relatione a beato Eusebio Strigoniensis canonico, postea Ordinis praefati primi in regno Hungariae provincialis erecti* (Rome, 1683); Gregorius Gyöngyösi, *Vitae fratrum eremitarum Ordinis sancti Pauli primi eremitae*, ed. F.L. Hervay (Budapest, 1988), 35ff.; my review of the volume in *Catholic Historical Review*, 76 (1990), 125f.; Michael Bene, "Kolostorok a Galga mentén" [Old Monasteries Along the Galga Stream], *Vigilia*, 46 (1981), 827ff.; Emil Kisbán, *A magyar Pálosrend története* [History of the Hungarian Paulist Order], 2 vols. (Budapest, 1938-40).

4. Cf. Pintér, I, 425; J. Horváth, *Irod. műv. megoszlása*, 561; Béla Iványi, "A Szent Domonkos Rend római központi levéltára"[The Central Archives of the Dominican Order in Rome], *Levéltári Közlemények*, 7 (1929), 1ff.

5. C. Horváth, *Régi irodalom*, 65, listed his publication at some length.

6. Ince Dám, "Andreas Pannonius ferrarai priorságának viszontagságai" [The Eventful Conventual Priorship of Andreas of Pannonia in Ferrara], *Civitas Dei*, 1 (1956), 101ff.; Antone Antore, in *Dictionnaire de théologie catholique*, 15 vols. (Paris, 1908-50), II, col. 2312; Jenő Ábel, *Analecta nova ad historiam renascentium in Hungaria litterarum spectantia* (Budapest, 1903), 158ff.; Cyrill Horváth, "Andreas Pannonius," *Egyetemes Philológiai Közlöny*, 66 (1946), 257ff.; Imre Várady, *La letteratura italiana e la sua influenza in Ungheria* (Rome, 1934), 80; on d'Este, see Egyed Hermann, *A katolikus egyház története Magyarországon 1914-ig* [History of the Catholic Church in Hungary Prior to 1914] (Munich, 1973), 196; Emil Békési, "Magyar írók Hunyadi Mátyás korából" [Hungarian Writers in the Age of Matthias Corvinus], *Katholikus Szemle*, 16 (1902), 134ff.

7. Cf. Mályusz, *Egyházi társadalom*, 282, n. 28, and 358; Pintér, I, 426 and 494; Béla Köpeczi et al. *Erdély története* [History of Transylvania], 3 vols. (Budapest, 1986), I, 376f.

8. Békési, *art. cit.*, 743, see above, n. 6; Mályusz, *op. cit.*, 357, see above, n. 7.

9. Adalbert wrote poetry about the Mother of God, the angels, and Paul the Hermit - Békési, *art. cit.*, 861 and 869; Pintér, I, 677ff.; Tíbor Kardos, *Középkori kultúra, középkori költészet* [Poetry in Medieval Culture: Beginnings of Hungarian Literature] (Budapest, n.d.), 236ff.

10. See László Dézsi, *Szent Agoston reguláinak magyar fordítása Caelius (Bánffy) Gergelytől, 1537* [The Hungarian Translation of Saint Augustine's Rule by Gregory Caelius (Bánffy), 1537] (Budapest, 1900), passim.

11. Compare his *Collectanea in Sacram Apocalypsin divi Joanni Apostoli et Evangelistae* (Paris, 1571), and known previous editions - in F. Stegmüller (ed.), *Repertorium biblicum medii aevi*, 4 vols. (Madrid, 1950), II, 363f., nn. 2623-24.

12. N. Benger, *Annualium eremocenobiticorum Ordinis Fratrum Eremitarum s. Pauli primi eremitae*, vol. I (Posonii, 1743), 181ff.

13. Cf. Dám, *op. cit.*, 46ff.; I. de Long, *Bibliotheca sacra in binos syllabos distincta* (Paris, 1723), 892; compare with Karl Hefele, *Der hl. Bernardin von Siena und die franziskanische Wanderpredigt in Italien während des XV Jahrhunderts* (Freiburg, 1912), 75 and 91.

14. See Richárd Horváth, *Laskai Osvát* (Budapest, 1932), 7; Kálmán Tímár, "Laskai Osvát és a bibliográfia" [The Bibliography on Osvát de Laska], *Magyar Könyvszemle*, 18 (1910), 122ff.; see further, Sándor V. Kovács (ed.), *Temesvári Pelbárt válogatott írásai* [Selected Writings of Pelbárt of Temesvár] (Budapest, 1982), 411ff.; Áron Szilády, *Temesvári Pelbárt élete és munkái* [Life and Works of Pelbárt of Temesvár] (Budapest, 1880), 3, note 1; János Karácsonyi, *Szent Ferenc rendjének története Magyarországon 1711-ig* [History of the Order of St. Francis in Hungary until 1711], 2 vols. (Budapest, 1922-23), II, 571; Gábriel Adriányi, "Pelbárt von Temesvár (ca. 1435-1504) und seine trinitarischen Predigtvorlagen," in *Im Gespräch mit dem Dreieinigen Gott: Elemente einer trinitarischen Theologie: Festschrift zum 65 Geburtstag von Wilhelm Breunig*, eds. M. Böhnke and H. Heinz (Düsseldorf, 1985), 276ff.

15. "Gewardus Ladislai de Themeswar," in *Album studiosorum Universitatis Cracoviensis*, 5 vols. (Cracow, 1887-1956), I, 156, in the year 1458, without further comment.

16. Pelbárt of Temesvár, *Sermones pomerii de sanctis* (Norimbergae, 1486), sermo 101; see also Alexander Gieysztor, *History of Poland* (Warsaw, 1968), 157f.; Cyrill Horváth, *Pomerius* (Budapest, 1894), 7f.; Paulus Pyczkowski, a known

philosopher-theologian served on the faculty - see Jenő Waldapfel, "A krakkói egyetem és a magyar-lengyel szellemi élet a renaissance korban" [Hungaro-Polish Intellectual Relations at the University of Cracow During the Renaissance Period], *Egyetemes Philológiai Közlöny*, 69 (1946), 26ff.; idem, "Le role de l'université de Cracovie dans la culture hongroise," *Annales Universitatis Budapestiensis*, sectio phil., 5 (1964), 3ff.

17. See Pelbárt's *Pomerium de sanctis* (Hagenau, 1499), pars hyemalis, sermo 39; Cyrill Horváth, *Temesvári Pelbárt és beszédei* [Pelbárt of Temesvár and his Sermons] (Budapest, 1899), 25f.; Imre Trencsény-Waldapfel, *Humanizmus és nemzeti irodalom* [Humanism and National Literature] (Budapest, 1966), 344ff.; Szilády, 33.

18. Cf. W. Wislocki (ed.), *Acta rectoralis Universitatis Cracoviensis* (Cracow, 1893), entries 3215 and 3224, dated February 10 and April 13, 1534, respectively; Békési, *art. cit.*, 332; Pelbárt Szalóczi, "Temesvári Pelbárt," *Vigilia*, 14 (1949), 721ff.

19. Cf. Pál Gulyás, *A könyv sorsa Magyarországon* [The Fate of Books in Hungary], 3 vols. (Budapest, 1961-65), I, 160ff. - a revised version of his *A könyvnyomtatás Magyarországon a XV és XVI században* [The Printing Press in Hungary During the 15th and 16th Centuries] (Budapest, 1931), 17f.; Joseph Fitz, "König Matthias und der Buchdruck," in Albert Humel (ed.), *Gutenberg Jahrbuch* (Mainz, 1939), 128ff.; idem, "Mátyás király a könyvbarát" [King Matthias, Lover of Books], in Lukinich, *Mátyás király*, II, 209ff.; József Balogh (ed.), *A művészet Mátyás király udvarában* [The Arts at the Court of King Matthias], vol. 1: *Adattár* [Documents] (Budapest, 1966), 644ff.

20. Gedeon Borsa, "A budai Hess nyomda új megvilágításban" [The Hess Press in Buda in the Light of Recent Research], *Magyar Könyvszemle*, 98 (1973), 138ff.; Mdme. Zoltán Soltész, "Milyen tervekkel és felszereléssel jöhetett Budára Hess András?" [What Were the Plans, What the Equipment of Andreas Hess Arriving in Buda?], *ibid.*, 90 (1974), 1ff.

21. Cf. Antoine Zawart, "The History of Franciscan Preaching and Franciscan Preachers," *Franciscan Studies*, old series, 7 (1928), 241ff., esp. 333-35.

22. In *Dictionnaire catholique*, XI, vols. 1657f.; Kálmán Tímár, "Laskai Osvát és a bibliográfia" [Bibliographical Data Concerning Oswald de Laska], *Magyar Könyvszemle*, 18 (1910), 122ff.; Hain, *Repertorium*, I, 113ff., nn. 9051-56; L. Wadding, *Scriptores ordinis minorum* (Rome, 1906), 181 and 183f.; R. Horváth, *Laskai Osvát*, 7f.; Zsolt Beöthy, *A magyar irodalom története* [History of Hungarian Literature], 2 vols., 3rd rev. ed., ed. Frigyes Badics (Budapest, 1901-03), I, 175ff.; Mályusz, *Egyházi társadalom*, 303, 354f.

23. R. Horváth, *Laskai Osvát*, 26f., 51ff.; Dám, 102.

24. "Solemnis praedicator at in theologia non mediocriter imbutus...in conventu Budensi legabat fratribus aptis super Sententiis;" compare B. de Zalka, "Chronica Fratrum Minorum de observantia provinciae Bosniae et Hungariae," in Ferenc Toldy (ed.), *Analecta*, vol. I (Pest, n.d.), 250; Hain, *Repertorium*, n. 12548, to the effect that Pelbárt's first book was published in 1483. On the educational background of the clergy, Békefi, *Káptalani iskolák*, 344f.; Mályusz, *Egyházi társadalom*, 35ff.

25. Karácsonyi, *Szent Ferenc rendje*, II, 567ff.; Ferenc Toldy's published university lecture notes, *A magyar nemzeti irodalom története* [History of National Hungarian Literature], 4th ed. (Budapest, 1878), 31f.; L.S. Domonkos, "Bildung und Wissenschaft," in Tíbor Klaniczay and Georg Stangler (eds.), *Schallaburg '82: Matthias Corvinus und die Renaissance in Ungarn, 1458-1541*. Landesmuseum of Lower Austria Catalogue 118 (Vienna, 1982), 48ff.

26. "Litterarum divinarum professor eximissimus," reads the reference to the 1498 edition of Pelbárt's sermons; W.A. Copinger (ed.), *Supplement to Hain's Repertorium bibilographicum*, 2 vols. (1895; repr., 2 vols. in 3, Milan, 1950), n. 4665.

Pelbárt was a professor at the Franciscan house of studies, and not at the "gymnasium generale" supported by the court; cf. Georgius Pray, *Annales regum Hungariae*, 5 vols. (Vienna, 1764-70), III, 315ff.; on Pray, see. C. Horváth, *Régi irodalom*, 696f. On schools of higher learning, see Jenő Ábel, *Egyetemeink a középkorban* [Medieval Hungarian Universities] (Budapest, 1881), 64, n. 31; idem, *Magyarországi humanisták és a Dunai Tudós Társaság* [Hungarian Humanists and the Danubian Learned Society] (Budapest, 1880), 3ff., and 124f.; Békefi, *Káptalani iskolák*, 290ff.; Elekes, 353f.; L.S. Domonkos, "The Origins of the University of Pozsony," *The New Review: Journal of East European History*, 9 (1969), 270ff.; Balogh, *Mátyás király*, 150f.; Denifle, 418ff.

27. "Quasi subridendo obdormivit in Domino;" F. Orban, *Historia, seu compendium decretorum provinciae Ordinis Minorum s. P. Francisici* (Kassoviae, 1759), 16.

28. Cf. Szilády, 16, 17.

29. Pelbárt, *Pomerium de sanctis* (Hagenau, 1499), pars hyemalis, sermo viii; Mályusz, 355f.

30. Pelbárt, *Pomerium de sanctis*, pars hyemalis, sermo xvii [Christmas homily]; or sermo lxix [for Good Friday]; Ferenc Toldy, *Magyar szentek legendái a carthausi névtelentől* [Lives of Hungarian Saints by the Anonymous Carthusian] (Pest, 1859), 3ff., and 33ff.

31. See his *Pomerium de sanctis*, pars aestivalis, sermo lii; Teodor Vida, "Temesvári Pelbárt kapcsolatai kora társadalmával" [Pelbárt's Social Contacts with his Contemporaries], *Vigilia*, 41 (1976), 671ff.

32. Pelbárt, *Pomerium de sanctis*, pars aestivalis, sermo xvii; Stegmüller, *Repertorium*, IV, 213f., n. 6371,1-4, though confusing him with Oswald de Laska! Békési, *art. cit.*, 331f.

33. Szalóczy, *art. cit.*, 721.

34. Pelbárt, *Pomerium de tempore* (Hagenau, 1498), pars paschalis, sermo xxxv, or his sermon on Gerard of Csanád (*ob.*, 1046), in Frigyes Brisits (ed.), *Temesvári Pelbárt műveiből* [Selections From the Writings of Pelbárt of Temesvár], vol. 6 of László Vajthó (ed.), *Magyar irodalmi ritkaságok* [Select Rare Pieces of Hungarian Literature] (Budapest, 1931), 108f., and compare with J. Bole and G. Polivka, *Anmerkungen zu den Kinder- und Hausmärchen der Brüder Grimm*, rev. ed., 5 vols. (Leipzig, 1915 etc.), V, 176ff.; on Gerard of Csanád, cf. Kosztolnyik, *Five Kings*, 46ff., and 161ff.

35. Compare Brisits, *Pelbárt műveiből*, 94ff.; Püskely, *Szent Erzsébet*, 38f.; Ijjas, *Szentek*, II, 111ff.

36. The Hagenau, 1498 edition, cited by Hain, *Repertorium*, n. 12563 (also n. 12566), or the Argentinae, 1496 edition, *ibid.*, n. 12565; G. Zolnai, *Nyelvemlékeink a könyvnyomtatás koráig* [Hungarian Linguist Remains Prior to the Age of Printing] (Budapest, 1894), 495ff.

37. His *Stellarium* (Hagenau, 1498), prologus; Hain, n. 12566; an earlier version, n. 12562; Ince Dám, "Kegyosztó társa Krisztusnak" [Mother of God, Co-Redeemer], *Vigilia*, 13 (1948), 1ff.

38. János Kudora, *A magyar katolikus egyházi beszéd irodalmának története* [History of the Development of Hungarian Sermon Literature] (Budapest, 1902), 68ff.; Lajos Katona and Ferenc Szinnyei, *Geschichte der ungarischen Literatur* (Leipzig, 1911), 16ff.; Klaniczay, *Irodalom*, 139f.; Mályusz, *Egyházi társadalom*, 355.

39. J. Horváth, *Irodalom kezdetei*, 57ff.; József Szinnyei, *Magyar írók élete és munkái* [Lives and Works of Hungarian Writers], 14 vols. (Budapest, 1891-1914), X, cols. 720ff.

APPENDIX II 423

40. Cyrill Horváth, "Temesvári Pelbárt beszédei" [Sermons by P.T.],
Egyetemes Philológiai Közlöny, Supplementum I (1899), 145ff.; Béla Menczer,
Commentary on Hungarian Literature (Castrop-Rauxel, 1956), 15f.
41. Pelbárt, *Stellarium* (Hagenau, 1498), vii:3,2; *Dictionnaire catholique*, XII,
cols. 715ff.
42. *Stellarium*, v:3; Dám, *op. cit.*, 24ff; idem, "Repertorium ex operibus
Pelbarti de Temesvár, O.F.M., aliorumque ab Angelo Elli Mediolanensi collectum,"
Scientiae artesque, 105ff. (repr., Rome, n.d.); H. Ameri, *Doctrina theologorum de
Immaculata B.M.V. Conceptione tempore Concilii Basiliensis* (Rome, 1954); Antal
Áldássy, "Mária ünnepek kérdése a bázeli zsinaton" [Questions Raised Concerning
the Feasts of Mary at the Synod of Basel], *Katholikus Szemle*, 44 (1930), 661ff.;
Hóman-Szekfű, IV, 122f., on the influence of Pelbárt in the Baroque age.
43. *Pomerium de tempore* (Hagenau, 1498), pars aestiva, sermo xx; *Sermones
pomerii* (Norimbergae, 1486); on the latter, cf. Hain, *Repertorium*, n. 12549.
44. Compare *Pomerium de sanctis*, pars hyemalis, sermo xxix; *Sermones de
tempore*, pars hyemalis et paschalis; on the latter, Hain, *Repertorium*, n. 12550.
45. Pelbárt, *Pomerium de sanctis*, pars aestivalis, sermo lii; Hóman-Szekfű, II,
562.
46. *Pomerium de tempore* (Hagenau, 1498), pars paschalis, sermo viii;
Sermones (Norimbergae, 1483) - Hain, *Repertorium*, n. 12548.
47. *Pomerium de tempore*, pars aestiva, sermo xlii; Pintér, I, 433ff.; exchange
of letters between King Matthias and Rome - cf. Vilmos Fraknói (ed.), *Mátyás király
levelei* [Correspondence of King Matthias], 2 vols. (Budapest, 1893-95), I, 259f., and
I, 33f.
48. *Pomerium de sanctis*, pars hyemalis, sermo xxix; Ferenc Galla, "Mátyás
király és a Szentszék" [King Matthias and the Holy See], in Lukinich, *Mátyás
emlékkönyv*, I, 95ff.; E. Mályusz, "Matthias Corvinus," in P.R. Rohden and Georg
Ostrogorsky, *Menschen die Geschichte machten*, 2 vols. (Vienna, 1931), II, 184ff.
49. The monarch used the Church as a political tool. He wrote to Pope Sixtus
IV that if His Holiness were to name the new bishop of Modrus - thereby to
ignore the privilege, "ius nostrum regium," claimed by the king - he and his
kingdom would secede from the Church. Cf. Marczali, *Enchiridion*, 275f.; compare
to Bonfini, IV, iv:40-41, and with Thurócz, c. 262 (iv:67); Mályusz, *Egyházi
társadalom*, 296ff.
50. Pelbárt, *Sermones de tempore*, pars aestiva, sermo xlii; also see the sermon
on the Feast of King St. Ladislas I of Hungary, in Brisits, *Pelbárt műveiből*, 59f. (On
Ladislas I, cf. Kosztolnyik, *Five Kings*, 92ff.) The letters of King Matthias may throw
some light on his relations with the Franciscans - Fraknói, *Mátyás levelei*, II, 2ff.,
229f.; or, *Monumenta Vaticana Hungariae: Matthiae Corvini epistolae ad Romanus
pontifices et ab eis acceptae*, ser. 1, vol. 6 (Budapest, 1891), 105f. The report of the
papal legate, Bishop Bertrand of Castello, about policies and the glory of the court of
Matthias, dated Fall, 1483, has a definite renaissance coloring - see Marczali,
Enchiridion, 277ff.
51. *Pomerium de sanctis*, pars aestiva, sermo xvii and sermo xv; Ransanus,
Epithoma, ind. xxxvii; for Matthias' reply to Rome, see Fraknói, *Mátyás levelei*, II, 26
and 49f.; Balogh, *Mátyás király*, 662ff.
52. Cf. Hain, II, 50ff., nn. 12548-60; Dám, *op. cit.*, 98ff.; Tivadar
Thienemann, "Temesvári Pelbárt német kortársai" [Pelbárt of Temesvár and his
German Contemporaries], *Egyetemes Philológiai Közlöny*, 44 (1920), 73ff.; Márta
Rozsondai, "Temesvári Pelbárt népszerűsége Európában: miről vallanak a
könyvkötések?" [Do the Bindings of his Works Bear Witness to the European
Popularity of Pelbárt of Temesvár], *Magyar Könyvszemle*, 100 (1984), 300ff.; E.
Weferich, "Bio-bibliographische Notizen über Franziskanerlehrer des 15 Jahr-

hunderts," *Franziskanische Studien*, 29 (1942), 190ff. The publishing record of Hungarian theologians seems to be unique by Hungarian standards only - cf. J.T. Welter, *L'exemplum dans la litttérature et didactique de moyen age* (Paris-Toulouse, 1927), 409 and 457f.
    53. Szilády, 53ff., mentions editions of 1504 and 1513; Hain, n. 12561, mentioned an Argentinae, 1487, edition.
    54. For detail, see Károly Szabó (ed.), *Régi magyar könyvtár* [Old Hungarian Library], 3 vols. in 4 (Budapest, 1879-98), II, 832ff.
    55. See Kovács, *Temesvári Pelbárt*, 415f.; Dám, *op. cit.*, 99; Mályusz, *Egyházi társadalom*, 356f.; compare with Wilhelm Goetz, "Franz von Assisi und die Entwicklung der mittelalterlichen Religiösität," *Archiv für Kulturgeschichte*, 17 (1927), 129ff.
    56. On Richardus de Mediavilla (Richard of Middleton), see Friedrich Überweg and Bernhard Geyer, *Die patristischen und scholastische Philosophie*, 11th ed. (Berlin, 1928), 489 and 762f.
    57. Pelbárt, *Stellarium*, iv:1,1; iv:2,2 (Venice, 1586), 81b, 83cd.
    58. *Ibid.*, iv:2,3, 91bc; Joseph Turmel, "Immaculate Conception," in *Encyclopaedia for Religion and Ethics*, ed. James Hastings, 13 vols. (1908-26; repr. New York, 1961), VII, cols. 165ff. If the year began with March 25, however, then the actual date ought to have been 1476 - see A. von Brandt, *Werkzeug des Historikers*, 2nd ed. (Stuttgart, 1960), 38.
    59. Pelbárt, *Rosarium*, pars viii (Venice, 1589), 106a-107c.
    60. Cf. Hieronimus de Montefortino (ed.), *Iohannis Duns Scoti Summa Theologica*, 6 vols. (Rome, 1900-04), V, 294ff., qu. 26, aa. 1-6; V, 310ff.; Gordon Leff, *Medieval Thought* (Baltimore, 1958), 194ff.
    61. See his *Summa Theologica*, ed. Petrus Caramello, 4 vols. (Turin-Rome, 1950-54), pars III, qu. 27, aa. 1-2.
    62. Cf. Thomas Aquinas'; *Commentarium in IV Libros Sententiarum Petri Lombardi*, in M.F. Moos (ed.), *Scriptum super Sententiis Magistri P. Lombardi*, 4 vols. (Paris, 1947), Sent. i:44,1,3.
    63. Pelbárt, *Stellarium*, iv:2,2 (Venice, 1586), 90bc.
    64. Cf. Friedberg, *Corpus Iuris Canonici*, II, cols. 1285f.; Batthyány, *Leges*, III, 609ff. and 650ff. - text from a *Csík* manuscript.
    65. See Wadding, *Scriptores*, 181 and 183f.; J.H. Sbaralea, *Supplementum et castigatio ad scriptores trium ordinum s. Francisci*, ed. L. Wadding, 2 vols. (Rome, 1906-08), II, 316f.
    66. Hóman-Szekfű, II, 600; Sándor Horváth, *Mulier amicta sole* (Budapest, 1948), 53ff.; on the author, a learned theologian, see András Szennay, "Horváth Sándor, O.P.," *Vigilia*, 49 (1984), 596f.; J. Horváth, *Irodalom kezdetei*, 229ff.
    67. Cyrill Horváth, "Kódexeink skolasztikus elemei" [Scholastic Features of Hungarian Codexes], *Irodalomtörténeti Közlemények*, 42 (1932), 121ff.; idem, "Temesvári Pelbárt és kódexeink" [Pelbárt of Temesvár and Hungarian Codex Literature], *Budapesti Szemle*, 65 (1891), 383ff.; 66 (1892), 21ff.; Zolnai, *Nyelvemlékek*, 239ff.; Edit Madas, "Az Érdy kódexről" [Some Remarks of the Érdy Codex], *Vigilia*, 50 (1985), 635ff.
    68. The material of thirty-nine codices has been edited and published by György Volf, *Nyelvemléktár: régi magyar kódexek és nyomtatványok* [Linguistic Remains: Old Hungarian Codices and Books], 15 vols. (Budapest, 1874-1908); Kálmán Tímár, "Magyar kódex családok" [Hungarian Codex Families], *Irodalomtörténeti Közlemények*, 36 (1927), 60ff., and 38 (1928), 52ff.; Pintér, I, 636ff.
    69. Hóman-Szekfű, II, 647; Beöthy, *Irodalomtörténet*, I, 169ff.; Kovács, *Temesvári Pelbárt*, 419ff.

APPENDIX II 425

70. King Matthias complained about the archbishop of Esztergom, and he had difficult relations with Janus Pannonius, bishop of Várad; cf. *VMH*, I, 158; Bonfini, IV, iv:31. On Janus Pannonius, cf. Georg Voigt, *Die Wiederbelebung des klassichen Altertums*, 2nd ed., 2 vols. (Berlin, 1880-81), II, 323, and Gábor Takács, "Janus Pannonius," *Vigilia*, 13 (1948), 660ff.; Kardos, *Humanizmus kora*, 150ff.

71. C. Horváth, *Régi irodalom*, 148ff.; Pintér, I, 480ff.; J. Horváth, *Irodalom megoszlása*, 75ff.; Békési, *art. cit.*, 242ff.; László Zolnay, *Ünnep és hétköznap a középkori Budán* [Holidays and Weekdays in Medieval Buda], 2nd ed. (Budapest, 1975), 205ff.

72. See the *Chronicles of the Reigns of Henry II and Richard I*, ed. William Stubbs, 2 vols. (London, 1867), I, 207 and 285; Henry II kept the Hungarian envoy waiting – *ibid.*, I, 346. Andreas Eckhardt, "Das Ungarnbild in Europa," *Ungarische Jahrbücher*, 22 (1942), 152ff.

73. Cf. Brisits, *Temesvári Pelbárt műveiből*, 3ff., and 59ff.; Kosztolnyik, *Five Kings*, 14ff., and 92ff.

74. Cf. Hermann, 138, 139; Dezső Csánki, "A renaissance és Mátyás király" [King Matthias and the Renaissance], *Budapesti Szemle*, 65 (1891), 393ff.; Beöthy, *Irodalomtörténet*, I, 140ff.; L. Zamba, *Bibliotheca Corvina: le bibliotheca di Mattia Corvino re di Ungheria* (Budapest, 1937), 7ff.; Edit Hoffmann, "Mátyás király könyvtára" [The Library of King Matthias], in Lukinich, *Mátyás emlékkönyv*, II, 209ff.; Tíbor Kardos, "Deákműveltség és a magyar renaissance" [Latin Culture and the Hungarian Renaissance], *Századok*, 72 (1939), 295ff.

BIBLIOGRAPHY

Jenő Ábel. *Analecta nova ad historiam renascentium in Hungaria litterarum spectantia* (Budapest, 1880).

_____. *Egyetemeink a középkorban* [Medieval Hungarian Universities] (Budapest, 1881).

Acta Sanctorum Bollandiana, 60 vols. to Oct. XI (Paris-Rome, 1864-76) - cited as *ASS*.

Acta Sanctorum Hungariae ex Bollandia et al. ...excerpta, 2 vols. (Tyrnaviae, 1743-44).

Ernst Adam. *Baukunst des Mittelalters*, 2 vols., vols. ix-x in *Ullstein Kunstgeschichte* (Frankfurt am Main-Berlin, 1963).

G.B. Adams. *Constitutional History of England* (New York, 1931).

G. Adriányi. "Pelbárt von Temesvár (ca. 1435-1504) und seine trinitarischen Predigtvorlagen," in *Im Gespräch mit dem Dreieinigen Gott: Elemente einer trinitarischen Theologie: Festschrift zum 65 Geburtstag von Wilhelm Breuning*, ed. M. Böhnke and H. Heinz (Düsseldorf, 1985), 276ff.

_____. "Die ungarischen Synoden," *Annuarium historiae conciliorum*, 8 (1976), 541ff.

Ibn Al-Athir. *Chronicon quod perfectissiumum inscribitur*, ed. K.J. Tornberg, 12 vols. (Leiden, 1851-76), vol. XII.

AföG = Archiv für österreichische Geschichte.

J. Alberigus, ed. *Conciliorum oecumenicorum decreta*, 2nd ed. (Freiburg, 1962).

Alberic. "Chronicon," *MGHSS*, XXIII.

Album studiosorum Universitatis Cracoviensis, 5 vols. (Cracow, 1887-1956).

Tíbor Almási and László Koszta. "Báncsa István bíboros, 1250k-1270" [Cardinal Stephen Báncsa, ca. 1250-1270], *Acta Historica*, Special Issue (Szeged, 1991), 9ff.

B. Altaner. *Die Dominikanermissionen des 13 Jahrhunderts* (Habelschwert, 1924).

A.M. Amnan. *Kirchenpolitische Wandlungen im Ostbaltikum bis zum Tode A. Newskirs* (Rome, 1936).

"Annales Placentenses," *MGHSS*, XVIII.

Annales Marbacenses qui dicuntur, ed. H. Bloch, SSrG (Hannover-Leipzig, 1907; repr. 1979).

Arnold of Lübeck. *Arnoldi Chronica Slavorum*, ed. G.H. Pertz, SSrG (Hannover, 1868; repr. 1978) - cited as Arnold, *Chronica*.

ASS = *Acta Sanctorum Bollandiana*.

H. Aubin. *Geschichte Silesiens*, vol. 1 (Bresslau, 1938).

ÁUO = Wenczel, *Árpádházi új Okmánytár*.

Roger Bacon. *Opus maius*, ed. J.H. Bridges, 2 vols. (Oxford, 1897).

F. Baethgen. "Zur Geschichte des Hauses Getani," *HZ*, 138 (1928), 47ff.

_____. "Kaiser Friedrich II, 1194-1250," *Stupor mundi: zur Geschichte Friedrichs II von Hohenstaufen*, ed. Günther G. Wolf (Darmstadt, 1982), 207ff.

Adolph Bachmann. "Die Völker an der Donau nach Attilas Tode," *Archiv für österreichische Geschichte*, 61 (1880), 189ff.

428 HUNGARY IN THE THIRTEENTH CENTURY

Gy. Balanyi. "Magyar szentek - szentéletű magyarok" [Hungarian Saints - Saintly Hungarians], *Katolius Szemle*, 15 (Rome, 1963), 100ff.

J.J. Baldwin. *The Government of Philip Augustus* (Berkeley-Oxford, 1986).

J. Balics. *A római katholikus egyház története Magyarországon* [History of the Roman Catholic Church in Hungary], 2 vols. in 3 (Budapest, 1885-90).

Sándor Bálint, ed. *Ünnepi kalendárium* [Holy Day Almanac], 2 vols. (Budapest, 1977).

J. Balogh. "Szent Gellért és a «Symphonia Ungarorum»" [St. Gerard and the «Symphonia Ungarorum»], *Magyar Nyelv*, 1926, offprint.

F. Banfi. "Vita di s. Gerardo de Venezia nel codice 1622 della Bibliotheca universitarie de Padova," *Benedictina*, 2 (1948), 262ff. - with text, *ibid.*, 288ff.

G. Bárczi. "A középkori vallon - magyar érintkezések" [Valoon-Hungarian Contacts in the Middle Ages], *Századok*, 71 (1937), 399ff.

G. Barna. "Remembering Sándor Bálint," *Vigilia*, 59 (1994), 577ff.

C. Baronius. *Annales ecclesiastici*, ed. A. Theiner, vols. XIX-XXIII (Barri Ducis, 1869-80).

Emma Bartoniek. "Az Árpádok trónöröklési joga" [The Right of Inheritance of the Árpáds], *Századok*, 60 (1926), 785ff.

Emma Bartoniek, ed. *Szent István törvényeinek XII századi kézirata: az admonti kódex* [The Twelfth Century Manuscript of the Laws of King St. Stephen, the Admont Codex], with reduced facsimile of Cod. med. aevi 433 of the Széchenyi National Library (Budapest, 1935).

Ignatius de Batthyány, ed. *Leges ecclesiasticae regni Hungariae et provinciarum adiacentium*, 3 vols., rev. ed. (Claudipoli, 1824, etc.) - cited as Batthyány, *Leges*.

Vincent de Beauvais. *Speculi maioris...qui speculum historiale inscribitur* (Venice, 1591).

Emil Békési. "Magyar írók Hunyadi Mátyás korából" [Hungarian Writers of the Age of Matthias Corvinus, 1458-90], *Katholikus Szemle*, 16 (1902), 134ff.

Remig Békefi. *A pilisi apátság története* [History of the Abbey of Pilis] (Pécs, 1891).

_____. *A káptalani iskolák története Magyarországon 1540-ig* [History of the Cathedral Schools in Hungary Prior to 1540] (Budapest, 1910).

_____. "Árpádkori közoktatásügy" [Public Education in the Árpádian Age], *Századok*, 30 (1896), 207ff., 310ff., and 413ff.

V. Belauer. *Instituciones y reyes de Aragon* (Bibl. Museo-Belaguer, 1896).

Matthias Bél. *Notitii Hungariae novae historico-geographica*, 4 vols. (Vienna, 1735-42; editio altera in 5 vols., Budapest, 1892).

L. Bella. "Scarabantiai emlékek" [Memories of Ancient Sopron], *Archaeologiai Értesítö*, 19 (1894), 74ff., and "Scarabantia sánca" [Fortifications of Ancient Sopron], *ibid.*, 16 (1896), 223f.

G.V. Below. "Zur Entstehung der deutschen Stadtverfassung," *HZ*, 58 (1887), 193ff.

M. Bene. "Kolostorok a Galga mentén" [Monasteries Along the Galga Stream], *Vigilia*, 46 (1981), 827ff.

N. Benger. *Annualium eremocenobiticorum Ordinis Fratrum Eremitarum s. Pauli primi eremitae*, vol. I (Posonii, 1743).

Loránd Benkő. "Maros- és Udvarhelyszék település- és népiség történetéhez" [Population Study of Székler Settlements in the Maros and Udvarhely Regions], *Századok*, 123 (1989), 343ff. - originally scheduled for publication in 1948!

J.F. Benton. "Individualism and Conformity in Medieval Western Europe," in *Culture, Power, and Personality in Medieval France*, ed. Th. N. Bisson (London-Rio Grande, 1991), 313ff.

Zsolt Beöthy. *A magyar irodalom története* [History of Hungarian Literature], 2 vols., 3rd. rev. ed., ed. Frigyes Badics (Budapest, 1901-03).

E. Bernheim. "Der Charakter Ottos von Freising und seine Werke," *MIÖG*, 6 (1885), 1ff.

Ilona Berkovits. *La miniatura ungherese nel periodo degli Angioni* (Rome, 1947).

W. Berthold, in *Enzyklopädie des Islam*, vol. I (Leipzig, 1913), 709ff.

A.V. Bethlen. *Geschichtliche Darstellungen des Deutschen Ordens in Siebenbürgen* (Vienna-Leipzig, 1831).

G.A. Bezzola. *Die Mongolen in abendländischer Sicht, 1220-70* (Bern-Munich, 1974).

A. Bielowski, ed. *Monumenta Poloniae historica*, 6 vols. (Lvov-Cracow, 1864-93; repr. Warsaw, 1960-61) - cited as *MPH*.

P. Binder. "A «Siebenbürgen» fogalom jelentésváltozásai" [Changes in the Meaning of the Concept of «Siebenbürgen», the German Equivalent of Transylvania], *Századok*, 126 (1992), 355ff.

Marc Bloch. *Feudal Society*, trans. L.A. Manyon (Chicago, 1961).

T.S.R. Boase. *Boniface the Eighth* (London, 1933).

Tamás Bogyay. "A 705 éves Aranybulla" [The 750th Anniversary of the Hungarian Golden Bull], *Katolikus Szemle*, 24 (Rome, 1971), 289ff.

Th. von Bogyay. "Die Kirchenorte der Conversio Bagoariorum et Carantenorum; Methoden und Möglichkeiten ihrer Lokalisierung," *Südostforschungen*, 19 (1960), 52ff.

H. Böhmer. *Kirche und Staat in England und in Normandie im 11 und 12 Jahrhundert* (Leipzig, 1899).

P. Boissonnade. *Life and Work in Medieval Europe*, trans. Eileen Power (repr. New York, 1987).

Kornél Bőle. *Árpádházi b. Margit szenttéavatási ügye és a legősibb "Margit legenda"* [Canonization process of Blessed Margaret of the House of Árpád, and the Earliest "Margaret-Legend"] (Budapest, 1937).

I.G. Bolla. "Az Aranybulla-kori mozgalmak a Váradi Regestrum megvilágításában" [Early Thirteenth Century Social Upheavals in Hungary in the Light of Entries in the Várad Register], *Acta Universitatis Budapestiensis*, sect. hist., 1 (1959), 84ff.

Ilona Bolla. *A jogilag egyeséges jobbágyosztály kialakulása Magyarországon* [Formation in Hungary of the Legally Unified Service Nobles' Stratum] (Budapest, 1983).

István Bóna. *A húnok és nagykirályaik* [The Huns and Their Great Kings] (Budapest, 1993).

_____. *Az Árpádok korai várairól* [Early Forts of the Árpádian Age] (Debrecen, 1995).

_____. *Der Anbruch des Mittelalters: Gepiden und Longobarden im Karpathenbecken* (Budapest, 1976).

A. de Bonfinis. *Rerum Hungaricum decades IV*, ed. J. Fógel, 4 vols. (Leipzig-Budapest, 1936-41).

György Bónis. "A székesfehérvári törvénynaptól az ország szabadságáig" [The Road From the Law Days at Fehérvár to the Country's Freedom], in *Székesfehérvár évszázadai* [Centuries of Székesfehérvár's History], ed. J. Fitz and A. Kralovanszky, 2 vols. (Székesfehérvár, 1967-72), vol. 2. (reprint).

_____. *A jogtudó értelmiség a Mohács előtti Magyarországon* [Der Juristenstand in Ungarn vor Mohács, 1526] (Budapest, 1971).

_____. "Die Entwicklung der geistlichen Gerichtsbarkeit in Ungarn vor 1526," *Zeitschrift der Savigny Stiftung für Rechtsgeschichte*, kan. Abt., 49 (1963), 174ff.

Gedeon Borsa. "A budai Hess nyomda új megvilágításban" [The Hess Press at Buda in Light of Recent Research], *MKSz*, 89 (1973), 138ff.

H. de Boor. *Die deutsche Literatur im späten Mittelalter, 1250-1350*, 3rd ed. (Munich, 1967).

_____. *Die höfische Literatur*, 7th ed. (Munich, 1966).

Arno Boorst. *Die Katharer* (Stuttgart, 1953).

_____. *Der Turmbau von Babel: Geschichte der Meinungen über Ursprung und Vielfalt der Sprachen und Völker*, 4 vols. in 6 (Stuttgart, 1957-63).

K. Bosl, et al. *Eastern and Western Europe in the Middle Ages* (London, 1970).

F.O. Brachfeld. *Dona Violante de Hungria, reina de Aragon* (Madrid, 1942).

A. Brackmann. "Die Anfänge der abendländischen Kulturbewegung in Osteuropa and deren Träger," in his *Gesammelte Aufsätze*, 2nd rev. ed. (Cologne-Graz, 1967).

A.V. Brandt. *Werkzeug des Historikers*, 2nd ed. (Stuttgart, 1960).

L. Bréhier. *L'eglise et l'orient au moyed age: les croisades*, 5th ed. (Paris, 1928).

J.S. Brundage. *Law, Sex and Christian Society in Medieval Europe* (Chicago-London, 1987).

Otto Brunner. *Structure and Government in Medieval Austria*, trans. and introduction by H. Kaminsky and J. Van Horn Melton (Philadelphia, 1992).

Max Buchner. "Um das Niebelungenlied - ein Beitrag, keine Lösung," *Ungarische Jahrbücher*, 9 (1929), 196ff.

Bullarium Magnum Romanum, editio Romana, vol. III-1 (Rome, 1733; repr. Graz, 1963, etc.).

Bullarium Franciscanum Romanorum Pontificum constitutiones, epistolae ac diplomata continens, tribus Odinibus Minorum...a s. Francisco insitutis concessa, 4 vols. (Rome, 1759-1904).

R.I. Burns, ed. *The Worlds of Alfonso the Learned and James the Conqueror* (Princeton, 1985).

Arnold Busson. "Der Krieg von 1278 und die Schlacht bei Dürnkrut. Eine kritische Untersuchung," *AfÖG*, 62 (1881), 3ff.

Pierce Butler. *Origins of Printing in Europe* (Chicago, 1940).

Ch. du Cange. *Glossarium ad scriptores medie et infime latinitatis*, ed. L. Favre, 10 vols. (Niort, 1893-88).

Plano Carpini's Travel Report, in Wyngaert, *Itinera*, I, 27ff.

E. Caspar, ed. *Das Register Gregors VII, MGH Epp. selectae*, 2 vols. (Berlin, 1920-23; repr. 1990).

H. v. Campenhausen. *Lateinische Kirchenväter* (Stuttgart, 1960).

CD = Fejér, *Codex diplomaticus*.

C.R. Cheney. *Innocent III and England*, vol. IX of *Päpste und Papsttum*, ed. G. Denzler (Stuttgart, 1976).

_____. "King John and the Papal Interdict," *Bulletin of the John Rylands Library*, 31 (1948), 295ff.

C.R. Cheney and W.H. Simple, eds. *Selected Letters of Innocent III Concerning England* (London, 1953).

Chronica Hungarorum impressa Budae, 1473, a facsimile of the original, with an introduction by Vilmos Franknói (Budapest, 1900).

Chronicon pictum: Képes Krónika, ed. Dezső Dercsényi, 2 vols. (Budapest, 1963), vol. 1: facsimile.

Chronica regia Coloniensis, ed. G. Waitz, SSrG (Hannover, 1880; repr. 1978).

F.W. Cleaver. *Secret History of the Mongols* (London, 1982).

"Continuatio Sancrucensis I-II-III," *MGHSS*, IX.

"Continuatio Vindobonensis," *MGHSS*, IX.

H. Conrad. "Gottesdienst und Heeresverfassung in der Zeit der Kreuzzüge," *Zeitschrift der Savigny Stiftung für Rechtsgeschichte*, kan. Abt., 61 (1941), 71ff.

Cortes de los antiguos reinos de Leon y de Castilla, ed. M. Colmeiro, 5 vols. (Madrid, 1861-94; repr. 1990) - cited as *Cortes*.

Corpus Iuris Civilis of Emperor Justinian the Great, eds. P. Kruger, Th. Thomsen, and R. Schoell, 3 vols. (Berlin, 1895-99), vol. III: *Institutiones*.

Cosmas of Prague. "Chronica Bohemorum," *MGHSS*, IX.

W.A. Copinger, ed. *Supplement to Hain's Repertorium bibliographicum*, 2 vols. (1895; repr. in 3 vols., Milan, 1950).

D. Csánki. "Matthias König der Ungarn," *Ungarische Rundschau*, 2 (1913), 85ff., and 316.

Dezső Csánki, ed. *Magyarország történelmi földrajza a Hunyadiak korában* [Hungarian Historical Geography in the Fifteenth Century], vols. 1-3 and 5 (Budapest, 1890-1913).

D. Csánki and A. Gárdonyi, eds. *Monumenta diplomatica civitatis Budapest, 1148-1301* (Budapest, 1936).

Csaba Csapodi. *A legrégibb magyar könyvtár benső rendje* [The Oldest Hungarian Library and its Inner Order] (Budapest, 1957).

J. Csemegi. *A budavári főtemplom középkori építéstörténete* [Medieval Architectural History of the Main Church in Buda] (Budapest, 1935).

L.J. Csóka. *A latin nyelvű történeti irodalom kialakulása Magyarországon a XI-XIV században* [Development of Latin Language Historical Literature in Hungary During the Eleventh-Fourteenth Centuries] (Budapest, 1967).

K. Csíky et al., eds. *Corpus Iuris Hungarici: Magyar Törvénytár, 1000-1895*, vol. I (Budapest, 1899).

Enikő Csukovits. "«Cum capsa,...cum bacillo»: középkori magyar zarándokok" [Hungarian Pilgrims in the Middle Ages', *Aetas*, 1994/1, 5ff.

A.S. Czermann. *Die Staatsidee des hl. Stephan* (Klagenfurt, 1953).

I. Dám. *A Szeplőtelen Fogantatás védelme Magyarországon a Hunyadiak és Jagiellók korában* [Defense of the Immaculate Conception in Hungary During the Reign of the Hunyadis and of the Jagiellos] (Rome, 1955).

_____. "Andreas Pannonius ferrarai priorságának viszontagságai" [The Eventful Conventual Priorship of Andreas of Pannonia in Ferrara], *Civitas Dei*, 1 (1956), 101ff.

_____. "Kegyosztó társa Krisztusnak" [Mother of God, Co-redeemer], *Vigilia*, 13 (1948), 1ff.

Christopher Dawson. "The Hungarian Middle Ages," *Hungarian Quarterly*, 5 (Budapest-New York, 1939), 585ff.

Christopher Dawson. *The Mongol Mission: Narratives and Letters of Franciscan Missionaries to Mongolia and China in the 13th and 14th Centuries* (New York, 1955).

_____. *Religion and the Rise of Western Culture* (New York: Doubleday, 1958).

Joseph Deér. *Die heilige Krone Ungarns* (Vienna, 1966).

_____. "Der Weg zur Goldenen Bulle Andreas II von 1222," *Schweizer Beiträge zur allgemeinen Geschichte*, 10 (1952), 104ff.

_____. "Közösségérzés és nemzettudat a XI-XIII századi Magyarországon" [Communal Identity and National Consciousness in Hungary During the 11th-13th Centuries], *Klébersberg Kúnó Történetkutató Intézet évkönyve* [Annual of the Kúnó Klébersberg Historical Research Institute], 4 (Budapest, 1934), 97ff.

Joseph Deér. "Szent István politikai és egyházi orientációja" [King St. Stephen's Political and Ecclesiastical Orientation], *Katolikus Szemle*, 1 (Rome, 1949), 27ff.

_____. "Aachen und die Herrschersitze der Árpáden," *MIÖG*, 79 (1971), 1ff.

A. Dempf. *Hauptform mittelalterlichen Weltanschauung* (Munich-Berlin, 1925).

_____. *Sacrum imperium: Geschichts- und Staatsphilosophie des Mittelalters und der politischen Renaissance*, 4th ed. (Stuttgart, 1973).

H. Denifle. *Die Entstehung der Universitäten des Mittelalters*, vol. I (repr. of the 1895 edition, Graz, 1956).

Odo de Deuil. *De profectione Ludovici VII in orientem*, ed. V.G. Berry [Latin-English] (New York, 1948).

Dezső Dercsényi, ed. *Chronicon pictum: Képes Krónika*, 2 vols. (Budapest, 1963), vol. 1: facsimile.

_____. *Nagy Lajos kora* [The Age of Louis the Great of Hungary] (Budapest, n.d. [1941]).

_____. *Nekcsei Dömötör bibliája a washingtoni Library of Congress-ben* [The Bible of Dömötör Nekcsei in the Library of Congress] (Budapest, 1942) - a reprint from *MKSz* (1942), 113ff.

_____. *Sopron és környéke műemlékei* [Artifacts in Sopron and in its Surroundings] , 2nd ed. (Budapest, 1956).

W. Dettloff. "Die Geistigkeit des hl. Franziskus in der Theologie der Franziskaner," *Wissenschaft und Weissheit*, 19 (1956), 197ff.

L. Dézsi. "Szent Agoston reguláinak magyar fordítása Caelius (Bánffy) Gergelytől, 1537" [The Hungarian Translations of the Rules of St. Augustine by Gregory Caelius (Bánffy)] (Budapest, 1900).

H. Dienst. *Die Schlacht an der Leitha, 1246* (Vienna, 1971).

H.J. Diesner. "Die 'Amibalenz' des Friedensgedanken und die Friedenspolitik bei Augustin," in his *Kirche und Staat im spätrömischen Reich* (Berlin, 1963), 46ff.

Diplomataria historiam Matthaei de genere Csák illustrantia, ed. Béla Karácsonyi and Gyula Kristó (Szeged, 1971).

F. Dölger. "Die mittelalterliche Kultur als byzantische Erbe," in his *Byzanz und die europäische Staatenwelt*, rev. ed. (Darmstadt, 1964).

Sándor Domanovszky. "A magyar király-krónika XIV századi folytatása" [The Fourteenth Century Continuator of the Hungarian Royal Chronicle], *Berzeviczy Emlékkönyv* (Budapest, 1934), 25ff.

B. Dombardt and A. Kalb, eds. *Sancti Augustini De civitate Dei* libri XXII, 2 vols., 5th ed., ed. J. Divjak (Stuttgart, 1931; repr. 1981).

L.S. Domonkos. "Bildung und Wissenschaft," in Tibor Klaniczay and Georg Stangler (eds.), *Schallaburg '82: Matthias Corvinus und die Renaissance in Ungarn, 1458-1541*, Landesmuseum of Lower Austria Catalogue, n.s. 118 (Vienna, 1982), 48ff.

J.P. Donovan. *Pelagius and the Fifth Crusade* (Philadelphia, 1950).

Alfons Dopsch. *Die Wirtschaftsentwicklung der Karolingerzeit*, 2 vols., 3rd rev. ed., ed. Erna Patzelt (Cologne-Graz, 1962).

F. Dőry, ed. *Decreta regni Hungariae* (Budapest, 1976).

G.M. Dreves and C. Blume. *Ein Jahrtausend lateinischer Dichtung* (Leipzig, 1909).

L. Duchesne, ed. *Liber pontificalis*, rev. ed., 3 vols. (Paris, 1957).

Bede Dudik, ed. *Iter Romanum*, in *Historische Forschungen* series, II: *Der päpstliche Registerwesen*, 2 vols. (Vienna, 1855).

E. Dümmler. *Geschichte des oströmischen Reiches*, 2nd ed., 3 vols. (Leipzig, 1887-88).

Thomas Ebendorfer. *Chronica Austriae*, ed. Alfons Lhotsky (Berlin-Zurich, 1967) - also in Pez, *SSRA*, II, 689ff.

A. Eckhardt. "Das Ungarnbild in Europa," *Ungarische Jahrbücher*, 22 (1942), 152ff.

F. Eckhart. "La diete corporative hongroise," *L'organisation corporative du moyen age* (Paris, 1939), 215ff.

_____. "Vita a leánynegyedröl" [Debate of the 'Filial Quarter'], *Századok*, 66 (1932), 408ff.

Ferenc Eckhart. *Magyarország története* [Lectures on Hungarian History] (repr. Buenos Aires, 1952).

EPhK = *Egyetemes Filolóiai Közlöny*

F. Ehrle. "Die Spiritualen, ihr Verhältnis zum Franziskanerorden und zu den Fratricellen," *Archiv für Literatur- und Kirchengeschichte des Mittelalters*, 3 (1887), 554ff.

Ekkehardt Eichdorff. "Einheit Europas im neuen gemeinsame Glauben," *Die Presse-Spectrum*, Vienna, July 18, 1987, i-ii.

Einhardi Vita Caroli Magni, ed. O. Holder-Egger, SSrG (Hannover, 1911).

St.L. Endlicher, ed. *Rerum Hungaricarum monumenta Arpadiana* (Sanktgallen, 1849; repr. Leipzig, 1931) - cited as *RHM*.

Pál Engel. "A 14 századi magyar pénztörténete néhány kérdése" [Questions Concerning Fourteenth Century Hungarian Monetary History], *Századok*, 124 (1990), 25ff.

_____. "Temetkezések a középkori székesfehérvári bazilikában" [Burials in the Medieval Cathedral of Székesfehérvár], *Századok*, 121 (1987), 613ff.

J. Erben and F. Embler, eds. *Regesta diplomatica necnon epistolaria Bohemiae et Moraviae*, 2 vols. (Prague, 1855-74).

L. Erdélyi, ed. *A pannonhalmi Szent-Benedek Rend története* [History of the Benedictines of Pannonhalma], 12 vols. (Budapest, 1902-07) - cited as *Rendtörténet*.

_____. *Magyar történet, művelődes és államtörténet* [Hungarian Cultural and Constitutional History], 2 vols. (Budapest, 1936-38).

Géza Érszegi. "Az Aranybulla" [The Golden Bull], *Fejér megyei történeti évkönyv* [Annual of Fejér County's History], 6 (1972), 5ff.

Conrad Eubel, ed. *Hierarchia catholica medii aevi*, 3 vols (Münster, 1910-1914; repr. 1960).

Georgius Fejér, ed. *Codex diplomaticus Hungariae ecclesiasticus ac civilis*, 42 vols. (Budae, 1828-44) - cited as *CD*.

László Feketekúty. *Christentum und Staat* (Cologne, 1953).

J. Félegyházy. "Történeti irodalmunk kezdetei" [The Beginnings of Hungarian Historical Literature], *Vigilia*, 34 (1969), 329ff.

J. Félegyházy. *A tatárjárás történetének és kútfőinek históriája* [A History of the Mongol Invasion and of its Sources] (Vác, 1941).

Felix Fellner, "The «Two Cities» of Otto of Friesing, and Its Influence Upon the Catholic Philosophy of History," *Catholic Historical Review*, 20 (1934-35), 154ff.

M. Ferdinándy. "Ludwig I von Ungarn," *Südost Forschungen*, 21 (1972), 41ff.

John V.A. Fine, Jr. "Was the Bosnian Banate Subjugated to Hungary in the Second Half of the Thirteenth Century?" *East European Quarterly*, 3 (1969), 167ff.

H. Finke, ed. *Acta Aragonensia: aus der diplomatischen Korrespondes Jaymes II*, vol. 3 (Berlin, 1922; repr. Aalen, 1966).

J. Fitz. "König Matthias und der Buchdruck," in Albert Humel (ed.), *Gutenberg Jahrbuch* (Mainz, 1939), 128ff.

K. Flasch. *Das philosophische Denken im Mittelalter, von Augustin zu Machiavelli* (Stuttgart, 1986).

A. Fliche and V. Martin. *Histoire de l'Eglise depuis des Origenes a nos Jours*, vol. 10 (Paris, 1950).

A. Folz. *Kaiser Friedrich II und Papst Innocenz IV* (Strassburg, 1905).

Fontes rerum Austricarum, Abt. 1: *Scriptores*, 10 vols. (Vienna, 1855, etc.) - cited as *FRA*.

M.F. Font. "Ungarn, Bulgarien und das Papsttum um die Wende vom 12 zum 13 Jahrhundert," repr. from *Hungaro-Slavica*, 1988, 259ff.

M.F. Font. "Politische Beziehungen zwischen Ungarn und der Kiever Rus' im 12 Jahrhundert," *Ungarn Jahrbuch*, 18 (1990), 1ff.

_____. "II András orosz politikája és hadjáratai" [Andrew II's Russian Policy and his Campaigns], *Századok*, 125 (1991), 107ff.

_____. "A Kievi Évkönyvek mint magyar történeti forrás" [The Kiev Annals as a Hungarian Historical Source], *Történelmi Szemle*, 33 (1991), 70ff.

_____. "Ungarische Vornehmen in der Halitisch im 13 Jahrhundert," *Specimina nova Universitatis de Iano Pannonio nominatae* (Pécs, 1990), 165ff.

Alan Forey. "The Military Orders in the Crusading Proposals of the Late-Thirteenth and Early-Fourteenth Centuries", *Traditio*, 36 (1980), 317ff.

_____. "The Militarisation of the Hospital of St. John," *Studia monastica*, 26 (1984), 75ff.

FRA = *Fontes rerum Austricarum*

Vilmos Fraknói. *Magyarország és a Szentszék* [Hungary and the Holy See], 3 vols. (Budapest, 1901-03).

Vilmos Fraknói, ed. *A veszprémi püspökség római levéltára* [Archives of the Diocese of Veszprém in Rome], 2 vols. (Budapest, 1896-99).

F.X. von Funk and K. Bihlmeyer. *Kirchengeschichte*, 2 vols., 8th rev. ed. (Paderborn, 1926-30).

E. Fügedi. *Castle and Society in Medieval Hungary*, trans. J.M. Bak (Budapest, 1986).

E. Függedi. "Das mittelalterliche Ungarn als Gastland," in W. Schlesinger (ed.), *Die deutsche Ostsiedlung des Mittelalters als Probleme der europäischen Geschichte* (Sigmaringen, 1975), 471ff.

_____. "Der Stadtplan von Stuhlweissenburg, und die Anfänge der Bürgertums in Ungarn," *Acta historica Academiae Scientiarum Hungaricae*, 15 (1969), 103ff.

Erik Függedi. "Sepelierunt corpus eius in proprio monasterio," *Századok*, 125 (1991), 35ff.

D. Fuxhoffer and M. Czínár, eds. *Monasteriologiae regni Hungariae libri II* (Pest, 1858-59).

Kirakos Gandzakecki. "Armenian History," in Ödön Schütz (ed.), *Tanulmányok az orientalisztika köréböl* [Studies Concerning the Orient] (Budapest, 1972), 255ff.

A. Garcia y Garcia. *Constitutiones Concilii quarti Lateranensis una cum commentariis glossatorum* (Vatican, 1981).

A. Gardner. *The Lascarids of Nicea: Story of an Empire in Exile* (London, 1922).

B. Gebhardt. *Handbuch der deutschen Geschichte*, 8th rev. ed., 4 vols. (Stuttgart, 1954-60), vol. I.

C.T. Gemeiner. *Chronik der Stadt Regensburg*, vol. 1 (Regensburg, 1800).

J. Gerics. "Adalékok a Kézai-krónika problémáinak megoldásához" [Some Remarks Concerning the Kéza Chronicle Question], *Annales Universitatis Budapestiensis*, sectio hist., 1 (1957), 106ff.

J. Gerics. "Az Aranybulla ellenállási záradékának értelmezéséhez" [Interpreting the Resistance Clause of the Golden Bull], *Ünnepi tanulmányok Sinkovics István 70 születésnapjára* [Studies in Honor of István Sinkovics on his 70th Birthday], ed. Iván Berendi (Budapest, 1980) - reprint.

József Gerics. *A korai rendiség Európában és Magyarországon* [Early Feudal Order in Europe and Hungary] (Budapest, 1987).

_____. "Krónikáink a III András-kori rendi intézmények friauli-aquileiai kapcsolatairól" [Hungarian Chronicles on the Relations of the Institutions of the Nobles' Estate with Friaul-Aquileia During the Reign of Andrew III], *Filológiai Közlöny*, 1975, 309ff.

József Gerics. "Domanovszky Sándor az árpádkori krónikakutatás úttörője" [Alexander Domanovszky, Pioneer in Research of the Chronicles of the Árpádian Age], *Századok*, 112 (1978), 235ff.

L. Gerevich, ed. *Towns in Medieval Hungary* (Budapest, 1990).

_____. "Hungary," in M.W. Barley (ed.), *European Towns: Their Archaeology and Early History* (London, 1977), 431ff.

E. Gerland. *Geschichte des lateinsichen Kaiserreiches von Konstantinople*, vol. 1 (Hamburg, 1905).

_____. "Der Vierte Kreuzzug und seine Probleme," *Neue Jahrbücher für das klassische Altertum*, 12 (1904), 505ff.

A. Gieysztor. *A History of Poland* (Warsaw, 1968).

E. Gilson. *History of Christian Philosophy in the Middle Ages* (London, 1955).

H. Göckenjan, ed. *Der Mongolensturm: Berichte von Augenzuegen und Zeitgenossen* (Graz-Cologne, 1985).

H. Göckenjan. "Stuhlweissenburg, eine ungarische Königsresidenz von 11-13 Jahrhundert," *Beiträge zur Stadt- und Regionalgeschichte Ost- und Nordeuropas*, ed. F. Zernack (Wiesbaden, 1971), 135ff.

Ransgerd Göckenjan. *Hilfsvölker und Grenzwächter im mittelalterlichen Ungarn* (Wiesbaden, 1972).

Wilhelm Goetz. "Franz von Assisi und die Entwicklung der mittelalterlichen Religiösität," *Archiv für Kulturgeschichte*, 17 (1927), 129ff.

Jacques le Goff. "Economie, morale et religion au XIIIe siècle," *Ricerche di storia sociale e religiosa*, 46 (1994), 7ff.

Zoltán Gombocz. "A magyar őshaza és a nemzeti hagyomány" [In Search of the Magyar Ur-country and the National Tradition], *Nyelvtudományi Közlemények*, 45 (1917-20), 129ff.; and 46 (1923-27), 1ff. and 168ff.

Kálmán Gouth. "Eszmény és valóság árpádkori királylegendáinkban" [The Ideal and the Real in the Royal Legends of the Árpád Age], *Erdélyi Múzeum*, 49 (1944), 304ff.

F. Gräfe. Die *Publizistik in der letzten Epoche Kaiser Friedrichs II* (Heidelberg, 1909).

K. Gránicz. "Az utolsó árpádházi királyleány emléke a tössi címerben" [Memory of the Last Royal Daughter of the House of Árpád in the Coat-of-Arms of Töss], *Vigilia*, 44 (1979), 319ff.

A. Gransden. *Historical Writing in England c. 550 to 1307* (Ithaca, NY, 1974).

S. Grayzel. *The Church and the Jews in the 13th Century* (Philadelphia, 1955).

J. Greven. *Die Anfänge der Beginnen*, vol. 8 of *Vor-Reformations-geschichtliche Forschungen* (Munster i.W., 1912).

H. Grotefend. *Zeitrechnung des deutschen Mittelalters und der Neuzeit*, 2 vols. (Hannover, 1891-92; repr. Aalen, 1984).

R. Grousset. *Histoire des croisades du royaume Franc de Jerusalem*, 3 vols. (Paris, 1936).

H. Grundmann. *Die religiöse Bewegungen im Mittelalter* (Berlin, 1935).

P. Gulyás. *A könvy sorsa Magyarországon* [The Fate of Books in Hungary], 3 vols. (Budapest, 1961-65) - a revised version of his *A könyvnyomtatás Magyarországon a XV és XVI században* [The Printing Press in Hungary During the 15th and 16th Centuries] (Budapest, 1931).

I. Gyárfás. *A jászkúnok története* [History of the Jaz(y)go Cumans], 2 vols. (Kecskemét, 1870-73).

Mátyás Gyóni. "A kievi ősévkönyv volochjai" [The Vlochs of the Ur-annals of Kiev], *Századok*, 123 (1989), 298ff. - scheduled for publication in 1948.

G. Gyöngyösi. *Vitae Fratrum eremitarum ordinis sancti Pauli primi eremitae*, ed. F.L. Hervay (Budapest, 1988).

György Györffy. "A magyar-szláv érintkezés kezdetei" [Origins of the Hungaro-Slavic Contacts], *Századok*, 127 (1993), 391ff.

_____. "A székelyek eredete" [In Search of Székler Origins], cf. Elemér Mályusz, *Erdély és népei* [Transylvania and its Peoples] (Kolozsvár, 1941).

György Györffy. "A székesfehérvári latinok betelepülésének kérdése" [Problems Concerning the Latin Settlement in Székesfehérvár], in A. Kralovánszky (ed.), *Székesfehérvár évszázadai* [Centuries of Székesfehérvár], 2 vols. (Székesfehérvár, 1972), II, 37ff.

_____. "Az árpádkori magyar krónikák" [Hungarian Chronicles of the Árpád Age], *Századok*, 127 (1993), 391ff.

_____. *A tatárjárás emlékezete* [Remembering the Mongol Invasion] (Budapest, 1987).

_____. *Einwohnerzahl und Bevölkerungsdichte in Ungarn bis zum Anfang des XIV Jahrhunderts* (Budapest, 1960).

_____. *Krónikáink és a magyar őstörténet* [Hungarian Chronicles on Early Hungarian History] (Budapest, 1948).

_____. *Napkelet felfedezése: Julianus, Plano Carpini és Rubruk utijelentései* [In Search of the Orient: Traveller Accounts of Julian, Plano Carpini and Rubruck] (Budapest, 1965).

_____. "Újabb adatok a tatárjárás történetéhez" [More Recent Data on the History of the Mongol Invasion], *Történelmi Szemle*, 33 (1991), 84ff.

_____. "Ungarn von 895 bis 1400," *Europäische Wirtschafts- und Sozialgeschichte im Mittelalter*, vol. 2 of H. Kellembenz (ed.), *Handbuch der europäischen Wirtschafts- und Sozialgeschichte* (Stuttgart, 1980), 625ff.

_____. *Wirtschaft und Gesellschaft in Ungarn um die Jahrtausendwende* (Vienna-Graz, 1983).

György Györffy, ed. *Geographia historica Hungariae tempore stirpis Arpadianae: Az árpádkori Magyarország történeti földrajza*, vol. 1, 3rd ed. (Budapest, 1987).

J. Győry. *Gesta regum - gesta nobilium* (Budapest, 1948).

O. Hagender. "Exkommunikation und Thronfolgerlust bei Innocenz III," *Römische historische Mitteilungen*, 2 (1959), 9ff.

O. Hagender and A. Haidacher, eds. *Die Register Innocenz' III, 1. Pontifikatsjahr* (1198-99); Publikationen des Österreichischen Kulturinstitutes in Rome, Abt. II, Reihe I, vol. I (Graz-Cologne, 1964) - cited as *Register 1*.

O. Hagender, W. Maleczek, and A. Strnad, eds. *Die Register Innocenz' III, 2. Pontifikatsjahr* (1199-1200); Publikationen des Österreichischen Kulturinstitutes in Rome, Abt. II, Reihe I, vol. II (Rome-Vienna, 1979) - cited as *Register 2*.

A. Haidacher. "Beiträge zur Kentniss der verlorenen Registerbände Innocenz' III," *Römische Mitteilungen*, 4 (1960-61), 37ff.

L. Hain. *Repertorium bibliographicum*, 2 vols. (Stuttgart-Tübingen, 1826-38; repr. in 4 vols., Milan, 1948).

István Hajnal. "Kézművesség, írásbeliség és európai fejlődés" [Handicrafts, Literacy and European Progress], *Századok*, 123 (1989), 407ff., scheduled for publication in 1948!

_____. "IV Béla király Kancelláriájáról" [The Chancery of Béla IV], *Turul*, 32 (1914), 1ff.

E.M. Hallam. *Capetian France* (London-New York, 1980).

Johann Haller. *Das Papsttum: Idee und Wirklichkeit*, 2nd ed., 5 vols. (Stuttgart, 1953-59).

Karl Hampe. *Das Hochmittelalter*, 5th rev. ed. (Cologne-Graz, 1963).

_____. "Kaiser Otto III und Rom," *HZ*, 140 (1929), 513ff.

_____. "Kaiser Friedrich II," *HZ*, 83 (1899), 1ff.

Karl Hampe. *Deutsche Kaisergeschichte*, 12th rev. ed., ed. F. Baethgen (Heidelberg, 1968).

H.R. Hanloser. *Villard de Honnecourt* (Vienna, 1935).

E. Hantos. *The Magna Carta and the Hungarian Constitution* (London, 1904).

Hugo Hantsch. *Geschichte Österreichs*, 2 vols., 5th rev. ed. (Vienna, 1969).

L. Hanzó. "A barcaság betelepítése és a Német Lovagrend" [Settlement of the Barca Region and the German Knights], *Századok*, 123 (1989), 359ff - originally scheduled for publication in 1948!

Ch. H. Haskins. "Latin Literature Under Frederick II," in his *Studies in Medieval Culture* (Oxford, 1929), 124ff.

H. Hauck, ed. *Geschichtsschreibung und geistiges Leben im Mittelalter: Festschrift für Heinz Löwe zum 65 Geburtstag* (Cologne-Vienna, 1978).

F. Hausmann. "Kaiser Friedrich II und Österreich," in *Probleme um Friedrich II*, ed. J. Fleckenstein (Sigmaringen, 1974).

J. Havet, ed. *Lettres de Gerbert* (Paris, 1889).

HO = Nagy, *Hazai Okmánytár*.

G. Bar Hebraeus. *Chronicon Syriacum*, ed. P. Bedjan (Paris, 1890).

Friedrich Heer. *Die Tragödie des hl. Reiches* (Stuttgart, 1952).

_____. *Europäische Geistesgeschichte*, 2nd ed. (Stuttgart, 1965).

C.J. v. Hefele. *Conziliengeschichte*, 2nd rev. ed., 6 vols. [vols. V-VI edited by A. Knöpfler] (Freiburg i. Br., 1873-90).

M. Heimbucher. *Orden und Kongregationen der katholischen Kirche*, 2 vols., 3rd ed. (Paderborn, 1933).

W. Heinemeyer. "Ottokar von Steier und die höfische Kultur," *Zeitschrift für deutsches Altertum und deutsche Literatur*, 73 (1936), 201ff.

A. Heisenberg. *Neue Quellen zur Geschichte des lateinischen Kaisertums* (Munich, 1932).

Erich Henisch. *Die Geheime Geschichte der Mongolen aus einer mongolischen Niederschrift des Jahres 1240 von der Insel Kode'e im Keluren Fluss* (Leipzig, 1941; rev. ed., 1948).

R. Hennig. *Terrae incognitae*, 4 vols. (Leiden, 1944-56).

H. Herding. "Geschichtsschreibung und Geschichtsdenken im Mittelalter," *Tübinger Theologische Zeitschrift*, 130 (1950), 129ff.

E. Hermann. *A katolikus egyház története Magyarországon 1914-ig* [History of the Catholic Church in Hungary until 1914] (Munich, 1973).

Julius Hermann. *Die italienischen Handschriften des Duecento und Trecento* (Vienna, 1930).

J.N. Hillgarth. *The Spanish Kingdoms, 1250-1516*, 2 vols. (Oxford, 1976).

Hincmar of Reims. *De ordine palatii*, ed. Th. Gross and R. Schieffer, *Fontes iuris Germanici antiqui*, III (Hannover, 1980).

_____. "De regis persona et regio ministerio," *MPL*, 125, cols. 833ff.

H. Hirsch, ed. *Scriptores rerum Prussicarum*, 5 vols. (Leipzig, 1861-74).

B. Hirsch-Reich. "Joachim von Fiore und das Judentum," in P. Wilpert (ed.), *Judentum im Mittelalter* (Berlin, 1966), 228ff.

HJb = *Historisches Jahrbuch*..

Antal Hodinka, ed. *Az orosz évkönyvek magyar vonakozásai* [Data in the Russian Annals Concerning Hungary] (Budapest, 1916) - cited as Hodinka.

_____. *Egyházunk küzdelme a bogomil eretnekekkel* [Struggle of the Church with the Bogomil Heretics], vol. 50 of *Studies by the Students of the Roman Catholic Major Seminary in Budapest* (Budapest, 1877).

H. Hoffmann. "Von Cluny zum Investiturstreit," *Archiv für Kulturgeschichte*, 45 (1963), 165ff.

I. Holl. "Sopron im Mittelalter," *Acta archaeological Hungarica*, 31 (1979), 105ff.

George Holmes. *Florence, Rome and the Origins of the Renaissance* (Oxford,1986).

J.C. Holt. *Magna Carta* (Cambridge, 1969).

_____. "The Barons and the Great Charter," *English Historical Review*, 70 (1955), 1ff.

Robert Holtzmann. *Geschichte der sächsischen Kaiserzeit*, 4th printing (Darmstadt, 1961).

W. Holtzmann. "XII századi pápai levelek kánoni gyüjteményekből" [Twelfth Century Papal Letters Taken from Canon Collections], *Századok*, 93 (1959), 404ff.

J. Holub. "La 'quarta puellaria' dans ancien droit hongrois," *Studi in memoria di Aldo Albertoni*, vol. 3 (Padua, 1935), 275ff.

H. Holzapfel. *Handbuch der Geschichte des Franziskanerordens* (Freiburg, i. Br., 1909).

Bálint Hóman. *Magyar pénztörténet, 1000-1325* [Hungarian Monetary History, 1000-1325] (Budapest, 1916).

_____. *Magyar városok az Árpádok korában* [Hungarian Towns in the Árpád Age] (Budapest, 1908).

Bálint [Valentine] Hóman. *Geschichte des ungarischen Mittelalters*, 2 vols. (Berlin, 1940-43).

Bálint Hóman and Gyula Szekfű. *Magyar történet* [Hungarian History], 5 vols., 6th ed. (Budapest, 1939).

C. Hopf, ed. *Chronista Novorednis*, in *Chroniques gréco-romanes inédites* series (Berlin, 1873).

J. Hormayr-Hortenburg, ed. *Die Goldene Chronik von Hochenschwangau*, 2 vols. (Munich, 1842).

O. v. Horneck. *Österreichische Reimchronik*, ed. J. Seemüller, *MGH scriptorum qui vernacula lingua usi sunt*, vol. V, 1-2 (Hannover, 1980-93) - cited as *Reimchronik*.

C.A. Horoy, ed. *Honorii III Romani Pontificis opera omnia*, 5 vols. (Paris, 1879-82).

Cyrill Horváth. *A régi magyar irodalom története* [History of Old Hungarian Literature] (Budapest, 1899).

_____. "Andreas Pannonius," *EPhK*, 66 (1946), 257ff.

_____. "Kódexeink skolasztikus elemei" [The Scholastic Element in Hungarian Codices], *ItK*, 42 (1932), 121ff.

Janós Horváth. *A magyar irodalmi műveltség kezdetei* [Beginnings of Hungarian Literary Culture], 2nd ed. (Budapest, 1944).

János Horváth. *Árpád-kori latinnyelvű irodalmunk stílusproblémái* [Stylistic Questions Concerning the Latin Language Literature of the Árpád Age] (Budapest, 1954).

_____. *A magyar irodalmi műveltség megoszlása* [Differentiation of Hungarian Literary Culture], 2nd ed. (Budapest, 1944).

_____. "Die ungarischen Chronisten aus der Angioveienzeit," *Acta linguistica Academiae Scientiarum Hungaricae*, 21 (1971), 324ff.

János Horváth. and György Székly, eds. *Középkori kútfőink kritikus kérdései* [Critical Problems Concerning Medieval Hungarian Historical Sources], vol. 1 of *Memoria saeculorum Hungariae* (Budapest, 1974) - cited as *Memoria Hungariae*, vol. 1.

P. Horváth. *Commentatio de initiis ac maioribus Jazygum et Cumanorum eorumque constitutionibus* (Pest, 1801).

Richard Horváth. *Laskai Osvát* [Life and Work of Oswald de Laska] (Budapest, 1932).

Sándor Horváth. *Mulier amicta sole* (Budapest, 1948).

H.H. Howorth. *History of the Mongols from the 9th to the 19th Century*, 3 vols. (London, 1876-88).

R.S. Hoyt. "The Coronation Oath of 1308: The Background of the 'Les leys et les customes'," *Traditio*, 11 (1955), 235ff.

Romualdus Hube, ed. *Antiquissimae constitutiones synodales provinciae Gneznenis* (Peterpolis, 1865).

A. Huber. *Geschichte Österreichs*, vol. 1 (Gotha, 1885).

_____. *Österreichische Rechtsgeschichte*, rev. ed., ed. A. Dopsch (Vienna, 1901).

A. Huber. "Studien über die Geschichte Ungarns in der Zeit der Árpáden," *Archiv für österreichische Geschichte*, 65 (1883-84), 153ff., esp. 170ff.

C.H. Hubertus. "The Codex," *Proceedings of the British Academy*, 40 (1954), 169ff.

Johan Huemer. "Rhythmus über die Schlacht auf dem Marchfelde (1278)," *Archiv für österreichische Geschichte*, 67 (1886), 183ff.

G. Hüffer. "Die Anfänge des Zweiten Kreuzzuges," *HJb*, 8 (1887), 391ff.

H. Hurter, ed. *Nomenclator literarium theologiae catholicae theologos exhibens aetate, natione, disciplinis distinctos*, 5 vols. (Oeniponte, 1903-13).

Lipót Hütter. *Korszerű-e a szentistváni világnézet?* [Is the Political Outlook of King St. Stephen Up-To-Date?] (Székesfehérvár, 1938).

HZ = Historische Zeitschrift.

Antal Ijjas. *Szentek élete* [Lives of the Saints], 2 vols. (Budapest, 1976).

Courtenay Ilbert. *Parliament, Its History, Constitution and Practice* (London, 1917).

W. Imkamp. *Das Kirchenbild Innocenz' III (1198-1216)*, vol. 22 of *Päpste und Papsttum* (Stuttgart, 1983).

A. Ipoly, ed. *Codex diplomaticus patrius Hungaricus*, vol. IV (Budapest, 1876).

ItK = Irodalomtörténeti Közlemények.

G. Itsványi. "XIII századi feljegyzés IV Bélának a tatárokhoz küldött követeségéről" [A Thirteenth Century Annotation on the Embassy Sent by Béla IV to the Mongols], *Századok*, 72 (1938), 270ff.

B. Iványi. "A Szent Domonkos Rend római központi levéltára" [The Central Archives of the Dominican Order in Rome], *Levéltári Közlemények*, 7 (1929), 1ff.

Gabriel Jackson. *The Making of Medieval Spain*, (London-New York, 1972).

R.A. Jackson. "Who Wrote Hincmar's Ordines?" *Viator*, 25 (1994), 31ff.

E. Jakubovich and D. Pais, eds. *Ó-magyar olvasókönyv* [Old Hungarian Reader] (Pécs, 1929).

Hans Jantzen. *Kunst der Gothik* (Hamburg, 1957).

Bede Jarrett. *Life of Saint Dominic*. (New York: Image Books, 1964).

H. Jedin, ed. *Handbuch der Kirchengeschichte*, 10 vols. (Freiburg i. Br., 1962, etc.).

E. Jekelius. *Das Burzenland*, 4 vols. (Kronstadt, 1928-29).

H. Jircek, ed. *Codex Iuris Bohemici*, vol. I (Prague, 1867).

C. Jirecek. *Die Handelstrassen und Bergwerke in Serbien und Bosnien des Mittelalters* (Prague, 1879).

_____. *Die Heerstrasse von Belgrad nach Konstantinople* (Prague, 1877).

Jean de Joinville. *Histoire de Saint Louis*, ed. N. de Wailly (Paris, 1874).

John of Salisbury. *Policraticus,* ed. C.C.J. Webb, 2 vols. (Oxford, 1909).

Jonas of Orleans. "De institutione regia," *MPL,* 106, cols. 279ff.

J. Jörgensen. *St. Francis of Assisi.* (New York: Image Books, 1935).

W. Ch. Jordan. *The French Monarchy and the Jews* (Philadelphia, 1989).

C. Juhász. *A csanádi püspökség története a tatárjárásig, 1030-1242* [History of the Csanád Diocese Until the Tartar Invasion, 1030-1242] (Makó, 1930).

R.F. Kaindl. "Studien zu den ungarischen Geschichtsquellen, I-II," *Archiv für österreichische Geschichte,* 81 (1895), 323ff.

E.H. Kantorowicz. "Kingship Under the Impact of Scientific Jurisprudence," in *Twelfth Century Europe and the Foundations of Modern Society,* ed. M. Clagett et al. (Madison, WI, 1966), 89ff.

_____. *The King's Two Bodies: A Study in Medieval Political Theology* (Princeton, 1957).

J. Karácsonyi. *Szent Ferenc Rendjének története Magyarországon 1711-ig* [History of the Franciscan Order in Hungary prior to 1711], 2 vols. (Budapest, 1922-24).

_____. *Szent Gellért élete és művei* [Life and Works of St. Gerard of Csanád] (Budapest, 1887).

János Karácsonyi. *Hamis oklevelek jegyzéke 1400-ig* [List of False Documents, with Supplement], ed. László Koszta (Aeta repr., Szeged, 1988).

Tíbor Kardos. *Középkori kultúra, középkori költészet* [Medieval Culture, Medieval Poetry] (Budapest, n.d.).

Tíbor Kardos. *A magyarság antík hagyományai* [The Magyars' Ancient Traditions] (Budapest, 1942).

J. Kárpát. "Die Lehre von der hl. Krone Ungarns im Lichte des Schrifttums," *Jahrbücher für die Geschichte Osteuropas*, 6 (1941), 1ff.

L. Katona and F. Szinnyei. *Geschichte der ungarischen Literatur* (Leipzig, 1911).

Stephanus Katona. *Historia critica regum Hungariae stirpis Arpadianae*, 7 vols. (Pest-Buda, 1779-81).

_____. *Historia critica regum Hungariae stirpis mixtae*, 12 vols. (Budae, 1787-92).

_____. *Historia pragmatica Hungariae*, 3 vols. (Budae, 1782, etc.)

J. Kaufmann. *Eine Studie über die Beziehungen der Habsburger zum Königtum Ungarn in den Jahren 1278 bis 1366* (Eisenstadt, 1970).

F. Kempf. *Die Register Innocenz' III, eine paläographische-diplomatische Untersuchung*, vol. IX of *Miscellanea historiae pontificiae* (Rome, 1945).

_____. *Papsttum und Kaisertum bei Innocenz III*, vol. XIX of *Miscellanea historiae pontificiae* (Rome, 1954).

W.P. Ker. *Medieval English Literature* (Oxford, 1948 - a reprint of the 1912 edition).

Fritz Kern. *Kingship and Law in the Middle Ages*, trans. S.B. Chrimes (Oxford, 1939).

A. Keutner. *Papsttum und Krieg unter dem Pontifikat des Papstes Honorius III (1216-27)* (Munster, 1935).

458   HUNGARY IN THE THIRTEENTH CENTURY

Pearl Kibre. "Intellectual Interests as Reflected in the Libraries of the Fourteenth and Fifteenth Centuries," *Journal of the History of Ideas*, 7 (1946), 257ff.

P. Kibre. *Nations in the Medieval Universities* (Cambridge, 1948).

W. Kienast. *Deutschland und Frankreich in der Kaiserzeit*, vol. III,1-3 in *Monographien zur Geschichte des Mittelalters*, ed. F. Prinze and K. Bosl (Stuttgart, 1952-75).

E.S. Kiss. "A királyi generális kongregáció kialakulásának történetéhez" [Comments on the History of the Development of the Royal Diet], *Acta historica Szegediensis*, 39 (1971), 3ff.

T. Klaniczay. *A magyar irodalom története 1660-ig* [History of Hungarian Literature Prior to 1660] (Budapest, 1964).

E. Klebel. "Die Ostgrenze des karolingischen Reiches," *Jahrbücher für Landeskunde von Niederösterreich*, n.s., 21 (1929), 348ff. - reprinted in *Die Entstehung des Deutschen Reiches, Wege der Forschung, Sammelband* (Darmstadt, 1955), 1ff.

Ferdinand Knauz. *Monumenta ecclesiae Strigoniensis*, 2 vols. (Strigonii, 1875-74).

Ferdinand Knauz, ed. *A nápolyi Margit-legenda* [The Margaret Legend of Naples] (Esztergom, 1868), 30ff.

D. Knowles. *The Evolution of Medieval Thought*, 2nd ed. (London-New York, 1988).

J. Koch. *Artes liberales* (Leiden-Cologne, 1959).

Sámuel Kohn. "Az 1279-es budai zsinat összes végzései" [A Comprehensive Listing of the Resolutions of the 1279 Synod of Buda], *TörténelmiTár* (Budapest, 1881), 543ff.

_____. *A zsidók története Magyarországon* [History of the Jews in Hungary], vol. I (Budapest, 1884).

Sámuel Kohn. "Héber források és adatok Magyarország történetéhez" [Hebrew Sources and Data Related to Hungarian History], *Történelmi tár* (Budapest, 1880), 99ff.

J. Koller. *Historia episcopatus Quinqueecclesiarum*, 3 vols. (Posonii, 1782-84); vol. 7 (Pest, 1801).

Zoltán Kordé. "A magyarországi besenyők az árpádkorban" [Petchenges in Hungary of the Árpád Age], *Acta historica Szegediensis*, 90 (1990), 3ff.

_____. "A székelyek a XII századi elbeszélő forrásokban" [The Széklers Mentioned in the 12th Century Narrative Sources], *Acta historica Szegediensis*, 92 (1991), 17ff.

László Koszta. "Az 1306-es pécsi püspökválasztás" [The 1306 Episcopal Election in Pécs], *Acta historica Szegediensis*, 98 (1993), 37ff.

_____. "Egy francia származású főpap Magyarországon: Bertalan pécsi püspök" [Bertalan of Pécs, a Hungarian Bishop of French Origin], *Aetas*, 1994/1, 64ff.

_____. "A pozsegai káptalan tagjai" [Members of the Pozsega Chapter of Canons], *Aetas*, 1991/3-4, 40ff.

_____. "Az esztergomi és a kalocsai érsekség viszonya a 13 század elején" [The Relationship Between the Esztergom and Kalocsa Archdioceses at the Beginning of the Thirteenth Century], *Essays in Church History in Hungary*, 3 (Budapest, 1992), 73ff.

Z.J. Kosztolnyik. *Five Eleventh Century Hungarian Kings: Their Policies and Their Relations with Rome* (New York, 1981).

_____. *From Coloman the Learned to Béla III (1095-1196): Hungarian Domestic Policies and Their Impact Upon Foreign Affairs* (New York, 1987).

Z.J. Kosztolnyik. "III András és a pápai udvar" [Andrew III of Hungary and the Roman See], *Századok*, 126 (1992), 646ff.

_____. "The Church and Béla III of Hungary (1172-96): The Role of Archbishop Lukács of Esztergom," *Church History*, 49 (1980), 375ff.

_____. "The Church and the Hungarian Court Under Coloman the Learned," *East European Quarterly*, 18 (1984), 129ff.

_____. "De facultate resistendi: Two Essential Characteristics of the Hungarian Golden Bull of 1222," *Studies in Medieval Culture*, 5 (1975), 97ff.

_____. "Did the Curia Intervene in the Struggle for the Hungarian Throne During the 1290's?" *Régi és új peregrináció: magyarok külföldön, külföldiek Magyarországon: Proceedings of the Third International Congress on Hungarian Studies, Szeged, 1991* (Budapest-Szeged, 1993), 140ff.

_____. "Did Géza of Hungary Send Delegates to the 'Synod' of Pavia, 1160?" *Annuarium historiae conciliorum*, 16 (1984), 40ff.

_____. "Esetleges spanyol: Leon-aragóniai, valamint nyugati behatás III András diétáinak összetételében" [Eventuelle spanische: leon-aragonische, und westliche Einflüsse auf die Zusammenstellung der ungarischen Landtage während der Herrschaft Andreas' III], *Aetas*, 1994/1, 49ff.

_____. "II Géza és a páviai zsinat" [Géza II of Hungary and the Synod of Pavia, 1160], *Történelmi Szemle*, 29 (1986), 237ff.

_____. "The Idea of the 'Body of the State' in John of Salisbury's *Policraticus*," *Specimina nova Universitatis de Iano Pannonio nominate*, 9 (1993), 229ff.

_____. "The Importance of Gerard of Csanád as the First Author in Hungary," *Traditio*, 25 (1969).

Z.J. Kosztolnyik. "In the European Mainstream: Hungarian Churchmen and Thirteenth Century Synods," *Catholic Historical Review*, 79 (1993), 413ff.

_____. "The Negative Results of the Enforced Missionary Policy of King St. Stephen of Hungary: The Uprising of 1046," *Catholic Historical Review*, 59 (1973-74), 569ff.

_____. "The Relations of Four Eleventh Century Hungarian Kings with Rome in the Light of Papal Letters," *Church History*, 46 (1977), 33ff.

_____. "Rome and the Church in Hungary in 1279: The Synod of Buda," *Annuarium historiae conciliorum*, 22 (1990), 68ff.

_____. "Triumphs of Ecclesiastical Politics in the 1231 *Decretum* of Andrew II of Hungary," *Studiosorum speculum: Studies in Honor of Louis J. Lekai, O. Cist.*, ed. F.R. Swietek and J.R. Sommerfeldt (Kalamazoo, MI, 1993), 155ff.

_____. "The Unforeseen Consequences of Charlemagne's Ecclesiastical Politics in the Mid-Danubian Region," *Proceedings of the Árpád Academy and of the Cleveland Hungarian Association, 1980* (Cleveland, Ohio, 1981), 175ff.

_____. "A View of History in the Writings of Gerhoch of Reichersberg and the Medieval Hungarian Chroniclers," *Die ungarische Sprache und Kultur im Donauraum: Vorlesungen des II International Kogresses für Hungarologie, Wien, 1986* (Vienna-Budapest, 1989), 513ff.

Aladár Kovács. "Der «Mongolenbrief» Béla IV schrieb an Papst Innocenz IV über einem zu erwartenden zweiten Einbruch der Mongolen im 1250," in *Überlieferung und Auftrag: Festschrift für M. de Ferdinándy zum 60 Geburtstag* (Wiesbaden, 1972), 495ff.

Aladár Kovács. "IV Béla levele a pápához" [The Writ of Béla IV to the Pope], *Uj Hungária Európa Évkönyv 1959* [The Uj Hungária Europe Calendar for 1959] (Munich, 1958), 43ff.

E.M. Kovács. "Signum crucis - lignum crucis: a magyar kettőskereszt ábrázolásai" [Depictions of the Hungarian Holy Cross," in Gy. Székely (ed.), *Eszmetörténeti tanulmányok a magyar középkorról* [Essays on the Hungarian Middle Ages] (Budapest, 1970).

S.V. Kovács, ed. *Temesvári Pelbárt válogatott írásai* [Select Writings of Pelbárt of Temesvár] (Budapest, 1982).

A. Kralovánszky. "Székesfehérvár X-XI századi településtörténeti kérdései" [Problems Concerning 10th-11th Century Settlements in Székesfehérvár], in his *Székesfehérvár*, I, 36f.

E.G. Krehbiel. *The Interdict, Its History and Operation* (Washington, D.C., 1909).

H. Kretschmayr. *Geschichte von Venedig*, vol. I (Gotha, 1905).

Gy. Kristó. *A feudális széttagoltság Magyarországon* [Feudal Particularism in Medieval Hungary] (Budapest, 1979).

_____. *A vármegyék kialakulása Magyarországon* [Development of the County Government in Medieval Hungary] (Budapest, 1988).

_____. *Az aranybullák évszázada* [Century of Golden Bulls] (Budapest, 1981).

_____. *Az Árpádkor háborúi* [Wars in the Árpádian Age] (Budapest, 1986).

_____. "Die Mach der Territorialherren in Ungarn am Anfang des 14 Jahrhunderts," *Études historiques hongroises, 1985*, 597ff., reprint.

Gy. Kristó. "Egy 1235 körüli Gesta Ungarorum körvonalairól" [The Outline of a «Gesta Ungarorum» of about 1235], separatum, *Memoria saeculorum Hungariae*, I, 229ff.

_____. "Magyar öntudat és idegenellenesség az Árpádkorban" [Hungarian Ethnic Consciousness and Hatred Toward Foreigners in the Age of the Árpáds], *ItK*, 94 (1990), 425ff.

_____. "Németek és latinok együttes szereplése a magyar krónikákban" [Germans and Latins Mentioned Together in the Hungarian Chronicles], *Acta Historica*, special issue (Szeged, 1991), 19ff.

_____. "Öt pondust fizetök és várhospesek" [Hospes de château et ceux qui payient cinq pondus], *Acta historica Szegediensis*, 92 (1991), 25ff.

_____. "Szempontok az Anonymus Gesta megvilágosításához" [Some Remarks on Anonymus' Gesta], *Acta historica Szegediensis*, 66 (1979), 45ff.

_____. *Szempontok korai helyneveink történeti tipológiájához* [Observations Concerning the Historical Typography of Early Hungarian Place Names] (Szeged, 1976).

Gy. Kristó, ed. *Anjoukori Oklevéltár* [Documents of the Angevin Age in Hungary] (Budapest-Szeged, 1990), vols. 1 and 2.

Gy. Kristó, F. Makk, and L. Szegfü. *Adatok «korai» helyneveink ismeretéhez* [Data Regarding «Early» Hungarian Place Names], 2 vols. (Szeged, 1973-74).

K. Krumbacher, ed. *Geschichte der byzantinischen Literatur*, 2nd ed. (Munich, 1897).

A. Kubinyi. "A mezőgazdaság történetéhez a Mohács előtti Magyarországon" [Hungarian Agricultural History Prior to 1526] - reprint from *Agrártörténeti Szemle*, 1964.

A. Kubinyi. "Burgstadt, Vorburgstadt und Stadtburg: zur Morphologie des mittelalterlichen Buda," *Acta archaeologica Academiae Scientiarum Hungaricae*, 33 (1981), 161ff.

_____. *Die Anfänge Ofens* (Berlin, 1972).

J. Kudora. *A magyar katolikus egyházi beszéd irodalmának története* [History of Catholic Hungarian Sermon Literature] (Budapest, 1902).

Flóris Kühár. "A Pray kódex rendeltetése, sorsa, szellemtörténeti emléke" [The Fate and Purpose, Intellectual Value of the Pray Codex], *MKSz*, 63 (1939), 213ff.

Hans Kühner. *Neues Papstlexion* (Frankfurt-Hamburg: Fischer Bücherei, 1965).

I. Kukuljevic, ed. *Codex diplomaticus Croatiae, Dalmatiae, Slavoniae*, 2 vols. (Zagreb, 1874-75).

Bernát L. Kumorovitz. "A középkori magyar írásbeliség kialakulása" [Development of Hungarian Literacy in the Middle Ages], *Századok*, 123 (1989), 381ff - originally scheduled for publication in 1948!

P. de Labriolle. *Histoire de la litterature latine-chrétienne* (Paris, 1920).

E. Ladányi. "Libera villa, civitas, oppidum; terminologische Fragen des 13 Jahrhunderts," *MIÖG*, 70 (1962).

J. Lampe. "Die Landesgrenze von 1254 und das steierische Ennstal," *Archiv für österreichische Geschichte*, 71 (1887), 297ff.

G. LeBras. "Canon Law," in C.G. Crump and E.F. Jacob, *Legacy of the Middle Ages* (Oxford, 1926; repr. 1951), 321ff.

J. Leclercq. "L'humanisme Bénédictine du VIIIe eu XIIe siècle," *Studia Anselmiana*, 20 (1948), 1ff.

J. Leclercq and H. Rochair, eds. *S. Bernardi opera*, vol. 3 (Rome, 1963).

Emma Lederer. "A tatárjárás Magyarországon és nemzetközi összefüggései" [The Mongol Invasion of Hungary in its International Context], *Századok*, 85 (1952), 327ff.

_____. "A legrégibb magyar iparososztály kialakulása" [Formation of the Oldest Segment of the Hungarian Craftsmen Class], *Századok*, 62 (1928), 494ff.

G. Leff. *Medieval Thought* (Baltimore, 1958).

L.J. Lekai. *The White Monks* (Okauchee, WI, 1953).

J. Lerner. *Italy in the Age of Dante and Petrarch* (London-New York, 1980).

E. Lewalter. "Eschatologie und Weltgeschichte in der Gedankenwelt Augustins," *Zeitschrift für Kirchengeschichte*, 55 (1934), 12ff.

B. Lewis. "The Mongol, the Turks, and Muslim Polity," *Transactions of the Royal Historical Society*, 5th ser., 18 (1968), 49ff.

F.R. Lewis. "Otakar II of Bohemia and the Double Election of 1257," *Speculum*, 12 (1937), 512ff.

Alfons Lhotsky. "Otto von Freising: seine Weltanschauung," in his *Europäisches Mittelalter* (Munich, 1970), 64ff.

_____. *Quellenkunde zur mittelalterlichen Geschichte Österreichs* (Cologne-Graz, 1963).

Hans Liebschütz. "Chartres und Bologna: Naturbegriff und Staatsgedanke bei Johann von Salisbury," *Archiv für Kulturgeschichte*, 50 (1968), 3ff.

_____. *Medieval Humanism in the Life and Writings of John of Salisbury* (London, 1950).

G. Lopez, ed. *La Siete partidas del Sabio Rey don Alfonso el Nono*, 3 vols. (Salamanca, 1555; repr. Madrid, 1974).

R. Lorenz. "Wissenschaftslehre Augustins," *Zeitschrift für Kirchengeschichte*, 67 (1955-56), 29ff. and 213ff.

J. Loserth. "Studien zu Cosmas von Prag: ein Beitrag zur Kritik der altböhmischen Geschichte," *Archiv für österreichische Geschichte*, 61 (1880), 1ff.

_____. *Geschichte des späten Mittelalters*, pt. II of *Handbuch der mittelalterlichen und neuren Geschichte*, ed. G. v. Below and F. Meinecke (Munich-Berlin, 1903).

Elemér Lovass. *Árpádházi Boldog Margit élete* [Life of Blessed Margaret of the House of Árpád] (Budapest, 1939).

Achille Luchaire. *Innocent III: la question l'orient* (Paris, 1907).

_____. *Social France in the Time of Philip Augustus*, ed. and trans. B. Krehbiel (New York, 1912; repr. 1967).

I. Lukinich, ed. *Mátyás király emlékkönyv születésének ötszázéves fordulójára* [Memorial Volume on the 500th Anniversary of the Birth of Matthias Corvinus], 2 vols. (Budapest, n.d. [1940]).

W.E. Lunt. "The Sources of the First Council of Lyons, 1245," *English Historical Review*, 33 (1918), 72ff.

K.E. Lupprian. *Die Beziehungen der Päpste zu islamischen und mongolischen Herrschern im 13 Jahrhundert* (Vatican City, 1981).

Bryce Lyon. *A Constitutional and Legal History of Medieval England* (New York-London, 1960).

C.A. Macartney. *The Medieval Hungarian Historians* (Cambridge, 1953).

M. Maccarone. *Chiesa e stato nella dottrina di Innocenzo III* (Rome, 1940).

T.F. Madden. "Vows and Contracts in the Fourth Crusade: The Treaty of Zara and the Attack on Constantinople in 1204," *International History Review*, 15 (1993), 441ff.

F.W. Maitland. *The Constitutional History of England* (Cambridge, 1911).

MKSz = *Magyar Könyvszemle*.

J. Major. "A magyar városok és városhálózat kialakulásának kezdetei" [Origins of Hungarian Towns and Town Network Formation], *Településtudományi Közlemények*, 18 (1968), 48ff.

Ferenc Makk. *Magyar külpolitika (896-1196)* [Hungarian Foreign Policy, 896-1196] (Szeged, 1993).

_____. *Magyarország a 12 században* [Hungary in the Twelfth Century] (Budapest, 1986).

_____. *The Árpáds and the Comneni* (Budapest, 1989).

_____. "Contributions à l'usage de la bulle d'or de l'époche de Géza II," *Acta historica Szegediensis*, 98 (1993), 29ff.

László Makkai. *A milkói püspökség* [The Milko Bishopric] (Debrecen, 1936).

L. Makkai and L. Mezey, eds. *Árpádkori és Anjoukori levelek, XI-XIV század* [Letters of the Árpád and of the Angevin Ages] (Budapest, 1960).

János Makkay. "Az uráli-finnugor őstörténet néhány kérdése az indóeurópai őstörténet szemszögéből" [Some Questions Concerning Finno-Ugrian Ur-history, Viewed from the Angle of Indo-European Ur-history], *Századok*, 125 (1991), 3ff.

F. Maksay. "Umwaldung der ungarischen Siedlungs- und Agrarstruktur in 11-14 Jahrhundert," *Zeitschrift für Agrargeschichte und Agrarsoziologie*, 23 (1975), 154ff.

Elemér Mályusz. "A magyar köznemesség kialakulása" [Formation of the Hungarian Service Nobility], *Századok*, 76 (1942), 272ff., and 407ff.

_____."A magyarság és a városélet a középkorban [Life in Medieval Hungarian Towns], *Századok*, 78 (1944).

_____. "A Pálosrend a középkor végén" [The Paulist Order at the End of the Middle Ages], *Egyháztörténet*, 3 (1945; published in 1947), 1ff.

_____.*A Thuróczy Krónika és forrásai* [The Thuróczy Chronicle and Its Sources] (Budapest, 1967).

_____. *Az V István kori gesta* [Hungarian Chronicle of the Reign of King Stephen V] (Budapest, 1971).

_____. "Die Entstehung der Stände in Ungarn," *L'organisation corporative du moyen age: Études préséntes a la commission internationale pour l'histoire des assemblées d'Étates* (Paris, 1939), 15ff.

_____. *Egyházi társadalom a középkori Magyarországon* [The Ecclesiastical Stratum in Medieval Hungary] (Budapest, 1971).

_____. "Entwicklung der ständischen Schichten im mittelalterlichen Ungarn," *Études historique hongroises, 1980*, 2 vols. (Budapest, 1980), I, 103ff.

_____. "Geschichte des Bürgertums in Ungarn," *Vierteljahrschrift für Sozial - und Wirtschaftsgeschichte*, 29 (1927-28), 365ff.

_____. *Túrócz megye kialakulása* [History of Túróc County] (Budapest, 1922).

J. Mandel. *József kazár király válaszlevelének hitelessége* [The Authenticity of the Letter of Response by the Khazar King Joseph] (Pécs, 1929).

Peter Manns, ed. *Die Heiligen*, 3rd rev. ed. (Mainz, 1977).

J.D. Mansi, ed. *Sacrorum conciliorum collectio*, 31 vols. (Florence-Venice, 1759-98).

Henrik Marczali, ed. *Enchiridion fontium historiae Hungarorum* (Budapest, 1901) - cited as *Enchiridion*.

H. Marczali. *Ungarns Geschichtsquellen im Zeitalter der Árpáden* (Berlin, 1882).

Maria Maresch, *Elisabeth, Landgräfin von Thüringen* (M. Gladbach, 1918).

G. Markovic. *Gli Slavi ed i Papai*, 2 vols. (Zagreb, 1897).

S.D. Márkus, et al., eds. *Corpus Iuris Hungarici: Magyar Törvénytár*, 10 vols. (Budapest, 1896, etc.), vol. I.

H.I. Marraou. *St. Augustine et la fin de la culture antique* (Paris, 1938).

Matthew of Paris. *Chronica maiora*, 7 vols. R.S. (London, 1872-83).

F.M. Mayer and R. Kaindl. *Geschichte und Kulturleben Österreichs*, 5th rev. ed., ed. H. Pirchegger, vol. I (Vienna, 1958).

H.E. Mayer. *Geschichte der Kreuzzüge*, 3rd rev. ed. (Stuttgart, 1973).

C.H. McIlwain. *The Growth of Political Thought in the West* (New York, 1932).

R. McKitterick, ed. *Carolingians and the Written Word* (Cambridge, 1989).

A.V. Meiller, "Österreichische Städrechte und Satzungen aus der Zeit der Babenberger," *Archiv für österreichischen Geschichtsquellen*, 10 (1853), 87ff.

Károly Mesterházy. "Régészeti adatok Magyarország 10-11 századi kereskedelméhez" [Archaeological Data in Support of Trading Activity in Hungary During the Tenth-Eleventh Centuries], *Századok*, 127 (1993), 450ff.

R.B. Merriman. *The Rise of the Spanish Empire*, vol. 1: *The Middle Ages* (New York, 1918; repr. 1962).

_____. "Cortes of the Spanish Kingdoms in the Later Middle Ages," *American Historical Review*, 16 (1911), 476ff.

László Mezey. *Irodalmi anyanyelvűségünk kezdetei az Árpádkor végén: a középkori női laikus mozgalom eredetkérdése* [Beginnings of Native Hungarian Literature at the End of the Reign of the Árpáds; The Origins of the Medieval Laywomen's Movement] (Budapest, 1955).

L. Mezey. "A Pray kódex keletkezése" [Origins of the Pray Codex], *ItK*, 75 (1971), 109ff.

_____. "Ungarn und Europa im 12 Jahrhundert," *Vorträge und Forschungen*, 12 (1968), 255ff.

L. Mezey, ed. *Athleta patriae; tanulmányok Szent László történetéhez* [Studies in the History of King St. Ladislas] (Budapest, 1980).

MGH Libelli de lite, ed. E. Dümmler, 3 vols. (Hannover, 1891-97) - cited as *LdL*.

MHSM = *Monumenta spectantia historiam Slavorum meriodionalium*.

A. Michnay and P. Lichner. *Ofener Stadrecht* (Pozsony, 1845).

W. Migg. "Heinrich Seuse und Elisabeth Stagel," *Neue Zürcher Zeitung*, January 22, 1966, 20.

J.P. Migne, ed. *Patrologiae cursus completus, series latina*, 221 vols. (Paris, 1844-55) - cited as *MPL*.

J.P. Migne, ed. *Patrologiae cursus completus, series graeca*, 166 vols. (Paris, 1857-66) - cited as *MPG*.

W. Miller. *The Latins in the Levant: A History of Frankish Greece, 1204-1566*. (London, 1908).

MIÖG = *Mitteilungen des Institutes für Österreichische Geschichtsforschung*.

H. Mitteis. *Der Staat des hohen Mittelalters*, 8th ed. (Weimar, 1968).

_____. *Lehnrecht und Staatsgewalt* (1933; repr. Weimar, 1958).

Otto Mittelstrass. *Beiträge zur Siedlungsgeschichte Siebenbürgens im Mittelalter* (Munich, 1961).

Ferenc Mónay. *Római magyar gyóntatók* [Hungarian Confessors at St. Peter's] (Rome, 1956).

Monumenta Erphesfurtensia, saec. XII, XIII, XIV, ed. O. Holder-Egger, SSrG (Hannover-Leipzig, 1899).

Monumenta Germaniae historica, Scriptores, ed. G.H. Pertz, 30 vols. (Hannover, 1854, etc.) - cited as *MGHSS*.

Monumenta spectantia historiam Slavorum meridionalium, ed. Southern Slavic Academy of Sciences, 43 vols. (Zagreb, 1868-1918), vol. XXVI - cited as *MHSM*.

J.C. Moore. "The Sermons of Pope Innocent III," *Römische Historische Mitteilungen*, 36 (1994), 81ff.

Gy. Moravcsik. *Byzantium and the Magyars* (Amsterdam-Budapest, 1970).

_____. "Die archaisierenden Namen der Ungarn in Byzanz," *Byzantinische Zeitschrift*, 30 (1929-30) 247ff.; reprinted in his *Studia Byzantina* (Budapest, 1967), 320ff.

_____. "Pour une alliance byzantino-hongroise (seconde moitié du XIIe siècle), *Byzantion*, 8 (1933), 555ff.

Gy. Moravcsik, ed. *Fontes byzantini historiae Hungaricae aevo dudum et regum ex stirpe Arpad descendentium* (Budapest, 1984).

Gy. Moravcsik, ed. Konstantinos Porphyrogennetos, *De administrando imperio* (Budapest, 1949; new ed., with English translation by R.J.H. Jenkins, London, 1962; rev. ed., Washington, D.C., 1967).

J. Morris. "Venice, The Triumphant City," in W.L. Langer (ed.), *Perspectives in Western Civilization*, 2 vols. (New York-London, 1979), I, 167ff.

G.E. Müller. "Die Ursache der Vertreibung des Deutschen Ordens aus dem Burzenland im Jahre 1225," *Korrespondenzblatt des Vereins für Siebenbürgische Landeskunde* (Hermannstadt, 1925) - xeroxed offprint.

A. Murarik. *Az ősiség alapintézményinek eredete* [Origins of 'aviticitas'] (Budapest, 1938).

L.A. Muratori, ed. *Rerum Italicarum scriptores*, 28 vols. (Milan, 1723-51, and recent reprint) - cited as *RISS*.

W. Näf. "Herrschftsverträge des Spätmittelalters," *Quellen zur neueren Geschichte* (Bern, 1951), 7ff.

Imre Nagy, et al., eds. *Anjoukori Okmánytár: Codex diplomaticus Hungaricus Andegavensis*, 6 vols. (Budapest, 1879-91) - cited as Nagy, *Anjou Okmánytár*.

Imre Nagy, et al., eds. *Hazai Okmánytár* [Collection of Domestic Writs and Documents], 8 vols. (Győr-Budapest, 1865-91) - cited as *HO*.

L. Nagy. "Székesfehérvár középkori topográfiája" [The Medieval Topography of Székesfehérvár], in Kralovánszky, *Székesfehérvár*, II, 199ff.

I.W. Nagl and J. Zeidler, eds. *Deutsch-österreichische Literaturgeschichte*, vol. 1 (Vienna, 1899).

A.N. Nasanov. *Mongol i Rus* (Moscow-Leningrad, 1940).

Gy. Németh. *A honfoglaló magyarság kialakulása* [Formation of the Magyars at the Time of the Conquest], 2nd ed., ed. Árpád Berta (Budapest, 1991).

Emil Niederhauser. "A cseh történetírás történetéből" [Observations on the Formation of Czech Historiography], *Századok*, 127 (1993), 201ff.

J.T. Noonan. "Gratian Slept Here: The Changing Identity of the Father of the Systematic Study of Canon Law," *Traditio*, 35 (1979), 145ff.

W. Norden. *Das Papsttum und Byzanz* (Berlin, 1903; repr. New York, n.d.).

Karl Oberleitner. "Die Stadt Enns im Mittelalter. Ein Beitrag zur Geschichte der deutschen Städte," *Archiv für österreichische Geschichte*, 27 (1861), 1ff.

J. F. O'Callaghan. "The Beginnings of the Cortes of Leon-Castile," *American Historical Review*, 74 (1969), 1503ff.

J.F. O'Callaghan. *A History of Medieval Spain* (Ithaca-London, 1975).

Odofriedus. *Commentary on the Code* (Lyon, 1550).

_____. *Commentary on the Digest* (Lyon, 1550).

Oefele. *Geschichte der Grafen von Andechs* (Innsbruck, 1877).

Martin Ohst. "Elisabeth von Thüringen in ihrem kirchengeschichtlichen Kontext, "*Zeitschrift für Theologie*, 91 (1994), 424ff.

Oliver of Cologne. *Historia Damiatina*, ed. Hermann Hoogweg. Vol. 202 of *Bibilothek des Literarischen Vereins in Stuttgart* (Tübingen, 1894).

F. Orban. *Historia, seu Compendium decretorum provinciae Ordinis Minorum s. P. Francisci* (Kassoviae, 1759).

J.F. O'Sullivan and J.F. Burns. *Medieval Europe* (New York, 1943).

Ottonis episcopi Frisingensis *Chronica sive Historia de duabus civitatibus*, ed. Adolfus Hofmeister, SSrG (Hannover-Leipzig, 1912; repr. 1984).

Ottonis et Rahewini *Gesta Friderici I Imperatoris*, ed. tertia, ed. G. Waitz and B. v. Simson, SSrG (Hannover-Leipzig, 1912; repr. Hannover, 1978).

G.R. Owst. *Preaching in Medieval England* (Cambridge, 1926).

Zs.P. Pach. "Egy évszázados történészvita: áthaladt-e a levantai kereskedelem útja a középkori Magyarországon?" [A Century Old Historical Debate: Did Levantine Trade Move Through Medieval Hungary?] *Századok*, 95 (1972), 849ff.

Zs. Pach. "Levantine Trade and Hungary During the Middle Ages," *Études historiques hongroises*, 1975, ed. D. Nemes, et. al., 2 vols. (Budapest, 1975), I, 283ff.

_____. "A Levante-történetírás fordulata" [Changing Views of the Historiography of Levantine Trade at the Turn of the Century], *Századok*, 127 (1993), 239ff.

S.R. Packard. *Europe and the Church Under Innocent III* (1927; repr. New York, 1986).

Lutz E. von Padberg. "Geschichtsschreibung und kulturelles Gedächtnis: Formen der Vergangenheitswahrnehmung in der hochmittelalterlich Historiographie am Beispiel von Thietmar von Merseburg, Adam von Bremen, und Helmold von Bosau," *Zeitschrift für Kirchengeschichte*, 105 (1994), 156ff.

Sidney Painter. *The Reign of King John* (Baltimore, 1949).

P. Palazzini. *Dizionario dei concili*, 6 vols. (Rome, 1963-68).

F. Palgrave, ed. *Parliamentary Writs*, vol. I (London, 1827).

F. Palacky. *Geschichte von Böhmen*, vols. I and II (Prague, 1844, etc.).

_____. *Würdigung der alten böhmischen Geschichtsschreiber*, rev. ed. (Prague, 1869).

Erwin Panofsky. *Gothic* (Meridian repr., 1985).

Erna Patzelt. *Die fränkische Kultur und der Islam* (Baden-Brünn, 1932).

_____. *Österreich bis zum Ausgang der Babenbergerzeit* (Vienna, 1947).

Pelbárt of Temesvár. *Pomerium de sanctis* (Hagenau, 1499).

Pelbárt of Temesvár. *Pomerium de tempore* (Hagenau, 1498).

_____. *Sermones pomerii de sanctis* (Norimbergae, 1486).

_____. *Stellarium* (Hagenau, 1498).

Jaroslav Pelikan. *The Growth of Medieval Theology, 600-1300* (Chicago-London, 1978).

P. Pelliot. "Les Mongols et la papauté," *Revue de l'Orient chrétien*, 23 (1922), 3ff.; 24 (1924), 225ff.; 28 (1931), 3ff.

_____. "Sung Kien, Jüan si," *Notes sur l'histoire de la Horde d'or* (Paris, 1949).

F. Pelsőczy. "Szent István, pap és király" [St. Stephen, Priest and King], *Vigilia*, 36 (1971), 513ff.

Kenneth Pennington. *Pope and Bishops: The Papal Monarchy in the Twelfth and Thirteenth Centuries* (Philadelphia, 1984).

J. Perényi. "Az orosz évkönyvek magyar vonatkozásai" [Data Concerning Hungary in the Russian Annals], in G. Kemény (ed.), *Tanulmányok a magyar-orosz irodalmi kapcsolatok köréből* [Studies Concerning Hungaro-Russian Literary Contacts] (Budapest, 1961).

G.P. Perfecky, ed. *The Hypathian Codex*, pt. 2: *The Galician-Volhynian Chronicle* (Munich, 1973) - cited as *GVC*.

Max Perlbach. "Der deutsche Orden in Siebenbürgen. Zur Kritik der neuesten polischen Literatur," *MIÖG*, 26 (1905), 415ff.

F. Pesty. *A magyarországi várispánságok története különösen a XIII században* [History of County Stewardships in Hungary Especially During the 13th Century] (Budapest, 1882).

Carolus Péterffy, ed. *Sacra concilia ecclesiae Romano-Catholicae in regno Hungariae celebrata*, 2 vols. (Vienna, 1742).

Ch. Petit-Dutaillis. *Feudal Monarchy in France and England*, trans. E.D. Hunt (London, 1936; repr. New York, 1964).

Ede Petrovich. "A pécsi egyetemi beszédgyüjtemény - a müncheni kódex" [The Literary Collection of the University of Pécs Library - The Munich Codex], *Jubileumi tanulmányok a Pécsi Egyetem történetéből* [Studies on the Jubilee of the University of Pécs], ed. A. Czizmadia, vol. I (Pécs, 1967), 163ff.

H. Pfeiffer. *Die Ungarische Dominikanerprovinz von ihrer Gründung 1221 bis zur Tartarenwüstung 1241-42* (Zurich, 1913).

Jenő Pintér. *A magyar irodalom története* [Synthesis of Hungarian Literature], 8 vols. (Budapest, 1930-41).

Henri Pirenne. *Medieval Cities* (Garden City: Doubleday-Anchor, 1956).

Ambrus Pleidell. "A magyar városfejlődés néhány fejezete" [Chapters on the Development of Town Life in Hungary] I-III, *Századok*, 68 (1934), 1ff., 158ff., and 276ff.

A.L. Poole. *Obligations of Society in the XII and XIII Centuries* (Oxford, 1946).

_____. *From Domesday Book to Magna Carta*, 2nd ed. (Oxford, 1955).

A. Potthast. *Bibliotheca historica medii aevi*, rev. ed., 2 vols. (Berlin, 1896).

_____. *Regesta pontificum Romanorum*, 2 vols. (Berlin, 1875).

J.M. Powell. *Anatomy of a Crusade, 1213-21* (Philadelphia, 1986).

E. Power. "The Opening of the Land Routes to Cathay," *Travel and Travellers of the Middle Ages*, ed. A.P. Newton (New York, 1926).

Georgius Pray. *Annales regum Hungariae ab anno 997 usque ad 1614 deductae*, 5 vols. (Vienna, 1764-79).

_____. *Dissertatio de sancto Ladislao rege Hungariae* (Posonii, 1774).

_____. *Vita s. Elisabeth viduae necnon b. Margarithae virginis* (Tyrnaviae, 1780).

F.K. Prümm. *Religiongeschichtliches für den Raum der altchristlichen Welt* (Rome, 1954).

Mária Püskely. *Árpádházi Szent Erzsébet* [St. Elizabeth of the House of Árpád] (Rome, 1981).

H.E. Queller. *The Fourth Crusade* (Philadelphia, 1977).

RA = Szentpétery, *Regesta regum stirpis Arpadianae.*

F.J.E. Raby. *A History of Christian Latin Poetry*, 2nd ed. (Oxford, 1953).

_____. *A History of Secular Latin Poetry*, 2nd ed., 2 vols. (Oxford, 1957).

Polycarp Radó. *Libri liturgici manu scripti bibliothaecarum Hungariae* (Budapest, 1947).

M.C. Rady. *Medieval Buda: A Study in Municipal Government and Jurisdiction in the Kingdom of Hungary*, vol. 182 of *East European Monographs* (New York, 1985).

I. Rákos. "IV Béla birtokrestaurációs politikája" [King Béla IV's Policy of Property Reconstruction], *Acta historica Szegediensis*, 47 (1974), 3ff.

E.K. Rand. "On the Composition of Boethius' *Consolatio philosophiae*," *Harvard Studies in Classical Philosophy*, 15 (1904), 1ff.

P. Ransanus. *Epithoma rerum Hungarorum* [the last book of his *Annales temporum omnium*], ed. P. Kulcsár (Budapest, 1977).

_____. "Vita b. Margarithae Hungaricae," *ASS*, Ian. II, 900ff.

RASS = *Rerum Austricarum Scriptores*.

Paul Ratchnevsky. *Genghis Khan: His Life and Legacy*, trans. and ed. Th. N. Haining (London, 1991).

A. Rauch, ed. *Rerum Austricarum scriptores*, 3 vols. (Vienna, 1793-94) - cited as *RASS*.

Ordericus Raynaldus. *Annales ecclesiastici*, 15 vols. (Lucca, 1738-56).

Regionis abbatis Prumensis *Chronicon*, ed. F. Kurze, SSrG (Hannover, 1890).

E. Reiszig. *A jeruzsálemi Szent János Lovagrend Magyarországon* [The Knight of St. John in Hungary], 2 vols. (Budapest, 1925-26).

D.R. Resnick. *Preaching in Medieval Florence* (Athens, GA, 1989).

Mihály Révész. "Andras Pannonius és Borino de Scala," *EPhK*, 59 (1935), 5ff.

H.G. Richardson. "The Coronation in Medieval England: The Evolution of the Office and the Oath," *Traditio*, 16 (1960), 111ff.

O. Riezler. "Der Kreuzzug Kaiser Friedrichs I," *Forschungen zur deutschen Geschichte*, 10 (1870), 1ff.

RISS = Muratori, *Rerum Italicarum Scriptores*.

Burkhard Roberg. "Der Konzilversuch von 1241," *Annuarium historiae conciliorum*, 24 (1992), 286ff.

C.H. Roberts. "The Codex," *Proceedings of the British Academy*, 40 (1954), 169ff.

W.W. Rockhill, ed. *The Journey of William Robruck to the Eastern Part of the World*, 1253-55, with two accounts of the earlier journeys of Plano Carpini (Hakulyt Society, 1910; repr. Lichtenstein, 1967).

C. Rodenberg. "Städegründungen Heinrichs I," *MIÖG*, 17 (1896), 161ff.

R. Röhricht. "Der Kreuzzug Königs Andreas II von Ungarn," *Forschungen zur deutschen Geschichte*, 16 (1876), 139ff.

_____. *Studien zur Geschichte des Fünften Kreuzzuges* (Innsbruck, 1891).

H. Röscher. *Papst Innocenz III und die Kreuzzüge* (Göttingen, 1969).

Norman Roth. "Bishops and Jews in the Middle Ages," *Catholic Historical Review*, 80 (1994), 1ff.

Márta Rozsondai. "Temesvári Pelbárt népszerűsége Európában: miről vallanak a könyvkötések?" [Do Bindings of His Works Bear Witness to the European Popularity of Pelbárt of Temesvár?], *MKSz*, 100 (1984), 300ff.

Rubruque's travel report, in Wyngaert, *Itinera*, I, 164ff.

Iohannes Saresberiensis. *Policraticus, sive de nubis curialem et vestigiis philosophorum*, libri octo, ed. C.C.I. Webb, 2 vols. (Oxford, 1909).

J.J. Saunders. "Matthew of Paris and the Mongols," in *Essays in Medieval History Presented to Bertie Wilkinson*, ed. A. Sanquist and M.R. Powicke (Toronto, 1969), 116ff.

J. v. Sawicki. "Zur Textkritik und Entstehungsgeschichte der Gesetze König Stephan des Heiligen," *Ungarische Jahrbücher*, 9 (1929), 395ff.

G.O. Sayles. *The King's Parliament of England* (New York, 1974).

_____. *The Medieval Foundations of England*, rev. repr. (London, 1966).

H.C. Scheeben. *Der hl. Dominikus* (Freiburg, 1927).

W. Scheck. *Geschichte Russlands*, rev. ed. (Munich, 1977).

Felix Schiller. "Das erste ungarische Gesetzbuch und das deutsche Recht," *Festschrift Heinrich Brunner* (Weimar, 1910), 379ff.

P.E. Schramm. *Kaiser, Rom und Renovatio*, 3rd rev. ed. (Darmstadt, 1962).

K. Schünemann. *Die Entstehung der Städtewesen in Südosteuropa* (Bresslau, 1929).

Antal Schütz, ed. *Szentek élete az év minden napjára* [Lives of the Saints for Every Day of the Year], 4 vols. (Budapest, 1932-34).

Ödön Schütz. "A mongol hódítás néhány problémája" [Some Questions Concerning the Mongol Conquest], *Századok*, 93 (1959), 209ff.

J. Schütze. "Bemerkungen zur Berufung und Vertreibung des deutschen Ordens durch Andreas II von Ungarn," *Siebenbürgisches Archiv*, 3rd ser. 8 (Cologne-Vienna, 1971) (offprint).

J.G. Schwandtner, ed. *Scriptores rerum Hungaricarum veteres ac genuini*, 3 vols. (Vienna, 1746-48).

Sedulus Scotus. *De rectoribus Christianis*, ed. S. Hellman (Munich, 1906).

Scriptores rerum Prussicarum: die Geschichtsquellen der Preuss-ischen Vorzeit bis zum Untergang der Ordengesellschaft ed. Th. Hirsch, M. Töppen, and E. Strehlke, 5 vols. (Leipzig, 1861-74).

E. Sebestyén. *A magyar királyok tartózkodási helyei* [Places of Residence of Hungarian Monarchs] (Budapest, 1938).

H.D. Sedwick. *Italy in the Thirteenth Century*, vol. 1 (Boston-New York, 1912).

Toru Senga. "Adalékok az 1236-évi magyar-osztrák kapcsolat történetéhez" [Data on the Hungaro-Austrian Relationship in 1236], *Acta historica Szegediensis*, 90 (1990), 63ff.

_____. "IV Béla külpolitikája és IV Ince pápához intézett 'tatár' levele" [The Foreign Policy of Béla IV and his "Mongol" Letter to the Pope], *Századok*, 121 (1987), 584ff.

F.X. Seppelt. *Geschichte des Päpste*, 5 vols. (Munich, 1949-57).

Siculus [sic!]. "A székelyek eredetéhez" [In Search of the Széklers], *Emlékkönyv a Székely Múzeum 50 éves jubileumára* [Memorial Volume on the 50th Anniversary of the Székler Museum], ed. V. Csutak (Sepsiszentgyörgy, 1929; repr. Budapest, 1988).

I. Sinka. *Magyaroszág árpádkori fő- és székvárosa* [Hungary's Capital City During the Árpád Age] (Szeged, 1936).

D. Sinor. "John of Monte Corvino's Return from the Mongols," repr. from *The Journal of the Royal Asiatic Society*, 1957.

_____. "The Mongols in Western Europe," in R.J. Wolf and H.W. Hazard (eds.), *The Later Crusades*, vol. III of *History of the Crusades*, ed. J.R. Strayer (Philadelphia, 1962, etc.), 513ff.

P. Simon. *Aurelius Augustinus: sein geistliches Profil* (Paderborn, 1954).

P.V. Simon. "A Niebelungének magyar vonatkozásai" [The Lay of Niebelung and its Hungarian Features], *Századok*, 112 (1978), 271ff.

H. Simonsfeld. *Jahrbücher des deutschen Reiches unter Friedrich I* (Leipzig, 1908).

Beryl Smalley, ed. *Trends in Medieval Thought* (Oxford, 1965).

T. Smiciklas, ed. *Codex diplomaticus regni Croatiae, Dalmatiae et Sloveniae*, vols. VI, VII, and XV (Zagreb, 1909, 1934) - cited as Smiciklas.

Zoltán Soltész (Mdme.). "Milyen tervekkel és felszereléssel jöhetett Budára Hess András?" [What Were the Plans, What Was the Equipment of Andreas Hess Arriving in Buda?] *MKSz*, 90 (1974), 1ff.

László Solymosi. "Árpád-kori okleveleink grafikus szimbólumai" [Graphic Symbols of Hungarian Documents in the Árpád Age], *Aetas*, 1991/3-4, 14ff.

_____. "Egyházi és világi (földesúri) mortuárium a 11-14 századi Magyarországon" [The Mortuaries of Spiritual and Secular (Land)lords in Eleventh-Fourteenth Century Hungary], *Századok*, 121 (1987), 547ff.

A. Somogyi. "La stuarotheque byzantine d'Esztergom," *Balkan Studies*, 9 (1968), 139ff.

Ferenc Somogyi. "The Constitutional Guarantee of 1351: The Decree of Louis the Great," in S.B. Vardy, et al. (eds.), *Louis the Great, King of Hungary and Poland* (New York, 1986), 429ff.

_____. *Küldetés: a magyarság története* [Destiny: A History of the Hungarians], 2nd rev. ed. (Cleveland, OH, 1978).

G. Soranzo. *Il papato, l'Europa cristiana e i tartari: un secolo dei penetrazione occidentale in Asia* (Milan, 1930).

P. Sörös, "Uriás pannonhalmi főapát levelei a tatárjárás idejéből" [The Correspondence of Abbot Urias of Pannonhalma During the Mongol Invasion], *A pannonhalmi főapátsági Főiskola Évkönyve az 1916/17-i tanévre* (Pannonhalma, 1917).

Thomas Spaleto. *Historia Salonitarum*, in Schwandtner, III, 532ff., and in *MHSM*, XXVI, 93ff.; and/or in *MGHSS*, XXIX, 570ff.

J. Spörl. "Das mittelalterliche Geschichtsdenken als Forschungsaufgabe," *HJb*, 53 (1933), 281ff.

B. Spuler. "Die Aussenpolitik der Goldenen Horde," *Jahrbücher für die Geschichte Osteuropas*, 5 (1940), 1ff.

B. Spuler. *Die Goldene Horde: die Mongolen in Russland, 1223-1502*, 2nd ed. (Wiesbaden, 1965).

_____. *Die Mongolen in Iran: Politik, Verwaltung und Kultur der Ilchanzeit, 1220-1350*, 3rd ed. (Berlin, 1968).

Peter Spufford. *Money and Its Use in Medieval Europe* (Cambridge, 1988).

SSH = Szentpétery, *Scriptores rerum Hungaricarum.*

V. Stagemann. *Augustins Gottesstaat* (Tübingen, 1928).

F. Stegmüller. *Repertorium biblicum medii aevi*, 4 vols. (Madrid, 1950).

Edith Stein. "Életalakítás Szent Erzsébet szellemében" [Life Formation in the Spirit of St. Elizabeth], *Szolgálat*, 32 (Munich, 1976), 41ff.

H.F. Steward and E.K. Rand, eds. *Consolatio philosophiae* and *Ouscula sacra* (London: Loeb Classics, 1918).

G. Stiassni. "Anonymi clerici Chronicon rythmicum: ein Beitrag zur Historiographie des XIII Jahrhunderts," doctoral dissertation (Vienna, 1955).

G. Stöckl. "Kanzler und Metropolit," *Wiener Archiv für Geschichte des Slawentums und Osteuropas*, 5 (1966), 163ff.

B. Stoll. *A magyar irodalomtörténet bibliográfiája* [Bibliography of Hungarian Literature] (Budapest, 1972).

K. Storck. *Deutsche Literaturgeschichte*, 10th rev. ed., ed. M. Rockenbach (Stuttgart, 1926).

G. Strakosch-Grassman. *Der Einfall der Mongolen in Mitteleuropa in den Jahren 1241 und 1242* (Innsbruck, 1893).

J.R. Strayer. "Feudalism in Western Europe," in *Feudalism in History*, ed. R. Coulborn (Princeton, 1956).

H. Svrita [J. Zurita]. *Indices rerum ab Aragonie regibus gestarum*, vol. I (Caesaroaugustae, 1578).

J.R. Sweeney. "Hungary in the Crusades, 1169-1218," *International History Review*, 3 (1981), 467ff.

F. von Sybel. "Über den zweiten Kreuzzug," *Zeitschrift für Geschichtswissen*, 4 (1845), 197ff.

Károly Szabó. "III Endre fogsága" [The Captivity of Andrew III], repr. from *Századok*,1884, 97ff.

_____. *Kún László* [King Ladislas the Cuman] (Budapest, 1886; repr. 1988).

_____. *Régi magyar könyvtár* [Library of Old Hungarian Publications], 3 vols. in 4 (Budapest, 1879-98).

K. Szabó and L. Szádeczky, eds. *Székely Oklevéltár* [Archives of Székler History], 3 vols. (Kolozsvár, 1872-98).

P. Szalóczi. "Temesvári Pelbárt," *Vigilia*, 14 (1949), 721ff.

A. Szilády. *Temesvári Pelbárt élete és munkái* [Life and Works of Pelbárt of Temesvár] (Budapest, 1880).

Loránd Szilágyi. "Az Anonymus-kutatás újabb erdeméneyi és problémái" [The Latest Problems and Results of Research Concerning the Identity of the Hungarian Anonymus], *Századok*, 123 (1989), 273ff. - scheduled for publication in 1948!

László Szegfü. "Gellért püspök halála" [The Death of Bishop Gerard of Csanád], *Acta historica Szegediensis*, 66 (1979), 19ff.

László Szegfü. "La missione politica ed ideologica di san-Gerardo in Ungheria," in Leo S. Olschki (ed.), *Venezia e Ungheria nel rinascimento* (Florence, 1973), 23ff.

Gy. Székely. "A polgári rend előzményeihez: a városi elit a 12-13 századi Európában" [Formation of the «Middle Class»: The Town Elite in Europe During the High Middle Ages], *Századok*, 126 (1992), 517ff.

_____. "Egy elfeljtett rettegés: a második tatárdúlás a magyar történei hagyományokban és egyetemes összefüggésekben" [A Forgotten Threat: The Second Mongol Invasion in Hungarian Historical Tradition and in its Universal Context], *Századok*, 122 (1988), 52ff.

Gy. Székely, ed. *Magyarország története: előzmények és magyar történet 1242-ig* [History of Hungary: Prehistory and Early History to 1242] (Budapest, 1984).

I. Szekfű. «*De servientibus et familiaribus,*» *Dissertationes hist. Academiae Scientarium Hungaricae*, XXIII-3 (Budapest, 1912), 5ff.

Szent István Emlékkönyv [Memorial Volume on the 900th Anniversary of the Death of King St. Stephen], ed. Jusztinián Serédi, 3 vols. (Budapest, 1938). One volume selective reprint, ed. J. Török (Budapest, 1988).

A. Szentirmai. "Die ungarische Diözesansynod im Spätmittelalter," *Zeitschrift der Savigny Stiftung für Rechtsgeschichte*, kan. Abt., 47 (1961), 266ff.

R. Szentivány. *Catalogus concinnus librorum manuscriptorum Bibliothecae Batthyanyianae Albae in Transylvania* (Szeged, 1958).

Emericus Szentpétery, ed. *Scriptores rerum Hungaricum*, 2 vols. (Budapest, 1937-38) - cited as *SSH*.

E. Szentpétery and I. Borsa, eds. *Regesta regum stirpis Arpadianae critico-diplomatica*, 2 vols. (Budapest, 1923-87), cited as *RA*.

F. Szinnyei. *Magyar írók élete és munkái* [Lives and Works of Hungarian Authors], 14 vols. (Budapest, 1891-1914).

Kornél Szlovák. "Wer war der Anonyme Notar? Zur Bestimmung des Verfassers der Gesta Ungarorum," *Ungarn Jahrbuch*, 19 (1991), 1ff.

Jenő Szűcs. "Az 1267-évi Decretum és háttere" [The Law of 1267 and its (Socio-Political) Background], *Mályusz Elemér emlékkönyv* [Studies in Honor of Elemér Mályusz], ed. É.H. Balázs (Budapest, 1984), 341ff.

_____. "Kézai problémák" [Questions Concerning the Work of Kéza], *Memoria saeculorum Hungariae*, I, 187ff.

_____. *Nation und Geschichte: Studien* (Vienna, 1981).

_____. "Nationalität und Nationalbewusstsein im Mittelalter," *Acta historica Academiae Scientiarum Hungaricae*, 18 (1972), 1ff., and 245ff.

Jenő Szűcs. "Theoretische Elemente in Meister Simon de Kezas Gesta Ungarorum," in his *Nation und Geschichte: Studien* (Vienna, 1981), 263ff.

H. Szvorényi. *Synopsis critico-historica decretorum pro Ecclesia Hungariae Catholica editorum* (Vesprimi, 1807).

G.L.F. Tafel and G.M. Thomas, eds. *Urkunden zur älteren Handelsgeschichte der Republik Venedig*, 2 vols. (Vienna, 1856), vol. 1.

M.M. Takács. *A budavári Mátyás templom* [The Matthias Church in Buda] (Budapest, 1940).

Olga R. Takács. "Róma ellenállhatatlan: vonások két századvégi paptudós portréjához [The Irresistible Eternal City: Some Remarks to the Portrait of Two Clerical Scholars - Vilmos Fraknói, 1843-1924, and Arnold Ipolyi, 1823-86], *Vigilia*, 57 (1992), 437ff.

N.P. Tanner, ed. *Decrees of the Ecumenical Councils*, 2 vols. (London-Washington, 1990).

Andor Tarnai. "A Képes Krónika forrásaihoz" [Some Remarks on the Sources of the Chronicle], *Memoria Hungariae*, I, 203ff.

_____. "A magyar nyelvet írni kezdék" [The Began to Write in Hungarian], *Irodalmi gondolkodás Magyarországon* [Literary Thinking in Medieval Hungary] (Budapest, 1984), 103ff.

M. von Taube, "Russische-liauische Fürsten an der Düna zur Zeit der deutschen Eroberung Livlands," *Jahrbücher für Kultur und Geschichte der Slawen*, n.s. 11 (1935), 367ff.

A.L. Tautu, ed. *Acta Honorii papae III et Gregorii IX (1216-27, 1227-41)* (Rome, 1950).

G. Templeman. "The Historiography of Parliament to 1400 in the Light of Recent Research," *University of Birmingham Historical Journal*, 1 (1948), 203ff.

F. Teutsch. *Geschichte der Siebenbürger Sachsen für das Sächsische Volk* (Hermannstadt, 1907).

G.D. Teutsch and F. Firnhaber, eds. *Urkundenbuch zur Geschichte Siebenbürgens*, in *FRA: Österreichische Geschichtsquellen*, Abt. 2, vol. XV (Vienna, 1857).

August Theiner, ed. *Vetera monumenta historiam Hungariae sacram illustrantia*, 2 vols. (Rome, 1859-60) - cited as *VMH*.

August Theiner, ed. *Vetera monumenta Slavorum meridionalium historica*, vol. 1 (Rome, 1863) - cited as *VMSH*.

Tivadar Thienemann. "Temesvári Pelbárt német kortársai" [German Contemporaries of Pelbárt of Temesvár], *EPhK*, 44 (1920), 73ff.

Thomas Aquinas' *Summa Theologiae*, ed. Petrus Caramello, 4 vols. (Turin-Rome, 1950-54).

Thomas Aquinas' *Commentarius in IV Libros Sententiarum Petri Lombardi*, in M.F. Moos (ed.), *Scriptum super Sententiis Magistri P. Lombardi*, 4 vols. (Paris, 1947).

Th. Thomsen, ed. Jordanis *Romana et Gotica*, in *MGHSS Auctores antiquissimi*, vol. 1 (Berlin, 1882).

S.E. Thorn. "What Magna Carta Was," in E.N. Griswold (ed.), *The Great Charter*, (New York-Toronto: Mentor Books, 1965), 11ff.

Helene Tillmann. *Papst Innocenz III* (Bonn, 1954).

K. Tímár. "Laskai Osvát és a bibliográfia" [Some Questions Concerning the Bibliography of Oswald Laska], *MKSz*, 18 (1910), 122ff.

Imre Timkó. *Keleti kereszténység, keleti egyházak* [Eastern Christianity - Eastern Churches] (Budapest, 1972).

Ákos v. Timon. *Ungarische Verfassungs- und Rechtsgeschichte*, trans. Felix Schiller, 2nd ed. (Berlin, 1904).

Johannes de Thurócz. *Chronica Hungarorum*, ed. E. Galánta and J. Kristó (Budapest, 1985).

J.B. Tkalcic, ed. *Monumenta historica liberae regiae civitatis Zagrabiae metropolis regni Dalmatiae, Croatiae et Slavoniae*, vol. 1 (Zagreb, 1889) - cited as *Monument Zagrabiae*.

J.B. Tkalcic, ed. *Monumenta historica episcopatus Zagrabiensis saec. XII-XIII*, 2 vols. (Zagreb, 1873-74) - cited as *Mon. ep. Zagr.*

F. Toldy, ed. *Chronicon Hungarorum Posoniense* (Budae, 1852).

Ferenc Toldy. *A magyar nemzeti irodalom története* [History of Hungarian National Literature], his published lecture notes, 4th ed. (Budapest, 1878).

_____. *Magyar szentek legendái a carthausi névtelentöl* [Lives of Hungarian Saints by the Anonymous Carthusian] (Pest, 1859).

S.L. Tóth. "A kabarok (kavarok) 9 századi magyar törzsszövetségben" [The Kabars's Position in the Hungarian [Magyar] Tribal Structure of the Ninth Century], *Századok*, 118 (1984), 92ff.

_____. *A 9 századi magyar törzsszövetség szervezete és kapcsolatai (838-96)* [Organizational Structure of the Magyar Tribal Association in the Ninth Century] - in typescript; publication forthcoming.

S.L. Tóth. "A «Liuntika» rejtély" [The «Liuntika» Mystery], *Magyar Nyelv*, 90 (1994), 168ff.

S.N. Troianos. "Die Wirkungsgeschichte der Trullaneuem (Quinisextum) in der byzantinischen Gestzgebung," *Annuarium historiae conciliorum*, 24 (1992), 95ff.

M. Tumler. *Der deutsche Orden im Westen, Wachsen und Wirken bis 1400, mit einer Abriss der Geschichte des Ordens von 1400 bis zur neuesten Zeit* (Vienna, 1954).

A. Turchányi. *Rogerius mester Siralmas Éneke a tatárjárásról* [Master Rogerius' *Carmen miserabile* on the Mongol Invasion] (Budapest, 1903).

Joseph Turmel. "Immaculate Conception," *Encyclopaedia for Religion and Ethics*, ed. James Hastings, 13 vols. (1908-26; repr. New York, 1961), VII, cols. 165ff.

Gábor Tüskés and Éva Knapp. "Europäische Verbindungen der mittelalterliche Heiligenverehrung in Ungarn," *Analecta Bollandiana*, 110 (1992), 31ff.

F. Überweg and B. Geyer. *Die patristische und scholastische Philosophie*, 11th ed. (Berlin, 1928).

I. Udvari. "Antal Hodinka - Forscher der ruthenischer Geschichte," *Studia Slavica Savariensia*, 2 (1992), 66ff.

Burchardi Urspergensis. *Chronicon*, ed. O. Holder-Egger and R. v. Simpson, SSrG (Hannover, 1916).

A. Vacant, ed. *Dictionnaire de théologie catholique*, 15 vols. (Paris, 1903-50).

Peter Váczy. *A középkor története* [History of the Middle Ages], vol. 2 of Bálint Hóman, et al. (eds.), *Egyetemes történet* [Universal History], 4 vols. (Budapest, 1935-37).

Peter Váczy. "A város az ókor és a középkor fordulóján" [Towns at the Threshold of the Middle Ages], in L. Dávid, et al. (eds.), Győr várostörténeti tanulmányok [Studies in the History of the Town of Győr] (Győr, 1971) - offprint.

_____. "Anonymus és kora" [The Hungarian Anonymus and his Age], Memoria Hungariae, I, 13ff.

Peter v. Váczy. Die erste Epoche des ungarischen Königtums (Pécs, 1935).

T.C. VanCleve. "The Fifth Crusade," in R.L. Wolf and H.W. Hazard (eds.), The Later Crusades, 1189-1311, vol. 2 of K.S. Setton (ed.), A History of the Crusades, 4 vols., 2nd ed. (Madison, WI, 1969, etc.).

_____. The Emperor Frederick II of Hohenstaufen (Oxford, 1972).

Anastasius van der Wyngaert, ed. Itinera et relationes Fratrum Minorum saeculi XII-XIV, vol. I of Sinica Franciscana (Quaracci-Florence, 1929).

Imre Várady. Docenti e scolari ungheresi nell'antico studio bolognese (Bologna, 1951).

_____. La letteratura italiana e la sua influenza in Ungheria (Rome 1934).

A.A. Vasiliev. History of the Byzantine State (Madison, WI, 1952).

E. Veress. Olasz egyetemeken járt magyarországi tanulók anyakönyve és iratai, 1221-1864 [Matriculation Entries of Students from Hungary in Italian Universities, 1221-1864] (Budapest, 1941).

G. Vernadsky. The Mongols and Russia (New Haven, CT, 1953).

M.H. Vicaire. Saint Dominic and his Times, trans. K. Pound (New York-London, 1964).

Iohannis Victoriensis. *Libri certarum historiarum*, ed. F. Schneider, SSrG (Hannover-Leipzig, 1909).

Jean de Villehardoin. *La conquête de Constantinople*, ed. Edmund Faral, 2 vols. (Paris, 1938-39).

Jacob de Vitry's "Epistolae," ed. R. Röhricht, in *Zeitschrift für Kirchengeschichte*, 15 (1895).

András Vízkelety. *«Világ világa, virágnak virágja...» (Ó-magyar siralom)* [«Light of Light, Flower of Flower...» Planctus: An Old Hungarian Marian Poem] (Budapest, 1986).

Andreas Vízkelety. "Die altungarische Marienklage und die mit ihr überlieferten Texte," *Acta litteraria*, 1986, 3ff., offprint.

G. Voigt. *Die Wiedebelebung des klassischen Altertums*, 2 vols., 2nd ed. (Berlin, 1880-81).

VMH = Theiner, *Monumenta Vaticana historiam Hungaricam illustrantia*.

György Volf, ed. *Nyelvemléktár: régi magyar kódexek és nyomtatványok* [Linguistic Remains in Old Hungarian Codices and Books], 15 vols. (Budapest, 1874-1908).

Lucas Wadding. *Annales Minorum seu trium Ordinum a s. Francisco institutorum*, 17 vols. (Quaracci, 1931-35).

Lucas Wadding, ed. *Scriptores Ordinis Minorum* (Rome, 1906).

J. Waldapfel. "A krakkói egyetem és a magyar-lengyel szellemi élet a renaissance korban" [The Influence of the University of Cracow upon Hungaro-Polish Intellectual Relations in the Renaissance], *EPhK*, 69 (1946), 26ff.

L. Waldmüller. *Die Synoden in Dalmatien, Kroatien und Ungarn von der Völkerwanderung bis zum Ende der Árpáden,* in *Konziliengeschichte,* ed. W. Brandmüller, Reihe A: *Darstellungen* (Paderborn, 1987).

Daniel Waley. *The Italian City Republics* (New York-Toronto, 1969).

_____. *The Papal State in the Thirteenth Century* (London, 1961).

J.J. Walsh. *The Thirteenth: Greatest of Centuries,* 5th ed. (New York, 1913).

W. Wattenbach. *Deutschlands Geschichtsquellen im Mittelalter,* 2 vols., 6th ed. (Berlin, 1893-94).

_____. "Ein Fragment über die Tartaren," *Archiv für österreichische Geschichte,* 42 (1870), 519ff.

F.X. Wegele. "Die hl. Elisabeth," *HZ,* 5 (1861), 351ff.

K. Wenck. "Die hl. Elisabeth v. Thüringen," *HZ,* 69 (1892), 209ff.

G. Wenczel. "Buda regeszták" [The Registers of Buda], *TörténelmiTár,* 1 (1855), 83f.

G. Wenczel, ed. *Anjoukori diplomáciai emlékek* [Diplomatic Correspondence of the Anjou Age], 3 vols. (Budapest, 1874-76) - cited as Wenczel, *Anjoukori diplomácia.*

G. Wenczel, ed. *Árpádkori új Okmánytár* [New Document Collection of the Árpádian Age], 12 vols. (Pest, 1860-74) - cited as *ÁUO.*

G. Wenczel, ed. *Magyar diplomáciai emlékek* [Documents Pertinent to Hungarian Diplomacy], 3 vols. (Budapest, 1872-76).

Stephanus Werbőczy. *Tripartitum opus iuris consuetudinarii incliti regni Hungariae*, anno 1517, in S. Kolozsváry and K. Óvári (eds.), *Werbőczy István Hármaskönyve* (Budapest, 1892).

Mór Werthner. *Az Árpádok családi története* [Family History of the Árpáds] (Nagybecskerek, 1892).

J.T. Welter. *L'exemplum dans la littérature et didactique de moyen age* (Paris-Toulouse, 1927).

Helene Wierunowski. *Vom Imperium zum nationalen Königtum* (Munich-Berlin, 1930).

P. Wilpert. *Judentum im Mittelalter* (Berlin, 1966).

W. Wislocki, ed. *Acta rectoralis Universitatis Cracoviensis* (Cracow, 1893).

R.L. Wolff. "The Second Bulgarian Empire to 1204," *Speculum*, 24 (1949), 167ff.

Heinrich Wölfflin. *Classic Art*, trans. Peter and Linda Murray, 5th ed. (London: Phaidon Books, 1994).

Th. Wright, ed. Gualteri Mapes, *De nugis curialium* distinctiones V (London, 1850).

Franz Zagiba. *Die altbayerische Kirchenprovinz Salzburg und die hll. Slawenlehrer Cyrill und Method* (Salzburg, 1963).

M. Zákonyi. "A Buda melletti szent Lőrinc pálos kolostor története" [History of the Paulist Abbey near Buda], *Századok*, 45 (1911), 686ff., and 764ff.

M. Zalán. "Árpádkori magyar vonatkozású kéziratok az osztrák könyvtárak kézirattáraiban" [Hungarian-related Manuscripts of the Árpád Age in the Austrian Libraries], *Pannonhalmi Szemle*, 1 (1926), 46ff.

Antoine Zawart. "The History of Franciscan Preaching and Franciscan Preachers," *Franciscan Studies*, old ser., 7 (1928), 241ff., esp. 333ff.

Levente Závodszky, ed. *A Szent István, Szent László és Kálmán korabeli törvények és zsinati határozatok forrásai* [Sources of the Legal Enactments and Synodical Acts During the Reigns of Kings St. Stephen, St. Ladislas, and Coloman] (Budapest, 1904).

H. Zeissberg. "Über das Rechtsverfahren Rudolfs von Habsburg gegen Ottokar von Böhmen," *Archiv für österreichische Geschichte*, 66 (1885), 1ff., and 69 (1867), 1ff.

_____. "Vincentius Kadlubek, Bischof von Krakau, 1208-18, +1223," (Bishop Kadlubek had died in 1223!) *Archiv für österreichische Geschichte*, 42 (1870), 1ff.

F. Zimmermann, C. Werner, and G. Müller, eds. *Urkundenbuch zur Geschichte der Deutschen in Siebenbürgen*, 3 vols. (Hermannstadt, 1892-1902).

K. Zimmert. "Der deutsch-byzantinische Konflikt von Juli 1189 bis Februar 1190," *Byzantinische Zeitschrift*, 12 (1902), 1ff., and 13 (1903), 42ff.

Erich Zöllner. *Geschichte Österreichs*, 4th ed. (Munich, 1970).

G. Zolnai. *Nyvelvemlékeink a könyvnyomtatás koráig* [Hungarian Linguistic Remains Prior to the Age of Printing] (Budapest, 1894).

László Zolnai. *Ünnep és hétköznap a középkori Budán* [Holydays and Weekdays in Medieval Buda], 2nd ed. (Budapest, 1975).

Irén Zoltvány. "A magyarországi bencés irodalom a tatárjárás előtt" [Benedictine Literature in Hungary Prior to the Mongol Invasion], in Erdélyi, *Rendtörténet*, I, 337ff.

Attila Zsoldos. "A várjobbágyi birtokolás megitélésének változásai a tatárjárást követő másfél évszázadban" [Variations of Judgments Handed Down on Inheritance Rights of the *iobagio castri* During the Thirteenth and Major Part of the Fourteenth Centuries], *Aetas*, 1990/3, 5ff.

Rózsa Zsótér. "Megjegyzések IV László itinerariumához" [Some Remarks on the Itinerary of King Ladislas IV], *Acta historica Szegediensis*, 92 (1991), 37ff.

INDEX

Adalbert of Csanád, Paulist and poet-humanist, 410, 420 n. 9.

Adrianum, 1224, Andrew II's charter for German settlers in Transylvania, 95-96, 101 nn. 16, 18-22, who were free to elect their own officials and were regarded as free landholders, 101 n. 21.

Aegidius, papal legate sent to Hungary, 103.

Andrew II, his early reign, 38-52; Innocent III to Andrew II in 1205, 38, 53 nn. 1-3; his coronation and the new coronation oath, 38, 39, 53 nn. 4, 8-10, 13, 16; his land (or, office) grant policy, 39, 40, 54 nn. 27-30; his grant of the Barca region to, and his relations with the German Knights, 40, 54 nn. 24-26; Queen Gertrud and her brother Berthold, 41, 54 nn. 34-36; Berthold to become archbishop of Kalocsa, Innocent III protests, 41, 54 nn. 36-40; Andrew II promotes Berthold to *ban[us]* and Grand Reeve, 42, 55 nn. 45-47; son Béla born, 40; Béla crowned "Junior King," 49; sends daughter Elizabeth to Thuringia, 40, 54 n. 31; relations with Bulgaria, 42-43; his church policy - supported by Rome, 43; troubles with Halich, 43-45, 50-52; trouble at home - conspiracy, the assassination of Queen Gertrud, her burial, 45-49, 56-59 nn. 87-102, 114, 125-29, 134-40, 146. Béla, Junior King, to change father's land-grant policy, 50; expressions such as *civiles*, *regis civiles, castranses* appear in legal usage; role of the *pristaldus*, 50, 59 nn. 151-52. Relations between father and son not always smooth, 86-87, 91 nn. 78-86.

Andrew II's crusade in 1217, 60-69, 72 n. 3, 73 n. 14; he went to fulfill the promise his father, Béla III, had made, 60, 72 n.4, and because he had hoped to gain the (Latin-)Byzantine throne, 60, 63, 74 n. 19 - a plan that did not meet his people's and the Esztergom archbishop's approval, 69, 70, 71, 75 nn. 55-56; he was not prepared for it, 62-63; during his absence, the archbishop of Esztergom became regent, together with the great officials of the realm, 62; the clergy unhappy with the tax they had to pay for the king's crusade, 62, 73 n. 9; the crusaders' route to the Holy Land, 63-64; the impression the troops created abroad, 65; the Holy See and the crusade, 61-62; the war council held in Accon in November, 1217 and the result that the papal crusade became a military venture of the princes of Palestine, 65, 74 n. 33; the King's military march, the "siege" of Mt. Tabor, 66-67, 75 nn. 37-38; by early 1218, the king returns home, 67, 75 n. 42; establishes personal and political contacts with regional rulers during the return journey, 60, 67-68, 75 nn. 49-50; has personal urge to impress his newly gained friends with his wealth, 68, 75 nn. 58-61, and to boast about his "accomplishments" to the papal curia, 69, 76 nn. 64-65; at home, social upheavals await, 68, 69, 75 nn. 56-57, and 78-79, 89 nn. 11-12.

Andrew II's power of government decreases because of parceling out the royal domain to less deserving recipients, 79; his *Decretum I* (Golden Bull) of 1222, 77-82, 82-85; and his *Decretum II* of 1231, 104-05, 117 nn. 5-20; military clash and agreement on western frontier with Frederick of Austria, 111-12. Marries, for the third time, 113-14, 119 nn. 86-87. Crusading expedition and Halich ventures were thoughtless, irrational, unproductive, 99. His unexpected death, 120 n. 105, and burial, at first at Várad, then at Egres Abbey, 116, 120 nn. 108-11.

Andrew, Andrew II's youngest son, whose claim over Halich involved his father in several military campaigns, 96, 101 nn. 33-34; 110, 118 n. 59, 111, 113.

Andrew III, last Árpád king, family
background, 342-43; claims the
throne as inheritance, 343; challenged by the Anjous of Naples,
344-45, 390-96; the Anjou claim
to the throne, 390, supported by
Rome, 391; papal claim for interference, *Unam sanctam*, 392, 400
nn. 17-18; 397, 402 nn. 56-60;
nobles ask Rome to replace him on
the throne, 392-93; Boniface VIII
very cautious, 393; controversy
between two candidates for the
archiepiscopal see of Esztergom,
393; the king appeals to Rome,
394; diplomatic move[s] before
the curia to deflate his opponents,
395-96; his coronation, 343-44,
348, 362 nn. 13-14; holds diet at
Óbuda in 1290 to enact articles in
support of the nobility, curtail
some prerogatives claimed by the
barons, and to clarify his attitude
toward the Church, 345-47; Saxons attend through representatives;
through the diet he establishes a
common tie with the lesser
nobility, 347; stresses representation in the diet, 348-49; Aragonese
family ties and examples in dietary
representation, 349, 381, 382; his
writ to James II of (Aragon-)Sicily,
382-83; the nobles' *estate* in
government, 350, 380; struggle for
the throne: the Anjou sympathizer
Kőszeg family; politics of, and
relations with Albert of Austria,
351,52; the Csáks turn against him;
dynastic division of the realm,
353-54; influence of the barons,
354; the diet of 1298 aims at
reconstruction, to support the
monarch, the nobles and the
Church, to regulate the issuance of
money, 354-56; royal advisors in
the Council to represent public
interest, 356-57; 380; power
struggle with the barons, 374-75;
constitutional developments, 374-
84; diet strengthens royal powers,
360; his foreign policy and the
goal of Albert of Austria, 358; his
mother Tomasina to have a role in
politics, 359-61; owes his crown to
the support (and resolutions) of
the high clergy and service nobility, 383, 389 n. 86; the 1299 diet
at Rákos, 394; confident that the
Royal Council would remain a
responsible body, 384; his death,
361, 373 nn. 201-202; 396, 401
nn. 41-42.

Andrew of Pannonia, theologian, 410,
420 n. 6.

Anjou claim to the throne of Andrew
III, 390, supported by the curia,
392; some Hungarian nobles ask
Rome to replace Andrew III, 392-
93; papal intervention - resented
by the Hungarian hierarchy, 393-
94; Andrew III to parry it before
the curia, 394-96; upon the death
of Andrew III, the Czech Vencel
enters the scene in the name of his
son, 396-97; the role of Cardinal
Boccassino, 397; in 1303 Boniface
VIII recognizes Charles Robert of
Anjou as king of Hungary, 398,
403 n. 63; Charles's coronation,
399.

Anonymus, chronicler of late twelfth
century, 5, 302; sources include
early history, peasant stories, 311
nn. 1-4; recorded folk poetry
recited by the bards - as verified
by Ekkehard of St. Gall, 302, 311
n. 5, and by the «Symphonia
Ungarorum» - heard by Bishop
Gerard of Csanád, 302, 311 n. 6;
wrote with loving care about Béla
III, but loses office upon the
king's death, 3. Recorded the
Blood Oath taken by Magyar tribal
heads in the 880's; cites the
responsibilities of the elected
Hungarian ruler (king), arguing
that the nobility had the right to
participate in the realm's government and in the deliberations of
the Royal Council, 3-5, 375, 385 n.
12; describes Árpád as a ruler with
unlimited power, 376.

Arnold of Lübeck on the meeting of
Béla III and Frederick Barbarossa
in Esztergom, referring to
Esztergom as "civitas,"
"metropolitis," the *centrum* of the
realm, 334; spoke of Aquincum,

where Béla III had entertained his imperial guests, as "Etzilburg": *urbs Adtile* (sic), 334.

Árpád dynasty, appraisal of their reign, 398-99, 403 n. 75.

Aurelius Augustinus: St. Augustine, 234; *De civitate Dei*, 223; his influence on Béla IV's Law for the Jews, 223-24, 231, 232, 233; belief that the "City of God" as reality that stood over time and space, 231; *De civitate Dei* known in Hungary, 224, 231; ideal of a ruler, 231-32; concept of the *republica Christiana* echoed in the introduction to Béla's Law for the Jews; 232; impact on the enactments of the 1252 synod of Esztergom, 232-33.

Frederick Babenburg of Austria, opponent of Andrew II and of Béla IV (Junior King), 111-12; killed in military action in 1246,201-02; continued unsettled situation with Austria, 202-03, 204; Rome and Otakar II intervene, 204-07; war, 205; conditions still unsettled in the 1250's, 210; his "Letter to the Jews" influences Béla IV's "Law for the Jews," 226, 236 n. 23.

Gregory Bánffy (Caelius Pannonius), bible scholar and translator of the Augustinian rule, 411, 420 nn. 10-13.

Béla IV, Andrew II's first born, to whom the nobles had free access; legal proceedings before him had to be completed at his court, 86; strained relations with his father, flees to Austria, and Rome intervenes, 86-87, 91 nn. 76-82; as governor of Transylvania, 97, 102 n. 28; plans to occupy Bulgaria, 96, 97; though unsuccessful, refers to himself as the Son of the King of Bulgaria, 96, 102 n. 47; ordered to recapture Halich and suffers heavy defeat, 98; urges forceful conversion of Cumans to the Christian faith - Cuman mission headed by Archbishop Robert of Esztergom leads to the formation

of the Milkovia bishopric, 97, 102 nn. 38-40, 43.

Béla IV, crowned for the second time at his succession, with a goal clearly set before him, 121; has to take a stand versus the nobles, many of whom had undeservedly received grants from his father, 121-22; has to be strict, but his timing was bad in repossessing grants and offices, 122, 124-25; nobles making a complaint had to do it in writing, through the chancery, 123; makes churchmen return unlawfully gained gifts, 123-24; refuses to pay tribute to Emperor Frederick II, 122. Relations with John II Asen of Bulgaria, 125-26; his letter to Rome and Gregory IX's reply, 125-27; his contact with the curia correct, but could not attend the synod that had been planned by the Pope, 127-128; his attitude toward the Cumans of King Kötény, 129, 130; does not answer the letter Batu Khan had sent to him, 130. The king's attitude toward the Dominican friars going east to find the *dent-maeger* ("Magyars at the Don"), 131; friar Julian and his journey to "Great Hungary" (1237), 132.

Béla declares state of emergency in early 1242 because of the Tartar threat - a call not taken seriously, 133; his nobles expect the arrival of (Kievan) Russians at the border, 136; Béla alone recognizes (too late) the danger of the situation, 136, but seems to play it down, 140; his nobles respond slowly to his call for mobilization, 137-38; out of sheer jealousy, the nobles force him to disassociate himself from the Cumans, 13738; first bloody clash with the Tartars at the Verecke Pass in March, 1241, 139. Because of the Tartar threat, Béla sends his family to the west and requests Austrian aid versus the Mongols, 140.

Béla caught in politics between Halich and Vienna, 200-35;

Rostislav Mihalovich, Danilo (Danyii) Romanovich of Kiev, 200-01; Danilo visits Batu's headquarters, 201; Patriarch Cyrill dispatched to Béla IV and to Nicea, 203, 214-15; Leo, Danilo's son, marries Constance, Béla's daughter; king and Danilo meet in Zólyom, 203-04; Béla supports papal politics with Danilo of Halich; the Rome-Halich-Kiev "union," 212-14.
Firm with Frederick of Austria, 201-02; claim to Frederick's inheritance leads to papal intervention, 204-05; compromises with Rome on the Babenberg estates, supports the curia's policy toward Danilo, 214; Austrian and Styrian nobles defeat Béla IV, 205; Czech invasion of Austrian lands leads to the Peace of Pozsony (1254), 205-06.
Béla IV and son, Stephen, Junior King (King Stephen V, 1270-72), 207-08, 209-10; war with Otakar II in 1260 leads to Otakar II's marriage to Constance, a granddaughter of Béla IV, 208-09; Stephen regards his father as someone first among the equals, 207; father vs. son, 207, 208, 209-10; peace between them: the Pacification of Poroszló, 239, 249 nn. 2-5; end of Béla IV's reign, his mental disposition before he died, 252 n. 67; characterization of the monarch, 248.
Benedict of Borsod county, tried for murder of his wife, 384.
Benedictines, role in the formation of early Hungarian Christian culture, 302; at Pannonhalma, 302, 311 n. 9, Czech monks had settled there, 303, 312, nn. 10-11; the abbey had some 80 books in its library by the 1080's, 302, 311 n. 9, 313 n. 18; their monasteries at Bakonybél, Pécsvárad, Ft. Zala (Zalavár), 303, 312 nn. 12-15. Latin as language of instruction in their schools, consequently, official writs, legal texts, historical narratives were composed in Latin, 303.

Bereg Agreement (1233), between Andrew II and Rome, negotiated by papal Legate Precorari, 110-11, 118 nn. 60-64, 119 nn. 65-66, 120, n. 70; less willingly agreed to by the monarch, 112-13, who had no intention of observing it, 114, 115, 120 nn. 96-97.
Beregszász (Luprechtzaz), its *hospites* obtained royal recognition of their duties and privileges in 1247, 322.
Bogomils (heretics), make headway in Szerém and Bosnia despite the efforts of Grand Reeve Kulin, 108; Archbishop Ugrin of Kalocsa instructed to deal with them (even established a bishopric to deal with them), but Rome, overcautious, calls upon Kajolan Angelos, who was in charge of the region, to lead a crusade against them, 108-109; papal legate replaced the bishop of Bosnia with a Dominican and the Church slowly regains ground, 109.
Brassó, Town of the Hungarian Crown (Kronstadt), built by German settlers during the 1220's, 96, 101 n. 31.
Byzantium and Béla IV, 246-47.

Charles of Anjou, brother of Louis IX of France, heir of the Byzantine (Latin) throne, wants to marry Margaret, Béla IV's daughter, but is turned down; arranges for a marriage between his son and Maria, Béla IV's granddaughter, 246-47.
Chronica regia Coloniensis, on Hungary, 334.
Church matters in Hungary, during the early 1230's, 103-16; report by Aegidius, papal legate, about conditions in the realm, 103, 117 nn. 1-2; reaction of the curia, 103, and of the royal court, 104, 117 n. 4; issuance of the Decree of 1231, 104-05, 117, nn. 6-18; strained relations between Andrew II and Robert of Esztergom; the interdict, 105-06, 117 nn. 21-26; interdict effective, 106, though the king responds with a new game of

diplomatic chess, 107, 117, nn. 29-31; church synod at Buda (1232), summoned by papal legate Precorari, 107-08; Andrew II's reluctance to meet with the legate, 108, 117 n. 38, 118 nn. 39-40; Precorari intervenes in the Bogomil question in Szerém, part of the royal domain and an area under the jurisdiction of Kalocsa, 108-09, 118 nn. 45-47; interferes in the dispute of Pannonhalma abbey with its servile folks, 109, 118 nn. 48-49. Precorari to initiate the canonization of Lukács, former archbishop of Esztergom, 109, 118 n. 52; to regulate election at Várad and to ease the burden of taxation of the parochial clergy, 110, 118 nn. 54-55. Archbishop Robert and the bishop of Bosnia, 114, the archbishop and legate Precorari, 114-15; the "Bereg Agreement" between the king and the Church, 110-11, 112-13; the king attempts to reassert his diplomatic initiative, 118 nn. 60-61, 119 n. 81; Andrew II unwilling to keep the agreement, and the curia's surprising response: Rome had canonized his daughter Elizabeth, 115-16, 120 nn. 107-08.

Coloman, Andrew II's younger son, governor of Slavonia, 96, 101 n. 32.

Cosmas of Prague, Czech chronicler, on towns in Hungary; spoke of Esztergom as *urbs*, where he was ordained a priest; called Esztergom an economic junction, 319-320, 333-34.

Cumans, led by their king, Kötény, fled to Hungary, 129-30, Béla IV had them settled down in the country - a plan opposed by the nobles, 129-30, who regard them as "Russian" spies, 136; common folk dislike them, 133; Béla IV needs the Cumans as his personal military contingent, 137; and yet, under pressure from the nobles, he has to keep them under surveillance, 138; still, in early 1241, he orders them to move their military force against the approaching Tartars.

Dám, Ince, on the doctrine of the Immaculata, 411, 419 n. 2, 420, n. 23; an authority on the writings of friars Pelbárt of Temesvár and Oswald de Laska, 411, 414.

Danilo (Danyii) of Halich, threatens position of Andrew, Andrew II's son, on its throne, 110, 111, 113, 118 n. 59; because of the intrigues with Mistislav, the prince only gained access to Przemysl, 96; visits Batu Khan in 1245, 200-01; recognizes Béla IV as prince of Halich, 201; sends Patriarch Cyrill to Béla IV's court, 203; son Leo marries Constance, daughter of Béla IV, 203; meets with Béla IV in Zólyom, 203-04; papal diplomatic plans with Danilo, 211-13.

Decretum I of 1222 (Golden Bull) by Andrew II, 77-82; date of issue, 77, 88 n.2; papal reaction, 83, 90 n. 42; referred to a social hierarchy of bishops, *iobagiones*, and nobles, 241; social position of the service nobility, 80-82, 91 n. 86; resolutions of the Bull mainly support the need for recognition of the status of the lesser (service) nobility, 82-85; had it been promulgated? - text came down only in a 1318 transcript, though a papal writ spoke of a "new law of the land," 85, 91 nn. 64-68.

Decretum II of 1231 by Andrew II, 104-05, 117 nn. 5-6[-20]; identical with *Decretum I* on essential points, but added nine new articles, 104-05; confirmed by king and his sons, 105, 117 n. 19; did he enact it in vain? 105; its use of the term *barones* replaced that of *iobagiones*, 241; threat of ecclesiastical excommunication, 105, 117 nn. 20-21.

Dénes, palatine, excommunicated by Archbishop Robert, 106-07; his dealings with papal legates, 107; met and defeated by the Tartars at the Verecke Pass in 1241, 130.

Diet of 1267, initiated by the lesser nobles, but resolutions submitted to the king, 377; lesser nobles separate themselves from the higher nobles, 375-76; Béla IV had recognized the nobles' *estate* (378), but Ladislas IV was less willing to accept it - Andrew III listens to their advice and places the government beyond the supervision of the barons, 379.

Diet of 1298, 354-65; *estates* of higher clergy and lesser nobility ordered by Andrew II to send representative delegates to the Royal Council, 379-80.

Elizabeth of Hungary, Saint, 404-07; daughter of Andrew II of Hungary, born in Sárospatak, 404, sent to Thuringia, 40; married to Louis of Thuringia, 405; upon her husband's death refuses to marry Emperor Frederick II, 406; Conrad of Marburg, her spiritual director, 405, 406, 407; her canonization, 116, 120 nn. 106-09, 407, 408. Bibliographical note, 408.

Emery, son of Béla III (*ob.* 1196), his record in the Chronicle, 1-2; why his son, Ladislas III, was referred to as Ladislas II in the record, 3; difficult relationship with brother Andrew, and provided the curia with the opportunity to intervene in Hungarian politics, 5-6; had the support of Esztergom, 6-7, and complains to Rome about his opponents, 7; displays an unworthy attitude toward his enemies, was no diplomat, 7-9; refuses to go on a crusade, 10, 28-29; his involvement in Serb politics might have led to a Rome-Serb understanding, 10-12, though he did not lose the support of the curia, 13-14.

Marriage to Constance of Aragon, daughter of Alfonso II, 28-29; brother Andrew marries Gertrud of Meran in order to reach an agreement with the anti-papal party in the German empire, 29. Gertrud wants Andrew to succeed Emery on the throne, 29, and Innocent III intervenes, 30. The Fourth Crusade leading to the Venetian capture of Zara, 24-27; Emery caught by surprise - he had been preoccupied by Bosnia and Serbia, 26; commander of the "crusaders" not involved in Zara affair; the crusade - a Frankish military move to promote Frankish-Byzantine political-business interests, 27; Hungaro-papal relations over the Balkans did not improve; in Germany, Emery aided Otto IV against Philip of Swabia, 28. Confronted brother Andrew, but by 1201, Emery was ill, 30-31, could not grasp political and personal matters clearly before his death, 32.

Esztergom, early settlement on Roman foundations, 318, 320; population included Franks and Lombards, 318, 327 n. 5; referred to as "*civitas*," "center" of the realm by Arnold of Lübeck, 334; mentioned by Odo de Deogilo and Cosmas of Prague as a marketing and trading center, seat of Prince Géza's court, 319-20, 334; public opinion regarded it as Attila's headquarters; as seat of government, 334, held tax-exempt status, 322, 325; merchants unperturbed about politics or "country values," 319.

German Knights and Andrew II, 93-95, 100 nn. 1-15, to invite them to settle in Barca land was a thoughtless decision on part of the king, 98.

Gesta Ungarorum, first one, of the 1090's, text lost, 305, 314 n. 39; the one by Anonymus "P. dictus magister," 305, 314 nn. 40-41; it preserved pagan legends, such as that of the "White Horse," or "The Tale of Emese," 305, 314 n. 44, narrated Hungarian history from the mid-ninth century to 997, 305, 314 nn. 45-49; originated ethnic Hungarian literature, 306, documented existence of ethnic folklore and poetry, 306, 314 nn. 51-52.

Guthkeled Bible, 336.

Győr, early town settlement since Roman times, 318; Stephen V exempted its *cives* from the jurisdiction of the regional reeve, retained privileges held by Fehérvár, 324; at Győr, St. Stephen issued the founding charter of the bishopric of Pécs in 1009, 325, 330 n. 64.

Halich, conflict between Mistislav, Danilo (aided by Conrad of Masovia), and Andrew, in whose interest Béla, Junior King, and later Andrew II himself, had to interfere, 98, 99, 102 nn. 49-51; in the diplomatic plans of Rome: a Rome-Halich-Kiev "union," 212-14.

Historiography, Hungarian, did not imitate German chronicles, but followed the form of Latin European *gesta*, 304, 314 n. 38; its scribes were well-educated clerics of the court, 304. First known "*gesta*" now lost, in the reign of Ladislas I; first surviving *gesta* by (the Hungarian) Anonymus under Béla III, 305, 314 nn. 40-41; he included pagan legends of "The White Horse" and "The Dream of Emese," in his narrative, 305; regarded the Árpáds as descendants of Attila the Hun, 305, 314 n. 44; recorded Hungarian events between the ninth and late tenth centuries, named Álmos as the first elected Magyar leader, 305; as a writer claimed to have strong literary European background; his histories in Latin became originators of ethnic national literature, 306. Simon de Keza, in the reign of Ladislas IV, combined Hun and Hungarian traditions; he felt he had to identify the Magyars with the threatening Huns, 306-07; he provided an outline, not a narrative, of events, 307. Mark de Kálta authored the *Chronicon pictum*, mid-fourteenth century, followed Keza's outline, but added more

information to it, 307-08. A "Gesta Ungarorum" of 1235, on the ur-history of the Magyars, 309, 316 nn. 76-77. Rogerius's *Carmen*, and Thomas of Spaleto on the Mongol devastation of Hungary in the early 1240's, 309, 316 nn. 79-82.

Holy Crown (*Corona sacra*), synonymous with *regia potestas, regnum*, 375-76; symbolizes constitutional royal power, 382-83.

Iobagio, had his social status on the periphery of the nobles' class, though within the structure of the nobility, like a service noble; lands he held in usufruct were small, 81; an "*iobagio castris*" assigned to fort defense was expected to uphold royal authority, 80.

Iura Iudaeorum, Béla IV's "Law of 1251," Law for the Jews, 224-32, 236 nn. 36-37; influenced by St. Augustine's *De civitate Dei*, 225, 235 n. 15, who argued that a monarch could not be conceited because he had to be merciful, maintain the law, rely on rational behavior, 225-26, 235 nn. 17-21; basic idea that Jews were guests in the realm, 226; example of Frederick Babenberg's "Letter to the Jews," 226, 236 n. 23; Otakar II also borrows from the Babenberg direction, 229; Jewish Laws regarded by some as an (the first) Austro-Czech law code, 229, 236 n. 41; establishes guidelines concerning mortgages, criminal cases, 227; Béla IV's protective policy of the Jewish stratum has a price, 226-27; Béla IV's law was his own - Jews in the country under his personal protection, 229, 236 n. 42; composition of law reflected the educational-intellectual background of clergy and royal advisors of the time, 229-230; copies of Augustine's works at library of the Veszprém cathedral school, 230.

Johann of Késmárk, theologian, 410.
Julian, Dominican friar, his reports on the Volga-Magyars, 309, 316 nn. 78-79.

Simon de Kéza, chronicler of the times of Ladislas IV, attributes rights to the nobles' *estate*, 375; on Árpád and the lesser nobles who assert themselves in the *communitas* of the country, 377.

Ladislas I, his *Vita*, 304, 313 n. 33; his legislative acts, 303; canonized under Béla III, 304, 313 n. 34.

Ladislas III (1204-1205), 32; son of Emery; Innocent III had to warn Prince Andrew, brother of King Emery, that upon the latter's death, it would be Ladislas who would succeed to the throne, 30; dies in Austria, buried in Fehérvár, 32.

Ladislas IV (the Cuman), succeeds Stephen V, whose widow became (an ineffective) regent, 255, 256-57; oligarchy becomes predominant, Henry of Kőszeg and Béla of Macho, 255-56, the Gútkeled-Kőszeg and the Csák families; between 1274 and 1284, the Csáks has control of the administration - except briefly in 1275 and 1281, 257; Hungaro-Czech military confrontations early in his reign, 256; filling the position of the see of Esztergom remains a problem for the king - candidates Benedict and Nicholas, 258; Rome has to intervene, 258-59; another invasion by Otakar II, 259; tragedy at Veszprém due to the personal feud with the bishop (who was of the Németújvár-Kőszeg family), 260-62; the king promises and provides compensation, 261; "Saxons" in Transylvania burn down the cathedral of Gyulafehérvár because of personal grievances, 262.

Ladislas IV and Rudolf of Habsburg, allied against Otakar II of Bohemia, the battle of Dürnkrutt, 262-63, 269 n. 75; the home front continues to deteriorate and Rome sends an envoy, Philip of Fermo, to investigate, 263-64; Ladislas convokes a diet of the three recognized estates: *praelati, barones et nobiles*, at Tétény, 264-65, 271 n. 91; the king opposes the gathering of the Synod of Buda in 1279 on political grounds (he resented the interference of the papal legate) and not because he led an immoral life, 276-78; Ladislas cannot accept the situation the curia had created - though, probably ill-advised, he may have acted thoughtlessly, 279-80.
Confrontation with the Cumans, Lake Hód, 284; possible cooperation between a Cuman leader "beyond" the Carpathians and the Cumans in the country - prelude to the 1285 Mongol invasion, 284-85; the Tartars once again reach Pest, 286-87; Ladislas has them expelled, 291; the king's emotional instability during the 1280's, his unfair public treatment of Queen Izabella, 291-92, and the reaction of the papal curia, 288-89, 290, 291, 294; the oligarchs conspire against him, 289-91, 292; the Diet of Rákos (1286), 292, 299 nn. 58-62; in fear of his life, changes places of residence constantly, 292-94; the oligarchs plan to dethrone, even kill, the king, 294-95; hired assassins murder him, 295, 301 nn. 99-101; reason for the plot, 295-96.
His reign was given a hostile appraisal by the *Chronicle*, but modern-day historians view him more positively, 33.

Law of 1267, 240-45, 249 nn. 1, 11-12; distinguished from the *Decretum I*, 1222, of Andrew II: in 1267, the nobles gathered together without royal summons, but Béla acted with the consent of the Royal Council, 240; use of the term *baro*, 241, 244; grants tax exemption to the service nobility, who could only be tried in royal court(s) of law, 242-43; modifies the nobles' military obligations; holdings of a nobleman who died in the line of duty could be inherited, 242, 243; every count to send at least two delegates to the annual law-day at Fehérvár, 243, 244; appeals and grievances of service nobles to be handled by the monarch, 243; service nobles could reclaim their confiscated lands, 243; *servientes regis*: service nobles who had administered the county in the 1260's; their judged gained a predominant position, 244-25; Béla IV increases their membership by elevating free knights to mounted "*servientes*"; emancipated *servientes* would do active duty under the king's standard, 245.

Laws of 1351 by Louis the Great of Hungary, 376.

Laws written down, 303, 312 n. 20; Laws and Admonitions of King St. Stephen, 303, 313 n. 23; under Ladislas I, 303, 313 nn. 24-27; Béla IV's Law for the Jews, 225-26; Béla IV's Law of 1267, 240-45.

Legends: pagan legends of "The White Horse" and "The Dream of Emese" recorded by the Hungarian Anonymus in his Hungarian *gesta*, 305; first Christian legends in Hungarian literature authored by Maurus of Pannonhalma (later, bishop of Pécs), dealt with Zoerard and Benedict of Zobor Hill, 303.

Literary remains (in Hungarian) include the charter of Tihany abbey (1055), the "Sermon over the Tomb," ca. 1200, an old Magyar versification, dated about 1300, of *Planctus Mariae* by Godfrey of St. Victor, 309-10, 316 nn. 84-85, 317 nn. 86-91.

Lives of first Hungarian Saints, 303, 312 n. 22; King Stephen's *Vita maior, Vita minor*, Hartvic's Life of King St. Stephen, 303-04, 313 n. 29; three lives (*vitae*) of King St. Stephen, 303-04; two lives of Bishop Gerard of Csanád, 304; the Life of King St. Ladislas, 304.

Margit (Margaret), Saint, daughter of Béla IV, 246-47, 253 nn. 79-80.

Marosini, Tomasina, mother of Andrew III, takes active role in the administrative politics of the realm, 359-61.

Merchant stratum, inactive in politics, 381, 383.

Michael of Hungary, theologian, 409, 419 n. 2.

Michael the Hungarian (Michael of Pannonia), theologian, 409-10, 419-20 nn. 3-5.

Mihalovich Rostislav, son of the Prince of Chernigov, flees to the court of Béla IV and marries his daughter Anna, 200; Béla makes him Grand Steward of Slovenia and Macho, 201.

Nicholas de Mirabilibus of Kolozsvár, theologian, 410, 420 n. 7.

Nyitra, its *cives* held certain liberties, 322-23; defended their fort from the Mongols, 323; mentioned, in 836, by the bishop of Salzburg, functioned as a bishop's see in the 880's, 323, 329 nn. 46-47.

Odo de Deogilo, accompanying Louis VII of France, wrote about Esztergom as a trade center, 319, the realm's capital, 334.

Oswald de Laska (Laskai Osvát), theologian, 411, 412, 415, author of *Biga salutis* and of *Gemma fidei*, 412, 420 n. 14, 421 nn. 21-23.

Otto of Freising, author of *Gesta Friderici Imperatoris*, wrote about Hungary, its land and people, admiring its riches; spoke of the Magyars as morose, wild, their language barbaric, their behavior crude and lacking cultural habits; the Magyars came from Scythia, 332; their king held high prestige, though he shared the care of government with his nobles, 333; witness to the dignity of Christian kingship among the Árpáds, 375; towns did not exist; their order of battle created a bad impression, 333, 339 nn. 2-9.

"Palace revolution," in early 1222, when new royal opponents forced the king's old allies from office? 81, 89 n. 26; Andrew II, upon his succession had dismissed his father's loyal advisors, 81, 90, n. 29, who, in turn, had caused the upheaval in 1222, 81-82; the concluding paragraph of the *Decretum I* (1222) would imply that the "multitude" had kept royal officials away from the King's Council, 82, 90 nn. 37-39; a letter of Pope Honorius III spoke of a social upheaval, 83, 90 n. 42.

Pelbárt of Temesvár, theologian, 411-18; his educational background, 411, 420 n. 15; his position in Hungary, 412-13, 421 nn. 24-26; his major works: *Stellarium* (on the Immaculate Conception), 413, 422 nn. 36-39, 423 n. 42; *Pomerium*, 413-14, 423, nn. 43-51; *Expositio psalmarum*, 415, 424 n. 53; *Rosarium* (on dogma), 415, 416, 420 n. 14, 424 nn. 54-55; published his works outside of Hungary, 411-12, 414, 417; manner of his sermons, 412-13; his death, 412, 422, nn. 27-28; Pelbárt on St. Thomas Aquinas, 415, 416; codices in which his works appear, 416, 424 nn. 66-68; his views of King St. Stephen's Laws, 414, 418, 423 nn. 51-52; his opinion of the court of Matthias Corvinus, 414, 417; Ince Dám on Pelbárt, 411f., 415; Pelbárt and Oswald de Laska, 412, 415; Pelbárt and Duns Scotus, 415; Sixtus IV's *Greve nimis* (on the Immaculata), 416, 424 nn. 63-65.

Pest, town, 322; and Buda, 322, 329 nn. 36-39; held tax-exempt status since the days of King St. Stephen, 322; earlier inhabited by Volga Bulgarians, 322.

Planctus, an anonymous elegy on the Tartar onslaught of Hungary in 1241-42, 309, 316 n. 82.

Planctus Mariae by Godfrey of St. Victor (*ob.* 1096), its Hungarian versification, «Mária siralom» of about 1300, 301, 317 nn. 89-91.

Poroszló, pacification of, between Béla IV and his son Stephen, 239; the country was divided in two, but legislatively it suffered no damage, 240.

Jacob Precorari, Cistercian, Cardinal of Praeneste and papal legate to Hungary, 107-10; summons synod in Buda (1231) to gain trust of the clergy, 107, 117 n. 35; takes firm stand toward members of the hierarchy and makes clergy pay for his expenses as papal envoy, 110; not received by Andrew II in person, 108, talks to the king only through his high officials, 108; meets with Andrew II only after the aborted Halich campaign, 111; deals effectively with the Bogomils in Szerém and in Bosnia, 109.

Reconstruction - the 1240's, settlement of foreign, mainly German, migrants, 186-87; 180-92, 193 n. 1; fear of a renewed Tartar attack, 180, 186, 187; Béla IV to Innocent IV, cry for help, 180-81, 193-94 nn. 2-10; date of the letter, 213, 222 n. 126-35; refers to the Danube as the line of military defense, *aqua contradictionis*, 181, 193 n. 7; the country suffers a devastating but not fateful defeat, 181, 194 n. 12; Béla meets the military threat from Austria head-on, 185-86; Béla has to build up the country's defense by fortifying cities, 187-90; construction of a fort at Buda Hill, 187, 188-89; Zagreb, 187-88, 189; Esztergom and Székesfehérvár, 189; Nyitra and Komárom, 190; Cumans recalled into royal military service, 190; fortifications along the Danube and the king's agreement with the Knights of St. John, 210-11; Béla IV concerned about the defense of the southeast, 211; royal diplomacy with Venice, 191-92; treatment of Trau, 191, 192, 199 nn. 127-28.

Robert, archbishop of Esztergom, his mission among the Cumans led to the formation of Milkovia bishopric, 97, 102 nn. 41-42; places country under interdict, 105, 117 nn. 21-23, with the exception of the king, 106; his working relationship with papal legate Precorari, 107; critical and yet supportive of Andrew II, would not cooperate with the bishop of Bosnia, 114.

Rogerius, archpriest of Várad, author of *Carmen*, on the 1241-42 Mongol invasion of Hungary, 309, 316 n. 79; an eyewitness, 133; his analysis of the country's domestic situation prior to the Tartar onslaught, 133-34, 148 nn. 136-39.

«Sermon and Prayer at the Tomb» (Halotti beszéd) - an early Hungarian sermon, 304, 313 nn. 36-37.

Servientes regis, service nobility, identical with land-holding social stratum and with formerly wealthy stratum that had declined socially, owed duties to the king, was not under the jurisdiction of the county reeve, 80.

Somogyvár abbey, founded by King St. Ladislas I in 1091, 303, 312 n. 17.

Sopron, town of Roman foundations, 318, and of Celtic origin, 320, bishop's residence in sixth century - in the eight, Einhard named it *deserta civitas* - Ödenburg, Pusztavár, 320.

St. Gerard [of Venice], Benedictine monk, advisor of King St. Stephen and tutor to his son, Emery; later bishop of Csanád (*ob.* 1046), his *vitae*, 304, 313 n. 31; author of *Deliberatio* on the Song of Daniel, 304, 313 n. 32; canonized in the reign of Ladislas I, 303.

St. Ladislas I (*ob.* 1095), his Life, 304, 314 nn. 33-34; his legislative acts, 303, 313 n. 24; first Hungarian history, now lost, composed during his reign, 302; canonized under Béla III, 304, 314, n. 34.

St. Stephen I (*ob.* 1038), his lives, *Vita minor*, *Vita maior*, and Life by Hartvic, 303, 313 n. 29; his Laws and Admonitions, 303, 312 n. 20,

313 n. 23; canonized in the reign of Ladislas I, 303.

Synod of Buda (1279), its resolutions, 272-76, 281 nn. 1-2; proposed articles not discussed in their entirety on account of royal opposition, 276; Ladislas IV resents the papal legate's interference in domestic politics, 276-77, and the legate forced to move to Pozsony; reaction of Nicholas III, 277; Ladislas IV's rather undiplomatic reaction, though he makes peace with the legate, 279-80, 283 nn. 78-79.

Székesfehérvár, settlement dating back to Roman times, 318, held tax-exempt status, 322, 324, 325; King St. Stephen had placed it under the jurisdiction of the bishop of Veszprém, 325-26.

Széklers, served as fort and border guards, originated from the Telegd region in Bihar county, 96; in a 1228 record, the first Székler reeve appeared by the name of Bagamér, 96, 101, n. 28. Organized settlements of the Kézdi and Sepsi Széklers by late 1220's, 96, 101 n. 23.

Tartars: invasion of Hungary, 154-60, 162 nn. 25-32; by mid-March, 1241, the Tartars were half a day's march from Pest, 151; the unruly behavior of Archbishop Ugrin of Kalocsa, 151-52; Frederick of Austria intervenes and wins engagement with the Tartars, 152-53; Béla loses support of his Cumans at a critical moments, 153; Béla IV to meet the enemy at Mohi, 154-55; mistakes made on the Hungarian side in planning and tactics, 155-56, 157; Batu's plan simple and effective, 156-57; encounter at the bridge across the Sajó, 157; Batu's planned surprise attack, 157-58; Batu's and Subutai's forces surround the Hungarian compound, 158-59; Béla IV escapes to Austria, 167; Duke Frederick demands payment the king could not meet, confiscates his gold reserves, and forces him to sign an agreement, 168,, 176 nn. 35-38; all equipment in camp at Mohi is lost, 159-60; the dead at Mohi, 159, 163 nn. 70-77. Batu's letter to the population, signed with the captured royal seal, encourages them to stay and carry on with their lives, 160, 163 nn. 82-84.

Tartar occupation of the land, 165-74, 175 nn. 1, 9-10; Kadar and Bedsak Khans enter Transylvania, devastating it, 165; Bedsak destroys Csanád; Lanad Khan moves toward Pereg and Egres, 166; Peta Khan enters country from the north-west, slowed down by many forts: Pozsony, Nyitra, Trencsén, Komárom, but demolishes the countryside and kills everyone in sight, 166-67. In occupied territory, villagers elect Tartar "mayors," 167.

Béla IV moves toward Zagreb in April, 1241, requesting aid from France, the Empire, and Rome, 168-69; the papal reply, 169; the Emperor instructs him to join imperial forces, and his son, Conrad, would defend him from the Tartars, 170; Frederick II totally misjudges the situation, 171; the king moves toward Dalmatia, places the Queen and her small court in Ft. Klissa on an island in the sea, 169; Judge Paul of the King's Court directs the home defense, holds on to the Danube as the line of resistance, 171; the Tartars cross the river and meet little resistance (except at fortified places), 172; Kadar Khan's forces take Esztergom and kill everyone, but is not successful in taking the fort; devastates the surroundings of Fehérvár, but cannot take the fort, 172; Arch-abbot Uriás of Pannonhalma describes the situation in a letter to Rome, 173; Kadar moves toward Dalmatia to capture the king; Béla IV moves to the island of Trau; Kadar besieges Klissa, and withdraws, 173-74; the king sus-

pects a ploy, but the news turns out to be correct, 174, 179 nn. 13-16. Tartar withdrawal - death of Ogotai, 182; did the onslaught of 1241 serve as a military reconnaissance mission for a well-planned future invasion of the west? 182, 194 n. 19; the role fortified places had played in the defense, 183; the withdrawal of Mongol divisions, 183; Rubruck on the Mongol treatment of prisoners, 183-84; Béla IV's return, rewarding his faithful supporters, 184; hunger and awful conditions in the realms, 184, 185; the king forced to secularize church wealth to obtain cash, 186; the king's attitude toward nobles and towns, 189, 190, 191.

Thomas of Spaleto, on the Tartars in Hungary, 134-35, 148 n. 149.

Tihany abbey, established by King Andrew I in 1055, 303, 312 n. 16.

Timothy, bishop of Zagreb, whose papal appointment to the see was opposed by Béla IV and his nobles on account of Timothy's social background, requiring papal intervention, 337, 341 n. 43.

Towns, town life, in 13th century Hungary, 318-26; according to Otto of Freising, it did not exist, 333; stagnant in the 13th century, 383; royal policy for establishing towns began with Béla IV, 318, his royal charter for Nagyszombat in 1238, 321, 328 n. 25; Béla IV wrote his letter of request to Rome from Zagreb in 1241, a bishop's see established by Ladislas I, 321, 328-29 nn. 27-28; the "new" town was established by Béla IV, 321-22; of earlier origin were Esztergom, Székesfehérvár, Győr, Sopron, Pest - as church and trading centers served defensive military purposes as well; by settling down foreigners, the king carried out economic and military defense policies, 323, 330 n. 54. Stephen V continued his father's town policy, 324; the king had further elevated fort personnel to the rank of *iobagiones*, 324-25.

Veszprém, episcopal town, 326, 331 n.
78; in early eleventh century, its
bishop held jurisdiction over
Székesfehérvár, 325-26; its cathedral and cathedral school, known
and held in esteem; (its library had
a copy of Augustine's works),
230; devastated by Peter Csák,
260-62, 268 nn. 58-60; Ladislas
IV wishes to rebuild it and reconstruct its curriculum to include the
study of law, 261, 269 n. 64.
vir militaris, omnino liber, mentioned
in the Várad Register, 80.
Vukovar, Croatia, its letter of liberties
for German, Saxon, Hungarian and
Slovene settlers, issued in 1231 by
Coloman, Béla IV's younger
brother, 325-26.

Zagreb, early town settlement, 318; in
1241, Béla IV dated his writ to
Pope Gregory IX from Zagreb,
321; its bishop's see was established by Ladislas I, 329 n. 28; the
earlier "Latin (bishop's) town"
and the "royal town" did not
form one unified township, 321;
kings Emery (1198) and Béla IV
(in 1266) on Zagreb, 321-22.
Zólyom, an early town whose charter
of liberties had to be confirmed by
Béla IV, 322, 329 n. 34.